Walt Whitman

A Literary Reference to His Life and Work

CHARLES M. OLIVER

Facts On File

An imprint of Infobase Publishing

Critical Companion to Walt Whitman:
A Literary Reference to His Life and Work

Facts On File, Inc.
An imprint of Infobase Publishing
132 West 31st Street
New York NY 10001

Library of Congress Cataloging-in-Publication Data

Oliver, Charles M.
Critical companion to Walt Whitman : a literary reference to his life and
work / Charles M. Oliver.
p. cm.
Includes bibliographical references and index.
ISBN 0-8160-5768-0 (hardcover : alk. paper)
1. Whitman, Walt, 1819–1892. 2. Poets, American—19th century—
Biography. I. Title.
PS3231.053 2005
811′.3—dc22   2005004172

Text design by Erika K. Arroyo
Cover design by Cathy Rincon
Chart by Sholto Ainslie

Printed in the United States of America

VB Hermitage 10 9 8 7 6 5 4 3 2 1

This book is printed on acid-free paper.

*This book is dedicated to the memory of Professor Fred
Eckman of Bowling Green State University and to the dozen
students in his graduate seminar on Walt Whitman in the
summer of 1966. He taught us to love more than the poetry.
Who among my colleagues in that class will ever forget the
telephone call on August 2 from Professor Eckman's
secretary, informing us that Fred's only son had been killed
the day before in the University of Texas Tower murders. The
shooter was Charles Whitman. We were told that Professor
Eckman was too distraught to finish the seminar and
that we would get our final exam in the mail.
But he changed his mind, and we met once more for two
hours of an emotional reading by Eckman of Walt Whitman's
poems. The emotions were mostly ours, and I can still hear
his sonorous voice, reciting some of the greatest of all
American poetry.*

CONTENTS

INTRODUCTION AND GUIDE TO USE

Walt Whitman is arguably America's greatest poet; his influence on poets both in the United States and around the world has been enormous. His free verse poetic form has become the touchstone for much of the poetry written in America since his final version of *Leaves of Grass* was published in 1892.

Critical Companion to Walt Whitman attempts to explain how and why Whitman's poetry still creates such an impact on readers. Part I presents a biographical essay on the poet; Part II presents entries on Whitman's works (with first publication information), including each of Whitman's nearly 400 published poems, his 24 short stories and one novel, and all of his important prose essays; Part III contains entries on the people, places, publications, and topics important to the poet; and Part IV contains appendices, including a Whitman chronology, a genealogy, bibliographies of Whitman's works and of secondary sources, addresses where he lived, newspapers at which he held paid positions and others in which he published articles, a glossary of terms particular to Whitman usage, and Whitman's will.

Most of the nearly 3,000 articles Whitman wrote for various newspapers are not included as separate entries, but many are mentioned as part of the discussion in other entries. Nearly all of the 80 newspapers and magazines that published Whitman's poetry *are* included as entries in Part III; each entry includes a list of the poems first printed in the publication. All 27 of the newspapers for which Whitman worked as a paid reporter or editor also have separate entries in Part III.

Each of the poems is listed as an entry in Part II in alphabetical order by the final title given by the poet in the sixth edition of *Leaves of Grass* (1881). Poems published in early editions or printings of *Leaves of Grass* but later excluded are also included here, as are poems published in newspapers or magazines before 1855 but not in *Leaves of Grass*. Also included are the 13 poems in "Old Age Echoes," which were added as an "Annex" by Whitman's friend and executor Horace Traubel in a new printing of *Leaves of Grass* (1897), Whitman having himself provided the title for the annexed poems.

Excluded from *Critical Companion to Walt Whitman* are unpublished poems, manuscript fragments, and lines of poems cut by Whitman. One can argue that these items found in Whitman manuscript materials are of interest to scholars as a way of understanding something of the poet's changing mind at work; but an argument can also be made that they add little or nothing to the general interest in *Leaves of Grass* as a major work of American poetry. Whitman was his own best editor.

Although Whitman stated that the 1892 ("Death-bed") printing of *Leaves of Grass* represented his final, definitive revisions and placement of poems, the sixth edition (1881) included all but minor revisions and so is, in this volume, the last date listed with a poem's publication information. The addition of poems in two "Annexes" ("Sands at Seventy" and *Good-Bye My Fancy*) were the only significant changes in editions after 1881, and publication information is provided for each of the individual poems in those groups.

Each entry on a published work has the date of first publication in parentheses following the title. All parenthetical dates for poetry entries are to editions or printings of *Leaves of Grass*, except as otherwise noted, for example those poems published in newspapers or magazines before they appeared in the major work; also, unless otherwise noted, the poem appeared in all editions and printings after and between the dates provided. For example: "Song of Myself" has the following publication information in *Critical Companion to Walt Whitman*: "First appeared as the opening poem in the first edition of *Leaves of Grass* (1855), untitled, as were each of the 12 poems in that edition; it was titled 'Poem of Walt Whitman, an American' for the second edition (1856); it became 'Walt Whitman' for the third edition (1860); it was finally presented as 'Song of Myself' for the sixth edition (1881)." Readers may assume, unless otherwise stated, that the poem appeared in all printings between the dates given and in all printings after the sixth and final edition in 1881.

The sometimes complicated changes in title (and nearly every poem had one or more title changes in its publication history) and the changing order of placement of each poem allows readers to understand something of Whitman's thinking as he moves from edition to edition of *Leaves of Grass*.

Whitman's final version of *Leaves* included 12 "clusters" of poems, 25 separate poems, and two annexes. Each cluster has its entry under the title of the cluster. The annexes are entered under the titles "First Annex . . ." and "Second Annex. . . ."

In both Part I and Part II of the book, any reference to a person, place, publication, or topic that is the subject of an entry in Part III is printed in SMALL CAPITAL LETTERS the first time it appears in a particular entry, in order to indicate a cross-reference. References to entries in Part II, Whitman's titles for poems and prose works, are *not* set in small capital letters. The inclusion of these titles as separate entries, in other words, may be assumed.

The articles "the" and "a" come at the end of the title; look for "A Sight in Camp in the Daybreak Gray and Dim," for example, under "Sight in Camp in the Daybreak Gray and Dim, A"; look for *The Brooklyn Daily Eagle* under *Brooklyn Daily Eagle, The*. In direct quotations from Whitman's works, spelling idiosyncrasies have been left as in the original.

The author acknowledges the generous assistance, suggestions, and encouragement of the following people: Ed Folsom, editor of *Walt Whitman Quarterly Review*; David Vander Muelin, Department of English at the University of Virginia; Lance Jones, Columbus, Ohio; Facts On File editor Jeff Soloway; and Fred Eckman (see Dedication).

—Charles M. (Tod) Oliver
Charlottesville, Virginia

PART I

Biography

Walt Whitman

(1819–1892)

Whitman was 6 feet tall, about 185 pounds, and 36 years old in 1855 when he produced one of the most important works of literature in American history. He was almost at the midpoint of the 73 years he would live. He had no idea at the time—nor did anyone else for that matter, with the possible exception of Ralph Waldo EMERSON—that his 95-page book of poetry would become such an influence not just on the future of American poetry but on the future idea of democracy.

Leaves of Grass contained a 10-page introduction and 12 untitled poems. The introduction would later be called a Preface, and the first and longest poem would be titled "Song of Myself." Those two items provided a definition of what Whitman thought America was and would become. He established a FREE VERSE style that still reverberates in poetry throughout the Western world, and, without preaching or condescension, he also established a tone for democracy that lasted for more than a hundred years.

Both the style and the ideas shocked and upset the few people who read the first edition of *Leaves of Grass.* Readers accustomed to the rhyme and rhythm of poetry popular in mid-19th century America were dismayed at Whitman's audacity. He was honest about himself, however, which won over some readers, and his vision for America was such that only the most pessimistic could fail to catch hold of the poet's dream. Who could not admire the writer of the following passage from "Song of Myself"?

> Walt Whitman, an American, one of the
>   roughs, a kosmos,
> Disorderly fleshy and sensual . . . eating
>   drinking and breeding,
> No sentimentalist . . . no stander above men
>   and women or apart from them . . . no more
>   modest than immodest. . . .
>
> I speak the password primeval. . . . I give the
>   sign of democracy;
> By God! I will accept nothing which all cannot
> have their counterpart of on the same terms.

Steel engraving of Whitman by Samuel Hollyer placed opposite the title page in the first edition of *Leaves of Grass,* 1855 *(Library of Congress, Prints and Photographs Division)*

As it turned out, a lot of people did *not* admire this passage. And many readers thought that Whitman's poems were meaningless, "filthy," atheistic. Only Emerson, luckily for Whitman the most influential American poet of the time, recognized something in *Leaves of Grass* that others seemed to have missed. What Emerson saw was the possibility that the author was the first truly American poet in the nation's short history. Other popular poets of the time, Emerson realized—BRYANT, Longfellow, Lowell, Whittier, perhaps especially Emerson himself—were old-stock English poets. Whitman was, on the other hand, raised not among the New England elite but among the farmers on Long Island, a mix of English and Dutch working-class blood, "one of the roughs." In a lifetime of writing poetry, he never left those roots.

PHYSICAL APPEARANCE

In *Journals of Bronson Alcott*, edited by Odell Shepard (1938), Bronson ALCOTT describes a visit to Whitman's home in 1856 and provides what is perhaps the best physical description of the poet available:

> Broad-shoulder, rouge-fleshed, Bacchus-browed, bearded like a satyr, and rank, he wears his man-Bloomer in defiance of everybody, having these as everything else after his own fashion, and for example to all men hereafter. Red flannel undershirt, open-breasted, exposing his brawny neck; striped calico jacket over this, the collar Byroneal, with coarse cloth overalls buttoned to it; cowhide boots, a heavy roundabout, with huge outside pockets and buttons to match; and a slouched hat, for house and street alike. Eyes gray, unimaginative, cautious yet sagacious; his voice deep, sharp, tender sometimes and almost melting. When talking will recline upon the couch at length, pillowing his head upon his bended arm, and informing you naïvely how lazy he is, and slow. Listens well; asks you to repeat what he has failed to catch at once, yet hesitates in speaking often, or gives over as if fearing to come short of the sharp, full, concrete meaning of his thought. Inquisitive, very; over-curious even; inviting criticism on himself, on his poems—pronouncing it "pomes."—In fine, an egotist, incapable of omitting, or suffering any one long to omit, noting Walt Whitman in discourse. Swaggy in his walk, burying both hands in his outside pockets. Has never been sick, he says, nor taken medicine, nor sinned; and so is quite innocent of repentance and man's fall.

Whitman's friend and one of the executors of his will, John BURROUGHS, wrote in his biography, *Whitman: A Study* (1896)—using information Walt had given him and which he even edited—that Whitman lived a

> poet's life from first to last,—free, unhampered, unworldly, unconventional, picturesque, simple, untouched by the craze of money-getting, unselfish, devoted to others, and was, on the whole, joyfully and contentedly lived. It was a

pleased and interested saunter through the world,—no hurry, no fever, no strife; hence no bitterness, no depletion, no wasted energies. A farm boy, then a school-teacher, then a printer, editor, writer, traveler, mechanic, nurse in the army hospitals, and lastly government clerk; large and picturesque of figure, slow of movement; tolerant, passive, receptive, and democratic,—of the people; in all his tastes and attractions, always aiming to walk abreast with the great laws and forces, and to live thoroughly in the free, nonchalant spirit of his own day and land.

With the possible exception of "farm boy" (Whitman disliked farming with some passion), this biographical summary by Burroughs holds up pretty well after more than 100 years. In writing about Whitman's appearance, Burroughs also retells the story that Emerson once handed a copy of *Leaves of Grass* to a friend and said to him, "Americans abroad may now come home: unto us a man is born."

THE EARLY YEARS

LONG ISLAND, approximately 120 miles long and from 12 to 20 miles wide, was a grand mix of people and ideas when Whitman was born there on May 31, 1819, in West Hills, a farming village in Huntington Township. His birthplace (now a museum) is located a mile south of what is now the village of South Huntington, on Walt Whitman Road, across from the Walt Whitman mall.

There had been people on Long Island for thousands of years. Tribes of hunters were probably the first settlers, arriving shortly after the ice age ended 10,000 years ago. Indian tribes were there when the first white settlers arrived in the 17th century. The Dutch came first and settled on the western half of the island; the English settled on the eastern half.

The first American Whitman, Zechariah, was an English farmer, who traveled to America on the *True Love* in 1635 and settled in Milford, Connecticut. His son, Joseph, moved to Huntington, Long Island, sometime "before 1660" and was still living in 1690. Another friend, and Walt's eventual executor, Dr. Richard BUCKE says in his biography,

Walt Whitman (1883), that "from him descended all the Long Island Whitmans," most of them farmers. Walt's father, Walter WHITMAN, SR., was born on July 14, 1789, the day French revolutionaries stormed the Paris Bastille. He had inherited 500 acres of farmland, what Walt would later refer to as "all good soil, gently sloping east and south, about one-tenth woods, plenty of grand old trees" and "two or three miles" from "West Hills, Suffolk County." The primary source of family information for both Burroughs and Bucke, as well as for Walt himself, is Savage's *Genealogical Dictionary,* which notes that there were Whitmans in Huntington township as early as 1664.

Whitman writes in *Specimen Days* (1882) that "it is quite certain that from that beginning (in the 1660s), and from Joseph, the West Hill Whitmans, and all others in Suffolk County, have since radiated, myself among the number." Whitman also notes, however, that a John Whitman, born in 1602, a nephew of Zechariah, "may well seem to be the ancestor of the larger portion of the thousands bearing that name in America."

Walter, Sr., worked as a carpenter's apprentice in New York City and then for a few years at paid carpentry jobs before he returned to his own Long Island territory, his inherited farmland in West Hills, and built a two-story, cedar-shingled house. He married Louisa Van Velsor (see WHITMAN, LOUISA VAN VELSOR) on June 8, 1816, and they moved into the new house. Louisa had grown up on a farm near Cold Spring, Long Island, on the Dutch side of the imaginary Dutch-English dividing line and about four miles from West Hills.

Louisa was of Dutch and Welsh ancestry and, for Walt, the stronger and more influential of his parents. Her parents, Cornelius VAN VELSOR and Naomi Williams VAN VELSOR, owned a horse farm near Cold Spring, about a mile from Cold Spring Harbor on the northern shore of Long Island. Walt often visited his grandparents in Cold Spring and remembered them fondly in his later years.

Walt was the second child born to Walter and Louisa. There were eight surviving children, six boys and two girls. Walt's brothers were Jesse WHITMAN, born in 1818, Andrew (Andy) Jackson WHITMAN (1827), George Washington WHITMAN (1829), Thomas Jefferson (Jeff) WHITMAN (1833), and Edward (Eddie) WHITMAN (1835). Their sisters were Mary Elizabeth WHITMAN, born in 1821, and Hannah Louisa WHITMAN (1823). Another child was born in 1825 but died, still unnamed, six months later.

The family was somewhat dysfunctional, and most of the weight for damage control fell on Louisa's shoulders. Three of Walt's brothers had lifelong psychological problems. Jesse and Eddie were both mentally retarded, and Eddie was physically handicapped as well. Andrew was not retarded, apparently, but unstable and in constant trouble, though he joined the Union army during the CIVIL WAR, perhaps in part to see if he could straighten himself out. He died of a throat ailment in 1863 in Washington, at age 36, one of thousands of soldiers who died during the war of diseases rather than of war wounds. Andy's wife, Nancy, meanwhile, was on the New York streets as a prostitute, and when Andy died, their two children were taken to their grandmother Louisa's in West Hills. She was 68 at the time and died five years later. She had led a full and generally happy life, notwithstanding the almost constant turmoil. Whitman referred to his mother's death as "the great dark cloud of my life."

For Walt, the most influential mix of ideas during his early years probably came in the variety of religious beliefs he encountered. There were a number of distinctive religious organizations on Long Island at the time, all of them powerful enough to have an influence on the population. One of the oldest Presbyterian churches was founded in Southold, Long Island, in 1640; one of the oldest Methodist societies was formed in Commack in 1783, and the first Methodist Church camp meeting was held in Glen Cove in 1805; the Protestant Episcopal Church of America was established in Setauket, Suffolk County; an African-American Episcopal church was founded in Breuckelen in 1815 (the town became BROOKLYN the next year); the first Catholic churches on Long Island were founded in the 1830s; Lutheran congregations were formed in Brooklyn during the period 1841–47; the first Jewish congregation was organized in Brooklyn in 1851; and there were the

Long Island Quakers, perhaps the most influential religious group of all on the developing Walt Whitman. After severe persecution by New England Puritans during the late 1640s, the Quakers settled first on Long Island in 1657 and then spread to the rest of the colonies.

Several of Walt's Van Velsor relatives were Quakers, and, although he did not himself become a Quaker, he certainly accepted many of the doctrines passed down to him from his Quaker ancestors, not the least doctrine of which was the moral value of brotherly love, which would become a major theme in his poetry. His grandmother, Naomi Van Velsor, whom Walt loved and admired, apparently was not a member of the Quakers (also known as the Religious Society of Friends) but passed on to him a number of Quaker ideals. They

were against slavery and were active in the underground railroad. They practiced democracy in church affairs and believed in equality of opportunity for the expression of religious ideas. This latter belief developed from their notion of "Inner Light," which Quakers believed illuminated the hearts of all people. They renounced ritual in church meetings, and there were no planned sermons, each member free to stand and speak when he or she felt moved to do so. Whitman must have liked this idea in particular; he wrote later of the need to rid the churches of preachers and priests. Each of these Quaker ideals showed up in the poet's work.

The first 30 years of the 19th century was a time of religious reawakening along the American east coast, and it had an impact on many religious organizations, perhaps especially on American

Walt Whitman's birthplace at West Hills in Huntington Township on Long Island, New York. He was born there on May 31, 1819. *(Library of Congress, Prints and Photographs Division)*

Quakerism. Along with a general revival of evangelism, there was at the same time a more liberal approach to biblical teachings. To combat this liberalism, Quaker leaders attempted to take away from members some democratic principles, which were historically a part of the Society of Friends' beliefs. One of the leaders on the liberal side against orthodoxy was Elias HICKS, the most popular Quaker preacher and orator of his time. The "Great Separation" within the society occurred in the period 1827–28, the Orthodox Quakers remaining evangelical, Hicks and his followers becoming unitarian and known as "Hicksites." Hicksville, a town on Long Island, is named for the preacher.

Whitman was taken as a 10-year-old to hear Hicks preach at the Morrison Hotel in Brooklyn. He probably did not understand much of Hicks's sermon, but he was impressed by his style of oratory; the understanding of Hicks's religious philosophy came later in Whitman's reading of the sermons and essays. The single most important idea Whitman got from Hicks may have been that God speaks directly to each person, connecting to the soul with Inner Light, which provided moments of spiritual exaltation, of direct contact with God. Whitman referred often in his poetry to the spiritual need for a direct link between the soul and God, a link as sensitive, perhaps, as the filament "launch'd forth" by a noiseless patient spider: "Till the bridge you will need be form'd, till the ductile anchor hold, / Till the gossamer thread you fling catch somewhere, O my soul."

Walter Sr. had moved back to West Hills from New York before his marriage to Louisa, thinking there would be a need for carpenters in central Long Island. There was not as much work as he expected, however, and he was not a skilled farmer, so after struggling for eight years in West Hills, he moved his growing family to Brooklyn. Louisa was three months pregnant with her fourth child, all four born during a period of less than six years.

On May 27, 1823, four days before Walt's fourth birthday, the Whitman family moved into a rented a house on Front Street in Brooklyn, near the FULTON FERRY settlement. May 27 was a historic day for Long Islanders and probably not a good day to move from West Hills to Brooklyn. It was the day of a famous horse race at the Union Race Track in the town of Jamaica between the Long Island favorite, Eclipse, and a horse from the south named Sir Henry. Eclipse won and celebrations were held over most of western Long Island, including in Brooklyn. Walter Sr. may have been unaware of the race, but Louisa, who had been raised on a horse farm, among horse breeders, was not unaware and probably rejoiced inwardly at least when she heard that Eclipse had won. The crowds of race fans heading for homes in Brooklyn may have passed the Whitmans, their wagon full of household goods and children en route to their new home. They arrived at the Front Street house in the midst of all-night celebrating. Six months later Hannah Louisa Whitman was born, on November 28.

Brooklyn, which had been Breuckelen until 1816 (named by Dutch settlers after a town in Holland), was still just a village of 7,000 people when the Whitmans moved there. It would not become a "city" until 1834, and when Walt published *Leaves of Grass* in Brooklyn in 1855, it was the third largest city in America, with a population of about 200,000. By 1870 it had 400,000 citizens and would become a borough of New York City in 1898; it is now the largest of the five boroughs with a population in 1990 of more than 2,200,000.

During the next 10 years (1823–33) the Whitmans would live in 10 different homes. Walter Sr. built two houses during 1824 and 1825, where the family lived for short periods of time, but Walt would report in *Specimen Days* that the houses "were mortgaged, and we lost them." For a list of places where Walt Whitman lived during his years in Brooklyn see "Brooklyn Addresses" in Part IV.

One of the most memorable events of Walt's early life occurred on July 4, 1825, when he was six. The marquis de Lafayette, the famous French general who had served with the Continental army during the AMERICAN REVOLUTION (1775–81), was on a 16-month tour of the United States in honor of his contributions during the war, and arrived in New York in time for Independence Day celebrations. He crossed to Brooklyn and was paraded up Fulton Street in order to lay a cornerstone for the Apprentices Library Building at the corner of Cranberry and Henry Streets. Schoolchildren followed the general's carriage, and, as Walt told the story later in newspaper articles as well as on many less formal occasions, Lafayette lifted him up over a fence and kissed him on the cheek before setting him down again.

PUBLIC SCHOOL

Walt began his formal education in the 1824–25 school year at District School Number 1 at the corner of Concord and Adams streets in Brooklyn. His schooling would end in 1830, in part because his father was having financial difficulties and the family needed whatever extra money the 11-year-old Walt could manage to earn on his own. He would take a job in the summer of 1830 as office boy in the James B. Clark & Son law firm on lower Fulton Street.

An English Quaker, Joseph Lancaster, organized the public school that Walt attended on the philosophy that one teacher, with older student monitors, could teach a number of students at one time by a system of rote learning. The District 1 School also emphasized social values and how to distinguish between good and evil. The teacher was strict, using whenever he thought it necessary a birch rod or cowhide strap on his pupils, or as Walt would suggest later, "other ingenious methods of child torture." The teacher may have inspired the character of Lugare in Whitman's short story "Death in the School-Room (A Fact)," published in 1841. It is not surprising, in any case, to learn from Walt later that the incident he remembered most during those years in public school was the steamship *Fulton* blowing up in the Brooklyn Navy Yard. The explosion on June 4, 1829—caused apparently by a disgruntled sailor, who set off a powder magazine—killed 40 of the ship's crew. Walt remembered that he attended the collective funeral a few days later and was moved to tears by the ceremony and by the parade to the cemetery afterward.

Brooklyn in the 1820s was a small village centered around Fulton Ferry, a fairly thriving community of houses, stores, shanties, stables, and taverns on the East River waterfront. It was still a farm community when the Whitmans lived there, and Walt remembered later how he "tramped freely about neighborhood and town." Small ferryboat

lines had been ferrying passengers across the half-mile to Manhattan for 150 years, most often in rowboats. Robert Fulton began his steamboat ferry service in 1814, running boats from the foot of what is now Old Fulton Street in Brooklyn to the present Pier 11 ferry stop in New York City. Even in Whitman's time the trip took only a few minutes. Several boat lines operated the run until the New York and Brooklyn Ferry Company formed in 1839 and bought up all the smaller companies. The BROOKLYN BRIDGE would be under construction from 1870 to 1883, beginning at Fulton Ferry and soon obliterating the village and forcing people and businesses further out into Kings County.

Edward, the "son" in the James B. Clark & Son law firm, gave their 11-year-old apprentice a subscription to a large circulation library to make up for the loss of his public education. Walt records that his first reading was *The Arabian Nights* and the Walter Scott novels; he also read the James Fenimore Cooper *Leatherstocking Tales.* Five years later he read Scott's *Complete Poems* and his three-volume *Minstrelsy of the Scottish Border,* which Walt later said he read several times. It must have been clear to him soon after leaving the public school system that he would learn more, and faster, working at various jobs and checking books out of the library than he had learned in school. Later in 1830 he worked in a doctor's office, and a few months into 1831 he would take his first newspaper job as a printer's devil, or printing apprentice, for the LONG ISLAND PATRIOT at 149 Fulton Street in Brooklyn.

JOURNALISM

Walt worked in paid positions for 28 newspapers between 1831 and 1859, mostly as a reporter or editor, and he would publish nearly 3,000 articles or editorials in 80 different papers during his lifetime. The longest he stayed as reporter or editor for any one newspaper, however, was about two and a half years. Mostly he disagreed with owners over political issues, and it was rarely clear whether he quit or was fired.

The editor of the *Patriot,* a Democratic newspaper, was Samuel E. Clements, who taught Walt the elements of printing and encouraged his growing interest in journalism. Walt stated later that he had written several "sentimental bits" for the *Patriot*, but there is no apparent evidence that they were published. In the fall of 1832 he took a job as an apprentice for the LONG ISLAND STAR under the editorship of Alden Spooner. The *Star* was a Whig newspaper, opposed to most of Clements's opinions at the *Patriot*, and the two contrasting points of view provided Walt with a good introduction to newspaper politics. Spooner was also involved in the temperance movement and may well have inspired Walt to write a novel and two short stories a few years later with moral lessons in each against drinking alcoholic beverages.

While working for the *Star* Walt published an article titled "In Olden Times" for the NEW-YORK MIRROR: A WEEKLY JOURNAL DEVOTED TO LITERA-TURE AND FINE ARTS (November 29, 1834). He was 15, and it was apparently the first publication known to be written by Whitman. He wrote later in *Specimen Days* about how excited he was, waiting "for the big, fat, red-faced, slow-moving, very old English carrier who distributed the *Mirror* in Brooklyn," and, finally getting it, opening the newspaper "with trembling fingers" to read his story.

CHOLERA reached the American East Coast in 1832, beginning in New York City on June 26. At its height in July the epidemic killed 100 people a day and a total of 3,500 by December, when it finally lessened; a third of the population left the coastal cities, carrying the disease into the countryside. Financial depression followed the cholera epidemic later that year, adding to Walter Sr.'s troubles. He moved his family back to Norwich, Long Island, near Oyster Bay, in May of the next year (1833). Walt stayed in Brooklyn to continue work for the *Star* and began what would become a lifelong interest in the theater, going often into New York to see productions. He later remembered that his first play was Richard Sheridan's *School for Scandal*. He also saw a number of Shakespeare's plays, including *Richard III* starring Junius Brutus Booth at the Bowery Theatre.

TEACHING

Walt left the *Star* in May 1835 to take a printing apprenticeship in New York and become a journey-man printer. An August fire that year destroyed nearly all of a central area of New York printing offices, creating a significant loss of printing jobs. Out of newspaper work temporarily, he moved in with his parents in the spring of 1836. They were living in Hempstead, Long Island, and Walt took a teaching position that June in Norwich (now East Norwich), near Cold Spring, where his 68-year-old grandfather Cornelius Van Velsor was still working his horse farm. Walt was 17, and this was his first of several short-term teaching positions.

Attitudes toward public education in central Long Island tended to be casual at best. Students attended school or not, depending on whether they were needed at the farm, and almost anyone who wanted to teach, could do so. Teachers were poorly paid, and they were expected to take room and board with the parents of their students, moving every few days to another pupil's home. Walt liked that aspect of his teaching experience, because it brought him into contact with a great variety of people and ideas.

In late summer 1836, the Whitman family moved to Babylon, Long Island, on Great South Bay, and Walt lived with them and taught a three-month fall term in a Babylon public school. In 1837 he taught at Long Swamp in the spring and at Smithtown in the fall. He had become involved in a debating group four years earlier in Brooklyn and so became active again in Smithtown, entering several debates, mostly on political issues of the time. But he was soon to return to journalism, where he could write out his beliefs for a larger audience.

THE *LONG-ISLANDER*

In early 1838, at age 19, Walt became the founder, publisher, and editor of the Huntington weekly the *LONG-ISLANDER*, a newspaper that still exists. The first issue was distributed on June 5, 1838. Apparently none of the issues from Whitman's one year as publisher-editor still exists, but seven of the articles he wrote that year were reprinted in either the *Hempstead Inquirer* or in the LONG ISLAND DEMOC-RAT. Three of the reprinted articles are two sentences long, and the longest is three paragraphs. Walt's earliest known poem, "Our Future Lot," was probably published in the *Long-Islander*. It was reprinted in the *Long Island Democrat* (October 31, 1838) and later retitled "Time to Come."

Walt bought a printing press and fonts of type in New York and hired some help. He did most of the work himself, writing the stories and editorials, setting type, and running the press. He even bought a horse and delivered the papers to subscribers. He wrote that deliveries took "one day and night" but that he "never had happier jaunts." He met the "old-fashioned farmers and their wives" and stopped by their hayfields; he was often invited to dinner and spent "occasional evenings" with his subscribers. It was clearly a happy memory as he wrote about it several years later. Not only did his casual habits delay delivery of the paper to subscribers, but he was also often late in merely getting the newspaper published, sometimes publishing the "weekly" newspaper only once every two or even three weeks.

Early in 1839 he quit the *Long-Islander,* or, as is more likely, was fired because his financial supporters gave up on his ability to get the paper out on time. He still remained friendly, however, with everyone involved with the continuation of the newspaper. Forty years later, as an old man who had already had a serious stroke, Whitman revisited the offices of the *Long-Islander* to a friendly reception. And a few years later the newspaper reported (December 29, 1888) that "We have received from our old friend, Walt Whitman, a Christmas present of his complete works, a gift which we appreciate very highly. Mr. Whitman is a grand old man with a good big heart, and while critics are debating about the quality of his poems, we advise any one who wants to have his heart touched with the poetic fire, to read his 'Ode to Lincoln!' We hope our aged friend may weather the blasts of many winters yet."

Walt's next job was with the *Long Island Democrat* in Jamaica, Long Island. The editor, James Brenton, knew and liked Whitman and had reprinted several poems and articles from the *Long-Islander.* Beginning in August 1839, he worked for two years as a typesetter, and Brenton published nine of Walt's new poems and several articles.

Whitman taught school in Jamaica at the same time, and his most important contribution to the *Democrat* was a series of articles under the general heading "Sun-Down Papers: From the Desk of a Schoolmaster." The essays had little to do with school teaching but are, instead, discourses on smoking, the difference between the death of an old person and the death of a young, the nature of philosophy, the search for truth, and other topics. There were 10 numbered essays in the series, the first three published in the *Hempstead Inquirer* (February and March 1840), the next six in the *Democrat* (April 1840–July 1841), and the 10th in the *Long Island Farmer and Queens County Advertiser* (July 1841).

Perhaps the best that came from the "Sun-Down Papers" was inspiration, if only from the title, for one of Whitman's greatest poems, titled "Sun-Down Poem," which later became "Crossing Brooklyn Ferry."

TEACHING II

By the fall of 1839 Whitman was teaching school again. He was fired at the *Democrat,* apparently not because Mr. Brenton didn't like his work but more likely because Mrs. Brenton thought him "slovenly" around her home, where she and her husband provided Walt with board and room. So he took another teaching job, this time at the Jamaica Academy at Flushing Hill, Long Island. By December he was teaching at Little Bay Side, near Jamaica. There is very little information about Whitman's teaching ability, but most of what is known comes from his experiences at Little Bay Side.

Fairly reliable information comes from the notes of one of his pupils, Charles Roe, who was elected a Flushing supervisor in 1860 and later was made Queens County treasurer. Roe told Whitman friend and biographer Horace TRAUBEL that Whitman had made a "powerful and peculiar effect on [him] as a boy. . . . Even back in the school-days, those of us who knew him, . . . felt, somehow, without knowing why, that here was a man out of the average, who strangely attracted our respect and affection." It is clear by Roe's account to Traubel that Whitman was dignified in the classroom but informal and experimental, constantly looking for new ways to hold his pupils' attention. Roe said that he often played the game of 20 questions in class as a way of stimulating the learning process. And he never used corporal punishment, according to Roe. If he caught a student cheating, Roe told Traubel, he would tell the class a moral tale that revealed no names but which made the main point clear to the culprit. Whitman would later publish a short story titled "Death in the School-Room (A Fact)," which confronts the moral issue of punishing pupils too severely.

Perhaps it was too much "informality," the casualness with which he taught, or the lack of discipline; whatever the reasons, Whitman's teaching contracts were rarely renewed.

By February 1840 Walt was teaching for the spring term at Trimming Square, Long Island, a small town which at that time was along the road from New York to Jamaica and about two miles from Hempstead; the town name was later changed to Washington Square. In May the Whitman family moved to Dix Hills, another return to the family's original roots. By summer Walt was teaching in Woodbury, just northwest of West Hills, where he was born. In a letter to a friend, Abraham Leech of Jamaica, Whitman wrote: "O, damnation, damnation! Thy other name is school-teaching and thy residence Woodbury," not a happy recommendation for the local public school. On the other hand, the teacher for whom he was a substitute at Woodbury returned in the fall and later wrote that Whitman must have spent most of his time writing poetry, because the "pupils had not gained a 'whit' in learning when he [the regular teacher] took them over again."

Walt taught the fall term in 1840 in Whitestone, near Jamaica, where he also participated in formal political debates in support of Martin Van Buren for president against William Henry Harrison. Van Buren lost.

Whitman was still teaching at Whitestone in early 1841, but by May he was back in journalism, working for the NEW WORLD, first as a printer but then as a writer and reporter.

JOURNALISM II

For the next 13 years, Whitman would edit nine different newspapers and contribute articles to several others. He left the New World to take a job for a few weeks in spring 1842 as editor of the NEW YORK AURORA. During the summer and fall of the same year he edited the NEW YORK EVENING TATTLER. By spring 1843 he was editor of the NEW YORK STATESMAN and was, at the same time, coeditor of the New York Sunday Times. During those two years he also contributed articles to BROTHER JONATHAN and the SUN.

In the summer and fall of 1844, he edited the NEW YORK DEMOCRAT, and for the next two years (1845–46), although he was not editing a newspaper, he continued to write articles and sold them to several papers, including the Broadway Journal, the United States Magazine and Democratic Review (known as the DEMOCRATIC REVIEW), and the AMERICAN REVIEW. He returned to Brooklyn in August 1845 and contributed 54 articles for the BROOKLYN EVENING STAR between September of that year and March 1846.

The editorial position for which Whitman is perhaps best known was with the BROOKLYN DAILY EAGLE, a job he held from March 1846 to January 1848. He wrote more than 1,000 articles and editorials for the Eagle during his tenure as editor. He wrote articles and editorials on, among other topics, democracy and patriotism, local and national politics and politicians, the U.S.-MEXICAN WAR (1846–48), the economy, prison reform, labor and labor organizations, local newspapers and their editors, and education and schools.

For the Eagle he also reviewed books and local theater performances, particularly OPERA, which had become for Whitman a lifelong passion. And he began a series of 25 articles he called "City Intelligence" ("Local Intelligence" for the final two), in which he wrote mostly upbeat stories about Brooklyn or New York: "City Intelligence: Fulton Street, Brooklyn" began the series on June 4, 1846.

He was dismissed as editor in January over political disagreements with the owners, Henry Cruse Murphy and Isaac Van Anden, who had founded the newspaper in 1841 as a Democratic Party organ. They supported James K. Polk in his successful 1844 campaign for the presidency, and they supported him when he declared war against Mexico. Polk submitted to Congress a deceitful war message, claiming that Mexico had started the war on American soil. It isn't clear whether Whitman was fired or quit over his editorial disagreement with the owners, but he was out of work by the end of January 1848.

Walt met the owner of the NEW ORLEANS CRES-CENT, J. E. McClure, during the intermission of a concert they were attending in New York, and McClure, who knew of Whitman's reputation, hired him on the spot to edit his newspaper. Whitman and his brother Jeff were in New Orleans, working for the *Crescent* for the next three months, from February to May 27, Walt as editor and Jeff as a job printer. He left, once again, for reasons of editorial disagreement with the owner.

He returned to Brooklyn to edit the *Brooklyn Freeman* from September 9, 1848, to September 11, 1849. For the remainder of 1849 and into 1854 he ran a print shop in Brooklyn and contributed articles for the *New York Sunday Dispatch*, the *Brooklyn Daily Advertiser*, the *National Era*, and the NEW YORK EVENING POST. In summer 1851 he edited the weekly *Statesman and Traveller's Director for Long Island*.

LEAVES OF GRASS

All of Whitman's previous experiences—on newspapers; in teaching; in a somewhat dysfunctional family; in contact with people of ideas and moral values, especially people like Emerson and Thoreau; with writing nearly 3,000 articles and editorials; even with writing a novel and 24 short stories, which were, by today's standards, pretty bad—all of this experience led to his thinking about, making notes for, and finally writing the first poems that would make their way into, and sometimes out from, *Leaves of Grass.*

There was so little in the short stories that prepared Whitman followers for *Leaves of Grass* that his contemporaries must have wondered if the same person wrote both. The stories are primarily moralistic, perhaps like the stories he told to his public school classes when someone had misbehaved. They are superficial and often poorly written. The poetry of *Leaves of Grass,* on the other hand, is philosophical, often with multiple layers of meaning. And though Whitman did not invent the free verse poetic style he used in *Leaves* (it is the verse form of much of the Old Testament), he developed it as the perfect form with which to

Walt Whitman, 1854 *(Library of Congress, Prints and Photographs Division)*

merge his own rich and optimistic belief in the American spirit: free, individual, and democratic.

The slim volume did not sell well, and the first reviews were a disappointment to Whitman. It was criticized both for its free-flowing style and for what reviewers saw as an exaltation of the human body in general and sexual love in particular. American readers favored rhyme and standard rhythm patterns, which were still the preference of poets in England and New England. And it was the free style and exaltation that Emerson liked, praising Whitman for his difference. "I find it the most extraordinary piece of wit & wisdom that America has yet contributed," Emerson wrote to him. "I am very happy in reading it, as great power makes us happy. . . . I rubbed my eyes a little to see if this sunbeam were no illusion; but the solid sense of the book is a sober certainty."

Whitman managed to have Emerson's letter published in the NEW YORK TRIBUNE without his permission and later in the second edition of *Leaves of Grass.* Whitman was wrong to take advantage of Emerson's kindness, but Emerson's praise of Whitman turned a number of heads, critics and readers alike, and no doubt made the second edition, published the next year, more popular and probably better read. Emerson met Whitman later on several occasions, apparently for the first time on December 11, 1855, at Whitman's home on Ryerson Street in Brooklyn. Bronson Alcott and Henry David THOREAU visited Whitman twice during the fall of 1856, the second time with Sarah Tyndale, an abolitionist and women's rights advocate from Philadelphia, who no doubt noted Whitman's equal treatment of women in his poems.

The influence of Emerson on Whitman was profound. Gay Wilson Allen, who wrote biographies of both men, summed them up as follows: "Walt Whitman, Emerson's disciple, later wanted to make his own life a poem. Emerson set the example by wanting to make his life a sermon." Whitman wrote about the Emerson influence in a letter to John Trowbridge in 1860, saying, in part, "I was simmering, simmering, simmering; Emerson brought me to a boil."

Whitman took a number of ideas from Emerson, including the importance of establishing an American poetry. Whitman saw himself as the nation's bard and proceeded to perpetuate that notion by writing some of the most American poems to that time (and perhaps since).

Readers of the 21st century are so familiar with free-verse poetry that it may be difficult to understand the mixed if not negative reception of the form in Whitman's 1855 poems. But what may seem more exceptional for today's reader is Whitman's concept of democracy, set down in some of the poet's clearest prose in an untitled introductory essay that served as a preface to the 1855 edition.

It would be difficult to find a better definition of democracy than Whitman's presentation of it in *Leaves of Grass,* as it appeared in the first edition and as it continued to develop through the next 37 years and 11 reprintings of his book. Even Alexis de Tocqueville, who had written a four-volume study titled *Democracy in America* (1835–40) to justify democracy to the rest of the world, did not explain it any better. Whitman's vision included, as a pri-

mary ingredient, equality for all Americans, regardless of sex, race, or ethnic background. He had some difficulty with racial equality as the threat of civil war began to loom large in the late 1850s, because as much as he hated slavery, preservation of the Union was more important to him. Once into the war, though, he realized that if the North won, slavery would be eliminated and the Union preserved.

For 150 years it seems as if nearly every political cause has embraced Whitman's dream for America. Early 20th-century Progressives, Franklin Roosevelt New Dealers as well as socialists in the 1930s, people for or against all of the wars beginning in the 1940s, and more recently feminists and gay rights activists have all found quotations from *Leaves of Grass* to promote their own ideas.

Whitman spent the rest of his life writing more poems for *Leaves of Grass,* constantly editing them, moving them around or removing some he had included in earlier editions. He had spent 36 years getting to the publication of his *Leaves;* he had 37 years left for polishing and promoting.

THE *BROOKLYN DAILY TIMES*

Following publication of the second edition of *Leaves of Grass* in September 1856 (copyright registration was September 11) and while working on and waiting for a third edition, Whitman accepted the editorship of the BROOKLYN DAILY TIMES on or about May 1, 1857. He had already written more than 60 new poems, but he needed a steadier income, and the *Times'* publisher, George C. Bennett, was looking for an editor who could give his newspaper a better circulation and reputation than its main competitor, the *Brooklyn Daily Eagle,* which Whitman had edited 10 years earlier. He was editor of the *Times* until sometime in the late spring or early summer 1859.

Whitman wrote more for the *Times* than he did in his nearly two-year tenure with the *Eagle,* yet it is generally his work for the latter newspaper that has received the most biographical interest. Nearly all editorials in all newspapers were unsigned (as they still are today), as well as many of the news and feature stories, so it is difficult for bibliographers to get an accurate count of Whitman items for any of the newspapers for which he worked. Scholars have had to rely on their recognition of Whitman's prose style, which has often left them unsure, especially with the earliest writing, in which case researchers have most often noted their doubts. If the generally accepted count is accurate, however, then Whitman wrote approximately 1,200 news items, feature stories, and editorials for the *Times* and about 1,000 for the *Eagle*.

He left the *Times* apparently of his own volition, but he had gotten in trouble with several Brooklyn ministers by suggesting rather liberal views on issues concerning prostitution and the sex lives of unmarried men and women. The most serious problem came, however, in an editorial titled "Beecherroyalty," in which he accused the famous preacher Henry Ward Beecher of encouraging his parishioners to worship their minister.

Sometime during the early months of 1859—perhaps as he was thinking about leaving the *Times* anyway—Whitman wrote a series of poems under the title "Live Oak with Moss." They would become part of the "Calamus" cluster of 39 poems for the third edition of *Leaves of Grass*, published the next year. The poems are about the love of men for other men. During the summer, having no paid employment, Whitman began in earnest to revise *Leaves of Grass* and to write additional poems for the new edition.

One of the new poems was titled "A Child's Reminiscence," published first in the Christmas issue of *Saturday Press* (December 24, 1859) and then as "A Word Out of the Sea" in the third edition of *Leaves of Grass*. The title was changed later to "Out of the Cradle Endlessly Rocking" and became one of Whitman's best-loved poems.

BOHEMIANISM

It was probably during the late spring or summer in 1859 that Whitman became a regular visitor to PFAFF'S CELLAR, a restaurant/chophouse at 653 Broadway in New York. It was a gathering place for freethinkers of all sorts: theater people and poets, but also newspaper reporters and editors, musicians, literary people, and critics of literary people.

Whitman joined in, usually after a theater performance or following a walk through lower Manhattan from Brooklyn. He even dressed the part and apparently carried it off as well as any, his dress usually including open-throated shirts and a large soft hat that gave him the look of someone with the ambition to become the poet of America. The affectations did not last long, however, because the very nature of the poems he was writing and of his personality were opposed to anything artificial. Since childhood he had been an observer of people—boatmen, bus drivers, pilots, fishermen, mechanics, newspapermen—always interested in their hardworking lives. He visited prisons and hospitals, and he is said to have spent a winter driving an omnibus for a disabled driver.

One of the "regulars" at Pfaff's described the poet among the Pfaffians as someone who would "sit by Pfaff's privy and eat sweet-breads and drink coffee, and listen to the intolerable wit of the crack-brains." Whitman must have enjoyed the variety of ideas he heard from such a diverse group of intelligent people.

The actress Ada CLARE, who was mistress of composer Louis Gottschalk at the time, was one of the more notorious frequenters of Pfaff's. She was known as the "Queen of Bohemia," while Henry CLAPP, editor of *Saturday Press*, was known as the "Prince of Bohemia." Clapp picked up a number of contributions to his paper through conversations with such writers as William Dean HOWELLS, John Swinton, Joseph E. Chamberlin, Fitz-Greene Halleck, William Winter, Charles D. Gardette, Thomas Bailey ALDRICH, and Fitz-James O'Brien, all frequenters of Pfaff's Cellar.

Whitman received a love letter from a "mysterious woman," addressed to him at Pfaff's, a woman believed to be an actress but about whom almost nothing else is known. See EYRE, ELLEN.

THE "QUICKSAND YEARS"

Out of work for most of 1859, Whitman must have been encouraged by the Christmas publication in *Saturday Press* of "A Child's Reminiscence," followed in February by a letter from Boston publishers THAYER & ELDRIDGE, who wanted to print the third edition of *Leaves of Grass*. The publishers were Whitman friends, and he accepted their offer immediately, arriving in Boston on March 15 to spend two months helping with the production.

Emerson called on Whitman while he was in Boston and tried to talk him out of including a few of his "Enfans d'Adam" poems that contained sexual images or connotations which Emerson felt were too explicit. At the end of the discussion, however, Emerson had not gained his point, and so—as the story goes—the two went out for dinner together at the American Hotel. It is interesting to note that Emerson did not, apparently, state objections to any of the "Calamus" poems, most of which carried sexual images of homosexual love.

The 456-page book, which included 124 new poems and considerable revision of old ones, was published in mid-May and sold its 1,000 copies by July. It was an attractive volume, and Whitman could not have been more pleased with its success. Thayer & Eldridge produced a pre-publication, 64-page pamphlet advertising the book, free of charge to Whitman. The pamphlet, plus other unexpected costs caused the Boston publishers to fall into bankruptcy by the end of the year, ending a relationship that all three men had hoped would be merely the beginning of something financially valuable for all of them. Whitman's royalties on the edition may have been as little as $250.

While in Boston, with the war drums beating further south, Whitman met a number of abolitionists, including William O'CONNOR and his wife, Ellen, who would become close friends. He had met Thoreau earlier in Brooklyn and must have known his essay on "Civil Disobedience" (1849) and the story of Thoreau's night in jail for failing to pay his taxes in protest of America's war with Mexico (1848–49). Whitman also became aware of the difference between the treatment of blacks in Boston and in Brooklyn; they held good jobs in Boston, ate in good restaurants, and served on juries. The poet was still ambiguous about the slavery question—in spite of the undoubted influence of his New England friends—feeling as he did that preservation of the Union was more important than the abolition of slavery. The O'Connors, however, along with other abolitionists he met in Boston, must have made an impression, yet there is no evidence that he had changed his mind by the time of the Civil War's beginning the next year.

Whitman would refer later to the time beginning with the publication of "A Child's Reminiscence" and the third edition of *Leaves of Grass* as "quicksand years." The war was coming, and there were also family problems ahead, including the death of Andrew.

THE CIVIL WAR

Whitman spent the evening of April 13, 1861, at the New York Academy of Music, hearing a performance of DONIZETTI's opera *Linda di Chamounix*. In *Speciman Days* the poet wrote that as he was walking down Broadway toward his home in Brooklyn after the opera, he heard newsboys shouting the headlines about the attack on Fort Sumter. A crowd formed near the Metropolitan Hotel at Prince Street, according to Whitman, and someone read aloud a telegram and newspaper stories about the outbreak of the war the day before. Sometime after midnight, Whitman made his way home to his Portland Avenue house.

Walt's brother George, age 31, joined Brooklyn's 13th Regiment on April 19 and spent his "100 days of enlistment" (no one seemed to think the war would last longer than that) in Washington protecting against Rebel forces. He reenlisted on October 30, this time in New York's 51st Volunteers, and was wounded on December 13, 1862, at Fredericksburg, Virginia. Walt saw the name "G. W. Whitmore" on a list of the regiment's wounded men in the *New York Herald,* assumed it was a misspelling of his brother's name, and went to Washington to see if he could get more details. By Christmas 1862 he was at the hospital in Falmouth, near Fredericksburg, where George had been taken.

It was Whitman's first taste of the war. He had been writing poetry and articles for various New York newspapers, and all he knew of the first year and a half of the war was what he had read in the city's newspapers or heard from returning soldiers.

When the war started, the only available hospital in Washington was the Infirmary at Judiciary Square (see CIVIL WAR HOSPITALS), but by the time Whitman was back in Washington in early 1863 there were a number of buildings being used as hospitals, and 85 structures would be converted before the war ended in 1865. Wounded soldiers were "maintained," Whitman wrote, "most on cots or makeshift beds, in rooms, in hallways, anywhere there was room, none of the buildings built for the purpose." Whitman's earlier experiences visiting hospital patients, or even men in prisons, made him a natural for helping wounded soldiers in Washington hospitals during the war.

But he had to have paid employment.

Walt had furnished most of the family income since the death of his father in 1855 (a week after publication of the first *Leaves of Grass*), and that income had been unreliable at best. And there was considerable trouble at home. His mother was 67 years old and had three sons, a daughter-in-law, and a daughter living with her in Brooklyn. Jesse, 44, had always been unstable and was now abusive as well; Edward, 27, required help with his lifelong physical disability; and Jeff, 29, was there also, with his wife, Martha, and their daughter, Mannahatta. Andrew, 25, and his wife, Nancy, lived near the Portland Avenue house, near enough to show up occasionally for Louisa's dinner; Andy was seriously ill and would die before the end of the year; Nancy either was already a prostitute or became one when Andy died, and their two children would be taken into Louisa's home in December.

Whitman wrote to a number of friends for letters of recommendation for jobs in Washington, including to Emerson and a few senators. He was living in a boardinghouse at 394 L Street at the time, where William and Ellen O'Connor also had rooms.

The poet held three jobs during the next few years in Washington, all as a government clerk. He worked for the paymaster general's office, under Major Lyman S. Hapgood; with the Bureau of Indian Affairs; and with the attorney general's office. He was fired from the Indian Affairs clerkship by James Harlan, a former senator from Iowa who was appointed secretary of the interior a month before Lincoln's assassination. Harlan led a campaign to purge government of all employees who had not displayed sufficient loyalty to the Union, and, when he searched for and found a copy of *Leaves of Grass* in Whitman's desk, he fired him for a lack of "decorum & propriety prescribed by a Christian Civilization." He also fired all

women employees because they "might be injurious to . . . the morals of the men."

Whitman got the job as clerk in the attorney general's office the day after he was dismissed by Harlan, thanks to friends, particularly William O'Connor, who saw through Harlan's obsessive behavior at the Department of the Interior. The position involved the copying of letters and legal opinions sent to the president, cabinet members, and other government officials. He complained of the pay, but he held the job for seven years.

Throughout the war, however, it was the hospital work that received most of his energy and resources. But the war eventually wore him down, and he became depressed enough over all the dead and dying soldiers he attended that he was finally told to take time off by hospital authorities.

After returning to Washington on January 2, 1863, with his brother and other wounded soldiers from Fredericksburg, Whitman spent the better part of the next two years serving as a self-appointed male nurse in many of the buildings that had been converted for the wounded. He assisted soldiers of both North and South, sympathizing with their wounds—meaning, for most of them, amputated limbs—listening to their war stories, and writing letters to their parents, wives, and sweethearts. On August 10, 1863, for example, he wrote to the parents of a soldier from Breesport, New York, about the death of their son. "He is one of the thousands of our unknown American young men in the ranks about whom there is no record or fame, no fuss made about their dying so unknown. . . . Poor dear son, though you were not my son, I felt to love you as a son."

Whitman kept notes of his observations and conversations and several years later turned them into the 62 short essays on the Civil War that appeared in his *Specimen Days* in 1882. Many of the soldiers wrote thank-you letters to him after the war, and at least one letter informed him that the letter writer had named his first child after the famous poet.

Many of his essays were reflections on the idea of war itself, and he wrote about the two days during the war that he would never forget: the "first Bull Run defeat and the day of Abraham Lincoln's death." He wrote that "all battles, and their results, are far more matters of accident than is generally thought. . . . Each side [at Bull Run] supposed it had won, till the last moment. . . . By a fiction, or series of fictions, the national forces at the last moment exploded in a panic and fled from the field." The retreating Federal troops began arriving in Washington early in the morning of July 22, the day after Bull Run. Whitman notes that at the Willard Hotel that evening a Northern colonel gave a speech in which he said he thought the North should capitulate. But luck plays a larger role in war, Whitman suggested, than is generally considered, perhaps especially by those who plan a battle and whose plans do not work. He was not in Washington when the first wounded soldiers arrived, nor did he hear the Northern officer's speech at the Willard Hotel, but his description of the events is as real as if he had been there. His descriptions of battles he only heard about also run true, much like the Civil War battle scenes in Stephen Crane's *The Red Badge of Courage* (1895), though Crane was not even born until six years after the war ended.

And the poet was never so eloquent as when writing about Lincoln. He wrote in *Specimen Days* that if there were nothing else for history to "stamp" Lincoln with, it would be enough just to remember "that he endured" that first battle of Bull Run, calling it "a crucifixion day," yet it "did not conquer him," Whitman said. Lincoln survived and "resolved to lift himself and the Union" out of that terrible and depressive defeat.

Whitman had returned to Washington with George and other wounded soldiers from Fredericksburg by landing at the foot of Sixth Street on what is now called the Washington Channel. He would return to the landing to help unload other boats with soldiers headed for Washington hospitals. In *Specimen Days* he describes meeting the boats after the battle of Chancellorsville (May 2–4, 1863), seeing "pale, helpless soldiers" lying around the wharfs or in the "neighborhood anywhere," on blankets or quilts, "with bloody rags bound round heads, arms, and legs." He said that there were often a thousand men a day brought in to the Sixth Street wharves. He reports seeing a procession of ambulances "passing up Fourteenth Street, on their way, probably, to Columbian, Carver, and Mount Pleasant Hospitals."

Disease was almost as fatal to the soldiers as enemy weapons, killing perhaps two-thirds of the 620,000 soldiers who died in the war. Whitman wrote that he protected himself from infection by "fortifying" himself with good rest, a bath and, apparently, clean clothes every day, and sufficient food to keep himself healthy. And he added that he tried to carry "as cheerful an appearance as possible."

Whitman made notes throughout the war that would aid him with details for his book *Specimen Days* written more than a decade later, but he also wrote articles for newspapers during the war, some of the articles critical of the treatment of wounded soldiers by poorly trained or incompetent medical personnel or simply by the military/medical bureaucracy. He also wrote about the differences between the treatment soldiers got in hospitals built during the early years of the war and the treatment in public buildings turned into hospital wards. The best-trained medical personnel were assigned to the former.

In early fall of 1863 Walt was in correspondence with his brother Jeff about the worsening health of Andrew and about the riots in New York City over Lincoln's announcement of a draft of more Union soldiers. Nearly 50,000 people went to the streets to protest the draft, and more than 100 were killed in the riots that followed. Whitman received leave from his government clerk duties and returned to Brooklyn on November 2, noting on the way the difference in prosperity between the cities of the north and of Washington.

Whitman arrived back in Washington on December 2, only to receive a telegram from Jeff the next day announcing the death of Andrew. Two weeks later Jeff wrote about their brother Jesse's increased emotional instability over the death of Andy, including threats of hurting other members of the family. Through all of the family's troubles, Louisa was apparently the only stabilizing influence.

In spite of constant preparations to stay healthy during his hospital work, Whitman became ill in early summer 1864, complaining in a letter home of a sore throat and a "bad feeling" in his head. He knew that he was finally feeling the effects of his work in the hospitals, the almost daily contact with badly wounded soldiers and often with their impending deaths. The doctors noticed the change in Whitman and suggested that he return to Brooklyn for some rest, which he did on June 22.

Adding to the weight of Whitman's concern for his family was the news in October 1864 that George had been captured and was in a prison somewhere in Virginia. And on December 5, Walt arranged to have Jesse committed to the Kings County Lunatic Asylum. Then the day after Christmas, George's trunk arrived at the Portland Avenue residence still with no word of where he was located. It must have been a chilling moment for Louisa and her family. George was later released from the Virginia prison, however, in a general exchange of prisoners, and he returned to Washington in late February. He had been captured in September 1864 at Poplar Grove Church, Virginia, and was a prisoner in Danville until his release on February 19, 1865.

April was another "quicksand" period for Whitman. He arranged for publication of a book of poems about the war, titled *Drum-Taps*, a book he

Whitman during the Civil War, 1863 *(Library of Congress, Prints and Photographs Division)*

had been working on for two years. But then Generals Lee and Grant signed papers at Appomattox on April 9 that ended the war, and the poet knew he would need to add more poems. When Lincoln was assassinated a few days later, Whitman wanted to delay publication even longer. Lincoln was shot on April 14 (Good Friday) and died the next morning. Whitman observed the mourning in New York and Brooklyn that weekend, perhaps especially on Easter Sunday morning, and then returned to Washington on Monday for the memorial services on Wednesday.

DRUM-TAPS

In spite of all his family and personal health concerns, Whitman had been working during late 1863 and 1864 on his poetry, particularly on the book of war poems. It was published in New York on October 28, 1865, along with the poems known as *Sequel to Drum-Taps* a little later in the year, an important addition, because it included "When Lilacs Last in the Dooryard Bloom'd," the elegy on Lincoln. All of the new poems were then included in the fourth (1867) edition of *Leaves of Grass.*

Drum-Taps (actually titled *Walt Whitman's Drum-Taps*) was not meant by the poet to glamorize the war but to emphasize for readers the emotional beat of the drums that had carried something of a thematic note for Whitman, perhaps not unlike the muffled drumbeats throughout the procession in Washington carrying President Kennedy's body to burial in Arlington Cemetery and which may still echo in the memory of the millions of people who heard it on television in 1963. Drummers were in every parade of soldiers in New York or Washington during the Civil War, and their constant drumbeat became ominous for Whitman, often an auditory sign of a death march for 620,000 killed in the war, North and South.

Whitman's principles for a democratic society had developed early in his life and were expressed in his preface to the first edition of *Leaves of Grass,* as well as in several early poems, but the Civil War gave enormous shape to those ideas and produced some of his greatest poems. One of his most popular poems, "O Captain! My Captain!," however, was *not* one of those. Whitman later spoke to

Horace Traubel about regretting having written the poem. It is certainly the most crassly sentimental of the Lincoln poems—yet, even today, the most anthologized.

The *Drum-Taps* poems did not receive particularly good early reviews. Henry James accused Whitman of cashing in on the war; William Dean Howells thought *Drum-Taps* was better than *Leaves of Grass* but still not "art." In early 1866, however, William O'Connor published his pamphlet *The Good Gray Poet,* which defended Whitman's poetic works. The essay was written in the summer of 1865, soon after Whitman was fired from his clerkship job by James Harlan. O'Connor accused Harlan of an inability to read poetry, but the pamphlet is more importantly an argument on the value of Whitman's poetry in general and of *Drum-Taps* in particular.

O'Connor argues that all great literature may contain material that seems offensive to some people, but that literature is deemed great in part because even those things that seem offensive to some are meant to be uplifting to all, to affirm rather than negate life.

O'Connor's pamphlet may have encouraged other readers to write more favorable reviews. John Burroughs's essay "Walt Whitman and His 'Drum-Taps'" was published in the important *Galaxy* magazine (December 1, 1866) and was a much more serious review, including, for example, an explication of the dramatic structure of "When Lilacs Last in the Dooryard Bloom'd." Burroughs published in May of the next year his *Notes on Walt Whitman, as Poet and Person,* which also contributed to a somewhat revitalized attitude toward the poet.

Whitman's discouragement, even depression, about the war showed up most emphatically in the notes he kept and then used in *Specimen Days,* written in the late 1870s and published in 1882. In an essay titled "The Million Dead, Too, Summed Up," the poet wrote about the Civil War dead:

> The dead in this war—there they lie, strewing
> the fields and woods and valleys and battlefields
> of the South—Virginia, the Peninsula—Malvern

Hill and Fair Oaks—the banks of the Chickahominy—the terraces of Fredericksburg—Antietam bridge—the grisly ravines of Manassas—the bloody promenade of the Wilderness—the varieties of the *strayed* dead (the estimate of the War Department is 25,000 national soldiers killed in battle and never buried at all, 5,000 drowned—15,000 inhumed by strangers, or on the march in haste, in hitherto unfound localities— . . . the crop reaped by the mighty reapers, typhoid, dysentery, inflammations—and blackest and loathesomest of all, the dead and living burial pits, the prison pens of Andersonville, Salisbury, Belle-Isle, etc. (not Dante's pictured hell and all its woes, its degradations, filthy torments, excelled those prisons)—the dead, the dead, the dead—*our* dead—or South or North, ours all (all, all, all, finally dear to me)— . . . somewhere they crawled to die, alone, in bushes, low gullies, or on the sides of hills (there, in secluded spots, their skeletons, bleached bones, tufts of hair, buttons, fragments of clothing, are occasionally found yet)—our young men once so handsome and so joyous, taken from us— . . . the corpses floated down the rivers, and caught and lodged (dozens, scores, floated down the upper Potomac, after the cavalry engagements, the pursuit of Lee, following Gettysburg) . . . the infinite dead (the land entire saturated, perfumed with their impalpable ashes' exhalation in Nature's chemistry distilled, and shall be so forever, in every future grain of wheat and ear of corn, and every flower that grows, and every breath we draw)—not only Northern dead leavening Southern soil—thousands, aye tens of thousands, of Southerners, crumble today in Northern earth. . . . UNKNOWN.

> (In some of the cemeteries nearly *all* the dead are unknown. At Salisbury, N.C., for instance, the known are only 85, while the unknown are 12,027, and 11,700 of these are buried in trenches.)

It is difficult to imagine American families in 2005 accepting such an outrage. Such, however, was the American Civil War.

NEW EDITIONS OF *LEAVES OF GRASS*

The fourth edition of *Leaves of Grass* included all of the poems from the third edition (1860), plus the poems from *Drum-Taps, Sequel to Drum-Taps,* and "Songs Before Parting," pages numbered separately for each of these sections. Whitman had worked hard since publication of *Leaves* in 1860 to revise the poems, change some titles, and edit out a few poems, including three from the "Calamus" cluster that he apparently thought were too sexually explicit.

In England, where Whitman had received generally more favorable reviews for each of his books than in America, English writer and critic William ROSSETTI wrote for the London *Chronicle* (May 6, 1867) of his great admiration for Whitman, that he was a poet of "great originality." And English writer Algernon Charles SWINBURNE wrote for publication in 1868 a book on William BLAKE's poetry that connected Blake with Whitman in such a way as to further enhance the American poet's reputation in England and Europe. A German reviewer would later the same year write that Whitman was nothing less than "mankind and the world." The Rossetti essay was reprinted in America, and it and other favorable criticism from Europe had an influence on American literary reviewers and readers in general.

The Civil War had a lasting impact on Whitman's attitude toward democracy, and the influence began to show in some of his later writings. He continued to defend democracy, but he acknowledged flaws in the system. The friction among politicians over reconstruction after the war discouraged him, though he still believed strongly in the democratic ideals he had been promoting. He wrote an essay titled "Democracy" for *Galaxy* (December 1867) and an 84-page pamphlet titled *Democratic Vistas* (1871), both of which works reconfirmed the poet's love for the democratic system.

Meanwhile, things were going badly for Louisa Whitman in Brooklyn. Walt began getting letters in mid-May (1868) describing a progressively out-of-control family situation. Andrew's wife, Nancy, had given birth to twins, one dead, and, according to reports to Louisa from Nancy's sister-in-law, the older children were on the streets, begging for money. Nancy's brother wanted the three children taken from their mother and placed in an orphanage. Louisa pleaded with Walt to help out by writing to a local judge on behalf of the children. She also wrote to him that Nancy was drinking and doing "everything else thats bad." Louisa was still writing letters to Walt in late June, but there is apparently no evidence that he did anything to help. It is difficult to believe, however, that he did nothing; he had for years been a constant factor in the welfare of the family and especially in helping his mother, whom he always credited as a constant influence on his own life.

Andrew's son, Andy, was run over by a cart and killed while playing in Hudson Avenue on September 1. Walt wrote to his mother that she should not mourn the child's death, since he was no longer in this world of "sin and trouble."

Also in September Whitman renewed a regular correspondence with Peter DOYLE, addressing him as "dearest boy" or "dear comrade" and writing letters as if from father to son. A year later Doyle was bothered by skin eruptions on his face, which he thought were a prelude to a serious illness, perhaps suggesting syphilis. He apparently hinted to Whitman the possibility of suicide, because Walt wrote back, criticizing him for thinking such thoughts and assuring him of help if he needed it.

Whitman was working on the next edition of *Leaves of Grass,* writing notices for newspapers in May 1869 and going home to Brooklyn in August to see his poems through the press. He suffered again from a sick spell, which might have been a minor stroke, similar to the illness he had gone through before.

The fifth edition of *Leaves of Grass* was published in 1871, the second issue of which included "Passage to India," a poem important for its contribution of exploration and discovery as a metaphor for the spiritual journey of the soul to union with God.

ILLNESSES AND STROKES

Whitman had been ill off and on for several years, perhaps mainly because of worry about his mother and her hardships in taking care of two members of a troubled family. But he was also worried about the lack of public response to his newest editions of *Leaves of Grass*.

These and other personal concerns were the probable causes of his first serious stroke during the night of January 22, 1873, a year that would turn out to be the worst of his life. He was well cared for by friends—particularly John and Ursula Burroughs, Ellen O'Connor, Charles ELDRIDGE, and Peter Doyle—who were in almost constant attendance on him at his rooming house at 535 Fifteenth Street in Washington. Walt's left leg was all but paralyzed, however, making it difficult to negotiate the stairs to his fourth-floor room.

On February 21 he wrote a letter to Abby Price, a good friend of Walt's mother from their earliest days in Brooklyn. He describes the stroke:

> My paralysis still leaves me extremely feeble— & with great distress in the head—but I shall certainly recover—mind just as clear as ever—I have lost my dear, dear sister [in-law] Martha, in St. Louis—I appreciate your kind letter Abby dear, and it is possible when I get better it may be just the thing for me to come on a few days—but at present I can hardly move ten steps with feeling sick—
>
> I am sitting here now in the rocking chair in my room writing this—most of the time alone which suits me best—it is paralysis of left side— Love to all. . . . Walt

It was three weeks before he managed to get out of the house, and he did not return to work at the solicitor's office until April 1. Even then, he still had dizzy spells and complained of headaches. And in spite of electric shock treatments by his regular doctor, William B. Drinkard, his leg was still of little use.

Whitman went to Camden, New Jersey, on May 20, where his seriously ill mother had moved to be with George and his wife, Louisa. His mother died on May 23, and Walt was devastated by "the great dark cloud of my life."

He was so depressed by her death and his own ailments that he made out a will and wrote to Peter Doyle that he didn't think he had long to live. John Burroughs was concerned enough to write to Charles Eldridge that he doubted "whether Walt is

going to recover. . . . He is a mere physical wreck to what he was. . . . It is a terrible misfortune, one of the saddest spectacles I have ever seen."

Yet he would live another 19 years.

He worked part-time at his clerk's job in Washington, but then decided to move in with George and Louisa at 322 Stevens Street, Camden. They moved to 431 Stevens Street in September, and Walt took a room on the third floor. Though he kept his room in Washington for a time, he would not be a resident there again. His job as clerk in the Treasury Department was terminated the next July.

CAMDEN, NEW JERSEY

Whitman was busy writing articles, poems, and letters to friends during 1874, his first full year in Camden. He wrote to Ellen O'Connor that he was having severe chest pains, which an autopsy at his death 18 years later proved to be an abscess that had spread eventually to his lungs.

He bought a piece of land for $450 at 460 Royden Street in July 1874, but the house he hoped eventually to build there was not built. On November 17 he attended the dedication of the Edgar Allan Poe memorial and the reburial service in the Westminster Churchyard in Baltimore; apparently, he was the only literary person to attend the ceremony.

George and Louisa were upset by all of Walt's visitors during the time he was with them. They—along with all other family members except Jeff—didn't understand *Leaves of Grass* and apparently understood his friends even less. Complicating the general friction was the death of George and Louisa's child, Walter, in 1876 and another child stillborn the following year. The earliest visitors to Camden included John Burroughs, Peter Doyle, and Walt and George's brother Jeff, on a visit from St. Louis. One of the most interesting visitors for Whitman but certainly a mystery for George and Louisa was Oscar WILDE, who stayed at the house and drank elderberry wine and hot toddies. He would later write to Walt that "there is no one in this great wide world of America whom I love and honor so much."

During the summer of 1875 Whitman worked to get two new books into print at the offices of the *Camden New Republic*. The books were *Two Rivulets*

Whitman in his 328 Mickle Street home in Camden, New Jersey, 1887 *(Library of Congress, Prints and Photographs Division)*

and *Memoranda During the War.* The latter was 68 pages of notebook and diary material from the war that would be reprinted in *Specimen Days* (1882). *Two Rivulets* would become the companion volume for the "Centennial Edition" of *Leaves of Grass,* to be published in 1876 and helping to celebrate the 100th anniversary of the birth of America. The first volume was titled *Leaves of Grass* and was an unchanged reprinting of the 1871 (fifth) edition; *Two Rivulets* included 14 new poems and seven essays.

The end of 1875 and January of 1876 produced a strange controversy indicating a certain paranoia on Whitman's part. He wrote a letter saying that

no American publisher would publish his work and that money from the sale of his books was being embezzled. Then he wrote an unsigned, third-person article for Camden's *West Jersey Press* (January 26, 1876), titled "Walt Whitman's Actual American Position," in which he states that Whitman was being neglected in his own country and that he was publishing the 1876 edition of *Leaves of Grass* in order "to keep the wolf from the door."

Walt then sent copies of the article to friends in England, which generated not only reprintings of the letter in various British publications but a large pre-sale subscription for the new edition of *Leaves.* Whitman wrote to William Rossetti trying to contain the poverty rumor, saying that he is "not" after all "in want" and that he hopes to continue living off his writing.

TIMBER CREEK

The year 1876 is also significant for two other Whitman events: his visits to the home of George and Susan Stafford and their five children above Timber Creek in southern New Jersey and the visit of Anne GILCHRIST, the English woman who had loved Whitman from across the Atlantic Ocean and wanted to better know the man. She and her three children rented a row house at 1629 North 22nd Street in Philadelphia.

Walt spent the better part of both 1876 and 1877 either at Timber Creek or with Mrs. Gilchrist in Philadelphia, who set aside a bedroom for him.

Timber Creek serves now as the border between Camden and Gloucester Counties and runs more or less parallel to the Atlantic City Expressway. It is still, 130 years after Whitman admired it, a tidal stream running through a beautiful, mostly wooded area, that empties into the Delaware River at Westville, about three miles south of Camden. The Stafford house was 12 or 13 miles upstream from Westville and about 400 yards above the creek. Walt made notes while he was at the Stafford farmhouse that would later become parts of several essays on Nature in *Specimen Days* (1882):

> After you have exhausted what there is in business, politics, conviviality, love, and so on—have found that none of these finally satisfy, or permanently wear—what remains? Nature remains: to bring out from their torpid recesses the affinities of a man or woman with the open air, the trees, fields, the changes of seasons—the sun by day and the stars of heaven by night.

After the illnesses of 1874 and 1875 and the awkward sharing of a house in Camden with his brother George and his wife, the two years during which he spent "half the time" along Timber Creek were just what Whitman needed to recover his physical and mental energies. He wrote about those "restoration hours" as if they were the beginning of a new life. He described the lane from the farmhouse down to the creek as his new "hobby, . . . a real farm lane fenced by old chestnut rails gray-green with dabs of moss and lichen, copious weeds and briers growing in spots athwart the heaps of stray-picked stones at the fence bases." And he wrote about the "spring under the willows—musical as soft-clinking glasses—pouring a sizable stream, thick as my neck, pure and clear . . . gurgling, gurgling ceaselessly—meaning, saying something . . . (if I could only translate it). . . ."

One of the Staffords' sons, Harry STAFFORD, 18 years old at the time, replaced Peter Doyle in Whitman's esteem during those years. Pete was working as a brakeman for the Baltimore and Potomac Railroad out of Washington, and although he still wrote occasional and loving letters to Walt, he was probably working longer hours than he had as a streetcar conductor. In any case, that relationship weakened for a time, and Harry Stafford and Walt became close friends. Harry was working for the print shop in Camden that was setting type for Whitman's *Two Rivulets,* so the two men saw each other often during that time. Walt introduced Harry to friends as "my son" or "my nephew," and Whitman told Burroughs that they shared a room and bed.

He later told Harry how much he regarded the Timber Creek experiences as a life-saving period of time for himself and that Harry was "the central figure of . . . all."

ANNE GILCHRIST

Anne Gilchrist was, next to his mother, the most loving woman in Whitman's life. She had been introduced to his poetry in England in June 1869 and fell in love with what she read and, apparently, with the poet himself. "I can read no other book," she wrote to her friend William Rossetti, who had lent her his copy of a selection of Whitman's poems; "it holds me entirely spellbound, and I go through it again and again with deepening delight and wonder."

Mrs. Gilchrist's husband had died in 1861, and when, 15 years later, her mother was dead and her oldest son had developed a career, she felt free to leave England and join Whitman in America. She wrote to him in August 1876 to tell him that she and three of her children would sail for Philadelphia on August 30. She wasn't vague about her purpose:

I passionately believe there are years in store for us, years of tranquil, tender happiness—me making your outward life serene & sweet—you making my inward life so rich—me learning, growing, loving—we shedding benign influences round us out of our happiness and fulfilled life—hold on but a little longer for me, my Walt—I am straining every nerve to hasten the day. I have enough for us all (with the simple unpretending ways we both love best).

The letter must have frightened Whitman, and he tried to discourage her from making the trip, but she had been reading his poetry and thinking about such a trip long enough to have made up her mind.

She and her children—Beatrice ("Bee"), 22; Herbert, 19; and Grace 17—were in the United States not quite three years, living the first two years in Philadelphia. Whitman visited the Gilchrists often from his residence across the river in Camden and from Timber Creek. Mrs. Gilchrist kept a spare bedroom for him in the rented house, which he used most of the fall of 1877. She was 49 at the time, he 58, and they established a special but apparently platonic relationship.

Grace, whom Whitman called "Giddy," wrote an article for the English periodical *Temple Bar* (February 1898) describing their evenings after supper, when they would take chairs out onto the sidewalk in front of the house and talk about literature.

FINAL EDITION OF *LEAVES*

The 1881–82 edition of *Leaves of Grass* proved to be the last one with any significant or "final" changes. Whitman added five more "cluster" titles to this sixth edition, making 12 clusters altogether, but the only additions after that would be in what he called annexes, placed at the back of any new printings of *Leaves*. He published *Specimen Days* in 1882 and *November Boughs* in 1888, the latter poems to be added to the "Death-bed" printing (1892) as "Sands at Seventy," the first annex.

November Boughs included a preface, "A Backward Glance O'er Travel'd Roads," which is both a reminiscence and a summary of Whitman's life in poetry. He asked that it be included at the end of all subsequent editions of *Leaves of Grass*. He obviously enjoyed looking back over his life, especially the poetry writing and revising part of it: "How the soul loves to float amid such reminiscences!"

The 1892 printing was virtually unchanged from the sixth (1881) edition, except for the addition of the two annexes. See the entries on editions in Part II.

SONGS OF PARTING

Whitman's health became progressively worse during the last three and a half years of his life. There were friends at his side almost constantly, however, especially Horace Traubel, who helped the poet get into print his last works, including *November Boughs, Good-Bye My Fancy,* and the 1892 printing of *Leaves of Grass.* Traubel made notes of conversations with Whitman that became a nine-volume biography, titled *With Walt Whitman in Camden,* a valuable transcription of almost daily conversations, beginning on March 28, 1888, almost exactly four years before Whitman's death.

Death was a major theme in Whitman's poetry almost from the beginning, and he had been thinking about his own death from his first serious illnesses in the early 1870s. *Songs of Parting,* the final cluster of poems in *Leaves of Grass,* contained 17 poems, eight of which had been published first in the 1860s, all of them concerned with the poet's own death and his "parting" from the poetry and from readers. In the cluster's opening poem, for example, written for the 1860 *Leaves,* he writes: "Perhaps soon some day or night while I am singing my voice will suddenly cease." The final poem in the cluster (and in *Leaves of Grass*), "So Long!," provides a vision of the poet's death and his mystical union with readers.

Whitman died at his home at 328 Mickle Street during the early evening of Saturday, March 26, 1892. He was buried at Harleigh Cemetery in a small mausoleum, using a design of William Blake, which Whitman had picked out himself. Several members of his family are buried there as well, including his mother and father.

The funeral was held on March 30, with several thousand people walking slowly past the coffin at the Mickle Street house and thousands following the procession to Harleigh Cemetery, about two

Whitman's tomb at the Harleigh Cemetery in Camden, New Jersey. The funeral was held on March 30, 1892.
(Library of Congress, Prints and Photographs Division)

miles away. A large tent was set up for the services, and, though there was no minister present, there were five speakers: Thomas B. HARNED, Robert G. INGERSOLL, Richard Maurice Bucke, Francis Howard Williams, and Daniel G. BRINTON. There were several short readings, including from "Out of the Cradle Endlessly Rocking," from Confucius and Plato, and from the Bible and the Koran.

Williams, a Philadelphia friend of Walt's and an amateur poet, gave the closing oration, stating in part,

He has lived, he has died, and death is less terrible than it was before. Thousands and millions will walk down into the "dark valley of the shadow" holding Walt Whitman by the hand. Long after we are dead the brave words he has spoken will sound like trumpets to the dying.

The thought is still valid more than 100 years later.

PART II

Works A–Z

"Aboard at a Ship's Helm" (1867)

First published as "Leaves of Grass, No. 3" in the fourth edition of *Leaves of Grass* (1867), then under its present title and in the *Sea-Shore Memories* cluster (1871–72); it was the fifth of 11 poems in the "Sea-Drift" cluster for the sixth edition (1881).

"A young steersman steering with care" hears a "warning bell" on the seacoast ahead and manages to turn the ship away from the danger. The most important thing saved, however, is not the ship itself but the "ship aboard the ship . . . the immortal ship"—the "soul," always traveling to distant lands: "But O the ship, the immortal ship! O ship aboard the ship! / Ship of the body, ship of the soul, voyaging, voyaging, voyaging."

The soul transcends the body in a number of Whitman's poems, but it is also considered equal with the body in others. See, for perhaps the best example, "Crossing Brooklyn Ferry."

"Abraham Lincoln, Born Feb. 12, 1809" (1888)

First published in the *New York Herald* (February 12, 1888), then in *November Boughs* (1888); it was the 17th of 65 poems in the "First Annex: Sands at Seventy" cluster for the "Death-bed" printing of *Leaves of Grass* (1892).

This couplet presents "a pulse of thought" in "memory of Him" on what would have been his 79th birthday.

"Adieu to a Soldier" (1871)

First appeared in a group of poems titled "Marches Now the War is Over" in the fifth edition of *Leaves of Grass* (1871); it was the 41st of 43 poems in the "Drum-Taps" cluster for the sixth edition (1881).

This poem compares what the soldier of the title has gone through with what the poet himself has gone through in writing poems about the war. The first stanza tells of the soldier's suffering: "rude campaigning," "the hot contention of opposing fronts," "Red battles with their slaughter," etc. The second stanza bids adieu to the "dear comrade, / Your mission is fulfill'd—but I, more warlike . . .

> Through untried roads with ambushes
>   opponents lined,
> Through many a sharp defeat and many a
>   crisis, often baffled,
> Here marching, ever marching on, a war fight
>   out—aye here,
> To fiercer, weightier battles give expression.

The poet is concerned, now that the war is over, with his own "weightier battles" of writing poetry. The soldier has no further obligation to his country, but Whitman believes that the poet must continue to "give expression" to battles yet to be fought, battles against forgetting too soon the horrors of the war.

"After an Interval" (1876)

First published in the *New York Tribune* (February 19, 1876); it then appeared in the fifth edition of *Leaves of Grass* (1876), but it was cut and did not appear again.

"After the Argument" (1891)

Cut from *Leaves of Grass* after appearing in *Good-Bye My Fancy* (1891).

"After the Dazzle of Day" (1888)

First published in the *New York Herald* (February 3, 1888), then in *November Boughs* (1888); it was the 16th of 65 poems in the "First Annex: Sands at Seventy" cluster for the "Death-bed" printing of *Leaves of Grass* (1892).

Just as the stars at night make the poet feel at ease after the "dazzle of day," so does "the symphony true" make him feel after the "clangor of organ majestic, or chorus, or perfect band."

"After the Sea-Ship" (1874)

First published as "In the Wake Following" in the *New York Daily Graphic* as part of "A Christmas Garland in Prose and Verse" (December 25, 1874); it received its present title in the fifth edition of *Leaves of Grass* (1876), later it was the last of 11 poems in the "Sea-Drift" cluster for the sixth edition (1881).

This is the second of two poems at the end of the "Sea-Drift" cluster, which describes objectively the sea, this one describing the wake following a "sea-ship. . . . / A motley procession with many a fleck of foam and many fragments, / Following the stately and rapid ship, in the wake following." See also "Patroling Barnegat."

"After the Supper and Talk" (1887)

First published in *Lippincott's Magazine* (November 1887); then in *November Boughs* (1888); and it was the last of 65 poems in the "First Annex: Sands at Seventy" cluster for the "Death-bed" printing of *Leaves of Grass* (1892).

This is one of Whitman's songs of departure, placed at the end of the "Sands at Seventy" cluster but also representing what he thinks may be his last poem of all. Just as a friend is reluctant to say Good-bye "after the supper and talk—after the day is done," so is Whitman "loth to depart! / Garrulous to the very last." He has some more talking and writing to do, but when he finished writing the poems for *November Boughs* he wasn't sure that this poem wouldn't be his last.

"Ages and Ages Returning at Intervals" (1860)

First appeared untitled as the 12th poem in the "Enfans d'Adam" cluster for the third edition of *Leaves of Grass* (1860); it received its present title and became the eighth of 16 poems in the "Children of Adam" cluster for the fourth (1867) and subsequent editions and printings.

The Adam of the Garden of Eden is, for the poet, "immortal": "Ages and ages returning at intervals, / Undestroy'd, wandering immortal." And sexual: "Lusty, phallic, with the potent original loins, perfectly sweet." And Adam has been reborn in America.

The poet reminds the reader that he himself is the "chanter of Adamic songs" for "the new garden the West." He sings the song of America and of its growing significance for the mid-19th century world. And he turns the sex act into a time of purification, a metaphor for a cleansing in the new garden from the stains of the Old World. "Bathing myself," he says, "bathing my songs in Sex."

For Whitman, here as in other Children of Adam poems, it is the suppression of sexual intercourse that is the sin, not the act itself. The act becomes a rebirth into a life free of sin.

"Ah Poverties, Wincings, and Sulky Retreats" (1865)

First appeared in the *Sequel to Drum-Taps* volume (1865); it was reprinted in the fourth edition of *Leaves of Grass* (1867), and it was the 10th of 22 poems in the "From Noon to Starry Night" cluster for the sixth edition (1881).

The poem seems to contradict in its pessimism the great optimism for the universal "I" in the immediately preceding poem in the cluster, "Excelsior." "Ah Poverties" is about the various "foes" that have "overcome" the speaker of the poem: "You degradations, you tussle with passions and appetites, / You smarts from dissatisfied friendships, (ah wounds the sharpest of all!)."

Yet at the end he feels that his "real self has yet to come forth, / It shall yet march forth o'ermastering, till all lies beneath me, / It shall yet stand up the soldier of ultimate victory." The poem was written near the end of the CIVIL WAR and so may reflect the depression Whitman felt during the war, but it shows that in the end one's "real self" must have hope for the future, "the soldier of ultimate victory."

"All is Truth" (1860)

First appeared as "Leaves of Grass, No. 18" in the third edition of *Leaves of Grass* (1860); then as "Leaves of Grass, No. 1" (1867); it received its present title in the fifth edition (1871); and it was the seventh of 22 poems in the "From Noon to Starry Night" cluster for the sixth edition (1881).

Truth and lies have an equality in this poem: ". . . there is no lie or form of lie, and can be none, but grows as inevitably upon itself as the truth does

Walt Whitman, photographed by Matthew Brady
(Library of Congress, Prints and Photographs Division)

upon itself." We are all capable of treating lies and truth the same, Whitman suggests, thus the poet's conclusion: "And henceforth I will go celebrate any thing I see or am, / And sing and laugh and deny nothing." Lies and truth are equals, as are good and evil; this is one of Whitman's poetic themes.

"Ambition" (1842)

First published in BROTHER JONATHAN (January 29, 1842); this is an "early poem" *not* later published in *Leaves of Grass*. It is most accessible now in Francis Murphy (editor), *Walt Whitman: The Complete Poems* (Penguin Books, 1996).

"America" (1888)

First published in the *NEW YORK HERALD* (February 11, 1888), then in *November Boughs* (1888); it was subsequently the 13th of 65 poems in the "First Annex: Sands at Seventy" cluster for the "Deathbed" printing of *Leaves of Grass* (1892).

Whitman was 69 years old when he wrote this poem, a six-line song of praise for America, "centre of equal daughters, equal sons. . . . A grand, sane, towering, seated Mother, / Chair'd in the adamant of Time." It is one of the shortest but most precisely descriptive statements in *Leaves of Grass* showing Whitman's love of America, as alive in his last years as in his more productive middle years.

American Primer, An (1904)

Published as a separate work in November 1904 by Small, Maynard & Company in Boston. Whitman's friend and one of his executors, Horace TRAUBEL, edited the manuscript and included "some facsimiles of the original manuscript."

Whitman was interested in language, and this essay is about the importance of what he refers to as "spiritual language." American English, which is made up of words from dozens of other languages, will one day be spoken by a "hundred millions of people. . . . The Americans are going to be the most fluent and melodious voiced people in the world—and the most perfect users of words." Words make up the "character" of individuals, Whitman says, implying that Americans will teach character to the rest of the world.

Traubel explains in his introduction to the booklet that *An American Primer* is made up of notes Whitman wrote to himself during the 1850s and that he "never intended them for publication. He should not be criticized, as he has been by certain American editors, for an act for which he is in no way responsible." Traubel has edited the notes into a coherent whole. It is a prose work that explains, in part, what Whitman attempted to do in his poetry. The difference between the two, however, is that in the essay he *tells* us about the importance of language; in the poetry he *shows* us.

"Among the Multitude"
(1860)

Titled "Calamus No. 41" in the third edition of *Leaves of Grass* (1860); it received its present title (1867); it was the 36th of 39 poems in the "Calamus" cluster for the sixth edition (1881).

In a "multitude" of people, the poet notices one person "among the men and women," picking him out and making "secret and divine signs" to him, letting him know he is like him in his desire for love. "That one knows me," he says.

> Ah lover and perfect equal,
> I meant that you should discover me so by faint
>   indirections,
> And I when I meet you mean to discover you
>   by the like in you.

Men and women who understand love in the way the poet does, are easily identified. See, for an example of people who do not get the secret signs, "O You Whom I Often and Silently Come," the next poem following this one in the "Calamus"

cluster. The "secret signs" may also be code words or signs understood between homosexuals.

"And Yet Not You Alone"
(1885)

First published with seven other poems under the heading "Fancies at Navesink" in *Nineteenth Century* magazine (August 1885); then in *November Boughs* (1888); and, finally, with the "Fancies at Navesink" group as an insert in the "First Annex: Sands at Seventy" cluster for the "Death-bed" printing of *Leaves of Grass* (1892).

The "twilight and burying ebb" tide is used in this poem as a metaphor for the despair caused by "failures, aspirations, . . . / Weaving from you, from Sleep, Night, Death itself, / The rhythmus of Birth eternal." The sea's nighttime ebb tide reminds the poet of the great rhythm of life, from birth to death and return to the sea.

"Angel of Tears, The"   (1842)

Short story, first published in the *United States Magazine and Democratic Review* (September 1842; see *Democratic Review, The*). The tale is most accessible now in *Walt Whitman: The Early Poems and the Fiction,* edited by Thomas L. Brasher (New York University Press, 1963).

The story's opening paragraph defines the "Angel of Tears": "High, high in space floated the angel Alza. Of the spirits who minister in heaven he is not the chief; neither is he employed in deeds of great import, or in the destinies of worlds and generations. Yet if it were possible for envy to enter among the Creatures Beautiful, many would have pined for the station of Alza. There are a million million invisible eyes which keep constant watch over the earth—each Child of Light having his separate duty. Alza is one of the Angels of Tears."

In the story, a man has killed his brother, and "the stamp of the guilt of Cain" is on him as he waits in prison for execution. The "Angel of Tears," appears to the man and reassures him that in the last day (at the end of the world), his sigh of repentance will overcome "the weight of the sum of [his] evil." God will forgive the sin of killing his brother. The last sentence reads: "Beautiful, to the Ear of God, is the sigh which ushers repentance!"

CHARACTER

Alza   "The Angel of Tears" in the short story of that title. Alza is a name made up by Whitman for the sake of this tale. The story's opening defines the angel as one who is "employed in deeds of great import" that involve the "destinies of worlds and generations." He is one of the angels who watches over the people of the earth, a "Child of Light," one of the "Angels of Tears." He informs a man who has killed his own brother and awaits execution that at the end of the world, God will forgive him.

"Apostroph" (1860)

Cut from *Leaves of Grass* after first appearing under its present title and as the introductory poem to the "Chants Democratic" cluster in the third edition (1860); the last 19 lines were retained and titled "Leaves of Grass, No. 1" (1867), and the poem was excluded thereafter.

The 65-line poem is an apostrophe, an evocation, to various people and things that are a part of Whitman's philosophic mind, telling each to what extent he depends on them for sustenance.

"Apparitions" (1891)

First published as the sixth of 31 poems in *Good-Bye My Fancy* (1891); it was then in "Second

Annex: Good-Bye My Fancy" for the "Death-bed" printing of *Leaves of Grass* (1892).

It is not clear whether the poet is reading his own "pages" or someone else's, but readers may infer that the "vague mist" creates the feeling that what were once "solid things" have become mere "apparitions."

There is evidence that these three lines were intended as the third stanza for another poem entitled "L. of G's Purport," in which case Whitman might have been thinking of his own earlier poems and wondering whether the meanings had changed since he first wrote them.

"Are You the New Person Drawn Toward Me?" (1860)

Titled "Calamus No. 12" in the third edition of *Leaves of Grass* (1860); it received its present title (1867); it was the 11th poem in the "Calamus" cluster for the sixth edition (1881).

Walt Whitman, photographed by Thomas Eakins or Samuel Murray, 1891 *(Library of Congress, Prints and Photographs Division)*

Whitman made a note to himself after publication of the 1860 edition to delete this poem from the next edition, but, instead, he changed some wording and cut the original ending. He apparently felt that the poem might be thought too obscene. The original opening line, for example, read, "Are you the new person drawn toward me, and asking something significant from me?" The last half of the line was cut, as was the ending: "O the next step may precipitate you! / O let some past deceived one hiss in your ears, how many have prest on the same as you are pressing now, / How many have fondly supposed what you are supposing now—only to be disappointed."

The poet seems to speak directly to the reader in this poem: "Are you the new person drawn toward me?" He sends a "warning": "I am surely far different from what you suppose." The warning is not directed merely to readers in his own time but to future readers as well, indicating, as in so many other poems, Whitman's placement of love as his key democratic principle. He offers a catalog of reasons readers might have for loving him, but the last line must certainly be intended to contradict reality: "Have you no thought O dreamer that it may be all maya, illusion?"

Maya is a Sanskrit word meaning "illusion." In Hindu philosophy, according to the *Oxford English Dictionary, maya* is used to teach "that only by looking on the world and the lust thereof as 'maya,' as illusion, vanity, deceptive appearance, can we get near to God."

Placed as it is in the "Calamus" cluster, the love Whitman speaks of must be between two men. Yet any love can be deceptive, the poet seems to be suggesting, because it can distract anyone from his or her nearness to God. If this seems contradictory to other poetic statements in *Leaves of Grass*, particularly in the "Children of Adam" and "Calamus" clusters, all of which poems are directed toward "lovers," it is important to remember that Whitman had sent another, emphatic "warning" in "Song of Myself":

> Do I contradict myself?
> Very well then I contradict myself,
> (I am large, I contain multitudes.)

"Army Corps on the March, An" (1865)

First appeared under the title "An Army on the March" in the *Sequel* to the *Drum-Taps* volume (1865) and in the fourth edition of *Leaves of Grass* (1867); it received its present title (1871); then it was the 12th of 43 poems in the "Drum-Taps" cluster for the sixth edition (1881).

Unlike several other descriptive poems in the "Drum-Taps" cluster which depict soldiers perhaps between battles but not in immediate danger, "An Army Corps on the March" describes "the sound of a single shot snapping like a whip" and the brigades moving forward toward the battle. The last four lines seem to suggest a peaceful enough scene of the army's advance, yet the soldiers are being shot at nevertheless, an ironic situation perhaps familiar to soldiers in any war.

But for a different kind of battle irony, see "Cavalry Crossing a Ford," "Bivouac on a Mountain Side," "By the Bivouac's Fitful Flame," "A Sight in Camp in the Daybreak Gray and Dim," "As Toilsome I Wandered Virginia's Woods," "I Saw Old General at Bay," and "Look Down Fair Moon."

"Arrow-Tip"

See "Half-Breed: A Tale of the Western Frontier, The."

"Artilleryman's Vision, The" (1865)

First entitled "The Veteran's Vision" in the *Drum-Taps* volume (1865), it then appeared under its present title in the fifth edition of *Leaves of Grass* (1871); it was the 27th of 43 poems in the "Drum-Taps" cluster for the sixth edition (1881).

The poem is in 25 lines but only two sentences, producing perhaps an early version of what William James would, a few years later, refer to as stream-of-consciousness.

The war is over, but the artilleryman, now back at home sleeping with his wife and listening to the breathing of his child, cannot sleep for his vision of battle experiences: "I hear the sounds of the different missiles, the short t-h-t! t-h-t! of the rifle-balls, / I see the shells exploding leaving small white clouds, I hear the great shells shrieking as they pass."

This soldier's waking nightmare defines the postwar trauma of a CIVIL WAR veteran—or of any soldier who, returned from war, cannot get the battles out of his mind.

"As Adam Early in the Morning" (1860)

First appearing untitled as the 15th poem in the "Enfans d'Adam" cluster for the third edition of *Leaves of Grass* (1860), it was the 16th and final poem in the "Children of Adam" cluster for the sixth edition (1881).

This five-line poem completes the circle of "Children of Adam" poems by returning to the Garden of Eden and to the first poem in the group, "To the Garden The World."

"As Adam Early in the Morning" urges once again in *Leaves of Grass* the idea of love, particularly sensual love, as a life force for good. He wants Adam to see him, "hear [his] voice," and, above all, he says to Adam: "Touch me, touch the palm of your hand to my body as I pass, / Be not afraid of my body."

The Children of Adam poems are about the love of men and women for each other, but this last line acts as a sort a transition into the next cluster of poems, the Calamus poems, which are about the love of men for other men.

As a Strong Bird on Pinions Free (1872)

A pamphlet of seven poems printed separately in 1872 and bound into the back of the *Two Rivulets*

volume for the third printing of the fifth edition of *Leaves of Grass* (1876). See *Preface 1872—As a Strong Bird on Pinions Free.*

"As at Thy Portals Also Death" (1881)

First published as the sixth of 17 poems in the "Songs of Parting" cluster for the sixth edition of *Leaves of Grass* (1881), it remained unchanged throughout its publication history.

The poem is Whitman's elegy to his mother, Louisa Van Velsor WHITMAN, who died May 23, 1873, at age 77: "To her, buried and gone, yet buried not, gone not from me." His poem is her "tombstone." She had the most influence on Whitman of any of his family members. He later referred to her death as the "great tragedy" of his life.

"As Consequent, Etc." (1881)

This poem was first published as the opening work in the "Autumn Rivulets" cluster for the sixth edition of *Leaves of Grass* (1881).

Just as all the "wayward rivulets," brooks, "subterranean sea-rills," and major rivers of America help form the idea of America, so do its people:

> In you whoe'er you are my book perusing,
> In I myself, in all the world, these currents
>   flowing,
> All, all toward the mystic ocean tending.

Whitman then deepens the metaphor: "Or from the sea of Time, . . . / A windrow-drift of weeds and shells." What is "As Consequent, Etc." is, the poet seems to be suggesting, that America is made up of people representing such diversity, both geographically and ethnically, that it can define for the world the nature of democracy. It does so by connecting all the "wayward rivulets" and major rivers into one ocean of consequent people.

This is the only poem in the "Autumn Rivulets" cluster that carries the rivulet metaphor throughout the poem.

"Ashes of Soldiers" (1865)

First published as "Hymn of Dead Soldiers" for the *Drum-Taps* volume (1865), it became the title poem for a cluster in the fifth edition of *Leaves of Grass* (1871); and it was the third of 17 poems in the "Songs of Parting" cluster for the sixth edition (1881).

This poem is a "chant," calling on the "Ashes of soldiers South or North," the "Phantoms of countless lost" in the CIVIL WAR to become his "companions": "Follow me ever—desert me not while I live."

Whitman wants to let the dead soldiers know that he has not forgotten them, that he loves them still: "Dearest comrades, all is over and long gone, / But love is not over—and what love, O comrades. . . ."

Whitman, who was no doubt emotionally touched by the Civil War more than by any other single event in his life, remained loyal to the memory of the Civil War dead to the end of his life.

"As I Ebb'd with the Ocean of Life" (1860)

First published under the title "Bardic Symbols" in the *ATLANTIC MONTHLY* magazine (April 1860), it was then titled "Leaves of Grass, No. 1" in the third edition of *Leaves of Grass* (1860), and "Elemental Drifts" (1867); then it appeared in a cluster of poems titled "Sea-Shore Memories" in the fifth edition of *Leaves of Grass* (1871); and it received its present title and was the second of 11 poems in the "Sea-Drift" cluster for the sixth edition (1881). It is written in four sections and 71 lines.

Whitman does not often in his poetry confess to moments of despair, but he seems to do so in this poem. He was 40 years old when he wrote the poem in 1859, and the immediate past four years had not been particularly happy or successful. The 795 copies of the first edition of *Leaves of Grass* (1855), had not sold well; and the second edition (1856), which included an additional 20 poems, had been an even greater disappointment. His father had died on July 11, 1855, a week after the first edition had gone on sale; although he had depended for moral support more from his mother, he nevertheless missed his father.

So perhaps it is not surprising that even the generally optimistic Walt Whitman would feel himself sometimes at ebb tide in "the ocean of life." He describes in Section 1 some of the tide's leavings: "Scum, scales from shining rocks, leaves of salt-lettuce," and so on.

In Section 2 the poet shows his depression over what he sees as personal failures, perhaps especially the lack of public enthusiasm for his poems.

> As I wend to the shores I know not, . . .
> I too but signify at the utmost a little wash'd-up
>   drift,
> A few sands and dead leaves to gather,
> Gather, and merge myself as part of the sands
>   and drift.

The "dead leaves" may be a weak reference to his own poems, but total discouragement certainly seems to enter the poet's thinking here, perhaps the result of so much tumult in his own life, though he keeps the images directed at himself and his work:

> I perceive I have not really understood any
>   thing, not a single object, and that no man
>   ever can,
> Nature here in sight of the sea taking advantage
>   of me to dart upon me and sting me,
> Because I have dared to open my mouth to sing
>   at all. . . .

This is a particularly interesting stanza in an especially pessimistic poem, coming as it does in the "Sea-Drift" cluster, placed immediately after "Out of the Cradle Endlessly Rocking," perhaps the most optimistic and upbeat poem in *Leaves of Grass*. The "old crone rocking the cradle" in the earlier poem becomes the "fierce old mother," in this poem, who "endlessly cries for her castaways," one of whom is the poet himself.

Section 3 offers the poet's feeling that he is a failure, as was his father. "I too am but a trail of drift and debris," he says; "I too leave little wrecks upon you, you fish-shaped island." The island is "Paumanok" (LONG ISLAND), where Whitman was born and where his father had difficulty keeping a job.

In the final stanzas of the poem (Section 4), he begins to regain a bit of hope. He realizes that if he is going to use the ocean as metaphor, as he does often in *Leaves of Grass*, he must acknowledge that there is both ebb and flow: "Ebb, ocean of life, (the flow will return,) / Cease not your moaning you fierce old mother, . . ." His "phantom" soul is "looking down" and perhaps criticizing him for his earlier, negative thoughts: "I gather for myself and for this phantom looking down where we lead, and following me and mine"; that is, the poetry he has written. He concludes, even so, with an image of drowning and an awareness of the contradictions in these thoughts.

> Me and mine, loose windrows [the dry leaves swept together], little corpses, . . .
> (See, from my dead lips the ooze exuding at last, . . .
> Buoy'd hither from many moods, one contradicting another,
> From the storm, the long calm, the darkness, the swell, . . .
> We, capricious, brought hither we know not whence, spread out before you,
> You up there walking or sitting,
> Whoever you are, we too lie in drifts at your feet.

The poet envisions himself and his poems as "loose windrows," dry leaves swept together like "little corpses," tossed up by the ocean along the shore and his own drowned body part of the drift. Readers may well tie the notion of ebb and flood tides into Whitman's *Leaves of Grass* theme of opposites being essential to equality in a democracy: men and women, black and white, good and evil, ebb tide and flood tide.

"As if a Phantom Caress'd Me" (1860)

This first appeared as the final section of the poem "Debris" in the third edition of *Leaves of Grass* (1860); it was revised through several editions, given its present title, and finally placed as the sixth of 18 poems in the "Whispers of Heavenly Death" cluster for the sixth edition (1881).

The poet may be suggesting a touch of paranoia in this five-line poem. He feels that a phantom has caressed him as he walks by the shore, but the phantom, perhaps a former lover, "utterly" disappears and he is left with others "that are hateful to me and mock me," the "others" perhaps people who criticize him and/or his poems for their sexual significance.

Placed, as this poem is, in a cluster titled "Whispers of Heavenly Death," one may also read it as including the "phantom" as a pleasant death image.

"As I Lay with My Head in Your Lap Camerado" (1865)

First appeared in the *Sequel to Drum-Taps* volume (1865); it was included in the "Leaves of Grass" cluster for the fifth edition of *Leaves of Grass* (1871) and subsequent printings; and it was the 36th of 43 poems in the "Drum-Taps" cluster for the sixth edition (1881). It was under this title throughout its publication history.

The poet thinks aloud in this poem about the aftermath of the CIVIL WAR, what his relationship will be with the "Camerado" to whom he has just confessed his love. The poem is so clearly homoerotic, readers may wonder why it was not included in the "Calamus" cluster.

He knows that his words "are weapons full of danger, full of death, / For I confront peace, security, and all the settled laws, to unsettle them." He will continue his nonconformity, and he assures readers that "the threat of what is call'd hell is little or nothing to me, / And the lure of what is call'd heaven is little or nothing to me." He does not know their "destination, / Or whether we shall be victorious, or utterly quell'd and defeated." By "victorious," Whitman suggests victory in his relationship with the "camerado," one that will be eventually accepted by other people.

"As in a Swoon" (1876)

First appearing in the third printing of the fifth edition of *Leaves of Grass* (1876), it was reprinted in *Good-Bye My Fancy* (1891), but was cut when that supplement was added as a cluster of poems for the "Death-bed" printing of *Leaves* (1892).

"As I Pondered in Silence" (1871)

First appeared in the fifth edition of *Leaves of Grass* (1871), it was the second of 24 poems in the "Inscriptions" cluster for the sixth edition (1881).

As the poet "ponders" the subject matter of his poetry, a "Phantom" rises before him to remind him that "*. . . there is but one theme for ever-enduring bards / And that is the theme of War, the fortune of battles, / The making of perfect soldiers.*" The Phantom's answers to the poet's questions are in italics.

The poet reminds the Phantom, "The genius of poets of old lands," that he, Walt Whitman, has sung also of war, "a longer and greater one than any" (the American CIVIL WAR) and that "Lo, I too am come, chanting the chant of battles, / I above all promote brave soldiers."

Whitman had served during most of the Civil War by visiting the wounded and dying soldiers of both North and South, primarily in Washington, D.C., hospitals and on the battlefields of northern Virginia. He wrote letters from the soldiers to their loved ones "back home," no matter where home was. The poem is an answer to such phantoms as may question his poetic subject matter.

"As I Sit Writing Here" (1888)

First published in the NEW YORK HERALD (May 14, 1888); then in *November Boughs* (1888); and it was the eighth of 65 poems in the "First Annex: Sands at Seventy" cluster for the "Death-bed" printing of *Leaves of Grass* (1892).

The poet, "sick and grown old," wishes in this four-line poem that all of his "querilities" (complaints)—his "glooms, aches, lethargy, constipation, whimpering *ennui*," may be "filter[ed]" from his "daily songs." He doesn't want to present to readers in his poems his personal life, especially his physically painful final years.

"As I Walk These Broad Majestic Days" (1860)

First appeared as "Chants Democratic, No. 21" in the third edition of *Leaves of Grass* (1860); then as "As I Walk Solitary, Unattended" in the fourth edition (1867); it received its present title and was placed in a cluster titled "Marches Now the War is Over" for the fifth edition (1871); and it was the 21st of 22 poems in the "From Noon to Starry Night" cluster for the sixth edition (1881). The poem was revised several times during its publication history, including editing for the 1871 edition that allowed references to the CIVIL WAR.

The days are "majestic" because the Civil War is over and times are peaceful again. The poet describes America's material gains but argues that ideas and ideals are more valuable, more real.

> Then my realities;
> What else is so real as mine?
> Libertad and the divine average, freedom to
>   every slave on the face of the earth,
> The rapt promises and luminé of seers, the
>   spiritual world, these centuries-lasting
>   songs, . . .
> And our visions, the visions of poets, the most
>   solid announcements of any.

Whitman uses "Libertad" here to mean liberty for all and "luminé of seers" to mean the illumination by poets of a better world. The ideas and ideals of poets are more "real" than material things, however important those things ("Science, ships, politics, cities, factories," and so on) may be.

"As I Watch'd the Ploughman Ploughing" (1871)

First appeared with the "Whispers of Heavenly Death" cluster in the "Passage to India" supplement to *Leaves of Grass* (1871); and it was the 17th of 18 poems in the "Whispers" cluster for the sixth edition (1881).

Whitman uses in this four-line poem the images of the "ploughman ploughing," the "sower sowing," and the "harvester harvesting," to get to what he sees as a general, parenthetical truth in the final line: "(Life, life is the tillage, and Death is the harvest according.)"

"Assurances" (1856)

First appeared under the title "Faith Poem" in the second edition of *Leaves of Grass* (1856); it was revised, given its present title, and placed with the "Songs Before Parting" cluster for the fourth edition (1867); it was then transferred to the "Whispers of Heavenly Death" cluster (1871); and it became the seventh of 18 poems in the "Whispers of Heavenly Death" cluster for the sixth edition (1881).

The opening line sets the tone for this poem: "I need no assurances, I am a man who is preoccupied of his own soul." He then CATALOGs things in life he does not doubt, but at the end he adds parentheses: "(Did you think Life was so well provided for, and Death, the purport of all Life, is not well provided for?)" Not only is Death provided for, the poet suggests, it is better situated than Life, the poem's last line reading: "I do not think Life provides for all and for Time and Space, but I believe Heavenly Death provides for all."

The preoccupation with his soul provides the poet with "Assurances" that Death will take greater care of him than has Life.

"As the Greek's Signal Flame" (1887)

First published in the *NEW YORK HERALD* (December 15, 1887); then in *November Boughs* (1888); and it was the 60th of 65 poems in the "First

Walt Whitman, 1860 *(Library of Congress, Prints and Photographs Division)*

Annex: Sands at Seventy" cluster for the "Death-bed" printing of *Leaves of Grass* (1892).

A parenthetical note under the title reads: "For Whittier's Eightieth Birthday, December 17, 1887." John Greenleaf Whittier was born on December 17, 1807, and died six months after Whitman in 1892. This six-line poem refers to Whittier as "the Greek's signal flame," and Whitman offers, "from Mannahatta's ship-fringed shore, . . . a kindled brand for thee, Old Poet."

"As the Time Draws Nigh" (1860)

First published as "To My Soul" in the third edition of *Leaves of Grass* (1860); then titled "As Nearing Departure" for the fourth edition (1867); it received its present title for the fifth edition (1871); and it became the opening poem of 17 in the "Songs of Parting" cluster for the sixth edition (1881). Whitman did a lot of revising over the publication history of the poem; the final version is half the length of the first.

The poet is thinking of his own mortality in this poem: "As the time draws nigh glooming a cloud, / A dread beyond of I know not what darkens me." This second line echoes Hamlet's "But the dread of something after death, / The undiscover'd country, from whose bourn / No traveler returns. . . ." It is the undiscovered country that bothers Whitman as well, yet he works his way out of the seeming concern.

In the end Hamlet chooses life, because he would prefer to "bear those ills we have / Than fly to others that we know not of . . ." and "Thus conscience does make cowards of us all." Whitman chooses life for what seems a more positive reason: "Must we barely arrive at this beginning in us?— and yet it is enough, O soul; / O soul, we have positively appear'd—that is enough." Whitman suggests here a cyclical movement in life, from birth to death, to a new life. It is enough for Whitman merely to have lived.

"As They Draw to a Close" (1871)

First published as "Thought" with a cluster of poems titled "Now Finalè to the Shore" in the fifth edition of *Leaves of Grass* (1871); and it was the 11th of 17 poems in the "Songs of Parting" cluster for the sixth edition (1881).

As Whitman sees the end of his poetic ability, he attempts here to explain his purpose for writing his poems, a need he says to "rapport," to harmonize Nature and his own soul: "To put rapport the mountains and rocks and streams, / And the winds of the north, and the forests of oak and pine, / With you O soul." His purpose has been to "compact" all of nature together with his own soul.

"As Toilsome I Wander'd Virginia's Woods" (1865)

First appeared in the *Drum-Taps* volume (1865) and under this title throughout its printing history; it was the 18th of 43 poems in the "Drum-Taps" cluster for the sixth edition of *Leaves of Grass* (1881).

While wandering in Virginia's woods, the poet sees the grave of a soldier, "mortally wounded he and buried on the retreat." The grave was made in a hurry, but a sign was left: "On a table scrawl'd and nail'd on the tree by the grave, / *Bold, cautious, true, and my loving comrade.*"

The poet continues his wandering, "through changeful season and scene, abrupt, alone, or in the crowded street," but he cannot get rid of the memory of the "tablet scrawl'd" and nailed to a tree somewhere in Virginia's woods. The epigraph is repeated, as the poem's refrain: "*Bold, cautious, true, and my loving comrade.*"

This is the third of three consecutive poems in the "Drum-Taps" cluster that present with greater emotional impact than any other poems in the group the theme of death in war. See also "A March in the Ranks Hard-Prest, and the Road Unknown" and "A Sight in Camp in the Daybreak Gray and Dim."

Walt Whitman, photographed by Mathew Brady, 1866
(Library of Congress, Prints and Photographs Division)

five from the second (1856), 12 from 1860, three from 1865, one from 1867, five from "Passage to India" (1871), one from *As a Strong Bird on Pinions Free and Other Poems* (1872), and four from *Two Rivulets* (1876).

The 38 poems are in the following order: "As Consequent, Etc.," "The Return of the Heroes," "There Was a Child Went Forth," "Old Ireland," "The City Dead-House," "This Compost," "To a Foil'd European Revolutionaire," "Unnamed Lands," "Song of Prudence," "The Singer in the Prison," "Warble for Lilac-Time," "Outlines for a Tomb," "Out from Behind This Mask," "Vocalism," "To Him That was Crucified," "You Felons on Trial in Courts," "Laws for Creations," "To a Common Prostitute," "I was Looking a Long While," "Thought" (Of Persons), "Miracles," "Sparkles from the Wheel," "To a Pupil," "Unfolded Out of the Folds," "What am I After All," "Kosmos," "Others May Praise What They Like," "Who Learns My Lesson Complete?," "Tests," "The Torch," "O Star of France," "The Ox-Tamer," "An Old Man's Thought of School," "Wandering at Morn," "Italian Music in Dakota," "With All Thy Gifts," "My Picture-Gallery," and "The Prairie States."

The careful selection and revising of the poems for this cluster and their collective placement immediately after the two CIVIL WAR clusters—"Drum-Taps" and "Memories of President Lincoln"—provide a sort of calm-after-the-storm presence in *Leaves of Grass*. Autumn suggests a comparatively quiet time of the year, and rivulets suggest quiet waters, the water imagery dominating the cluster.

"As Toilsome I Wander'd Virginia's Woods" is also one of seven poems within "Drum-Taps" that describe isolated, yet universal, incidents of war, descriptions that seem to stop time, perhaps as in a painting, and yet which also carry larger, thematic ideas. See also "Cavalry Crossing a Ford," "Bivouac on a Mountain Side," "By the Bivouac's Fitful Flame," "A Sight in Camp in the Daybreak Gray and Dim," "I Saw Old General at Bay," and "Look Down Fair Moon."

"Autumn Rivulets" (1881)

This cluster of 38 poems appeared for the first time in the sixth edition of *Leaves of Grass* (1881). Four new poems were added to 34 pulled together out of several earlier editions, gathered by Whitman clearly with a great deal of thought and revision. There are two poems from the first edition (1855),

"Backward Glance O'er Travel'd Roads, A" (1888)

Title for the introductory essay in *November Boughs* (1888), a pamphlet that included 20 other literary essays and 64 poems. "A Backward Glance" became the closing essay for the final "printings" of *Leaves of Grass* (1889 and 1892).

This "Backward Glance" is both a reminiscence and a summary of the poet's life and work, and Whitman said that he would prefer that it be included at the end of all subsequent editions of *Leaves of Grass.* He obviously enjoyed looking back over his life, especially the poetry-writing and revising part of it: "How the soul loves to float amid such reminiscences!" He notes that a recent article on Wordsworth in an English journal quotes a French critic who had argued that "owing to the special tendency to science and to its all-devouring force, poetry would cease to be read in five years." Whitman's answer to this in "Backward Glance" is that "only a firmer, vastly broader, new area begins to exist—nay, is already form'd—to which the poetic genius must emigrate. . . . Without that ultimate vivification—which the poet or other artist alone can give—reality would seem incomplete, and science, democracy, and life itself, finally in vain."

Whitman mentions, nevertheless, those writers from the "Old World" who most influenced him: "Walter Scott's poetry entire," the Old and New Testaments, "Shakespere," Ossian, Homer, "Eschylus," Sophocles, the "old German Nibelungen," the "ancient Hindoo poems," Dante, and "The Iliad (Buckley's prose version)." But Whitman says that, although the "New World receives with joy the poems of the antique," and "though the dawn-dazzle of the sun of literature is in those poems for us of to-day—though perhaps the best parts of current character in nations, social groups, or any man's or woman's individuality, Old World or New, are from them—. . ." he wonders if "there [is] one whose underlying basis is not a denial and insult to democracy? Even Shakespere, who so suffuses current letters and art (which indeed have in most degrees grown out of him,) belongs essentially to the buried past." It is for the America of the present time, Whitman suggests here, and for American poets to bring a new body of poetry to the world, the Old world as well as the New. This was certainly one of the ideas that attracted EMERSON from his first reading of *Leaves of Grass* in 1855. Emerson understood Whitman's argument that America's New England poets were still too English and that before America could make an impression on the

old world it would have to develop a poetry of its own.

Whitman sums up what he believes to have been his primary purposes for writing *Leaves of Grass.* He says that the "word" he would use to describe his poetry is

Suggestiveness. I round and finish little, if anything; and could not, consistently with my scheme. The reader will always have his or her part to do, just as much as I have had mine. I seek less to state or display any theme or thought, and more to bring you, reader, into the atmosphere of the theme or thought—there to pursue your own flight. Another impetus-word is Comradeship as for all lands, and in a more commanding and acknowledg'd sense than hitherto. Other word-signs would be Good Cheer, Content, and Hope.

It may be up to the poet to "suggest" themes and thoughts, Whitman says, but the reader shares responsibility for making poetry work. It is the reader who must pursue his or her "flight" to theme or thought. It is in the imagination of the reader where poetry matters most.

In summing up his poetic theme of democracy in "A Backward Glance," he makes the following statement:

One main genesis-motive of the "Leaves" was my conviction (just as strong to-day as ever) that the crowning growth of the United States is to be spiritual and heroic. To help start and favor that growth—or even to call attention to it, or the need of it—is the beginning, middle and final purpose of the poems. (In fact, when really cipher'd out and summ'd to the last, plowing up in earnest the interminable average fallows of humanity—not "good government" merely, in the common sense—is the justification and main purpose of these United States.)

It is up to the people to plant the seeds of democracy, not government. And, as one might expect from the poet of democracy, his closing paragraph offers an additional thought for one of his constant themes in *Leaves of Grass:*

Concluding with two items for the imaginative genius of the West, when it worthily rises—First, what Herder taught to the young Goethe, that really great poetry is always (like the Homeric or Biblical canticles) the result of a national spirit, and not the privilege of a pol-ish'd and select few; Second, that the strongest and sweetest songs yet remain to be sung.

It is in the national spirit that the best American poetry is to be written and in that same spirit in which it is to be read.

This essay of reminiscence appeared, as Whit-man planned and requested, in the final printings of *Leaves of Grass* and especially in the "Death-bed" printing (1892). And most 20th-century edi-tors, in reprinting editions of *Leaves,* have followed his wishes, both in the ordering of poems as Whit-man wanted them and in the inclusion of "A Back-ward Glance O'er Travel'd Roads" as a final prose statement of purpose.

Banner at Daybreak

Title of a planned book of poems that Whitman never published. See "Song of the Banner at Day-break."

"Base of All Metaphysics, The" (1871)

First appeared as the eighth poem in the "Calamus" cluster for the fifth edition of *Leaves of Grass* (1871); it was the eighth of 39 Calamus poems for the sixth edition (1881).

After all the great philosophers have had their say—"Greek and Germanic systems," (Socrates, Plato, Kant, Fichte, Schelling, Hegel), even after Christ—Whitman still sees the need for people lov-ing one another as the basis for all metaphysics.

The dear love of man for his comrade, the
    attraction of friend to friend.

Of the well-married husband and wife, of
    children and parents,
Of city for city and land for land.

The "base for all metaphysics"—which, in part, attempts to explain the nature of all things—is still the love of human beings for one another and for nature. The poem is placed in the "Calamus" clus-ter, which suggests homosexual love for its primary subject, and it is addressed "And now gentlemen"; but the poet makes it clear to the men of his imagi-nation that there are other love relationships that are of equal importance.

"Bathed in War's Perfume" (1865)

First appeared in the *Drum-Taps* volume (1865), then in the fourth edition of *Leaves of Grass* (1867), it was the first poem in the "Bathed in War's Per-fume" cluster (1871) and published again as a sepa-rate poem in the fifth edition of *Leaves* (1876). After that, it was cut from *Leaves.*

"Beat! Beat! Drums!" (1861)

First published simultaneously in HARPER'S WEEKLY and in the NEW YORK LEADER (September 28, 1861); then in the *Drum-Taps* volume (1865); and it was the third of 43 poems in the "Drum-Taps" cluster for the sixth edition of *Leaves of Grass* (1881).

Whitman wrote this dramatic poem sometime after the first battle of Bull Run, (April 21–22, 1861), but before he saw any actual combat. It is both an upbeat invitation to arms and a sorrowful, perhaps sarcastic comment on the impact of war, the drums and bugles a metaphor for the canons and rifles drowning out all other noises, even the shouts of men running, wounded, and dying. The refrain line, "Beat! beat! drums!—blow! bugles! blow!," is both an evocation of the drums and bugles and an aid in establishing the poem's rhythm. Whitman calls on the drums and bugles to do their duty, which is to call the soldiers to battle and drown out all everyday noises that might distract them from their duty.

The first two stanzas present the call to arms. The drums and bugles represent the call to battle, which "burst" "through the windows" and doors "like a ruthless force." The marching beat is heard also in churches and schools and in the home of the "bridegroom quiet—no happiness must he have now with his bride." It is loud enough to be heard "over the traffic of cities—over the rumble of wheels in the streets." No regular business is carried on, "no brokers or speculators" are at work, everyday activities are at a standstill. Even the lawyer hesitates to take his case to court. The second stanza ends: "Then rattle quicker, heavier drums—you bugles wilder blow."

Following the call to battle of the first two stanzas, the last stanza carries the full weight of the war, the bloody results of which Whitman witnessed firsthand in the hospitals of New York and Washington.

But the poet is now sarcastic, urging the drums and bugles to cover the sounds of men dying, asking the drummers and buglers to pay no attention to "expostulation"; not from the "timid—mind not the weeper or prayer, . . . / Let not the child's voice be heard, nor the mother's entreaties." Do your duty drums and bugles, the poet says, let nothing get in the way of the battle, of the killing and maiming of otherwise healthy men, young and old alike, North and South alike: "So strong you thump O terrible drums—so loud you bugles blow." Let no one hear the sounds of the soldiers screaming.

This is one of the more popular *Drum-Taps* poems because of its rhythmic, exciting beat and its haunting refrain.

"Beautiful Women" (1860)

First published as two lines in "Debris" in the third edition of *Leaves of Grass* (1860); it was reprinted as "Picture" (1867); then it received its present title in the fifth edition (1871); and it was the 18th

of 29 poems in the "By The Roadside" cluster for the sixth edition (1881).

This two-line poem has 12 syllables in the first line and 17 in the second but five syllables accented in each, an example of how Whitman used ACCENTUAL VERSE to create a pattern of rhythm.

The poem is a description of beautiful women, "some old some young," but, he says, "the old are more beautiful than the young," suggesting that age brings on a different kind of beauty.

"Beauty of the Ship, The" (1876)

First published in the NEW YORK TRIBUNE (February 19, 1876); it was then pasted into the endpapers of several copies of the fifth edition of *Leaves of Grass* (1876), but it did not appear again.

"Beginners" (1860)

First appeared in the third edition of *Leaves of Grass* (1860); it was the 11th of 24 poems in the "Inscriptions" cluster for the sixth edition (1881).

"Beginners" have a difficult life: "How dear and dreadful they are to the earth . . . / How all times mischoose the objects of their adulation and reward, / And how the same inexorable price must still be paid for the same great purchase."

There is ambiguity in this seven-line poem because these "beginners" are not novices but special people, born sometimes at the right time and sometimes not, sometimes understood and sometimes not, but, nevertheless, always important for their various and unique contributions to the social order.

There is nothing in this poem to indicate a certain person, yet Whitman spent so much time during the late 1850s walking the streets of BROOKLYN and New York observing people and talking to them, that he must have had some of these individuals in mind when he wrote this poem.

"Beginning My Studies"
(1867)

First appeared in the fourth edition of *Leaves of Grass* (1867); it was the 10th of 24 poems in the "Inscriptions" cluster for the sixth edition (1881).

In this six-line poem the poet expresses the excitement he felt with "fact consciousness," which he encountered at the beginning of his studies of natural things. "The least insect" he saw raised his consciousness of the facts of life, accentuated his "senses, eyesight, love" for the things of Nature. He felt so "awed" by what he saw that he "hardly wish'd to go any farther." He wanted to stop time perhaps in order to absorb all that was happening to his sense of the meaning of Nature and in order "to sing it in ecstatic songs."

Nature was one of his poetic subjects, one of his "ecstatic songs."

"Behold This Swarthy Face"
(1860)

Titled "Calamus No. 19" in the third edition of *Leaves of Grass* (1860), it received its present title (1867); and it was the 16th of 39 poems in the "Calamus" cluster for the sixth edition (1881).

In this poem it is the kiss of masculine friends that has such meaning for the poet's great image of the brotherhood of men: "Yet comes one a Manhattanese and ever at parting kisses me lightly on the lips with robust love." It is the common "salute of American comrades land and sea, / We are those two natural and nonchalant persons."

See also "City of Orgies," the poem immediately preceding "Behold This Swarthy Face" in the "Calamus" cluster.

"Bervance: or, Father
and Son" (1841)

Short story, first published in the *United States Magazine and Democratic Review* (December 1841; see

DEMOCRATIC REVIEW, THE). The story is most accessible now in *Walt Whitman: The Early Poems and the Fiction*, edited by Thomas L. Brasher (New York University Press, 1963).

The story is told as a first-person confessional, a father (Mr. Bervance) narrating his mostly unexplained "positive aversion" for his second son, Luke. It is an antipathy that leads to horrifying results, the son forced into an insane asylum, only to be made worse psychologically by the hospital. After several weeks, Luke sneaks away from the hospital and returns home unannounced, frightening his father, cursing him for putting him in the institution, and then leaving, never to be seen by the family again.

On his deathbed the narrator-father pours his guilt out to the reader, explaining that "occasions seemed continually to arise wherein [Luke] felt disposed to thwart me, and make himself disagreeable to me. Every time I saw him, I was conscious of something evil in his conduct or disposition." The father further confesses that he was "conscious of something evil in his [own] conduct or disposition. I have since thought that a great deal of all this existed only in my own imagination, warped and darkened as it was, and disposed to look upon him with an 'evil eye.'"

Following a particularly horrifying evening, when Luke deliberately disobeys his father's command that he not attend a theater performance but does and makes a scene, Mr. Bervance orders that Luke be placed in the asylum. Bervance explains that he was afraid the theater would be too much excitement for the boy, whom he considered too "sensitive." Whether Luke was seriously deranged is not clear to the reader, but Bervance clearly feels guilty for his aversion to his son and for his lifelong mistreatment of him.

In an introductory paragraph Whitman warns readers that this a "strange story—the true solution of which will probably be found in the supposition of a certain degree of unsoundness of mind, on the one part, manifesting itself in the morbid and unnatural paternal antipathy; and of its reproduction on the other, by the well known though mysterious law of hereditary transmission."

This statement makes clear the author's ambivalence about where to place the blame. Readers in the 21st century, however, who know more about genetics than Whitman or his contemporaries, may well have a better feel for "blame" than the author himself. Another interesting factor is that the reader does not get Luke's side of the story. He is not quoted nor mentioned in any way other than through his father's confession of having mistreated him.

CHARACTERS

Bervance   The narrator of the story and the father of the title "Bervance: or, Father and Son." He confesses that he has a "positive aversion" for his son Luke but cannot explain it either to himself or to the reader. He tells the story from the position of a guilty man on his deathbed, trying to understand why he felt the way he did toward his son.

Luke   The "son" in the short story "Bervance: or, Father and Son." Because the story is told by the father, Mr. Bervance, the reader does not get Luke's side, nor is he described in any objective way, only through the father's rather distorted viewpoint.

"Birds of Passage" (1881)

Cluster title for seven poems in the sixth edition of *Leaves of Grass* (1881). Each poem appeared in earlier editions, but they were brought together under this cluster title, all of the poems presenting images of movement.

In America we are all "birds of passage," Whitman seems to suggest, moving from one place to another, replacing others and being replaced by others. The final poem in the cluster, "With Antecedents," registers the importance of holding respect for the past—which is how we arrived at where we are now—and hope for the future, while acknowledging at the same time that the present moment is where life is lived.

The poems in this cluster are published in *Leaves of Grass* in the following order: "Song of the Universal," "Pioneers! O Pioneers!," "To You," "France, The 18th Year of These States," "Myself and Mine," "Year of Meteors (1859–60)," and "With Antecedents."

"Bivouac on a Mountain Side" (1865)

First appeared in the *Drum-Taps* volume (1865) and kept its title throughout its *Leaves of Grass* printing history; it was the 11th of 43 poems in the "Drum-Taps" cluster for the sixth edition (1881).

This is one of several poems descriptive of CIVIL WAR scenes of men at war but not in battle. The scene here is almost pastoral, soldiers halted for the night on the "terraced sides of a mountain," the "camp-fires scatter'd near and far, some away up on the mountain." The poet describes the "shadowy forms of men and horses," all the details creating an effect of a peaceful camp, the sky "studded" with the "eternal stars."

There doesn't seem to be any obvious attempt on Whitman's part to create a metaphor in this poem, although readers may feel some ironic tension between this peaceful scene of time stopped for a moment, as in a painting, and the coming battle when lives may be lost.

See also "Cavalry Crossing a Ford," "By The Bivouac's Fitful Flame," "A Sight in Camp in the Daybreak Gray and Dim," "As Toilsome I Wandered Virginia's Woods," "I Saw Old General at Bay," and "Look Down Fair Moon."

"Blood-Money" (1850)

First published in the NEW YORK TRIBUNE (March 22, 1850); an "early poem" *not* later published in *Leaves of Grass*. It is most accessible now in Francis Murphy (editor), *Walt Whitman: The Complete Poems* (Penguin Books, 1996).

"Boston Ballad, A" (1854)

First published as the ninth of 12 untitled poems in the first edition of *Leaves of Grass* (1855); then as "Poem of Apparitions in Boston, the 78th Year of These States" (1856); as "A Boston Ballad" (1860);

Walt Whitman, photographed by Alexander Gardner, 1864 *(Library of Congress, Prints and Photographs Division)*

as "To Get Betimes in Boston Town" (1867); then under its present title for the fifth edition (1871); and as the first of 29 poems in the "By The Road-side" cluster for the sixth edition (1881).

The poem was composed during the public uproar over the arrest and trial in Boston of the fugitive slave Anthony Burns, which took place shortly after the passage in Congress of the Kansas-Nebraska bill in 1854, repealing the Missouri Compromise and encouraging southerners in their effort to avoid antislavery legislation.

Whitman was incensed by the news of Burns's arrest and wrote "A Boston Ballad" as a satirical protest against the incident, one of only a few such satires in *Leaves of Grass.* In the poem he raises from their graves the American soldiers who had died during the Revolutionary War and King George III of England as well, so the poet could explain to the soldiers that they had died in vain and to the king that he had won the war after all.

The FUGITIVE SLAVE ACT of 1850 was an attempt by southern congressmen to strengthen laws against helping slaves escape to the North. Anyone "harboring, concealing or rescuing" a runaway slave could, according to the congressional bill, be fined $1,000 and put in jail for six months. On May 26, 1854, a vigilance committee tried to rescue Anthony Burns from the Boston courthouse, killing a marshall in the process. U.S. commissioner Edward G. Loring remanded Burns to his Virginia owner in spite of the protests, and he was sent back to Alexandria on June 2. Boston citizens collected $1,300 and bought Burns back in 1855.

The poet envisions a parade in Boston: "I love to look on the Stars and Stripes, I hope the fifes will play Yankee Doodle. . . ." It is a parade of

> Phantoms! phantoms countless by flank and
>   rear!
> Cock'd hats of mothy mould—crutches made
>   of mist!
> Arms in slings—old men leaning on young
>   men's shoulders.

Revolutionary War soldiers are resurrected in order to march in the parade in Whitman's mock celebration of the Fugitive Slave Act in general and of the recent Anthony Burns case in particular—though neither the act nor Burns is mentioned in the poem. To King George, the poet says: "You have got your revenge, old buster—the crown is come to its own, and more than its own. . . ." The British won the war after all.

"Boy Lover, The" (1845)

Short story, first published in AMERICAN REVIEW (May 1845); it was reprinted in the BROOKLYN DAILY EAGLE (January 4–5, 1848), then revised by

Whitman for reprinting in *Specimen Days & Collect.* The story is most accessible now in *Walt Whitman: The Early Poems and the Fiction,* edited by Thomas L. Brasher (New York University Press, 1963).

The title is ambiguous. It does not mean the lover of boys, but, rather, a boy who is in love.

The narrator begins his moral tale by stating that it is a "chronicle for the young." He warns that youth fades, that "old age takes everyone to the grave who has not already died in youth." And he warns that "Love! . . . with its cankerseed of decay within, has sent young men and maidens to a long'd-for, but too premature burial." This is a story, readers are told, that took place several years ago when the narrator was a law student.

He and his 16-year-old brother, Matthew, and two other students of law, Wheaton and Frank Brown, go to a tavern owned by a widow, whose daughter, Ninon, is a waitress. She is about 16 as well, and Matthew, we are told, "is troubled [at meeting the waitress] with an inward illness." The narrator tells us that Ninon is the most fascinating but "artless creature" he had ever seen. "She had blue eyes and light hair, and an expression of childish simplicity which was charming indeed." He says that within a half an hour of seeing Ninon, he, his brother, and their friends were all in love with her "to the very depth of passion." The boys return every Wednesday for several weeks; each time they have beer and conversation with Ninon.

One Wednesday she fails to show up, and the boys discover that she has died of a mysterious illness. Although all four of the boys are saddened by her death, it becomes apparent that it is Matthew who suffers most. He dies a week later of a broken heart over his love of Ninon, who, as was suggested by the narrator's opening warning to young readers, has also died of love, perhaps even of her love for Matthew, though that element of the story is left unclear.

CHARACTERS

Matthew Brother of the narrator in the short story "The Boy Lover." He is 16 and "troubled" with what the narrator refers to as an inward illness," the result of falling in love with a waitress, Ninon, in a tavern owned by her mother and to which his brother and friends take him. All four boys are "in love" with her, but for them it is mere infatuation, which they will get over. Matthew, on the other hand, dies at the end of the story—of his love for the beautiful Ninon. She had died also the week before of some mysterious illness, perhaps, though we are not told, of her love for Matthew.

Widow Owner of an ale-house in the short story "The Boy Lover" and the mother of Ninon, with whom the four boys of the story fall in love.

Margery "[S]ober, stately old woman, half companion, half servant" to the widow in the story.

Ninon Daughter of the widow in "The Boy Lover." She is about 16, the age of the narrator's brother, Matthew, who falls in love with her. She is a "fascinating" but "artless creature," the narrator says, with a "simplicity" that was charming. All four of the boys who visit her parents' tavern for beer fall in love with her, though it is Matthew who falls the hardest. She dies of a mysterious illness, and, although all four boys are saddened by her death, Matthew dies of a broken heart—caused by his love for Ninon.

"Bravest Soldiers, The" (1888)

First published in the NEW YORK HERALD (March 18, 1888); then in *November Boughs* (1888); and it was the sixth of 65 poems in the "First Annex: Sands at Seventy" cluster for the "Death-bed" printing of *Leaves of Grass* (1892).

This is a two-line epitaph for the soldiers who fought in the CIVIL WAR (the war is not named), especially the "bravest" of all, those who "fell, unnamed, unknown." The poet mentions that the soldiers were "high named to-day," implying an actual ceremony for them on March 18, 1888, the date the *Herald* published the poem.

"Bravo, Paris Exposition!"
(1889)

First published in *HARPER'S WEEKLY* (September 28, 1889); it was the 13th of 31 poems in *Good-Bye My Fancy* (1891); then in "Second Annex: Good-Bye My Fancy" for the "Death-bed" printing of *Leaves of Grass* (1892).

Though Whitman did not attend, this poem is in honor of the Paris Exposition, which was held from May 6 to November 6, 1889. The most famous exhibit at the event was the newly constructed Eiffel Tower.

The poet sends, "before [the exposition] close[s]," the "good-will" of the American "grand-sons and great-grand-sons" of their French "grand-sires" for the success of the summerlong celebration in Paris.

"Broadway" (1888)

First published in the *NEW YORK HERALD* (April 10, 1888), then in *November Boughs* (1888), and as the 34th of 65 poems in the "First Annex: Sands at Seventy" cluster for the "Death-bed" printing of *Leaves of Grass* (1892).

This is a song of joy for one of the poet's favorite streets of his favorite city: "What hurrying human tides . . . / What passions, winnings, losses, ardors, swim thy waters! / What whirls of evil, bliss and sorrow, stem thee!" Good and evil are present on Broadway, the "portal" to all the best and worst of what the poet believes makes the city great.

"Broadway Pageant, A"
(1860)

First published as "The Errand-Bearers" in the *NEW YORK TIMES* (June 27, 1860); it was then published under its present title in the *Drum-Taps* volume (1865); and it was placed as a separate poem between the "Birds of Passage" and "Sea-Drift" clusters for the sixth edition of *Leaves of Grass*

(1881). There was a subtitle for the 1865 version: "(Reception Japanese Embassy, June 16, 1860)." The final version, without the subtitle, is in three sections and 81 lines.

Whitman witnessed the arrival of a Japanese delegation in New York, in the United States to negotiate a treaty between the two countries. Whitman wrote the poem after seeing huge crowds of people waiting at the docks. According to the *New York Times* report, the crowds watched a "mammoth parade" up Broadway, led by 5,000 American troops. Section 1 describes the New York parade and reception.

In Section 2 Whitman calls up the history of the Orient, which the Japanese delegation represents. "Confucius himself, the great poets and heroes, the warriors, the castes, all, / Trooping up, crowding from all directions from the Altay mountains." The Altai Mountains are in the Northwest corner of China and may represent for Whitman the westernmost boundary of the Orient. He envisions the opening of commerce with the East, "races reborn, refresh'd, / Lives, works resumed . . . / Commencing from this day surrounded by the world."

The poem then takes on a metaphorical significance in Section 3, the poet wishing that the "Libertad" available to Americans would also be made available to people all over the world. The word "Libertad" is used nine times in the poem, taken by Whitman from the Spanish and meaning liberty or freedom, as in *libertad de palabra*, freedom of speech. Asia has come to America, Whitman believes, seeking to learn what the New World has to offer. The circle is complete:

> The sign is reversing, the orb is enclosed,
> The ring is circled, the journey is done,
> The box-lid is but perceptibly open'd,
>   nevertheless the perfume pours copiously out
>   of the whole box.

The visit by the Japanese is just the first step.

In the final stanza the poet evokes "Libertad," asking it to be humble and to respect the great historic significance of the Orient: "Bend your proud neck to the long-off mother now sending messages over the archipelagoes to you, / Bend your proud neck low for once, young Libertad." The Orient, mother of great nations, is seeking liberty for its people and looking to America for guidance.

In the past it was America looking across the seas east and west to other great countries, now the entire world is looking to America, the "mistress" of democracy.

"By Blue Ontario's Shore" (1856)

First appeared as "Poem of Many in One," one of 20 new poems for the second edition of *Leaves of Grass* (1856); it became "Chants Democratic No. 1" (1860); it was then titled "As I Sat Alone by Blue Ontario's Shore" (1867); and it received its present title and was a separate poem for the sixth edition (1881). The poem and title were revised often during its publication history, especially for the 1867 edition after the CIVIL WAR. The final version is in 20 sections and 335 lines.

Whitman repeats many of the thematic ideas from his "preface" to the first edition (see "Preface" [*Leaves of Grass*, 1855]). More than 60 lines, in fact, are taken almost directly from the preface. In both works the poet identifies the themes of *Leaves of Grass* plus his purpose in writing the poems: to reveal his vision for America, including the dangers following the Civil War, and the role for himself and other national poets in revealing democracy to the world.

Whitman opens the poem by describing an experience—strolling along "blue Ontario's shore" and thinking about "warlike days and of peace return'd." A "Phantom gigantic superb, with stern visage" interrupts the poet's thoughts and, acting as a momentary muse, asks (in italics) that the poet write a poem *"that comes from the soul of America, . . . a carol of victory."* But the Phantom also asks for a *"song"* that includes the *"throes of Democracy,"* the problems the Nation faces now that the war is over. The poet thinks of the "treacherous lip-smiles everywhere [lip-smiles suggests hypocrisy], / And death and infidelity at every step."

Sections 2 and 3 present America's immediate past victories on its way to becoming the world's standard for democracy ("A breed whose proof is in time and deeds"), but the poet also issues warnings. "We are powerful and tremendous in ourselves, / Nothing is sinful to us outside of ourselves." Whitman often wrote of his belief that the only sin was a belief in sin, and here he notes that if America fails it will be because of internal failures, not because somebody from outside has somehow intervened. He ends the third section with the thought that if America can "Produce great Persons, the rest follows." Great people produce great world leadership.

The next several sections are devoted to the role of the poet in a democratic society. Whitman takes up the stance he had first created for himself in the short *Inscriptions* poem "One's-Self I Sing" and later worked out in more detail in "Song of Myself." It is "One's-self I sing, a simple separate person, / Yet utter the word Democratic, the word En-Masse." He says in Section 4 of "By Blue Ontario's Shore": "I am he who walks the States with a barb'd tongue, questioning every one I meet." The new American "Bard" should be prepared to ask questions of everyone he or she meets. Whitman warns against a failure of citizens to think for themselves. If you are only interested in what you already know, he says, or in what you get from books, then you are of little help in a democratic society. These things "precede the decay of the ruggedness of states and men." America did not get where it is without a lot of people capable of thinking for themselves.

In Section 5 Whitman discusses what America needs in its poets. If the Nation got where it is through the ruggedness of its people, then it must bring to its poetry its own ruggedness, "its own styles." America's poets must surpass poets from all other countries: "The immortal poets of Asia and Europe have done their work and pass'd to other spheres, / A work remains, the work of surpassing all they have done." And the subject is America itself; America is its own greatest poem:

> These States are the amplest poem,
> Here is not merely a nation but a teeming
>   Nation of nations,
> Here the doings of men correspond with the
>   broadcast doings of the day and night, . . .

Here are the flowing trains, here the crowds,
 equality, diversity, the soul loves.

Equality and diversity are two key elements in a democracy, Whitman continues to say, and two of the subjects for the poets of America.

In Section 6 the poet CATALOGs some particular aspects of American life that need to be included in the nation's poetry: "Making its cities, beginnings, events, diversities, wars, vocal in him, / Making its rivers, lakes, bays, embouchure in him." Embouchure means, according to *Cassell's French Dictionary*, "to put to one's mouth," or "to sound," as with a wind instrument. The American poet must voice to the world those things about the nation that make it great.

The haughty defiance of the Year One, war,
 peace, the formation of the Constitution,
The separate States, the simple elastic scheme,
 the immigrants,
The Union always swarming with blatherers
 and always sure and impregnable. . . .
Manhattan firemen, the Yankee swap, southern
 plantation life,
Slavery—the murderous, treacherous
 conspiracy to raise it upon the ruins of all
 the rest.

The good with the bad, everything is a part of democracy and essential for inclusion as part of the national poetry.

The "new aureola" is described in Section 7, an encircling radiance around the idea of Liberty ("Libertad"), not the "soft astral" radiance of before the Civil War but, since the war, "dazzling and fierce, / With war's flames and the lambent lightnings playing." The war sharpened America's instincts for making itself better.

Whitman suggests in Section 8 the need to let go of the past, even though it may continue to provide subject matter for poets: let "Others adorn the past, but you O days of the present, I adorn you." Yet his true feelings are for the future of the nation; "I believe in you," he says, "I isolate myself for your sake, / O America because you build for mankind I build for you." The Civil War was a depressing time for the poet of democracy, but Whitman kept his

hopes up for the future; and certainly most of the poems for the final printings of *Leaves of Grass* show this optimism.

In Section 9, Whitman suggests that America needs poets rather than governments: "Of all races and eras these States with veins full of poetical stuff most need poets, and are to have the greatest, and use them the greatest, / Their Presidents shall not be their common referee so much as their poets shall." Americans are born with poetry in their blood, but they need poets to bring out that poetic spirit in the people. People and their poets are more important than presidents, because presidents (and other politicians) work for the people, Whitman believed, not the other way around.

After presenting a definition of poets in Section 10 ("the equable man" and "leader of leaders") and then their mission in Section 11 ("For the great Idea, / That . . . is the mission of poets"), Whitman offers a challenge in Section 12 to those Americans who might feel some of the poet's poetic urges. But hard work is required:

Who are you indeed who would talk or sing to
 America?
Have you studied out the land, its idioms and
 men?
Have you learn'd the physiology, phrenology,
 politics, geography, pride, freedom,
 friendship of the land? . . .
Have you possess'd yourself of the Federal
 Constitution?

The poet of America must have all of this knowledge, plus the ability to be "faithful to things," immune "against all seductions, follies, whirls, fierce contentions," and "of the whole people." Whitman is naming attributes that he believes he himself has, and which, most 21st-century readers believe, his poetry does not dispute.

Section 13 continues the thematic definition of poetry and of the kind of person it takes to be a great American Bard: "He or she is greatest who contributes the greatest original practical example." Whitman's ego seems at work again in Section 14, except, as in earlier poems, he is bragging not for himself but for humankind. "Fall behind me States! / A man before all—myself, typical, before all." All poets with potential for writing the poetry of America must feel this way, he argues, and be comfortable that the ego speaks for all. He claims "nothing to myself which I have not carefully claim'd for others on the same terms." And as a transition to the final sections of the poem, he adds a parenthetical question at the end of the section: "(Say O Mother, have I not to your thought been faithful? / Have I not through life kept you and yours before me?)"

Mother-Democracy then becomes the chief thematic element in the final six sections of the poem. It is as if Whitman has come to realize, in the process of writing this poem, of thinking about all of these things along blue Ontario's shore that it is the "individual" who is important in America and in democracy; in fact, he believes that is America's "compact" with its people:

Underneath all, individuals,
I swear nothing is good to me now that ignores
   individuals,
The American compact is altogether with
   individuals,
The only government is that which makes
   minute of individuals,
The whole theory of the universe is directed
   unerringly to one single individual—namely
   to You.

At the end of Section 16 the poet adds, "Underneath all to me is myself, to you yourself, (the same monotonous old song.)" Monotonous perhaps, but this is the great Whitman theme: each individual is larger, more important than the government or any aspect of the government. It is the individual citizen who creates democracy.

Whitman begins Section 17 by continuing with the idea that "America is only you and me" and adds a catalog of ideas and people that are the responsibility of all Americans but of each one individually— of, as he says, "you and me."

Its power, weapons, testimony, are you and me,
Its crimes, lies, thefts, defections, are you and
   me,
Its Congress is you and me, the officers,
   capitols, armies, ships, are you and me, . . .

Freedom, language, poems, employments, are
   you and me,
Past, present, future, are you and me.

Yet the worst as well as the best must be each individual's responsibility, as he indicates near the end of Section 18: "I know now why the earth is gross, tantalizing, wicked, it is for my sake, / I take you specially to be mine, you terrible, rude forms."

He summarizes the idea of America in the final two sections by returning to earlier themes. He sees the "bards" of the past once again "trooping toward me," but they are no longer important, even in their criticism of him. Only the present is important and what he and all other American bards do now and for the future. He calls on

Bards of the great Idea! Bards of the peaceful
   inventions! . . .
Bards with songs as from burning coals or the
   lightning's fork'd stripes!
. . . bards of California! inland bards . . .
You by my charm I invoke.

Whitman would, through his own poetic charm, conjure up all of the bards of America. He sees his own role as one of mentor for poets yet to come, poets who will have the same vision for democracy that he has.

Whitman presents in this poem his vision for America—which he has been inspired to observe while "By Blue Ontario's Shore"—but also his role and that of all America's poets in the presentation of that vision to the nation and the world.

"By Broad Potomac's Shore" (1871)

First published in *As a Strong Bird on Pinions Free*, the supplementary volume to the fifth edition of *Leaves of Grass* (1871); it was not printed again until it appeared as the 15th of 22 poems in the "From Noon to Starry Night" cluster for the sixth edition (1881).

The poem comes out of Whitman's return to Washington in 1865 as a clerk in the Department of the Interior. He was eager to return to the capital city, but postwar Washington was depressing and is reflected in the eighth line of the poem: "Perfume this book of mine O blood-red roses!" He would like his poem to be more optimistic than he himself is feeling. He was working on his fourth edition of *Leaves of Grass* at the time (1867), which may account for the poem's mixed images.

The poem has a sonnet-like frame; not the traditional stanzas of eight and six lines (Italian) or three quatrains and a couplet (English) and an iambic pentameter rhythm but of seven and five lines and in an ACCENTUAL VERSE form, the number of accented syllables carrying the rhythm. It has short lines at the beginning and end of each stanza with longer lines in the middle, the number of accents per line as follows: 5-5-9-9-4-6-4 and 5-5-8-6-3.

"By That Long Scan of Waves" (1885)

First published with seven other poems under the heading "Fancies at Navesink" in NINETEENTH CENTURY magazine (August 1885); then in *November Boughs* (1888); and, finally, with the "Fancies at Navesink" group as an insert in the "First Annex: Sands at Seventy" cluster for the "Death-bed" printing of *Leaves of Grass* (1892). The "scan of waves" represents for Whitman a sort of retrospective on his own life: "Joys, travels, studies, silent panoramas—scenes ephemeral," all "summ'd up" as "intentionless, the whole a nothing." Yet in the last two lines he recognizes an element of hope for a life that may have been worth living after all: "And haply yet some drop within God's scheme's ensemble—some wave, or part of wave, / Like one of yours, ye multitudinous ocean." Like the movement of the waves at sea, he perhaps sees his own life as having a similar chaotic ebb and flow.

"By the Bivouac's Fitful Flame" (1865)

First appeared in the *Drum-Taps* volume (1865) and was under this title throughout its printing his-

tory in *Leaves of Grass*; it was the 13th of 43 poems in the "Drum-Taps" cluster for the sixth edition (1881).

The poet places himself in the mind of a soldier seated at a fire during a troop bivouac. Most of the army sleeps, but the poet can see the "fields' and woods' dim outline," and "an occasional figure moving." He feels the thoughts of the soldiers, "tender and wondrous thoughts, / Of life and death, of home and the past and loved, and of those that are far away." All of this he feels or thinks about while he sits by the "bivouac's fitful flame."

There doesn't seem to be any attempt on Whitman's part to create anything more than a peaceful scene in time of war, yet readers may feel some tension between this scene and the potential for coming battles and the killing that follows, an irony that soldiers who have been in battle will not miss.

See also "Cavalry Crossing a Ford," "Bivouac on a Mountain Side," "A Sight in Camp in the Daybreak Gray and Dim," "As Toilsome I Wandered Virginia's Woods," "I Saw Old General at Bay," and "Look Down Fair Moon."

"By The Roadside" (1881)

Cluster title for 29 poems in the sixth edition of *Leaves of Grass* (1881). The first two poems in the cluster, "A Boston Ballad (1854)" and "Europe, The 72d and 73d Years of These States," had appeared with 10 other untitled poems in the first edition (1855); 24 of the poems appeared in editions and printings published during the next 20 years, and three were new to *Leaves of Grass*.

The 29 poems are connected not by theme so much (as poems tend to be in other *Leaves of Grass* clusters) but by Whitman's own observations of life, as if he were seated "by the roadside" making notes as people and events pass by, notes that he later turned into these poems.

More than half of the poems in the cluster are short, 17 of them four lines or less, and most are one sentence in length.

The poems appear in the following order: "A Boston Ballad (1854)," "Europe, The 72d and 73d

Years of These States," "A Hand-Mirror," "Gods," "Germs," "Thoughts" [Of ownership], "When I Heard the Learn'd Astronomer," "Perfections," "O Me! O Life!," "To a President," "I Sit and Look Out," "To Rich Givers," "The Dalliance of the Eagles," "Roaming in Thought," "A Farm Picture," "A Child's Amaze," "The Runner," "Beautiful Women," "Mother and Babe," "Thought" [Of obedience], "Visor'd," "Thought" [Of Justice], "Gliding o'er All," "Hast Never Come to Thee an Hour," "Thought" [Of Equality], "To Old Age," "Locations and Times," "Offerings," and "To the States: To Identify the 16th, 17th or 18th Presidentiad."

"Calamus" (1860)

Cluster title for 45 untitled but numbered poems in the third edition of *Leaves of Grass* (1860); Whitman reduced the number to 42 for the fourth edition (1867) and gave them titles; by the fifth edition (1871) he had reduced the number of Calamus poems to 39 and made no further changes in the number or ordering of the poems.

Webster's New World Dictionary (1980), the second college edition, defines the Calamus plant as "any of a genus (*Calamus*) of climbing palms of the old World that yield rattan." Known popularly as Sweetflag, it grows near ponds with a stem about three feet high. It also has a phallic-shaped bloom, no doubt important in Whitman's choice of the plant for his final title. Whitman wrote a letter to an English acquaintance, "M. D. Conway," dated November 1, 1867, in which he says that "Calamus is a common word here [in Washington]; . . . The recherché or ethereal sense, as used in my book, arises probably from it, Calamus presenting the biggest and hardiest kind of spears of grass, and from its fresh, aromatic, pungent bouquet."

The "Children of Adam" cluster of poems—which appears just before the Calamus cluster in *Leaves of Grass*—celebrates heterosexual love; the Calamus poems celebrate homosexual love. Whitman, who most biographers believe was homosexual, or perhaps bisexual, made a distinction between the two kinds of love that is important to

an understanding of these poems. He used the term *amativeness* to describe the love between men and women, and he used the term *adhesiveness* to describe the love between two men. The latter term is used to describe the brotherhood of man, a love sometimes physical (which may be, though not necessarily, sexual) but most often spiritual, a love he uses as a metaphor for democracy; he believed that love was one of the essential ingredients for the America he envisioned. The *Oxford English Dictionary* defines *amativeness*, on the other hand, as a "propensity to love, or sexual passions," for Whitman a more limited definition.

The need for adhesiveness, then, which Whitman often refers to in his poems as "comradeship," is more important to the poet because it generates the larger concept of love. Several of the Calamus poems are overtly sexual, but they too carry the larger idea of the need in a democratic society for love among all people—perhaps the single most important theme in *Leaves of Grass*.

In *Democratic Vistas*, Whitman discusses the ambiguity in a society that encourages individualism while, at the same time, encouraging the love of one's friends and fellow beings. He writes that democracy "alone can bind, and ever seeks to bind, all nations, all men, of however various and distant lands, into a brotherhood, a family. It is the old, yet ever-modern dream of earth, out of her eldest and her youngest, her fond philosophers and poets. Not that half only, individualism, which isolates. There is another half, which is adhesiveness or love, that fuses, ties, and aggregates, making the races comrades, and fraternizing all."

In arguing against critics who tend to emphasize the homosexual interpretations of the Calamus poems, James E. Miller, Jr., argues in his *Critical Guide to Leaves of Grass* that "there are only two ways of reading 'Calamus' as a proclamation of . . . unwholesome [love]: superficially, without going beneath the surface meanings, without attention to the intentional ambiguity; or psychoanalytically, with no attention whatever to either surface or symbolic meaning, but with intensive (and wild) speculation as to personal motives and unintended revelations." The Calamus poems become then some of the most important poems in *Leaves of*

Grass for understanding Whitman's concept of democracy.

The cluster's 39 poems are in the following order: "In the Paths Untrodden," "Scented Herbage of My Breast," "Whoever You Are Holding Me Now in Hand," "For You O Democracy," "These I Singing in Spring," "Not Heaving from my Ribb'd Breast Only," "Of the Terrible Doubt of Appearances," "The Base of All Metaphysics," "Recorders Ages Hence," "When I Heard at the Close of the Day," "Are You the New Person Drawn Toward Me?" "Roots and Leaves Themselves Alone," "Not Heat Flames Up and Consumes," "Trickle Drops," "City of Orgies," "Behold This Swarthy Face," "I Saw in Louisiana a Live-Oak Growing," "To a Stranger," "This Moment Yearning and Thoughtful," "I Hear It was Charged against Me," "The Prairie-Grass Dividing," "When I Peruse the Conquer'd Fame," "We Two Boys Together Clinging," "A Promise to California," "Here the Frailest Leaves of Me," "No Labor-Saving Machine," "A Glimpse," "A Leaf for Hand in Hand," "Earth, My Likeness," "I Dream'd in a Dream," "What Think You I Take My Pen in Hand?" "To the East and to the West," "Sometimes with One I Love," "To a Western Boy," "Fast-Anchor'd Eternal O Love!" "Among the Multitude," "O You Whom I Often and Silently Come," "That Shadow My Likeness," and "Full of Life Now."

"Calming Thought of All, The" (1888)

First published in the NEW YORK HERALD (May 27, 1888); then in *November Boughs* (1888); and it was the 45th of 65 poems in the "First Annex: Sands at Seventy" cluster for the "Death-bed" printing of *Leaves of Grass* (1892).

Whatever the "speculations," the poet suggests in these four lines, the most "calming thought of all" is that the "round earth's silent vital laws, facts, modes continue." No matter what habits humans develop over time, the earth survives.

"Camps of Green" (1871)

First appeared in the *Drum-Taps* volume (1865); then in the "Ashes of Soldiers" cluster for the fifth edition of *Leaves of Grass* (1871); and it was the ninth of 17 poems in the "Songs of Parting" cluster for the sixth edition (1881).

It is the green tents that make the camps green in this poem, but the alive camps of the first stanza, which Whitman had observed, become metaphoric in the second stanza. The green tents become monuments for the soldiers dead and buried across the battlegrounds of the Civil War.

> Now in those camps of green, in their tents
>   dotting the world, . . .
> Sleeping under the sunlight, sleeping under the
>   moonlight, content and silent there at last, . . .
> For presently O soldiers, we too camp in our
>   place in the bivouac-camps of green,

Walt Whitman, 1871 *(Library of Congress, Prints and Photographs Division)*

But we need not provide for outposts, nor word
for the counter-sign,
Nor drummer to beat the morning drum.

For those soldiers who died in the war—more than 600,000 all together—there is no longer a need for an awakening by the "morning drum," nor a need to pack up and move on to the next battle site. The war is over for them. Yet the poet reassures the dead soldiers that "we too camp in our place in the bivouac-camps of green," that we too die or are dead and in the camps of green. As John Donne had written in a sermon 200 years before, "any man's death diminishes me, because I am involved in Mankinde." Every American died a little with each dead soldier in the CIVIL WAR, North and South.

"Carol Closing Sixty-Nine, A" (1888)

First published in the NEW YORK HERALD (May 21, 1888); then in *November Boughs* (1888); and it was the fifth of 65 poems in the "First Annex: Sands at Seventy" cluster for the "Death-bed" printing of *Leaves of Grass* (1892).

Whitman turned 69 in 1888, and this poem, first published 10 days before his birthday, is a "carol" to the things he remembers and loves best: "God, Life, Nature, Freedom, Poetry." And America: "Of you, my Land—your rivers, prairies, States . . . north, south, east and west, your items all."

And himself, "the jocund heart yet beating in my breast, . . . the burning fires down in my sluggish blood not yet extinct." And his "undiminish'd faith . . . [in] loving friends."

"Cavalry Crossing a Ford" (1865)

First appeared in the *Drum-Taps* volume (1865); it then appeared in the fourth edition of *Leaves of Grass* (1867); it was the 10th of 43 poems in the "Drum-Taps" cluster for the sixth edition of *Leaves* (1881). It was published under this title throughout its printing history.

This is the first of several poems descriptive of CIVIL WAR scenes of men at war but not in battle. "Cavalry Crossing a Ford" describes the movement of soldiers across a "silvery river," the "splashing horses" stopping to drink, suntanned soldiers, some resting on their saddles, some moving up onto the shore, others just entering the river, "The guidon flags flutter[ing] gayly in the wind." Whitman doesn't seem to suggest any particular metaphoric significance in this poem, although readers may well feel the tension, perhaps even irony, between the scene of time stopped momentarily for these soldiers and a coming battle in which they know men will be killed.

There are other poems following "Cavalry Crossing a Ford" in the "Drum-Taps" cluster that present similar, seemingly peaceful descriptions of men at war. See "Bivouac on a Mountain Side," "By the Bivouac's Fitful Flame," "A Sight in Camp in the Daybreak Gray and Dim," "As Toilsome I Wandered Virginia's Woods," "I Saw Old General at Bay," and "Look Down Fair Moon."

"Centenarian's Story, The" (1865)

First appeared in the *Drum-Taps* volume (1865); it was the ninth of 43 poems in the "Drum-Taps" cluster for the sixth edition of *Leaves of Grass* (1881), and it was under this title throughout its printing history in *Leaves of Grass*. It was originally titled "Washington's First Battle" and was to appear in a separate volume titled *Banner at Daybreak*, but the book was not published. The poem's subtitle is "Volunteer of 1861–2 (at Washington Park, BROOKLYN, assisting the Centenarian)."

"The Centenarian's Story" is a dramatic conversation between the poet and a veteran of the Revolutionary War, a man of a "hundred and extra years." The narrative takes place in Brooklyn's

Washington Park, the site of an old Revolutionary War battleground as young soldiers prepare 89 years later to leave for the CIVIL WAR. The Centenarian had fought on the same ground against the British on August 27, 1776. Although the battle is not named, the fighting that took place on that date was later referred to as the "Battle of Long Island."

The poem is in three sections and 112 lines. Section 1 sets the scene: the Centenarian is watching young soldiers preparing to go to war; Section 2 describes the old veteran's story of how his brigade held off the British long enough to allow General Washington to escape with his remaining troops across the East River to New York City; and in Section 3, titled "Terminus," the poet envisions the scene of the British landing 80 years ago and sums up the significance of Brooklyn's Civil War encampment.

The poet takes the Centenarian by the hand at the beginning of the poem, helping him walk to the top of the hill where they can watch the soldiers preparing for war. He explains to the nearly blind old soldier that the "recruits are drilling and exercising" and that one of the regiments will depart the next day for the South. The old man is emotional at the scene, and the poet asks him why: "Why what comes over you now old man? / Why do you tremble and clutch my hand so convulsively?" It is a "splendid" summer afternoon, and when the drilling is over, the troops march back to their quarters to the applause of the people watching. The poet and the old soldier remain: "Not for nothing have I brought you hither," the poet says, "we must remain, / You to speak in your turn, and I to listen and tell."

The Centenarian tells the poet that the scene has reminded him of the horror of fighting against the British along the same hillside during the war for independence:

Aye, this is the ground,
My blind eyes even as I speak behold it
   re-peopled from graves,
The years recede, pavements and stately
   houses disappear,
Rude forts appear again, the old hoop'd guns
   are mounted, . . .

Here we lay encamp'd, it was this time in
   summer also.

He remembers that General Washington had read the Declaration of Independence to the troops on the same ground; the Declaration had been signed on August 2, 1876, less than a month before the Battle of Long Island. "Twas a bold act then," he says, because they could see the English warships on the river "at anchor, / And the transports swarming with soldiers." The battle began a few days later: "Twenty thousand were brought against us, / A veteran force furnish'd with good artillery."

It sickens me yet, that slaughter!
I saw the moisture gather in drops on the face
   of the General.
I saw how he wrung his hands in anguish. . . .

General Washington's troops were fighting along Brooklyn Heights, one of the first battles of the Revolutionary War. "And then he left us," the old soldier says, and a Virginia and Maryland brigade of 2,000 men was left to hold off the British while Washington took the remainder of his troops across the East River to safety. Of the 2,000, most "remain in Brooklyn," the veteran says, only a few survived. The old vet refers to Washington as "my General" and describes seeing him as a man not ready for "capitulation."

It is not the memory of the lost battle that frightens the Centenarian. Even as the Civil War soldiers prepare for war they turn and smile at their wives and sweethearts, full of confidence that they will return safely from the coming battles. It is that confidence which frightens the old man.

In the final, "Terminus," section, the poet says that with the end of the Centenarian's story, the two scenes, "past and present, have interchanged." He sees himself as the "connector," telling the story and bringing the two dramatic scenes together: "I must copy the story, and send it eastward and westward." In the second to last stanza he sums up the old soldier's story of the futile battle, concluding:

Ah, hills and slopes of Brooklyn! I perceive you
   are more valuable than your owners supposed;
In the midst of you stands an encampment very
   old,
Stands forever the camp of that dead brigade.

There is significant irony involved in the difference between the two stories told in this poem. There is the horrifying story of the old Revolutionary War soldier reminded of the battle he had been in 89 years before on the same Brooklyn hillside and telling about the slaughter by the British of most of the soldiers in his brigade. That story is placed against the young soldiers preparing to go off to another battle, this one against the South in the Civil War, the soldiers full of confidence and cheered on by their women and children as if the battle would be nothing for the soldiers or their loved ones to worry about.

"Chanting the Square Deific" (1865)

First appeared in the *Sequel to Drum-Taps* volume (1865); it was then placed in the "Passage to India" supplement to the fifth edition of *Leaves of Grass* (1871); it was the third of 18 poems in the "Whispers of Heavenly Death" cluster for the sixth edition (1881).

In this poem God is not a trinity, as generally accepted in the Christian church, but a quaternity. There are four stanzas, each 10 to 13 lines and each presenting one of the four sides to Whitman's "Square Deific," and each told from the speaker's point of view, first God, then Christ, then Satan, and, finally, the Soul ("Santa Spirita").

God describes himself as Jehovah, but also as "Old Brahm" (god of Hindu mythology), "Saturnius" (god of Roman mythology), and Kronos (youngest of the Titan gods). God describes himself as merciless: "Relentless I forgive no man—whoever sins dies—I will have that man's life; / . . . I dispense from this side judgments inexorable without the least remorse."

Christ, the second side of the square deific, is the "Consolator," the comforter. He says he is the "mightier God"; he takes "All sorrow, labor, suffering" onto his own shoulders. He "absorbs" all sin in himself. He is also the "cheer-bringing God, with hope and all-enclosing charity." Charity "has no death," Christ says: "My wisdom dies not, . . . /

And my sweet love bequeath'd here and elsewhere never dies."

Satan is, on the other hand, "Aloof, dissatisfied, plotting revolt." He is the "Comrade of criminals," but at the same time a "brother of slaves," indicating a soft heart for the downtrodden. He is with "sudra," a member of the lowest Hindu class. Satan is "Defiant" and "Permanent . . . warlike, equal with any, real as any," and nothing will change him or his words. Satan is opposite God in the Square Deific, creating, Whitman may be suggesting here, a balance between good and evil, both necessary, he believed, in the lives of human beings and in all of Nature.

The fourth side is "Santa Spirita, breather, life," the Holy Spirit, the unifying spirit of the universe, the "general soul," opposite Christ in the square but more "solid," because the Soul includes all three of the other sides: God, Satan, and Christ. The Soul reconciles the other three:

> Life of the great round world, the sun and stars,
>   and of man, I, the general soul,
> Here the square finishing, the solid, I the most
>   solid,
> Breathe my breath also through these songs.

The last line suggests that the poet himself represents the Santa Spirita, singing not just this "Chant" of the "Square Deific," but all the songs of *Leaves of Grass.*

"Child and the Profligate, The" (1841)

Short story, first published in the NEW WORLD (November 20, 1841) under the title "The Child's Champion." The tale underwent a number of revisions in four reprintings during the next few years, including the change of title. The story is most accessible now in *Walt Whitman: The Early Poems and the Fiction,* edited by Thomas L. Brasher (New York University Press, 1963).

It is the story of the 13-year-old Charley, the "child" of the story's title, who with his widowed mother is rescued from poverty by the "profligate," John Langton. The boy is mistreated by farmer

Ellis, for whom he works, and Charley threatens to run away from the job and would if it weren't for his mother's pleading. She tries to reassure him about the importance of the money he is earning for the two of them.

The story's narrator describes Langton as "a dissipated young man—a brawler—one whose too frequent companions were rowdies, blacklegs [gamblers who cheat], and swindlers. The New York police offices were not strangers to his countenance." He had, however, "been bred to the profession of medicine" and "he had a very respectable income, and his house was in a pleasant street on the west side of the city." He left the city for a time and finds himself in a small village with a tavern, which suits his dissipation. He is extremely unhappy at who he has become, however, yet continues to drink away the sorrow.

His life is turned around when he and Charley meet in the tavern, now full of drunken sailors. Charley has been attracted to the bar by some music and is listening at one of the windows. A "one-eyed sailor" invites Charley into the bar—in fact, lifts him through the window—and then threatens the boy when he refuses to drink a glass of brandy the sailor is trying to force on him. The one-eyed sailor is thrashed by Langton, who then befriends the boy and promises to help him and his mother.

The "profligate" rescues Charley and his widowed mother from their life of poverty. The story's last paragraph sums up the new life for both Charley and the profligate: "It needs not that I [the narrator] should particularize the subsequent events of Langton's and the boy's history—how the reformation of the profligate might be dated to begin from that time—how he gradually sever'd the guilty ties that had so long gall'd him—how he enjoy'd his own home again—how the friendship of Charles and himself grew not slack with time—and how, when in the course of seasons he became head of a family of his own, he would shudder at the remembrance of his early dangers and his escapes."

This story, along with the novel, *Franklin Evans; or The Inebriate: A Tale of the Times*, presents a rather too obvious moral tale meant to discourage intemperance on the part of its readers.

CHARACTERS

John Langton   Young man of 21 or 22 years, the "profligate" of the short story "The Child and the Profligate." He has a medical degree and a "respectable income," yet is squandering his life away with alcohol. The story's narrator describes him as "intelligent" with an "air of city life and society." He owns a nice house in a pleasant neighborhood on the west side of a city, probably New York. He is, in short, a gentleman. But he has become "a dissipated young man," who often finds himself in drunken fights and associated with the wrong people. He is in the tavern of a small village 50 miles from the city when he meets Charley.

Charley   The 13-year-old only child of his widowed mother. Charley wants to quit his job as an apprentice to farmer Ellis who treats him like a "slave." The boy's mother reminds him, however, of their poverty and of the importance of his income. On his way back to Ellis's farm, Charley is attracted by some tavern music. A one-eyed sailor invites him in for a drink—even lifts him through the window—and threatens him when he refuses a brandy. Langton, the story's main character, rescues the boy, befriends him, and helps him and his mother out of their poverty.

Ellis   Farmer to whom Charley is apprenticed in "The Child and the Profligate." He doesn't appear in the story, but his treatment of the boy is crucial to the reader's understanding of why Charley continues to work for him.

"Child-Ghost: A Story of the Last Loyalist, The"

See "Last Loyalist, The."

"Children of Adam"   (1881)

Cluster title for 16 poems in the sixth edition of *Leaves of Grass* (1881). The cluster was originally titled "Enfans d'Adam" with 15 poems in the third edition of *Leaves* (1860); 12 of the poems were new to that edition; the fourth edition (1867) carried the present cluster title and 14 poems; the fifth edition (1871) included the 14 poems from the preceding edition and two poems that had appeared originally in the *Drum-Taps* volume (1865).

Each of the Children of Adam poems affirms the Garden of Eden myth. Whitman called these "amative" poems because of their collective concern for the physical love of a man for a woman. The "Calamus" cluster, which Whitman placed next in his ordering of poems for *Leaves of Grass,* is collectively concerned with the love of a man for another man, "paths untrodden."

In the Children of Adam poems, all people are the children of Adam. EMERSON, who had praised the first edition of *Leaves of Grass,* argued against publication of the Children of Adam poems in a conversation with Whitman. Emerson may have seen the poems while still in their handwritten stage, and his main argument, which Whitman later recorded, was that the poems "would lose sales"—probably because of their sexual imagery and innuendo. Even before these poems were published, Whitman had had difficulty with censorship. He had been forced to move publication of the second edition of *Leaves of Grass* (1860) to BROOKLYN because Boston authorities wanted to cut some lines or whole poems from the book. Emerson apparently lost the loss-of-sales argument, after which, according to Whitman, the two men went out to dinner. It is interesting to note that Emerson did not complain about the Calamus poems, apparently because he believed that Whitman was using the love of one man for another as a metaphor for brotherly love.

Whitman makes the distinction between *amativeness* and *adhesiveness,* the former term used to describe the love between men and women, the latter used to describe the love of men for men. Poems in both clusters also may be read as images of love that encompass the larger and, Whitman believed, more significant concept of the brotherhood of man, of comradeship, friendship, a love sometimes physical (though not necessarily sexual) but most often spiritual, a love he used often as a metaphor for democracy. Democracy demands equality, he believed, which can only be secured with love. And

for Whitman, the only sin was a belief in sin. God excluded Adam and Eve from the Garden of Eden, Whitman believed, not because they had sinned but because they believed they had.

The order of the 16 poems in the 1881 "Children of Adam" cluster is as follows: "To the Garden the World," "From Pent-up Aching Rivers," "I Sing the Body Electric," "A Woman Waits for Me," "Spontaneous Me," "One Hour to Madness and Joy," "Out of the Rolling Ocean the Crowd," "Ages and Ages Returning at Intervals," "We Two, How Long We Were Fool'd," "O Hymen! O Hymenee!" "I Am He that Aches with Love," "Native Moments," "Once I Pass'd through a Populous City," "I Heard You Solemn-Sweet Pipes of the Organ," "Facing West from California's Shores," and "As Adam Early in the Morning."

Three of these poems had been published in earlier editions: "I Sing the Body Electric," untitled in the first edition (1855); "A Woman Waits for Me," titled "Poem of Procreation" (1856); and "Spontaneous Me," titled "Bunch Poem" (1856).

"Child's Amaze, A" (1865)

First published in the *Drum-Taps* volume (1865); it was in the fourth edition of *Leaves of Grass* (1867); it was published as a separate poem (1871); then it was the 16th of 29 poems in the "By The Roadside" cluster for the sixth edition (1881).

The child's "amaze" in this three-line poem concerns the preacher's "statements" about God. For the preacher, God was always "contending against some being or influence." For the child, the preacher described a negative God, one unsatisfactory to the natural optimism that a child (or poet) would feel about life.

"Christmas Greeting, A" (1891)

First published as the 17th of 31 poems in *Good-Bye My Fancy* (1891); and it was in "Second Annex: Good-Bye My Fancy" for the "Death-bed" printing of *Leaves of Grass* (1892).

The "greeting" is, according to the parenthetical epigraph, from a "Northern Star-Group to a Southern, 1889–90," the former indicating America, the latter Brazil, or perhaps all of Latin America. Whitman suggests that America is, in "1889–'90," already as bright a star shining in the Northern Hemisphere as the "Cross" and the "Crown" are in the Southern. The Cross ("Crux") is the Southern Cross, the Crown ("Corona Australis") is the Southern Crown, two of the brightest constellations in the Southern Hemisphere. America is "cluster free," the poet says, a "brilliant lustrous [single star]," the "height" of which is "superb humanity."

"City Dead-House, The" (1867)

First appeared in the fourth edition of *Leaves of Grass* (1867); it was the fifth of 38 poems in the "Autumn Rivulets" cluster for the sixth edition (1881). It remained virtually unrevised during its publication history.

Many of the poems of the 1867 edition of *Leaves* showed Whitman's concern with the social upheaval following the CIVIL WAR. There was a great deal of nationwide tension over several issues, mostly racial tensions but other issues as well. When Whitman published these poems Congress was discussing and in the process of passing the Fourteenth Amendment to the Constitution (passed in the summer of 1868), which made all people born in the United States citizens and which forbade any state from making a law that would take away any person's rights of citizenship. That meant that former slaves became U.S. citizens immediately, and that idea did not go down well with a number of southern states.

For Whitman, the "poor dead prostitute," whose body was unceremoniously dumped at the gate of "The City Dead-House," became a symbol for all the invincible people in America, who, like the prostitute, went through life unnamed and, in death, were unclaimed. The Dead-House itself became a symbol of the "tenement of a soul," more important to society than "all the rows of dwellings

ever built! . . ." more important than the "white-domed capitol . . . or all the old high-spired cathedrals." Not even churches mattered to Whitman if the Dead-House continued to survive as a place to dump the bodies of unidentified citizens.

If a nation cannot take care of its poor, then it is doomed to the same "invincibility" as the dead prostitute ("dead, dead, dead") or the former slave trying to cope with sudden freedom and finding invisibility.

"City of Orgies" (1860)

Titled "Calamus No. 18" in the third edition of *Leaves of Grass* (1860); it was given its present title (1867), which remained unchanged throughout the remainder of its publication history; it was the 15th of 39 poems in the "Calamus" cluster for the sixth edition (1881).

The "city of orgies" is New York, which offers "orgies" but also "walks and joys." The city offers great variety—pageants, tableaus, "interminable rows" of houses, "ships at the wharves," street processions, bright store windows, and so forth; but it is not these to which the poet responds. It is instead the city's "swift flash of eyes offering me love." It is the signal given on the street, perhaps, one man to another, the offer of love, perhaps sexual love, that Whitman responds to—at least in this poem.

The poet believes that his poems of Manhattan will make the city "illustrious," but it is not the variety of "spectacles" that will repay the poet; "lovers, continual lovers, only repay me."

See also "Behold This Swarthy Face," the next poem following "City of Orgies" in the "Calamus" cluster.

"City of Ships" (1865)

First appeared in the *Drum-Taps* volume (1865); it was under this title throughout its printing history and not revised; it was the eighth of 43 poems in the "Drum-Taps" cluster for the sixth edition of *Leaves of Grass* (1881).

The poem is a memorial to New York, city of ships and "City of the world! (for all races are here, / All the lands of the earth make contributions here)." Every ship of importance stopped in New York, and Whitman enjoyed thinking of the diversity brought to the city by these ships, representing all the great nations of the world.

In the early 1860s, however, it was a city at war, and this poem expresses Whitman's love for the city still, even though "warlike." It was, for the poet, a "proud and passionate city—mettlesome" and a "mad, extravagant city."

> I chant and celebrate all that is yours—yet
>   peace no more,
> In peace I chanted peace, but now the drum of
>   war is mine,
> War, red war is my song through your streets,
>   O city!

The poem presents Whitman's ambiguity toward the CIVIL WAR. He thought the war was necessary in order to preserve the Union, but he spent much of the war working in Washington, D.C., hospitals, and he hated what he saw the war do to the soldiers of both North and South. In this poem he shows his love for New York, in spite of the war, always willing to take the bad with the good.

"Clear Midnight, A" (1881)

First appeared as the last of 22 poems in the "From Noon to Starry Night" cluster for the sixth edition of *Leaves of Grass* (1881).

This four-line poem is a coda to the "From Noon to Starry Night" cluster and a transition into the next group of poems, "Songs of Parting." The midnight is clear because "This is the hour O Soul, [for] thy free flight into the wordless."

Collected Writings of Walt Whitman, The (1961)

The most complete and comprehensive collection of Whitman's writing available. New York Univer-

sity Press began publishing the collection in 1961. The general editors for the project are Gay Wilson Allen and Sculley Bradley. Twenty-two volumes have been published to date, but they are not numbered sequentially.

In order of publication, the collection is as follows: *Correspondence*, edited by Edwin Haviland Miller in six volumes, 1961–1977; *The Early Poems and the Fiction*, edited by Thomas L. Brasher in one volume, 1963; *Prose Works 1892*, edited by Floyd Stovall in two volumes, 1963–1964; *Leaves of Grass: Comprehensive Reader's Edition*, edited by Harold W. Blodgett and Sculley Bradley, 1965; *Daybooks and Notebooks*, edited by William White in three volumes, 1978; *Leaves of Grass: A Textual Variorum of the Printed Poems*, edited by Sculley Bradley, Harold W. Blodgett, Arthur Golden, and William White in three volumes, 1980; *Notebooks and Unpublished Prose Manuscripts*, edited by Edward F. Grier in six volumes, 1984; and *The Correspondence*, vol. 7, edited by Ted Genoways, 2004. For more up-to-date information about this collection, see the Walt Whitman Archive on the Internet at http://www.whitmanarchive.org.

"Columbian's Song, The" (1840)

First published in the LONG ISLAND DEMOCRAT (October 27, 1840); an "early poem" *not* later published in *Leaves of Grass*. It is most accessible now in Francis Murphy (editor), *Walt Whitman: The Complete Poems* (Penguin Books, 1996).

"Come, Said My Soul" (1874)

Not a title but the first line of an untitled, nine-line poem that became the epigraph, appearing before the title page for *Leaves of Grass* beginning with the sixth edition (1876). It was first published in the NEW YORK DAILY GRAPHIC (December 1874).

The poet informs readers that he wishes to write "verses" that would be pleasing "should I after death invisibly return" and see the name "Walt Whitman" credited for the poems. This futuristic imagery appears in a number of Whitman's poems. He often envisions future readers, and he sometimes sees himself walking with them and he wishes them well.

"Come up from the Fields Father" (1865)

First appeared in the *Drum-Taps* volume (1865) and under this title throughout its printing history in *Leaves of Grass*; it was the 14th of 43 poems in the "Drum-Taps" cluster for the sixth edition (1881).

The poem opens with a letter home from a soldier during the war:

> Come up from the fields father, here's a letter
>   from our Pete,
> And come to the front door mother, here's a
>   letter from thy dear son.

The letter is written by a stranger but signed by the son. The family—father, mother, a "just-grown daughter" and "little sisters"—gather around the front door to hear the letter read. It tells of the son's wounding but reassures the family that he will be okay. Then the omniscient poet tells the reader:

> Alas poor boy, he will never be better,
>   (nor may-be needs to be better, that brave
>   and simple soul,)
> While they stand at home at the door he is
>   dead already,
> The only son is dead.

This poem comes directly from Whitman's own experiences of such potential scenes. While working as an assistant at various Washington CIVIL WAR HOSPITALS, he often wrote letters home to families of soldiers—North and South—perhaps even knowing that by the time the family received the letter, their son would be dead.

"Commonplace, The" (1891)

First published as a manuscript facsimile in *Munson's Magazine* (March 1891); it was the 24th of 31 poems in *Good-Bye My Fancy* (1891); and in "Second Annex: Good-Bye My Fancy" for the "Deathbed" printing of *Leaves of Grass* (1892).

Whitman "sings" here "the commonplace, . . . the open air . . . freedom, toleration." Democratic "wisdom" is "underneath" the commonplace, "like solid ground for all." The democratic theme of freedom, toleration, and equality permeates the poet's work here and throughout *Leaves of Grass*.

Complete Poems and Prose: 1855 . . . 1888 (1888)

Published by David McKAY in Philadelphia late in 1888, printed by Ferguson Brothers & Co. The 900 pages of text included the sixth edition of *Leaves of Grass* (1881), *Specimen Days & Collect*, and *November Boughs*.

In a "Note at Beginning," Whitman writes about his illness ("paralysis, continued yet—which will have to serve as excuse for many faults both of omission and commission . . ."). But he adds: "But I would not let the great and momentous Era of these years [1855–88], these States, slip away without attempting to arrest in a special printed book . . . some few specimens—even vital throbs, breaths—as representations of it all—from my point of view, and right from the midst of it, jotted at the time."

The years he refers to are some of the most important years in the history of the United States, history that was determined primarily by the CIVIL WAR and by new attitudes toward democracy that developed during those years. Whitman's six editions of *Leaves of Grass* had a large influence on America's attitudes toward those years, even though most people might not have recognized it at the time.

Walt Whitman at 71, June 1890 *(Library of Congress, Prints and Photographs Division)*

"Continuities" (1888)

First published in the NEW YORK HERALD (March 20, 1888); then in *November Boughs* (1888); and it was the 38th of 65 poems in the "First Annex: Sands at Seventy" cluster for the "Death-bed" printing of *Leaves of Grass* (1892).

Whitman identifies the source of this poem as a talk he had had "lately with a German spiritualist," the gist of which was that "nothing is ever really lost, or can be lost." There is "continuity," a connectedness among all things that keeps those things alive: "The body, sluggish, aged, cold—the embers left from earlier fires, / The light in the eye grown dim, shall duly flame again." But everything returns, just as does the spring "grass and flowers and summer fruits and corn."

The idea of "continuities" ties in with two of Whitman's thematic ideas: that from life there is death, but then rebirth, and that the spirit of God is in all things and that all things reflect that spirit (see PANTHEISM).

"Crossing Brooklyn Ferry" (1856)

Published first as "Sun-Down Poem" in the second edition of *Leaves of Grass* (1856); then under its present title and as a separate poem (1860); it became the third of 12 separate poems that followed the "Calamus" cluster in the sixth edition (1881). "Crossing Brooklyn Ferry" is generally considered to be one of the greatest of Whitman's poems.

The poet takes a mystical journey, not to a union with God as in "Song of Myself," but to a union with people outside the normal limits of time or space. Even during Whitman's life, the actual ferry service for the half-mile run across the East River from BROOKLYN to New York took only a few minutes, so it must have been the crowds of people who made the trip daily that influenced the poet to think of it as a metaphor for the movement of time. People had been taking the ferry since the beginning of the service in 1642 (using rowboats), and were, during Whitman's years in Brooklyn, using the steamboat service of the New York and Brooklyn Ferry Company. The poet took the ferry frequently, even if just to walk the streets of the lower part of the city. He wrote the poem several years before the BROOKLYN BRIDGE was built (1870–83), but the bridge didn't matter in Whitman's mystical vision.

Whitman refers to it as the Brooklyn Ferry, but during most of its history it has been called the FULTON FERRY, because it began at Fulton Landing, a waterfront village on the Brooklyn side of the river. Robert Fulton was in 1807 the first to make steam navigation a success, and in 1814 he began his steamboat ferry service across the East River, running boats from the foot of what is now Old Fulton Street in Brooklyn to the present Pier 11 ferry stop in New York City. The Fulton Ferry still runs every half hour most of the day from Fulton Ferry Landing beneath the Brooklyn Bridge to five landing stations on the New York side of the East River.

"Crossing Brooklyn Ferry" brings together several of Whitman's poetic skills, not the least of which is one of the clearest examples of the rhythm of his FREE VERSE style. Free verse was a shock to mid-19th-century readers of poetry, accustomed as they were to a uniform metrical pattern and a rhyme scheme. Whitman presented instead large stanzaic patterns, similar to those in ancient Hebrew poetry, especially in the Psalms of the Old Testament.

Because of the merging of past, present, and future verb tenses and a gradual shift from a narrative "I" to "you" and then to "we," the reader and the poet become one in this mystical voyage across the river. The poet warps time in order to merge himself with people, past, present, and future, the ferry crossing only a starting point for his journey.

SECTIONS 1–3

The poem contains nine sections and 133 lines. The first three sections describe, through a series of verb tense shifts, the movement of people across the river to and from work or pleasure, the people no different, Whitman insists, from people in any other part of the world or in any historic time. In every moment of the earth's daily passage around the sun, people are moving from one place to another, and a few hours later back again.

The Brooklyn Ferry is established by Whitman as a sort of touchstone in Section 1, meant to do two things: first, to create a moment in time present, the time in which Whitman lives, rides the ferry himself, and writes this poem; and second, to create a link between time present and time future when readers—for example 21st-century readers, 150 or more years after the poem's creation—will meditate about Whitman meditating about us. This mystical, transcendent moment comes at the end of the section: "On the ferry-boats the hundreds and hundreds that cross, returning home, are more curious to me than you suppose, / And you that shall cross from shore to shore years hence are more to me, and more in my meditations, than you might suppose." As we read these lines and those that follow, we find ourselves traveling in both his time and ours.

The present tense at the end of Section 1 shifts to an indefinite verb tense in the first stanza of Sec-

tion 2, a transitional seven lines to the future tense of the seven-line second stanza, where the poet can say of the ferryboat passengers: "A hundred years hence, or ever so many hundred years hence, others will see them, / Will enjoy the sunset, the pouring-in of the flood-tide, the falling-back to the sea of the ebb-tide."

In Section 3 the poet transcends time and place in order to join the future reader, even those living "A hundred years hence"—or 150 years hence. Whitman insists that "It avails not, time nor place—distance avails not." And, as we will understand beginning in Section 4, neither the East River nor the Brooklyn Ferry matter. Any avenue of travel will do. "I am with you," he says to us, "you men and women of a generation, or ever so many generations hence." And we are "refresh'd" by what we see on our voyage just as he was "refresh'd."

The poet even looks back on himself from his new place in the future, remembering how he "cross'd the river of old" and had his "eyes dazzled" by all that he saw.

> Just as you feel when you look on the river and
> sky, so I felt,
> Just as any of you is one of a living crowd, I was
> one of a crowd, . . .
> Just as you stand and lean on the rail, yet hurry
> with the swift current, I stood yet was
> hurried. . . .

The poet has left his own time and place to join readers in their time and place, no matter when or where that is. And he feels the luxury of looking back on his own time and place: "I too many and many a time cross'd the river of old," and he then CATALOGs all the things he "saw" (past tense).

Midway through the long second stanza of Section 3 he turns the catalog of things he "saw" on the ferry journey into a spiritual vision: He "Look'd at the fine centrifugal spokes of light round the shape of [his] head in the sunlit water." This image of "centrifugal spokes" around the shadow of his own head in the water suggests a kind of divinity shared, he believes, by all people and makes stronger the connection of the poet with the "hundreds and hundreds" who cross on the ferry, or who travel anywhere—past, present, or future.

SECTIONS 4–6

The Brooklyn Ferry's symbolic importance becomes clear in the rest of the poem as the poet moves from the ferry-crossing imagery to the feeling he has for his spiritual closeness with the reader. He represents this closeness by merging past and present tense verbs in the first line of the five-line Section 4: "These and all else *were* to me the same as they *are* to you" (verb emphasis added). It was the image of the halo he saw around the shadow of his head on the water in Section 3 that sets up this emotional closeness to readers in the later sections. He thinks of the "others who look back on me," he says, "because I look'd forward to them."

At the beginning of Section 5 he wonders what it is "then between us, / What is the count of the scores or hundreds of years between us?" What is it that, in spite of time and space, binds us together. The bonds imagined in Section 5 are external, while the bonds of Section 6 are internal. "I too lived," he says. "I too walk'd the streets" of Brooklyn, of Manhattan. "I too" was curious about all the people and events. Then, in further description, he uses the word "float" to describe the state of his body as it transcends from the physical state to the spiritual. "Float" is used here and in other Whitman poems to indicate a state of suspension, of levitation, that the poet feels in this mystical merging of his body and soul with the bodies and souls of others. "I too had receiv'd identity by my body, / That I was I knew was of my body, and what I should be I knew I should be of my body." Our identities come from an awareness of the physical being. But it is the spiritual being, Whitman believed, that matters more.

In Section 6 the poet continues to think about this experience and, perhaps realizing that readers may be concerned with a comparison of their lives with his, Whitman lists some of his "sins" so others can feel better about their own. And he continues to use the present/past verb tense switches:

Nor is it you alone who know what it is to be evil,
I am he who knew what it was to be evil,
I too knitted the old knot of contrariety.

The "old knot of contrariety" may be the mythical knot of Satan working in mankind, tying us to evil. And Whitman catalogs a few of these Satanic workings in his own life, things he had done: "blabb'd, blush'd, resented, lied, stole, grudg'd, / Had guile, anger, lust, hot wishes I dared not speak," etc. This was/is his life, and he has no regrets; nor should anyone reading the poem regret his or her sins. They are, the poet believed, a manifestation of who he is, who we are. The only sin, Whitman suggests in "Song of Myself," is awareness of sin, one of the poet's larger themes in *Leaves of Grass*.

The "old knot of contrariety" may also refer to the difficult knot of body and soul tied together, the body sometimes acting contrary to the wishes of the soul.

SECTIONS 7–9

The spiritual union of the poet with his readers takes place in the six-line Section 7. The poet tells us that he *was* thinking "long and seriously" about us before we were born. "Who knows but I am enjoying this," he says. And now we—if we are reading well—may think long and seriously about the poet, and perhaps we are enjoying ourselves as well. The section's last line reads, "Who knows, for all the distance, but I am as good as looking at you now, for all you cannot see me?" Only the truly skeptical can keep from looking, figuratively, over his or her shoulder; the images allow us to "float" also, in spiritual union with the poet and, perhaps, with everyone who has read this poem. "It avails not, time nor place—distance avails not." (See also, for similar imagery, the endings to "Song of Myself" and "So Long.")

Section 8 reminds the reader of the imagery of the poem's opening sections: "Ah, what can ever be more stately and admirable to me than masthemm'd Manhattan? / River and sunset and scallop-edg'd waves of flood-tide?" This reminder then brings the poet to the climactic moment in the spiritual merger of poet and reader: "What is more subtle than this which ties me to the woman or man that looks in my face? / Which fuses me into you now, and pours my meaning into you?"

And the merger of the "I" into the "you" now merges with the "we." "We understand then do we not?" We understand the mystical merging of bodies and souls, ours not just with his, he insists, but with those of people in all time and space. Although "democracy" is not an overt thematic element in "Crossing Brooklyn Ferry," this merging of bodies and souls carries with it Whitman's often used definition of democracy: the perfect equality of all people. It is now "we" and not "you" or "I." The spiritual union is complete, and one's spiritual identity provides mystical knowledge. Readers who have difficulty with "Song of Myself" or "One's-self I Sing" because of the seeming egotism at work in the poet may understand from "Crossing Brooklyn Ferry" that the "I" is always obliterated by Whitman's insistence on the "we."

The poem's final stanzas (Section 9) present a catalogued review of images from previous sections and present what amounts to a hymn of praise for all he and his readers have seen on this mystical journey on the "Brooklyn Ferry." "Flow on, river," he says. And perhaps to add dramatic intensity, the poet begins 23 of the 25 lines of the section's first stanza with a verb: "Flow on," "Frolic on," "Cross," etc. Whitman summarizes the poem's key thematic idea that through an appreciation for the things in our respective physical worlds that help to identify who we are, we may be led to a greater understanding of our spiritual world.

The "dumb, beautiful ministers" of the poem's final, seven-line stanza are the physical elements that permeate the lives of all people. There is no "I" in this final stanza and the use of the "you" refers to the "ministers" which "we receive." The pronouns "we" or "us" are used seven times, as if to place a final emphasis on the merger of all souls into one: "Flow on, river!"

This journey into spiritual discoveries may be found in several other poems as well, but Whitman is perhaps never so forceful with the idea as in "Crossing Brooklyn Ferry."

"Dalliance of the Eagles, The" (1880)

First published in *Cope's Tobacco Plant* magazine (November 1880); then as one of three new poems

and the 13th of 29 poems in the "By The Roadside" cluster for the sixth edition of *Leaves of Grass* (1881).

This 10-line poem describes two eagles in flight and in the act of copulation, of "dalliance," which become a metaphor for one of Whitman's largest *Leaves of Grass* themes:

> The rushing amorous contact high in space
>   together,
> The clinching interlocking claws, a living,
>   fierce, gyrating wheel,
> Four beating wings, two beaks, a swirling mass
>   tight grappling, . . .
>
> Till o'er the river pois'd, the twain yet one, a
>   moment's lull,
> A motionless still balance in the air, then parting,
>   talons loosing,
> Upward again on slow-firm pinions slanting, their
>   separate diverse flight,
> She hers, he his, pursuing.

The poet presents in this poem an answer to the baffling question of how one retains individual "freedom" in the midst of the democratic "en masse," a term Whitman uses in "Song of Myself" to mean people together as a unified force. In this poem, the eagles are "twain yet one," locked together in their "dalliance," afterwards in a "separate diverse flight," she her way, "he his, pursuing."

Democracy involves a person being at once part of the great social group but at the same time an individual, capable of thinking and acting for him or her self.

"Darest Thou Now O Soul" (1868)

First published in the (London) BROADWAY MAGAZINE (October 1868), where it was the second of five poems under the general heading "Whispers of Heavenly Death"; it first appeared in *Leaves of Grass* in the fifth edition (1871); in the *Two Rivulets* volume of *Leaves* (1876); and as the first of 18 poems in the "Whispers of Heavenly Death" cluster for the sixth edition (1881). It has one of the few regular patterns in *Leaves*, consisting of five stanzas with three lines each.

The poem is a dramatic monologue in which the poet addresses his own soul: "Darest thou now O soul, / Walk out with me toward the unknown region, . . ." That is, toward "death," the "blank" in front of the individual and his or her soul. Once there, however, in "that inaccessible land, . . . we burst forth, we float"—float in the sense of being suspended in "Time and Space." This poem and nearly all others in the "Whispers of Heavenly Death" cluster bridge the narrow gap between life and death and honor death as one of the key life experiences.

"Dead Emperor, The" (1888)

First published in the NEW YORK HERALD (March 10, 1888); then in *November Boughs* (1888); and it was the 59th of 65 poems in the "First Annex: Sands at Seventy" cluster for the "Death-bed" printing of *Leaves of Grass* (1892). The emperor is Germany's Wilhelm I, who died in Berlin on March 9, 1888; he was the first ruler of the reunited Germany, after Bismarck.

This is a four-line poem in honor of the German emperor, "a good old man—a faithful shepherd, patriot."

"Dead Tenor, The" (1884)

First published in the CRITIC (November 8, 1884); then in *November Boughs* (1888); and it was the 37th of 65 poems in the "First Annex: Sands at Seventy" cluster for the "Death-bed" printing of *Leaves of Grass* (1892). The unnamed tenor is Pasquale BRIGNOLE, whose funeral was November 3, 1884, and whom Whitman identified as the subject of the poem in a letter to William O'CONNOR. He was one of Whitman's favorite OPERA tenors.

This poem is a memorial tribute to Brignole, one of the many singers he had heard in New York opera houses before he began to lose his hearing late in life. He writes of the "liquid-soft" voice, "that tremulous, manly timbre, the perfect singing voice." Whitman names in the poem four of Brignole's roles he had heard him sing in New York: Fernando in *La Favorita*, Manrico in *Il Trovatore*, the lead role in *Ernani*, and Gennaro in *Lucrezia Borgia*.

"Death and Burial of McDonald Clarke, The" (1842)

First published in the NEW YORK AURORA (March 18, 1842); an "early poem" *not* later published in *Leaves of Grass*. It is most accessible now in Francis Murphy (editor), *Walt Whitman: The Complete Poems* (Penguin Books, 1996).

"Death-bed Edition"

See *Leaves of Grass* (1892).

"Death in the School-Room (A Fact)" (1841)

Short story, believed to be Whitman's first published work of fiction. It appeared in the *United States Magazine and Democratic Review* (August 1841; see DEMOCRATIC REVIEW, THE) and was reprinted six times during Whitman's lifetime, more than any other of his short stories. It is most accessible now in *Walt Whitman: The Early Poems and the Fiction*, edited by Thomas L. Brasher (New York University Press, 1963).

Tim Barker is a student in a schoolroom taught by a tyrannical man named Lugare, "one little fitted for his important and responsible office. Hasty to decide, and inflexibly severe, he was the terror of the little world he ruled so despotically. Punishment he seemed to delight in." Lugare falsely accuses Tim of stealing fruit from a neighbor's garden, but the bag that Tim was seen carrying was full of potatoes given to him for his widowed mother by a farmer friend.

Lugare refuses to accept Tim's explanation and threatens him with a beating in front of his classmates. The teacher gives Tim an hour to reflect upon his "crime" and to prepare a confession. At the end of the hour Lugare calls for the confession, and when Tim fails to raise his head from his desk, Lugare thinks the boy has been sleeping. Tim has been so disturbed by the false accusation, however, that when Lugare tries at the end of the hour to get the confession, first by beating him with his rattan and then by lifting his head, Tim is discovered to be dead.

The story's final sentence reads: "Death was in the school-room, and Lugare had been flogging a corpse."

Whitman was a schoolteacher on LONG ISLAND for three or four years, beginning at age 16. He was 22 when this story was first appeared, and he was apparently pleased with its popularity, writing to a friend later that he had written the story to show how terrible it was to use in the schools the rod as punishment.

CHARACTERS

Tim Barker   Mr. Lugare's student in the story "Death in the School-Room." Tim is falsely accused by his teacher of having stolen some fruit from a garden on his way to school the day of the story's action. Lugare gives Tim an hour to admit to the crime before receiving a "deserved" beating in front of his classmates as the penalty for lying. He is so frightened by the threat of an unjust punishment that his heart gives out before the hour is up, and he is dead when Lugare begins to flog him.

Lugare   A teacher in "Death in the School-Room." He is described by the narrator as "tyrannical, . . . [a person] little fitted for his important and responsible office" as schoolteacher. He falsely accuses one of his students, Tim Barker, of stealing

some fruit from a neighbor's garden, and he threatens a beating in front of his classmates if Tim does not decide to confess to the crime within the hour. At the end of the hour Lugare begins to beat Tim, who seems to be asleep with his head resting on his arms, but Lugare soon discovers that he has "been flogging a corpse."

"Death of General Grant" (1885)

First published in HARPER'S WEEKLY (May 16, 1885); then in *November Boughs* (1888); and it was the 30th of 65 poems in the "First Annex: Sands at Seventy" cluster for the "Death-bed" printing of *Leaves of Grass* (1892).

This poem is interesting if for no other reason than that it was first published in May 1885, and President Grant died two months later (July 23, 1885). It does, however, bemoan the death of all CIVIL WAR heroes as "one by one" the "lofty actors" withdraw, victors and vanquished—LINCOLN and Lee and now Grant with the rest. The poem is in effect, then, in honor of all Civil War soldiers.

"Death of the Nature-Lover, The" (1843)

First published in BROTHER JONATHAN (March 11, 1843); an "early poem" *not* later published in *Leaves of Grass*. It is most accessible now in Francis Murphy (editor), *Walt Whitman: The Complete Poems* (Penguin Books, 1996).

"Death of Wind-Foot, The" (1845)

Story, originally embedded in Whitman's novel, *Franklin Evans*. When he reprinted the novel in the

BROOKLYN DAILY EAGLE (November 16–30, 1846), however, he took out the "Wind-Foot" segment and sold it separately to the AMERICAN REVIEW (June 1845).

The story is from chapter 2 of *Franklin Evans* and was considerably revised when published separately, but the basic story remains and is arguably better than the novel as a whole or many of Whitman's other short stories.

"Wind-Foot" is the last son of "Unrelenting," chief of a tribe of LONG ISLAND Indians. His other sons and their mother had been killed in one of the many wars fought by the tribes of that time (300 years ago). An Indian stranger comes into the camp, looking for food and rest, and is invited to stay the night. During the time before sleep, "Unrelenting" tells the story of how he had come on two Indians of the Kansi Nation, archenemies of his own tribe and killers of his sons and wife. He had saved the life of the younger of the two men, a teenager, but killed the other. He wanted one of the two left alive to return to his tribe with the story.

"Unrelenting" goes off the next day to take care of business, leaving the stranger in the care of Wind-Foot. When the chief returns late the same evening he discovers that the stranger and Wind-Foot are gone.

The stranger is the Kansi teenager whom "Unrelenting" had not killed years ago. Now realizing that he had stumbled into the camp of the very person who had killed his friend, the stranger determines to take revenge. He escapes with Wind-Foot as his captive. Once "Unrelenting" returns to camp and realizes what has happened, he trails the stranger and Wind-Foot, catching up to them just as the stranger prepares to kill the boy. The stranger is killed by a poison arrow from Unrelenting's bow but still manages—"as the death-rattle shook in his throat"—to kill Wind-Foot with an ax blow to the head.

CHARACTERS

Unrelenting   Americanized name of the Long Island Indian chief in the story. He returns to camp to discover that an Indian who had entered the camp in the morning had kidnapped the chief's son. He caught up to the two just as the Indian

stranger was about to kill the boy; he managed to kill the Indian but not before the Indian killed his son.

Wind-Foot   Indian teenage son of "Unrelenting," the chief of the Long Island tribe. He is kidnapped by an Indian who had determined that Wind-Foot was the son of the tribal chief who had killed a friend of his years before. Wind-Foot is killed just as his father attempts to rescue him at the end of the story.

Indian stranger   A mysterious character, who turns out to be the Kansi teenager whom Unrelenting had felt sorry for and so released when Unrelenting had killed a friend of the stranger's years ago.

"Death's Valley"   (1892)

First published in HARPER'S NEW MONTHLY MAGAZINE (April 1892); it was the 11th of 13 poems in the "Old Age Echoes" cluster for the reprinting of *Leaves of Grass* in 1897 by Whitman's executor Horace TRAUBEL.

An epigraph requests that the poem accompany a painting entitled *The Valley of the Shadow of Death*, by George Inness (1824–94). Inness was a well-known American painter of landscapes during the 19th century. Whitman evidently felt that the painter had "portray'd . . . [The] theme entire," that is, the theme of "Death's Valley." The poet evokes death and tells it that he is unafraid of its power and that he welcomes it: "Rich, florid, loosener of the stricture-knot call'd life, / Sweet, peaceful, welcome death."

"Debris"   (1860)

Cut from *Leaves of Grass* after appearing only in the third edition (1860), this poem has, nevertheless, an interesting publication history. It had 60 lines in its only appearance under its original title, but Whitman took almost half the lines and published them later either as separate poems or as parts of other poems.

The word *debris* implies that the original poem was broken into pieces of various materials, which may account for the poet's recognition of the value of lines worth saving for later placement in *Leaves of Grass;* some pieces were more valuable than others. Several stanzas, for example, are epigrams: "He is wisest who has the most caution, / He only wins who goes far enough." "Any thing is as good as established, when that is established that will produce it and continue it." Those are the original poem's first three lines, lines the poet chose not to publish again.

Two other "Debris" examples show how Whitman used the ideas in later poems. Here are lines 34 and 35 in the original: "Women sit, or move to and fro—some old, some young, / The young are beautiful—but the old are more beautiful than the young." These lines appeared as a separate poem titled "Picture" in the fourth edition of *Leaves* (1867), then as "Beautiful Women" in the fifth edition (1871), and finally, with the same title in the "By The Roadside" cluster in the sixth and final edition (1881). The last four lines (57–60) of the original "Debris" read as follows:

> I thought I was not alone, walking here by the
>   shore,
> But the one I thought was with me, as now I
>   walk by the shore,
> As I lean and look through the glimmering
>   light—that one has utterly disappeared,
> And those appear that perplex me.

Those lines appear in later editions of *Leaves,* only slightly altered, as the last four lines of a five-line poem titled "As if a Phantom Caress'd Me."

"Delicate Cluster" (1871)

First appeared in a group titled "Bathed in War's Perfume" in the fifth edition of *Leaves of Grass* (1871); it was the 37th of 43 poems in the "Drum-Taps" cluster for the sixth edition (1881).

The "Delicate Cluster" in this poem is the "flag of teeming life," representing for the poet "all my lands—all my seashores lining!" The word *cluster* suggests the stars on their blue background in the American flag. It was the flag of death during the CIVIL WAR, but now it is the "Flag cerulean," a heavenly flag, a "sunny flag, with the orbs of night dappled!" Whitman says at the end: "Ah to sing the song of you, my matron mighty! / My sacred one, my mother." America, the poet believed, is the mother of us all.

"Democracy" (1867)

Essay first published in the GALAXY (December 1867).

See also *Democratic Vistas.*

Democratic Vistas (1871)

An 84-page pamphlet on the subject of democracy and literature, published in New York by J. S. Redfield (1871); reprinted in *Specimen Days & Collect* (1882). Whitman is best known as a poet for good reasons, but *Democratic Vistas* is arguably the clearest statement he made about his theory of democracy and literature and the connection between the two.

The Scottish essayist Thomas CARLYLE had written an antidemocracy article, published in the NEW YORK TRIBUNE (August 16, 1867) and titled "Shooting Niagara: And After?" He argued that democracy would destroy civilization.

The editors of the GALAXY, who had just published a poem of Whitman's, asked him if he would like to write a response to "Shooting Niagara." Whitman, the leading American spokesman for democracy, clearly could not refuse the assignment. He wrote three articles for the *Galaxy:* "Democracy," "Personalism," and "Literature." The first two were accepted and published in the magazine in its December 1867 and May 1868 issues respectively, but "Literature" was rejected by the editors for reasons of vague reader dissatisfaction with the first two articles.

Democratic Vistas brought together the three essays as one and, although it is a significant statement about the importance of democracy, it also shows for the first time Whitman's concern for the future of America's political system.

Even into the 21st century, Whitman is not known for his prose style. He wrote and published 25 short stories—which few people know about and fewer still have read. He wrote nearly 3,000 news items, features, or editorials for 80 newspapers, and he wrote a number of essays about American democracy and poetry, including "prefaces" to various editions of *Leaves of Grass,* many of which are available in the most recent reprintings of *Leaves.* Yet most of Whitman's prose, including the "prefaces," seem off-the-cuff, as if he were hurrying to meet a newspaper deadline, which was often a factor. The prose may be judged by comparison with the poetry, which he was constantly revising, never quite satisfied with the wording or punctuation, style of presentation, or rhythm. The revisions account for the great differences among the six distinct editions of *Leaves of Grass.* The uneasy quality of his prose may be accounted for by his lack of revising. The poetry remains the best source for Whitman's perception of democracy and is arguably the best source by anyone for an explanation of democratic principles; but *Democratic Vistas* remains one of the best prose statements about democracy written by an American.

Whitman's thesis in *Democratic Vistas* is that America cannot become a world leader if there is not a first-class national literature.

> The problems of the achievements of this crowning stage through future first-class National Singers, Orators, Artists, and others—of creating in literature an *imaginative* New World, the correspondent and counterpart of the current Scientific and Political New Worlds—and the perhaps distant, but still delightful prospect, (for our children, if not in our own day,) of delivering America, and, indeed, all Christian lands everywhere, from the thin, moribund, and watery, but appallingly extensive nuisance of conventional poetry—by putting something really alive and substantial in its place—I have

undertaken to grapple with, and argue, in Democratic Vistas.

This is a long and somewhat convoluted one-sentence statement, a PERIODIC SENTENCE at that (although the stanzas in many of Whitman's poems are also written in one sentence, often periodic; that is, with the grammatical subject at the end of the stanza), yet it is sufficient in summary of *Democratic Vistas.*

Whitman defends democracy in *Democratic Vistas,* but he also shows great disappointment at the directions some aspects of democracy have taken. He sees selfishness among the people, for example, and a materialism that runs counter to the democratic principles he supports.

DEMOCRACY

By "democracy" Whitman means "political democracy." Democracy is achieved, he believed, through an equal mix of individualism and "adhesiveness," a word he got from his interest in phrenology, but which comes from "adhere"—that is, to stick together, as in a devoted attachment to someone or to a group of people. Democracy requires the perfect blending of the two ingredients. In the poetry Whitman refers to the equal importance of the individual and the "en-masse," the adhesiveness of individuals within the whole population.

The problem in Europe, he suggests, is the lack of such "solidarity." "Of all dangers to a nation as things exist in our day, there can be no greater one than having certain portions of the people set off from the rest by a line drawn—[some people] not privileged as others, but degraded, humiliated, made of no account."

It is the "average man of a land at last" that is important, Whitman argues, and it is the "average" individual who is of greatest concern only in a democratic society. "We shall, it is true, quickly and continually find the origin-idea of the singleness of man, individualism, asserting itself, and cropping forth, even from the opposite ideas. But the mass, or lump character, for imperative reasons, is to be ever carefully weigh'd, borne in mind, and provided for. Only from it, and from its proper regulation and potency, comes the other, comes the chance of individualism. . . . This idea of perfect individualism it is indeed that deepest tinges and gives character to the idea of the aggregate. For it is mainly or altogether to serve independent separatism that we favor a strong generalization, consolidation."

In other words, individualism plus adhesiveness equals democracy.

PERSONALISM

The "second principle is individuality, the pride and centripetal isolation of a human being in himself—identity—personalism." Whatever the word is that best describes it, Whitman says, the idea is that in order for the adhesiveness half of the democratic equation to work well, the individual must accept as important the growth and development of his or her own personality. What does "civilization itself rest upon," he asks, "and what object has it, with its religions, arts, schools, etc., but rich, luxuriant, varied personalism?"

He does not use the word "diversity," as he might if he were writing the essay today, but that is what he suggests. Democracy demands diversity, otherwise the equation falls into imbalance. One reason Whitman places so much emphasis on literature, both in discussing PERSONALISM and in the final third of *Democratic Vistas,* is that literature (imaginative literature) offers the best "models" for emulation. "The literature," he says in discussing personalism, "songs, aesthetics, etc., of a country are of importance principally because they furnish the materials and suggestions of personality for the women and men of that country, and enforce them in a thousand effective ways."

In a footnote to this idea, he lists several "models" from literature for men and several for women. For the men, he lists, among others, Yudishtura, Rama, Solomon (and "most" Old and New Testament characters), Achilles, Ulysses, Hercules, Aeneas, Arthur and his knights, Don Quixote, and Hamlet. For the women, he lists, among others, the goddesses of the Egyptian, Indian, and Greek mythologies, certain Bible characters, Cleopatra, Penelope, and "Walter Scott's Jeanie and Effie Deans." He adds, parenthetically, that a woman at her "best, or as perfect mother, does not hitherto, it seems to me, fully appear in literature." But, he

argues, none of these literary models for either men *or* women may be found yet in American literature as he knew it in the 19th century.

At the core of the original equation—individualism plus adhesiveness equals democracy—there is what Whitman refers to as the "religious element." Religion is an important ingredient for individual improvement, but Whitman suggests that the religion he means cannot be found in churches. The "identified soul," he says, "can really confront Religion [only] when it extricates itself entirely from the churches, and not before."

> Alone, and silent thought and awe, and aspiration—and then the interior consciousness, like a hitherto unseen inscription, in magic ink, beams out its wondrous lines to the sense. Bibles may convey, and priests expound, but it is exclusively for the noiseless operation of one's isolated Self, to enter the pure ether of veneration, reach the divine levels, and commune with the unutterable.

The individual must get off by him or her "Self" and confront his or her own conscience to find "the pure ether of veneration" and come to grips with the mysteries of God. Individuals must learn to think for themselves.

But the words *Democracy* and *Nature* are, like religion, mysteries too:

> We have frequently printed the word Democracy. Yet I cannot too often repeat that it is a word the real gist of which still sleeps, quite unawaken'd, notwithstanding the resonance and the many angry tempests out of which its syllables have come, from pen or tongue. . . . It is, in some sort, younger brother of another great and often-used word, Nature, whose history also waits unwritten. . . . It is . . . good to reduce the whole matter [of religion] to the consideration of a single self, a man, a woman, on permanent grounds. Even for the treatment of the universal, in politics, metaphysics, or anything, sooner or later we come down to one single, solitary soul.

The idea of the "solitary soul" brings the reader back not to religion but to the importance of the individual—the "one single, solitary soul"—working to improve his or her own personalism in order to improve the union, the "adhesiveness," with the neighborhood, the state, the nation.

LITERATURE

In discussing the value of imaginative literature in a democracy and why America has not yet produced the literary culture he would like, Whitman lists three stages in the development of American literature. The first is "the planning and putting on record the political foundation rights of immense masses of people." These writings include, for Whitman, the "Declaration of Independence," the federal Constitution, and other books and essays that helped form America's historical record. The second stage "relates to [essays about America's] material prosperity, wealth, produce, laborsaving machines," etc., writings that helped improve the Nation's material wellbeing and that helped generate capitalism.

The third stage in the development of American literature is still in the future, Whitman suggests. It is to be made up of "American personalities, plenty of them, male and female, traversing the States, none excepted . . . and by a sublime and serious Religious Democracy sternly taking command, dissolving the old, sloughing off surfaces, and from its own interior and vital principles, reconstructing, democratizing society."

America is still mostly European, he reminds readers, and needs to break that bond by creating its own national literature, especially in poetry. He does not want to "insult the reader's intelligence . . . by supposing it necessary to show, in detail, why the copious dribble, either of our little or well-known rhymesters, does not fulfill, in any respect, the needs and august occasions of this land. America demands a poetry that is bold, modern, and all-surrounding and kosmical, as she is herself." The "Soul" of a nation, he says a few pages later, is in its "Literature." The American poets at the time were still English, living in New England but not yet American. One of the things about Whitman's poetry that had so caught EMERSON's attention in 1855 was his Americanism, the "first" American poet, Emerson said. And *Democratic Vistas* was published just five years before *Huckleberry Finn*, generally considered now to be the first truly American novel and Mark Twain the first American novelist.

In summarizing the value of literature in a democratic culture, Whitman says a "new theory of literary composition for imaginative works of the very first class, and especially for highest poems, is the sole course open to these States. Books are to be call'd for, and supplied, on the assumption that the process of reading is not a half-sleep, but, in highest sense, an exercise, a gymnast's struggle; that the reader is to do something for himself, must be on the alert, must himself or herself construct indeed the poem, argument, history, metaphysical essay— the text furnishing the hints, the clue, the start or framework." The great imaginative literature offers truths of the human condition, Whitman suggests with this idea, that cannot be found elsewhere.

It is not enough, in other words, for the writer to attempt to stimulate the imagination of the reader; the reader must be awake to imaginative possibilities and work to read with understanding. As the Imagist poets (for example, Ezra Pound and Amy Lowell) would declare 40 years later, whatever happens in the imagination of the reader of a poem *is the poem*. Failure to understand this about imaginative literature is to read, as Whitman says, in a "half-sleep." Democracy cannot survive, he is saying, with half-asleep readers.

"Literature," the third of the three original essays from which *Democratic Vistas* evolved, was essential to Whitman's overall thesis, because it is the imaginative writer who supplies the examples of democracy at work. Other artists could provide similar examples to those in literature, but Whitman believed that it is the individual character in literature, the "hero" in an imaginative work, that has the best opportunity for presenting case studies. Whitman had in mind characters who represented the "ideals" of democracy, perhaps characters too "romantic" or sentimental for 21st-century tastes; that is, not the human condition as it is, but as it should be. On the other hand, the character he created out of himself in *Leaves of Grass*, particularly in "Song of Myself," presents a democratic ideal that America has never actually achieved but for which many may feel it is still worth striving.

DEMOCRATIC VISTAS AS A WHOLE

Democratic Vistas is basically optimistic, as is nearly all of Whitman's work. He sees the America of the future as a leader of nations, and Americans as leaders of the world's people. But if Whitman's "means" were to come true, the "end" would still be Utopian, and the reader notes a certain amount of disillusionment in Whitman's long, narrow view of America's future. Perhaps he begins to realize just how utopian is his idea.

In summary, Whitman says that people ("personalism") will make America great and that its literature ("the soul of a nation") will make the people great. In the part of *Democratic Vistas* that was originally published as the essay "Personalism," Whitman names three elements that make up the model personality of human beings: "selfhood," "conscience," and "religiousness." Selfhood is the result of "strong-fibered physique" and "in youth, fresh, ardent, emotional, aspiring, full of adventure; at maturity, brave, perceptive, under control, neither too talkative nor too reticent, neither flippant nor somber." Conscience is "the primary moral element," he says. "If I were asked to specify in what quarter lie the grounds of darkest dread, respecting the America of our hopes, I should have to point to this particular [conscience]." By religiousness, Whitman means "the identified soul, which can really confront religion when it extricates itself entirely from the churches, and not before." The churches and their priests and preachers get in the way of religion, primarily because they keep their people from thinking for themselves. Whitman also believed that people should develop their own system of moral values, rather than depend on ministers of particular faiths, who always have biases.

Whitman takes pride in his picture of the ideal American, but the description is not offered without a certain amount of concern. It is at this point then, according to the poet, that "literature" becomes important; it is literature that must set the heroic example for the "model personality. . . . America . . . must, for her purposes, cease to recognize a theory of character grown of feudal aristocracies, or form'd by merely literary standards, or from any ultramarine full-dress formulas of culture, pol-

ish, caste, etc., and must sternly promulgate her own new standard."

The American Poet of Democracy says that the great literature of the past was grown "not for America, but rather for her foes, the feudal and the old—while [America's] genius is democratic and modern." In spite of what he says about the need to overthrow the literature of the past in order to arrive at a new, healthier literature for America, Whitman nevertheless evokes often the great literary leaders of the past: "Yet could ye, indeed, but breathe your breath of life into our New World's nostrils—not to enslave us, as now, but, for our needs, to breed a spirit like your own—perhaps (dare we to say it?) to dominate, even destroy, what you yourselves have left!"

The heart of the matter is not reliance on the great literature of the past, whether from Europe or from early Americans, but on contemporary and future literature. Whitman says that the current contributions of American writers to their nation's literature is "useless and a mockery": "They strengthen and nourish no one, express nothing characteristic, give decision and purpose to no one, and suffice only the lowest level of vacant minds."

Magazine production flourished in America from the mid-1830s through the rest of the century, publishing fiction, poetry, plays, and essays for thousands of readers. HARPER'S NEW MONTHLY MAGAZINE had a circulation of 200,000 shortly after its founding in 1850, featuring short stories and novels with woodcut illustrations. *Godey's Lady's Book* was founded in 1830 and had a circulation of 25,000 in 1839, but 150,000 in 1860 at the beginning of the CIVIL WAR. It seemed as if everyone who took up a pen could get published in one or more of the hundreds of magazines available and cheap. It is this proliferation of publications that Whitman criticizes. He worries that it is those magazines that will determine the nation's literary future.

In a more optimistic note, Whitman says in *Democratic Vistas*: "What an age! What a land! Where, elsewhere, one so great? The individuality of one nation must then, as always, lead the world. Can there be any doubt who the leader ought to be? Bear in mind, though, that nothing less than the mightiest original non-supordinated SOUL has ever really, gloriously led, or ever can lead. (This SOUL—its other name, in these Vistas, is LITERATURE.)" The Soul of America is its Literature.

According to Whitman, then, "The true question to ask respecting a book, is *has it help'd any human soul?*" Whitman is disillusioned by contemporary literature, which he says has not, but, at the same time, he strikes out for a time in the future when American literature will bring forth the "model personality" in a fictional hero who will then act as a touchstone for all Americans.

Readers may wonder if Whitman had forgotten such unique and particularly American works as *The Scarlet Letter, Moby-Dick,* THOREAU's *Walden,* and *Uncle Tom's Cabin,* all of which had been published in the early 1850s, just before the first edition of *Leaves of Grass.*

"Dirge for Two Veterans" (1865)

First appeared in the sequel to the *Drum-Taps* volume (1865) and unchanged throughout its printing history; it was the 24th of 43 poems in the "Drum-Taps" cluster for the sixth edition (1881).

The two veterans are a father and son killed together in the CIVIL WAR: "the double grave awaits them, . . . / And the strong dead-march enwraps me." As with nearly all of the "Drum-Taps" poems, Whitman here shows his sympathy for the wounded and dead soldiers in the War. And he rarely identifies them as soldiers of the North or South.

> The moon gives you light,
> And the bugles and the drums give you music,
> And my heart, O my soldiers, my veterans,
> My heart gives you love.

This poem also offers an example of ACCENTUAL VERSE which Whitman used frequently in *Leaves of Grass.* In each stanza there are two accented syllables in the first and fourth lines and three in the

second and third, providing the beat of a dead-march.

"Dismantled Ship, The" (1888)

First printed in the NEW YORK HERALD (February 23, 1888); then in *November Boughs* (1888); and it was the 61st of 65 poems in the "First Annex: Sands at Seventy" cluster for the "Death-bed" printing of *Leaves of Grass* (1892).

This five-line poem is a song of praise for the dismantled ship, any old ship that has been dumped in "some nameless bay" in "lonesome waters," a "gray and batter'd ship . . . rusting, mouldering" and clearly due more respect than it has received.

Drum-Taps (1865)

First published in 1865 as a separate, 72-page book containing 53 poems, followed later that year by *Sequel to Drum-Taps,* a 24-page pamphlet that contained an additional 18 poems, including "When Lilacs Last in the Dooryard Bloom'd." The Sequel was later bound into a second issue of *Drum-Taps.* All 71 of these poems were incorporated into the fourth edition of *Leaves* (1867). "Drum-Taps" was then made the cluster title for 43 poems in the sixth edition of *Leaves of Grass* (1881). For that edition, "When Lilacs Last in the Dooryard Bloom'd" was moved with three other LINCOLN poems to a cluster titled "Memories of President Lincoln."

All of the final selection of "Drum-Taps" poems (1881) were written between 1861 and 1865 and came out of Whitman's experiences during the CIVIL WAR.

The first few poems in the cluster reflect Whitman's reserved attitude about the war, which probably would not last more than a few weeks. He was ambivalent about the war, because he hated SLAVERY but hated worse the thought of a divided Union. Several of the middle poems show Whitman's growing depression because of all the wounded and dying soldiers he was seeing in Washington hospitals. The late poems in the cluster tend to look toward a brighter postwar future for America, perhaps even that the war strengthened a democracy by creating closer regional ties.

The final, 1881 selection of 43 "Drum-Taps" poems is in the following order: "First O Songs for a Prelude," "Eighteen Sixty-One," "Beat! Beat! Drums!," "From Paumanok Starting I Fly like a Bird," "Song of the Banner at Daybreak," "Rise O Days from Your Fathomless Deeps," "Virginia—the West," "City of Ships," "The Centenarian's Story," "Cavalry Crossing a Ford," "Bivouac on a Mountain Side," "An Army Corps on the March," "By the Bivouac's Fitful Flame," "Come up from the Fields Father," "Vigil Strange I Kept on the Field One Night," "A March in the Ranks Hard-Prest, and the Road Unknown," "A Sight in Camp in the Daybreak Gray and Dim," "As Toilsome I Wander'd Virginia's Woods," "Not the Pilot," "Year that Trembled and Reel'd beneath Me," "The Wound-Dresser," "Long, too Long America," "Give Me the Splendid Silent Sun," "Dirge for Two Veterans," "Over the Carnage Rose Prophetic a Voice," "I Saw Old General at Bay," "The Artilleryman's Vision," "Ethiopia Saluting the Colors," "Not Youth Pertains to Me," "Race of Veterans," "World Take Good Notice," "O Tan-Faced Prairie-Boy," "Look Down Fair Moon," "Reconciliation," "How Solemn as One by One," "As I Lay with My Head in Your Lap Camerado," "Delicate Cluster," "To a Certain Civilian," "Lo, Victress on the Peaks," "Spirit Whose Work is Done," "Adieu to a Soldier," "Turn O Libertad," and "To the Leaven'd Soil They Trod."

Drum-Taps, Sequel to (1865)

Whitman had begun planning for the addition of several poems to the Drum-Taps collection upon the death of President LINCOLN on April 15, 1865. After a few copies of the first book had been published, a second issue was printed that included the additional poems, including one of the poet's greatest works, "When Lilacs Last in the Dooryard Bloom'd."

The title page for this additional insert presents "When Lilacs Last in the Dooryard Bloom'd and other pieces" as the title for the sequel, although at the top of the page in a smaller and lighter type face are the words "Sequel to Drum-Taps," and tradition has kept "Sequel" as the reference title.

Printing was done in New York in early October 1865 by the Gibson Brothers who billed Whitman for 1,000 copies, all of which were inserted into the back of the second issue of Drum-Taps.

What is most significant about the Sequel is that Whitman stopped publication of Drum-Taps in order to include with the CIVIL WAR poems his elegies to Lincoln.

The Drum-Taps poems and those in the Sequel were incorporated into the fourth edition of Leaves of Grass (1867), along with "Songs Before Parting." "Drum-Taps" was later used as the cluster title for 43 poems in the sixth edition of Leaves of Grass (1881). For that edition, "When Lilacs Last in the Dooryard Bloom'd" was moved with three other Lincoln poems from the Sequel to a cluster titled "Memories of President Lincoln."

"Dumb Kate" (1844)

Short story, first published in COLUMBIAN MAGAZINE as "Dumb Kate: An Early Death" (May 1844). The story is most accessible now in Walt Whitman: The Early Poems and the Fiction, edited by Thomas L. Brasher (New York University Press, 1963).

The story is about the betrayal of Kate, "dumb" from birth but "gentle" and "beautiful" and who "attracted the admiration" of many of the strangers who stopped by the "old-fashion'd tavern." The tavern, readers are told, is located between Amboy village and "the metropolis of our republic"—no doubt New York City—a tavern which her parents own and at which Kate works as a waitress. The narrator describes her as "the landlord's lovely daughter, who kept everything so clean and bright" at the tavern. "Kate had been dumb from her birth. Though she could not talk, she was, nevertheless, a good waitress, one liked by patrons and the pride of her parents and her friends. She is described as being beautiful like the lilies she grew in her garden.

A young, unnamed man, the son of a "wealthy farmer" falls in love with Kate and determines to win her love in return, which he does. His feelings of love "wore away," however, "and he made up his mind to become the betrayer of poor Kate." He was a handsome young man, and Kate was an easy victim of his sexual nature.

The villain moves away, and shortly thereafter "did sickness of the heart wear into the life and happiness of Dumb Kate." She dies and is buried by the villagers on a hill in the nearby churchyard, her grave visited "by gossips, sometimes of a Sabbath afternoon," attracted by a "dumb girl's hapless story." She had died of a broken heart.

CHARACTER

Kate   Main character in the short story "Dumb Kate." She was "the landlord's lovely daughter, who kept everything so clean and bright" at a tavern, the setting for the story. Kate had been unable to speak from birth. She is described by the narrator as gentle, timid, and affectionate, a good waitress in spite of her inability to talk with patrons, and "beautiful as the lilies of which she loved to cultivate so many every summer in her garden." The young son of a "wealthy farmer" fell in love with Kate and set out to win her love, only to then betray her. The lover leaves for the big city, and Kate dies of a broken heart.

"Dying Veteran, The" (1887)

First published in *McClure's Magazine* (July 1887); then in *November Boughs* (1888); and it was the 51st of 65 poems in the "First Annex: Sands at Seventy" cluster for the "Death-bed" printing of *Leaves of Grass* (1892).

There is a parenthetical epigraph to this poem that reads "*A Long Island incident—early part of the nineteenth century.*" The incident concerns a veteran of the Revolutionary War, a "queer old savage man," who fought under General Washington and who on his deathbed, surrounded by family and

friends, tells them, "Away with your life of peace!— your joys of peace! / Give me my old wild battle-life again!" Twenty or more years after the war, the veteran still shows signs of what we today would call "post-traumatic stress disorder."

early poems

In this *Critical Companion,* Whitman's "early poems" are those poems published in newspapers and magazines before 1855 but which are not in any of the editions of *Leaves of Grass.*

The following 25 poems are included in this volume, each with a brief publication history: "Our Future Lot," "Young Grimes," "Fame's Vanity," "My Departure," "The Death of the Nature-Lover," "The Inca's Daughter," "The Love That Is Hereafter," "We All Shall Rest at Last," "The Spanish Lady," "The End of All," "The Columbian's Song," "The Punishment of Pride," "Ambition," "The Death and Burial of McDonald Clarke," "Time to Come," "The Play-Ground," "Ode," "New Year's Day," "The House of Friends," "Resurgemus," "The Mississippi at Midnight," "Song for Certain Congressmen," "Blood-Money," "Pictures," and "Isle of La Belle Riviere."

"Earth, My Likeness" (1860)

Titled "Calamus No. 36" in the third edition of *Leaves of Grass* (1860); it received its present title for the fourth edition (1867); it was the 29th of 39 poems in the "Calamus" cluster for the sixth edition (1881).

In seven lines Whitman evokes the Earth, telling it that though it looks "impassive, ample and spheric there," like himself, he feels that that is "not all; / I now suspect there is something fierce in you eligible to burst forth."

An athlete and the poet are "enamour'd" of one another, and the poet tells Earth that, like it, the poet feels "something fierce and terrible" is about to "burst forth." He says, however, that he cannot tell about it, not even in his poems.

"Earth, My Likeness" is interesting because it seems to show Whitman as hesitant in talking about his sexual ambiguity; yet he has been extremely explicit in other Calamus poems. See, in particular, "We Two Boys Together Clinging" and "A Glimpse."

"Eidólons" (1876)

First published in the NEW YORK TRIBUNE (February 19, 1876); it then appeared in Leaves of Grass as the seventh and longest of the 24 poems in the "Inscriptions" cluster for the sixth edition (1881). It was also the only poem in the cluster with a regular stanzaic form, with its 24 four-line stanzas.

An eidolon [eye-DOE-lun] is, according to the Oxford English Dictionary, from a Greek word and means an "unsubstantial image, spectre, phantom." It is the phantom ideal attached to every "real" object, experience, or idea.

> I met a seer,
> Passing the hues and objects of the world,
> The fields of art and learning, pleasure, sense,
> To glean eidólons.

For Whitman a "seer" was someone who had the ability to see clearly. He believed that one of the functions of poet-prophets throughout history had been to explain phantom ideals to listeners or readers. Greek poets explained the illusive thoughts and actions of immortal gods and goddesses to believing mortals; modern poets explain the ideals of their own times.

> The present now and here
> America's busy, teeming, intricate whirl,
> Of aggregate and segregate for only thence
>   releasing,
> To-day's eidólons.

He refers to the "prophet" and "bard" who "shall mediate to the Modern, to Democracy, interpret yet to them [the people], / God and eidólons." It takes a poet, Whitman believed, to explain God and to interpret the ideal. It is this, his explanation of the ideal America, for which Whitman feels called to be a national poet.

"Eighteen Sixty-One" (1865)

First appeared titled "1861" in the Drum-Taps volume (1865) and retained that title in Leaves of Grass until it received its present title and became the second of 43 poems in the "Drum-Taps" cluster for the sixth edition (1881).

The poem is an evocation of the year 1861, the year the CIVIL WAR began: "Arm'd year—year of the struggle, / No dainty rhymes or sentimental love verses for you terrible year, . . ." After the excitement of seeing men marching in the streets of New York, heading off to war (see "First O Songs for a Prelude," the poem immediately preceding this one in the 1881 edition), Whitman now expresses a much more somber view of the war.

He compares the year to the "strong men erect" with rifles on their shoulders fighting in the war. It was, for Whitman a "strong" but "terrible" year. As a hospital attendant in Washington, D.C., he saw these men weakened or killed by wounds and sickness. He ends the poem with the following saddened note:

> Saw I your gait and saw I your sinewy limbs
>   clothed in blue, bearing weapons, robust year,
> Heard your determin'd voice launch'd forth
>   again and again,
> Year that suddenly sang by the mouths of the
>   round-lipp'd cannon,
> I repeat you, hurrying, crashing, sad, distracted
>   year.

Whitman saw firsthand the terrible conditions under which doctors were forced to treat the soldiers. He was impressed by the equal treatment dealt to soldiers from both northern and southern armies, but he never got over the hospital conditions during that first "sad, distracted year." See CIVIL WAR HOSPITALS.

"Eighteenth Presidency, The" (1928)

An essay written by Whitman in 1856 but not published until January 1928 when Causse, Graille, and Castelnau printed a limited edition in Montpellier, France. It was reprinted in 1956 by the University of Kansas Press, edited by Edward F. Grier. The subtitle is "Voice of Walt Whitman to each Young Man in the Nation, North, South, East, and West."

The essay is an indictment of Presidents Millard Fillmore (1850–53) and James Buchanan (1857–61) for their support of "three hundred and fifty thousand owners of slaves." They were the 13th and 15th presidents respectively, and led Whitman to support the first Republican presidential candidate, John C. Fremont, in the 1856 presidential campaign. The Republican platform opposed SLAVERY expansion against Buchanan and his Democratic Party's conservative platform, which favored states' rights and a larger federal government.

"Election Day, November, 1884" (1884)

First published in the PHILADELPHIA PRESS (October 26, 1884); then in *November Boughs* (1888); and it was the 28th of 65 poems in the "First Annex: Sands at Seventy" cluster for the "Death-bed" printing of *Leaves of Grass* (1892).

The presidential candidates for the election of November 1884 were Republican James G. Blaine and Democrat Grover Cleveland. It was one of the most fiercely fought elections in United States history, both candidates and their parties turning the campaign into personal attacks. Blaine was accused of taking money from big business and Cleveland was accused of fathering an illegitimate child.

Whitman does not mention the campaign, but he may have had it in mind when he wrote this 14-line poem, declaring that it is the "choosing day" itself that matters most—democracy in action—and not the candidates.

He states in the poem that if he were to name the Western world's "powerfulest scene and show," it would not be Niagara Falls or the "limitless prairies" or the Colorado canyons or Yosemite or Yellowstone, but "*the still small voice* vibrating— America's choosing day, / (The heart of it not in the chosen—the act itself the main, the quadrennial choosing,)." It is the election itself that makes America the democracy it is. The "chosen" that year was Cleveland.

"Ended Day, An" (1891)

First published as the eighth of 31 poems in *Good-Bye My Fancy* (1891); then in "Second Annex: Good-Bye My Fancy" for the "Death-bed" printing of *Leaves of Grass* (1892).

Whitman added a long footnote to this three-line poem about the "triumph" and beauty of the evening hours, explaining how he had always felt that there was more joy in the late afternoon or evening than in the morning sunrise. He felt that birds, especially the thrush, provided their best singing in the late afternoon. And he remembered the calmness of CIVIL WAR battle zones in the evening; he quotes a surgeon describing an old sailor's death: "He went out with the tide and the sunset."

Another reference to his experiences nursing soldiers during the Civil War includes the note that in the late afternoon or evening hours, "the badly wounded would get some ease, and would like to talk a little, or be talk'd to. Intellectual and emotional natures would be at their best: Deaths were always easier; medicines seem'd to have better effect when given then, and a lulling atmosphere would pervade the wards."

"End of All, The" (1840)

First published in the LONG ISLAND DEMOCRAT (September 22, 1840); an "early poem" *not* later published in *Leaves of Grass*. It is most accessible now in Francis Murphy (editor), *Walt Whitman: The Complete Poems* (Penguin Books, 1996).

"Enfans d'Adam"

See "Children of Adam."

"Ethiopia Saluting the Colors" (1871)

First appeared as "Ethiopia Commenting" in the fifth edition of *Leaves of Grass* (1871); then under its present title but with a subtitle ("A Reminiscence of 1864") and in a group titled "Bathed in War's Perfume" for the fifth edition (1876); it then became the 28th of 43 poems in the "Drum-Taps" cluster for the sixth edition (1881).

The speaker in this poem, marching with Sherman to the Carolina sea, notices at the side of the road a "dusky woman, so ancient hardly human" and wonders what she thinks of the war. She tells him about being caught like a "savage beast is caught" and brought across the sea in a "slaver" ship. In the poem's last line, thinking about her still, he says: "Are the things so strange and marvelous you see or have seen?"

This poem is unusual in *Leaves of Grass* because it has a distinctively classical poetic form. It is made up of five stanzas of three lines each, the lines in a basic iambic pattern, and each line of 13 or 14 syllables. And there is a rhyme scheme. The middle accented syllable of each stanza's first line rhymes with the last syllable in the line (for example, "woman . . . human") and the last syllables of the second and third lines rhyme (for example, "feet . . . greet").

"Europe" (1850)

First published as "Resurgemus" in the *New York Tribune* (June 21, 1850); then as the eighth of 12 untitled poems in the first edition of *Leaves of Grass* (1855); as "Poem of the Dead Young Men of Europe, the 72d and 73d Years of These States" (1856); under the present title, with the subtitle "The 72d and 73d Years of These States" for the third edition (1860); and it was the second of 29 poems in the "By The Roadside" cluster for the sixth edition (1881).

The poem was written to celebrate the European revolutions of 1848–49, taking place 72 years after the American Revolution of 1776—"the 72d and 73d years of these states." A second French Republic was set up in 1848, after revolutionists had taken away Louis-Philippe's throne; Ferdinand I of Austria abdicated during the same year, and his nephew Franz Josef became emperor; and there were other European revolutions taking place as well that included Hungary, Ireland, Venice, Germany, and Denmark.

"Resurgemus," the original title for this poem, means resurgence (probably from the Latin word *resurgo*), as in the rising up of citizens against unjust governments: "Suddenly out of its stale and drowsy lair, the lair of slaves, / Like lightning it le'pt forth half startled at itself." Even the citizen-soldiers were surprised at their successes, at the ease with which they took down their own governments.

Whitman shows in this poem his enthusiasm for the liberty of people everywhere where there are tyrannical governments enslaving the people. The poet was aware of the seeming contradiction between his ambivalence over SLAVERY in America and what he felt to be the more important need to preserve the Union. He ends this poem, however, clearly in favor of Liberty for all people:

> Liberty, let others despair of you—I never
>   despair of you.
> Is the house shut? is the master away?
> Nevertheless, be ready, be not weary of watching,
> He will soon return, his messengers come anon.

Whitman nourishes his love of liberty in this final stanza but warns that tyrants can take it away.

"Evening Lull, An" (1888)

First appearing in *November Boughs* (1888), it was the 63rd of 65 poems in the "First Annex: Sands at Seventy" cluster for the "Death-bed" printing of *Leaves of Grass* (1892).

This four-line poem describes "three hours of peace and soothing rest of brain" at the end of a week of "physical anguish, / Unrest and pain."

Whitman wrote a footnote meant to explain this poem and "Now Precedent Songs, Farewell," on the same page in *November Boughs*, saying that the poems were "eked out during an afternoon, June, 1888, in my seventieth year, at a critical spell of illness. . . . I feel in them an end and close of all." He would live another three years, but it is clear from this and other similar notes he wrote during the late 1880s that he believed the illness he was then suffering would end in death.

"Excelsior" (1856)

First appeared as "Poem of the Heart of the Son of Manhattan Island" in the second edition of *Leaves of Grass* (1856); it was "Chants Democratic, No. 15" in the third edition (1860); it received its present title (1867); and it was the ninth of 22 poems in the "From Noon to Starry Night" cluster for the sixth edition (1881).

Excelsior means "lofty," "higher," ever upward; the word is used on the seal of the state of New York, though there is no evidence that Whitman had the seal in mind when he wrote the poem.

The poet brags in the poem about being the best at everything: the "most cautious," the "happiest," the "proudest," the most "benevolent," the most "loved" and with the most "friends," and having the "perfect and enamour'd body," etc. But, as with other seemingly ego-driven poems, Whitman uses the universal "I" here. He is bragging for all people, saying perhaps (it is not actually stated as it is, for example, in "Song of Myself"), that we can all be better, happier, prouder, more loved, than we are.

In spite of the optimism here, see the next poem in the cluster, "Ah Poverties, Wincings, and Sulky Retreats," a poem of seeming pessimism.

"Executor's Diary Note, 1891, An" (1891)

Written by Horace TRAUBEL, one of Whitman's three estate executors. The short note is a "Preface" to "Old Age Echoes," a cluster of 13 poems published at the end of the 10th edition of *Leaves of Grass* (1897).

Traubel writes that Whitman gave him permission to add the poems to the 1892 *Leaves of Grass* for the 1897 printing and suggested the title, "Old Age Echoes." Traubel also says that Whitman told him that he hoped that succeeding printings of *Leaves* would keep the same ordering of poems as in the final edition. "In the long run the world will do as it pleases with the book. I am determined to have the world know what I was pleased to do."

"Faces" (1855)

This was the sixth of 12 untitled poems in the first edition of *Leaves of Grass* (1855); it was titled "Poem of Faces" in the second edition (1856), "Leaf of Faces" (1860), "A Leaf of Faces" (1867), and it received its present title in the fifth edition (1871); it became the second of 22 poems in the "From Noon to Starry Night" cluster for the sixth edition (1881). The poem is in five sections and 84 lines.

Section 1 describes some of the beautiful faces the poet recognizes: "Faces of friendship, precision, caution, suavity, ideality, / The spiritual-prescient face, the always welcome common benevolent face, . . ." But Whitman nearly always balances good and bad, beautiful and ugly; so Section 2 describes ugly faces: "This face is a dog's snout sniffing for garbage, . . . / This face is an epilepsy, . . . / This face is bitten by vermin and worms, . . ." The poet loves them all, beautiful and ugly alike.

In Section 3 the poet recognizes the inward beauty of even the ugliest of faces. "Well, you cannot trick me," he says; in a "score or two of ages, . . . I shall meet the real landlord . . . perfect and unharm'd, every inch as good as myself." The poet evokes the image of God in Section 4, suggesting that all faces "show their descent from the Master himself."

Section 5 presents the face of one whom Whitman might consider the most important of all, "The old face of the mother of many children, . . . / She looks out from her quaker cap, her face is clearer and more beautiful than the sky." And at the end of the poem, he turns the woman into a metaphor for the mythical earth mother, the most fruitful of all:

The melodious character of the earth,
The finish beyond which philosophy cannot go
   and does not wish to go,
The justified mother of men.

Whitman always seems to find a balance between good and evil, between the real and ideal; and there is most often a metaphor, as in "Faces," where the Quaker woman, "her face . . . more beautiful than the sky," becomes the mother of us all.

"Facing West from California's Shores" (1860)

First appeared untitled as the 10th poem in the "Enfans d'Adam" cluster for the third edition of *Leaves of Grass* (1860); and it became the 15th of 16 poems in the "Children of Adam" cluster for the sixth edition (1881).

The "I" of this poem is an explorer who, having reached "California's Shores," looks toward "Hindustan," "Kashmere," and "Asia" and sees "the circle almost circled"; he faces "home again, very pleas'd and joyous," but he wonders why what he had been looking for is yet "unfound."

"Home" for the explorer is Asia, from where thousands of native people migrated eastward to North America. According to the poet, they have yet to find whatever it was they were looking for.

"Fame's Vanity" (1840)

First published in the LONG ISLAND DEMOCRAT (October 23, 1839), an "early poem" *not* later published in *Leaves of Grass*. It is most accessible now in Francis Murphy (editor), *Walt Whitman: The Complete Poems* (Penguin Books, 1996).

"Fancies at Navesink" (1885)

Cluster title for eight poems published first in NINETEENTH CENTURY magazine (August 1885);

then, with a cluster of 57 poems entitled "Sands at Seventy" in *November Boughs* (1888); and as an insert in the "First Annex: Sands at Seventy" cluster for the "Death-bed" printing of *Leaves of Grass* (1892).

A Whitman note refers to Navesink as a "seaside mountain" at the lower entrance to New York Bay. On current maps it is a small town about a mile from the New Jersey coast, across lower New York Bay from BROOKLYN. It is four miles inland from Highlands Beach, at the southern end of what is now Gateway National Recreation Area, Sandy Hook Unit.

All eight poems in the Navesink group use the sea as a metaphor for the lives of humankind. Whitman thinks of the ebb tide, especially the one coming late each day, as a metaphor for human despair; the flood tide, on the other hand, represents hope. In his eighth and final Navesink poem Whitman recognizes the need for both in the full lives of people, even in himself.

The poems are in the following order: "The Pilot in the Mist," "Had I the Choice," "You Tides with Ceaseless Swell," "Last of Ebb, and Daylight Waning," "And Yet Not You Alone," "Proudly the Flood Comes In," "By That Long Scan of Waves," and "The Last of All."

"Farm Picture, A" (1865)

First published in *Drum-Taps* (1865); then in the fourth edition of *Leaves of Grass* (1867); it was printed as a separate poem in *Leaves* (1871); then it was the 15th of 29 poems in the "By The Roadside" cluster for the sixth edition (1881).

This three-line poem presents a pastoral "farm picture."

"Fast-Anchor'd Eternal O Love!" (1860)

Titled "Calamus No. 38" in the third edition of *Leaves of Grass* (1860); it received its present title for the fourth edition (1867); it was the 35th of 39 poems in the "Calamus" cluster for the sixth edition (1881).

This six-line poem shows the emotional differences between the physical love of a man for a woman and the spiritual love of a man for another man. The former is "Fast-anchor'd eternal . . . more resistless than I can tell." The love of one man for another is, on the other hand, "Ethereal, the last athletic reality." The love of another man shares the "roving life."

This is a poetic example of Whitman's concept of the difference between love for a woman, amativeness, and love for a man, adhesiveness. The former may be found in his "Children of Adam" poems, the latter in his "Calamus" poems. See the main entries for each of these clusters.

"Few Drops Known, The" (1897)

First published as the third of 13 poems in the "Old Age Echoes" cluster for the first posthumous printing of *Leaves of Grass* (1897), added by one of Whitman's executors, Horace TRAUBEL.

This five-line poem presents one of Whitman's secondary themes in *Leaves*, that of the importance of the unknown. The "few drops known [of the ancient Greeks and Romans, for example] must stand for oceans of the unknown." We have only bits and pieces of the "long and copious retrospect of antiquity."

"First Annex: Sands At Seventy" (1892)

In 1888 Whitman published *November Boughs*, a book separate from *Leaves of Grass*, which included a group of 65 poems in two clusters: "Sands at Seventy" and "Fancies at Navesink." The book also included 21 prose essays, including "A Backward Glance O'er Travel'd Roads." The latter essay is

both a reminiscence and a summation of Whitman's ideas about poetry and America, and he asked that it be included at the end of subsequent editions of *Leaves of Grass*. He clearly enjoyed looking back over his life and what he considered his most important accomplishments.

For the "Death-bed" printing of *Leaves of Grass* (1892) the poems were placed together under the title "First Annex: Sands at Seventy" and added at the end of the book, making it actually an "annex" to the sixth edition of *Leaves* (1881), which was otherwise unchanged in 1892. Thirty-two of the poems were first published in the NEW YORK HERALD during the early months of 1888. He placed the group of poems under the heading "Fancies at Navesink" in the middle of the "Sands at Seventy" grouping. The poems tend to be short and are reflections on Whitman's old age.

The ordering of the poems is as follows:

"Sands at Seventy": "Mannahatta," "Paumanok," "From Montauk Point," "To Those Who've Fail'd," "A Carol Closing Sixty-Nine," "The Bravest Soldiers," "A Font of Type," "As I Sit Writing Here," "My Canary Bird," "Queries to My Seventieth Year," "The Wallabout Martyrs," "The First Dandelion," "America," "Memories," "To-day and Thee," "After the Dazzle of Day," "Abraham LINCOLN, Born Feb. 12, 1809," "Out of May's Shows Selected," and "Halcyon Days."

"Fancies at Navesink": "The Pilot in the Mist," "Had I the Choice," "You Tides with Ceaseless Swell," "Last of Ebb, and Daylight Waning," "And Yet Not You Alone," "Proudly the Flood Comes In," "By That Long Scan of Waves," and "Then Last of All."

"Sands at Seventy" (continued): "Election Day, November, 1884," "With Husky-Haughty Lips, O Sea!," "Death of General Grant," "Red Jacket (from Aloft)," "Washington's Monument, February, 1885," "Of That Blithe Throat of Thine," "Broadway," "To Get the Final Lilt of Songs," "Old Salt Kossabone," "The Dead Tenor," "Continuities," "Yonnondio," "Life," "Going Somewhere," "Small the Theme of My Chant," "True Conquerors," "The United States to Old World Critics,"

"The Calming Thought of All," "Thanks in Old Age," "Life and Death," "The Voice of the Rain," "Soon Shall the Winter's Foil Be Here," "While Not the Past Forgetting," "The Dying Veteran," "Stronger Lessons," "A Prairie Sunset," "Twenty Years," "Orange Buds by Mail from Florida," "Twilight," "You Lingering Sparse Leaves of Me," "Not Meagre, Latent Boughs Alone," "The Dead Emperor," "As the Greek's Signal Flame," "The Dismantled Ship," "Now Precedent Songs, Farewell," "An Evening Lull," "Old Age's Lambent Peaks," and "After the Supper and Talk."

"First Dandelion, The" (1888)

First published in the NEW YORK HERALD (March 12, 1888); then in *November Boughs* (1888); and it was the 12th of 65 poems in the "First Annex: Sands at Seventy" cluster for the "Death-bed" printing of *Leaves of Grass* (1892).

This poem is a four-line song of praise for the first dandelion in spring, come "Forth from its sunny nook of shelter'd grass—innocent, golden, calm as the dawn," with its "trustful face"—trustful that other dandelions will follow and the rest of spring.

"First O Songs for a Prelude" (1865)

This poem was titled "Drum-Taps" in the *Drum-Taps* volume (1865) and for the fourth edition of *Leaves of Grass* (1867); then it was used as an epigraph or "prelude" for the "Drum-Taps" cluster (1871); it was under its present title and the first of 43 poems in the revised "Drum-Taps" cluster for the sixth edition of *Leaves* (1881). A four-line stanza was added at the beginning of the poem for the 1871 and 1876 printings but then dropped.

In *Specimen Days* Whitman writes about first hearing the news of the outbreak of CIVIL WAR:

I had been to the OPERA in Fourteenth Street that night [April 13, 1861], and after the performance was walking down Broadway toward 12 o'clock, on my way to BROOKLYN, when I heard in the distance the loud cries of the newsboys, who came presently tearing and yelling up the street, rushing from side to side even more furiously than usual. I bought an extra and crossed to the Metropolitan Hotel (Niblo's), where the great lamps were still brightly blazing, and, with a crowd of others, who gathered impromptu, read the news, which was evidently authentic.

Whitman's "Prelude" poem to *Drum-Taps* reflects the poet's horror at what was happening in the South: "At dead of night, at news from the south, / Incens'd struck with clinch'd hand the pavement." He watched the parade of "incens'd" New York citizens angry at the South and signing up to go to war, a war they were told could last only a few weeks. The poet is clearly pleased that his New Yorkers ("O Manhattan, my own, my peerless") were going to war. It was not that Whitman favored SLAVERY but that he hated the possibility that a Southern victory would break up the Union. So he was proud of the "young men falling in and arming." He CATALOGs others, all preparing to go to war: mechanics, lawyers, wagon drivers, salesmen "leaving the store, the boss, book-keeper, portrer, all leaving. . . ." They heard the "drum-taps" and gathered in the streets of New York.

Whitman, perhaps the greatest of all spokesmen for democracy, is nevertheless completely enthralled by the activity of men going off to fight a war against their own countrymen: "(How good they look as they tramp down to the river, sweaty, with their guns on their shoulders! / How I love them! how I could hug them, with their brown faces and their clothes and knapsacks cover'd with dust!)." There was a "tearful parting" as mothers kissed their sons good-bye.

The poet's description makes clear how exciting the scene must have been, men marching toward the river where boats waited to haul them to points south. The artillery was moving too, "silent cannons bright as gold, drawn along, rumbl[ing] lightly over the stones, / (Silent cannons, soon to cease [their] silence. . . .)" The poem's final line reflects Whitman's view of the city's attitude: "[N]ow you smile with joy exulting old Mannahatta."

The poet was in Washington, D.C., in time to see the casualties from both North and South brought into the Washington hospitals from the first battle at Bull Run, near Manassas, Virginia, July 20–21, 1861. He spent most of the war working in those hospitals; as he says in the initial four-line stanza—the lines later dropped—his job was "To sit by the wounded and soothe them, or silently watch the dead." Soldiers of both sides dictated letters to Whitman, who then mailed them to loved ones at home.

"Font of Type, A" (1888)

Appeared first in *November Boughs* (1888); and it was the seventh of 65 poems in the "First Annex: Sands at Seventy" cluster for the "Death-bed" printing of *Leaves of Grass* (1892).

Whitman often set type for his own books, and this poem seems to be in praise of the "passionate powers" of fonts of type, "these unlaunch'd voices . . . the pallid slivers slumbering," waiting for the printer.

"For Him I Sing" (1871)

First appeared in the fifth edition of *Leaves of Grass* (1871); it was the eighth of 24 poems in the "Inscriptions" cluster for the sixth edition (1881).

The "him" is not identified in this five-line poem, but it is one of several poems in which Whitman "sings" not of people but of ideas. "I raise the present on the past, . . . / To make himself by them the law unto himself." The present is a law unto itself, fused to the past by "immortal laws." Certain "laws" of the past are immortal, because they are right for all times and, ideally, we have learned from them, yet the present is still more important than the past.

"For Queen Victoria's Birthday" (1890)

First published in the PHILADELPHIA PUBLIC LEDGER (May 22, 1890); it then appeared in *Good-Bye My Fancy* (1891) but was not in the "Death-bed" printing of *Leaves of Grass* (1892).

"For Us Two, Reader Dear" (1891)

Cut from *Leaves of Grass* after appearing in *Good-Bye My Fancy* (1891).

"For You O Democracy" (1860)

Titled "Calamus No. 5" in the third edition of *Leaves of Grass* (1860); it was published as a separate poem titled "A Song" (1867); it received the present title and was the fourth of 39 poems in the "Calamus" cluster for the sixth edition (1881).

The key word in this seven-line poem is "comrades," repeated four times in two refrains. The love the poet feels for "comrades" is equated with the love he has for democracy, for the love and friendship he feels for all people. He refers to democracy as "ma femme" (meaning my woman, my wife), and it is for this intimacy with democracy that he is "trilling these songs." See also "These I Singing in Spring."

"France, The 18th Year of These States" (1860)

First published in the third edition of *Leaves of Grass* (1860); it was published with a cluster of poems titled "Songs of Insurrection" in the fifth edition (1871); then as the fourth of seven poems in the "Birds of Passage" cluster for the sixth edition (1881).

The influence for this poem was the French Revolution, especially one of the war's key years, 1794—"The 18th Year of These States"—and France's ongoing struggle for Liberty. Whitman uses the French "*battues* of death" (the wholesale slaughter of citizens) and the idea that good people must sometimes fight for Liberty as metaphors for the Liberty sought in the American CIVIL WAR, a liberty for which every American must fight. "O Liberty! O mate for me! / Here too the blaze, the grape-shot and the axe, in reserve, to fetch them out in case of need."

The Civil War began 11 months after the first appearance in public of this poem. He calls on other "chansonniers," other singer/poets to join him in the cause of Liberty. In the poem's last line Whitman refers to singing "a song for you ma femme," a personification of Liberty.

Franklin Evans; or The Inebriate: A Tale of the Times (1842)

Whitman's only novel, first published in the NEW WORLD (November 1842), the work taking up the magazine's entire issue of 31 pages. After a great amount of advertising by the editor (one ad stating that the story was written "by one of the best Novelists of this country, with a view to aid the great work of Reform"), the first issue may have sold as many as 20,000 copies. It was reprinted by the *New World* a year later, under a slightly different title: *Franklin Evans; or the Merchant's Clerk: A Tale of the Times* (August 13, 1843). It was later published by J. Winchester in New York (no date) as an off-print from *The New World*, and retitled, *Franklin Evans: Knowledge is Power. The Merchant's Clerk, in New York; or Career as a Young Man from the Country.*

Franklin Evans is most accessible now in *Walt Whitman: The Early Poems and the Fiction*, edited by

Thomas L. Brasher (New York University Press, 1963).

A prepublication blurb in *The New World* magazine advertised the novel as an "Original Temperance Novel." In his introduction, Whitman states:

> The story I am going to tell you, reader, will be somewhat aside from the ordinary track of the novelist. It will not abound, either with profound reflections, or sentimental remarks. Yet its moral—for I flatter myself it has one, and one which it were well to engrave on the heart of each person who scans its pages—will be taught by its own incidents, and the current of the narrative.

Whitman often wrote not only blurbs advertising his stories but also his own reviews, including a few years later for the poems of *Leaves of Grass*. The "teaser" is applied to *Franklin Evans,* a novel whose moral theme is shamefully clear even for mid-19th century American tastes, tastes that often favored romantic, even sentimental, stories and novels.

The 20-year-old Franklin Evans is a "country boy," full of promise as a businessman, until, led by his friend John Colby, he gets in with the wrong crowd and gradually becomes an alcoholic. It is Colby who gets Evans drunk the first time and so is the constant figure to blame for Evans's life of inebriation. Evans narrates the story of his own fall into alcoholism.

Every incident is described as resulting from Evans's "intemperance." There are minor crimes committed; there are friends and even family members who die; and there is a robbery in which Evans plays a part, is arrested and imprisoned. There are a dozen or more of such incidents, each one blamed on Evans's intemperance; the "moral," for which Whitman "flatters" himself, is obvious enough to be insulting to readers.

There is one twist in Evans's moral favor, however, which may be credited with saving the story just a little. He had saved the life of a little girl, and four years later, while he is in prison for the robbery, the father of the girl, a lawyer, takes Evans's case and gets him acquitted. The lawyer, his wife, and especially the little girl, become an influence for good, and Evans is saved finally from intemperance, does not take another drink of alcohol, and lives out the rest of his life, we are led to believe, helping others resolve their problems, especially problems of intemperance.

As with a number of his short stories, Whitman states that the novel "is not a work of fiction, as the term is used. I narrate occurrences that have had a far more substantial existence, than in my fancy." The incidents described, he says, are based on fact. Readers might argue that nearly all fiction comes from incidents in the life of the writer and that it's what happens to the incident in his imagination that determines the story's quality.

Evans ends the novel by stating: "I have desired, amid the path we [he and the reader] have travelled together, and which is now at an end—that a few seeds of wholesome instruction might be dropped at the same time that we gathered the fruits and the flowers." Since Evans seems to have ended his story, it must be Whitman himself who steps in to provide "Chapter XXV . . . Conclusion": "As works of fiction have often been made the vehicle of morality, I have adopted the novel experiment of making one of the sort a messenger of the cause of Temperance."

Even Whitman recognized the story as "rot." He told his friend and biographer Horace TRAUBEL that one of the temperance people asked him to write an anti-drinking story and that the money was too good to turn down—$75, he told Traubel, and another $50 later from royalties. "I was hard up at the time," he told the biographer. Whitman said he finished the book in "three days of constant work," with the help, he added, of "a bottle of port." He remembered the novel as "damned rot—rot of the worst sort—not insincere perhaps, but rot, nevertheless."

CHARACTERS

John Colby The villain in Whitman's novel. There are antagonists in other Whitman stories but rarely a villain. Colby is a "friend" to Franklin Evans but introduces him to alcohol and continues to encourage him to drink until he becomes an alcoholic. He is certainly to blame for Evans's problems, but it doesn't take Evans long to become his own worst enemy.

Franklin Evans The 20-year-old narrator of the novel, Evans describes his fall into alcoholism and his subsequent life of minor crimes, including a robbery for which he spends time in prison, all the result of his intemperance. He is eventually acquitted of further crimes, however, by a lawyer who turns out to be the father of a little girl whose life Evans had saved several years ago.

"From Far Dakota's Cañons" (1876)

First published under the title "A Death Sonnet for Custer" in the NEW YORK TRIBUNE (June 10, 1876); it appeared in the 1876 printing of *Leaves of Grass;* then with its present title and as the 16th of 22 poems in the "From Noon to Starry Night" cluster for the sixth edition (1881). It carried a subtitle, "June 25, 1876," the date of the battle at Little Big Horn River.

The poem commemorates George Armstrong Custer's death at the battle of the Little Big Horn. The poet places himself in the Dakota setting, watching the battle, and honoring the general:

> Thou of the tawny flowing hair in battle,
> I erewhile saw, with erect head, pressing ever in
>   front, bearing a bright sword in thy hand,
> Now ending well in death the splendid fever of
>   thy deeds,
> (I bring no dirge for it or thee, I bring a glad
>   triumphal sonnet,) . . .

Whitman romanticizes the battle in favor of the soldiers, who were under orders to chase the Indians out of the Dakota territory.

"From Montauk Point" (1888)

First published in the NEW YORK HERALD (March 1, 1888); then in *November Boughs* (1888); and it was the third of 65 poems in the "First Annex: Sands at

Seventy" cluster for the "Death-bed" printing of *Leaves of Grass* (1892).

Montauk Point is at the eastern end of LONG ISLAND, at the end of what is today Montauk Point State Park. Looking eastward, Whitman says in the five-line, descriptive poem, there is "nothing but sea and sky." He writes of the "wild unrest" of the sea, "that inbound urge and urge of waves, / Seeking the shores forever."

"From My Last Years" (1876)

Cut from *Leaves of Grass* after appearing in the sixth edition (1876).

"From Noon To Starry Night" (1881)

Cluster title for 22 poems in the sixth edition of *Leaves of Grass* (1881). The only unifying element in the cluster is that the setting of the opening poem, "Thou Orb Aloft Full-Dazzling," is noontime, and the setting for the final poem, "A Clear Midnight," is 12 hours later. Seventeen of the poems were clustered together for the first time in the sixth edition, having been transferred from earlier editions; five of the poems were new to *Leaves of Grass*.

Here are the 22 poems in their ordering by Whitman for the sixth edition and subsequent printings of *Leaves:* "Thou Orb Aloft Full-Dazzling," "Faces," "The Mystic Trumpeter," "To a Locomotive in Winter," "O Magnet-South," "Mannahatta." "All is Truth," "A Riddle Song," "Excelsior," "Ah Poverties, Wincings, and Sulky Retreats," "Thoughts" (Of Public Opinion), "Mediums," "Weave in, My Hardy Life," "Spain," "By Broad Potomac's Shore," "From Far Dakota's Cañons (June 25, 1876)," "Old War-Dreams," "Thick-Sprinkled Bunting," "What Best I See in Thee," "Spirit That Form'd This Scene," "As I Walk These Broad Majestic Days," and "A Clear Midnight."

"From Paumanok Starting I Fly Like a Bird" (1865)

First appeared in the *Drum-Taps* volume (1865) and it carried this title there and in all editions of *Leaves of Grass;* it was the fourth of 43 poems in the "Drum-Taps" cluster for the sixth edition (1881).

The poet visualizes himself flying "like a bird" in order to "sing the idea of all" during the CIVIL WAR. It is Whitman's idea of democracy, a concept of equality for all Americans regardless of regional origin and in spite of the fighting between North and South during the Civil War—though the war is barely mentioned in this poem. As if to emphasize the need for democracy, he CATALOGs the people of "Michigan" and "Wisconsin," among other northern and midwestern states, as well as people from "Tennessee and Kentucky . . . the Carolinas and Georgia" and other southern states. All of these people are equal in a democratic society.

He ends with the following notion:

> To sing first, (to the tap of the war-drum if
>   need be,)
> The idea of all, of the Western world one and
>   inseparable,
> And then the song of each member of these
>   States.

In this and other poems Whitman shows his concern that equality be the first principle of a democratic society. This is why he was so ambivalent about SLAVERY; he was against slavery at any cost save one: the Union of the states was more important to him than the issue of slavery. Democracy could withstand slavery for awhile longer, he felt, but if the northern forces won the war, not only would the Union be preserved but slavery would also then be abolished.

"From Pent-up Aching Rivers" (1860)

Second poem in the "Enfans d'Adam" cluster of the third edition of *Leaves of Grass* (1860); it was the second of 16 poems in the "Children of Adam" cluster for the sixth edition (1881).

The poem celebrates the divinity of sexual intercourse:

> . . . singing the phallus,
> Singing the song of procreation,
> Singing the need of superb children and
> therein superb grown people, . . .

Whitman uses a series of provocative images in this 57-line poem that leave little room for misunderstanding: "muscular urge," "blending," "resistless yearning," "hungry gnaw," "love-flesh tremulous aching." But he refers to this as the "divine list," suggesting that the divinity comes from the notion that God made us in his own image.

Whitman also ties this idea into the nature of all things: "Two hawks in the air, two fishes swimming in the sea not more lawless than we." It is in the nature of all things to procreate. At the end he celebrates "you act divine and you children prepared for, / And you stalwart loins." It is not difficult to see why some city officials in Whitman's time, particularly in Boston, wanted to censor some of the lines or even whole poems from the "Children of Adam" and "Calamus" clusters.

"From Pent-up Aching Rivers" serves as an emotional outline for the remaining poems in the "Children of Adam" group.

"Full of Life Now" (1860)

Titled "Calamus No. 45" in the third edition of *Leaves of Grass* (1860); received its present title (1867); it was the 39th and final poem in the "Calamus" cluster for the sixth edition (1881).

This is one of several poems in *Leaves of Grass* where Whitman speaks to future readers, reading the poetry long after the poet's death:

> When you read these I that was visible am
> become invisible,
> Now it is you, compact, visible, realizing my
> poems, seeking me,
> Fancying how happy you were if I could be with
> you and become your comrade;

> Be it as if I were with you. (Be not too certain
> but I am now with you.)

We readers, living a century and a half or more later, know Whitman died in 1892, but we may look over our shoulders nevertheless.

"Germs" (1860)

First published as "Leaves of Grass, No. 19" in the third edition of *Leaves of Grass* (1860); then as "Leaves of Grass, No. 2" (1867); it received its present title (1871); and it was the fifth of 29 poems in the "By The Roadside" cluster for the sixth edition (1881).

The "Germs" are "qualities, lives, humanity, language, thoughts," all the various seeds planted in people before birth. Even the Sun and Moon have an influence on our lives.

> Splendid suns, the moons and rings, . . .
> Such-like, and as good as such-like, visible here
> or anywhere, stand provided for in
> a handful of space, which I extend my arm and
> half enclose with my hand,
> That containing the start of each and all, the
> virtue, the germs of all.

All things in Nature are in the "germs" from which each person begins.

"Give Me the Splendid Silent Sun" (1865)

First appeared in the *Drum-Taps* volume (1865) and under this title throughout its printing history in *Leaves of Grass*; it was the 23rd of 43 poems in the "Drum-Taps" cluster for the sixth edition (1881).

The first of two sections in this poem is devoted to a CATALOG of things the poet loves about Nature's pastoral scenes: the "splendid silent sun," the "field where the unmow'd grass grows," the "sweet-breath'd woman of whom I should never tire," the "perfect child." But at the end of the section the poet rejects the pastoral life for the city, especially in time of war.

"Keep your splendid silent sun," he says in the opening line of Section 2. Keep your Nature, he says; "Give me faces and streets . . . give me the streets of Manhattan! / Give me Broadway, with the soldiers marching—give me the sound of the trumpets and drums!"

This rejection of Nature in favor of city life seems incongruous for a poet like Whitman, especially in a poem titled "Give Me the Splendid Silent Sun." He may feel the effect of the war in this case, that the natural elements of the countryside were an illusion, one that seemed inappropriate.

It's not just the city but the people in it and the city sounds ("People endless, streaming, with strong voices, passions, pageants") that make the poet aware of what he misses when he's away, and which make him feel more at home during the war. Perhaps it is inappropriate to appreciate nature in time of war.

"Gliding o'er All" (1871)

First published as the epigraph on the title page of the *Passage to India* supplement to the fifth edition of *Leaves of Grass* in the period 1871–72; it was the 23rd of 29 poems in the "By The Roadside" cluster for the sixth edition (1881).

In this five-line poem the poet envisions floating above "Nature, Time, and Space" in a "voyage of the soul." He writes of the constancy of death and that he will yet sing of "many deaths." Whitman often writes of this supremacy of the soul and of its transcendent nature.

"Glimpse, A" (1860)

Titled "Calamus No. 29" in the third edition of *Leaves of Grass* (1860); it received its present title (1867); and it was the 27th of 39 poems in the "Calamus" cluster for the sixth edition (1881).

This poem describes the spiritual emotions that come with holding another man's hand. The poet

enters a barroom and sees another "youth who loves me and whom I love." They sit together and hold hands and pay little attention to the "smutty jest[s]" they hear from others in the room, "content, happy in being together, speaking little, perhaps not a word." See also "A Leaf for Hand in Hand," the next poem after "A Glimpse" in the "Calamus" cluster.

"Gods" (1871)

First published in the fifth edition of *Leaves of Grass* (1871); and it was the fourth of 29 poems in the "By The Roadside" cluster for the sixth edition (1881).

Whitman did not accept the idea of belief in a single god, or a nation ruled by any single set of religious beliefs. There were many gods, according to Whitman, and the poet worships them all. He believed that God could be found in other people, men and women, or in one's own Self:

> Lover divine and perfect Comrade,
> Waiting content, invisible yet, but certain,
> Be thou my God.

The poet CATALOGs other gods in the 21-line poem: "Ideal Man," "Death," "soul," "ideas," "the races' aspirations," "heroisms," "rapt enthusiasts," "Time and Space," etc. And each verse ends with the refrain: "Be thou my God" or "Be ye my Gods." That Whitman capitalizes the word God only emphasizes the importance of each of the various gods he worships.

"Going Somewhere" (1887)

First published in LIPPINCOTT'S MAGAZINE (November 1887); then in *November Boughs* (1888); and it was the 41st of 65 poems in the "First Annex: Sands at Seventy" cluster for the "Death-bed" printing of *Leaves of Grass* (1892).

The "science-friend" and "noblest woman-friend" of the poem was Anne GILCHRIST, from

England, who fell in love with Whitman long-distance, visited him from 1876 to 1879 and who wanted to marry him and/or have his children. She died in 1885, and this is a "memory-leaf for her dear sake."

Whitman quotes her in the poem, indicating her vast knowledge and "intuitions deep" and her belief that all things are bound together and "surely going somewhere," a pantheistic idea that the poet also accepted and that helped form the bond between the two.

Good-Bye My Fancy
(1891)

Published as a separate volume of 66 pages by David McKay in Philadelphia, uniform in format and style with *November Boughs*. The 32 poems would become the "Second Annex" to the final printing of *Leaves of Grass* (1892). *Good-Bye My Fancy* also included a preface and, at the end of the volume, the essay "A Backward Glance O'er Travel'd Roads," which had appeared as the preface to *November Boughs* (1888).

Whitman was ill when he put this slim book together in 1891, and he writes nostalgically about what he has accomplished in his life. He is concerned that readers will care more about his late poetry than about the early. In a footnote to the first of two poems entitled "Good-Bye My Fancy," he passes this concern on to readers: "Why do folks dwell so fondly on the last words, advice, appearance, of the departing? Those last words are not samples of the best, which involve vitality at its full, and balance, and perfect control and scope. But they are valuable beyond measure to confirm and endorse the varied train, facts, theories and faith of the whole preceding life."

The final poem in the collection is titled "Good-Bye My Fancy!" and the final line reads, "Good-Bye—and hail! my Fancy," a summing up of the nostalgia but indicating a hope for the future. See "Second Annex: Good-Bye My Fancy."

"Good-Bye My Fancy" [1]
(1891)

First published as the third of 31 poems in *Good-Bye My Fancy* (1891); then in "Second Annex: Good-Bye My Fancy" for the "Death-bed" printing of *Leaves of Grass* (1892).

This four-line poem is the first of two with this title, the second one at the end of the cluster and a more potent statement about the poet's "good-bye" to poetry and to life itself. Whitman uses the word *fancy* to mean the "creative imagination," implying in the title that he is near the end of his creative powers.

He provides a footnote to this poem, on the other hand, in which he wonders why "folks dwell so fondly on the last words, advice, appearance, of the departing." He would prefer that readers focus on the best of what he has done rather than merely on the last, referring to the poems in the "Sands at Seventy" and "Good-Bye My Fancy" annexes.

He seems discouraged by the quality of these last poems, but in "You Lingering Sparse Leaves of Me" in "Sands at Seventy," he feels that these final poems are the "faithfulest—hardiest," as well as the "last."

"Good-Bye My Fancy!" [2]
(1891)

First published as the last of 31 poems in *Good-Bye My Fancy* (1891); then in "Second Annex: Good-Bye My Fancy" for the "Death-bed" printing of *Leaves of Grass* (1892).

Whitman's placement of this poem last in the final edition of *Leaves* brings the reader's attention full circle. The poem is a statement of good-bye from the self to the self's "fancy," meaning his creative imagination—a definition now obsolete but used often by 19th-century writers. The self is the physical being, while the imagination transcends the physical in order to get to the metaphysical, the spiritual, the inner self. The idea is thematic in *Leaves of Grass,* and now that the poet is facing his own death, he turns the idea in on himself.

"Long have we lived, joy'd, caress'd together," he says, speaking for the relationship of the physical self to the metaphysical, but foreseeing that death will now separate them. But then he rethinks "separation" ("Let me not be too hasty") and decides that he and his "fancy" have "lived, slept, filter'd, become really blended into one" and that they would, therefore, "die together, (yes, we'll remain one,) / If we go anywhere we'll go together to meet what happens." So now, "finally," he says in the last line of both this poem and *Leaves of Grass:* "Goodbye—and hail! my Fancy."

"Grand is the Seen" (1891)

First published as the 29th of 31 poems in *Good-Bye My Fancy* (1891); then in "Second Annex: Good-Bye My Fancy" for the "Death-bed" printing of *Leaves of Grass* (1892).

"Grand are the sky and stars, . . . the earth, . . . time and space." But "grander far," Whitman says in this poem, is "the unseen soul of me." The soul allows for the comprehension of "seen" things; it is "more evolutionary, vast, puzzling, . . . / More multiform far—more lasting" than things seen by mere eyes. Whitman may be aware of the idea of things seen and unseen at the time of writing this poem because he's concerned with losing his eyesight. But one of his poetic themes is that of the soul's immortality, and several of his last poems reflect his personal interest in this idea.

"Great Are the Myths" (1855)

Appeared first untitled in the first edition of *Leaves of Grass* (1855); it was titled "Poem of a Few Greatnesses" (1856), titled "Leaves of Grass, No. 2" (1860), and under its present title for the fourth edi-

tion (1867) and a few later printings. It was cut after the 1876 printing, however, and did not reappear.

Four lines of the 71-line original poem were saved and titled "Youth, Day, Old Age and Night" for publication as a separate poem in the final printing of Whitman's book (1892).

The poet writes of the "greatness" of the classical myths, including Adam and Eve, but then he CATALOGs also the myths of Liberty, of Youth, of wealth, of Truth, of Language, of Justice, and of Life itself.

"Had I the Choice" (1885)

First published with seven other poems under the heading "Fancies at Navesink" in NINETEENTH CENTURY magazine (August 1885); then in *November Boughs* (1888); and, finally, with the "Fancies at Navesink" group as an insert in the "First Annex: Sands at Seventy" cluster for the "Death-bed" printing of *Leaves of Grass* (1892). Whitman writes that he would give up all the "greatest" literary figures (Homer, Hector, Achilles, Ajax, Shakespeare, Hamlet, Lear, Othello, and Tennyson's "fair ladies") if "O sea . . . you the undulation of one wave, its trick to me transfer, / Or breathe one breath of yours upon my verse, / And leave its odor there." The poet is asking questions about the secrets of the universe and offers to trade history's greatest literary figures for an answer. See also "You Tides with Ceaseless Swell."

"Halcyon Days" (1888)

First published in the NEW YORK HERALD (January 29, 1888); then in *November Boughs (1888);* and it was the 19th of 65 poems in the "First Annex: Sands at Seventy" cluster for the "Death-bed" printing of *Leaves of Grass* (1892).

The "happiest days of all," the poet writes, are the "brooding and blissful halcyon days," the nostalgic memories in old age of earlier times.

"Half-Breed: A Tale of the Western Frontier, The" (1845)

Short story first published as "Arrow-Tip" in the ARIS-TIDEAN (March 1845) and reprinted as "The Half-Breed: A Tale of the Western Frontier" in the BROOKLYN DAILY EAGLE (June 1–6, 8, and 9, 1846). The 27-year-old Whitman was editor of the *Eagle* at the time; the story appeared under the by-line "by a Brooklynite." The change of title is significant, because it switches the blame for the tale's outcome from Arrow-Tip to Boddo, the half-breed of the later title.

The original story was written in nine titled "chapters," but titles were left out of the reprinted version. An advertisement for the story, which appeared in the May 30, 1846, issue of the *Eagle,* calls the story an "Original Novelette." It is most accessible now in *Walt Whitman: The Early Poems and the Fiction,* edited by Thomas L. Brasher (New York University Press, 1963).

Arrow-Tip, an Indian who lives near the village of Warren on the "upper branches" of the Mississippi River, is a friend of the local whites and a personable member of the community. Arrow-Tip and another villager, Peter Brown, a blacksmith and recently married member of the community, get into what begins as a friendly altercation while on a hunting trip but which turns into the apparent death of Brown. Brown's "death" is reported to the town's authorities, who arrest Arrow-Tip and hold him for the murder even though, when they go to the hunting site to get Brown's body, the body is gone.

Brown, badly wounded but aware that he is as much to blame for the altercation and for his own injuries as is Arrow-Tip, is found by "Boddo," the "half-breed" of the story's revised title and helped to the hut of a local priest, Father Luke, who attempts to heal Brown's wounds. Father Luke sends Boddo to town in order to let the authorities know that Brown is alive and equally to blame for his injuries.

Boddo is a hunchback and much abused by the townspeople for his ugliness and for his unfriendly nature, much the result of the abuse. He decides to seek some revenge on the town by not carrying the priest's message to authorities. Father Luke, called "the Monk" and the "Lonesome Man" by townspeople, had conducted the wedding of Peter Brown and his unnamed bride and confides in her shortly after the wedding that he is the father of Boddo. The act of trusting his son to carry the message, even though he is aware of the town's treatment of Boddo, turns into disaster. Arrow-Tip is hung just as Brown himself rushes in to take part of the blame for the fight and to stop the execution. He is too late.

The tale ends with the following narrative statement: "Scorned and abhorred by man, woman, and child, the half-breed, through whose malicious disposition the fatal termination took place . . . fled the settlement of Warren."

The narrator clearly places the blame for the ugly incident on Boddo, in other words, even though blame could be shared among several other characters. The townspeople are certainly to blame for longtime mistreatment of Boddo, and the authorities had no evidence of a murder, other than what Arrow-Tip himself had told them. And Father Luke could have been his own best messenger, had it not been for his fear of being discovered as the father of Boddo. And Brown himself could have made a better effort to get to town in time to save Arrow-Tip's life.

CHARACTERS

Arrow-Tip   Main character in the story. Arrow-Tip is an Indian, living a pleasant life in a village on the "upper reaches" of the Mississippi River. He is a personable member of the white community but gets into what starts out as a friendly fight with Peter Brown, the town's blacksmith. Arrow-Tip thinks he has killed Brown and reports the incident to the town authorities.

Even though Brown's body cannot be found at the site of the fight, the town accuses Arrow-Tip of murder and sentences him to hang. Brown, who knows he is as much to blame for the fight as Arrow-Tip, confesses to Father Luke, who immediately sends the hunchback and much abused Boddo into town to stop the hanging. Father Luke sends the wounded Brown as well, but neither messenger gets to town in time, and Arrow-Tip is hung.

Boddo   A hunchback and half-breed. He is bullied by the townspeople for his odd physical nature and mixed parenthood and decides to take a bit of revenge on the town by failing to carry Father Luke's message to the town authorities that Peter Brown is alive and just as much to blame for a fight with Arrow-Tip as is the Indian. Boddo's delay is cause for Arrow-Tip's execution.

Father Luke   After a fight between Arrow-Tip and Peter Brown, in which Arrow-Tip thinks he has killed Brown, the latter goes to the local priest, Father Luke, who has recently conducted the ceremony of marriage between Brown and a local girl. The priest gets the news that the authorities have accused Arrow-Tip of murder and have sentenced him to be hung. Father Luke sends Boddo into town with a message that would save Arrow-Tip's life. Boddo does not deliver the message.

There is an understated twist near the end of the story as readers discover that Father Luke is Boddo's biological father. Perhaps he has placed too much trust on his son to deliver the message.

Peter Brown   The town's blacksmith. He and Arrow-Tip have an altercation which turns into the apparent death of Brown. Brown's body is not found when Arrow-Tip takes the town authorities to the place of the fight, but the Indian is accused of the crime nevertheless and sentenced to hang. Brown is culpable in the execution of Arrow-Tip, as are Father Luke and the townspeople themselves.

"Hand-Mirror, A" (1860)

First published in the third edition of *Leaves of Grass* (1860); and it was the third of 29 poems in the "By The Roadside" cluster for the sixth edition (1881). It remained unchanged throughout its publication history.

The poet asks about the importance of people showing character. The "hand-mirror" shows only the outside, he says: "Hold it up sternly—see this it sends back, (who is it? is it you?) / Outside fair costume, within ashes and filth." Whitman then connects the "ashes and filth" with the various superficial characteristics we see in "some slaves's eye," or in a "drunkard's breath," or a "venerealee's flesh."

So he warns that looks can deceive and that there is a difference in the mirror's reflection between outside and inside, beyond as merely that between handsome and ugly or between youth and old age. "Such from one look in this looking-glass ere you go hence, / Such a result so soon—and from such a beginning!" Looks, in other words, can be deceiving.

"Hast Never Come to Thee an Hour" (1881)

First published as the 24th of 29 poems in the "By The Roadside" cluster for the sixth edition of *Leaves of Grass* (1881), one of three new poems.

The poet asks in this four-line poem whether it ever occurs to the reader, during an occasional hour's thinking, that things that happen to us— "these bubbles, fashions, wealth," even "books, politics, art, amours"—ever amount to more than "utter nothingness."

"Here the Frailest Leaves of Me" (1860)

Titled "Calamus No. 44" in the third edition of *Leaves of Grass* (1860); it received its present title (1867); it was the 25th of 39 poems in the "Calamus" cluster for the sixth edition (1881).

The importance of ambiguity in the "Calamus" poems is evident in this three-line poem. They are about the love of men for other men. Whitman is sexually ambiguous himself and aware that the ambiguity is in these poems and may cause readers difficulty in understanding them or him. And yet, he says in the last line, "they expose me more than all my other poems."

The "Calamus" poems certainly brought the poet out of the closet, which no doubt bothered readers in his time (and no doubt bothers readers still), but he also worried that he would be misunderstood (represented by the "frailest leaves"), that readers would not see the depth of these poems (the "strongest lasting" leaves). To miss the ambiguity, in other words, the images of HOMOSEXUALITY as representative of the brotherhood of men, for example, was to miss the meaning of the poem.

"[Hours Continuing Long, Sore And Heavy-Hearted]" (1860)

Cut from *Leaves of Grass* after first appearing as "Calamus, No. 9" in the third edition (1860). The brackets indicate the poem's first line.

As with the poem "[I Thought That Knowledge Alone Would Suffice]," this poem may have been dropped by Whitman because of the criticism he received from publication of the "Calamus" collection. He might also have cut the poems, however, because they reflect a dejection in the poet that does not show in the cluster's other poems.

"House of Friends, The" (1850)

First published in the NEW YORK TRIBUNE (June 14, 1850); an "early poem" *not* later published in *Leaves of Grass*. It is most accessible now in Francis Murphy (editor), *Walt Whitman: The Complete Poems* (Penguin Books, 1996).

"How Solemn as One by One" (1865)

First appeared in the *Sequel to Drum-Taps* volume (1865) and under this title throughout its publication history in *Leaves of Grass*; it was the 35th of 43 poems in the "Drum-Taps" cluster for the sixth edition (1881). The poem's parenthetical subtitle, "(*Washington City, 1865*)," was added for the 1871 edition.

In contrast with the earliest poems in the "Drum-Taps" group, which celebrated the marching off to the CIVIL WAR of Northern soldiers, this poem honors the "solemn" returning of the survivors.

The poet watches "the men file by" and sees "behind each mask . . . a kindred soul, / O the bullet could never kill what you really are, dear friend, / Nor the bayonet stab what you really are." Whitman believed that bullets and bayonets were not enough to kill the soul of these men.

"Hush'd Be the Camps To-Day" (1865)

First appeared in the *Drum-Taps* volume (1865); then with three other LINCOLN poems under the general heading "President Lincoln's Burial Hymn" for the fifth edition of *Leaves of Grass* (1871); finally, it was the third of four poems under the new heading "Memories of President Lincoln" for the sixth edition (1881). Whitman was under the impression that Lincoln was to be buried in Washington on April 19, so the subheading note for the *Drum-Taps* version read "(A. L. Buried April 19, 1865)." The note was revised for the 1871 and later printings to read "(May 4, 1865)," the date of the president's burial in Springfield, Illinois. Like "O Captain! My Captain!," this poem was an "occasional" poem, written sometime between April 15, the day Lincoln died, and April 19, the day Whitman thought the president was to be buried.

The CIVIL WAR ended with the surrender of Lee to Grant on April 9, 1865, and of Johnston to Sherman on April 26, so the "Hush'd Camps" in this poem refer to the camps of soldiers after the war is over. Whitman asks the soldiers to "drape" with him "our war-worn weapons, / And each with musing soul retire to celebrate, / Our dear commander's death." The poet did not include Southern soldiers in this poem as he did in most other Civil War poems, because Lincoln's determination to free slaves did not make him a popular figure in the South.

"I Am He that Aches with Love" (1860)

First appeared untitled as the 14th poem in the "Enfans d'Adam" cluster in the third edition of *Leaves of Grass* (1860); it received its present title and became the 11th of 16 poems in the "Children of Adam" cluster for the fourth edition (1867) and for all subsequent printings.

This three-line poem connects—as do all of the "Children of Adam" poems—man with his sexual nature: ". . . . does not all matter, aching, attract all matter? / So the body of me to all I meet or know." See also "I Sing the Body Electric."

"I Dream'd in a Dream" (1860)

Titled "Calamus No. 34" in the third edition of *Leaves of Grass* (1860); it received its present title (1867) and remained unrevised during the rest of its publication history; it was the 30th of 39 poems in the "Calamus" cluster for the sixth edition (1881).

The poet's dream is of "a city invincible to the attacks of the whole of the rest of the earth," a city of friends of "robust love," a reference to homosexual love. If a city were composed of friends like this, "robust" love would prevail, and the city could

withstand the criticism from any other city. In several of the Calamus poems Whitman offers subtle attempts to calm the fears of those who do not understand homosexual love.

"I Hear America Singing" (1860)

First appeared as "Chants Democratic No. 20" in the third edition of *Leaves of Grass* (1860); it received its present title for the fourth edition (1867); it was the 18th of 24 poems in the "Inscriptions" cluster for the sixth edition (1881).

One of the most popular of Whitman's poems—often sung by choruses—"I Hear America Singing" presents the poet's vision of the democratic ideal, with each citizen contributing to the welfare of America. No matter the occupation, each person contributes to the nation's "varied carols," showing the joy with which individuals create what Whitman envisions as the perfect nation.

The poet creates in 11 lines one of his most powerful and beautiful images of the America he envisions and wishes to pass on to other Americans—that is, to readers in his time and ours. The "singers" he describes are mechanics, carpenters, masons, boatmen, deckhands, shoemakers, hatters, woodcutters, ploughboys, mothers, young wives, and a girl sewing or washing:

> I hear America singing, the varied carols I hear,
> Those of mechanics, each one singing his as it
>   should be blithe and strong,
> The carpenter singing his . . .

Ending with the following image:

> Each singing what belongs to him or her and to
>   none else,
> The day what belongs to the day—at night the
>   party of young fellows, robust, friendly,
> Singing with open mouths their strong
>   melodious songs.

Though each song "belongs to him or her and to none else," Whitman hears all of the songs—and others he doesn't identify in the poem—and passes them on to his readers. It is not just the idea itself, however, that makes the poem so popular. It is also the rhythm of the lines, the music. All good poems should be read aloud for their musical sounds, but some poems demand to be sung.

The theme of the democratic ideal is introduced in "I Hear America Singing" and runs through many other poems that follow this one in *Leaves of Grass*.

The Library of Congress's Bicentennial, a three-year series of concerts beginning in the period 1999–2000 and celebrating its collection of American music, was named "I Hear America Singing."

"I Heard You Solemn-Sweet Pipes of the Organ" (1861)

First published in the *NEW YORK LEADER* (October 12, 1861), titled "Little Bells Last Night"; it then appeared in the fourth edition of *Leaves of Grass* (1867); it was the 14th of 16 poems in the "Children of Adam" cluster for the sixth edition (1881).

The poet here feels the merger of music with his sensual nature. He hears the "solemn-sweet pipes of the organ" as he passes a church; he hears "the perfect Italian tenor singing at the opera" and the "soprano in the midst of a quartet singing."

And he thinks of his lover—a woman probably, since this is a "Children of Adam" poem: "Heart of my love! you too I heard murmuring low through one of the wrists around my head, / Heard the pulse of you when all was still ringing little bells last night under my ear." See also "Once I Pass'd Through a Populous City."

"I Hear It was Charged against Me" (1860)

Titled "Calamus No. 24" in the third edition of *Leaves of Grass* (1860); it received its title for the

fourth edition (1867), and Whitman made no changes thereafter; it was the 20th of 39 poems in the "Calamus" cluster for the sixth edition (1881).

This is the poet's response to criticism that he was against the "institutions," perhaps particularly the institution of love. Few critics found favor with Whitman's poems about the love of men for other men—the Calamus poems. But the poet argues that he is "neither for nor against institutions." What he is *for* is "the institution of the dear love of comrades." He favors the brotherhood of men, believing it to be one of the keys to the fulfillment of his vision for democracy.

"In Cabin'd Ships at Sea" (1871)

First appeared in the fifth edition of *Leaves of Grass* (1871); it was the third of 24 poems in the "Inscriptions" cluster for the sixth edition (1881). The Inscription poems were at the beginning of *Leaves*.

This is the first of several poems in which Whitman uses the sea as a metaphor for life experiences. He feels the movement of the sea in his own poetry. He feels its undulation, its "long pulsation, ebb and flow of endless motion." And this is Whitman's wish as he begins his book of poems:

> Speed on my book! spread your white sails my
>   little bark athwart the imperious waves,
> Chant on, sail on, bear o'er the boundless blue
>   from me to every sea,
> This song for mariners and all their ships.

The irregular beat of waves against a sandy shore reminds him of the irregular beat of his own FREE VERSE poetic style, a merger of form and meaning he would like to continue. See, for two of the best examples of this merger, "Out of the Cradle Endlessly Rocking" and "As I Ebb'd with the Ocean of Life."

"Inca's Daughter, The" (1840)

First published in the LONG ISLAND DEMOCRAT (May 5, 1840); an "early poem" *not* later published in *Leaves of Grass*. It is most accessible now in Francis Murphy (editor), *Walt Whitman: The Complete Poems* (Penguin Books, 1996).

"In Former Songs" (1876)

Cut from *Leaves of Grass* after appearing in the sixth edition (1876).

"In Paths Untrodden" (1860)

The first "Calamus" poem in the third edition of *Leaves of Grass* (1860); it took its present title in the fourth edition (1867); it was the first of 39 poems in the final ordering of the Calamus cluster for the sixth edition (1881).

In this poem, the poet "celebrate[s] the need for comrades":

> Afternoon this delicious Ninth-month in my
> forty-first year,
> I proceed for all who are or have been young
> men,
> To tell the secret of my nights and days,
> To celebrate the need of comrades.

The poem is both a description of the Calamus plant, found "in paths untrodden, . . . by margins of pond-waters, . . . aromatic" and a celebration of a man's "need for comrades."

The "secret" thoughts or actions which he wishes to "tell" are the "paths untrodden" in the love relationship of men for one another. In the tradition of mysticism, the mystic always meditates in some quiet place and then makes his thoughts public—through preaching or publication. The poet relates to the calamus plant, which too is "secluded" and which has "escaped from the life that exhibits itself."

The poem was written in September 1859, which was for Whitman the "Ninth-month in my forty-first year."

"Inscriptions" (1871)

Cluster title for the nine opening poems in the fifth edition of *Leaves of Grass* (1871); increased to 24 poems for the sixth edition (1881).

The word *inscriptions* is used here as a sort of Whitman signature to the world—an offering of ideas and images that evoke an intimacy between the poet and reader, an invitation to join in an adventure to discover and experience possible aspects of the human condition, some of the experiences to be mystical. The poems in "Inscriptions" are an introduction to this world.

The poems appear in the following order in the "Death-bed" printing: "One's Self I Sing," "As I Pondered in Silence," "In Cabin'd Ships at Sea," "To Foreign Lands," "To a Historian," "To Thee Old Cause," "Eidólons," "For Him I Sing," "When I Read the Book," "Beginning My Studies," "Beginners," "To the States," "On Journeys Through the States," "To a Certain Cantatrice," "Me Imperturbe," "Savantism," "The Ship Starting," "I Hear America Singing," "What Place is Besieged?" "Still Though the One I Sing," "Shut not Your Doors," "Poets to Come," "To You," and "Thou Reader."

"Interpolation Sounds" (1888)

First published in the NEW YORK HERALD (August 12, 1888); it was the 14th of 31 poems in *Good-Bye My Fancy* (1891); then in "Second Annex: Good-Bye My Fancy" for the "Death-bed" printing of *Leaves of Grass* (1892).

The poem is in honor of General Philip SHERIDAN who died August 5, 1888. An epigraph to the poem explains that Sheridan had died and had been buried at the Washington, D.C., cathedral in early August. The eight-line poem is a "burial chant" and "solemn service" causing Whitman to relive ("interpolate") CIVIL WAR battle noises: the cracks of rifles, "the cannon thud," the "clank of cavalry," and so on, all of the sounds that Whitman recalled from the war while he sat through the services at the National Cathedral.

In a letter to the *New York Herald,* which accompanied the poem, Whitman added to the poetic tribute by saying that Sherman would go down in history as one of the "bright" lights of the Civil War.

"[In the New Garden]"
(1860)

Cut from *Leaves of Grass* after first appearing as "Enfans d'Adam, No. 11" in the third edition (1860). The brackets indicate the poem's first line.

"I Saw in Louisiana a Live-Oak Growing" (1860)

Titled "Calamus No. 20" in the third edition of *Leaves of Grass* (1860); it received its title for the fourth edition (1867); and it was the 17th of 39 poems in the "Calamus" cluster for the sixth edition (1881).

The "live-oak" is symbolic, Whitman believes, of the poet himself, a solitary singer. The tree has "joyous leaves of dark green," and its rude look, "unbending, lusty, made me think of myself."

The poet wonders, however, about the tree's need for friends, "how it could utter joyous leaves standing alone there without its friend near, for I knew I could not." Whitman mentions the joyous leaves three times in this 13-line poem, placing an emphasis on the relationship he feels with the live-oak.

The poet identifies here as elsewhere in *Leaves of Grass* with solitary objects in Nature. For perhaps

the best example of this identification with Nature, see "When Lilacs Last in the Dooryard Bloom'd."

"I Saw Old General at Bay"
(1865)

First appeared in the *Drum-Taps* volume (1865) and remained unchanged throughout its printing history; it was the 26th of 43 poems in the "Drum-Taps" cluster for the sixth edition of *Leaves of Grass* (1881).

The omniscient speaker of this seven-line poem watches as a General, "hemm'd in" with his "small force" of men, asks for "volunteers to run the enemy's lines," and, of a "hundred and more" who stepped forward, "two or three were selected" and given orders. In the last line, the poet tells us: "I saw them depart with cheerfulness, freely risking their lives." There is irony here in the friction apparent in the peaceful nature of the scene and the reality of two soldiers going off to their likely deaths.

There are other poems in the "Drum-Taps" cluster that present similar, seemingly peaceful yet potentially horrifying descriptions of men at war. See "Cavalry Crossing a Ford," "Bivouac on a Mountain Side," "By the Bivouac's Fitful Flame," "A Sight in Camp in the Daybreak Gray and Dim," "As Toilsome I Wander'd Virginia's Woods," and "Look Down Fair Moon."

"I Sing the Body Electric"
(1855)

The fifth of 12 untitled poems in the first edition of *Leaves of Grass* (1855); titled "Poem of the Body" for the second edition (1856); then it was the third poem in the "Enfans d'Adam" cluster (1860); it received its present title and was the third of 16 poems in the "Children of Adam" cluster for the sixth edition (1881). The final version is in nine sections and 164 lines, the longest of the Children of Adam poems.

The "body electric" in physical love is generated by the electricity of the soul, according to the poet, and is related to a mystical journey. The opening lines provide the poem's theme and tone.

> I sing the body electric,
> The armies of those I love engirth me and I
>   engirth them,
> They will not let me off till I go with them,
>   respond to them,
> And discorrupt them, and charge them full
>   with the charge of the soul.

Physical love is as innocent ("discorrupt") now, Whitman suggests, as it was with Adam and Eve, and our bodies are "perfect": "The love of the body of man or woman balks account, the body itself balks account, / That of the male is perfect, and that of the female is perfect." And this unaccountable electricity creates the mystical union.

In Section 3, Whitman describes a "common farmer," who may stand for the ideal man, charged "with the charge of the soul." He is "the father of five sons, / And in them the fathers of sons, and in them the fathers of sons." Everything about the farmer is good and "wise." And all his children, grandchildren, and great grandchildren loved him and all who met him. In the last line of the section the poet writes: "You would wish long and long to be with him, you would wish to sit by him in the boat that you and he might touch each other." He represents the ultimate result of the love which Whitman is defining in this poem and in others of the "Children of Adam" cluster.

Love "is enough," he states in Section 4: "To pass among them [those he 'likes'] or touch any one, or rest my arm ever so lightly round his or her neck for a moment, what is this then? / I do not ask any more delight, I swim in it as in a sea."

The next two sections present the ideal woman-child of Adam and the ideal man-child. The "nucleus" of love is this, Whitman says: "after the child is born of woman, man is born of woman." The male is born of woman and, as a man, comes back to her for her love and for procreation. Women "are the gates of the body," the poet says in the next line, "and [women] are the gates of the soul."

And "the male is not less the soul nor more, he too is in his place, / He too is all qualities, he is action and power." The bodies of men and women are "sacred," even that of "the meanest one in the laborers' gang" or those bodies of the "dull-faced immigrants just landed on the wharf." Each person "has his or her place in the procession." And the poet asks at the end of the section, "Do you think . . . water runs and vegetation sprouts, / For you only, and not for him and her?" We are all sacred in this mystical "procession."

Sections 7 and 8 observe society's corruption of the body when it is sold at auction, when black men and women are sold at auction. Whitman describes the sale of a black slave:

> Within there runs blood,
> The same old blood! the same red-running
>   blood! . . .
> How do you know who shall come from the
>   offspring of his offspring through the
>   centuries?
> Who might you find you have come from
>   yourself, if you could trace back through the
>   centuries? . . .
> If any thing is sacred the human body is sacred.

Bodies are sacred because, as Whitman suggested in "Song of Myself" and repeated here in the final lines of "I Sing the Body Electric," the body and soul are joined together as one. He writes in the final two lines: "O I say these are not the parts and poems of the body only, but of the soul, / O I say now these are the soul."

The poem describes the physical as the origin of the spiritual in human beings, and corruption of the body is corruption of the soul. But if there is sin, Whitman says, it is not from the physical love of a man for a woman but from the separation of human beings according to gender or skin color or occupation.

"I Sit and Look Out" (1860)

First published as "Leaves of Grass, No. 17" for the third edition of *Leaves of Grass* (1860); it was "Leaves of Grass, No. 5" in the fourth edition

(1867); it received its present title (1871); and it was the 11th of 29 poems in the "By The Roadside" cluster for the sixth edition (1881).

"I sit and look out upon all the sorrows of the world, and upon all oppression and shame, . . ." He presents a catalog of evils that he hears about or sees, and in the end, he says, "All these—all the meanness and agony without end I sitting look out upon, / See, hear, and am silent."

This is one of a few poems in which Whitman suggests silence as an answer to what he sees as America's problems, one of the few poems in which he seems so depressed. The poet may be accused of contradiction in this idea, since he makes it clear throughout *Leaves of Grass* that democracy is made up of both good and evil and that both are equally important to the survival of his own principles of democracy. The poem was written, however, as it was becoming clear that a war between North and South was imminent.

"Italian Music in Dakota" (1881)

First appeared as the 35th of 38 poems in the "Autumn Rivulets" cluster for the sixth edition (1881).

The subtitle for this poem is "(*The Seventeenth— the finest Regimental Band I ever heard*)." Whitman may have heard this regimental band, but he did not visit the Dakotas during his western trip in 1879.

Scenes from three OPERAS are briefly mentioned, although it isn't clear whether the poet saw performers singing or only the band playing the music. The scenes are from Vincenzo BELLINI's *La Sonnambula*, from Bellini's *Norma*, and from Gaetano DONIZETTI's *Poliuto*. What is important in the poem, however, is Whitman's awareness of the "rapport however far remov'd" between Nature (of the Dakotas or of the Western States that he was visiting) and beautiful music. He says in the last line that Nature "Listens well pleas'd."

"I Was Looking a Long While" (1860)

First appeared as "Chants Democratic, No. 19" in the third edition of *Leaves of Grass* (1860); then under its present title in the fourth edition (1867); and as the 19th of 38 poems in the "Autumn Rivulets" cluster for the sixth edition (1881).

The opening line of this 10-line poem reads, "I was looking a long while for Intentions." Whitman suggests that the "clew to the history of the past" may be found not in "libraries" or "legends" but "in this earth to-day, / It is in Democracy—(the purport and aim of all the past)." Everything that has happened in the past was intended "All for the modern—all for the average man of to-day." Everything was *intended* to make the nation the democracy he, Walt Whitman, envisions.

"Joy, Shipmate, Joy!" (1871)

First appeared in the fifth edition of *Leaves of Grass* (1871); and it was the 12th of 17 poems in the "Songs of Parting" cluster for the sixth edition (1881).

Using the ship as a metaphor for life, Whitman in these seven lines brings his own ship to shore. The ACCENTUAL VERSE form is almost perfect, the lines having the following number of accented syllables: 2-4-4-4-3-3.

"Kiss to the Bride, A" (1874)

First published in the NEW YORK DAILY GRAPHIC (May 21, 1874); it was the sixth of 13 poems in the "Old Age Echoes" cluster for the first posthumous printing of *Leaves of Grass* (1897), added by one of Whitman's executors, Horace TRAUBEL.

Subtitled "*Marriage of Nelly Grant, May 21, 1874*," this poem is in honor of the marriage of President Grant's daughter to a Mr. Sartoris, and was published on the day of the marriage. The "kiss to the bride" is from America: "Yield thy red cheeks, thy lips, to-day, / Unto a Nation's loving kiss."

"Kosmos" (1860)

First appeared in the third edition of *Leaves of Grass* (1860); and it was the 26th of 38 poems in the "Autumn Rivulets" cluster for the sixth edition (1881).

"Kosmos" in this poem means being in harmony with Nature. Whitman had used the term in "Song of Myself," declaring himself a "kosmos, . . . / Turbulent, fleshy, sensual, eating, drinking and breeding." Human beings are, he declares in "Kosmos," part of the kosmos. They are "the amplitude of the earth, and the coarseness and sexuality of the earth," all things that are natural.

The poet sums up this idea in the final two lines: "Who, constructing the house of himself or herself, not for a day but for all time, sees races, eras, dates, generations, / The past, the future, dwelling there, like space, inseparable together." Everything that people do is in harmony with the natural order.

"Last Invocation, The" (1868)

First published as the fourth of five poems under the general title "Whispers of Heavenly Death" in the (London) BROADWAY MAGAZINE (October 1868); then with the "Whispers of Heavenly Death" cluster in the "Passage to India" supplement to *Leaves of Grass* (1871); and it was the 16th of 18 poems in the Whispers cluster for the sixth edition of *Leaves* (1881).

The "last invocation" is provided by the poet for the dead within the "walls of the powerful fortress'd house"—the vaults where the dead are buried. It isn't clear whether the poet would call on God or the Muse to help him write more poems for the dead, more "whispers of heavenly death."

In a note to this poem in the Norton Critical Edition of *Leaves of Grass*, Bradley and Blodgett write: "Of superb lyrical skill, it has often been set to music by modern composers—among them, Frank Bridge (1919), Percival Garratt (1920) and James H. Rogers (1919). In the words of John Livingston Lowes (*Convention and Revolt in Poetry*, 1919), the reader who will 'let the words beat their own time' may find the clue to WW's practice of constructing stanzas on the basis of repetitive accentual patterns of rhythm."

See also ACCENTUAL VERSE.

"Last Loyalist, The" (1842)

Short story, first published under the title "The Child-Ghost: A Story of the Last Loyalist" in the *United States Magazine and Democratic Review* (May 1842; see DEMOCRATIC REVIEW, THE). "The Last Loyalist" is most accessible now in *Walt Whitman: The Early Poems and the Fiction*, edited by Thomas L. Brasher (New York University Press, 1963).

The story takes place during the time of the AMERICAN REVOLUTION. Just before the war, a man named Vanhome, the story's main character, inherited from a brother a "country-residence" just east of New York City. Vanhome had been a loyal supporter of the British king. He had fought on the side of the British, because he thought, ironically as it turned out, that the British would take his home away if he didn't support their cause.

He had also been given responsibility for his brother's child, a 10-year-old boy. He is a "stern" taskmaster for the child, and the boy dies after two years with the uncle, the death resulting from unspecified causes but causes the neighbors believe might have been the result of the uncle's mistreatment.

Because of his loyalty to the British, Vanhome had become known by neighbors to have engaged "in the cruelist outrages, the boldest inroads, or the most determin'd attacks upon the army of his countrymen or their peaceful settlements." He had done everything he could to disrupt his American neighbors in their efforts to rid themselves of British tyranny.

Shortly after the war he returned as a "stranger" to the old farmstead, now tenanted by an old couple, the Gills. Vanhome decides to spend the night at his old homestead but is awakened by the ghost of his nephew, whom he had mistreated. The ghost frightens Vanhome to such an extent that he rushes off to New York and barely manages to catch the last of the British boats leaving the harbor for England, taking on board the last survivors of a lost war. The story's last line informs us that "the Last Soldier of King George had left the American shores."

CHARACTER

Vanhome   The main character in "The Last Loyalist." He remained loyal to the British crown during the American turmoil before and during its Revolutionary War. He had inherited from a brother both his home and his 10-year-old boy. He is harsh with the boy, hoping to bring him up as he thought his brother would, but the boy dies of what the neighbors think is abuse by Vanhome. After the war he returns to the homestead, now owned by a couple named Gills, stays the night, and is tormented by the ghost of his nephew. He leaves immediately for New York and manages to catch the last boat leaving for England.

"Last of Ebb, and Daylight Waning" (1885)

First published with seven other poems under the heading "Fancies at Navesink" in NINETEENTH CENTURY magazine (August 1885); then in *November Boughs* (1888); and, finally, with the "Fancies at Navesink" group as an insert in the "First Annex: Sands at Seventy" cluster for the "Death-bed" printing of *Leaves of Grass* (1892). Whitman uses the ebb tide at the end of day as a metaphor for the last sighs of the dying, "love's unresponse . . . hope's last words, / Some suicide's despairing cry. . . ." There are many "half-caught" voices "sent up from the eddies," all desperate to be heard, perhaps the voice of artists most of all. At the end, the poet accepts the inevitability of Nature:

On to oblivion then!
On, on, and do your part, ye burying, ebbing
   tide!
On for your time, ye furious debouché!

There is some scholarly debate over the meaning of *debouché*. It probably refers to a place where a narrow opening becomes wider, suggesting in this poem the great expanse of "oblivion."

"Last of the Sacred Army, The" (1842)

Short story, first published in the *United States Magazine and Democratic Review* (March 1842; see DEMOCRATIC REVIEW, THE). The tale is most accessible now in *Walt Whitman: The Early Poems and the Fiction*, edited by Thomas L. Brasher (New York University Press, 1963). The story was reprinted as the dream scene in chapter 20 of Whitman's novel, *Franklin Evans*, published in November 1842.

Nearly half of this moralistic story is an essay on the importance of our "memory of the Warriors of our Freedom!—let us guard it with a holy care." On a July 4th of an unidentified year, the narrator is staying at a farmhouse near a "thriving country town." He has lost some sleep because the townspeople began shooting off their muskets early in the morning in celebration of the holiday. During the "warm and drowsy afternoon," while watching at the window some of the celebration, he falls asleep and dreams.

He dreams that he was at a festival celebrating "the Last of the Sacred Army," that is, the last of the soldiers who fought for American independence. There was one soldier in particular, an old man, who was being honored, even worshipped, by the younger men and women present at the celebration; he had a medal that had been given to him by the "Chief" of all those soldiers who had fought "for liberty." The medal had on it the initials "G. W."

The narrator is told by a "philosopher" in the crowd that it is good for people to see such veneration as the old man received. No nation can become enslaved by another, the narrator is told, as long as people are occasionally reminded of the efforts of past generations to insure the nation's freedom and independence.

"Laws for Creations" (1860)

First appeared as "Chants Democratic, No. 13" in the third edition of *Leaves of Grass* (1860); seven of its 18 lines were cut for the fourth edition (1867); the remaining 11 lines, under the same title, then became the 17th of 38 poems in the "Autumn Rivulets" cluster for the sixth edition (1881).

The "laws for creations," for creative people— "strong artists and leaders, for fresh broods of teachers and perfect literats for America"—require the freedom to seek "the compact truth of the world." The poet asks, "What do you suppose creation is?" and answers by asking more questions out of his PANTHEISM: ". . . that man or woman is as good as God."

> And that there is no God any more divine than
> Yourself?
> And that that is what the oldest and newest
> myths finally mean?
> And that you or any one must approach
> creations through such laws?

For Whitman the spirit of God is in all people and things; and, therefore, all people and things are a manifestation of God. To be creative requires the freedom to believe in such "laws."

"Leaf for Hand in Hand, A" (1860)

Titled "Calamus No. 37" in the third edition of *Leaves of Grass* (1860), it received its present title (1867); and it was the 28th of 39 poems in the "Calamus" cluster for the sixth edition (1881).

The poet presents here a "leaf" (a poem) as a gift to "natural persons old and young," to encourage the holding of hands. He also encourages men

everywhere to hold hands—along "the Mississippi and on all the branches and bayous of the Mississippi, . . . you roughs." The word *roughs* is one of Whitman's code words for "homosexual."

Don't be ashamed to show your love, he is saying: "I wish to infuse myself among you till I see it common for you to walk hand in hand." See also "A Glimpse," the poem immediately preceding this poem in the "Calamus" cluster.

"Leaflets" (1860)

This two-line poem first appeared in the third edition of *Leaves of Grass* (1860) as two lines in a poem titled "Debris." It was cut from *Leaves* after appearing separately in the fourth edition (1867).

Leaves of Grass

Whitman's major work of poetry; first published with an untitled "preface" and 12 untitled poems (1855); the second edition (1856); third edition (1860); fourth edition (1867); fifth edition, including the "Passage to India" supplement (1871); a third printing in two volumes of the fifth edition (unchanged from 1871), with *Two Rivulets* as volume 2 (1876); the sixth and final edition (1881); and a printing, often referred to as the "Death-bed Edition" (1891 and 1892) that included two annexes, "Sands at Seventy" and "Good-Bye My Fancy." There was also a printing in 1897, published after the poet's death by Horace TRAUBEL, one of Whitman's friends and biographers, who added, at Whitman's request, "Old Age Echoes," a cluster of 13 new poems. (For information on the difference between "editions" and "printings," see "*Leaves of Grass* editions," the next entry following. And for information on each separate edition, see entries immediately following "*Leaves of Grass* editions"—for example, "*Leaves of Grass*, First Edition [1855].")

The *BOSTON DAILY GLOBE* ran an item (August 24, 1881), about Whitman's visit to Boston, in which Whitman answered a question about the history of *Leaves of Grass*.

It is now, I believe twenty-six years since I began to work upon the structure; and this edition [sixth and final edition] will complete the design which I had in my mind when I began to write. The whole affair is like one of those old architectural edifices, some of which were hundreds of years building, and the designer of which has the whole idea in his mind from the first. His plans are pretty ambitious, and, as means or time permits, he adds part after part, perhaps at quite wide intervals. To a casual observer it looks in the course of its construction odd enough. Only after the whole is completed, one catches the idea which inspired the designer, in whose mind the relation of each part to the whole had existed all along. That is the way it has been with my book. It has been twenty-six years building. There have been seven different hitches at it. Seven different times have part of the edifice been constructed,—sometimes in BROOKLYN, sometimes in Washington, sometimes in Boston, and at other places. The book has been built partially in every part of the United States; and this edition is the completed edifice.

DEMOCRACY AND *LEAVES OF GRASS*

Whitman's final version of *Leaves of Grass*, with 389 poems, proclaims the beauty and value of democracy as has no other writer in poetry or prose. Not even Alexis de Tocqueville, the great French politician who wrote the four-volume *Democracy in America* (1835–40), which justified democracy to the rest of the world and predicted its survival and success, defined America's purposes and direction as well as Whitman. Three items provide the best access to Whitman's vision for America: the preface to the first edition of *Leaves of Grass* (see "Preface" [*Leaves of Grass*, 1855]); his longest poem, "Song of Myself"; and *Democratic Vistas*, an 84-page pamphlet published separately in 1871.

Democracy is an almost constant theme in *Leaves of Grass*, permeating several other thematic ideas, including the following: 1, the soul's relation-

ship with the "Self"; 2, the importance of respect for Nature; 3, the equality of all people as essential for a stable society; 4, the mystical path to transcendental experience; 5, the need for poets to enlighten the people; and 6, the idea that Whitman himself might be that poet. The clusters of poems in *Leaves of Grass* as well as individual poems reflect in various ways one or more of these themes.

Readers, however, have sometimes so confused Whitman's seeming egotism in referring to himself in his poetry that they have failed to grasp his vision for the nation. The opening poem in *Leaves of Grass* is titled "One's-Self I Sing." The opening lines define the poet's "Self" as a speaker for America.

One's-Self I sing, a simple separate person,
Yet utter the word Democratic, the word
    En-Masse.

A few lines later he says, "The female equally with the Male I sing." Whitman rarely uses the word "man" or any of its derivations without also using "woman" or its derivations: "And I say to any man or woman, / Let your soul stand cool and composed before a million universes."

It is not that Whitman foresees the gender equality of the late 20th and early 21st centuries, because, for Whitman, the word democracy *requires* equality—not just of men and women but of all Americans. In his personal life Whitman was torn between his wish to abolish SLAVERY and his greater wish to preserve the Union. This "contrariety" appears in the poems, and he answers this criticism of himself by saying near the end of "Song of Myself,"

Do I contradict myself?
Very well then I contradict myself,
(I am large, I contain multitudes.)

And so do we all, according to the poet.

In "I Hear America Singing," he CATALOGs the variety of people and their vocations that make up the nation's great diversity and that, therefore, helps define "these United States." He includes mechanics, carpenters, masons, boatmans, shoemakers, woodcutters, and ploughboys, as well as "the delicious singing of the mother, or of the young wife at work, or of the girl sewing or washing." He says that they are "Each singing what belongs to him or her and to none else." Throughout *Leaves of Grass* the poem *is* the song. If Whitman seems to be bragging in the above lines, it is not for himself that he does so but for humankind. This is his vision for democracy; anything he is capable of doing, others can do as well.

The first three lines of "Song of Myself," the first major poem in *Leaves of Grass* and the longest, is intended to remind us that every American can and should celebrate his or her Self, for in celebrating one's own Self, we celebrate, Whitman suggests, "the word Democratic, the word En-masse."

> I celebrate myself, and sing myself,
> And what I assume you shall assume,
> For every atom belonging to me as good
>   belongs to you.

Democracy is nothing more nor less, Whitman says here, than the people who, while individual Selves, are also a part of the whole, the "en masse." Democracy is always inclusive, he suggests, never exclusive. No one who wants to be a part of the whole is left out. He says in *Democratic Vistas* that an understanding of "individualism" is impossible without an understanding of the concept of the social whole. The two concepts are "contradictory," he says, "but our task is to reconcile them." Democracy would not work, he felt, unless individuals could learn to celebrate themselves while celebrating their role in the social fabric. And this reconciling of two seemingly contradictory concepts is what he attempts to do in *Leaves of Grass*.

In Section 15 of "Song of Myself," the poet catalogs for almost 100 lines Americans at their various lives: the ship pilot, his mate, the duck-shooter, the ordained deacon, the spinning girl, the farmer, the lunatic, the quadroon girl, the drover, the peddler, the opium-eater, the prostitute, the President, and so on and so forth. And at the end of the section, he offers the following summation:

> And these tend inward to me, and I tend
>   outward to them,
> And such as it is to be of these more or less I am,
> And of these one and all I weave the song of
>   myself.

It would be difficult to find a clearer definition of democracy than Whitman's in "Song of Myself." But see also, among the poems, "By Blue Ontario's Shore," or, as is suggested above, the whole of *Leaves of Grass*.

It is no wonder that people around the world have been impressed by Whitman's book. He speaks to the urge of individuals everywhere for the freedom that democracy offers. In the preface to the first edition of *Leaves of Grass* (1855), he writes: "The United States themselves are essentially the greatest poem. . . . Here is not merely a nation but a teeming nation of nations. . . . The attitude of great poets is to cheer up slaves and horrify despots. . . . Liberty relies upon itself, invites no one, promises nothing, sits in calmness and light, is positive and composed, and knows no discouragement."

All of this, Whitman says, he tried to present in the poems of *Leaves of Grass*.

Leaves of Grass "editions"

Whitman and many of his biographers have used the term "edition" to describe any new volume or set of volumes printed that included his *Leaves of Grass* poems. He counted nine editions altogether—the "ninth" published in the period 1891–92—and that number was generally accepted through much of the 20th century. But modern bibliographical standards suggest there were only six editions, an edition defined as any number of copies of a book printed from a single setting-up of type.

There is no dispute with Whitman over the first five editions of *Leaves of Grass*: 1855, 1856, 1860, 1867, and 1871. Each of these volumes contained new poems, revisions of poems previously published, and new organizational patterns; so each of these editions involved the setting of new type.

The two-volume set published in 1876, however—sometimes referred to as "Author's Edition" or "Centennial Edition"—which Whitman called the "sixth edition," is not in modern terms an edition but a new "printing" of the 1871 edition, actually the third printing. Volume 1 is titled *Leaves of Grass* and was printed from the same plates used in the 1871 book. Volume 2 was titled *Two Rivulets* and contains several new poems that were later incorporated into the sixth edition.

The sixth edition was published in 1881 and is the last of the legitimate editions. The poems received their final arrangement. The remainder of the volumes published after 1881 were printed from the 1881 plates and so are "printings" and not editions, including the volume often referred to as the "Death-bed Edition," published in the period 1891–92.

Current bibliographical terms are used throughout this *Critical Companion* but without an attempt to identify the various printings other than by date of publication. For further details on the more than 50 printings of *Leaves of Grass,* see Joel Myerson's *Walt Whitman: A Descriptive Bibliography* (University of Pittsburgh Press, 1993).

Leaves of Grass, First Edition (1855)

One of the most famous first editions in American literary history was published in BROOKLYN, paid for by Whitman himself, and printed by James and Thomas ROME at their job printing shop on the southwest corner of Fulton and Cranberry Streets in Brooklyn. According to the bookbinder's statement, there were 795 copies printed in at least three different bindings. The book had a large format, not quite 8 by 11 inches.

Whitman's name appears only on the copyright page and in the untitled first poem, which would later be titled "Song of Myself." The famous Samuel Hollyer engraving of the author, unidentified, appears opposite the title page (see page 3). Whitman registered the copyright on May 15, 1855.

Although there are several printings of facsimile copies of the first edition, the first edition itself is one of the rarest of American collector's items. It is clear that none of the participants in the printing, including Whitman, had much thought for the future of the book. Type was handset by the Rome

brothers, with Whitman's help, and, after the book was printed, the type was dumped. Even the original handwritten manuscript gathered dust in the Rome Brothers office for two or three years and was then—apparently accidentally—burned.

There was so much controversy about the poems that some New Yorkers threatened to sue Whitman for publishing an obscene book. It is not clear what stopped them, although it was no doubt in part because Whitman was popular on the streets of the city. And whatever the threat actually was, it ended entirely upon publication of Ralph Waldo EMERSON's letter, first in the NEW YORK TRIBUNE (October 10, 1855), and then in the second edition of *Leaves of Grass* the next year.

The early reviewers were somewhat mystified by the poems, as were most other readers. One reviewer wrote about the "indecent language" that came "from a naïve unconsciousness rather than from an impure mind." Another wrote about the "curious collection of poems" written "in a sort of excited prose." He said the author strayed from polite standards. Another reviewer wrote about the longest poem (which would be later titled "Song of Myself") but said that some grossness bars the poem from reading in mixed company.

Whitman wrote some of his own reviews, stating in one, "An American bard at last!" In another he wrote that the poet would appear "very devilish to some" but "very divine" to others, in his rude and vital American qualities.

In discussing the poor reviews Whitman received for the poems, Richard Maurice BUCKE states in his 1883 biography that the "first reception . . . was in fact about as disheartening as it could be. Of the thousand copies of this 1855 edition [there were actually 795 copies], some were given away, most of them were lost, abandoned, or destroyed." Bucke also wrote that "the book quite universally, wherever it was read, excited ridicule, disgust, horror, and anger. It was considered meaningless, badly written, filthy, atheistical, and utterly reprehensible." But then there was Emerson's response, and Bucke reprinted the favorable letter, stating that the editor of the *Tribune,* Charles A. Dana, asked to publish the letter, "at first refused by Walt Whitman, but on a second and pressing application he consented." Apparently, however, Whitman had asked Dana to publish the letter, and the editor agreed.

The first edition contains a preface and 12 poems. The poems were untitled but would become in their final form the following: "Song of Myself," "A Song of Occupations," "To Think of Time," "The Sleepers," "I Sing the Body Electric," "Faces," "Song of the Answerer," "Europe, the 72d and 73d Years of These States," "A Boston Ballad," "There Was a Child Went Forth," "Who Learns My Lesson Complete," and "Great Are the Myths."

Leaves of Grass, Second Edition (1856)

This volume is well known for Whitman's presentation of a letter Ralph Waldo EMERSON sent to him in congratulations for the first edition, published the year before. On the spine of the new edition, Whitman offered in gold type "I Greet you at the / Beginning of A Great Career / R. W. Emerson." But the second edition is probably better known for the first presentation of one of Whitman's greatest poems, "Crossing Brooklyn Ferry."

Emerson's letter and Whitman's "Thank you" note are at the back of the volume. Whitman's note begins: "Here are thirty-two poems, which I send you, dear Friend and Master, not having found how I could satisfy myself with sending any usual acknowledgment of your letter." The poet had not asked Emerson for permission to use his letter.

The second edition was much smaller in format than the first, barely 4 by 6 inches compared with an almost 8-by-11-inch format for the first. There are 20 new poems, plus the 12 from the first edition, all of them this time with titles, plus the two letters and 26 pages of criticism, all the prose under the heading "Leaves Droppings"—324 pages in all. It was published in late August or early September 1856.

The book was published by FOWLER & WELLS, at 308 Broadway in New York, but, because the first edition had been considered immoral, they took no credit in print for the work.

Among the new poems are the following: "Salut au Monde"; "By Blue Ontario's Shore"; "Sun-Down Poem," which would later be entitled "Crossing Brooklyn Ferry"; "Song of the Open Road"; "A Woman Waits for Me"; "Song of Prudence"; "Spontaneous Me"; and "Song of the Rolling Earth."

Leaves of Grass, Third Edition (1860)

Whitman wrote a letter to an unidentified person on July 20, 1857, indicating his dissatisfaction with FOWLER & WELLS, publishers of his second edition of *Leaves of Grass* (1856). He refers to them as "bad persons for me—They retard my book very much. . . ."

More important, however, is the information in the letter that the poet wants to bring out a new edition, with a total of 100 poems. And "no other matter but poems," he says, still reacting no doubt to the adverse publicity he received from publishing in the second edition, without permission, Emerson's letter to him, stating, "I greet you at the beginning of a great career."

Perhaps most important of all about the third edition, however, is its presentation of two of Whitman's greatest poems, "Crossing Brooklyn Ferry" (first printed in the second edition) and "Out of the Cradle Endlessly Rocking," the latter poem under the title "A Word Out of the Sea," and both to be considerably revised before their final versions for the sixth edition of *Leaves of Grass* (1881).

The Boston publishers THAYER & ELDRIDGE wrote to Whitman on February 10, 1860, not asking but telling the poet that they wanted "to be publishers of Walt. Whitman's poems—Leaves of Grass.—When the book was first issued we were clerks in the establishment we now own. We read the book with profit and pleasure. It is a true poem and writ by a true man." The letter ends with this plea: "Are you writing other poems? Are they ready for the press? Will you let us read them? Will you write us? Please give us your residence." And signed, "Yours Fraternally, Thayer & Eldridge."

Not surprisingly, Whitman chose them as publishers for the third edition, and Charles ELDRIDGE became one of Whitman's lifelong friends. Whitman had been thinking about the new edition probably since publication of the 1856 edition, which proved to be so troublesome. And he had more than the total of 100 poems—including the 32 from the second edition—that he had written about in his 1857 letter.

When Thayer & Eldridge heard, in fact, that the poet had more than 100 previously unpublished poems and a plan of arrangement for the new edition of *Leaves*, they offered him the chance to design and supervise the printing of the book and with the standard 10 percent royalty. Whitman went to Boston in March and stayed until the first printing of 1,000 copies in mid-May. Letters indicate that the publication date was probably May 19; review copies were mailed May 24. The issue was sold out by the end of July and there was a second printing of about another 1,000 copies.

The 456-page book was almost the same size as the second edition, not quite 4 by 6 inches. There are 146 new poems, plus major revisions of the 32 poems from the second edition. For the first time, Whitman has a clear plan for his *Leaves of Grass*. There is an introductory poem entitled "Proto-Leaf," which is meant to present thematic elements for the entire book. Whitman changed the title to "Starting from Paumanok" in the fourth edition and revised it into a more successful statement of theme. The problem in the second edition, however, was that "Proto-Leaf" was considerably upstaged by the second poem, "Walt Whitman," which would later become "Song of Myself."

The second element of interest in Whitman's plan for the book is the presentation of "clusters" of poems, a term Whitman chose to describe the ordering of poems into special groups. Besides the separate poems such as "Walt Whitman" and "Salut au Monde" (also from the second edition), there are "clusters" which contain poems on a similar theme. Some of the clusters were "Chants Democratic," "Leaves of Grass," "Enfans D'Adam" (later titled "Children of Adam"), "Calamus," "Messenger Leaves," and "Thoughts." Only the "Messenger Leaves" poems had titles; poems in the other clusters were merely numbered.

The most important separate poems included "A Word Out of the Sea," which would become "Out of the Cradle Endlessly Rocking"; "Poem of the Road," which would become "Song of the Open Road"; and "Crossing Brooklyn Ferry." The final poem in the edition is "So Long," a poem that, with a few others in the volume, suggest that Whitman might have thought this edition to be his last.

Leaves of Grass, **Fourth Edition** (1867)

Published by Whitman, printed by William E. Chapin & Co., 24 Beekman Street in New York (late November 1866), the publication page the only place in the book, other than in the poetry itself, where Whitman's name appears. The copyright date is 1866, but the date on the title page is 1867. The size of the book is slightly smaller than 5 by 8 inches.

There are three known issues for the edition. First, there is the new issue of *Leaves of Grass*, with a lot of revising and rearranging of poems but with only six new poems; second, there is *Leaves of Grass* with the addition of the "Drum-Taps" and "Sequel to Drum-Taps" poems, printed from their original plates and bound in at the back of the new volume; and, third, there is an issue with all of the above plus "Songs Before Parting."

Leaves of Grass, **Fifth Edition** (1871)

Published in New York by J. S. Redfield, 140 Fulton St., "(up stairs)." There were two printings of the edition, each with two issues: the first "issue" carried the poems of the fourth edition (1867) with a number of alterations; the second "issue" contained the 384 pages from the first issue, plus a 120-page annex that included 74 poems, 24 new, including "Passage to India." The size of the book is $5^5/_8$ by $3^3/_{16}$ inches.

Whitman rearranged the order of many of the poems for this edition, and he broke up the *Drum-Taps* poems—which he had published as a separate volume in 1865—dividing the war poems into three clusters: "Drum-Taps," "Marches Now the War is Over," and "Bathed in War's Perfume."

Leaves of Grass (1876)

Published in two volumes: *Leaves of Grass* and *Two Rivulets*. This is technically not a new "edition," because the first volume is a reprint of the 1871 edition of *Leaves* (using the same plates), and the second volume is a collection of some of his other writings, including *Democratic Vistas, Passage to India,* and a group of poems he called "Centennial Songs." "Two Rivulets" refers, according to Whitman, to the dual nature of prose and poetry working together.

It is clearly a rush job on the poet's part; he wanted to help celebrate the 100th anniversary of the nation's founding. The two-volume set is referred to as the "Centennial Edition" and as the "Author's Edition."

This edition was electrotyped by Smith and McDougal of New York, printed by Samuel W. Green of New York, and bound by James Arnold of Philadelphia. The format size is not quite 5 by 8 inches. Copies were ready for circulation on September 1, 1876.

Leaves of Grass, Sixth Edition (1881)

James R. Osgood of Boston published the first 2,000 copies of the new edition, but Osgood felt forced to stop the work when the Boston district attorney notified him that *Leaves* had been officially classified as "obscene."

Following some negotiating with Whitman over the deletion of certain words, Osgood wrote Whit-man that he must eliminate two poems altogether, "A Woman Waits for Me" and "Ode to a Common Prostitute." The poet rejected the suggestion and fired the publisher. They came to an agreement on the terms of the split, including that Whitman would receive "the plates, dies, steel portrait [of the poet], and 225 copies (more or less), in sheets of *Leaves of Grass,* and pay W. W. the sum of $100 in cash."

Whitman offered the continuing publication to David McKAY, who worked for Rees Welsh & Co., No. 23 South Ninth Street, in Philadelphia. Rees Welsh printed six more issues of the sixth edition (dated 1882). McKay then bought out Rees Welsh and began publishing under his own imprint and would continue as Whitman's publisher for the rest of the poet's life. It is ironic that the sixth edition of *Leaves of Grass* is often referred to as the "Osgood Edition."

In spite of all the confusion over printing issues, the sixth edition is significant more because Whitman made no changes in the ordering of poems after this edition. He was finally satisfied with the placement and titles of all the poems and decided that it would simply be easier to add new poems in "annexes" for subsequent editions.

Leaves of Grass (1889)

As with the 1876 volume this was called an "edition" by Whitman and many biographers but technically is not. It is an additional "printing" of the sixth edition (1881). Whitman had wanted for several years to publish a pocket-sized copy of *Leaves of Grass,* one that readers could carry around with them. This is that volume.

Leaves of Grass (Death-bed Edition) (1892)

This was called the "Death-bed Edition" by Whitman and many biographers, but, as with the 1876 and 1889 volumes of *Leaves of Grass,* this too was an additional "printing" of the sixth edition (1881).

One of the interesting facts about this "Death-bed" printing is that although it was rushed to press in December 1891 so Whitman could have a copy in hand "before he died," thereby providing what would be called today a "proof copy," the issue as formally published in the late spring of 1892 by David McKay is the best and clearest presentation of what Whitman wanted for his *Leaves of Grass*. And it is the version still most often reprinted and read today.

Whitman probably received copies on December 6, 1891. He wrote letters on December 5 and 6 to his friend and biographer Richard Maurice Bucke with no mention of the new book in the first letter but with a copy and the following comment in the latter:

> Send same time with this first copy, (rude, flimsy cover, but good paper, print & stitching) of L. of G. *at last complete*—after 33 y'rs of hackling at it, all times & moods of my life, fair weather & foul, all parts of the land, and peace & war, young & old—the wonder to me that I have carried it on to accomplish as essentially as it is, tho' I see well enough its numerous deficiencies & faults—(At any rate "From waiting long & long delay Johnny comes marching home")
>
> The cumulus character of the book is a great factor—perhaps even the jaggedness, or what might be call'd so f'm the conventional & tidy principles of "art"—probably *is* so anyhow—Bad days & nights with me, no hour without its suffering—
>
> Walt Whitman

In a letter to Richard Bucke on December 10, he added another comment about the final *Leaves*. "As I now consider it as *finished* as I propose & laid out—even its deficiencies are provided for, or plainly hinted at—to me its best points are its unmistakable *atmosphere* and with any maturity or stamina or the like its *being in process* (or evolution) qualities f'm first to last—"

McKay dated the printed book "1891–92," even though the December unbound proof sheets could

hardly be considered "publication." And Whitman's death, which precipitated the hurry, did not occur until March 26, 1892.

It was technically *not* a new edition; it would be called an "issue" today. Most of the poetry is a reprinting of the 1881 edition from the original plates set in Boston by James R. Osgood, who had sold them to Whitman after a Boston district attorney had called the book "obscene" and threatened prosecution. Whitman added two "annexes" to the poetry volume, also from earlier plates: the "cluster" of poems entitled "Sands at Seventy" from *November Boughs* (1888) and the "cluster" entitled "Good-Bye My Fancy" from *Good-Bye My Fancy* (1891).

McKay also published a second, matching volume of Whitman's prose, taken from the 1882 plates of *Specimen Days & Collect*.

Dr. Richard Bucke, one of Whitman's executors, was instrumental in the publication of Whitman's announcement about the "completion" of *Leaves of Grass*, written for Bucke in January 1892 and published as an advertisement in the NEW YORK HERALD.

> Walt Whitman wishes respectfully to notify the public that the book Leaves of Grass, which he has been working on at great intervals and partially issued for the past thirty-five or forty years, is now completed, so to call it, and he would like this new 1892 edition to absolutely supersed all previous ones. Faulty as it is, he decides it as by far his speciall and entire self-chosen poetic utterance.

Whitman added a particularly poignant note to this just before he died, saying that "In the long run, the world will do as it pleases with the book. I am determined to have the world know what I was pleased to do."

McKay included in the 1892 *Leaves of Grass* another statement from Whitman to all future editors, urging them to honor his request that this be the final order and revision of his poems.

> As there are now several editions of L. of G., different texts and dates, I wish to say that I prefer and recommend this present one, com-

plete, for future printing, if there should be any; a copy and fac-simile, indeed, of the text of these 438 pages. The subsequent adjusting interval which is so important to form'd and launch'd work, books especiall, has pass'd; and waiting till fully after that, I have given (pages 423–438) my concluding words.

Nearly all editors of reprinted editions of *Leaves of Grass* have accepted and followed this injunction. Most editors have added at the back of the book, however, sections that included poems which Whitman had excluded from the final *Leaves*, if not from earlier editions, plus the "early" poems, those published before the first edition (1855) and considered unworthy by the author.

Leaves of Grass (1897)

The Boston publishers Small, Maynard, and Co. printed a posthumous volume of *Leaves of Grass* (1897), poems written by Whitman and included under the cluster title "Old Age Echoes" in what is generally referred to as the 10th "edition" of *Leaves of Grass*.

The volume, which friend and biographer Horace TRAUBEL saw through the press, included all the poetry from the "Death-bed" printing and in the same order, plus 13 short poems that Whitman had approved for publication after his death. He told Traubel that he had held them in "reserve." The poet also provided, according to Traubel, the title "Old Age Echoes."

"Legend of Life and Love, A" (1842)

Short story, first published in the *United States Magazine and Democratic Review* (July 1842; see DEMOCRATIC REVIEW, THE). The tale is most accessible now in *Walt Whitman: The Early Poems and the Fic-*

tion, edited by Thomas L. Brasher (New York University Press, 1963).

A character referred to in the story only as an "Ancient Man" provides deathbed advice for his two orphaned grandsons, Nathan and Mark: "The world, my children, is full of deceit. Evil men swarm in every place, and sorrow and disappointment are the fruits of intercourse with them." He tells the boys that because life is made up of "shadows, passing like the darkness of a cloud," do not allow love to come in your life. Love is the "ficklest" of all things in life. "The object of affection dies," he says, or perhaps love itself dies; either way, both are painful and worth avoidance.

Further, the "Ancient Man" advises, it is better to avoid confiding in any man. "It is well to keep aloof from the follies and impurities of earth," he tells the boys; "let there be no links between you and others." Dependence upon others can only lead to a loss of happiness. All of these truths, he tells the boys, he has learned "by bitter experience."

The grandfather dies and the boys separate, not meeting again for 50 years, at which time they exchange their life stories.

Mark tells of a life that followed his grandfather's advice: he had rejected love, he had "looked upon everything with suspicious eyes," he had "found it but too true that iniquity and deceit are the ruling spirits of men." He had been a "success" in business, but he had not been happy.

He tells his brother that "if few glittering pleasures ministered to me on my journey, equally few were the disappointments." He describes "hopes" that were "blighted" and "trusts betrayed." Ah, my brother, he says, in conclusion, "the world is full of misery!"

Nathan then tells of his life story, of his love for a beautiful woman, his marriage to her, of their family of "brave boys and fair girls. Oh, Mark, that, *that* is a pleasure—that swelling of tenderness for our offspring. . . ."

He too had "engaged in trade." He tells his brother: "Various fortune followed my path. I will not deny but that some in whom I thought virtue was strong, proved cunning hypocrites, and worthy no man's trust. Yet are there many I have known, spotless as far as humanity may be spotless."

He says that it was true that his "life has been alternately dark and fair," but that he has been generally happy. No one is ever completely happy, he says, "it is never for mortals to be so. . . . But I can lay my hand upon my heart, and thank the Great Master, that the sunshine has been far oftener than the darkness of the clouds."

"Dear brother," he says in conclusion, the world is not a perfect place; there is misery, "but it is a pleasant world still, and affords much joy to the dwellers!"

Nathan finishes the story of his past 50 years, and the omniscient narrator tells the reader: "As Nathan ceased, his brother looked up in his face, like a man unto whom a simple truth had been for the first time revealed."

CHARACTERS

Ancient Man   He is the grandfather of Nathan and Mark in the short story "A Legend of Life and Love." He dies early in the story but not before he passes on some advice about life to the two boys. He is the consummate pessimist, who believes that the world is full of evil people, whose main goal in life, apparently, is to cheat others. He tells his sons that they should not marry, because all women are untrustworthy. He has learned all of this from "bitter experience," he says, and he insists that the lessons from his life represent a "truth" that his sons must believe. He is a bitter, "ancient" old man.

Mark   Younger grandson of the "Ancient Man" and one year younger than his brother, Nathan, in the short story "A Legend of Life and Love." He receives the advice of his dying grandfather to love nobody, to trust nobody. He heeds the advice: he rejected the love he had for a young woman, he had "looked upon everything with suspicious eyes," he had "found it but too true," as his grandfather had said, "that iniquity and deceit are the ruling spirits of men." He had been a "success" in business, but he had not been happy. When Mark meets his brother after 50 years, he tells of a life of "misery" and unhappiness.

Nathan   Older grandson of the "Ancient Man" and brother to Mark. He receives the advice of his dying grandfather to love nobody, to trust nobody, the same advice given to Mark. But, unlike Mark, Nathan has taken the opposite tack during the past 50 years: he had fallen in love and married, he had raised a family of "brave boys and fair girls," he had both failures and successes in business, but Nathan can look back on a happy and successful life. He had *not* taken his grandfather's advice, and now that he has heard his brother's life story, he is glad that he had not.

"Lessons" (1871)

Cut from *Leaves of Grass* after appearing in the "Passage to India" supplement to the fifth edition (1871).

Letters of Anne Gilchrist and Walt Whitman, The (1918)

Various letters written between Whitman and GILCHRIST and edited by Thomas B. Harned, one of Whitman's literary executors, and published in New York by Doubleday, Page & Company in 1918.

Letters Written by Walt Whitman to his Mother from 1866–1872 (1902)

Edited by Thomas B. Harned, one of Whitman's literary executors, and published in 1902 by G. P. Putnam's Sons. There are 70 pages of letters, plus three essays by Harned: "Whitman and Oratory," "Walt Whitman and Physique," and "Walt Whitman and His Second Boston Publishers." This material is most accessible now in a volume of *The Collected Writings of Walt Whitman*, edited by Gay Wilson Allen and Sculley Bradley.

"Life" (1888)

First published in the NEW YORK HERALD (April 15, 1888); then in *November Boughs* (1888); and it was the 40th of 65 poems in the "First Annex: Sands at Seventy" cluster for the "Death-bed" printing of *Leaves of Grass* (1892).

The "soul of man" is in a constant struggle with life, ever "dissatisfied, curious, unconvinc'd at last" with the way things are. If armies fail, the poet says, then "we send fresh armies." The soul battles the same, at work with the "grappled mystery of all earth's ages old or new."

"Life and Death" (1888)

First published in the NEW YORK HERALD (May 23, 1888); then in *November Boughs* (1888); and it was the 47th of 65 poems in the "First Annex: Sands at Seventy" cluster for the "Death-bed" printing of *Leaves of Grass* (1892).

This four-line poem reminds readers of the "two old, simple problems ever intertwined"—life and death. They are the two "insoluble" problems inevitable for each generation and passed on from one to the next.

"Lingave's Temptation"
(c. 1841–1847)

Short story, first publication and date unknown. The tale is most accessible now in *Walt Whitman: The Early Poems and the Fiction*, edited by Thomas L. Brasher (New York University Press, 1963). According to Brasher, the story has not been identified by place or date of publication but is thought to have been published between 1841 and 1847. According to Brasher, there is a clipping of this story in the Charles E. Feinberg Collection of Whitman manuscript materials and first editions.

Lingave is a poor poet struggling to keep food on his table and a fresh spirit in his life. He believes that he has the quality of genius, but he knows "genius is not apparel and food."

He is offered the chance to make a lot of money and perhaps get a permanent position by writing for a *"money-maker."* The job would require a loss of virtue and therefore dignity; he would "labor for the advancement of what he felt to be unholy—he was to inculcate what would lower the perfection of man." Lingave turns down the job. The specific job he is asked to do is not made clear, but the narrator does make clear that it would be dishonest.

"Virtue," the reader is informed, "is ever the sinew of true genius. Together, the two in one, they are endow'd with immortal strength, and approach loftily to Him from whom both spring." So Lingave turns down the job and then continues as he had before the offer, plodding along in his poverty, remaining at the end both honest and poor.

CHARACTER

Lingave   Main character in the short story "Lingave's Temptation." He is a poor poet and believes that he has the quality of genius, but he knows "genius is not apparel and food." He is offered the chance to make a living writing for a *"money-maker,"* but it would require so much dishonesty that he decides to give up the opportunity. Virtue is more important to him, the moral is made clear, than money.

"Lingering Last Drops"
(1891)

First published as the second of 31 poems in *Good-Bye My Fancy* (1891); then in "Second Annex: Good-Bye My Fancy" for the "Death-bed" printing of *Leaves of Grass* (1892).

The poet asks the lingering rain drops "whence and why" they come last. The drops answer that they don't know, that they merely "wafted at last" and are now making "the passing shower's concluding drops." It is just rain, after all, another part of nature than transcends human understanding.

"Literature"

Essay written for publication in GALAXY magazine to go with two other essays, "Democracy" and "Personalism," which the magazine published in December 1867 and May 1868 respectively. "Literature," however, was rejected by the editor following complaints from readers about the first two essays in the series. Whitman then combined "Literature" with the first two essays for *Democratic Vistas*, one of the most important essays Whitman wrote on the value of literature in a democratic society. See *Democratic Vistas*.

"Little Jane" (1846)

Short story, originally embedded in chapter 14 of Whitman's novel, *Franklin Evans*. When the author reprinted the novel in the BROOKLYN DAILY EAGLE (November 16–30, 1846), however, he took out the "Little Jane" segment and published it separately in the *Eagle* (December 7, 1846) as a short story. It is one of the more sentimental of Whitman's short stories.

Little Jane is the youngest child in her family and is dying of an unnamed illness. Her brother Mike, an alcoholic, is off drinking in a local tavern even as Jane is on her deathbed. Feeling guilty that he is not more sympathetic to her cause, Mike at last staggers home and witnesses the last few minutes of Jane's life.

Jane has been giving each of her parents and her brothers and sisters small gifts, meant to be something by which they will remember her. She has saved for Mike a "small, much-thumbed book—a religious story for infants, given her by her mother when she had first learned to read." When Mike enters the room, Jane immediately takes his hand, and, as she dies, lays the religious token in his hand. The story ends with the moral statement: "From that night, the young man stepped no more in his wild courses, but was reformed."

See also "The Death of Wind-Foot," another segment of *Franklin Evans*, later published as a separate short story.

CHARACTERS

Little Jane   A young child, dying from an unnamed illness. Her brother Mike, an inebriate, is the last member of her family to arrive at her deathbed. She has been distributing small gifts to each member of her family and has saved a favorite memento for Mike—a little religious story for children, which had been given to her by her mother.

Mike   The alcoholic brother of Jane in Whitman's "Little Jane." He shows up at her deathbed just in time to receive from her a small token by which he may remember her. It is a little booklet, a religious story that her mother had given to her as a child. The gift so moves Mike that readers are told that he will never again enter a tavern or take a drink of alcohol.

"Little Sleighers, The" (1844)

Nonfiction sketch, first published in COLUMBIAN MAGAZINE (September 1844). The sketch is most accessible now in *Walt Whitman: The Early Poems and the Fiction*, edited by Thomas L. Brasher (New York University Press, 1963).

Subtitled "A Sketch of a Winter Morning on the Battery," this piece describes a walk Whitman took on a cold day in New York, probably during January or February of 1844, his encounter with several young boys sledding on the sidewalks, and the moral that occurs to him as he wonders what will happen to these boys. "Who can foretell their destinies? Some will die early. . . . Some will plod onward in the path of gain. . . . Some will love. . . . But all, all will repose at last."

He ends the moral piece by acknowledging that he has wandered away in his thinking from his original intention, which was to write a merely descriptive piece about the joy of walking in New York on a beautiful wintry afternoon.

"Lo, Victress on the Peaks" (1865)

First appeared in the "Sequel to Drum-Taps" segment (1865); then with a group titled "Bathed in War's Perfume" in the fifth edition of *Leaves of Grass* (1871); it appeared under its present title throughout its publication history and was the 39th of 43 poems in the "Drum-Taps" cluster for the sixth edition (1881).

The "Victress" in the CIVIL WAR was Liberty ("Libertad"), and the poet wants to sing it to the world: "No poem proud, I chanting bring to thee, nor mastery's rapturous verse, / But a cluster containing night's darkness and blood-dripping wounds." He won't glorify the war, the poet says, but will sing instead "psalms of the dead."

There is an interesting accentual rhythm pattern also at work in this poem (see ACCENTUAL VERSE). The first two lines have two and five accented syllables respectively, and the last two lines reverse the pattern with five and two. The middle line of the nine-line poem has four accented syllables, the line suggesting perhaps a moment of doubt, which Whitman certainly felt from the results of the war. He wanted to show pride in the Union's new liberty, yet at the same time acknowledge the horror left by the dead and wounded in the war.

"Locations and Times" (1860)

First published as "Leaves of Grass, No. 22" in the third edition of *Leaves of Grass* (1860); it was one of the "Songs Before Parting" poems (1867); it received its present title and was one of the "Passage to India" poems (1871); and it was the 27th of 29 poems in the "By The Roadside" cluster for the sixth edition (1881).

This two-line poem is a revision of four lines taken out of the "Sun-Down Poem" (later titled "Crossing Brooklyn Ferry") for the second edition of *Leaves of Grass* (1856). Whitman seems to be looking for things that makes him feel at ease with

"locations and times," or that "correspond" with "forms, color, densities, odors." By "correspond," he probably means things which are in agreement with or harmonize with other things.

"L. of G.'s Purport" (1891)

First published as the 27th of 31 poems in *Good-Bye My Fancy* (1891); then in "Second Annex: Good-Bye My Fancy" for the "Death-bed" printing of *Leaves of Grass* (1892).

Whitman summarizes in this poem the history of *Leaves of Grass*, the "Evolution—the cumulative—growths and generations." It was begun, he says, "in ripen'd youth and steadily pursued, . . . dallying with all—war, peace, day and night absorbing, / Never even for one brief hour abandoning my task."

As with all of the poems in the "Good-Bye My Fancy" cluster, Whitman feels that he is near the end of his life and poetry, and, as he says, "I end it here in sickness, poverty, and old age." He had been writing "farewell songs" for several years, but, in this case, he would be dead before the end of another year. He concludes the poem: "I sing of life, yet mind me well of death." Death "dogs" his steps and is sometimes as close as "face to face."

"Long, Long Hence" (1891)

First published as the 12th of 31 poems in *Good-Bye My Fancy* (1891); then in "Second Annex: Good-Bye My Fancy" for the "Death-bed" printing of *Leaves of Grass* (1892).

Only after "myriads of readers, . . . [and] after ages' and ages' encrustations, / Then only may these songs reach fruition." Whitman suffered unpopularity as a poet throughout his life, and the suffering is evident in this poem as he suggests that it will be "long, long hence" before his poems can be appreciated.

"Long, too Long America" (1865)

First appeared as "Long, Too Long, O Land" in the *Drum-Taps* volume (1865) and in *Leaves of Grass*; it received its present title and was the 22nd of 43 poems in the "Drum-Taps" cluster for the sixth edition (1881).

For too long the speaker says in this five-line poem, America has been satisfied with its "joys and prosperity," but now that the CIVIL WAR has begun—this "crises [crisis] of anguish, advancing, grappling with direst fate and recoiling not"—we must "show to the world what your children enmasse really are."

The poet brags that only he "has yet conceiv'd what [American] children enmasse really are." He has experienced firsthand the bravery of the soldiers both North and South, and he is writing these poems in order to describe the significance of what he has learned.

"[Long I Thought That Knowledge Alone Would Suffice]" (1860)

Cut from *Leaves of Grass* after first appearing as "Calamus, No. 8" in the third edition (1860). The brackets indicate the poem's first line. The last two lines of this 12-line poem may have seemed too sexually explicit to Whitman, who was criticized for several of the "Calamus" poems, poems devoted to homosexual love. The original lines read as follows: "I will go with him I love, / It is to be enough for us that we are together—We never separate again." See also "[Hours Continuing Long]," another poem cut after the 1860 edition.

"Look Down Fair Moon" (1865)

First appeared in the *Drum-Taps* volume (1865) and under this title throughout its publication his-

tory in *Leaves of Grass*; it was the 33rd of 43 poems in the "Drum-Taps" cluster for the sixth edition (1881).

In four lines the poet makes a reverent request to the moon: "Look down fair moon . . . / On the dead on their backs with arms toss'd wide, / Pour down your unstinted nimbus sacred moon." The word *nimbus* suggests a request for divine halos to be placed over the heads of the dead soldiers in spite of (or maybe because of) the otherwise horrifying scene.

There are other poems in the "Drum-Taps" cluster that present similar, seemingly peaceful yet potentially horrifying descriptions of men at war. See "Cavalry Crossing a Ford," "Bivouac on a Mountain Side," "By the Bivouac's Fitful Flame," "A Sight in Camp in the Daybreak Gray and Dim," "As Toilsome I Wander'd Virginia's Woods," and "I Saw Old General at Bay."

"Love of Eris: A Spirit Record, The" (1844)

A fairy tale, though most often referred to as a short story. It was first published in the COLUMBIAN MAGAZINE as "Eris: A Spirit Record" (March 1844). Whitman retitled it for reprinting in the BROOKLYN DAILY EAGLE (August 18, 1846) while he was the editor. The tale is most accessible now in *Walt Whitman: The Early Poems and the Fiction*, edited by Thomas L. Brasher (New York University Press, 1963).

The angel Dai hovers over the mortal beauty Eris, who lies ill on a couch in her home in the care of her betrothed. Dai is there because the "office of this spirit is to keep a sleepless watch, and fill the heart of his charge with strange and mysterious and lovely thoughts." But Dai makes the mistake of falling in love with the girl himself, which exceeds his heavenly duties, so when Eris dies and ascends to heaven Dai is made blind by God so he will not be able to find her.

While Dai wanders through heaven seeking his beloved Eris, she, who loves a mortal man, waits at the door to paradise for her earthly betrothed, who yearns for death even as he continues to live into old age.

The narrator ends the fairy tale with the following moral imperative: "Thus the tale is told in Heaven, how the pure love of two human beings is a sacred thing, which the immortals themselves must not dare to cross." Readers are told that Dai unhappily represents "the destiny of those whose selfishness would seek to mar the peace of gentle hearts, by their own intrusive and unhallowed passion."

CHARACTERS

Dai   An immortal being in "The Love of Eris: A Spirit Record." He exceeds his angelic charge, which is to watch over the beautiful Eris in her illness and provide her "with strange and mysterious and lovely thoughts." The angel falls in love with her instead.

Eris   Loved by the immortal Dai in "The Love of Eris: A Spirit Record." She, however, loves another mortal, a man to whom she is betrothed. She dies, but while Dai, who has been blinded by God for "selfishness," wanders heaven calling for Eris, she stands at heaven's gate waiting for her betrothed to arrive.

"Love That Is Hereafter, The" (1840)

First published in the LONG ISLAND DEMOCRAT (May 19, 1840); an "early poem" *not* later published in *Leaves of Grass*. It is most accessible now in Francis Murphy (editor), *Walt Whitman: The Complete Poems* (Penguin Books, 1996).

Madman, The (1843)

Short story fragment of a longer piece of fiction—probably a novel since there is a "Chapter II," at the end of which is a note, "to be continued." It was first published in the New York *Washingtonian and Organ* (January 28, 1843), formerly the WASHINGTONIAN. The unfinished tale is most accessible now in *Walt Whitman: The Early Poems and the Fiction*, edited by Thomas L. Brasher (New York University Press, 1963). According to Brasher, the story was discovered by Whitman biographer Emory Holloway but no further installments of the story beyond chapter 2 have been found.

All readers have in the first two chapters are brief introductions to two men, the "hero," Richard Arden, and a Frenchman, Pierre Barcoure. They become friends, but neither is described in such a way as to indicate "madness," so even the story's title is obscure—at least without further material.

"Mannahatta" [1]   (1860)

First appeared in the third edition of *Leaves of Grass* (1860); it was part of a "Leaves of Grass" cluster (1871); and it was the sixth of 22 poems in the "From Noon to Starry Night" cluster for the sixth edition (1881).

"Mannahatta" is an aboriginal word for "large island," from which New Yorkers get Manhattan, a borough of New York City. Apparently the Algonquian Indians named the island Manhattan and Whitman's "Mannahatta" is his own term. In his poetry the word *Manhattan* stood for the entire city rather than for one of the city's five boroughs.

The poem is descriptive of New York but also about the name "Mannahatta" itself:

> I was asking for something specific and perfect
>   for my city,
> Whereupon lo! upsprang the aboriginal name.
> Now I see what there is in a name, a word,
>   liquid, sane, unruly, musical, self-sufficient, . . .
> City of hurried and sparkling waters! city of
>   spires and masts!
> City nested in bays! my city!

The 20-line poem is one of the great lyrical tributes to New York.

"Mannahatta" [2] (1888)

First published in the NEW YORK HERALD (February 22, 1888); then in *November Boughs* (1888); and it was the first of 65 poems in the "First Annex: Sands at Seventy" cluster for the "Death-bed" printing of *Leaves of Grass* (1892).

Mannahatta is the Algonquian Indian tribal name for Manhattan (see "Mannahatta" [1]), a "choice aboriginal name," Whitman says in this poem, *"a rocky founded island."* It is a three-line picture of New York City's most famous borough.

"March in the Ranks Hard-Prest, and the Road Unknown, A" (1865)

First appeared in the *Drum-Taps* volume (1865) and under this title throughout its printing history; it was the 16th of 43 poems in the "Drum-Taps" cluster for the sixth edition of *Leaves of Grass* (1881).

In this poem the CIVIL WAR soldiers are in retreat after heavy losses in the day's battle. They come to "an open space in the woods" where there is a "dim-lighted" church at a crossroads, "now an impromptu hospital." The narrator enters the church and sees "a sight beyond all the pictures and poems ever made." He describes the darkness of the church, the "moving candles and lamps" creating "shadows of the deepest, deepest black." He sees a soldier, "shot in the abdomen," and tries to help him: "I stanch the blood temporarily, (the youngster's face is white as a lily.)"

The narrator, his eyes apparently adapting to the poor light, looks around the church, "fain to absorb it all." There are "surgeons operating, attendants holding lights, the smell of ether, the odor of blood, . . . / Some [of the wounded] on bare ground, some on planks or stretchers, some in the death-spasm sweating." For the narrator it is a terrifying scene.

Orders are given for his army unit to leave the church and continue their march. The narrator bends over the first soldier he had seen, who gives him a "half-smile" and then dies. The poem's last three lines both sum up the incident and confirm the horror of war.

> Then the eyes close, calmly close, and I speed
> forth to the darkness,
> Resuming, marching, ever in darkness
> marching, on in the ranks,
> The unknown road still marching.

Whitman was familiar with such scenes; he had worked in hospitals during much of the war, helping the wounded on both sides.

This is the first of three consecutive poems in the "Drum-Taps" cluster that present with greater intensity than other poems in the group the theme of death in war. See also "A Sight in Camp in the Daybreak Gray and Dim" and "As Toilsome I Wander'd Virginia's Woods."

"Mediums" (1860)

First appeared as "Chants Democratic, No. 16" in the third edition of *Leaves of Grass* (1860); it received its present title (1867); and it was the 12th of 22 poems in the "From Noon to Starry Night" cluster for the sixth edition (1881).

The "Mediums" are those who in a democracy have a vision of what the nation can become. They are the poets, yet not only poets, Whitman says; they are also the "orators and oratresses" whose "poems and materials of poems shall come from their lives, they shall be makers and finders."

"Me Imperturbe" (1860)

First appeared as "Chants Democratic, No. 18" for the third edition of *Leaves of Grass* (1860); it received its present title (1867); and it was the 15th of 24 poems in the "Inscriptions" cluster for the sixth edition (1881).

The most common reading of the key word here is "imperturbable," that is, not easily disturbed or excited. In this poem Whitman means not easily disturbed with Nature or with natural things.

The opening lines suggest the speaker's confidence at being imperturbable:

Me imperturbe, standing at ease in Nature,
Master of all or mistress of all, aplomb in the
    midst of irrational things,
Imbued as they, passive, receptive, silent as
    they, . . .

I am comfortable with my life, he suggests, and others can be as well. As with nearly all of the poems in *Leaves of Grass* Whitman does not fail to acknowledge that what he is capable of doing as a male can also be accomplished by a female. Anyone can be as I am, he says: "A river man, or a man of the woods or of any farm-life of these States or of the coast, or the lakes of Kanada, . . ." All of us can be imperturbable.

Memoranda During the War (1875–1876)

Book of 68 pages published as an "Author's Edition" in the print shop of the Camden, New Jersey, *New Republic*. There were about 1,000 copies printed, 750 of which were bound. It was Whitman's notebook and diary material from the CIVIL WAR, most of which later appeared in *Specimen Days & Collect* (1882).

Whitman had proposed a book of war "memoranda" to a Boston publisher in 1863 but was turned down. Ten years later he published a series of six essays—"papers," he called them—in the NEW YORK WEEKLY GRAPHIC, from January 24 to March 7, 1874. Each essay was titled " 'Tis But Ten Years Since"; they were later published as separate items in *Memoranda During the War.*

Whitman was in New York when he read the names of wounded soldiers in the NEW YORK HERALD in December 1862 and found a "G. W. Whitmore," which he assumed correctly was his brother

George. Walt rushed off to Washington and found that George was in a hospital at Falmouth, Virginia, near Fredericksburg. Whitman went to Falmouth to help his brother. George was wounded but managed to be in a group of exchange prisoners and so returned to BROOKLYN in late February. While Walt was taking care of his brother at the Falmouth hospital, he helped other wounded soldiers as well and liked being able to assist the wounded and dying. He talked to them, wrote letters home for them, and listened to them talk about their families and home life.

This was the beginning of Whitman's primary work for most of the next three years. He went back to Washington and got a paid job as a government clerk, but he spent most of his time in the hospitals—mostly old buildings in the process of being turned

Walt Whitman, photographed by Mathew Brady, 1875
(Library of Congress, Prints and Photographs Division)

into hospitals, a total of 85 before the end of the war (see CIVIL WAR HOSPITALS, which includes a complete list of the "hospitals").

He started making notes about his experiences. In the introduction to *Memoranda During the War*, a shortened version of which appears as a footnote to the first entry in *Specimen Days*, he provides information about the "memoranda":

> From the first I kept little note-books for impromptu jottings in pencil to refresh my memory of names and circumstances, and what was specially wanted, &c. In these I brief'd cases, persons, sights, occurrences in camp, by the bedside, and not seldom by the corpses of the dead. Of the present Volume most of its pages are *verbatim* renderings from such pencillings on the spot. Some were scratch'd down from narratives I heard and itemized while watching, or waiting, or tending somebody amid those scenes. I have perhaps forty such little note-books left, forming a special history of those years, for myself alone, full of associations never to be possibly said or sung. I wish I could convey to the reader the associations that attach to these soil'd and creas'd little livraisons, each composed of a sheet or two of paper, folded small to carry in the pocket, and fasten'd with a pin. I leave them just as I threw them by during the War, blotch'd here and there with more than one blood-stain, hurriedly written, sometimes at the clinique, not seldom amid the excitement of uncertainty, or defeat, or of action, or getting ready for it, or a march. . . . [The notes] summon up, even in this silent and vacant room as I write, not only the sinewy regiments and brigades, marching or in camp, but the countless phantoms of those who fell and were hastily buried by wholesale in the battle-pits, or whose dust and bones have been since removed to the National Cemeteries of the land, especially through Virginia and Tennessee.

He writes that he assisted not only Northern soldiers but Southern as well; it did not matter to Whitman, who believed that the preservation of the Union was more important than the slavery issue that brought about the war. His daily contact with "Carolinian, Georgian, Alabamian, Louisianian, Virginian" soldiers no doubt gave Whitman a chance to mend not only the physical wounds of Southern soldiers but the psychological wounds as well. As he writes 10 years later of these experiences, he says in *Memoranda* that they were

> Vivid as life, they recall and identify the long Hospital Wards, with their myriad-varied scenes of day or night—the graphic incidents of field or camp—the night before the battle, with many solemn yet cool preparations—the changeful exaltations and depressions of those four years, North and South—the convulsive memories, (let but a word, a broken sentence, serve to recall them)—the clues already quite vanish'd, like some old dream, and yet the list significant enough to soldiers—the scrawl'd, worn slips of paper that came up by bushels from the Southern prisons, Salisbury or Andersonville, by the hands of exchanged prisoners—the clank of crutches on the pavements or floors of Washington, or up and down the stairs of the Paymasters' offices—the Grand Review of homebound veterans at the close of the War, cheerily marching day after day by the President's house, one brigade succeeding another until it seem'd as if they would never end. . . .

The "bushels" of "worn slips of paper" are letters he received later from soldiers he had helped, letters from North and South. He also writes of seeing "the tall form of President LINCOLN with his face of deep-cut lines, with the large, kind, canny eyes, the complexion of dark brown, and the tinge of weird melancholy saturating all." Whitman was impressed by the "Common People, . . . thousands of specimens of first-class Heroism, steadily accumulating, (no regiment, no company, hardly a file of men, North or South, the last three years, without such first-class specimens.)" He refers often to the bravery of men who fought in the war and who suffered with wounds, disease, or impending death.

> To me, the points illustrating the latent Personal Character and eligibilities of These States, in the two or three millions of American

young and middle-aged men, North and South, embodied in the armies—and especially the one-third or one-fourth of their number, stricken by wounds or disease at some time in the course of the contest—were of more significance even than the Political interests involved. (As so much of a Race depends on what it thinks of death, and how it stands personal anguish and sickness. As, in the glints of emotions under emergencies, and the indirect traits and asides in Plutarch, &c., we get far profounder clues to the antique world than all its more formal history.)

Historians, Whitman believed, could not describe the war except in abstractions. He does not refer to poets specifically as better equipped for describing war, but it may well have been on his mind, and he certainly uses the idea in his poetry. It is the poet, he believed, who must tell the story of America. "Future years will never know," he wrote in *Memorada,* "the seething hell and the black infernal background of countless minor scenes and interiors, (not the few great battles) of the Secession War; and it is best they should not."

It may be "best" that no one should know about the horrors of the war, but the memoranda nevertheless include grisly scenes of the capturing and torturing of soldiers by both Northern and Southern troops (see, in particular, "A Glimpse of War's Hell-Scenes" in *Specimen Days*).

War is never a "quadrille in a ball-room" as Whitman says, and he was certainly correct in suggesting that no one, perhaps not even poets, could recreate for readers "the seething hell and the black infernal background" of a battle or its aftermath.

He sums up, however, in one last long statement in his memoranda "Introduction," the cost of the war in lives and money:

Of that many-threaded drama, with its sudden and strange surprises, its confounding of prophecies, its moments of despair, the dread of foreign interference, the interminable campaigns, the bloody battles, the mighty and cumbrous and green armies, the drafts and bounties—the immense money expenditure, like a heavy pouring constant rain—with, over the whole land,

the last three years of the struggle, an unending, universal mourning-wail of women, parents, orphans—the marrow of the tragedy concentrated in those Hospitals—(it seem'd sometimes as if the whole interest of the land, North and South, was one vast central Hospital, and all the rest of the affair but flanges)—those forming the Untold and Unwritten History of the War—infinitely greater (like Life's) than the few scraps and distortions that are ever told or written. Think how much, and of importance, will be—how much, civic and military, has already been—buried in the grave, in eternal darkness!

Counting the dead on both sides in the CIVIL WAR—nearly 620,000 soldiers killed in battle or from disease—no war involving the United States has cost more in lives lost. Whitman saw the great cost, yet, if the *Memoranda* are a fair indication of his internal feelings throughout the war, he seemed continually optimistic about the prospects for democracy. What he had written in his earliest editions of *Leaves of Grass* about America's future seemed undeterred by whatever discouragement he must have felt at times during the three years he served in Washington as an attendant for thousands of soldiers in the hospitals.

"Memories" (1888)

First appeared in *November Boughs* (1888); it was the 14th of 65 poems in the "First Annex: Sands at Seventy" cluster for the "Death-bed" printing of *Leaves of Grass* (1892). This brief poem extols the joys of looking back on one's life.

Memories of President Lincoln (1881)

Cluster title for four poems: "When Lilacs Last in the Dooryard Bloom'd," "O Captain! My Captain!," "Hush'd Be the Camps To-day," and "This Dust

Was Once the Man." These poems were brought together under the collective title "President LIN-COLN's Burial Hymn" for the fifth edition of *Leaves of Grass* (1871); and they were grouped under the title "Memories of President Lincoln" for the sixth edition (1881).

"Miracles" (1856)

First appeared as "Poem of Perfect Miracles" in the second edition of *Leaves of Grass* (1856); then as "Leaves of Grass, No. 8" (1860); it received its present title (1867); and it was the 21st of 38 poems in the "Autumn Rivulets" cluster for the sixth edition (1881).

"Why, who makes much of a miracle? / As to me I know of nothing else but miracles." The poet CAT-ALOGs in this poem several of the particular miracles he has in mind: walking "the streets of Manhattan," a "day with any one I love," a "look at strangers opposite me riding in the car," "the exquisite delicate thin curve of the new moon in spring," and more. It doesn't take long for a reader of Whitman's poetry to realize that this is an idea that permeates his work. Life itself is the greatest of all the miracles.

"Mirages" (1891)

First published as the 26th of 31 poems in *Good-Bye My Fancy* (1891); then in "Second Annex: Good-Bye My Fancy" for the "Death-bed" printing of *Leaves of Grass* (1892).

A parenthetical note following the title states that the poem is remembered "verbatim after a supper-talk out doors in Nevada with two old miners." The mirages are scenes one of the miners describes to Whitman, everything from weddings and funerals to trials in courts and "returns of long-absent sons," all seen by Nevada miners "in the sky-edge" or "on the hill-tops," scenes imagined perhaps but real enough to the miners.

The fact that Whitman was never in Nevada does not detract from the story he tells in this poem.

"Mississippi at Midnight, The" (1848)

First published in the NEW ORLEANS CRESCENT (March 6, 1848); an "early poem" *not* later published in *Leaves of Grass*. It is most accessible now in Francis Murphy (editor), *Walt Whitman: The Complete Poems* (Penguin Books, 1996).

"Mother and Babe" (1865)

First published in *Drum-Taps* (1865); then in the "Drum-Taps" annex to *Leaves of Grass* (1867); it was then printed separately (1871); and it was the 19th of 29 poems in the "By The Roadside" cluster for the sixth edition (1881).

The poet was caught by the impression left on him in seeing a "sleeping babe nestling the breast of its mother." He studies "them long and long," moved by the life-giving forces at work in the scene.

"My Boys and Girls" (1844)

Nonfiction sketch, first published in the ROVER (April 20, 1844). The essay is most accessible now in *Walt Whitman: The Early Poems and the Fiction*, edited by Thomas L. Brasher (New York University Press, 1963).

Brasher refers to the piece as a "somewhat allegorical sketch," but the "boys and girls" Whitman writes about are his own brothers and sisters or young friends. The closest he comes to extended meaning is in wishing at the end of the piece that as we grow older we can still retain our love for children, "can yet keep *the within* cheerful and youthful." That, Whitman says, is "the great secret of warding off all that is unenviable in old age."

"My Canary Bird" (1888)

First published in the NEW YORK HERALD (March 2, 1888); then in *November Boughs* (1888); and it was the ninth of 65 poems in the "First Annex: Sands at Seventy" cluster for the "Death-bed" printing of *Leaves of Grass* (1892).

In his old age Whitman refers to his soul as a "caged bird," yet feels that the songs he still "warble[s]" are—"from thee to me" (just between you and me)—as "great" as the songs he sang in the earlier "mighty books." The poet likes to believe that these numerous small poems, written during the last four years of his life, are as good as any of the earlier ones. The next poem in "Sands at Seventy," however, is much more pessimistic. He thinks his singing voice may be cracking. See "Queries to My Seventieth Year."

"My Departure" (1839)

First published in the LONG ISLAND DEMOCRAT (November 27, 1839); an "early poem" *not* later published in *Leaves of Grass*. It is most accessible now in Francis Murphy (editor), *Walt Whitman: The Complete Poems* (Penguin Books, 1996).

"My Legacy" (1872)

First published as an epigraph titled "Souvenirs of Democracy" in the pamphlet *As a Strong Bird on Pinions Free* (1872); it received its present title and was the seventh of 17 poems in the "Songs of Parting" cluster for the sixth edition of *Leaves of Grass* (1881).

The "business man" has a legacy to leave to family and friends, but the poet has "Nor houses nor lands, nor tokens of gems or gold for my friends," yet with his love, he says in the last line, "I bind together and bequeath in this bundle of songs." Whitman always believed his poems were his greatest legacy, even his best biography.

"My Picture-Gallery" (1880)

First published in the AMERICAN magazine (October 30, 1880); then as the 37th of 38 poems in the "Autumn Rivulets" cluster for the sixth edition of *Leaves of Grass* (1881).

The "Picture-Gallery" is the mind of the poet: "In a little house keep I pictures suspended, it is not a fix'd house, / It is round, it is only a few inches from one side to the other; . . ." The gallery is full of pictures, "the tableaus of life . . . and . . . the groupings of death; . . ." And from these pictures are developed the poems.

"Myself and Mine" (1860)

First published as "Leaves of Grass, No. 10" in the third edition of *Leaves of Grass* (1860); then as "Leaves of Grass, No. 2" (1867); it received its present title for the fifth edition (1871); and it was the fifth of seven poems in the "Birds of Passage" cluster for the sixth edition (1881). The poem is in 35 lines.

By declaring for himself independence and self-assurance, the poet expresses the need for all people to be independent and self-assured. And he argues for the revolutionary spirit: "Let others praise eminent men and hold up peace," he says, "I hold up agitation and conflict, / I praise no eminent man, I rebuke to his face the one that was thought most worthy." Whitman is revolutionary in the sense that he believes loyalty comes best from criticism, even of the most popular men of the time. He would go even further by aiming his criticism precisely at those most "eminent," perhaps merely to keep them honest.

He says a few lines later that he would also let others "dispose of questions." He would prefer to "arouse unanswerable questions." For the true philosopher, only unanswerable questions are worth asking. And he suggests that the world would be better off if people listened to their "enemies" rather than to their "friends." Friends have the same basic beliefs or they wouldn't be friends;

enemies can present different, and perhaps even better, beliefs.

This revolutionary spirit requires, however, that the poet urges that no one should follow him, that everyone should be as independent, as capable of thinking for him or her self as he is. "I charge that there be no theory or school founded out of me, / I charge you to leave all free, as I have left all free."

"My 71st Year" (1889)

First published in CENTURY MAGAZINE (November 1889); it was the fifth of 31 poems in *Good-Bye My Fancy* (1891); then in "Second Annex: Good-Bye My Fancy" for the "Death-bed" printing of *Leaves of Grass* (1892).

"After surmounting" 70 years, with all its "chances, changes, losses, sorrows," the poet now, in old age and like some "broken soldier" after the CIVIL WAR, yet with "vital voice," is prepared to report to and salute the "Officer over all," the supreme commander.

"Mystic Trumpeter, The" (1872)

First published in KANSAS MAGAZINE (February 1872); it then appeared in the small volume of poems titled *As a Strong Bird on Pinions Free*, a supplement to the *Two Rivulets* volume of *Leaves of Grass* (1876); it was the third of 22 poems in the "From Noon to Starry Night" cluster for the sixth edition (1881). It is in eight sections and 76 lines.

The poem is about the inspiring and mystical nature of music, and Whitman may have picked the trumpet because of its long history as a musical instrument, dating back to at least the 14th century. "Bring the old pageants, show the feudal world." The poem's first two lines provide the mystical element: "Hark, some wild trumpeter, some strange musician, / Hovering unseen in air, vibrates capricious tunes to-night."

The poet wants to "translate" the trumpeter's music, telling him at the beginning of Section 3:

> Blow trumpeter free and clear, I follow
>   thee, . . .
> Thy song expands my numb'd imbonded spirit,
>   thou freest, launchest me,
> Floating and basking upon heaven's lake.

He sees the mystic trumpeter as one who has played his instrument over and above the whole of human history, including over the extremes of love and war: "Blow again trumpeter—conjure war's alarums" (Section 6).

At the beginning of Section 7, the poem becomes metaphoric: "methinks I am myself the instrument thou playest." The rest of the section shows the sometimes depressed feelings of the poet: "And now thy sullen notes send darkness through me." The poet visualizes all the evil of history, "the enslaved, the overthrown, the hurt, the opprest of the whole earth." The "foe," evil, seems "victorious." Yet even then the poet feels his own Pride, Endurance, and Resolution "unshaken to the last."

As so often happens in Whitman's poems, the final section here (Section 8) brings hope out of despair, and the poet summarizes the mystical experience and looks once more at the joy of living.

> Joy! joy! in freedom, worship, love! joy in the
>   ecstasy of life!
> Enough to merely be! enough to breathe!
> Joy! joy! all over joy!

The reader is reminded of earlier *Leaves of Grass* themes, particularly that in life it is "Enough to merely be."

"Native Moments" (1860)

First appeared as the eighth poem in the "Enfans d'Adam" cluster for the third edition of *Leaves of Grass* (1860); it received its present title and became the 12th of 16 poems in the "Children of Adam" cluster for the fourth edition (1867) and for all subsequent editions.

"Native" in the title suggests the natural in all people; the poet would shun the moral values forced on him by society in favor of "libidinous joys only." He prefers to "consort with Nature's darlings," those who are "coarse and rank"; he believes in "loose delights" and "midnight orgies." And he ends the poem by repeating a thematic element for all of *Leaves of Grass;* he would be the poet for all of the world's "shunn'd" people. "I will play a part no longer," he says; "why should I exile myself from my companions?" And he promises to be more to them "than to any of the rest."

Navesink

See "Fancies at Navesink."

"Nay, Tell Me Not To-day the Publish'd Shame"   (1873)

First published in the NEW YORK DAILY GRAPHIC (March 5, 1873); it was the seventh of 13 poems in the "Old Age Echoes" cluster for the first posthumous printing of *Leaves of Grass* (1897), added by one of Whitman's executors, Horace TRAUBEL.

Subtitled *"Winter of 1873, Congress in Session,"* this poem is about the scandals of the Crédit Mobilier of America and the involvement of the U.S. Congress in the scandal. The Crédit Mobilier was a group of leaders of the Union Pacific Railroad who, in the mid-1860s and early 1870s, made huge profits during the building of rail lines and then paid off members of Congress in case there were questions of illegal or unethical practices involved. Congress then raised the salaries of the president and other government officials in what looked also like a further unethical act.

Whitman was clearly appalled at reading in the local newspapers about the "publish'd shame." He seems most concerned, however, for the "noiseless mothers, sisters, [and] wives" of the shamed members of Congress.

"New Year's Day"   (1892)

First published in the HOME JOURNAL (March 30, 1892); an "early poem" not published until the year of the poet's death and *not* published in *Leaves of Grass.* It is most accessible now in Francis Murphy (editor), *Walt Whitman: The Complete Poems* (Penguin Books, 1996).

"Night on the Prairies" (1860)

First appeared as "Leaves of Grass, No. 15" in the third edition of *Leaves of Grass* (1860); it became "Leaves of Grass, No. 3" in the fourth edition (1867); it received its present title in the "Passage to India" supplement to the fifth edition (1871); and it was the 14th of 18 poems in the "Whispers of Heavenly Death" cluster for the sixth edition (1881).

Although Whitman had not been to the prairies when he wrote this poem, he nevertheless uses the image of a "night on the prairies" as a metaphor for even larger thoughts: "Now I absorb immortality and peace, / I admire death and test propositions." The poem's last two lines sum up what the poet has learned: "O I see now that life cannot exhibit all to me, as the day cannot, / I see that I am to wait for what will be exhibited by death."

It is not just the vastness of the prairies but also the seemingly enhanced vastness of the night that inspires the poet's largest thoughts, especially the thought of death. He will have to wait for death to understand death's mystery.

"Noiseless Patient Spider, A" (1868)

First published in the BROADWAY MAGAZINE (London) (October 1868), the third of five poems under the general title "Whispers of Heavenly Death"; it then appeared with the "Whispers of Heavenly Death" cluster in the "Passage to India" supplement to *Leaves of Grass* (1871); and it was the 11th of 18 poems in the "Whispers" cluster for the sixth edition (1881).

"A Noiseless Patient Spider" is in two stanzas, five lines each, in an accentual rhythm pattern, the second stanza mirroring the form of the first (see ACCENTUAL VERSE). The first stanza describes the spider, which patiently "launched forth filament, filament, filament, out of itself, / Ever unreeling them, ever tirelessly speeding them," the result of its natural instinct. In the second stanza, this image is turned into a metaphor for the poet's soul, which "stand[s]"

> Surrounded, detached, in measureless oceans
>   of space,
> Ceaselessly musing, venturing, throwing,
>   seeking the spheres to connect them,
> Till the bridge you will need be form'd, till the
>   ductile anchor hold,
> Till the gossamer thread you fling catch
>   somewhere, O my soul.

Whatever the instincts of the spider, the soul also reaches out into "oceans of space": for faith, for security, for companionship, perhaps for God, something to "anchor" to. It is as close to perfection as poetic comparisons get, both the spider and the soul seeking out of patience, noiselessness, and, above all, loneliness, for security in an insecure world.

"No Labor-Saving Machine" (1860)

Titled "Calamus No. 33" in the third edition of *Leaves of Grass* (1860); it received its present title (1867); it was the 26th of 39 poems in the "Calamus" cluster for the sixth edition (1881).

Whitman shows a bit of false humility in this poem, concerned as he seems to be that he has never produced a "labor-saving machine" or made a "discovery," nor will he "leave behind . . . any

wealthy bequest to found a hospital or library." He has merely produced, he writes, "a few carols vibrating through the air I leave, / For comrades and lovers."

Whitman certainly knew the value of his poetry, but he was no doubt discouraged by the poor public reception of his poems during the 1850s, and he seems to suggest in this poem that he would be satisfied if his poems were appreciated merely by his few personal friends, his "comrades and lovers."

"Not Heat Flames Up and Consumes" (1860)

Titled "Calamus No. 14" in the third edition of *Leaves of Grass* (1860); it received its present title for the fourth edition (1867); and it was the 13th of 39 poems in the "Calamus" cluster for the sixth edition (1881).

Nothing "flames up and consumes," the poet suggests in this 10-line poem, "more than the flames of me, consuming, burning for his love whom I love." Like the tide at sea, he never gives up, he says. He is like the clouds, "borne through the open air, . . . / Wafted in all directions O love, for friendship, for you." Placement in the "Calamus" cluster makes this poem one of the most romantic of the poems of love between one man and another.

"Not Heaving from my Ribb'd Breast Only" (1860)

Titled "Calamus No. 6" in the third edition of *Leaves of Grass* (1860); it received the present title (1867); and it was the sixth of 39 poems in the "Calamus" cluster for the sixth edition (1881).

The source of "adhesiveness" is the central thought in this poem, which provides a catalog of sources for love that adhesiveness is "Not." It is, instead, according to Whitman, comradeship, fraternal love, and a love that lasts beyond the grave.

"Not in any or all of them [ideas of other kinds of love] O adhesiveness! O pulse of my life! / Need I that you exist and show yourself any more than in these songs."

Adhesiveness, the adhering nature of love between two men, the friendship that grows among men, that is the chief source of both male love and of the brotherhood of men. And it is in these "songs," these poetic leaves that show the poet's lasting friendship, his adhesiveness.

"Not Meagre, Latent Boughs Alone" (1887)

First published in LIPPINCOTT'S MAGAZINE (November 1887); then in *November Boughs* (1888); and it was the 58th of 65 poems in the "First Annex: Sands at Seventy" cluster for the "Death-bed" printing of *Leaves of Grass* (1892).

Whitman envisions in this five-line poem a time when his poems, his "verdant leaves," would "some future spring, some summer—[burst] forth . . . like scented roses blooming." The poet's vision of America's future included people reading his poems.

"Not My Enemies Ever Invade Me" (1865)

Cut from *Leaves of Grass* after first appearing in the *Sequel to Drum-Taps* (1865) and in the fourth edition of *Leaves* (1867).

"Not the Pilot" (1860)

First appeared untitled as part of a group of poems titled "Debris" in the third edition of *Leaves of Grass* (1860); it then became a separate poem with its present title (1867); and it was the 19th of 43 poems in the "Drum-Taps" cluster for the sixth edition (1881).

Whitman suggests in this five-line poem that neither a ship's pilot trying to bring his ship into port, "though beaten back and many times baffled," nor a "pathfinder penetrating inland weary and long," has a greater charge on himself than the poet of America; he is thinking of himself here: "More than I have charged myself, heeded or unheeded, to compose a march for these States, / For a battle-call, rousing to arms if need be, years, centuries hence."

The poet's path to poetry is fraught with as many difficulties as is that of a ship's pilot or that of a pathfinder. Although this idea may be true there is more of the poet's ego showing in this poem than in "Song of Myself," where he is bragging for all of humanity, rather than for just for himself.

"Not Youth Pertains to Me" (1865)

First appeared in the *Drum-Taps* volume (1865) and under this title throughout its publication history in *Leaves of Grass;* it was the 29th of 43 poems in the "Drum-Taps" cluster for the sixth edition (1881).

In the middle lines of this eight-line poem, Whitman uses a form of the word *inure* three times, the word indicating that he has toughened his senses toward the CIVIL WAR and its casualties. He has become accustomed to the violence.

"In the learn'd coterie sitting constrain'd and still, for learning inures not to me, / Beauty, knowledge, inure not to me—yet there are two or three things inure to me." He has done three things that have toughened him to the war: he has "nourished the wounded," he has "sooth'd many a dying soldier," and he has "composed these songs." He has overcome the shock of seeing wounded and dying youths by specializing in these three occupations.

November Boughs (1888)

A large-format book of 140 pages, published separately by David MCKAY at 23 South Ninth Street in Philadelphia (1888). It is uniform in format and style with *Good-Bye My Fancy,* published two years later. *November Boughs* consisted of a "Preface" entitled "A Backward Glance O'er Travel'd Roads," 20 essays on literature and life, and 65 poems in two clusters: "Sands at Seventy" and "Fancies at Navesink." The prose works included essays on Shakespeare, Robert Burns, Tennyson, and Abraham LINCOLN.

The poems became "First Annex: Sands at Seventy" in the "Death-bed" printing of *Leaves of Grass* (1892). It was titled "First Annex" because *Leaves* was unchanged from the sixth edition (1881) and Whitman wanted any additions to the 1881 text to be included at the back of any new printings. See "First Annex: Sands at Seventy."

The *November Boughs* poems and essays clearly reflect Whitman's concern that he is in the "November" of his years, writing about his life, happy with what he has accomplished as a poet but not quite satisfied with his success in getting across his ideas about democracy and his hopes for the future of America. He reminds readers of his originally stated purpose in the *Leaves of Grass* poems: to use his own personality as a touchstone for showing what Americans are capable of accomplishing through the power of democracy.

Whitman was not popular as a poet, in part because 19th-century readers could not grasp his FREE VERSE technique, even though the very freedom of his style merged comfortably with the "meaning" of his poems, especially those poems that spoke to American democracy.

"Now Finalè to the Shore" (1871)

First appeared in the fifth edition of *Leaves of Grass* (1871); it was the 16th of 17 poems in the "Songs of Parting" cluster for the sixth edition (1881).

This poem is Whitman's vision of his "finalè and farewell, / Now Voyager depart, (much, much for thee is yet in store,) . . ." What is ahead for the poet is death and its adventures, experiences that the poet has been looking forward to throughout the poems in the "Songs of Parting" cluster.

"Now Lift Me Close" (1860)

Cut from *Leaves of Grass* after first appearing as "Leaves of Grass, No. 24" in the third edition (1860), and under its present title (1867).

"Now Precedent Songs, Farewell" (1888)

First appeared in *November Boughs* (1888); and it was the 62nd of 65 poems in the "First Annex: Sands at Seventy" cluster for the "Death-bed" printing of *Leaves of Grass* (1892).

Whitman lists several of his "precedent songs," poems published during his more prolific years as a poet. He gives 14 titles, including "Song of Myself," "Calamus," and "Beat! Beat! Drums." These poems represent for the poet his "life's hot pulsing blood."

Whitman wrote a footnote meant to explain this poem and the next ("An Evening Lull") on the same page in *November Boughs,* saying that these two poems were "eked out during an afternoon, June, 1888, in my seventieth year, at a critical spell of illness. . . . I feel in them an end and close of all." He would live another three years, but it is clear from this and other similar notes he wrote during the late 1880s that he believed the illness he was then suffering would end in death.

"O Captain! My Captain!" (1865)

First published in the (New York) SATURDAY PRESS (November 4, 1865); in the "Sequel to Drum-Taps" pamphlet (1865); then with three other LINCOLN poems in the "Passage to India" supplement under the general heading "President Lincoln's Burial Hymn" for the fifth edition of *Leaves of Grass* (1871); and it was the second of four poems under the new heading "Memories of President Lincoln" for the sixth edition (1881). It was considerably revised between 1865 and 1871.

This is probably the most recognized of all of Whitman's poems but also one of the most sentimental and one of the least satisfactory. It was an "occasional" poem, written in a hurry following Lincoln's assassination, and Whitman regretted its popularity for the rest of his life. He told his friend and biographer Horace TRAUBEL, "I'm almost sorry I ever wrote the poem." In contrast, "When Lilacs Last in the Dooryard Bloom'd" was written over a six-month period following the president's death and became one of Whitman's greatest poems.

Each of the three stanzas of "O Captain!" is composed of four lines of 12 or 13 syllables rhyming a-a-b-b, followed by four lines of five or six syllables rhyming x-c-x-c—the poem is one of the few rhyming poems in *Leaves of Grass*.

"Ode" (1846)

First published in the *BROOKLYN DAILY EAGLE* (July 2, 1846); an "early poem" *not* later published in *Leaves of Grass*. It is most accessible now in Francis Murphy (editor), *Walt Whitman: The Complete Poems* (Penguin Books, 1996).

"Offerings" (1860)

First published as the seventh stanza of "Debris" in the third edition of *Leaves of Grass* (1860); it was titled "Picture" (1867); and it received its present title and was part of the "Passage to India" cluster (1871); and it was the 28th of 29 poems in the "By The Roadside" cluster for the sixth edition (1881).

The poem is about the "offerings" given freely by each of a "thousand perfect men and women" to each other and to their own "cluster of friends"; it is no doubt the gift of love, because this special gift is mentioned in a number of other Whitman poems.

"Of Him I Love Day and Night" (1860)

First published as "Calamus No. 17" in the third edition of *Leaves of Grass* (1860); under its present title and with the "Calamus" cluster for the fourth edition (1867); it was then moved to the "Whispers of Heavenly Death" cluster (1871); and it was the fourth of 18 poems in the "Whispers" cluster for the sixth edition (1881).

In a dream the poet searches for "Him I love" but discovers that nothing is as it should be. The one he searches for is not where he was buried, and the "houses full of life were equally full of death, . . . / The streets, the shipping, the places of amusement, the Chicago, Boston, Philadelphia, the Mannahatta, were as full of the dead as of the living."

So he disregards "burial-places" and is more satisfied with the confusion of the life and death images he has in his imagination than in places of either life or death.

"Of Many a Smutch'd Deed Reminiscent" (1897)

First published as the ninth of 13 poems in the "Old Age Echoes" cluster for the first posthumous printing of *Leaves of Grass* (1897), added by one of Whitman's executors, Horace TRAUBEL.

In this three-line poem Whitman suggests that in spite of his memories of "wickedness" and "smutch'd" deeds, he also remembers his experiences with "joys of life," and he awaits death "with perfect equanimity," knowing that he loves "him" and is loved in return. Death is not to be dreaded when one has love for someone whose "boundless love" is returned.

"Of That Blithe Throat of Thine" (1885)

First published in *HARPER'S NEW MONTHLY MAGAZINE* (January 1885); then in *November Boughs*

(1888); and it was the 33rd of 65 poems in the "First Annex: Sands at Seventy" cluster for the "Death-bed" printing of *Leaves of Grass* (1892).

In an epigraph to this poem Whitman says that while "Greely the explorer" was searching for a route to the North Pole he heard "the song of a single snow-bird merrily sounding over the desolation." It is a reference to a disastrous trip made by the great Arctic explorer Major Adolfus Washington Greely (1844–1935), leader of a group of 25 Americans sent to set up an observation base at 81° latitude north in Franklin Bay.

After two years of scientific work, a supply ship failed to show up, and Greely and his men started south in a flotilla of small boats. On June 20, 1884, the seven survivors, including Greely, were found in a tent, rescued and described as "veritable zombies." The story made the front pages of American newspapers.

In this nine-line poem Whitman places himself in Greely's place, hearing the "solitary bird" and learning from it something of the nature of the Arctic's "chilling drifts." If Greely actually heard the snow-bird it must have been one of the few pleasures of the three-year trip.

"Of the Terrible Doubt of Appearances" (1860)

Titled "Calamus No. 7" in the third edition of *Leaves of Grass* (1860); it received its present title (1867); and it was the seventh of 39 poems in the "Calamus" cluster for the sixth edition (1881).

Whitman's thought in this poem is we are too easily "deluded" by appearances: "Of the uncertainty after all, that we may be deluded, / reliance and hope are but speculations after all." What is "real" and whether there is life after death are questions that, because they cannot be answered, should be treated with indifference. It is too often impossible to separate reality from the appearance of reality.

> I cannot answer the question of appearances or
> that of identity beyond the grave,

But I walk or sit indifferent, I am satisfied,
He ahold of my hand has completely satisfied
  me.

What matters, he says, is the love of comrades. "Indifference," however, to unanswerable questions contradicts Whitman's belief that, for the philosopher, only unanswerable questions are worth thinking about.

"O Hymen! O Hymenee!" (1860)

First appeared as "No. 13" in the "Enfans d'Adam" poems for the third edition of *Leaves of Grass* (1860); it received its present title in the fourth edition (1867); it was the 10th of 16 poems in the "Children of Adam" cluster for the sixth edition (1881). The poem's title may be translated unpoetically from the French as "O married man! O married woman!" Hymen was the Greek god of marriage.

This four-line poem is an evocation to marriage: ". . . why do you tantalize me thus? / O why sting me for a swift moment only?" Is it that marriage is such a blissful time that it seems to last a moment only and that anything beyond that would suggest death?

More likely, however, since nearly all of the poems in the "Children of Adam" cluster carry images of sexual intercourse, Whitman is probably making a play on the word "hymen," which means also a virgin's maidenhead. The image then is of the briefness of the "sting" at the loss of virginity. "Is it because if you continued beyond the swift moment you would soon certainly kill me?" The sex act and death are often paired in literary analogies.

"Old Age Echoes" (1897)

Cluster title for 13 poems added by Whitman executor Horace TRAUBEL for the first posthumous printing of *Leaves of Grass* (1897). It is parenthetically subtitled (*Posthumous Additions*). Most if not all of the poems seem to be fragments of other works and cut or rejected by Whitman for his final version of *Leaves of Grass*.

Traubel wrote "An Executor's Diary Note, 1891" to go with the additional poems. In the "Note" Traubel quotes a conversation he had with Whitman on an unspecified date in 1891 during which the poet gave the biographer permission to publish additional poems and provided Traubel with the title, "Old Age Echoes." Whitman made it clear, however, that poems added to *Leaves of Grass* after he died should be called "supplementary, . . . leaving the book complete as I left it, consecutive to the point I left off, marking always an unmistakable, deep down, unobliteratable division line."

The most important thought in this short essay is, however, in another statement Traubel quotes Whitman as making, this concerning the future printings of *Leaves of Grass:* "In the long run the world will do as it pleases with the book. I am determined to have the world know what I was pleased to do." Interestingly enough, the "world" has kept reprintings of the "complete" poems the way Whitman wished them to be, the ordering of poems the same and very little editing of language or style. Except for the addition by editors of poems "rejected" by Whitman or poems removed by him after a second or third thought, reprintings of the complete *Leaves of Grass* are exactly like the 1892 edition, the additional or "supplementary" poems always printed at the back of the book.

Nine of the 13 poems in "Old Age Echoes" are new to *Leaves of Grass,* and one poem, "To Be at All," may be an early and rejected version or part of Section 27 of "Song of Myself" for the 1855 edition of *Leaves of Grass.*

The order for the 13 poems is as follows: "To Soar in Freedom and in Fullness of Power," "Then Shall Perceive," "The Few Drops Known," "One Thought Ever at the Fore," "While Behind All, Firm and Erect," "A Kiss to the Bride," "Nay, Tell Me Not To-day the Publish'd Shame," "Supplement Hours," "Of Many a Smutch'd Deed Reminiscent," "To Be at All," "Death's Valley," "On the Same Picture," and "A Thought of Columbus."

Traubel says that "there is no reason for doubt that 'A Thought of Columbus,' closing 'Old Age Echoes,' was W. W.'s last deliberate composition, dating December, 1891."

"Old Age's Lambent Peaks" (1888)

First published in CENTURY MAGAZINE (September 1888); then in *November Boughs* (1888); and it was the 64th of 65 poems in the "First Annex: Sands at Seventy" cluster for the "Death-bed" printing of *Leaves of Grass* (1892).

There are a few times, Whitman suggests in this poem, when old age has "lambent peaks," times when there is a soft, clear light shining on something important: "Objects and groups, bearings, faces, reminiscences," perhaps an "atmosphere," a "point of view," or a "situation." Whitman is referring to the "soft, clear light" he feels shining on his impending death.

"Old Age's Ship; and Crafty Death's" (1890)

First published in CENTURY MAGAZINE (February 1890); it was the eighth of 31 poems in *Good-Bye My Fancy* (1891); then in "Second Annex: Good-Bye My Fancy" for the "Death-bed" printing of *Leaves of Grass* (1892).

In spite of the ship's "old age," it can still put on "top-sail, top-gallant and royal studding-sails," and "take to the open! . . . the deepest, freest waters" in racing away from death. This is a race that Whitman feels he is himself now making. This idea contradicts the theme of "Sail Out for Good, Eidólon Yacht!," the first poem in the "Good-Bye My Fancy" cluster, in which the poet envisions with pleasure his final voyage out to sea, *toward* death.

"Old Chants" (1891)

First published in the New York TRUTH (March 19, 1891); it was the 16th of 31 poems in *Good-Bye My Fancy* (1891); then in "Second Annex: Good-Bye My Fancy" for the "Death-bed" printing of *Leaves of Grass* (1892).

All the "old chants" and chanters are cataloged in this poem: Egyptian priests, Hindu epics, biblical books and prophets, the *Iliad* and *Odyssey*, Hesiod, Sophocles, Merlin, Arthur, Roland, the Nibelungen, and so forth.

Whitman is responding to the "Mother of All" muses, who has asked him to name for her, "before thou goest [before he dies] each ancient poet." Whitman writes, as part of his response: "(Of many debts incalculable, / Haply our New World's chiefest debt is to old poems.)"

Whitman envisions the "great shadowy groups gathering around" the "Mother of All," who is watching and pleased with what she sees of his review of the greatest of all poets.

(1865); and it was the fourth of 38 poems in the "Autumn Rivulets" cluster for the sixth edition (1881). The 18-line poem remained unchanged throughout its *Leaves of Grass* printing history.

Ireland, "an isle of wondrous beauty," is "mourning her shrouded hope and heir," a country devastated by the potato famine (1846–50) and "Once a queen, now lean and tatter'd seated on the ground." But Whitman urges the Irish to not despair, because "What you wept for was translated, pass'd from the grave, . . . / And now with rosy and new blood, / Moves to-day in a new country."

More than a million Irish, faced with the poverty of their homeland, emigrated to America during the 1850s and now, as Whitman suggests in the last line, are helping to build a new republic.

"Old Ireland" (1861)

First published in the NEW YORK LEADER (November 2, 1861); it appeared in the *Drum-Taps* volume

Whitman with his nurse, Warren Fritzenger, in Camden, New Jersey, 1890 *(Library of Congress, Prints and Photographs Division)*

"Old Man's Thought of School, An" (1874)

First published in the NEW YORK DAILY GRAPHIC (November 3, 1874), it was then in the *Two Rivulets* volume of *Leaves of Grass* (1876), and later the 33rd of 38 poems in the "Autumn Rivulets" cluster for the sixth edition (1881).

A headnote for the *Daily Graphic* printing reads, "The following poem was recited personally by the author Saturday afternoon, October 31, at the inauguration of the fine new COOPER PUBLIC SCHOOL, Camden, New Jersey." The subtitle in the final version reads, *"For the Inauguration of a Public School, Camden, New Jersey, 1874."*

Whitman was 55 when he read this poem at the Cooper School: "An old man's thought of school, / An old man gathering youthful memories and blooms that youth itself cannot." It is a new public school in Camden, so the poet reminds his listeners that just as a church is not a "pile of brick and mortar," but the preacher and the people, so a school is not the building but the teacher and pupils. The George FOX he quotes concerning the church is the founder of the Society of Friends, beginning on Cape Cod in 1657.

"Old Salt Kossabone" (1888)

First published in the *New York Herald* (February 25, 1888); then in *November Boughs* (1888); and it was the 36th of 65 poems in the "First Annex: Sands at Seventy" cluster for the "Death-bed" printing of *Leaves of Grass* (1892). Kossabone was Whitman's great-grandfather on his mother's side.

Whitman writes about the death of the 90-year-old "old salt." He lived with his "married grandchild, Jenny" in a house on a hill overlooking a bay and a distant cape. Every day the old sailor watches the ships sail by, and one afternoon he watches a ship struggle to make it around the cape. It finally does, with a change of breeze and luck. He sees that "she's free" and then dies in his "great arm chair," perhaps from the tension he had felt and remembered.

"Old War-Dreams" (1865)

First appeared as "Clouds Descending, in Midnight Sleep" in the *Drum-Taps* volume (1865); then titled "In Midnight Sleep" as part of the "Ashes of Soldiers" cluster in the fifth edition of *Leaves of Grass* (1871); it received its present title and was the 17th of 22 poems in the "From Noon to Starry Night" cluster for the sixth edition (1881).

Originally a "Drum-Taps" poem, this descriptive "dream" is more like a postwar nightmare: "Of the dead on their backs with arms extended wide, / I dream, I dream, I dream." Whitman certainly had firsthand knowledge of soldiers dead or dying, the poem following as it did his experiences working in Washington hospitals during the Civil War.

"O Living Always, Always Dying" (1860)

First appeared as "Calamus No. 27" in the third edition of *Leaves of Grass* (1860); it received its present title for the fourth edition (1867); and it was the 12th of 18 poems in the "Whispers of Heavenly Death" cluster for the sixth edition (1881).

The poet becomes the living, the dying, and the dead in this six-line poem that reflects the image of the constancy of life and death, "living always, always dying!"

"O Magnet-South" (1860)

First published as "Longings for Home" in the *Southern Literary Messenger* (July 15, 1860); then, unchanged, in the third edition of *Leaves of Grass* (1860); it received its present title and was the fifth of 22 poems in the "From Noon to Starry Night" cluster for the sixth edition (1881).

Whitman liked the South, especially after his trip to New Orleans in 1848, and it became a "magnet" for his thinking and his poetry for the rest of his life.

> O magnet-South! O glistening perfumed South! my South!
> O quick mettle, rich blood, impulse and love! good and evil! O all dear to me!
> O dear to me my birth-things—all moving things and the trees where I was born—the grains, plants, rivers, . . .

Whitman was born on Long Island and lived nearly all of his life in New York or New Jersey, so the lines above tend to give the poem universality. It is personal only in the way so many of his poems are personal; the poet *becomes* what he is writing about. In this poem he *becomes* a Southerner, in love with the people and places, the rivers and fields. This universal quality helps to explain his caring for soldiers of both South and North during his Civil War work in Washington hospitals.

See also "Mannahatta," the next poem in the "From Noon to Starry Night" cluster and one of his love poems to New York City.

"O Me! O Life!" (1865)

First published in the *Drum-Taps* volume (1865); it was the ninth of 29 poems in the "By The Roadside" cluster for the sixth edition of *Leaves of Grass* (1881). It remained virtually unchanged throughout its publication history, with one significant exception, noted below.

Whitman says in this poem that with all that happens during one's lifetime, there is always the question: ". . . O me! so sad, recurring—what good amid these, O me, O life?" And his "Answer": "That you are here—that life exists and identity, / That the powerful play goes on, and you may contribute a verse."

The poet suggests that even with occasional moments of self-pity or depression, life *is* worth living. One "may" even "contribute" a small part in the play; one "verse" would be sufficient.

It is interesting to note that Whitman changed one word for the final, 1881, version. The word "may" in "may contribute" in the last line had been "will" in all previous printings, an indication of a slight loss of confidence on the part of the poet.

"Once I pass'd Through a Populous City" (1860)

First appeared untitled as the ninth poem in the "Enfans d'Adam" cluster for the third edition of *Leaves of Grass* (1860); it received its title and became the 13th of 16 poems in the "Children of Adam" cluster for the fourth edition (1867) and for all subsequent editions.

The city is not identified in this seven-line poem—although it is probably New Orleans, which Whitman visited in 1848—but the poet tells what he remembers most about the city: "a woman I casually met there who detain'd me for love of me," and that she is still on his mind. "I see her close beside me with silent lips sad and tremulous."

According to unattributed Whitman mythology, the poet once spoke of an affair with a Creole woman in New Orleans, by whom he had one or more children. But he gave out no names, and the only biographer who attempted to locate Whitman progeny found none.

"One Hour to Madness and Joy" (1860)

Sixth poem for the "Enfans d'Adam" cluster in the third edition of *Leaves of Grass* (1860); it became the sixth of 16 poems in the "Children of Adam" cluster for the sixth edition (1881).

The "one hour" is devoted to the sex act, the "mystic deliria," and to a wish "to return to Paradise," to the Garden of Eden, where sex was not a sin. The act of sex is a force for freedom from the sin imposed on it by society: "To drive free! to love free! to dash reckless and dangerous! . . . / To be lost if it must be so!" It is an hour of freedom from sin, and it helps also to make one feel more psychologically "sufficient."

The poet returns to the title imagery in the final two lines: "To feed the remainder of life with one hour of fulness and freedom! / With one brief hour of madness and joy." This may be read, perhaps, as Whitman's poetic plea for a more liberal attitude toward freer sexual relations between men and women. See also "I Sing the Body Electric."

"One Song, America, Before I Go" (1872)

First appeared as the first of two introductory poems in *As a Strong Bird on Pinions Free* (1872) and in the 1876 printing of *Leaves of Grass*; it was then revised and became the opening section of "Thou Mother with Thy Equal Brood" for the sixth edition (1881), but it was cut from that poem and did not appear again.

"One's-Self I Sing" (1867)

First appeared in a shorter version as the frontispiece in the fourth edition of *Leaves of Grass*

(1867); the present version, under its present title, was the first poem in the "Inscriptions" cluster for the fifth edition (1871); and it remained in that position throughout the remainder of its publication history.

This eight-line poem presents the central theme for the entire *Leaves of Grass:*

> One's-self I sing, a simple separate person,
> Yet utter the word Democratic, the word
>   En-Masse.

There are two Walt Whitmans in this and other "Inscriptions" poems: the poet himself and a third-person character created as a metaphor for all people in all space and time. Who I am, Whitman seems to be saying, may be taken as a mere image of all people in all time, all equal, as they must be in a democracy; these thoughts that I have may be your (the reader's) thoughts as well; if I seem to be bragging, it is not for myself alone that I brag but for all people, the "En-Masse." Everyone is capable of having the same thoughts, of having the confidence (or egoism) required for equality. In later poems this second Walt Whitman will take readers into both past and future and into all parts of the world, providing mystical examples of how this bragging on behalf of the en-masse works.

The poet sees himself as a representative of all people but also as a poet, a "singer," of their equality: "The Female equally with the Male I Sing. . . . / The Modern Man I Sing." There is also a spiritual element that grows of the mystical and which will become thematic later also. No one who has ever lived or will live is better than I, nor am I better than they.

"One Thought Ever at the Fore" (1897)

First published as the fourth of 13 poems in the "Old Age Echoes" cluster for the first posthumous printing of *Leaves of Grass* (1897), added by one of Whitman's executors, Horace TRAUBEL.

This three-line poem supports Whitman's theme of the value of death, one of the major themes in *Leaves of Grass.* The great voyage is to death. It is a voyage on which all people in all time sail in a "Divine Ship," all "bound to the same destination." See—for perhaps the best example in *Leaves* of the same theme at work—"Passage to India."

"One Wicked Impulse!" (1845)

Short story, first published in the *United States Magazine and Democratic Review* (July–August 1845; see DEMOCRATIC REVIEW, THE), under the title "Revenge and Requital: A Tale of a Murderer Escaped." The tale is most accessible now in *Walt Whitman: The Early Poems and the Fiction,* edited by Thomas L. Brasher (New York University Press, 1963).

Marsh, a distant relative and client of Adam Covert's, dies "somewhat suddenly" and leaves his children, Philip and Esther, "and some little property," in the care of Covert. He is described as a New York lawyer, "tolerably well-known" among other lawyers, middle-aged but not particularly successful because most of what he has gained he has done by "trickery," rather than by "the legitimate and honorable exercise of his profession."

Marsh writes his own will, but Covert inserts provisions that give him "an almost arbitrary control over the property and over those for whom it was designed." Covert feels so in control that he tries to seduce Marsh's daughter, Esther, into marrying him, since he had changed the will to include marriage for Esther as essential to receiving her share of her father's money. Esther is described as "a plain, and somewhat devotional young woman." Nevertheless, she has the sense to reject Covert's offer.

Esther's brother, Philip, is outraged by what his sister tells him, and, together with his own suspicions of Covert's attempts to cheat them, Philip accuses Covert of fraud and later, during a moment of "wicked impulse," murders him.

Whitman provides two endings to this story. In the original version, Philip, after traveling the world trying to escape his guilty conscience, returns to New York and helps in the care of cholera victims and, coincidentally, saves the life of one of Covert's orphaned children. In the revised version, the last paragraph reads: "Though against all the rules of story-writing, we continue our narrative . . . no further. Only to say that *the murderer* soon departed for a new field of action—that he is still living—and that this is but one of thousands of cases of unravel'd, unpunish'd crime—left, not to the tribunals of man, but to a wider power and judgment."

CHARACTERS

Adam Covert   According to the narrator, he is a New York lawyer, "tolerably well-known" among other lawyers, "a middle-aged man of rather limited means, who . . . gained more by trickery than he did in the legitimate and honorable exercise of his profession."

Covert attempts to cheat a client named Marsh and his children by adding provisions to his will that give Covert "an almost arbitrary control over the property and over those for whom it was designed." Covert even tries to seduce Marsh's daughter, Esther, into marrying him, since marriage for Esther would assure her of her share of her father's money. But she rejects Covert's offer.

Her brother, Philip, is outraged when his sister tells him about Covert's overtures, and because he already has suspicions of Covert's attempts to cheat them, Philip accuses Covert of fraud and later, during a moment of "wicked impulse," murders him.

Philip Marsh   Son of a distant relative and client of lawyer Adam Covert, his antagonist in the short story "One Wicked Impulse!" Covert cheats Marsh and his sister, Esther, of their inheritance. When Covert attempts to seduce Esther into marrying him, Philip angrily accuses him of fraud and later, during a moment of "wicked impulse," murders him.

Esther Marsh   She is described as "a plain, and somewhat devotional young woman . . . in her nineteenth year." The lawyer Covert attempts to seduce her into marrying him, having changed her father's will to include marriage as necessary for her

receiving her share of the inheritance. She rejects him and tells her brother about Covert's insult.

"On Journeys Through the States" (1860)

First appeared in the third edition of *Leaves of Grass* (1860); it was dropped from the fourth edition (1867); it was the 13th of 24 poems in the "Inscriptions" cluster for the sixth edition (1881).

Exploratory "journeys" are used often in *Leaves of Grass*, the images usually conveying a mystical experience for the traveler and reader.

> On journeys through the States we start,
> (Ay through the world, urged by these songs,
> Sailing henceforth to every land, to every sea,)
> We willing learners of all, teachers of all, and
>   lovers of all. . . .

The poems in these "leaves of grass" provide images of experience even if the reader hasn't had and will not likely have the actual experiences. "And what you effuse [what you gain] may then return as the seasons return, / And may be just as much as the seasons." Whatever comes from the experience will return in the mind of the traveler just as do the seasons. The poet might have said that the best travelers need no cameras to enhance their memories, because the mental and sense images are powerful and will suffice. See also "Starting from Paumanok" and "A Backward Glance o'er Travel'd Roads."

"On, on the Same, Ye Jocund Twain!" (1891)

First published as the fourth of 31 poems in *Good-Bye My Fancy* (1891); then in "Second Annex: Good-Bye My Fancy" for the "Death-bed" printing of *Leaves of Grass* (1892).

The jocund, pleasant or cheerful "twain" are the poet's "life and recitative," both now in songs of old age: "(My verses, written first for forenoon life, and for the summer's, autumn's spread, / I pass to snow-white hairs the same, and give to pulses winter-cool'd the same). . ." Both he and his "recitatives" are in their winter phases. In the last line, he imagines his life and poetry continuing on, even after his life has stopped and his last poems are written.

"On the Beach at Night" (1871)

First published in the "Sea-Shore Memories" cluster in the fifth edition of *Leaves of Grass* (1871); and it was the sixth of 11 poems in the "Sea-Drift" cluster for the sixth edition (1881).

This poem describes a little girl "on the beach at night," weeping because the "lord-star Jupiter" and the stars of the "delicate sisters the Pleiades," which her father has pointed out to her and described, are disappearing behind some "ravening clouds." The little girl's father has to assure her that the clouds will go away eventually and that she will see the stars again.

The poet encourages the child to wipe her tears, because the stars are "immortal, . . . they endure." For the reader, however, this scene on the beach is a metaphor for a much larger idea; "Something there is," the poet says,

> Something that shall endure longer even than
> lustrous Jupiter,
> Longer than sun or any revolving satellite,
> Or the radiant sisters the Pleiades.

Something more immortal "even than the stars . . . longer even than lustrous Jupiter." Readers are not told what that "something" is, but because the other poems in the "Sea-Drift" cluster have evoked the poet's thoughts of the soul and its meanings, readers can assume that the poet has the soul and its spiritual meanings in mind here too.

"On the Beach at Night Alone" (1856)

First published as "Clef Poem" in the second edition of *Leaves of Grass* (1856); then as "Leaves of Grass, No. 12" (1860); as "Leaves of Grass, No. 1" and thoroughly revised (1867); it then received its present title and was placed with the "Sea-Shore Memories" cluster in the *Passage to India* volume of the two-volume fifth edition (1871); and, finally, it was the eighth of 11 poems in the "Sea-Drift" cluster for the sixth edition (1881).

Whitman walked often "on the beach" as a way of creating personal thoughts which might then be turned into poems. This poem describes that process. "As I watch the bright stars shining, I think a thought of the clef of the universes and of the future." The word *clef* is not clear here, but *The Oxford English Dictionary* offers the word as an obsolete form of "cliff," indicating perhaps in this case the border between the "universes" or between the present and future, a metaphor Whitman uses in other poems as well. Or perhaps it refers to notes of music and, in this case, to the music of the spheres, which, if we could hear it, he seems to suggest, would sing of the future.

> A vast similitude interlocks all, . . .
> All souls, all living bodies though they be ever
> so different, or in different worlds, . . .
> All lives and deaths, all of the past, present,
> future,
> This vast similitude spans them, and always has
> spann'd,
> And shall forever span them and compactly
> hold and enclose them.

All things, places, and people have "similitude" (a counterpart or resemblance to others of the species), and ever have had and will continue to have. It is this interlocking of all things—equality—which the poet visualizes for the future of America.

"On the Same Picture" (1897)

First published as the 12th of 13 poems in the "Old Age Echoes" cluster for the first posthumous printing of *Leaves of Grass* (1897), added by one of Whitman's executors, Horace TRAUBEL.

As the subtitle indicates, this eight-line poem was "Intended for [the] first Stanza of 'Death's Valley,'" which preceded it in the cluster. Both poems are meant to accompany a painting titled *The Valley of the Shadow of Death,* by George Inness, at the time a well-known painter of landscapes.

"Orange Buds by Mail from Florida" (1888)

First published in the *NEW YORK HERALD* (March 19, 1888); then in *November Boughs* (1888); and it was the 55th of 65 poems in the "First Annex: Sands at Seventy" cluster for the "Death-bed" printing of *Leaves of Grass* (1892).

There is a parenthetical epigraph to this poem citing Voltaire's argument that "a ship of war and the grand OPERA were proofs enough of civilization's and France's progress." Whitman offers in this seven-line poem an even "greater" proof of civilization in that he had just received at his "plain Northern hut" in America a package from a thousand miles away, "a bunch of orange buds by mail from Florida." Whitman is bragging about America and of what it is capable, even through the mail.

"Or, from That Sea of Time" (1876)

Cut from *Leaves of Grass* after appearing in the 1876 printing.

"Osceola" (1890)

First published in *Munson's Illustrated World* (April 1890); it was the 21st of 31 poems in *Good-Bye My Fancy* (1891); then in "Second Annex: Good-Bye My Fancy" for the "Death-bed" printing of *Leaves of Grass* (1892).

Osceola was a leader among the Seminole Indians, captured during the FLORIDA WAR (1836–43), begun by the U.S. government in order to move Florida Indians to land west of the Mississippi River. Osceola died of what Whitman called a broken heart at Fort Moultrie on Sullivan's Island in Charleston, South Carolina, January 30, 1838.

A long, parenthetical epigraph to this poem describes Whitman's memory of a conversation with a U.S. Marine, returned from the Florida war in 1838, who told the poet about Osceola's death in prison at Fort Moultrie. This poem describes the last hour of the Indian's life, how he put on his "war-dress" and painted his face; he takes a final look at his wife and children and dies. This poem is, Whitman says in the last line, "a line in memory of his name and death."

"O Star of France" (1871)

First published in the *GALAXY* (June 1871); it appeared in *As a Strong Bird on Pinions Free and Other Poems* (1872); was reprinted in the *Two Rivulets* volume of the 1876 printing of *Leaves of Grass*; and it was the 31st of 38 poems in the "Autumn Rivulets" cluster for the sixth edition (1881).

Subtitled "1870–1871," this poem provides Whitman's reflections on the beauty of the France that was, the France before the Franco-Prussian War that led to the defeat of the French Army, the end of the Napoleanic empire, and the establishment of the Third Republic—plus the rise of Germany as an empire under imperialistic Prussia.

Whitman is aware that France itself was not blameless for its own losses:

> Star crucified—by traitors sold,
> Star panting o'er a land of death, heroic land,
> Strange, passionate, mocking, frivolous land. . . .

> Miserable! yet for thy errors, vanities, sins, I will
>   not now rebuke thee,
> Thy unexampled woes and pangs have quell'd
>   them all,
> And left thee sacred.

But he sees the rebirth of an even greater France:

> Again thy star O France, fair lustrous star,
> In heavenly peace, clearer, more bright than ever,
> Shall beam immortal.

In the early manuscripts, the poem's last line reads, "Shall rise immortal," providing the image of a phoenix-like revival for the nation which, Whitman remembers, was an American ally during the Revolutionary War.

"O Sun of Real Peace" (1871)

Cut from *Leaves of Grass* after first appearing under its present title in the fifth edition (1871). It had appeared first in the third edition (1860) as a 13-line revision of the final 19 lines of "Apostroph," a poem also cut after the 1876 printing of *Leaves*.

"O Tan-Faced Prairie-Boy" (1865)

First appeared in the *Drum-Taps* volume (1865), under this title and unrevised throughout its publication history in *Leaves of Grass;* it was the 32nd of 43 poems in the "Drum-Taps" cluster for the sixth edition (1881).

The "Prairie-Boy" came to the CIVIL WAR camp "with nothing to give . . . / When lo! more than all the gifts of the world you gave me." He gave the poet love. Whitman often wrote of the love he felt coming to him from the men he took care of during the war.

"Others May Praise What They Like" (1865)

First appeared in the *Drum-Taps* volume (1865); then with the "Passage to India" poems for the fifth edition (1871); and it was the 27th of 38 poems in the "Autumn Rivulets" cluster for the sixth edition (1881).

Whitman writes in this four-line poem about the value of visiting the Missouri River and the West (as he did twice), that nothing is praiseworthy "in art or aught else" unless "it has well inhaled the atmosphere of this river, also the western prairie-scent."

"Our Future Lot" (1839)

First published in the LONG ISLAND DEMOCRAT (October 31, 1839); an "early poem" *not* later published in *Leaves of Grass*. It is most accessible now in Francis Murphy (editor), *Walt Whitman: The Complete Poems* (Penguin Books, 1996). It is generally considered to be Whitman's first published poem.

"Our Old Feuillage" (1860)

First published as "Chants Democratic, No. 4" in the third edition of *Leaves of Grass* (1860); then as "American Feuillage" (1867); it received its present title and was printed as a separate poem in the sixth edition (1881).

Feuillage is, according to the *Oxford English Dictionary*, a "rare" French word meaning "foliage." Whitman certainly means "leaves" or perhaps "branches of leaves" or even "clusters of leaves." The poem seems to be both a summing up of some images he has presented in earlier poems and an invitation to readers to join in the gathering of these "leaves" of America. He is no doubt also inviting readers to discover and enjoy his own *Leaves of Grass*.

Feuillage is the foliage of America, the great and plentiful places available, much of it yet to be explored and sampled.

> Always our old feuillage!
> Always Florida's green peninsula—always the
>   priceless delta of Louisiana—always the
>   cotton-fields of Alabama and Texas,
> Always California's golden hills and hollows,
>   and the silver mountains of New Mexico—
>   always soft-breath'd Cuba, . . .

The poem is an invitation to visit these clusters of places, an invitation to Americans but also to the "old world," which is becoming more and more enchanted by the possibilities of adventures in the New World.

The poem is 83 lines long, almost entirely a catalog of places and things that remind the reader of other *Leaves of Grass* poems: "the mocking-bird . . . singing in the Great Dismal Swamp"; the "Southern fisherman fishing"; "California life, the miner, bearded, dress'd in his rude costume, . . ."; "All these states compact"; "The hawk sailing where men have not yet sail'd. . . ." The poet loves these lands and the images conjured up by his thinking about America: "O lands! all so dear to me—what you are, (whatever it is,) I putting it at random in these songs, become a part of that, whatever it is." He isn't sure what the lands are, but now he has them in his songs. And in the cataloging he often becomes part of the image: "Southward there, I screaming, with wings slow flapping, with the myriads of gulls wintering along the coasts of Florida. . . ."

Whitman summarizes the lengthy catalog at the end: "How can I but as here chanting, invite you for yourself to collect bouquets of the incomparable feuillage of these States?" He invites readers to explore for themselves and collect the foliage of America.

"Out from Behind This Mask" (1876)

First published in the *New York Tribune* (February 19, 1876); it was in the *Two Rivulets* volume for the fifth edition of *Leaves of Grass* (1876); it was the 13th of 38 poems in the "Autumn Rivulets" cluster for the sixth edition (1881). It has a parenthetical note in 1876, "(To confront My Portrait, illustrating 'the Wound-Dresser' in Leaves of Grass.)," changed to read "(To Confront a Portrait.)" for the 1881 edition.

"Portrait" refers to the W. J. Linton engraving of a photograph of Whitman by G. C. Potter, taken in 1871 and printed in the 1876 edition of *Leaves*.

The revised subtitle-note is significant, showing perhaps more humility in its final form. But the poem suggests Whitman's preference for his own poetic version of his face and self than that represented by the engraving. He also told one of his early biographers that he preferred to let his poems be his life history.

"Outlines for a Tomb" (1870)

First published under the title "Brother of all, with Generous Hand" in the *Galaxy* (January 1870); then in the fifth edition of *Leaves of Grass* (1871); it received its present title and was the 12th of 38 poems in the "Autumn Rivulets" cluster for the sixth edition (1881). Thirty of the poem's original 79 lines were cut from the final version.

The subtitle-note for this poem reads, "(G. P., Buried 1870.)." G. P. is George Peabody (1795–1869), who in 1867 established the "Peabody Fund," a $2 million endowment to aid the South in the aftermath of the Civil War. Peabody was a London banker when he died in 1869; he was returned to America for burial in January 1870.

The poem is directed to his tomb in Danvers, Massachusetts, and suggests that a "millionaire" too can live a good and exemplary life. At the end the poet wants "to the high seas launch" his "thought" of Peabody's "memory."

"Out of May's Shows Selected" (1888)

First published in the *New York Herald* (May 10, 1888); then in *November Boughs* (1888); and it was the 18th of 65 poems in the "First Annex: Sands at Seventy" cluster for the "Death-bed" printing of *Leaves of Grass* (1892).

This five-line poem is the poet's reflection on one of the "shows" of May—apple orchards, wheat fields—the "eternal, exhaustless freshness of each early morning."

"Out of the Cradle Endlessly Rocking" (1859)

Generally acknowledged to be one of Whitman's greatest poems, "Out of the Cradle Endlessly Rocking" was first published as "A Child's Reminiscence" in the SATURDAY PRESS (December 24, 1859); then as "A Word Out of the Sea" in the third edition of *Leaves of Grass* (1860); under the present title in the fifth edition (1871); and, finally, Whitman placed it first of 11 poems in the "Sea-Drift" cluster for the sixth edition (1881). It is a poem of 183 lines.

It is perhaps the most musical poem in all of *Leaves of Grass*. Whitman was influenced by Old Testament poetry and by OPERA, and "Out of the Cradle" is made up of operatic-like recitatives and arias, plus rhythm patterns taken from ancient Hebrew poetry, typically accentual stanzas where the number of accents per line provides the rhythm (see ACCENTUAL VERSE).

A "cradle endlessly rocking" evokes images of the continually repeating life cycle, the baby rocked by its mother and the old man or woman in a rocking chair. But it also evokes the sea—one of Whitman's favorite metaphors—the sea constantly repeating its rocking motion and reminding readers of the inevitability of their journey through life to inevitable death. This is thematic in "Out of the Cradle," and Whitman pushes the idea to an extreme. He suggests that death ought to be welcomed, because of all life experiences it is the most life-affirming. The poet suggests that as death approaches, the dying person becomes more focused on his or her life, even on the present moment, a focus so powerful as to make the impending death more significant and even pleasant as yet another important life experience.

Whitman has been accused of sentimentalism in "Out of the Cradle," especially for this life/death-affirmation theme. But, as Edwin H. Miller writes in *Walt Whitman's Poetry: A Psychological Journey*, "It is scarcely sentimental to recognize that life is constructed upon death (there is no other foundation), and that whatever order an artist discovers or assumes is an order in which death (that final

Portrait of Whitman known as the "Quaker Photograph," 1870 *(Library of Congress, Prints and Photographs Division)*

order) must be accounted for. Whitman's position is not only tenable but also basically sane and life-affirming."

"Out of the Cradle" has a storyline. Whitman explains how, from a childhood experience of watching a pair of mockingbirds along the seashore, he came to understand the cycle of life, love, and death, and says that he was determined from that visionary moment to become a poet and to take "death" as his poetic theme.

LINES 1–40

The poem begins with the poet's memory of that childhood experience of watching the pair of birds along the "Paumanok" seashore, Paumanok the Indian name for LONG ISLAND:

> Out of the cradle endlessly rocking,
> Out of the mocking-bird's throat, the musical
>   shuttle, . . .

From the memories of the bird that chanted to
me, . . .
A man, yet by these tears a little boy again, . . .
I, chanter of pains and joys, uniter of here and
hereafter,
Taking all hints to use them, but swiftly leaping
beyond them,
A reminiscence sing.

The mockingbirds provided the child with an
image of love in a natural setting, a love so natural
that he felt it intuitively, perhaps from his experiences of love within his own family. The poet
remembers himself as the "little boy" daily observing the two "feathered guests from Alabama," first
building their nest in some of the seashore's
"briers," then with "four light-green eggs spotted
with brown," the female covering the eggs, "silent,
with bright eyes," and the male "to and fro near at
hand," watchful and protective.

The birds "sing" of their love (lines 33–40), and
the boy learns from their song about the quality of
natural love, fulfilled in the extreme, the boy "cau-
tiously peering, absorbing, translating." Whitman
had the mockingbirds' songs printed in italic type
throughout the poem, providing the operatic form
of recitatives and arias in a somewhat alternating
pattern as the poet recites his tale of this life-form-
ing, life-affirming childhood experience.

The English poet William Wordsworth had written in 1815 a three-line epigraph to his poem "Inti-
mations Of Immortality from Recollections of Early
Childhood," the first line of which is "The child is
father of the man." Whitman's "Out of the Cradle
Endlessly Rocking" exemplifies this idea, the poet
describing how his childhood experience along the
Paumanok shore "fathered" his life as a poet with a
fascination for death.

LINES 41–131

Then, "of a sudden," the female mockingbird disappears:

One forenoon the she-bird crouch'd not on the
nest,
Nor return'd that afternoon, nor the next,
Nor ever appear'd again.

The child sees the male mockingbird alone, searching "all summer in the sound of the sea" for its
mate, the "lone singer wonderful causing tears." It
is the disappearance of this bird's mate that makes
the child wonder, perhaps for the first time, at the
mystery of death; but it is the man/poet who realizes that it was this childhood experience that
would make him aware of death and that he would
become a poet, a singer of songs. The male mockingbird "call'd on his mate," a call that the poet
now recognizes: "He pour'd forth the meanings
which I of all men know."

The next 60 lines are devoted to the male
mockingbird's "sorrowful" attempt to find his mate,
the lines personifying the hope the bird still has of
finding her; but ultimately, she gives in to the
inevitability of death. Whitman uses a number of
images in these lines to evoke the grief felt by the
boy, now a man recalling the boy's feelings: "the
stars glisten'd . . . on the prong of a moss-scallop'd
stake"; "the slapping waves" mixed with the boy's
tears; "obscure shapes"; "the white arms out in the
breakers tirelessly tossing"; the boy who "listen'd
long and long" in order to translate the sounds into
meaning for himself.

The poet also establishes a rhythmic refrain that
will be echoed throughout the poem. It begins with
"Shine! shine! shine!" (line 32) and continues:
"Blow! blow! blow!" (53), "Soothe! soothe! soothe!"
(71), "Loud! loud! loud!" (81), and "Land! land! O
land!" (90). All of these lines are in the song of the
mockingbird as he sings of his lost love, culminating with his final aria which includes "Loved!
loved! loved! loved! loved." The final repetition of
this rhythmic refrain comes from the summing up
by the boy/poet near the end of the poem: "Death!
death! death! death! death!"

LINES 132–192

The boy is made aware that life goes on, represented for the reader in a sonnet-length passage
containing 18 verbs with "-ing" endings, the continuous present tense enhancing images of the constantly rocking sea.

The aria sinking,
All else continuing, the stars shining,
The winds blowing, the notes of the bird
continuous echoing,

With angry moans the fierce old mother
   incessantly moaning,
On the sands of Paumanok's shore gray and
   rustling, . . .
The yellow half-moon enlarged, sagging down,
   drooping, the face of the sea almost touching,
The boy ecstatic, with his bare feet the waves,
   with his hair the atmosphere dallying,
The love in the heart long pent, now loose,
   now at last tumultuously bursting,
The aria's meaning, the ears, the soul, swiftly
   depositing,
The strange tears down the cheeks coursing,
The colloquy there, the trio, each uttering,
The undertone, the savage old mother
   incessantly crying,
To the boy's soul's questions sullenly timing,
   some drown'd secret hissing,
To the outsetting bard.

This FREE VERSE sonnet is one of the best examples in *Leaves of Grass* of Whitman's ability to merge poetic form and meaning. The effect of the lines expanding toward the middle of the passage and growing shorter again at the end mimics a wave and merges with the significance of the images of "winds blowing" and the sea (the "fierce old mother") constantly rocking in its inevitable way the cradle, suggesting for the boy/man/poet the cycle of life, love, and death.

The "outsetting bard" has become aware—through the "love in the heart" he feels for the mockingbirds, the "strange tears," the happiness generated by the experience, and, above all, the "colloquy" (mystical communication) of the trio of boy, bird, and sea—that his concentrated thoughts of death have made him more alert to the possibilities of life. He sees in the bird's loss of his mate the greatness of life, because the inevitability of death makes him want to live more fully the life that he has. And it is this knowledge, he believes, that frees him to sing.

The poet now knows the answer to what Whitman believed to be the greatest of all philosophical questions: Why was I born? Just as the male mockingbird has become a solitary singer, so will the poet be. It is this answer, this "drown'd secret hissing" from the sea, which is gradually recognized by "the outsetting bard."

O you singer solitary, singing by yourself,
   projecting me, . . .
Never again leave me to be the peaceful child I
   was before what there in the night,
By the sea under the yellow and sagging moon,
The messenger there arous'd, the fire, the
   sweet hell within,
The unknown want, the destiny of me. . . .

The poet hears the voice of the boy he once was, "projecting" himself as "father to the man." The "sweet hell within" suggests the poet's continuing awareness of the paradox present in his involuntary drive to be a solitary singer; it is a life at once beautiful and frightening—beautiful because he now knows why he exists, yet frightening because of the daunting task ahead.

The poet then asks for a "clew" to subject matter for his poetry, and the answer comes to him out of the sea: "Are you whispering it, and have been all the time, you sea-waves? / Is that it from your liquid rims and wet sands?" And the sea

Whisper'd me through the night, . . .
Lisp'd to me the low and delicious word death,
And again death, death, death, death,
Hissing melodious, neither like the bird nor
   like my arous'd child's heart,
But edging near as privately for me rustling at
   my feet,
Creeping thence steadily up to my ears and
   laving me softly all over,
Death, death, death, death, death.

Edith Wharton records in her autobiography, *A Backward Glance* (1934), "a memorable moment in the history of American literature—Henry JAMES reading the poetry of Walt Whitman." Wharton says that James thought Whitman was the "greatest of American poets." At a gathering of friends James read aloud from "Song of Myself," and "When Lilacs Last In The Dooryard Bloom'd." Wharton says that "when he read 'Lovely and soothing Death' his voice filled the hushed room like an organ adagio," and James "thence let himself be lured on to the mysterious music of 'Out of the Cradle,' reading, or rather crooning it in a mood of subdued ecstasy till the fivefold invocation of Death tolled out like the knocks in the opening bars of the Fifth Symphony." This passage in Wharton's autobiography reminds readers that Whitman's poems need to be read aloud.

The poet discovers in the repetition of the sea's word "death" his own affirmation of life. He has the echo of the line in the mockingbird's song "Loved! loved! loved! loved! loved!" And he has the "whispered" word from the sea's "liquid rims and wet sands," this latter image representing perhaps the narrow line between life and death, between the physical and the spiritual, between the intellectual and the TRANSCENDENTAL. The poem's final lines sum up the poet's memory of the childhood experience along Paumanok's shore and his summary interpretation of its meaning:

> My own songs awaked from that hour,
> And with them the key, the word up from the
>   waves,
> The word of the sweetest song and all songs,
> That strong and delicious word which,
>   creeping to my feet,
> (Or like some old crone rocking the cradle,
>   swathed in sweet garments, bending aside,)
> The sea whisper'd me.

The image here of the sea waves as an "old crone rocking the cradle" reminds readers of the theme of the constantly repeating life-cycle suggested in the poem's opening lines and which is imitated throughout in the very form and rhythmic movement of the poem.

"Out of the Rolling Ocean the Crowd" (1865)

First published as a poem in *Drum-Taps* (1865); it was transferred to *Leaves of Grass* for the fifth edition (1871) and became the seventh of 16 poems in the "Children of Adam" cluster for the sixth edition (1881).

This is a love poem, and, although Whitman first placed it in his *Drum-Taps* volume of war poems—perhaps only because the 1865 book was the next published after he wrote the poem—he realized that it tied in more closely to the "Children of Adam" poems.

The rolling ocean is used here as a metaphor for the merger of all things: "I too am part of that ocean my love, we are not so much separated, / Behold the great rondure, the cohesion of all, how perfect!" The "great rondure," the circular nature of all things, even including perhaps the return to the Garden of Eden, cannot separate two people in love: "Be not impatient—a little space—know you I salute the air, the ocean and the land, / Every day at sundown for your dear sake my love."

Whitman may have directed this poem at a particular woman. Ellen O'CONNOR, a Whitman friend, is quoted by biographers as stating that this poem was written to "a certain lady," who angered her husband by answering the poem with a love letter and by continuing correspondence with him. Whitman biographer John Burroughs apparently identified the woman as Juliette Beach, but she refused his request to publish her exchange of letters with the poet. Apparently as a response to an unfavorable review her husband had written of the 1856 edition of *Leaves of Grass*, Mrs. Beach wrote a favorable review, and there was apparently some evidence of a love letter she wrote to Whitman in response to his poems. That he wrote this poem to Mrs. Beach is part of Whitman lore.

"Over the Carnage Rose Prophetic a Voice" (1860)

First appeared as "Calamus No. 5" in the third edition of *Leaves of Grass* (1860); then under its present title for the *Drum-Taps* volume (1865); it was the 25th of 43 poems in the "Drum-Taps" cluster for the sixth edition of *Leaves of Grass* (1881).

Originally a "Calamus" poem, Whitman here voices the prophecy that the love of men for one another will overcome the "carnage" of the CIVIL WAR:

> Over the carnage rose prophetic a voice,
> Be not dishearten'd, affection shall solve the
>   problems of freedom yet,
> Those who love each other shall become
>   invincible,
> They shall yet make Columbia victorious. . . .

The poet visualizes an America after the war where "One from Massachusetts shall be a Missourian's comrade" and where men from Maine, Carolina, and Oregon "shall be friends triune, / More precious to each other than all the riches of the earth."

"The dependence of Liberty shall be lovers, / The continuance of Equality shall be comrades," and it is this Liberty and Equality that will tie the group of men closer together "than hoops of iron." In spite of all the wartime carnage, Whitman believes that the war will make the nation stronger in part through the bonding of men with men.

"Ox-Tamer, The" (1874)

First published in the NEW YORK DAILY GRAPHIC (December 1874); then in the *Two Rivulets* volume of *Leaves of Grass* (1876); and as the 32nd of 38 poems in the "Autumn Rivulets" cluster for the sixth edition (1881).

The "Ox-Tamer" holds the attention and affection of "a hundred oxen young and old," to such an extent that the poet envies the "illiterate" Ox-Tamer, "(books, politics, poems, depart—all else departs,)." Some things get more attention than books.

"O You Whom I Often and Silently Come" (1860)

Titled "Calamus No. 43" in the third edition of *Leaves of Grass* (1860); it received its present title 1867); it was the 37th of 39 poems in the "Calamus" cluster for the sixth edition (1881).

This poem envisions a contrasting scene to the one presented in "Among the Multitude," the immediately preceding poem in the "Calamus" cluster. The latter poem explains how easy it is, through "secret and divine signs," to spot those men in a crowd who think about love relationships in the way the poet does.

In "O You Whom I Often and Silently Come," Whitman describes how easy it is to be with someone who does *not* get the "secret" signs. He writes of someone (unidentified) who walks by his side or

remains in the same room with him, and he thinks, "Little you know the subtle electric fire that for your sake is playing within me."

"Pallid Wreath, The" (1891)

First published in the CRITIC (January 1891); it was the seventh of 31 poems in *Good-Bye My Fancy* (1891); then in "Second Annex: Good-Bye My Fancy" for the "Death-bed" printing of *Leaves of Grass* (1892).

The poet is not yet willing to "let go" of the funeral wreath still hanging on the wall, in honor of a "dear friend," and he wonders if the friend has "faded" in the grave the same as the wreath has faded on the wall. But let the pallid wreath hang on the wall; his memory of the friend is neither faded nor dead.

"Passage to India" (1871)

First published as the title poem in a supplement to the fifth edition of *Leaves of Grass* (1871); the supplement was a 120-page pamphlet of 75 poems, 23 of which were new; the poems were then bound into a reprinting of the fifth edition and were incorporated into later printings; "Passage to India" became a separate poem for the sixth edition (1881), one of six separate poems placed between the "Autumn Rivulets" and "Whispers of Heavenly Death" clusters. The poem is in nine sections and 255 lines.

"Passage to India" is one of Whitman's most rhythmic poems, the lines basically accentual and using a "wave" pattern—that is, the number of accented syllables per line determines the rhythm, and most of the stanzas begin and end with shorter lines (fewer accented syllables) than lines in the middle of the stanza, creating an overall effect of wave movement throughout (see ACCENTUAL VERSE). Merely looking at the separate stanzas as printed on the page makes the pattern apparent in most of the poem's sections.

Whitman was motivated to write the poem, in part at least, by three historic events, all occurring during 1868–69: the completion of the Suez Canal and the American transcontinental railroad and the laying of the Atlantic Ocean cable. As with nearly all of Whitman's major poems, however, the historic events are used metaphorically, in this case as a collective metaphor for the importance of exploration, of time as well as space, and of the spiritual journey of the soul to union with God—often a theme in separate poems.

SECTIONS 1–3

The first six of the nine sections in "Passage to India" use the three historic events as touchstones for showing the importance of human exploration and discovery as part of God's purpose for human beings and as a way of enriching the soul: "Passage to India! / Lo, soul, seest thou not God's purpose from the first?" The poet marvels at "Our modern wonders," how they have "outvied" the "antique" original Seven Wonders of the World, because those wonders have merely "impell'd" the present, which is, "after all but a growth out of the past." Past "wonders" have merely encouraged the creation of even greater ones, "the cry with thee O soul, / The Past! The Past! The Past!"

At the beginning of Section 2, Whitman uses the French word "Eclaircise," which means clarification and is perhaps a reference to a period of Enlightenment. He connects Asiatic mythology and "primitive fables" to the notion that humans can make a spiritual passage to India: "Passage O soul to India! / Eclaircise the myths Asiatic, the primitive fables." We can transcend the world of space and time, the poet believes, in order to make the spiritual journey in search of God. He asks rhetorically whether this isn't, in fact, "God's purpose from the first." At the end of the section he suggests a new kind of worship, "not for trade or transportation only"; that is, not just for the sake of new explorations, "But in God's name," and for the soul's sake.

Section 3 develops the importance of the Suez canal and the "Pacific railroad" (but does not include, interestingly enough, the "eloquent gentle wires" of the Atlantic cable, which the poet had mentioned in Section 1 and which was a historical advance in international communication). The Suez canal ties "the Eastern to the Western sea, / The road between Europe and Asia." The poet evokes Columbus, whose dream, when he landed on America's shores, was to find a passage to the fabled East:

(Ah Genoese thy dream! thy dream!
Centuries after thou are laid in thy grave,
The shore thou foundest verifies thy dream.)

The railroad across America became the passage that Columbus could not find. America itself became then the passage to India. Whitman believes that the further away we are in time from Columbus's reaching the eastern coast of the Americas, the more significant is his "dream" of finding the passage to India.

SECTIONS 4–6

In Section 4 Whitman recalls all of the voyages that failed to achieve goals: "Struggles of many a captain, tales of many a sailor dead, / Over my mood stealing and spreading they come." Time and space are merged in the poet's thinking. A few lines later Whitman evokes Vasco da Gama, the Portuguese navigator who discovered the sea route to India in 1497–99: "The rondure of the world at last accomplish'd."

Rondure is a reference to the spinning earth, "swimming in space" as Whitman says in the first line of Section 5. The section presents a view of the earth as if from outer space, or as a poet-God's eye view, and the poet offers a glimpse of human exploration from the Garden of Eden to the present: "Down from the gardens of Asia descending radiating, / Adam and Eve appear, then their myriad progeny after them." The poet asks, what next for explorers? "Ah who shall soothe these feverish children? / Who justify these restless explorations?"

After the seas are all cross'd, (as they seem
    already cross'd,)
After the great captains and engineers have
    accomplish'd their work,
After the noble inventors, after the scientists,
    the chemist, the geologist, ethnologist, . . .

What then? Part of the answer, Whitman believes, is in the power of poetry to record and explain: "Finally shall come the poet worthy that name, / The true son of God shall come singing his songs." The idea of the poet as a son of God should not surprise readers of Whitman's poetry; he believed we are all sons and daughters of God. One of the tenets of Whitman's religion is that God is in all things. But it is the power of the poet's work that is important here; the poet fuses all of Nature into one entity.

> (He shall indeed pass the straits and conquer
>   the mountains,
> He shall double the cape of Good Hope to
>   some purpose,)
> Nature and Man shall be disjoin'd and diffused
>   no more,
> The true son of God shall absolutely fuse them.

Vasco da Gama "doubled" the cape of Good Hope—that is, he sailed around the point of land, the southern tip of Africa, in this case—to get into the Indian Ocean, the first sea-passage to India and one connecting west with east just five years after Columbus's voyage to the Americas. That then is the task of the poet, the "true son of God," to be an explorer of the imagination "to some purpose." For Whitman that "purpose" is to fulfill a spiritual journey and then to create poetry out of the experience.

In Section 6 Whitman presents the historian's more concrete view of history, beginning in his own time, 1867–69: "Year at whose wide-flung door I sing!"

> Passage to India!
> Cooling airs from Caucasus far, soothing cradle
>   of man,
> The river Euphrates flowing, the past lit up
>   again.

And he names people and places—Alexander, for example, "on his warlike marches suddenly dying, / On one side China and on the other side Persia and Arabia, / To the south the great seas and the bay of Bengal."

Poets are the best historians, Whitman believed, because of their "visionary" perspective. The poet can *become* the military conqueror, the explorer, the discoverer, as so often Whitman *becomes* the very people he evokes in *Leaves of Grass.*

> And who are thou sad shade?
> Gigantic, visionary, thyself a visionary, . . .

> Spreading around with every look of thine a
>   golden world,
> Enhuing it with gorgeous hues.

"Enhuing" means to anoint with oil. It is the poet who anoints the "golden world" with "gorgeous hues," suggesting that it is the poet who can present better than others the stories of discovery and the places discovered, even the religion of the people of the new lands. Gay Wilson Allen compares "Passage to India" with Milton's "Paradise Lost," stating that Whitman's theology is more optimistic than Milton's Puritan predestination. "Whitman's subject," Allen says, "was not the fall of man but the human soul's triumph over Time, Space, and Death."

SECTIONS 7–9

The first six sections of "Passage to India" present images of the importance of time and space in the human experiences of exploration and discovery. In the final three sections, these images are turned into metaphors for the soul's voyage through Time and Space: "O soul, repressless, I with thee and thou with me, / Thy circumnavigation of the world begin." The soul's travel is timeless and spaceless, and, as happens elsewhere in Whitman's poetry, the movement is from the physical—in "Passage to India" the geographical—to the spiritual. The poet visualizes a journey for himself and his soul "Back, back to wisdom's birth, to innocent intuitions," back he believes to the beginning of time.

Whitman builds in Section 8 toward an emotional climax in the soul's ultimate aim, union with God. Whitman believed that on such a voyage the soul would conquer Time and Space, even Death.

> Thoughts, silent thoughts, of Time and Space
>   and Death, like waters flowing,
> Bear me indeed as through the regions infinite,
> Whose air I breathe, whose ripples hear, lave
>   me all over,
> Bathe me O God in thee, mounting to thee,
> I and my soul to range in range of thee.

The "I" and the Soul are now one: "O soul, thou actual Me, . . . / Thou matest Time, smilest content at Death, / And fillest, swellest full the vastnesses of Space." The poet achieves finally that which he has wished for, the merger of the "I" and soul in Time and Space. The physical "Passage to India" has become a metaphor for the human discovery and exploration of the soul's merger with God. This then is the subject of the poem.

Section 9 opens with a direct statement of poetic purpose: "Passage to more than India!" The spiritual "passage" transcends the physical. He wonders aloud, in the second and third lines, if his soul is up for such a voyage: "Are thy wings plumed indeed for such far flights? / O soul, voyagest thou indeed on voyages like those?" Is it prepared to move from its own physical setting to the spiritual? Whitman envisions this voyage as the human's way of overcoming death, through the soul's merger with God.

But enough of this talk of voyaging, the poet says to his soul, we have planned long enough—in spite of the risks, it is time to go!

> Have we not darken'd and dazed ourselves with
>   books long enough?
> Sail forth—steer for the deep waters only,
> Reckless O soul, exploring, I with thee, and
>   thou with me,
> For we are bound where mariner has not yet
>   dared to go,
> And we will risk the ship, ourselves and all.

The waters are never deeper than in Whitman's vision of the soul's voyage to a union with God. "Passage to India" is not about the seeming physical passage suggested by the title but about the soul's spiritual transcending of time, space, and death, in order to become united with God.

In the 15 years Whitman had been writing and revising *Leaves of Grass* up to the publication of *Passage to India*, this mystical insight had been one of the poet's main thematic concerns. This poem helps define Whitman's religious beliefs, which are also evident in "Out of the Cradle Endlessly Rocking," "Crossing Brooklyn Ferry," "When Lilacs Last in the Dooryard Bloom'd," and "Prayer of Columbus."

"Patroling Barnegat" (1880)

First published in the AMERICAN (June 1880); reprinted in HARPER'S NEW MONTHLY MAGAZINE

(April 1881) and in the *Philadelphia American* (May 1881); then it was the 10th of 11 poems in the "Sea-Drift" cluster for the sixth edition of *Leaves of Grass* (1881). Barnegat Bay is a long inlet, part of the intracoastal waterway along the New Jersey coast, north of Atlantic City.

This is the first of two poems at the end of the "Sea-Drift" cluster that describe the sea, this one of a winter storm along the Barnegat inlet:

> Wild, wild the storm, and the sea high
>   running, . . .
> Waves, air, midnight, their savagest trinity
>   lashing,
> Out in the shadows there milk-white combs
>   careering, . . .
> A group of dim, weird forms, struggling, the
>   night confronting,
> That savage trinity warily watching.

Very little is more frightening for a sailor that the "trinity" of "waves, air, [and] midnight," the air in this case an "easterly death-wind breasting. " See also "After the Sea-Ship."

"Paumanok" (1888)

First published in the NEW YORK HERALD (February 29, 1888); then in *November Boughs* (1888); and it was the second of 65 poems in the "First Annex: Sands at Seventy" cluster for the "Death-bed" printing of *Leaves of Grass* (1892).

Paumanok is the Indian name for LONG ISLAND. Whitman was born in West Hills, Long Island, and knew the surrounding country well. In this five-line, descriptive poem he refers to it as an "Isle of sweet brooks of drinking-water—healthy air and soil! / Isle of the salty shore and breeze and brine!"

"Paumanok Picture, A" (1856)

This seven-line poem, including an opening line later cut, was first published as Canto 8 of "Salut au

Monde!" in the second edition of *Leaves of Grass* (1856); it was transferred, with few revisions from the original version, and as a separate poem, to the sixth edition (1881).

The poem is descriptive of a fishing scene off Paumanok's (LONG ISLAND's) "sea-beach." Ten fishermen cast an expansive net, then drag it onto the beach full of "green-back'd spotted mossbonkers," which *Webster's New World Dictionary* spells with a "u" and defines as "menhaden," a member of the herring family and used as bait or for making oil and fertilizer.

"Pensive and Faltering" (1868)

First appeared as the last of five numbered poems under the general title "Whispers of Heavenly Death" in the (London) BROADWAY MAGAZINE (October 1868); it became part of the "Whispers of Heavenly Death" cluster in the "Passage to India" supplement to the fifth edition of *Leaves of Grass* (1871); and it was the last of 18 poems in the "Whispers" cluster for the sixth edition (1881).

This five-line poem is about the Dead being alive: "For living are the Dead, . . ." It is the poet who keeps them alive through the "spectre" of his poems: "(Haply the only living, only real, / And I the apparition, I the spectre.)" The dead are still alive in the memories of some people.

It is interesting to note that the poem's title and first line reflect a sense of the poet's hesitation about the idea expressed in the poem.

"Pensive on Her Dead Gazing" (1865)

First published in the *Drum-Taps* volume (1865); then in the "Ashes of Soldiers" cluster in the fifth edition of *Leaves of Grass* (1871); and it received its present title and was the eighth of 17 poems in the "Songs of Parting" cluster for the sixth edition (1881).

This is melancholy ("pensive") thinking by the poet about the CIVIL WAR dead and about the "Mother of All" gazing down on her children as the earth absorbs their bodies and blood. And she wishes for the perpetuation of the memories of the dead: "O years and graves! O air and soil! O my dead, an aroma sweet! / Exhale them perennial sweet death, years, centuries hence." Protect them through eternity.

"Perfections" (1860)

First published in the third edition of *Leaves of Grass* (1860); and it was the eighth of 29 poems in the "By The Roadside" cluster for the sixth edition (1881). It remained unchanged throughout its publication history.

This is a two-line poem about the sources of "perfection." Only "perfection" understands perfection, just as only "souls" understand souls. Whitman is suggesting here that there are some things that transcend a person's understanding of them.

"Persian Lesson, A" (1891)

First published as the 23rd of 31 poems in *Good-Bye My Fancy* (1891); then in "Second Annex: Good-Bye My Fancy" for the "Death-bed" printing of *Leaves of Grass* (1892).

The "greybeard sufi," a Persian mystic and teacher, is described by Whitman as teaching his "last lesson." The sufi's message to the "young priests and students" is that "Allah is all, all, all— immanent in every life and object."

Whitman would have been impressed by this message, because it is what he too believed: God is in all things, and all things are a manifestation of God; it is, he says near the end of the poem, "the central urge in every atom." See PANTHEISM.

"Personalism" (1868)

Essay first published in GALAXY (May 1868).
See also *Democratic Vistas*.

"Pilot in the Mist, The"
(1885)

First published with seven other poems under the heading "Fancies at Navesink" in NINETEENTH CENTURY magazine (August 1885); then in *November Boughs* (1888); and, finally, with the "Fancies at Navesink" cluster as an insert in the "First Annex: Sands at Seventy" cluster for the "Death-bed" printing of *Leaves of Grass* (1892).

The poem is descriptive of an "Indian helmsman" guiding his boat through the morning mist near Navesink, the pilot "elate," proud and exalted at his accomplishment. Navesink is about a mile from the New Jersey coast, across lower New York Bay from BROOKLYN.

"Pioneers! O Pioneers!"
(1865)

First published as one of the *Drum-Taps* poems (1865); it was reprinted with a cluster of poems titled "Marches Now the War is Over" in the next three editions of *Leaves of Grass* (1867, 1871, and 1876); and it was the second of seven poems in the "Birds of Passage" cluster for the sixth edition (1881).

This is one of a few poems in *Leaves of Grass* with a consistent stanzaic pattern: 26 stanzas of four lines each, with the first and fourth lines shorter than the middle two lines and beginning from a wider margin; each fourth line carries the refrain, "Pioneers! O pioneers!" The rhythm of the poem is basically trochaic, a stressed syllable followed by an unstressed one.

The idea of "Pioneers" is used in this poem to identify not just the explorers, the first people to discover the eastern shores of America or the far West, but to celebrate the pioneer spirit of all Americans, a "resistless restless race!"

> All the pulses of the world
> Falling in they beat for us, with the Western
>   movement beat,
> Holding single or together, steady moving to
>   the front, all of us,
> Pioneers! O pioneers!"

The American "race" sets an example for a worldwide movement toward the democratic principles, which encourage the pioneering spirit. It is only when people feel of equal importance to all others that they are motivated by that spirit. All pioneers have the same spirit of adventure, each one containing, according to Whitman, "a curious trio"—the mind, body, and soul of a poet.

The "curious trio"—I, soul, and body—is described in the following stanza:

> I too with my soul and body,
> We, a curious trio, picking, wandering on our
>   way,
> Through these shores amid the shadows, with
>   the apparitions pressing,
> Pioneers! O pioneers!

It takes an awareness of the Self, as well as of the soul and the body, to make a pioneer, someone curious and energetic and alert to the ghosts ("apparitions") of those pioneers who have gone before.

The poem concludes with a series of images evoked in the thought of America's westward movement, which included women, "daughters of the West"; and minstrels, taking the place of the "bards of other lands," no longer needed. For Whitman, they and all the others moving west represent the best of the American race.

"Play-Ground, The" (1846)

First published in the BROOKLYN DAILY EAGLE (June 1, 1846); an "early poem" *not* later published in *Leaves of Grass*. It is most accessible now in Francis Murphy (editor), *Walt Whitman: The Complete Poems* (Penguin Books, 1996).

"Poem of Remembrances for a Girl or a Boy of These States" (1856)

Cut from *Leaves of Grass* after first appearing with its present title in the second edition (1856); the first half of the original poem, titled "Chants Democratic, No. 6" was reprinted in the third edition (1860), and the second half titled "Leaves of Grass, No. 1" was reprinted in the fourth edition (1867); the poem was together again and retitled "Think of the Soul" (1871) and excluded thereafter.

poems cut from *Leaves of Grass*

Forty-five poems appeared in one or more of the early editions of *Leaves of Grass* but not in either the sixth edition (1881) or in the final printing of the book (1892). They are indexed in this *Critical Companion to Whitman* by their final title but usually with a minimum of publication history.

These poems show something of Whitman's thinking as he began to give a final form to his book. Most are fragments of earlier poems, beginnings of poems or complete poems that somehow failed to work out in the way Whitman had planned. Some of the poems, however, are of particular interest. "Great Are the Myths," was untitled and the 12th and last poem in the first edition of *Leaves of Grass* (1855); and four poems were cut from the "Calamus" cluster: "[Long I Thought That Knowledge]," "[Hours Continuing Long, Sore and Heavy-Hearted]," "[Who is Now Reading This?]" and "[States!]" Brackets indicate that the poem's first line was used as a title, either by Whitman himself or later editors.

Following is the order in which these "excluded" poems are printed in most current texts of *Leaves of Grass*: "Great Are the Myths," "Poem of Remembrances for a Girl or a Boy of These States," "Think of the Soul," "Respondez!" "[In the New Garden]" "[Who is Now Reading This?]," "[I Thought That Knowledge Alone Would Suffice]," "[Hours Continuing Long]," "[So Far, and So Far, and On Toward the End]," "Thoughts—1: Visages," "Leaflets," "Thoughts—6: 'Of What I Write,'" "Says," "Apostroph," "O Sun of Real Peace," "To You," "Now Lift Me Close," "To the Reader at Parting," "Debris," "[States!]" "Thoughts—2: 'Of Waters, Forests, Hills,'" "Thought—4: 'Of Owner-ship . . .,'" "Bathed in War's Perfume," "Solid, Ironical, Rolling Orb," "Up, Lurid Stars!" "Not My Enemies Ever Invade Me," "This Day, O Soul," "When I Read the Book," "Lessons," "Ashes of Soldiers: Epigraph," "One Song, America, Before I Go," "Souvenirs of Democracy," "From My Last Years," "In Former Songs," "The Beauty of the Ship," "After an Interval," "Two Rivulets," "Or, from That Sea of Time," "As in a Swoon," "[Last Droplets]," "Ship Ahoy!" "For Queen Victoria's Birthday," "L of G," "After the Argument," and "For Us Two, Reader Dear."

"Poets to Come" (1860)

First appeared as "Chants Democratic, No. 14" in the third edition of *Leaves of Grass* (1860); it received its present title (1867); it was part of "The Answerer" cluster (1871); finally it was the 22nd of 24 poems in the "Inscriptions" cluster for the sixth edition (1881).

Whitman seeks justification from "Poets to come!":

> Not to-day is to justify me and answer what I
>   am for,
> But you, a new brood, native, athletic,
>   continental, greater than before known,
> Arouse! for you must justify me. . . .

He wishes to have his poetry "justified" by the next generations of poets. The *free verse* poetic form used by Whitman certainly dominated 20th-century poetry, not just in America but throughout western Europe as well, a justification with which Whitman would no doubt feel pleased.

"Portals" (1871)

First published in the fifth edition of *Leaves of Grass* (1871); and it was the 14th of 17 poems in the "Songs of Parting" cluster for the sixth edition (1881).

In this two-line poem the poet recognizes that only by traveling through the "portals" into death can one know what, throughout life, is "unknown."

"Prairie-Grass Dividing, The" (1860)

Titled "Calamus No. 25" in the third edition of *Leaves of Grass* (1860); it received its title in the fourth edition (1867); it was the 21st of 39 poems in the "Calamus" cluster for the sixth (1881).

"Prairie-grass" becomes here a "spiritual corresponding" symbol connecting "inland America" with the larger meaning of his *Leaves of Grass* for a democratic society.

The poet "demands . . . the close companionship of men," and the blades of grass become "words, acts, beings," representing an "open atmosphere, [the] coarse, sunlit, fresh, nutritious" grasses allowing for all people to "look carelessly in the faces of Presidents and governors" and to say, with audacity, "Who are you?" It is this atmosphere that allows for a society in which men are allowed the freedom to love one another.

Democracy is like the prairie-grass, the poet suggests—open, coarse, fresh, and nutritious.

"Prairie States, The" (1880)

First published in facsimile in the ART AUTOGRAPH magazine (May 1880); and it was the last of 38 poems in the "Autumn Rivulets" cluster for the sixth edition of *Leaves of Grass* (1881).

This six-line poem is a descriptive tribute to the prairie states, written shortly after Whitman's trip to several western states in 1879: "A newer garden of creation . . . / Dense, joyous, modern, populous millions, cities and farms, . . ."

"Prairie Sunset, A" (1888)

First published in the NEW YORK HERALD (March 9, 1888); then in *November Boughs* (1888); and it was

the 53rd of 65 poems in the "First Annex: Sands at Seventy" cluster for the "Death-bed" printing of *Leaves of Grass* (1892).

Nature's "multiform power" is "consign'd for once to colors," Whitman says in this five-line poem. They are "colors till now unknown, . . . fighting the silent shadows to the last." The day's magnificent colors fight to stay alive into the night.

"Prayer of Columbus" (1874)

First published in HARPER'S NEW MONTHLY MAGAZINE (March 1874); it then appeared in the *Two Rivulets* volume of the sixth edition of *Leaves of Grass* (1876); and it was printed as a separate poem, following "Passage to India," in the sixth edition (1881).

This "Prayer of Columbus" is, on the surface, the plausible prayer of the 51-year-old Columbus on his last voyage, "A batter'd, wreck'd old man, / Thrown on this savage shore, far, far from home." But it is primarily Whitman's prayer for himself, however parallel he felt his life might be to that of Columbus.

Whitman wrote the poem in 1874 at age 55, the age of Columbus when he died. The poet is at an extremely discouraging time in his life. He had suffered a paralytic stroke on January 23, 1873; his mother had died on May 23 of that year, a week before his 54th birthday; and, in spite of his good feeling about the *Passage to India* poems published in 1871 and prospects for a second volume (*Autumn Rivulets*) for his 1876 edition of *Leaves of Grass*, he was going through a period of what he thought was a general loss of public esteem. "I am too full of woe," he says to God; "Haply I may not live another day." He would live another 18 years, but at the time of writing this poem he felt that he, like Columbus who died poor and alone, was on his last voyage.

His English friend Anne GILCHRIST wrote a short letter to him, dated March 9, 1874, in which she tells him she has just read, with "tears of joy," the "sacred poem," a reference to "Prayer of Columbus": "O august Columbus! Whose sorrows, sufferings, struggles are more to be envied than any triumph of conquering warrior—as I see him in your poem his figure merges into yours, brother of Columbus. Completer of his work, discoverer of the spiritual, the ideal America—you too have sailed over stormy seas to your goal—surrounded with mocking disbelievers—you too have paid the great price of health—our Columbus."

One of the reasons Whitman was so fond of Gilchrist, even from long distance—he didn't meet her until her three-year visit beginning two years later—was that she seemed to understand his poetry as well as, if not better than, most of his American critics. Her letters to him reporting on her reading of his poems must have been a constant and pleasant surprise.

"Prefaces," *Leaves of Grass*

Whitman wrote essays on his poetical theories that function as prefaces for five of the various printings of *Leaves of Grass*. Only the essay for the first edition, however ("Preface 1855"), may be considered a true preface—that is, an essay of introduction to the work, printed at the beginning. All five essays, however, describe or expand on Whitman's poetic theory and plans for his book of poems. And most of these ideas are reflected in the poems, the wording sometimes taken directly from the essays.

His ideas changed considerably as the book developed, and, although these changes may be seen in the differences between the early and late individual poems, they may also be seen as part of his overall vision for his poetry of America. For more information on each preface, see the following four entries.

"Preface 1855" is an untitled introduction to the 12 untitled poems in the first edition. It would be difficult to overstate the importance of this essay in understanding Whitman's dream for the future of poetry, his own and America's.

"Preface 1856," titled "Prefatory Letter to Ralph Waldo Emerson," which appeared in the appendix of the second edition (1856), was Whitman's answer to a letter EMERSON had written shortly

after reading the first edition. Emerson had stated, in part, "Dear Sir—I am not blind to the worth of the wonderful gift of 'Leaves of Grass.' . . . I greet you at the beginning of a great career. . . ." Whitman's essay is a thank-you note of sorts, but only by way of letting readers know that Emerson had written a glowing report of the first *Leaves of Grass*.

"Preface 1872—As a Strong Bird on Pinions Free" was printed at the beginning of a separate volume titled *As a Strong Bird on Pinions Free*, which was later transferred to *Leaves of Grass* and retitled "Thou Mother with Thy Equal Brood."

"Preface 1876" was published in *Two Rivulets*, the second of two volumes for the 1876 printing of *Leaves of Grass*.

See also "A Backward Glance O'er Travel'd Roads," which appeared at the end of the 1889 reprinting of *Leaves of Grass* and is often referred to as a preface.

"Preface" (*Leaves of Grass*) (1855)

First published, untitled but with pages marked in roman numerals (iii–xii) in the first edition of *Leaves of Grass* (1855). It was not reprinted until the publication of *Specimen Days & Collect* (1882), when it was included with *Democratic Vistas* as part of the "Collect" essays. It was later printed in *Complete Poems & Prose of Walt Whitman, 1855–1888* (1888) and in *Whitman: Complete Prose Works* (1892). Quotations below are from the 1855 edition, including the caesura breaks, though Whitman revised it for later editions.

It would be difficult to overstate the importance of this essay, which is both an explanation of Whitman's vision for American democracy and for a national poetry. It would be difficult to find anywhere in our written history a clearer, more detailed explanation of America's democratic principles and the sort of poetry that can develop under those principles: "The Americans of all nations at any time upon the earth have probably the fullest poetical nature. The United States themselves are essentially the greatest poem. . . . Here is not merely a nation but a teeming nation of nations."

It is as if Whitman feels a direct relationship between democracy and FREE VERSE, the form most of his own poetry takes. We are, to Whitman, a nation of common people, all of whom are more important individually and collectively than all the politicians who run the country.

> The genius of the United States is not best or most in its executives or legislatures, nor in its ambassadors or authors or colleges or churches or parlors, nor even in its newspapers or inventors . . . but always most in the common people. Their manners speech dress friendships—the freshness and candor of their physiognomy— the picturesque looseness of their carriage . . . their deathless attachment to freedom—their aversion to anything indecorous or soft or mean—the practical acknowledgment of the citizens of one state by the citizens of all other states . . . the air they have of persons who never knew how it felt to stand in the presence of superiors . . . the terrible significance of their elections—the President's taking off his hat to them not they to him—these too are unrhymed poetry. It awaits the gigantic and generous treatment worthy of it.

It is clear that Whitman has himself in mind as the Poet of America, but his poetry lives up to his own ideal of America's poetic spirit. Nearly every one of the ideas presented in this preface essay may be found in *Leaves of Grass*. See, for example, "By Blue Ontario's Shore," for which more than 60 lines of the final version (1881) are taken almost directly from this 1855 preface.

The caesura breaks in the following quotation from the "Preface" show that Whitman is already thinking about the poetry to come: "He [the American poet] is the seer . . . he is individual . . . he is complete in himself . . . the others are as good as he, only he sees it and they do not. He is not one of the chorus . . . he does not stop for any regulations . . . he is the president of regulation." It is almost as if Whitman were, in the thought here, warning readers that his poetry is to be different,

that it establishes new "regulations," which open poetry to larger, greater verse possibilities.

But there are important qualifications, ideas that keep what would later be known as "free verse" from allowing the poet to feel "free" to do anything he or she wants—an idea that some critics have suggested and that some poets have accomplished. Robert Frost's doubtlessly tongue-in-cheek statement that free verse was like playing tennis with the net down is perhaps closest to a workable analogy for "free verse." The lack of a net allows the player great freedom, but he or she still plays within the lines laid down on the court, even though it is the poet who determines where the lines go.

This freedom is the "soul" of America, Whitman says in the 1855 Preface: "The poetic quality is not marshaled in rhyme or uniformity or abstract addresses to things nor in melancholy complaints or good precepts, but is the life of these and much else and is in the soul."

Emphasizing the importance of the soul, he says later that "the greatest poet does not moralize or make applications of morals . . . he knows the soul. The soul has that measureless pride which consists in never acknowledging any lessons but its own. . . . The greatest poet has less a marked style and is more the channel of thoughts and things without increase or diminution, and is the free channel of himself. . . . [The greatest artist is he] who contributes the greatest original practical example. The cleanest expression is that which finds no sphere worthy of itself and makes one."

But because of the importance of the individuality that America encourages, Whitman says, there will always be more than one poet, more than one "bard." "The American bards shall be marked for generosity and affection and for encouraging competitors. . . . hungry for equals night and day. . . . The American bard shall delineate no class of persons nor one or two out of the strata of interests nor love most nor truth most nor the soul most nor the body most . . . and not be for the eastern states more than the western or the northern states more than the southern."

Whitman's vision for the subject of America's poets could not be clearer: The treatment of all elements of society as equals is primary. And it is an essential ingredient for poetry, Whitman suggests; that is, the poet must present his subjects without bias. All things in Nature too must be treated as fair and equal parts of any democratic society. This is Whitman's meaning for the term "prudence" in his poem "Song of Prudence."

> Little or big, learned or unlearned, white or black, legal or illegal, sick or well, from the first inspiration down the windpipe to the last expiration out of it, all that a male or female does that is vigorous and benevolent and clean is so much sure profit to him or her in the unshakable order of the universe and through the whole scope of it forever. If the savage or felon is wise it is well . . . if the greatest poet or savan is wise it is simply the same . . . if the President or chief justice is wise it is the same . . . if the young mechanic or farmer is wise it is no more or less . . . if the prostitute is wise it is no more nor less. The interest will come round . . . all will come round.

He writes that the "final test of poems or any character or work" still remains to be discussed. The poem, the character, the work in a democracy must have lasting value and encourage poets of the world (the "kosmos") to create also out of their love for democracy. In this ideal social order, there will be no need of priests, because everyone will provide his or her own moral values.

> Is he [the poet] beloved long and long after he is buried? Does the young man think often of him? and the young woman think often of him? and do the middle-aged and the old think of him?
>
> A great poem is for ages and ages in common and for all degrees and complexions and all departments and sects and for a woman as much as a man and a man as much as a woman. A great poem is no finish to a man or woman but rather a beginning. . . .
>
> There will soon be no more priests. Their work is done. They may wait awhile . . . perhaps a generation or two . . . dropping off by degrees. A superior breed shall take their place . . . the

gangs of kosmos and prophets en masse shall take their place. A new order shall arise and they shall be the priests of man, and every man shall be his own priest. The churches built under their umbrage shall be the churches of men and women. Through the divinity of themselves shall the kosmos and the new breed of poets be interpreters of men and women and of all events and things. They shall find their inspiration in real objects today, symptoms of the past and future. . . . They shall not deign to defend immortality or God or the perfection of things or liberty or the exquisite beauty and reality of the soul. They shall arise in America and be responded to from the remainder of the earth.

The poet who does not think of his or her future reader—perhaps the reader living under despotic rulers and who might be encouraged by the poet of democracy—is not worthy of the name "poet." Whitman knows that he is writing about his own vision for himself, his own wish to be the very poet, the Bard, he describes in this preface to the 1855 edition of *Leaves of Grass.*

Whitman's vision is of a poet who has accumulated all the wisdom of past generations and is able to see also—through some mystical system further developed in the poetry—the future, especially the future of a nation motivated by the democratic principles he understands and has attempted to lay down, both in the prefaces and in the poetry.

"Preface" (*Leaves of Grass*) (1856)

Not technically a "preface" because it appeared as part of an appendix to the second edition of *Leaves of Grass* (1856), it nevertheless is most often referred to as a preface. It is a letter to Ralph Waldo EMERSON, thanking him for his letter of praise for the copy of *Leaves* that Whitman had mailed to him a few months before. This letter-essay nevertheless adds to what Whitman had established as important to the canon of American poetry in his "preface" to the first edition (1855).

The second edition's "preface" is probably better known, however, for Whitman's publishing Emerson's letter without his permission and for trading on Emerson's kind words: "I am not blind to the worth of the wonderful gift of *Leaves of Grass*. I find it the most extraordinary piece of wit and wisdom that America has yet contributed. I am very happy in reading it, as great power makes us happy. . . . I greet you at the beginning of a great career, which yet must have had a long foreground somewhere, for such a start. . . ."

Whitman even had the words "I greet you at the beginning of a great career" printed on the spine of the 1856 edition. And he had given the letter to Charles A. Dana for publication in his NEW YORK TRIBUNE, and had sent clippings from the *Tribune* to friends, all without even notifying Emerson of his intentions.

Not only was Emerson surprised to see his own letter published in the *Tribune* and in the second edition of *Leaves*, he had not even seen Whitman's thank-you letter, which followed his own letter in the book's appendix. Only the first and last two paragraphs of Whitman's letter to Emerson are actually directed to the Concord writer. The rest can stand as repetition of or additional material for Whitman's personal vision for America and for its poetry. He adds, for example, to his earlier prophecy about the future of the American habit of reading: "What a progress popular reading and writing has made in fifty years! What a progress fifty years hence! The time is at hand when inherent literature will be a main part of These States, as general and real as steam-power, iron, corn, beef, fish. First-rate American persons are to be supplied. . . . America is to be kept coarse and broad. What is to be done is to withdraw from precedents, and be directed to men and women—also to The States in their federalness; for the union of the parts of the body is not more necessary to their life than the union These States is to its life."

Whitman wrote this during one of the most prolific times in the history of American literature. The list of books published in the four years before *Leaves of Grass* (1855) reads like a "what's what" of great American literature: Hawthorne's *The Scarlet Letter* (1850), Emerson's *Representative Man* (1850),

Melville's *Moby-Dick* (1851), Stowe's *Uncle Tom's Cabin* (1852), and THOREAU's *Walden* (1854). There is no following of "precedents" in these works; they are, to quote Whitman from another context, themselves precedents.

Whitman also makes clear in his 1856 essay his attitude toward sex. He writes against the mostly unwritten laws prohibiting from literature what "speakers and writers fraudulently [assume] as always dead what every one knows to be always alive. . . . Women in These States approach the day of that organic equality with men, without which, I see, men cannot have organic equality among themselves. This empty dish, gallantry, will then be filled with something. . . . Of bards for These States, if it come to a question, it is whether they shall celebrate in poems the eternal decency of amativeness of Nature, the motherhood of all, or whether they shall be the bards of the fashionable delusion of the inherent nastiness of sex, and of the feeble and querulous modesty of deprivation."

Amativeness, is a term Whitman used more in poetry than in prose. In the above context he seems to mean the love of Nature for everything in nature—Nature as mother of us all. In the poems he uses the word to mean sexual passion for someone of the opposite sex. It is *amativeness* that is the key word in the "Children of Adam" cluster of poems; parallel to *adhesiveness*, the key word in the "Calamus" poems about homosexual love, the adhering nature of one man for another.

"Preface 1872—As a Strong Bird on Pinions Free" (1872)

This "preface" appeared at the beginning of the pamphlet publication of *As a Strong Bird on Pinions Free* (1872). The pamphlet also included seven poems that were later bound at the back of the *Two Rivulets* volume for the 1876 printing of *Leaves of Grass*. The pamphlet's title poem later became "Thou Mother with Thy Equal Brood" and was published in the sixth edition of *Leaves of Grass* (1881). The poem "As a Strong Bird on Pinions

Free" was delivered by Whitman as a commence-ment poem for the Dartmouth College graduation, June 26, 1872.

The preface was reprinted in *Specimen Days & Collect* (1882), included with *Democratic Vistas* as part of the "Collect" essays. It was later printed in *Complete Poems & Prose of Walt Whitman, 1855–1888* (1888) and in *Whitman: Complete Prose Works* (1892). It is the 1872 text that is quoted below.

The opening sentence states the purpose of the preface: "The impetus and ideas urging me, for some years past, to an utterance, or attempt at utterance, of New World songs, and an epic of Democracy, having already had their published expression, as well as I can expect to give it, in *Leaves of Grass,* the present and any future pieces from me are really but the surplusage forming after that Volume, or the wake eddying behind it."

He has no plans for retirement from the writing of poetry. He writes here of the present "colossal drama" facing the United States, which he believes will play the "leading parts" in current world history.

In them [the United States] History and Humanity seem to seek to culminate. . . .

The leading parts. . . . Not to be acted, emu-lated here, by us again, that role till now fore-most in History—Not to become a conqueror nation, or to achieve the glory of mere military, or diplomatic, or commercial superiority—but to become the grand Producing Land of nobler Men and Women—of copious races, cheerful, healthy, tolerant, free—To become the most friendly Nation, (the United States indeed,)— the modern composite Nation, formed from all, with room for all, welcoming all immigrants— accepting the work of our own interior develop-ment, as the work fitly filling ages and ages to come;—the leading Nation of peace, but nei-ther ignorant nor incapable of being the leading Nation of war;—not the Man's Nation only, but the Woman's Nation—a land of splendid moth-ers, daughters, sisters, wives.

Whitman also clarifies in this essay what he calls "the Religious purpose" underlying *Leaves of Grass.*

He refers to it as "the New Theology—heir of the West—lusty and loving, and wondrous beautiful. . . . As there can be, in my opinion, no sane and com-plete Personality, nor any grand and electric Nationality, without the stock element of Religion imbuing all the other elements, (like heat in chem-istry, invisible itself, but the life of all visible life,) so there can be no Poetry worthy the name without that element behind all. . . ." And Religion, as he made clear in his Preface to the first edition of *Leaves of Grass,* must be taken out of the church, away from ministers and priests and given back to the people: "It [Religion] is, indeed, too important to the power and perpetuity of the New World to be consigned any longer to the churches, old or new, Catholic or Protestant—Saint this, or Saint that. . . . It must be consigned henceforth to Democracy *en masse,* and to Literature. It must enter into the Poems of the Nation."

This latter idea is not new to *Leaves of Grass;* it has been filtered through the poetry all along, and this is one of several statements Whitman makes which help define his religious beliefs. If men and women know how to think for themselves, there is then no need for churches or priests/ministers. The individual is capable of working out moral values on his or her own.

"Preface" (*Leaves of Grass*) (1876)

Titled "Preface," this essay appeared at the begin-ning of the second volume (*Two Rivulets*) for the "Centennial Edition" of *Leaves of Grass* (1876), actually just a later printing of the fifth edition (1871). For later collections the title was changed to "PREFACE, 1876/to the two-volume Centen-nial Edition/of L. of G. and 'Two Rivulets.'" Whit-man added a footnote to the first page of the 1876 essay, stating that the "Preface" is intended for both volumes of the edition: Volume I, *Leaves of Grass;* Volume II, *Two Rivulets.*

Whitman devotes as much space to explanatory notes in this essay as he does to the ideas expressed.

Most of the notes refer to earlier ways of saying what he says here.

Perhaps the most important statement in this preface, however, is his discussion of his poems as "Experiments, under the urge of powerful, quite irresistible, perhaps wilful influences, (even escapades,) to see how such things will eventually turn out—and have been recited, as it were, by my Soul, to the special audience of Myself, far more than to the world's audience. . . . Till now, by far the best part of the whole business is, that, these days, in leisure, in sickness and old age, my Spirit, by which they were written or permitted erewhile, does not go back on them, but still and in cabinet hours, fully, deliberately allows them."

It is as if he is saying that he tried out this or that poetic idea or style and then took a look at it to decide if he liked it, changing it in the next printing of *Leaves of Grass* if he didn't like it. The essay was written during Whitman's illness of the mid-1870s, and he is clearly thinking of his impending death (he would live until 1892). The mood is one of clarification of original intentions in the writing of *Leaves of Grass* and of the *Two Rivulets* volume to which this preface is attached.

"Preface Note to 2d Annex" (1891)

This short essay was subtitled "Concluding L. of G.—1891." Whitman was 72 years old, ill and near the end of his life. He says in this "Preface," "certainly I have nothing fresh to write." Yet he is concerned as always for his reputation as a poet, and he is concerned about the future of American democracy. He wonders if his poetry, the "Last droplets of and after spontaneous rain, . . . / Will they filter to any deep emotions? any heart and brain?" He has published his poems for almost 40 years, poems that reflect his love for America and its people, and he can only hope that his words have filtered into the American psyche.

He wonders also at the end of the essay, whether Americans will ever understand the "sad, wrenching times" of the CIVIL WAR, and he asks: "Will the America of the future—will this vast rich Union ever realize what itself cost, back there after all? . . . Those times of which, O faroff reader, this whole book is indeed finally but a reminiscent memorial from thence by me to you?" Throughout his writing career Whitman kept future readers in mind, wondering even, perhaps, what impact his late 19th-century poems might have on 21st century readers.

"Promise to California, A" (1860)

Titled "Calamus No. 30" in the third edition of *Leaves of Grass* (1860); it received its present title (1867); it was the 24th of 39 poems in the "Calamus" cluster for the sixth edition (1881).

The "promise" to California is for robust love from the poet, and not just to California but to "the great pastoral Plains, and on to Puget sound and Oregon." And he promises to visit the West (Whitman was never west of Denver), for, he says, "I know very well that I and robust love belong among you, inland, and along the Western sea." Robust was a term the poet used most often in referring to homosexual love.

"Proudly the Flood Comes In" (1885)

First published with seven other poems under the heading "Fancies at Navesink" in NINETEENTH CENTURY magazine (August 1885); then in *November Boughs* (1888); and, finally, with the "Fancies at Navesink" group as an insert in the "First Annex: Sands at Seventy" cluster for the "Death-bed" printing of *Leaves of Grass* (1892). See "First Annex: Sands at Seventy."

This is one of two poems in the "Navesink" group that uses the sea's flood tide as a metaphor for hope. The flood tide comes in "proudly, . . . shouting, foaming, advancing." The poet refers to it as "outswelling," as if in pride at its accomplishment, the pride felt by people at work—on farms, in woods, on city streets, or on sailing ships and steamboats, all who feel the joy of work well done.

"Proud Music of the Storm" (1869)

First published as "Proud Music of the Sea-Storm" in the ATLANTIC MONTHLY (February 1869); it appeared under its present title in the "Passage to India" annex to the fifth edition of *Leaves of Grass* (1871); then in the *Two Rivulets* volume of the 1876 printing; and it was a separate poem, following the "Autumn Rivulets" cluster for the sixth edition (1881). The poem is in six sections and 164 lines.

"Proud Music of the Storm," itself one of Whitman's most musical poems, describes a source for a rededication to poetry that he hears in music.

The poem begins with a 13-line PERIODIC SENTENCE: "Proud music of the storm . . . why have you seiz'd me?" Between the subject and verb is a description of the storm raging, a "dream" from which the speaker wakes only in the poem's last section. The middle sections are devoted to the kinds of music he hears, the significance of which becomes clear only after he wakes and realizes inspiration from the music that leads to his rededication.

In Section 2 the poet urges his soul to "Come forward" to listen to the diversity of music: the "duet of the bridegroom and the bride," the "flutes' clear notes and sounding harps' cantabile," the "approaching drums." There are also unpleasant sounds: the "sobs of women, the wounded [in war] groaning in agony, / The dirge and desolation of mankind." There is the music "Of winds and woods and mighty ocean waves." And there are the "tongues of violins."

The first stanza of Section 3 reveals the poet's memory of the music he heard as a child: his mother's voice, but also the rain, growing corn, the "breeze among the long-leav'd corn," the sea-surf, wild-fowl's notes, lowing cattle, etc. The second

Walt Whitman, photographed by Goldsmith, April 1869 *(Library of Congress, Prints and Photographs Division)*

stanza lists the popular folk music of various countries he may have heard during his early maturity, "German airs of friendship, wine and love," Irish ballads, English "warbles," French chansons, Scotch tunes, and "Italia's peerless compositions."

Thoughts of Italy's MUSIC lead then into a series of seven OPERA vignettes, remarkable for their clarity of scene description: the climactic scene in BELLINI's *Norma;* the "mad scene" in DONIZETTI's *Lucia di Lammermoor;* the climactic moment as the hero realizes he has lost his lover in Verdi's *Ernani;* the famous trombone duet from Bellini's *I Puritani;* Fernando in despair in Donizetti's *La Favorita* because he thinks his lover, Leonora, has become the king's mistress; and the awakening scene from Bellini's *La Sonnambula* ("The Sleepwalker"), with one of Whitman's favorite singers, Marietta ALBONI, named in the final line as the lead contralto.

From hearing—still in his dream—the music of specific opera scenes, he then hears in Section 4, all in present tense recitation, "odes, symphonies" and other operas: Rossini's *William Tell*; Meyerbeer's *The Huguenots, The Prophet*, and *Robert the Devil*; Gounod's *Faust* and Mozart's *Don Juan*. He hears the "dance-music of all nations," the waltz, the bolero, and "religious dances old and new," the Hebrew lyre, etc.

He sees Roman youth with their flageolets, and their long swords, throwing and catching them. He hears the muezzin calling in the mosque and sees the worshippers; he hears the Egyptian harp, the chants of Nile boatmen, Hindu flutes, and a band of bayaderes, Indian dancing girls.

All of this music he hears in his dream.

After listing the nations and continents from which yet other music comes and which he hears in his dream, including the *Agnus Dei* and *Gloria in Excelsis* from the Latin Mass, the poet then sums up what he has heard in the final lines of Section 5:

Give me to hold all sounds, (I madly struggling
   cry,)
Fill me with all the voices of the universe,
Endow me with their throbbings, Nature's also,
The tempests, waters, winds, operas and
   chants, marches and dances,
Utter, pour in, for I would take them all!

He wakes in the first line of Section 6 and questions the significance of the dream. Just as he had received a similar "clew" to his future as a poet in "Out of the Cradle Endlessly Rocking," so he does in "Proud Music of the Storm":

I said to my silent curious soul out of the bed of
   the slumber-chamber,
Come, for I have found the clew I sought so
   long,
Let us go forth refresh'd amid the day,
Cheerfully tallying life, walking the world, the
   real,
Nourish'd henceforth by our celestial dream.

And, after reviewing the dream images, he tells his soul, for whom the music is intended, that he now has

. . . a new rhythmus fitted for thee,
Poems bridging the way from Life to Death,
   vaguely wafted in night air, uncaught,
   unwritten,
Which let us go forth in the bold day and
   write.

The music of the storm of his dream has provided the poet with a new "rhythmus," new rhythms from which he will write his new songs. The *Oxford English Dictionary* connects "rhythmus," in its second definition, to musical rhythms: "the assemblage or union of tunes in music which are joined together with a certain order and in certain proportions."

Gay Wilson Allen, in *The New Walt Whitman Handbook*, has this to say about the music of "Proud Music of the Storm": "It is not one of Whitman's most famous works, but nowhere else did he use his characteristic symphonic structure with greater unity of effect or with richer symbolism. It is his only poem which is literally a symphony of sound. . . . The orchestration of the storm ranges through the elemental sounds of all creation and the music of humanity."

"Punishment of Pride, The" (1841)

First published in the (New York) *World* (December 18, 1841); an "early poem" *not* later published in *Leaves of Grass*. It is most accessible now in Francis Murphy (editor), *Walt Whitman: The Complete Poems* (Penguin Books, 1996).

"Queries to My Seventieth Year" (1888)

First published in the NEW YORK HERALD (May 2, 1888); then in *November Boughs* (1888); it was the 10th of 65 poems in the "First Annex: Sands at Seventy" cluster for the "Death-bed" printing of *Leaves of Grass* (1892).

Whitman turned 69 in 1888, and the "query" concerns what he thought of as the "uncertain spectre" of his 70th year. He wonders if the "placid skies and sun" will "stir the waters yet" or if he will be left "as now, / Dull, parrot-like and old, with crack'd voice harping, screeching." The idea that the singer's voice is cracking in these last poems is out of character for the poet's more normal grandiose optimism, yet pessimism creeps in often during the last three or four years of his life.

Whitman is far more negative here as he thinks about the poetry he is writing in his last years than he was in the immediately preceding poem in *Leaves of Grass*, "My Canary Bird," in which he believes these final poems are as good as any he had written.

"Quicksand Years" (1865)

First appeared in the *Drum-Taps* volume (1865); it was transferred under its present title to the "Whispers of Heavenly Death" cluster for the fifth edition of *Leaves of Grass* (1871); and it became the eighth of 18 poems in the "Whispers" cluster for the sixth edition (1881).

"Quicksand" is a metaphor for life; only the "great and strong-possess'd soul," escapes the quicksand. "When shows break up what but One's-Self is sure?" The word *shows* suggests everything that is external to the Self; when all those things let us down, all that is left is the Self.

It is an accentual poem, the rhythmic frame in a rough "pyramid" form; the lines are in the following pattern of accented syllables: 5-8-8-9-8-5 (see ACCENTUAL VERSE).

"Race of Veterans" (1865)

First appeared in the "Sequel to Drum-Taps" volume (1865); then as one of the poems in the group titled "Marches Now the War is Over" for the fifth edition of *Leaves of Grass* (1871); and it was the

30th of 43 poems in the Drum-Taps cluster for the sixth edition (1881).

"Race of Veterans" refers to the generation of men who fought during the CIVIL WAR. It was a "Race of passion and the storm," soldiers devoted to a cause, no matter what the outcome.

"Reconciliation" (1865)

First appeared in the "Sequel to Drum-Taps" volume (1865) and under this title throughout its publication history in *Leaves of Grass;* it was the 34th of 43 poems in the "Drum-Taps" cluster for the sixth edition (1881).

The "reconciliation" between the North and South after the Civil War comes from an awareness of the beauty of Nature: "Beautiful that war and all its deeds of carnage must in time be utterly lost, / That the hands of the sisters Death and Night incessantly softly wash again, and ever again, this soil'd world."

The "enemy is dead," the South represented for the poet by one "man divine as myself" dead; "I look where he lies white-faced and still in the coffin—I draw near, / Bend down and touch lightly with my lips the white face in the coffin." Reconciliation comes through the recognition of the divinity of each soldier, no matter his origins or beliefs. For another poem with a similar theme, see "A Sight in Camp in the Daybreak Gray and Dim."

"Recorders Ages Hence"
(1860)

Titled "Calamus No. 10" in the third edition of *Leaves of Grass* (1860); it received its present title in the 1867 printing; and it was the ninth of 39 poems in the "Calamus" cluster for the sixth edition (1881).

The poet wants to tell the "recorders ages hence" what to say about him as a poet and as a man: "Publish my name and hang up my picture as that of the tenderest lover, / The friend the lover's portrait, of whom his friend his lover was fondest." He was not proud of his songs, Whitman says, but he *was* proud "of the measureless ocean of love within him" and that he "freely pour'd it forth."

The particular examples the poet uses of this love he feels are, in this and most of the other Calamus poems, clearly a love for another man—or men, as in the brotherhood of men.

Whitman wrote a number of poems intended to help future biographers with personal information, not—perhaps he thought—readily available elsewhere. He told those friends of his, however, who wanted to write biographies, that he preferred that they get his life story from his poetry. See also the next poem after this one in the "Calamus" cluster, "When I Heard at the Close of the Day."

"Red Jacket (from Aloft)" ## (1884)

First published in the PHILADELPHIA PRESS (October 10, 1884); then in *November Boughs* (1888); and it was the 31st of 65 poems in the "First Annex: Sands at Seventy" cluster for the "Death-bed" printing of *Leaves of Grass* (1892).

A parenthetical headnote for this poem reads, "(Impromptu on Buffalo City's monument to, and re-burial of the old Iroquois orator, October 9, 1884)." Red Jacket was the "grand sachem" of the Iroquois tribe and is credited for generating Iroquois support for the American side in the War of 1812.

Whitman envisions the great Indian "orator" looking down "(from Aloft)" on the scene of his monument and reburial in Buffalo, New York, "Like one of Ossian's ghosts." This latter reference is to Ossian's poems about the heroes of Scottish mythology—though the Ossian poems were later discovered to have been written by James Macpherson (1736–96). In one of the Ossian poems, it seems traditional for military heroes to retire at night to their own "hill of ghosts," in order to decide who would win the next day's battles.

Whitman may have connected this Scottish myth to that of American Indians, especially the superior ones, as was Red Jacket.

"Respondez!" ## (1876)

Cut from *Leaves of Grass* after first appearing as "Poem of the Propositions of Nakedness" in the second edition (1856), as "Chants Democratic, No. 5" in the third edition (1860), and under its present title through the 1876 printing.

Whitman revised the earlier versions of the poem in order to get in lines about the Civil War. The second and third lines of the 1876 version, for example, read: "(The war is completed—the price is paid—the title is settled beyond recall;) / Let every one answer! let those who sleep be waked! let none evade!" Everyone is to blame for the war, he is saying here, let no person evade that responsibility. This idea fits in with Whitman's philosophy of the importance of equality in a democratic society. There are other, similar lines: "Let the priest still play at immortality! / Let death be inaugurated!" "Let there be no God! . . . / Let insanity still have charge of sanity."

Whitman dropped "Respondez!" before publication of the sixth edition (1881), but he took several lines from the poem and moved them to other poems. Lines 6–8 and 65–66 in "Respondez," for example, were merged and became, with few other changes, the six-line poem "Reversals," following "By Blue Ontario's Shore" in the sixth edition.

"Return of the Heroes, The" ## (1867)

First published under the title "A Carol of Harvest for 1867" in the GALAXY magazine (September 1867); reprinted in *Tinsley's Magazine* (London) (October 1867); then with the "Passage to India" poems in the fifth edition of *Leaves of Grass* (1871); it was under its present title and as the second of 38 poems in the "Autumn Rivulets" cluster for the sixth edition (1881). At 132 lines in eight sections, this is the longest of the "Autumn Rivulets" poems.

"The Return of the Heroes" is both a memorial to those men, from both North and South, who fought and died in the just-ended (when he wrote the poem) CIVIL WAR, but the poem also describes the new role for those soldiers who returned.

> But now I sing not war,
> Nor the measur'd march of soldiers, nor the
>   tents of camps,
> Nor the regiments hastily coming up deploying
>   in line of battle;
> No more the sad, unnatural shows of war.

Whitman begins Section 5 with lines of hope for a new Nation: "But on these days of brightness, . . . / Should the dead intrude?" Though the heroes who did not return should not be forgotten, those who did return have an obligation to repair the damage of the war by going to the fields to plant and harvest.

Near the beginning of Section 8 the poet urges returning soldiers to "Toil on heroes! toil well! Handle the weapons well!" The weapons are new farming machinery, "crawling monsters," "labor-saving implements," "steam-power reaping-machines," a "newer saw-mill," "southern cotton-gin[s]," a "rice-cleanser."

These returning heroes have a new commitment; they must "All gather and all harvest . . . the wheat of Ohio, Illinois, Wisconsin, . . . the buckwheat of Michigan, . . . the cotton in Mississippi or Alabama, . . . the golden sweet potato of Georgia and the Carolinas." The harvesting of crops is envisioned by Whitman as a way for the returning soldiers to begin the reconstruction of America and of their own lives.

"Reuben's Last Wish" (1842)

Short story, first published in a New York temperance newspaper, the WASHINGTONIAN (May 2, 1842), this according to Emory Holloway in *American Literature* (January 1956). The tale is most accessible now in *Walt Whitman: The Early Poems*

and the Fiction, edited by Thomas L. Brasher (New York University Press, 1963). The publication date of the story is at issue, because Brasher writes in a note to the story that the date on page 1 of the *Washingtonian* where the story was printed is May 2, but page 2 gives the date of the newspaper as May 21.

This is one of several Whitman temperance stories, each moralizing about the evils of alcohol. The author warns readers at the beginning that the story is without plot, interest, or excitement, and he merely wishes that his story "may haply teach a moral and plant a seed of wholesome instruction."

Franklin Slade becomes an alcoholic after years of leading a nonalcoholic, more "normal," farmer's life. He is "a handsome, healthy American farmer," 30 years old, living a comfortable life with a "fair" reputation, making good money without debts. His wife is "prudent," and they have two sons, eight and three years old. Slade seems to have everything a man of his age could possibly want.

Ten years later, however, at the age of 40, and as the direct result of alcohol, Slade is "a bloated, red faced fellow," his estate is "mortgaged for half its value," he is without a dollar to his name, he has lost all of his friends, his wife has lost all of her energy and beauty, and his family is overtaken by poverty. Slade's older son, who is just at the age to be good help on the farm, leaves home, and his younger son, Reuben, has died, apparently of pneumonia—all of this as the direct result of Slade's drinking habits. Slade's motivation to drink is vague, the narrator saying only that he was the victim "through one of the thousand painted snares, which ministers of sin ever stand ready to tempt frailty withal." The motivation, in other words, doesn't matter.

Reuben had helped his father home from a drunken spree late one night during a cold rainstorm, the storm resulting in an illness from which the boy did not recover. During his illness, Reuben made an elaborate copy of a temperance pledge he had seen and copied during a meeting he had attended with his father, Slade's willingness to go to the meeting with his son indicating some hope for his recovery. Reuben had decorated the pledge by adding a silk border "and a fine ribbon bow at the top."

On his deathbed Reuben pulls from under his pillow the elaborate pledge he had made and shows it to his father, pointing to the vacant signature line as he dies. The reader is left to hope that Franklin Slade, perhaps through tears, is himself moved enough to sign the pledge.

CHARACTERS

Franklin Slade   Main character in the short story "Reuben's Last Wish." He is described by the story's narrator as "a handsome, healthy American farmer, [who] possessed at the age of thirty years, a comfortable estate, a fair reputation, a tolerably well filled purse—and could boast that he owed no debts which he was not able to pay on the instant. He had a prudent, good tempered wife, and two children, sons, one eight years old and the other three." By the age of 40 and as a direct result of alcohol, Slade has lost everything, and his family is overtaken by poverty. His older son leaves home, his wife loses all of her "former energy and good looks," and his younger son dies of pneumonia.

Reuben   The invalid son of the alcoholic Franklin Slade in the short story "Reuben's Last Wish." Reuben is kept out one "cold, rainy" night helping his father home from a drunken spree; the child becomes ill from the event and never recovers. He had made an elaborate copy of a temperance pledge that he had seen and copied during a meeting he had attended with his father. On his death bed the boy pulls from under his pillow the pledge and shows it to his father, pointing to the vacant signature line as he dies. Reuben's "last wish" is that his father would stop drinking and take care of his family.

"Reversals"   (1856)

First appeared as part of a 57-line poem titled "Poem of the Propositions of Nakedness" in the second edition of *Leaves of Grass* (1856); the longer poem then appeared as "Chants Democratic, No.

5" (1860); was retitled "Respondez!" (1867); then was dropped from the sixth edition (1881), except for six lines, which appeared as a separate poem titled "Reversals."

The poem follows "By Blue Ontario's Shore" in *Leaves of Grass*, the two separate poems coming in Whitman's final editions between two major clusters of poems, "Memories of President Lincoln" and "Autumn Rivulets."

The title of this poem refers to Whitman's suggestion that those things that have been first should now "go behind," that ideas should be reversed: "Let bigots, fools, unclean persons, offer new propositions, / Let the old propositions be postponed." This is an ironic contradiction to the poet's own poetic values, which he spent a lifetime establishing and around which he built the whole of *Leaves of Grass*.

"Richard Parker's Widow" (1845)

Short story, first published in the Aristidean (April 1845). The story is most accessible now in *Walt Whitman: The Early Poems and the Fiction*, edited by Thomas L. Brasher (New York University Press, 1963).

The story of British admiral Richard Parker's mutiny at the Nore in the Thames River estuary in 1797 is known to history, and Whitman's version is the same as most others, especially Camden Pelham's in his *Chronicles of Crime; or, The New Newgate Calendar*, published in London (1841). According to Thomas Ollive Mabbott in his introduction to *The Half-Breed and Other Stories by Walt Whitman*, Whitman's story is a mere paraphrase of Pelham's account. What makes Whitman's story fiction, however, and more interesting than the historical account, is that Parker's wife is placed at the center of events and that it is told in the first person singular, providing freshness as a more intimate account.

Mrs. Parker is pointed out to the narrator by a friend. "That woman . . . is the widow of a man whose name, forty years ago, rang for many weeks like a death-knell through England, and shook with terror the foundations of the throne itself!" Her husband, he explains, was Admiral Richard Parker, who headed the sailors' rebellion at the Nore.

The narrator then relates both the story of the mutiny and Parker's hanging as a traitor. But the heart of Whitman's story is Mrs. Parker's arrival on the scene, her struggle to say good-bye to her husband, her stealing his body from the grave with help from strangers, and its subsequent burial in Whitechapel churchyard in London. It is an amazing feat of love and loyalty, both by Parker's wife and by his friends for her sake.

At the end of the narration, readers are told that in 1836, nearly 40 years after the event of the Nore, the narrator had seen her again. She was "nearly blind . . . [and] was making application for some public aid." She received the aid, but the narrator does not know whether she is still alive.

CHARACTERS

Richard Parker   Admiral of the British navy, accused of mutiny at the Nore anchorage of the Thames River in 1797 and hung for treason. Whitman's short story "Richard Parker's Widow" is based on the incident.

Mrs. Richard Parker   The main character in the short story. Whitman based his story on a historical event, but chose to emphasize the wife of Admiral Parker, the leader of a mutiny on the Thames River in 1797 who was hung for treason. Mrs. Parker, with the help of friends and strangers, steals the body and reburies it in London's Whitechapel churchyard.

"Riddle Song, A" (1880)

First published in Philadelphia's FORNEY'S PROGRESS (April 17, 1880); it was the eighth of 22 poems in the "From Noon to Starry Night" cluster for the sixth edition of Leaves of Grass (1881).

The riddle is not resolved in this poem. It is two words only: "Two little breaths of words comprising it, / Two words, yet all from first to last comprised in

it." A few biographers and critics have provided guesses, but Whitman remained steadfast in his refusal to say more than is in the poem.

Early biographer and close friend during Whitman's last years, Horace TRAUBEL, writes that the poet once told him, "I made the puzzle, it is for others to solve." And so it remains.

"Rise O Days from Your Fathomless Deeps" (1865)

First appeared under this title for the Drum-Taps volume (1865), and Whitman did not revise it; the poem was the sixth of 43 poems in the "Drum-Taps" cluster for the sixth edition of Leaves of Grass (1881).

Whitman shows a great deal of frustration in this poem over the bickering among political leaders of some "unchain'd" American cities, while soldiers born and raised in those cities fought and died in the CIVIL WAR: "Manhattan rising, advancing with menacing front—Cincinnati, Chicago, unchain'd; . . ." But in the final section (Section 3) he feels that democracy will survive in spite of the seeming passive attitude toward the war by city politicians: "Thunder on! stride on, Democracy! strike with vengeful stroke! / And do you rise higher than ever yet O days, O cities!" America will survive even these politicians.

Democracy will "rise . . . from [its] fathomless deeps" in spite of the "storms" of war and the seeming lack of interest by those less involved than the soldiers wounded and dying in the fields. Whitman was upset by the seeming apathy of other citizens also, those not close enough to the war to be directly affected. He tries to convince Americans that for democracy to work everyone must be involved, even politicians.

> I have lived to behold man burst forth and
>   warlike America rise,
> Hence I will seek no more the food of the
>   northern solitary wilds,
> No more the mountains roam or sail the stormy
>   sea.

I will become the poet of all America, Whitman seems to be saying here, as he does in a number of other poems; I will become the poet of North and South, cities and country, the good of the nation, and the evil.

"Roaming in Thought" (1881)

Subtitled "(After Reading Hegel)" this was first published as the 14th of 29 poems in the "By The Roadside" cluster for the sixth edition of *Leaves of Grass* (1881), one of three new poems for this edition.

Georg Wilhelm Friedrich Hegel (1770–1831) was a German philosopher who argued that there is a unifying nature in all things, that there is always "thesis, antithesis, and synthesis." Whitman agreed and wrote this two-line poem, perhaps as an example: "Roaming in thought over the Universe, I saw the little that is Good steadily hastening towards immortality, / And the vast all that is call'd Evil I saw hastening to merge itself and become lost and dead."

Good and Evil "merge" in Nature, but Good is immortal, while Evil becomes "lost and dead." This idea seems to contradict Whitman's earlier philosophy that good and evil are of equal importance in a democratic society, as equal as men and women, as blacks and whites.

"Roots and Leaves Themselves Alone" (1860)

Titled "Calamus No. 13" in the third edition of *Leaves of Grass* (1860); it received the present title for the fourth edition (1867); and it was the 12th of 39 poems in the "Calamus" cluster for the sixth edition (1881).

The "roots and leaves" are the poem itself, Whitman suggests here, one of the clearest uses of leaves-symbolism in *Leaves of Grass*. And if readers allow "the warmth of the sun" to nourish their

understanding, the leaves of this poem and of all others will "open and bring form, color, perfume to you, . . . they will become flowers, fruits, tall branches and trees."

Whitman is offering a way for readers to have a greater understanding of and appreciation for his poems, particularly the Calamus poems, which he feels have been misunderstood. The "warmth" may come from a reader's developing love for the poet.

"'Rounded Catalogue Divine Complete, The'" (1891)

First published as the 25th of 31 poems in *Good-Bye My Fancy* (1891); then in "Second Annex: Good-Bye My Fancy" for the "Death-bed" printing of *Leaves of Grass* (1892).

In a parenthetical epigraph, Whitman describes his hearing in a Sunday sermon the expression, "the rounded catalogue divine complete." The speaker had in mind, the poet says, "only the esthetic things, and [he] entirely ignored what I name in the following." And Whitman lists things from the "devilish and the dark, the dying and diseas'd." The poet believes, in other words, that no catalogue is either round or divinely complete without describing the evil in the world as well as the good.

The equality of good and evil is one of Whitman's important themes in *Leaves of Grass*. See also "Song of the Universal" and "Chanting the Square Diefic."

"Runner, The" (1867)

First published as a separate poem in the fourth edition of *Leaves of Grass* (1867); and it was published separately thereafter until it became the 17th of 29 poems in the "By The Roadside" cluster for the sixth edition (1881).

The four-line poem describes a "well-train'd runner" running. It is one of the thoughts he has while "by the roadside."

"Sail Out for Good, Eidólon Yacht!" (1891)

First published in LIPPINCOTT'S MAGAZINE (March 1891); it was the first of 31 poems in *Good-Bye My Fancy* (1891); then in "Second Annex: Good-Bye My Fancy" for the "Death-bed" printing of *Leaves of Grass* (1892).

Whitman uses the word *eidólon* here and elsewhere in *Leaves* to mean an image of something real, the spiritual manifestation of a "real" object. In this case it is the spiritual or perhaps phantom image of the "little white-hull'd sloop." The poet envisions the yacht leaving port for "deep waters"; though he says he "will not call it our concluding voyage," he nevertheless says there will be "no more returning to these shores."

Whitman's last poems, those in both *Good-Bye My Fancy* and in "Sands at Seventy" are all poems of farewell to his readers. In "Sail Out for Good, Eidólon Yacht!," he envisions himself on the phantom yacht sailing out to sea for the last time and into eternity, perhaps into immortality.

"Sail out for good," he says, "eidólon yacht of me!" The yacht he envisions carries him out to the sea's deep waters, on to his ultimate destination. The "concluding voyage" will be the one he takes after death.

See also the poem "Eidólons."

"Salut au Monde!" (1860)

Published first as "Poem of Salutation" in the third edition of *Leaves of Grass* (1860); then under its present title and as a separate poem in the fourth edition (1867); and it became the first of 12 separate poems that followed the "Calamus" cluster in the sixth edition (1881). There are 13 sections and 226 lines in this poem of democracy.

"Salut" is French for "salute" or "salutation," but, perhaps more appropriately for this poem, the title means "Greetings to the World"—greetings from these United States to all the people of the world. The poem offers readers a clear explanation of the distinction between Walt Whitman the poet and Walt Whitman a character *in* the poem, a distinction the poet-Whitman wants the reader to make throughout *Leaves of Grass*.

The poet-Whitman is *not* the same persona as the character-Whitman. This is understandably confusing on first meeting the idea in *Leaves of Grass* and perhaps best understood by quoting THOREAU on the subject. He says in *Walden*, published in 1854, a year before *Leaves of Grass*: "If I seem to boast more than is becoming, my excuse is that I brag for humanity rather than for myself; and my shortcomings and inconsistencies do not affect the truth of this statement." Whitman is making the same point in *Leaves of Grass*, most conspicuously in "Song of Myself" and "Salut au Monde!" My ego is not as large as readers may think, Whitman seems to be saying to readers; all people are capable of having the same sensations, the same vision for the world, the same love for others, that I have.

He makes the distinction between poet and character four times in the first four sections of this poem:

> O take my hand Walt Whitman! . . .
> What widens within you Walt Whitman? . . .
> What do you hear Walt Whitman? . . .
> What do you see Walt Whitman?

The speaker may be taken in the first line as the poet-muse for the main character, named Walt Whitman. Section 3 is devoted to the things Whitman "hears," and Sections 4–10 are dominated by a catalog of the things he "sees." After the poet-muse asks, "What do you hear Walt Whitman?" the Whitman character answers with 18 lines, a catalog of sensations, each beginning "I hear." What he "sees" is dealt with in a similar fashion. The impact of all of these sensations is that with the poet-muse as encourager and the character as observer, readers may feel the transcendent spirit at work in Whitman as he travels through time and space, hearing the sounds: "a Spanish dance with castanets," "the Italian boat-sculler," "Christian priests at the altars," "the cry of the Cossack," "the Hindoo teaching his favorite pupil," and so on. And seeing the sights: "distant lands," "Vesuvius and Etna," "Antarctic icebergs," "the old empire of Assyria," and so forth.

Whitman hears and sees all the unique sounds of these worldly places—past, present, and future—and he CATALOGs the places and types of people he encounters on this mystical tour.

What "widens within" Whitman then—to answer the poet's question in the fifth line of the opening section—is an awareness of the importance of the great diversity offered by the world's places and people to America and of the diversity offered by America to the world. He envisions a new world for democracy: "Within me latitude widens, longitude lengthens, . . . / Within me zones, seas, cataracts, forests, volcanoes, groups. . . ." In the last line of Section 10, following the long catalog of things seen, Whitman says: "And I salute all the inhabitants of the earth." *Salut au monde!*

Whitman speaks directly to the world's citizens in Sections 11 and 12: "You daughter or son of England! / You of the mighty Slavic tribes . . . / divine-soul'd African. . . ." He speaks to people "centuries hence" and even to those people not specifically mentioned, "but [which I] include just the same!" We are all equals, he says at the end of Section 11:

> Each of us inevitable,
> Each of us limitless—each of us with his or her
>   right upon the earth,
> Each of us allow'd the eternal purports of the
>   earth,
> Each of us here as divinely as any is here.

And to the "have-nots" he catalogs in Section 12, he speaks of his kinship with them: "I do not say one word against you, away back there where you stand [with your complexes, he may be suggesting], / (You will come forward in due time to my side.)"

Whitman presents in Section 13 a summary of what he has learned from his mystical, sensuous tour of the world and his vision for a completely new and democratic society. He has traveled the world, he says: "I have look'd for equals and lovers and found them ready for me in all lands, / I think some divine rapport has equalized me with them."

He is still in the hand of his poet-muse at the end of the poem, still sending greetings to the rest of the world and passing on his own "light and warmth" to the "haunts and homes of men" everywhere.

Salut au monde!
> What cities the light or warmth penetrates I
>   penetrate those cities myself,
> All islands to which birds wing their way I wing
>   my way myself.

> Toward you all, in America's name,
> I raise high the perpendicular hand, I make the
>   signal,
> To remain after me in sight forever,
> For all the haunts and homes of men.

There is no other poem in all of *Leaves of Grass* that is any better at presenting Whitman's vision for a democratic world as in *"Salut au Monde!"* He wants the entire world to see the democracy of his vision.

"Sands at Seventy"

See "First Annex: Sands at Seventy."

"Savantism" (1860)

First appeared in the third edition of *Leaves of Grass* (1860); it became the 16th of 24 poems in the "Inscriptions" cluster for the sixth edition (1881).

The word *savantism* is not in the *Oxford English Dictionary.* Whitman probably made up the term to refer to someone with the qualities of a savant; that is, a learned or wise person. The poet wants his "leaves and songs [to be] trustful, admirant"—poems to be trusted as truthful and, therefore, admired.

"Says" (1860)

Cut from *Leaves of Grass* after first appearing under its present title in the third edition (1860), then with only stanzas 1, 5, 7, and 8 retained (1867), and retitled "Suggestions" (1871 and 1876). This is a philosophic poem, with the grammatical subject and verb of each stanza, "I say." Each stanza presents one of Whitman's key ideas about the importance of American democracy, especially of the individual and his or her social responsibility.

"Scented Herbage of My Breast" (1860)

Titled "Calamus No. 2" in the third edition of *Leaves of Grass* (1860); it received its present title in 1867; it was the second of 39 poems in the "Calamus" cluster for the sixth edition (1881).

The poem introduces the love/death theme in *Leaves of Grass*. The poet directs his thoughts to the calamus plant: "Scented herbage of my breast, / Leaves from you I glean. . . ." He writes of the beauty of the plant, yet the "faint odor" and "faint-tinged roots" make him think of death, and he visualizes himself dead under its "tomb leaves, body-leaves, growing up above me above death."

"Death is beautiful from you," he says, and he is reminded that nothing is "finally beautiful except death and love."

The leaves of the calamus plant remind the poet of the relationship of love and death, the two most important ingredients of life, inexplicably joined, "beautiful," according to the poet, because love lasts beyond death. "Give me your tone therefore O death, . . . / Give me yourself, for I see that you belong to me now above all, and are folded inseparably together, you love and death are."

These thoughts inspire the poet to connect them with the idea of democracy. He says that he will send the poem's "immortal reverberations through the States," providing "an example to lovers" of the importance of their love in the full scheme of democracy.

"Sea-Drift" (1881)

Cluster title for 11 poems in the sixth edition of *Leaves of Grass* (1881). Seven of the poems are from the "Sea-Shore Memories" cluster (1871),

two are from the 1876 printing, and two of the poems are new.

These poems use the sea and its constant ebb and flow as image and metaphor for the meanings of life and death. The 11 poems are in the following order: "Out of the Cradle Endlessly Rocking," "As I Ebb'd with the Ocean of Life," "Tears," "To the Man-of-War Bird," "Aboard at a Ship's Helm," "On the Beach at Night," "The World Below the Brine," "On the Beach at Night Alone," "Song for All Seas, All Ships," "Patroling Barnegat," and "After the Sea-Ship."

"Second Annex: Good-Bye My Fancy" (1892)

A cluster of 31 poems transferred without revision from *Good-Bye My Fancy* (1891) to the "Death-bed" printing of *Leaves of Grass* (1892), where it, like "Sands at Seventy," became an "annex." *Good-Bye My Fancy* had been published separately the year before as a pamphlet of 66 pages that included a preface ("Preface Note to the Second Annex") and a few other essays. Fourteen of the poems had been published for the first time in *Good-Bye My Fancy*. Like the poems in "Sands at Seventy," these poems reflect Whitman's thinking about "old age" and death and whether his poems will last. See also "Preface Note to 2d Annex."

The poems appear in the following order: "Sail Out for Good, Eidólon Yacht!," "Lingering Last Drops," "Good-Bye My Fancy" [1], "On, on the Same, Ye Jocund Twain!," "My 71st Year," "Apparitions," "The Pallid Wreath," "An Ended Day," "Old Age's Ship and Crafty Death's," "To the Pending Year," "Shakspere—Bacon's Cipher," "Long, Long Hence," "Bravo, Paris Exposition!," "Interpolation Sounds," "To the Sun-set Breeze," "Old Chants," "A Christmas Greeting," "Sounds of the Winter," "A Twilight Song," "When the Full-Grown Poet Came," "Osceola," "A Voice from Death," "A Persian Lesson," "The Commonplace," "The Rounded Catalogue Divine Complete," "Mirages," "L. of G.'s Purport," "The

Unexpress'd," "Grand is the Seen," "Unseen Buds," and "Good-Bye My Fancy!" [2].

Sequel to Drum-Taps

See *Drum-Taps, Sequel to.*

"Shadow and the Light of a Young Man's Soul, The" (1848)

Short story—although termed "fact" by the narrator—first published in UNION MAGAZINE OF LITERATURE AND ART (June 1848). The tale is most accessible now in *Walt Whitman: The Early Poems and the Fiction,* edited by Thomas L. Brasher (New York University Press, 1963).

The Deans are a poor family living in New York and trying to survive hard times. The widow Dean hears of a teaching job in a little district school out in the country and sends her older son Archie to get the job. He is described as "unstable as water," with a "want of energy and resolution." Archie has an inferiority complex—he worries constantly about his "deficiencies"—and is depressed by his faults; but he was also "unflinchingly honest" and would have done anything to help make his mother's life more comfortable.

There is "a refreshing influence in open-air nature," readers are reminded by the narrator, and "the country life begins to have an influence on Archie's psychic makeup."

He meets "an ancient, bony, yellow-faced maiden," an outgoing woman who gets along with everyone. She too had lived a childhood of poverty. Her father's large farm had been lost and sold to pay debts incurred by his "extravagance and dissipation." Instead of giving up on life, however, as Archie Dean seems to be doing, she resolves to get the farm back, and "this determination" tends to determine how she lives. She works hard for the lit-

tle money she received—less for women than for men doing the same sort of work—but she persists. After "long—long—long years" of this hard work and determination, she clears the debt on the farm and furnishes her old father with a comfortable place to live out his last years.

Archie Dean "felt the narrative of this old maid's doings as a rebuke—a sharp-pointed moral to himself and his infirmity of purpose." It made him realize that he would have to change, and the seeds were sown for a renewed interest in life. He is called home to the deathbed of his little brother, David, and he stays to take care of his mother. He is described as developing an "iron will," and the narrator says that Archie "substituted action and cheerfulness for despondency and a fretful tongue."

The story's moral is stated fully in the final paragraph: "Ah, for how many the morose habit which Archie rooted *out* from his nature, becomes by long usage and indulgence rooted *in,* and spreads its bitterness over their existence, and darkens the peace of their families, and carries them through the spring and early summer of life with no inhalement of sweets, and no plucking of flowers!"

CHARACTER

Archie Dean   Main character in the short story "The Shadow and the Light of a Young Man's Soul." After nearly giving up on himself and his family because of extreme poverty and something of an inferiority complex, he meets an old woman who becomes for him an example of someone who has turned her life of poverty around to become content with herself and a friend to her neighbors. Archie learns from her and returns home to help his mother in her old age and to become satisfied at last with his own life.

"Shakspere-Bacon's Cipher" (1887)

First published in COSMOPOLITAN (October 1887); it was the 11th of 31 poems in *Good-Bye My Fancy* (1891); then in "Second Annex: Good-Bye My Fancy" for the "Death-bed" printing of *Leaves of*

Grass (1892). A few critics have argued that Francis Bacon (1561–1626) is the author of plays generally attributed to Shakespeare.

Whitman seems to be suggesting in this poem that the mystery of authorship is still unclear. In a letter to one of his biographers, Richard Maurice BUCKE, dated November 18, 1891, Whitman says, in part, that "the Bacon attribution & cypher are too thin yet—too 'got up' at best—But we will see what time brings out further—at any rate 'probable' or even 'likely' wont do in science or history."

See also BACONIAN THEORY.

"Ship Ahoy!" (1891)

Cut from *Leaves of Grass* after appearing in *Good-Bye My Fancy* (1891).

"Ship Starting, The" (1865)

First appeared in *Drum-Taps* (1865); it was one of the "Paumanok" poems (1871 and 1876); and it was the 17th of 24 poems in the "Inscriptions" cluster for the sixth edition of *Leaves* (1881).

This four-line poem exalts the power of a ship "spreading all sails" as it starts a voyage on "the unbounded sea." The ship's sails make "emulous waves"; that is, the sails in the wind are imitative of the waves.

"Shirval: A Tale of Jerusalem" (1845)

Short story first published in the ARISTIDEAN (March 1845). It is an almost exact rendering of the biblical story of Jesus raising from the dead the only son of a widowed woman of Nain (Luke 7:11–18). Whitman's story is most accessible now in *Walt Whitman: The Early Poems and the Fiction*, edited by Thomas L. Brasher (New York University Press, 1963).

The 24-year old Shirval is the only son of the widow Unni, and he has "been forsaken, by the angels of Life," and now lies dead in his mother's "house of tears." Unni and Zar, Shirval's beloved and bereaved, prepare the body for burial in the town's sepulcher. Unni wept while the two women waited for other mourners to arrive and carry the body to the gravesite. She shouted to heaven, "O, God of Judgments, what am I that thou hast afflicted me thus!"

There was a strange response from the townspeople of Nain. Hundreds of them joined the walk to the graveyard. "Yet none spoke, or understood what mysterious impulse led him thus to honour the funeral-march of the poor widow's son."

Just at the edge of town, at the gate to the city, the townspeople met another group of people, travelers of a different sort. The two groups paused as they merged together. Among the travelers was a small group, at the center of which was a strange-appearing man who now held the attention of everyone close enough to see him; he had "an undefinable presence, more than mortal. . . . His face was beautifully clear, and his eyes, blue as the sky above them, beamed forth benevolence and love." All the mourners of Nain were awed by this man.

He stood over the body of Shirval for only a moment, showing a "mortal look of sympathy" as he looked down on the body. "He spoke,—and his voice, musical and manly, thrilled to the fine chords of every soul in that multitude," he touched the bier and said to Shirval, "Live! thou who are dead!—Arise, and speak to the woman, thy mother!"

Shirval comes to life, and "the awe of the presence of the Stranger gathered like a mantle upon him—and the three [Shirval, Unni, and Zar] knelt upon the ground and bent their faces on the earth-worn sandals of the Man of Wo."

The "Man of Wo," a name no doubt made up by Whitman, is in this fable a Christ-figure. Whitman names the main characters in his story, but the biblical plot remains unchanged.

CHARACTERS

Shirval He is like the unnamed biblical "dead man" of Nain, raised from the dead by Jesus, who, with his disciples and a crowd of followers, meet the mourners of Nain as they walk toward the city graveyard. In Whitman's story, however, he is brought back to life not by Jesus but by a "Stranger," another kind of "undefinable presence," the "Man of Wo."

"Man of Wo" God, or at least some kind of supreme power, labeled by Whitman "an undefinable presence," who raises Shirval from the dead in Whitman's short story "Shirval: A Tale of Jerusalem." The name is undoubtedly made up by Whitman for a character meant as a Christ-figure.

"Shut not Your Doors" (1867)

First appeared in the fourth edition of *Leaves of Grass* (1867); it became the 21st of 24 poems in the "Inscriptions" cluster for the sixth edition (1881).

This six-line poem is Whitman's plea for acceptance by common readers, perhaps because some of his earlier poems were criticized for their sexual imagery: "Shut not your doors to me proud libraries, / For that which was lacking on all your well-fill'd shelves, yet needed most, I bring, . . ."

He says that the words of his book are "nothing, the drift of it every thing." Although the words Whitman refers to, which were criticized and sometimes censored in the mid 19th century, seem rather harmless for 21st-century readers, the poet insists that it is the idea that matters, not the words.

"Sight in Camp in the Daybreak Gray and Dim, A" (1865)

First appeared in the *Drum-Taps* volume (1865) and under this title throughout its printing history; it was the 17th of 43 poems in the "Drum-Taps" cluster for the sixth edition of *Leaves of Grass* (1881).

The poet leaves his tent "in the daybreak gray and dim" to find three "untended" soldiers, dead on stretchers near the hospital, a "gray and heavy blan-

ket, folding, covering all." He lifts the blanket off the face of each in turn, the first an "elderly man so gaunt and grim, with well-gray'd hair, and flesh all sunken about the eyes." The second is a boy: "Who are you sweet boy with cheeks yet blooming?"

> Then to the third—a face nor child nor old,
>   very calm, as of beautiful yellow-white ivory;
> Young man I think I know you—I think this
>   face is the face of the Christ himself,
> Dead and divine and brother of all, and here
>   again he lies.

It is this image of Christ, crucified again, that stuns the poet and makes him aware that we are all "brothers" to those who die in war and that they are Christ-like in their sacrifice for what they hope to be the better good of humankind. Christ, crucified again, represents for the poet the universal significance of a soldier's death.

The title for this poem comes from the poet's simple-early morning awakening from a "sleepless" night to the horrors of war. The poem offers the feeling of the incomprehensible futility of it all. He sees Christ, "Dead and divine and brother of all"— not just once again, but every time a soldier dies in such a sacrificial way. The tone of the poem is as serious as Whitman gets, yet the contrast between his initial "sight in camp" and the sudden, universal impact of the final stanza is ironic in its horror. We have crucified Christ yet again.

The very structure of the poem lends support to its theme. There are four groups of lines. In the first group of six lines, the scene sets up the later irony; the narrator leaves his tent and walks "in the cool fresh air the path near by the hospital tent" and sees "three forms" covered with blankets. In each of the next three groups (four, two, and three lines respectively), the poet uncovers a dead soldier, with the third "a face nor child nor old, very calm, as of beautiful yellow-white ivory . . . / Christ himself." The movement from the relative innocence of the initial impression to curiosity ("Curious I halt and silent stand") to the shock of recognition as he sees Christ in the face of the third soldier shows tremendous structural control in the understatement of the emotions the narrator is going through as he inspects each of the three dead soldiers.

Besides the Christ-imagery, there are also a number of color images that add to the oppressive tone. The words "gray and dim" in the title and first line set the tone. The "brownish wollen" blanket, which becomes "Gray and heavy" on closer inspection, continues the imagery, and "covering all" foreshadows the universal appeal of the final group of lines. (It may also remind readers of the grass in "Song of Myself" which "covers all" of the dead, everywhere.) The "well-gray'd hair" of the first uncovered soldier, the "cheeks yet blooming" of the second face, and the "yellow-white ivory" of the third all enhance the color imagery of the opening lines.

The emotion of curiosity at the beginning, which becomes almost obsessive as the poet takes a look at each of the "untended" soldiers, becomes the emotion of horror as he realizes at the end that each of these men has been "crucified"—for Whitman the ultimate sacrifice of soldiers at war.

This is the second of three consecutive poems in the "Drum-Taps" cluster that present with greater impact than any other poems in the group the theme of death in war. See also "A March in the Ranks Hard-Prest, and the Road Unknown," which immediately precedes this poem in the 1881 edition, and "As Toilsome I Wander'd Virginia's Woods."

The "Drum-Taps" cluster suggests a chronology of the CIVIL WAR, from the initial drum beats of "Beat! Beat! Drums!" as confident soldiers march south, to the muffled drums of the "dead march" as they return home. "A Sight in Camp in the Daybreak Gray and Dim" is one of seven poems within Drum-Taps that describe isolated, yet universal, incidents; "A Sight in Camp" stops time for the moment and yet offers an eternal theme. See also, for similar moments, "Cavalry Crossing a Ford," "Bivouac on a Mountain Side," "By the Bivouac's Fitful Flame," "As Toilsome I Wander'd Virginia's Woods," "I Saw Old General at Bay," and "Look Down Fair Moon."

"Singer in the Prison, The" (1869)

First published in the Washington, D.C., *Saturday Evening Visitor* (December 25, 1869); then it was published in the fifth edition of *Leaves of Grass* (1871); it was the 10th of 38 poems in the "Autumn Rivulets" cluster for the sixth edition (1881).

Whitman heard a concert performance by Euphrosyne Parepa-Rosa at Sing Sing prison in 1869 and was moved by the response of the prisoners to Ms. Parepa-Rosa's singing.

It's one of Whitman's few "occasional" poems, this one to narrate the prisoners' response to the singer's "quaint old hymn" about "A soul confined by bars and bands." The prisoners were "bow'd and moved to weeping" by the song's refrain which could be heard still "Years after" in that place: *"O sight of pity, shame and dole! / O fearful thought—a convict soul."*

Whitman quotes what is apparently the entire song within his own poem.

"Sleepers, The" (1855)

First published as the fourth of 12 untitled poems in the first edition of *Leaves of Grass* (1855); it was titled "Night Poem" in the second edition (1856); and "Sleep Chasings" in the third (1860); it received its present title in the fifth edition (1871); and it was a separate poem, following "Prayer of Columbus," in the sixth edition (1881). The final version is in eight sections and 184 lines.

"The Sleepers" presents the poet's "vision" of hovering over others while they sleep and dream; he then enters the dreams and becomes the dreamer. In Section 1 he CATALOGs some of people he envisions, some dead and some still alive: the bored ("ennuyés"), corpses, drunkards, "onanists," battlefield dead, the insane, the blind and the deaf and dumb; "the married couple sleep calmly in their bed, he with his palm on the hip of the wife, and she with her palm on the hip of the husband."

"I dream in my dream all the dreams of the other dreamers, / And I become the other dreamers." He *becomes* "the actor, the actress, the voter, the politician, / The emigrant and the exile, the criminal that stood in the box," etc. At the end of Section 1 the poet becomes the woman "who adorn'd herself and folded her hair expectantly," waiting for her lover, but it is the "darkness" whom she takes as a lover, suggesting perhaps the distinction she makes between her physical and spiritual lovers: "He whom I call answers me and takes the place of my lover." The darkness is "gentler than my lover," she says; "his flesh was sweaty and panting, / I feel the hot moisture yet that he left me." At the end, she thinks that the darkness and her lover have become one and the same, and she "fade[s] away," apparently into sleep.

Whitman continues the cataloging of sleepers through the next five sections, focusing on particular people: "the sleepless widow" (Section 2); the "beautiful gigantic swimmer swimming naked through the eddies of the sea," later drowned (Section 3); the sailors from a shipwreck, their "howls of dismay" and their washing ashore during the night, dead (Section 4); General Washington saying goodbye to his troops in "the old tavern, the well-belov'd soldiers all pass through" (Section 5); and the poet's mother who welcomed a beautiful "red squaw" into her old homestead and loved and remembered her long after she had gone away (Section 6).

In Section 7 the images of "darkness" and "sleep" become for the poet a metaphor for death—the great "averager" for all the sleepers he has imagined:

I swear they are averaged now—one is no
    better than the other,
The night and sleep have liken'd them and
    restored them,
I swear they are all beautiful,
Everyone that sleeps is beautiful, every thing in
    the dim light is beautiful,
The wildest and bloodiest is over, and all is
    peace.

For the sleeper, while he or she is asleep, "The universe is duly in order, every thing is in its place." The same may be said for the dead.

In the final two stanzas (Section 8), the sleepers "flow hand in hand over the whole earth." The "Asiatic and African are hand in hand, the European and American are hand in hand." All of them are equal in sleep or death; in death the "felon steps forth from the prison, the insane becomes sane, the suffering of sick persons is reliev'd."

Death becomes, for Whitman, little more than sleep. "Why should I be afraid to trust myself to you?" he asks of death. "I am not afraid, I have been well brought forward by you." He does not know how he came to be hand in hand with death, but "I know I came well and shall go well." He is not afraid of the darkness.

In the poem's last line, the poet evokes life-cycle imagery by returning to the mother: "I will duly pass the day O my mother, and duly return to you." Whitman suggests here, most likely, that it is the earth mother to whom he returns; but it may also be a return in the final sleep to his biological mother. Both readings represent the return of sleepers to their beginnings.

"Small the Theme of My Chant" (1867)

First appeared on the flyleaf of the fourth edition of *Leaves of Grass* (1867); then in *November Boughs* (1888); and it was the 42nd of 65 poems in the "First Annex: Sands at Seventy" cluster for the "Deathbed" printing of *Leaves of Grass* (1892). The poem is subtitled "(From the 1867 edition of 'L. of G.')."

Another version of this poem is "One's-Self I Sing," which appeared as the first poem in the "Inscriptions" cluster for the fifth edition of *Leaves* (1871). The meaning of both poems concerns the importance of the "Self," a "simple, separate person," yet part of the whole, the "En-Masse." In this poem Whitman refers to the theme of "One's-Self" as small, "yet the greatest." It is the poet's leading democratic principle: Only out of a knowledge of and love for one's self can anyone come to love others and recognize their equality.

"Sobbing of the Bells, The" (1881)

First published in the *BOSTON DAILY GLOBE* (September 27, 1881); and it was the 10th of 17 poems in the "Songs of Parting" cluster for the sixth edition of *Leaves of Grass* (1881). The poem is subtitled "(*Midnight, Sept. 19–20, 1881.*)"

The poem is a memorial to President James Garfield, who had been shot by an assassin on July 2, 1881, and died September 19. Whitman was in Boston at the time of Garfield's death and wrote the six-line poem for publication in the *Globe* and as a last-minute addition to the 1881 edition of *Leaves of Grass* that he was supervising through the press.

Gay Wilson Allen writes in *The Solitary Singer* (1955) that Whitman had known Garfield "while the young politician was an inexperienced Congressman from Ohio. After the poet's New York Exhibition performance, Garfield would always greet him by shouting, 'After all not to create only,' and Walt was very fond of him. Therefore as the bells tolled on the night of September 19–20, the poet's thoughts naturally went back to those days in Washington when he had ridden on the streetcar and walked with Garfield on the streets of the capital."

"[So Far, and So Far, and On Toward the End]" (1860)

Cut from *Leaves of Grass* after first appearing as "Leaves of Grass, No. 20" in the third edition (1860).

"Solid, Ironical, Rolling Orb" (1865)

Cut from *Leaves of Grass* after first appearing in the *Drum-Taps* volume (1865) and in the next three printings of *Leaves* but cut before the final version (1881).

"So Long!" (1860)

First published in the third edition of *Leaves of Grass* (1860); it was the last of 17 poems in the

"Songs of Parting" cluster for the sixth edition (1881). "So Long!" was the final poem in every edition of *Leaves* from the third on, although it was heavily revised throughout its publication history.

Whitman is given credit in the *Oxford English Dictionary* for using the expression "So Long" (meaning an informal "good-bye") in 1868, only after an English writer had used it in 1865. But the *OED* editors have it wrong. As noted above, Whitman first used the expression, at least in print, in 1860.

"So Long!" is in 71 lines and is both a review of some of Whitman's poetic themes and a friendly good-bye to his readers. "To conclude," he says in the opening line, "I announce what comes after me." What comes after is a description of the poet's vision of his own death and a mystical union with readers.

In reviewing his poems Whitman reminds readers of some of his subjects:

> I have sung the body and the soul, war and
>   peace have I sung, and the songs of life and
>   death,
> And the songs of birth, and shown that there
>   are many births.
> I have offer'd my style to every one, I have
>   journey'd with confident step;
> While my pleasure is yet at the full I whisper *So
>   long!*

He reminds readers of the importance of "adhesiveness"—lasting friendships—one of the themes of *Leaves of Grass*. It refers both to the spiritual relationships he has with readers and to the physical relationships ("love") he has for friends, particularly men (see the "Calamus" poems), but for women as well and, perhaps above all, for the union of the states, his vision for the collective brotherhood of all Americans.

The "songs cease," the poet says, and he abandons them in order to come out from "behind the screen" of his life to face the reader and to tell him:

> Camerado, this is no book,
> Who touches this touches a man, . . .
> It is I you hold and who holds you,
> I spring from the pages into your arms—
>   decease calls me forth.

Whitman did not believe in the Christian concept of death but in the greater value of immortality. This union of the poet with his readers will, he believes, continue after his death—as, in fact, it does:

Dear friend whoever you are take this kiss,
I give it especially to you, do not forget me, . . .
An unknown sphere more real than I dream'd,
    more direct, darts awakening rays about me,
    So long!
Remember my words, I may again return, . . .

He returns again every time someone picks up his book to read his poems. The above quotation's last line may remind readers of the final stanza of "Song of Myself":

Failing to fetch me at first keep encouraged,
Missing me one place search another,
I stop somewhere waiting for you.

Whitman's concept of the cycle of life, death, and life again (in immortality) is constant throughout *Leaves of Grass*. Every time someone picks up my book, Whitman is saying, I am there; every time someone reads one of my poems, I am there.

"Some Fact-Romances" (1845)

A work of fiction containing five untitled "incidents," told as "fact-romances," first published in the ARISTIDEAN (December 1845). It was reprinted as "The Old Black Widow" in the BROOKLYN DAILY EAGLE (November 12, 1846). Each of the five incidents was reprinted separately, but they are reprinted together in *Walt Whitman: The Early Poems and the Fiction*, edited by Thomas L. Brasher (New York University Press, 1963).

In the two introductory paragraphs, the narrator assures the reader that he "has the pledged personal veracity of the writer . . . but [also] as a man" that the incidents are true.

In the first incident, a beach party on the Huntington south shore of LONG ISLAND is interrupted by a storm. A young man saves his sister from drowning, but just before he gets to shore with her, he sees that his "beloved" is still with the overturned boat yelling for help. He abandons his sister in order to save his lover, but his sister then drowns. The two lovers marry, but he is never the same, constantly dreaming of "his sister's dripping hair . . . against his cheek." He dies, and the "story is yet told among the people thereabouts. . . ."

In the second incident, a black widow-woman of nearly 70 years lives opposite a "row of stables for horses and public vehicles," from where the old woman heard "coarse oaths and indecent ribaldry." She notices a barefoot girl of 12 or 13 years "strolling about" the stables and is afraid for her. The girl is "a deaf mute, the daughter of a wretched intemperate couple in the neighborhood, who were letting her grow up as the weeds grow." The old woman devotes the next several months collecting from neighbors and strangers the $200 necessary to enroll the girl in an institution provided for the deaf and dumb. The woman is successful finally, and, although the narrator has lost track of both the old woman and the girl, he concludes by saying, "surely a purer or more elevated deed of disinterested love and kindness never was performed!"

In the third incident, a French immigrant, who lives in a country town near New York is wealthy but eccentric, and his neighbors think him "deranged." But he is harmless and so they let him alone. One day, he takes his wife into the city for medical advice about her ailments, and, against the insistence of several doctors that she be kept under observation, he loads her into his covered wagon again, on a bed he had made for her in the back, and starts for home. Out in the countryside, he turns the wagon over to a hired man who accompanies them and starts off on foot for their farm. After a couple of miles the hired man stops the wagon to have a look at the woman, and discovers that she is dead. He unhitches the horses and rides one as fast as he can to catch up with the husband. Instead of returning to the wagon the man walks on, even past his home and into a large "swampy wood," where he wanders alone "for three days and nights, and when found at the end of that time, all pale, ragged, weak and bloody, [he] is a confirmed maniac."

In the fourth, a young boy named Saunders is imprisoned for forgeries on his employers. He might have gotten away with the crime except that he went to a pawnbrokers' shop in the Bowery in New York in order to retrieve a little piece of jewelry he had left with the pawnbroker, a keepsake from his dead mother. "That half hour cost him the doom" that was then "meted out to him" by the authorities.

In the fifth, the narrator tells a story about his own mother and grandmother worrying one stormy night when the horse that his grandfather had ridden on business that day returns late at night with an empty saddle. The two women then hear "something" in a spare garden room that frightens them and keeps them awake the rest of the night. The next morning grandfather returns, explaining that the horse had broken its bridle and had run off. When the three of them look in the spare room to see what the noise had been, they discover the peach-tree limbs that had been stored in the room had dropped peaches one at a time, making the noise of someone walking.

"Sometimes with One I Love" (1860)

Titled "Calamus No. 39" in the third edition of *Leaves of Grass* (1860); it received its present title (1867); it was the 33rd of 39 poems in the "Calamus" cluster for the sixth edition (1881).

This four-line poem expresses the value even in "unreturn'd love": "I loved a certain person ardently and my love was not return'd, / Yet out of that I have written these songs."

Whitman had moments of depression and it shows sometimes in his poems; but far more often he responded with optimism to life's setbacks.

"Song at Sunset" (1860)

First published as "Chants Democratic, No. 8" for the third edition of *Leaves of Grass* (1860); it received its present title in the fourth edition (1867); and it was

the fifth of 17 poems in the "Songs of Parting" cluster for the sixth edition (1881).

As with other poems in this cluster, Whitman writes of his love of both life and death: "Wonderful to depart! / Wonderful to be here." It is wonderful to "celebrate" others and himself, and he celebrates Nature as well: "Surely there is something more in each of the trees, some living soul."

He is concerned about departing from all of this that he loves, but he will "sing to the last the equalities modern or old, / I sing the endless finalés of things." He was not yet concerned about his own death in 1860, but this is another of many poems by Whitman declaring his affirmation of life, even in death.

"Song for All Seas, All Ships" (1873)

First published as "Sea Captains Young or Old" in the *NEW YORK DAILY GRAPHIC* (April 4, 1873); then under its present title as one of four "Centennial Songs" in a third printing of the fifth edition of *Leaves of Grass* (1876); and it was the ninth of 11 poems in the "Sea-Drift" cluster for the sixth edition (1881). The poem was written originally to honor the crews and more than 800 passengers of two steamships (the *NORTHFLEET* and the *ATLANTIC*), lost at sea in 1873.

There is no mention of any ship or captain in this poem, because it is meant to be universal, a "song for all seas, all ships." And Whitman presents his "rude brief recitative" as a "chant for the sailors of all nations."

> But do you reserve especially for yourself and
>   for the soul of man one flag above all the
>   rest, . . .
> A pennant universal, subtly waving all time,
>   o'er all brave sailors,
> All seas, all ships.

Just as the sea treats all ships equally, so should we treat equally the nations represented by the flags of these ships.

The "Butterfly Photograph," by Phillips and Taylor, 1873
(Library of Congress, Prints and Photographs Division)

"Song for Certain Congressmen" (1850)

First published in the NEW YORK EVENING POST (March 2, 1850); an "early poem" not later published in *Leaves of Grass*. It is most accessible now in Francis Murphy (editor), *Walt Whitman: The Complete Poems* (Penguin Books, 1996).

The satirical, rhyming poem argues against the move in Congress to compromise on the question of SLAVERY.

"Song for Occupations, A" (1855)

First appeared untitled as the second of 12 poems in the first edition of *Leaves of Grass* (1855); it was given the title "Poem of the Daily Work of the Workmen and Workwomen of these States" for the second edition (1856); then "Chants Democratic, No. 3" (1860); then "To Workingmen" (1867); it was "Carol of Occupations" in the fifth edition (1871); finally under its present title and as the 10th separate poem following the "Calamus" cluster in the sixth edition (1881). Often revised, the "finished" poem is in six sections and 151 lines.

"A Song for Occupations" is one of Whitman's many poems on the theme of equality, an essential ingredient for democracy. All occupations are equal in importance, as are all people. The "eternal meanings" may be found in occupations. The poet addresses "Workmen and Workwomen" everywhere. "Neither a servant nor a master I," he says in Section 1. "If you stand at work in a shop I stand as nigh as the nighest in the same shop, . . . / If you become degraded, criminal, ill, then I become so for your sake." Equality requires empathy, the poet suggests here; we become one another in our outward manifestation of this equality; he says then, parenthetically:

(Because you are greasy or pimpled, or were
   once drunk, or a thief,
Or that you are diseas'd, or rheumatic, or a
   prostitute,
Or from frivolity or impotence, or that you are
   no scholar and never saw your name in
   print,
Do you give in that you are any less immortal?)

The poet turns in Section 3 to the idea of equality of occupations as an argument for the importance of each person's unique perception of the world, particularly with the idea that all people are connected to Nature and all of its manifestations, and regardless of religious or ethnic background: "We consider bibles and religions divine . . . / I say they have all grown out of you, . . . It is not they who give the life, it is you who give the life." Whitman believed in the importance of all religious beliefs, that all of them lead to God.

Section 4 considers the president and other politicians; the president, secretaries, and Congress, he says, are all "here for you, . . . it is not you who are here for [them]." And this equality goes for scholars, architects, and musicians as well; they are all the same, all equal with the rest: "All architecture is what you do to it when you look upon it, . . . / All music is what awakes from you when you are reminded by the instruments." The music uplifts us, but the composer is no better in Whitman's philosophy than anyone else.

Whitman takes us in Section 5 to yet a third level of understanding by suggesting that this unique perception available in everyone comes from deep within the soul. "Can each [person] see signs of the best by a look in the looking-glass? is there nothing greater or more? / Does all sit there with you, with the mystic unseen soul?" Whitman admits to a "paradox" here, because, he says, "Objects gross and the unseen soul are one."

He offers examples of this paradox by cataloging "occupations" through the rest of Section 5, the poet reminding the reader near the end that it is the person, not the occupation, that is important: "The hourly routine of your own or any man's life, the shop, yard, store, or factory, / These shows all near you by day and night—workman! whoever you are, your daily life!" Regardless of the "shows" of occupations, it is the workman's "daily life" that matters.

In summary (Section 6) Whitman reminds readers that what is important in democracy is the singer not the song, the preacher not the "script," the wood carver not the desk—and the "men and women like you."

> When the psalm sings instead of the singer,
> When the script preaches instead of the
>   preacher,
> When the pulpit descends and goes instead of
>   the carver that carved the supporting
>   desk, . . .
> I intend to reach them my hand, and make as
>   much of them as I do of men and women
>   like you.

As Ezra Pound and other poets would say in defining imagistic poetry 60 years after this poem was written, "the image *is* the poem." Whatever happens in one's unique sensual response to art, music, poetry, (and architecture, or anything else, Whitman seems to be saying), it is in that sensual response where the beauty may be found.

Just as all people are equal regardless of gender, race, or creed, so are all occupations equal, because it is the people working the occupations that matter. And it is this unity of occupations that makes the workers feel the unity of themselves with others.

"Song of Joys, A" (1860)

First published as "Poem of Joys" in the third edition of *Leaves of Grass* (1860); it received its present title and was the sixth separate poem following the "Calamus" cluster in the sixth edition (1881). Whitman made several revisions in the poem before it reached its final form of 161 lines.

"A Song of Joys" is about all the various "joys" available in life. Life can be lived to the fullest no matter the activity:

> O to make the most jubilant song!
> Full of music—full of manhood, womanhood,
>   infancy!
> Full of common employments—full of grain
>   and trees.

It is as if Whitman is speaking to himself in these opening lines, wishing for the right words and music with which to complete the poem. "Grain and trees," the symbols of life and leaves, are the stuff of his songs.

There is a catalog of examples of Americans at work or play, all of the items providing images of "joy." The poet envies each of the people he describes: "O the engineer's joys! to go with a locomotive! / To hear the hiss of steam, the merry shriek, the steam-whistle, the laughing locomotive!" The catalog of people includes the horseman and horsewoman, the fireman, the "strong-brawn'd fighter," the mother, the miner, the whaleman, the orator, the farmer, the soldier, the dying man.

Other joys are catalogued: "the joy of that vast elemental sympathy which only the human soul is capable of generating and emitting in steady and limitless floods." There are also the joys of youth, of pensive thought, the thought of death, and the joy of death; the joys of "dear companions and of the merry word and laughing face."

Ever the optimist, Whitman leaves little room here for unhappiness. America is for the poet a land of happiness, of joy available for everyone who seeks it. Very little is left out of Whitman's catalog of life's joys, not even Death. "Death" is life-affirming, he believes, because the earth and all that lives benefits from the body's "returning to the purifications."

And in the final stanza, he provides a summing up:

O to have life henceforth a poem of new joys!
To dance, clap hands, exult, shout, skip, leap,
    roll on, float on!
To be a sailor of the world bound for all ports,
A ship itself, (see indeed these sails I spread to
    the sun and air,)
A swift and swelling ship full of rich words, full
    of joys.

"A Song of Joy" presents Whitman's vision of an America of independent and free individuals proud of themselves and happy to be alive in such a country.

"Song of Myself" (1855)

First appeared as the opening and longest poem in the first edition of *Leaves of Grass* (1855), untitled, as were each of the 12 poems in that edition; it was titled "Poem of Walt Whitman, an American" for the second edition (1856); it became "Walt Whitman" for the third edition (1860); it was not titled "Song of Myself" until the sixth edition (1881).

The poem was in a constant state of revision throughout the six editions of *Leaves of Grass*, although the first version is only 10 lines shorter than the last. The final version contains 1,346 lines in 52 sections. It is arguably the most important poem in *Leaves of Grass*, partly because of its placement by Whitman near the beginning of the book, making it introductory, but also because it presents most of the book's themes, especially his vision for a democratic America and of its connection to the union of human beings with God.

First-time readers of "Song of Myself" are often turned off by the seeming egotism of a poet narcissistic enough to "celebrate" and "sing" himself. The poet is singing, however, of a simple faith in democracy and of an America made up of individuals each assuming faith in a nation as diverse as any on earth, everyone an independent self, yet free and equal. "Song of Myself" could stand as the country's national poem, so packed is it with the poet's idealistic vision for America.

I celebrate myself, and sing myself,
And what I assume you shall assume,
For every atom belonging to me as good
    belongs to you.

I will "sing myself," the poet says to the reader in these opening lines, but I will also "sing you"; and the first of the major themes of the poem is introduced. He "sings" of the equality of all Americans—the single most important democratic principle upon which the nation is built.

Throughout the poem he offers CATALOGs (lists) of people he identifies with as equals in the America of his vision. In Section 15, for example, he provides one-line pictures of Americans at work: "The pure contralto sings in the organ loft, / The carpenter dresses his plank, the tongue of his foreplane whistles its wild ascending lisp."

And he continues this catalog with more than 50 other one-line descriptions, including "children" home for Thanksgiving dinner, the boat "Pilot," his "mate," the "duck-shooter," "deacons . . . at the altar," the "spinning-girl," the "farmer," the "lunatic," the "quadroon girl" (sold at auction), the "drunkard," the "machinist," the "policeman," the "gatekeeper," the "half-breed," the "marksman," the "newly-come immigrants," the "squaw," the "connoisseur," the "one-year wife," the "clean-hair'd Yankee girl," the "pedler," the "President," the "Missourian," the "flatboatman," etc., each worker described as doing what he or she does.

Whitman is not out to bore readers with this long list but to show the diversity of working people in the America of the mid-19th century and, more important, to argue for their individual value to the nation. At the end of this lengthy catalog, the poet reminds us of the poem's opening, celebratory thought:

> And these tend inward to me, and I tend
> outward to them,
> And such as it is to be of these more or less I
> am,
> And of these one and all I weave the song of
> myself.

The "I" of "Song of Myself," in other words, is each of these working people and each of them is the narrator of the poem. Each is important, first to him or her self and then to one another. Whitman cannot provide a line for every working man and woman in America, but he can provide enough to remind readers of the greatness of diversity and that in a democracy all occupations are valuable and that there is no second class.

SECTIONS 1–4

The "weaving" of this "song" of the self involves the mystical experience of union with God, a thematic element not only in "Song of Myself" but in other poems in *Leaves of Grass*. In "Song of Myself," the theme is introduced in the second stanza of the first section: "I loafe and invite my soul,/ I lean and loafe at my ease observing a spear of summer grass." Whitman invites readers to an understanding of the mystical journey he takes in order to arrive at his vision of democracy. It is a journey of the poet's self and soul to a merger with God. The idea introduces readers to Whitman's pantheistic belief that God is in all creatures and in all the forces of nature, "Nature without check," as he says in the section's last line (see PANTHEISM). The "spear of summer grass" is the symbol of such a union; "leaves of grass" is used in a similar way throughout the book.

An awareness of one's sensual responses to everyday things is God-given and not to be ashamed of, not even sexual responses (Section 2). He breathes in the perfumes made by human beings, but he prefers the smells of nature, and he celebrates in stanza three each of the five "natural" senses: the "smoke" of his own breath; the "buzz'd whispers" he hears; the smell of "hay in the barn"; the touch of a lover in a "few light kisses" or in a

"reaching round of arms"; and the sight of the "play of shine and shade" on the trees.

He feels his own strength in his "health," and healthy senses, he says, are essential to a healthy individual, suggesting that it also produces a healthy nation. He brags about his own health in Section 2, but he is still merely bragging for humankind:

> Stop this day and night with me and you shall
> possess the origin of all poems,
> You shall possess the good of the earth and
> sun, . . .
> You shall no longer take things at second or
> third hand, . . .
> You shall not look through my eyes either, nor
> take things from me,
> You shall listen to all sides and filter them from
> your self.

The individual aware of his or her sensual response to natural things is also one who can think for him or her self and takes nothing at "second or third hand."

In Section 3 the poet suggests that there is too much talking about the past and future and too little action. There is no better moment for living than the present moment. There is no more "heaven or hell than there is now," he says, so live now. "Urge and urge and urge, . . . Always sex . . . always a breed of life." Whitman got in trouble with readers and critics for his liberal thinking about sex, but he believed that sex was so much a part of the "natural" life that to ignore it was unhealthy, for the individual and for society. Both the spiritual and the physical are important to the self, and to ignore either jeopardizes the health of both.

Whitman catalogs in Section 4 some of the things that make up the character of the poem's narrator; "but," he says, "they are not the Me myself." Others can think they know the "Me," and even he himself does not have the full picture yet. So he watches and waits. "I witness and wait," he says in the section's last line. He waits for union with the soul to teach him more about himself.

SECTION 5

The union of the body and soul is central to the mystical experience. Whitman suggests this in addressing the soul at the beginning of Section 5: "I believe in you my soul, the other 'I am' must not abase itself to you, / And you must not be abased to the other." The other "I am" is the self, which the poet keeps separate from but equal to the soul.

The poet reminds the soul of a previous "sexual" experience:

> I mind how once we lay such a transparent
>   summer morning,
> How you settled your head athwart my hips
>   and gently turn'd over upon me,
> And parted the shirt from my bosom-bone, and
>   plunged your tongue to my bare-stript heart,
> And reach'd till you felt my beard, and reach'd
>   till you held my feet.

Whitman uses sexual experiences metaphorically here as a way of attempting to explain in human terms a complex spiritual union. The poem's first four sections are meant to prepare readers for this union of body and soul. It is a union, Whitman says, that offers also union with God ("the spirit of God is the brother of my own" [spirit]). And it is a union with "all the men ever born" who are his brothers and with all women, who are his "sisters and lovers."

This is arguably the clearest statement of Whitman's theme of "brotherhood" anywhere in *Leaves of Grass*. And it is not just that we are brothers and sisters of all men and women living at any given moment but at any time, past or future. (See also "Crossing Brooklyn Ferry," where, in Section 8, the "I" of the poem is obliterated by the "we.")

The final stanza of Section 5 describes the emotional effect of this moment of union of body and soul with God: "Swiftly arose and spread around me the peace and knowledge that pass all the argument of the earth, / And I know that the hand of God is the promise of my own." It is the New Testament's "peace of God, which passeth all understanding," also a mystery.

Since God is now in me, the poet seems to be saying, I must pass along to others this knowledge of how God works in the human spirit. And readers are then reminded of the poet's vision for democracy: "And that all the men ever born are also my brothers, and the women my sisters and lovers, /

And that a Kelson of the creation is love." A "kelson" is the long beam running the length of a ship's hull, providing structural strength, and "love" provides the structural strength in the relations among people. Even that is not quite enough. Whitman's democratic principles include also the things of Nature:

> And limitless are leaves stiff or drooping in the
>   fields,
> And brown ants in the little wells beneath
>   them,
> And mossy scabs of the worm fence, heap'd
>   stones, elder, mullein and poke-weed.

Gay Wilson Allen calls the eight-line stanza at the end of Section 5 "one of the most magnificent passages in the literature of mysticism, conveying a sense of union with God, brotherhood with men and women, and sympathy with all living things, however small, lowly, or common."

The most significant single image of a common living thing in "Song of Myself" is "the grass," used by Whitman both as a unifying device in this poem and for the whole of *Leaves of Grass*.

SECTIONS 6–8

In Section 6 the poet imagines the grass as a metaphor for the eternal circle of life, death, and resurrection. He opens the section, however, denying his own understanding of how the metaphor works: "A child said *What is the grass?* fetching it to me with full hands, / How could I answer the child? I do not know what it is any more than he." The poet suggests several possible answers, each image of which is woven later into other stanzas. He says,

> I guess it must be the flag of my disposition, out
>   of hopeful green stuff woven.
>
> Or I guess it is the handkerchief of the Lord,
> A scented gift and remembrancer designedly
>   dropt, . . .
>
> Or I guess the grass is itself a child, the produced
>   babe of the vegetation.
>
> Or I guess it is a uniform hieroglyphic,
> And it means, Sprouting alike in broad zones and
>   narrow zones,

Growing among black folks as among white,
Kanuck, Tuckahoe, Congressman, Cuff, I give
 them the same, I receive them the same.

And now it seems to me the beautiful uncut hair
 of graves.

The last image ("the beautiful uncut hair of graves") reveals Whitman's developing fascination with death, especially with the idea that death is the ultimate affirmation of life. The last stanza of Section 6 pushes this grass/death image a bit further:

The smallest sprout shows there is really no
 death,
And if ever there was it led forward life, and
 does not wait at the end to arrest it,
And ceas'd the moment life appear'd.

The idea that there is "no death" is pantheistic: God is not a personality, he believes; the spirit of God is in all of Nature, including human nature, and all things reflect that spirit. The section ends with this couplet: "All goes onward and outward, nothing collapses, / And to die is different from what any one supposed, and luckier."

Section 7 begins with this death-as-life imagery: "Has any one supposed it lucky to be born? / I hasten to inform him or her it is just as lucky to die, and I know it." He "knows" because it is part of his discovery of what the "self" is and how "love" is used by God as a force in society. The poet "passes" over, levitates above, the dying and the newly born and begins to wake to the cycle of life.

The cycle is evident in the three couplets at the beginning of Section 8: "life" with the newborn; "love" with the "youngster and the red-faced girl"; and "death" with the suicide. The poet provides several examples of the cycle of life at work in what he sees as he passes over various moments in the lives of people at various periods in history. He sees "the hounded slave," for example, a man who "wince[s] at the bite of dogs"; he is with "an old artillerist" at his "fort's bombardment"; he is with a Texas child listening to the horror tales of massacre at the Alamo; he is with a sailor who hears his captain say: "We have not struck, . . . we have just begun our part of the fighting." In Section 9 he helps a farmer deposit a load of "dried grass" in his barn, unseen by the farmer at harvest time.

SECTIONS 10–14

Whitman provides a catalog of lonely or isolated people at work in Sections 10–14. They are people sometimes isolated by their own opinion of themselves. The poet is still in his levitated state or perhaps only in a dream, like a boy "asleep on the gather'd leaves with [his] dog and gun by [his] side." He is on a "Yankee clipper" under "sky-sails"; he's with a "runaway slave" who stops by the poet's house, tired and awkward (Section 10); he "loiters" with a "butcher-boy" and enjoys the "repartee" and he watches a blacksmith (Section 12), each of whom "hits in his place"; he sees a negro, driving a team of horses, the sun falling "on the black of his polish'd and perfect limbs" (Section 13). The poet loves them all: "In me the caresser of life wherever moving, . . . not a person or object missing, / Absorbing all to myself and for this song." All of this, too, is open to the poet and makes him even more aware of himself. And he does "not call the tortoise unworthy because she is not something else, / And the jay in the woods never studied the gamut, yet trills pretty well to me." Whitman uses the word "gamut" here to mean the musical scale; it doesn't matter that the jay manages only a shrill, harsh scream (Section 13).

The poet too is who he is (Section 14). He sees all of these things in nature, and he sees "in them and myself the same old law."

What is commonest, cheapest, nearest, easiest,
 is Me,
Me going in for my chances, spending for vast
 returns,
Adorning myself to bestow myself on the first
 that will take me,
Not asking the sky to come down to my good
 will,
Scattering it freely forever.

He asks nothing from anyone, not even God. They are all a part of him already, and he is part of them.

Section 11, perhaps the most written-about section of "Song of Myself," fits with the cataloging of isolated people in Sections 10–14, except that Section 11 offers an extremely sensual scene of a lonely woman, 28 years old, looking out from her seaside house at "Twenty-eight young men" bathing "by the shore, / Twenty-eight young men and all so friendly." The poet sees the woman become the 29th bather while staying "stock still" in her room. He sees her "dancing and laughing along the beach . . . / The rest did not see her, but she saw them and loved them." They do not see the trembling hand as it passes over their bodies; nor do they "ask who seizes fast to them," or "who puffs and declines with pendant and bending arch." The poet understands why the lonely woman imagines this sexual fantasy. It is one of the most lyrical sections in all of *Leaves of Grass*.

SECTIONS 15–19

Section 15 is a lengthy catalog (as described earlier in this essay), more than 50 one- or two-line descriptions of Americans at work doing whatever they do best. The poet continues to look outward to these people, connecting to them out of love and respect, and recognizing their equality with each other and with him, out of which he "weaves," as he says in the section's last line, "the song of myself." They have all added to his knowledge of himself.

As he continues on this mystical journey, however, he becomes more and more aware of his union with the people he sees. In Section 16 he no longer merely observes them, he becomes them. "I am of old and young," he says in the opening line, "of the foolish as much as the wise, / Regardless of others, ever regardful of others." He is "A Southerner soon as a Northerner, a planter nonchalant and hospitable down by the Oconee I live." He is "A Yankee bound my own way ready for trade"; "A Kentuckian walking the vale of the Elkhorn"; "a Louisianian or Georgian"; a "Comrade of Californians, comrade of free North-Westerners"; "Comrade of raftsmen and coalmen, comrade of all who shake hands and welcome to drink and meat"; "A learner with the simplest, a teacher of the thoughtfullest"; "Of every hue and caste am I, of every rank and religion."

He pictures democracy at work in this great diversity of people and in his newfound ability to become them. He has become diverse himself and will later announce this in his claim of being America's poet. It is what EMERSON recognized in Whitman's poetry from his first reading of *Leaves of Grass*, and he willingly ceded him the honor.

"I resist any thing better than my own diversity," Whitman says, "And am not stuck up, and am in my place." Whitman acknowledged late in life his own egotism and no doubt rightly so, but this is not an example of his ego at work. As is made clear in the opening stanza of "Song of Myself," it is not for himself alone that he is bragging but for all of man- and womankind; everyone is capable of arriving at the same point, of acknowledging his or her own importance in the scheme of things, especially in the scheme of American democracy. The "diversity" is from the mystical merging of all variant personalities into the poet's own personality. He knows his equal place in society, and, as he says in the section's last three lines, everything is in its proper place:

(The moth and the fish-eggs are in their place,
The bright suns I see and the dark suns I
   cannot see are in their place,
The palpable is in its place and the impalpable
   in its place.)

All is right with the world of democracy.

At the beginning of Section 17, the poet provides a reminder that this vision he describes is not his alone. "These are really the thoughts of all men in all ages and lands, they are not original with me." Early criticism of Whitman's poetic form notwithstanding, he is also using a FREE VERSE form that is as old as the Old Testament, a poetic rhythm familiar to the Hebrew of the Psalms or Ecclesiastes. And he ends the section with a further note of pantheism: "This is the grass that grows wherever the land is and the water is, / This the common air that bathes the globe." Awareness of selfhood comes when one recognizes the equality of all things. It is a humbling but necessary process in the soul's purification.

Another part of the purification process involves recognition of the importance of opposites. Section 18 introduces this idea: "Have you heard that it was good to gain the day?/ I also say it is good to fall, battles are lost in the same spirit in which they are won." The victor and vanquished are of equal importance, Whitman believed. He offers honor "to those who have failed"; to "war-vessels sank in the sea"; and to "the numberless unknown heroes equal to the greatest heroes known!" In Section 19 he adds the examples of the "wicked" who are "just the same as the righteous"; and he names the "kept-woman," the "thief," the "heavy-lipp'd slave," and the "venerealee." They are of equal importance with the righteous, and the poet makes "appointments" with them all.

Whitman says through these examples that we cannot know "good" without knowing "evil" just as well. A person's greatest sin, Whitman suggests, is his or her sense of sin. Purification of the soul involves acceptance of sin, acceptance of all things on which society tends to frown. Those who frown do not understand this concept of purification.

SECTIONS 20–30

In Section 20, the poet returns to the self, further examining the idea of purification of the soul. "All I mark as my own," he says, "you shall offset it with your own, / Else it were time lost listening to me." You must learn to think for yourself, to purify your own soul. "In all people I see myself, none more and not one a barley-corn less, / And the good or bad I say of myself I say of them." The poet knows who he is, and he urges others to know themselves as well.

The rest of Section 20 and Sections 21–24 are devoted to the poet's description of himself, perhaps as proof of how well he knows who he is and what his role in society is. He begins with his physical fitness in the last half of Section 20 as preparation for the opening line of Section 21: "I am the poet of the Body and I am the poet of the Soul." He is acquainted with the "pleasures" of both heaven and hell, two more opposites. He is also "the poet of the woman same as the man, / And I say it is as great to be a woman as to be a man." There are few times in *Leaves of Grass* when Whitman fails to include WOMEN in a line that states something about men. Awareness of equality, Whitman suggests in these sections, leads also to a purification of the soul.

At the end of Section 21 he offers a lyrical and passionate invocation to the earth to be his "lover." "Smile O voluptuous cool-breath'd earth! . . . Smile, for your lover comes." In between these first and last lines of the eight-line stanza, he defines the earth in all its natural majesty.

In Section 22 he turns to the Sea and its "crooked inviting fingers" and recognizes that he and the sea are also lovers: "Cushion me soft, rock me in billowy drowse, / Dash me with amorous wet, I can repay you." He will "repay" the sea by being its poet too, "partaker of influx and efflux, extoller of hate and conciliation"; he is the poet of both goodness and wickedness, virtue and vice. Just as the sea plays no favorites, the poet plays no favorites; all are equal in importance. And he will continue to use the sea as metaphor throughout *Leaves of Grass.*

Whitman turns in Section 23 to two other opposites: time past vs. time present and reality vs. spirituality. He accepts time "absolutely." Time is "without flaw," he says, "it alone rounds and completes all." He accepts "Reality." And he honors "positive science" for all it has accomplished and catalogs lexicographers, chemists, mariners ("who put the ship through dangerous unknown seas"), geologists, doctors, mathematicians. But he says to them,

> Gentlemen, to you the first honors always!
> Your facts are useful, and yet they are not my
>   dwelling,
> I but enter by them to an area of my dwelling.

The poet's dwelling is "of life untold," life imagined perhaps rather than proved by science. Facts only provide a way into the world of the poet, Whitman suggests, where dwells the imagination, a world of the mystic perhaps but a world available to all.

The lengthy Section 24 offers the relations of the poet to other people, repeating the seemingly egotistical impact of the poem's first section yet arguing for the capability of all people to do exactly the same thing; that is, to know him or her self and to bask in the mental picture.

> Walt Whitman, a kosmos, of Manhattan the son,
> Turbulent, fleshy, sensual, eating, drinking and
>   breeding,
> No sentimentalist, no stander above men and
>   women or apart from them,
> No more modest than immodest.

He says, "Whoever degrades another degrades me, / And whatever is done or said returns at last to me." No man is an island, the English poet John Donne insisted in one of his sermons, and "any man's death diminishes me, for I am a part of mankind." Whitman insists on the truth of this idea: "By God! I will accept nothing which all cannot have their counterpart of on the same terms."

People who, because of "dumb voices," cannot otherwise make themselves heard, can be heard through the poet of America: "Through me forbidden voices" may be heard, he says. He will speak for all people who, for whatever reason, cannot make themselves heard.

He believes "in the flesh and the appetites," and he "dotes" on his own sexuality; and his is "divine . . . inside and out, and I make holy whatever I touch or am touch'd from." This is God in the human being, where both heaven and hell may be found. Why shouldn't he "dote" then? Why shouldn't he feel the pride of self?

It is the responsibility of the poet, Whitman suggests then in Section 25, to pass this philosophy on to others; and that is the purpose of "Song of Myself" and of other poems in *Leaves of Grass.* "Speech is the twin of my vision," he says. But he has already talked enough, he suggests at the beginning of Section 26; "Now I will do nothing but listen." Nevertheless, he continues to talk, offering to the reader a catalog of the sounds he hears when he "listens," all of which generate knowledge, everything from the "bravuras of birds" to the train's "steam-whistle" and the "violoncello," more than 25 sounds cataloged, all of which help to solve the "puzzle of puzzles," the act of "Being."

Sections 25 and 26 are devoted to the poet's sensual responses to sight and sound respectively; Sections 27–30 are devoted to the sense of touch, a sensitivity that Whitman uses as a physical manifestation of a spiritual truth. The sense of touch is sexually powerful for Whitman. "To touch my person to some one else's is about as much as I can stand." Touch is strong enough to drive his other senses away; "I am given up by traitors, / I talk wildly, I have lost my wits," but he quickly acknowledges that he alone is his own worst traitor. He refers to his sense of touch as a "villain. . . . / Unclench your floodgates, you are too much for me."

But just as water seeks its own level, so does truth; "All truths wait in all things," he says in the opening line of Section 30. "Logic and sermons never convince. . . . Only what proves itself to every man and woman is so." Truth lies in the sense of touch as it does in all the senses; self-identification lies in one's sensual response to all that life brings.

SECTIONS 31–33

Whitman returns in the lyrical Section 31 to the relationship of common things to the miracles they represent. He has gone far enough now in his mystical journey to feel better able to define the "grass," not so much for the child of Section 6 as for himself. The first line provides a new definition: "I believe a leaf of grass is no less than the journeywork of the stars"—the common and the miraculous. He lists other common things in the section's 21-line catalog, including the "mouse," which, he says, "is miracle enough to stagger sextillions of infidels." He wonders here how anyone can look at the mouse, or any common thing, and fail to acknowledge the presence of God.

"I think I could turn and live with animals," the poet writes at the beginning of Section 32; "they're so placid and self-contain'd." He separates humans from other animals for the sake of his argument here. Animals "do not sweat and whine about their condition, / They do not lie awake in the dark and weep for their sins, / They do not make me sick discussing their duty to God." God is in all things, Whitman believes; the greater "duty" of the human animal, therefore, is to one's self and the purification of the soul. This *is* their duty to God.

The poet's vision becomes progressively clearer in the next five sections. In Section 33 he is "afoot with [his] vision." "Space and Time! Now I see it is true, what I guess'd at, / What I guess'd when I loaf'd on the grass." Space and time become one at this point, inseparable in his "vision." Whitman catalogs in the long third stanza events that are all going on at the same time. He sees the active life of the country at work or play: "Scorch'd ankle-deep by the hot sand, hauling my boat down the shallow river," he becomes the people he sees. He sees "where the panther walks to and fro on a limb overhead; . . . Where the brook puts out of the roots of the old tree and flows to the meadow; . . . Where the she-whale swims with her calf and never forsakes it"; and so on. "I visit the orchards of spheres and look at the product; . . . I go hunting polar furs and the seal." The poet wonders at the life going on in each new scene he visits in his vision. He treads "day and night such roads."

He is "pleas'd" initially with what he sees "speeding through space." But the catalog of people and places begins to change, and he sees things that are not so pleasing: the scene of a "feverish patient," for example, to whom he hands a glass of lemonade. Later he encounters "The mother of old, condemn'd for a witch, burnt with dry wood, her children gazing on, / The hounded slave that flags in the race . . . / The twinges that sting like needles his legs and neck, the murderous buckshot and the bullets." And the poet becomes this slave:

> I am the hounded slave, I wince at the bite of
> the dogs,
> Hell and despair are upon me, crack and again
> crack the marksmen,
> I clutch the rails of the fence, my gore dribs,
> thinn'd with the ooze of my skin,
> I fall on the weeds and stones,
> The riders spur their unwilling horses, haul
> close,
> Taunt my dizzy ears and beat me violently over
> the head with whip-stocks.

Still traveling in simultaneous time and space, the poet also becomes a "mash'd fireman with breast-bone broken," after fighting a fire; and an "old artillerist," taking part in a battle, watching an army "ambulanza slowly passing trailing its red drip," and watching his own "dying general" issuing his last orders to his troops.

SECTIONS 34–37

The next three sections continue the poet's now bewildered vision of the impact of war on the soldiers who fight, citing two battles, separated by history and geography, but not in the poet's vision; there they are simultaneous in space and time. And war is tragic in this vision, whether in defeat as described in the first battle or victory as described in the second.

He describes in Section 34 the massacring "in cold blood of four hundred and 12 young men." They are described as "rangers," no doubt Texas Rangers, since the narrator makes clear in the section's opening lines that this is a tale he "knew in Texas in my early youth," but not of the "fall of Alamo." The 412 men, the "glory of the race of rangers," had killed twice their own number in a battle the day before but were now surrounded, outnumbered, and without ammunition. "They treated for an honorable capitulation, receiv'd writing and seal, gave up their arms and march'd back prisoners of war."

The surrender papers notwithstanding, the prisoners are marched out in the morning and massacred ("it was beautiful early summer"). Following horrible and bloody details, the poet ends by casually stating: "That is the tale of the murder of the four hundred and 12 young men."

The second battle (Sections 35–36) describes the naval battle during the AMERICAN REVOLUTION of the *Bonhomme Richard* and *Serapis* on September 23, 1779, in which John Paul Jones issued the famous line, "I have not yet begun to fight." The battle was more important, however, as one of the first major American naval victories over England's usually superior navy.

In the poet's vision, he is one of the sailors aboard the *Bonhomme Richard* and describes the battle as he "saw" it. "Our frigate takes fire," he says, and "the other asks if we demand quarter?" He laughs as he recalls the "voice of my little captain," who says—in Whitman's version of the famous line (which may be as accurate as any)— "we have just begun our part of the fighting."

Section 36 describes the aftermath of the battle, the *Bonhomme Richard* sinking slowly and the American sailors scrambling aboard the defeated British ship. His captain has a "countenance white as a sheet," the flames are "flickering aloft and below," and everywhere are "formless stacks of bodies and bodies by themselves, dabs of flesh upon the masts and spars." No victory here either.

It is as if God has disappeared from the poet's vision. In Section 37 the narrator envisions himself in "prison shaped like another man, / And feel the dull unintermitted pain." He feels as if he has two bodies, one kept in the prison and the other "let out in the morning and barr'd at night." During the day, he sees other convicts: a "mutineer," who is on his way to jail, "but I am handcuff'd to him and walk by his side." He also goes with the "youngster" accused of larceny and with a "cholera patient" who "lies at the last gasp." Once again, the poet feels the enormous power of his own responsibility to other people and especially those who have little other help.

SECTIONS 38–40

There is a significant break in thought at the beginning of Section 38. "Enough! enough! enough!" the poet exclaims. His vision ends abruptly, and he awakes "stunn'd." He finds himself "on the verge of a usual mistake." He has forgotten God, or rather the God within himself: "That I could forget the mockers and insults! / That I could look with a separate look on my own crucifixion and bloody crowning!" Just as the crucifixion of Christ meant eternal life, so do all the horrors and deaths he envisioned in the worst of his dream—the crucifixion of men everywhere, especially in war—carry with them an affirmation of the God within.

He wakes to the joy of sudden intuitive understanding—an epiphany. It is he as poet of America who must take on the Christ-role as healer of the people.

He exemplifies this role beginning in Section 39, where he calls attention to the "friendly and flowing savage," whoever he is and whether a "Southwesterner" or "Kanadian"; whether from Iowa, Oregon, or California; and no matter his vocation. He is called "savage," perhaps because it is not clear whether he is "waiting for civilization, or past it and mastering it." Perhaps he offers a new kind of civilization that attracts people to him. Whatever it is, he is mysterious and therefore accepted and desired by both men and women. Like the poet himself, the savage has "Behavior lawless as snowflakes, words simple as grass, uncomb'd head, laughter, and naivetè."

In Sections 40 and 41, Whitman returns as a first-person narrator and to his role as the omniscient poet-Christ of Section 38. "Behold," he says, "I do not give lectures or a little charity, / When I give I give myself." He gives of himself entirely, even sexually, to everyone he meets: "I have stores plenty and to spare, / And any thing I have I bestow." To "women fit for conception," he starts "bigger and nimbler babes"; to the dying, he changes the "bed-clothes" and sends the physician and priest from the room; to the sleeper he stands guard during the night. It is the poet-Christ figure at work.

SECTIONS 41–45

In Section 41, he suggests a different sort of reconciliation with the world. He has "heard what [has been] said of the universe," and he wonders at its "middling" qualities; "is that all?" he asks. He argues for the acceptance of the best thoughts from all religions and the avoidance of religious "hucksters."

> Taking myself the exact dimensions of Jehovah,
> Lithographing Kronos, Zeus his son, and
>   Hercules his grandson,
> Buying drafts of Osiris, Isis, Belus, Brahma,
>   Buddha,
> In my portfolio placing Manito loose, Allah on
>   a leaf, the crucifix engraved,
> With Odin and the hideous-faced Mexitli and
>   every idol and image,
> Taking them all for what they are worth and
>   not a cent more,
> Admitting they were alive and did the work of
>   their days,
> (They bore mites as for unfledg'd birds who
>   have now to rise and fly and sing for
>   themselves.)

None of the beliefs of any single religion is accepted at face value but must have its "exact dimensions" taken before acceptance. And the last line of the quoted passage sums up Whitman's own attitude toward religion: in a democracy, people must learn, like the "unfledg'd birds," to "rise" from the nest and "sing" for themselves.

In Section 42 the poet offers a lyrical passage on his relationship with the people around him: "This is the city and I am one of the citizens, / Whatever interests the rest interests me, politics, wars, markets, newspapers, schools," etc. "I acknowledge the duplicates of myself," he says a few lines later; "the weakest and shallowest is deathless with me, / What I do and say the same waits for them." And he repeats the idea from the beginning of "Song of Myself" about the purpose of his seeming ego.

> I know perfectly well my own egotism,
> Know my omnivorous lines and must not write
>   any less,
> And would fetch you whoever you are flush
>   with myself.

If I seem to be bragging it is not for myself alone but for all people; "What I do and say the same waits for them." He sums this up in the last lines of the section: "The saints and sages in history" are no more than "you yourself"; the "fathomless human brain" is capable of "sermons, creeds, theology" and of answering questions concerning reason, love, and life.

At the beginning of Section 43, the poet sums up his faith in a God of all religions: "My faith is the greatest of faiths and the least of faiths, / Enclosing worship ancient and modern and all between ancient and modern."

Perhaps the most important knowledge, however, that comes from the poet's mystical journey and which is central to "Song of Myself," is that of the poet's understanding of the equality of all things. He has told readers from the beginning that this is not just a "song of myself" but a song that everyone can and must sing. As he says in the couplet from Section 17 quoted above, "These are really the thoughts of all men in all ages and lands, they are not original with me, / If they are not yours as much as mine they are nothing, or next to nothing." It takes someone with extreme faith in himself and in the human condition to write such a couplet. But, as he says midway through Section 43, this is a poem for

> Down-hearted doubters, dull and excluded,
> Frivolous, sullen, moping, angry, affected,
>   disheartend, atheistical,
> I know every one of you, I know the sea of
>   torment, doubt, despair and unbelief.

Whitman has been there himself, and it is only through this mystical journey of the self and soul to a merger with God that he has worked his way out

of the "torment, doubt, despair and unbelief." And "Song of Myself" offers this to its readers.

He returns to further ideas about death at the end of Section 43. "I do not know what is untried and afterward, / But I know it will in its turn prove sufficient, and cannot fail." He catalogs in the last 10 lines of the section people who have died or are dying, most of them "excluded" during their lives, and he assures them that whatever occurs after death will be "sufficient, and cannot fail"; that is, cannot fail to be right for the person who dies.

Section 44 offers a return to description of the mystical experience; or rather, as he says in the opening line: "It is time to explain myself—let us stand up." And for the next six sections he places an emphasis on the difference between the mystic and the others in their respective perceptions of the world.

"What is known I strip away," he says in the second line; "I launch all men and women forward with me into the Unknown." The "known" is an illusion to the poet, who is more interested in the "unknown." The latter transcends what others call reality, and the knowledge gained leads to reliance on the Self. Little is gained toward self-knowledge from accepting what is already known. The Self matures from explorations into the unknown, the road less, or not at all, traveled. Whitman ends the section by suggesting once again that he did not invent this idea.

> Before I was born out of my mother
>   generations guided me,
> My embryo has never been torpid, nothing
>   could overlay it. . . .
> All forces have been steadily employ'd to
>   complete and delight me,
> Now on this spot I stand with my robust soul.

There is joy in the present moment, Whitman seems here to suggest. Where else is it going to be better?

He continues this stream of thought in Section 45 where he describes the various ages of man and their respective attitudes toward living in the present moment as against the idea of eternity. "There is no stoppage and never can be stoppage" to time or space, he says, reminding us of his philosophy of the merger of time and space beginning in Section 33. And, in the long run, none of it makes much difference. "If I, you, and the worlds, and all beneath or upon their surfaces, were this moment reduced back to a pallid float, it would not avail in the long run." Whitman uses the word "float" here and elsewhere to mean a floating object, suspended in air. If the world as we know it were taken back "a few quadrillions of eras" (time) or "a few octillions of cubic leagues" (space) and started over, "We should surely bring up again where we now stand." Not only would we come back to where we are now, he says, but we would "surely go as much farther, and then farther and farther" than we have here and now.

Time and space matter little; what matters is the individual human being, self-assured of his or her small but significant importance (to the self at least) in the whole scheme of things and of union with the transcendent God, both in life and in death. "My rendezvous is appointed," he says.

SECTIONS 46–47

Whitman begins Section 46 by reiterating this theme of SELF-RELIANCE: "I tramp a perpetual journey, (come listen all!) / My signs are a rain-proof coat, good shoes, and a staff cut from the woods." And then he presents what may be his definitive statement not just on self-reliance but on the awareness of self as well.

> No friend of mine takes his ease in my chair,
> I have no chair, no church, no philosophy,
> I lead no man to a dinner-table, library,
>   exchange,
> But each man and each woman of you I lead
>   upon a knoll,
> My left hand hooking you round the waist,
> My right hand pointing to landscapes of
>   continents and the public road.
>
> Not I, not any one else can travel that road for
>   you,
> You must travel it for yourself.

The poet can only point the way "to landscapes of continents and the public road" that will take us to other places; he must then turn us loose to travel

on our own. He can tell us about his own experiences of union with the transcendent, but we must travel there alone.

He adds what might be taken as a discouraging note. There is no end to the journey. He says to his own "spirit" (the question is italicized because it is conversation with a being who transcends reality): *"When we become the enfolders of those orbs, and the pleasure and knowledge of every thing in them, shall we be fill'd and satisfied then?"* And the answer is *"No, we but level that lift to pass and continue beyond."* The poet then says to his readers: "You are also asking me questions and I hear you, / I answer that I cannot answer, you must find out for yourself." There is contradiction here, because the poet has certainly answered key questions concerning the mystical journey and whether there is ever an end to it.

And at the beginning of Section 47, Whitman provides another warning to the reader: "He most honors my style who learns under it to destroy the teacher." This is perhaps the ultimate sign of self-reliance. He is still speaking for humankind when he says a few lines later: "If you would understand me go to the heights or water-shore, / The nearest gnat is an explanation, and a drop or motion of waves a key." One's perception of the world may come from the simplest objects—the "motion of waves," for example, or from the grass under one's feet. One must pay attention, that is all. The "young mechanic" or "woodman" understands the poet, Whitman suggests, because they work daily with things that touch the transcendent. The poet's catalog includes the "young mother and old mother," the "girl and the wife," all of whom also, perhaps intuitively, understand the poet. But, he suggests, everyone is capable of understanding.

SECTIONS 48–49

Sections 48 and 49 sum up the pantheistic theme of transcendent reality: God is no more important than any human Self.

> I have said that the soul is not more than the
>   body,
> And I have said that the body is not more than
>   the soul,

And nothing, not God, is greater to one than
   one's self is, . . .

I hear and behold God in every object, yet
   understand God not in the least,
Nor do I understand who there can be more
   wonderful than myself.

Because in Whitman's philosophy God is everywhere, his spirit encompassing everyone and everything, the poet wishes instead to focus on the love
for all things that he feels as a result of that spirit.
"Why should I wish to see God better than this day,"
he asks. The day is the very reflection of God: he
sees God "in the faces of men and women" and in his
own "face in the glass"; he "finds letters from God
dropt in the street, and every one is sign'd by God's
name." For the poet, God is no greater than this.

He invokes death in Section 49, telling it that
he is not afraid: "you bitter bug of mortality, it is
idle to try to alarm me." And he is not offended by
a "corpse," because it is "good manure" for the
"white roses sweet-scented and growing." This suggests Whitman's search in Section 6 for the meaning of simple things as a clue to Life:

The smallest sprout shows there is really no
   death,
And if ever there was it led forward life, and
   does not wait at the end to arrest it,
And ceas'd the moment life appear'd.

He says to Life, "I reckon you are the leavings of
many deaths, / (No doubt I have died myself ten
thousand times before.)" This is one of the few
times Whitman uses in *Leaves of Grass* the Hindu
religious belief in reincarnation, but he presents it
here in support of his belief in the idea of death as
life-affirming.

SECTIONS 50–52

"Happiness" is the key word in Section 50 as the
poet comes to grips with the meaning of all that he
has been through and described. The mystical journey is over, but now he must find the key to its
meaning. "Do you see O my brothers and sisters? /
It is not chaos or death—it is form, union, plan—it
is eternal life—it is Happiness."

Socrates argued that happiness was the ultimate
aim of man, and Whitman seems to suggest the
same philosophy in this passage. Chaos and death
are illusory in Whitman's thinking, because he has
transcended their "reality." It is "form, union, plan"
and the knowledge of "eternal life" that is the transcendent reality. Such a self rooted in such a faith
may indeed sing the poetry of *Leaves of Grass.*

Whitman recognizes the ambiguity of much of
what he says, especially in the later sections of this
poem, but he covers it in Section 51:

Do I contradict myself?
Very well then I contradict myself,
(I am large, I contain multitudes.)

Even if I contradict myself, he says, it is because "I
am large," but so are all the "selves" of humankind;
everyone is capable of being "large," of containing
"multitudes." This may seem to be a quarrel with
himself at this point, however, and William Butler
Yeats would answer several years later that "out of
our quarrel with others we get rhetoric; out of our
quarrel with ourselves we get poetry." Perhaps the
whole of *Leaves of Grass* may be seen as a quarrel
between the poet and himself.

At the end of "Song of Myself" (Section 52),
Whitman continues to reassure readers: "I too am
not a bit tamed, I too am untranslatable, / I sound
my barbaric yawp over the roofs of the world."

He returns in the final eight lines to the poem's
basic symbol and the further reassurance that everyone can achieve all that has been demonstrated.

I bequeath myself to the dirt to grow from the
   grass I love,
If you want me again look for me under your
   boot-soles.

You will hardly know who I am or what I mean,
But I shall be good health to you nevertheless,
And filter and fibre your blood.

Failing to fetch me at first keep encouraged,
Missing me one place search another,
I stop somewhere waiting for you.

Even those readers who remain skeptical of the
poet's idealistic vision for a democracy formed of

citizens who can think for themselves or of a religion that elevates human beings to an equal status with God—even those readers, in reading the final lines of "Song of Myself," may tend to look over their shoulders "nevertheless," wondering perhaps if the poet might be waiting yet, his "barbaric yawp" still reverberating over "the roofs of the world."

"Song of Prudence" (1856)

First appeared under the title "Poem of the Last Explanation of Prudence" in the second edition of *Leaves of Grass* (1856); it was titled "Leaves of Grass, No. 5" (1860); the first line became its title (1867); it was given its present title and placed as the ninth of 38 poems in the "Autumn Rivulets" cluster for the sixth edition (1881).

Equated with "Time, Space, Reality" in the second line of the poem, it is "prudence that suits immortality."

> All that a person does, says, thinks, is of
>   consequence,
> Not a move can a man or woman make, that
>   affects him or her in a day, month, any part
>   of the direct lifetime, or the hour of death,
> But the same affects him or her onward
>   afterward through the indirect lifetime. . . .

The "indirect" life involves spiritual prudence and is just as important as the prudence of the direct, physical life, because the former is of the soul. "Whatever satisfies souls is true," the poet says; the inner life transcends the outer. See also "Unnamed Lands," the poem that immediately preceded "Song of Prudence" in the 1881 edition of *Leaves of Grass*.

"Song of the Answerer" (1855)

This poem is in two sections. The first (lines 3–53) was the seventh of 12 untitled poems in the first edition of *Leaves of Grass* (1855); it was titled

"Poem of the Poet" in the second edition (1856), "Leaves of Grass, No. 3" in the third (1860), and "Now List to My Morning Romanza" in the fourth (1867), the new title taken from the first of two lines added at the beginning of the poem.

The second section of "Song of the Answerer" (lines 54–83) was printed as a separate poem, titled "Poem of The Singers and of The Words of Poems" (1856), "Leaves of Grass, No. 6" (1860), and "The Indications" (1867). The two poems were then combined and placed under the present title in the sixth edition (1881). Whitman placed it as the fourth of 12 separate poems following the "Calamus" cluster in the sixth edition (1881).

The "Answerer" of the title is the poet himself, any poet. The poet's self-proclaimed mission is to answer questions and change the world for the better.

Section 1 explains what, according to Whitman, a poet does; Section 2 explains why.

"Now list to my morning's romanza," the poet says in the first line. *Romanza* is Italian for romance, song, or, perhaps more appropriate in this poem, a ballad. In this ballad then, the poet says, "I tell the signs of the Answerer . . . and I answer for him that answers for all, and send these signs." The "signs" are not identified, but they may refer to the poet's gift for touching the minds and emotions of readers. The poet "is the Answerer, / What can be answer'd he answers, and what cannot be answer'd he shows how it cannot be answer'd." This is a heavy load for a poet, but Whitman clearly feels himself up to the task.

In his "preface" to the first edition of *Leaves of Grass*—see "Preface" (*Leaves of Grass*, 1855)—Whitman writes extensively about the poet's mission. He says, for example, that the poet is a "seer . . . he is individual . . . he is complete in himself . . . the others are as good as he, only he sees it and they do not. He is not one of the chorus . . . he does not stop for any regulations . . . he is the president of regulation." And Whitman, free of regulations, shocked poetry readers everywhere with his "barbaric yawp over the rooftops of the world." He adds later in the Preface that the poet knows that there is nothing "in the known universe more divine than men and women." He refers to "poets of the kosmos"—poets anywhere, without politics, without loyalty to anything or anybody other than to their own souls. "Whatever satisfies the soul," he says, "is truth." These poetic elements are the "signs" of the "Answerer." It is how he or she is identified.

In the second section, not added until the sixth edition of *Leaves of Grass* (1881), Whitman explains *why* the poet is the answerer. First he distinguishes "singers" from "poets":

> The words of the singers are the hours or
>   minutes of the light or dark, but the words of
>   the maker of poems are the general light and
>   dark,
> The maker of poems settles justice, reality,
>   immortality, . . .
> The singers do not beget, only the Poet begets,
> The singers are welcom'd, understood, appear
>   often enough, but rare has the day been,
>   likewise the spot, of the birth of the maker of
>   poems, the Answerer. . . .

The poet "begets" answers to sometimes unanswerable questions, and this is his or her apparent role. "Singers do not beget." What is perhaps most interesting in this passage is the seeming contradiction in Whitman's more normal use of the words "poems" and "songs" in *Leaves of Grass*. He uses them interchangeably throughout, and often refers to himself as a "singer."

"Song of the Banner at Daybreak" (1865)

Under the title "Banner at Daybreak," this poem was meant originally as the opening poem in a book of poems titled *Banner at Daybreak* that Whitman was working on before the CIVIL WAR—a book never completed. The poem was first published under the present title in the *Drum-Taps* volume (1865); it was part of a group of poems titled "Bathed in War's Perfume" for the 1871 edition of *Leaves of Grass;* and it was the fifth of 43 poems in the "Drum-Taps" cluster for the sixth edition (1881).

The poem is in 14 sections and 144 lines. It is a dramatic conversation among five characters: the "Poet," a "Pennant," a "Child," the child's "Father," and the "Banner" of the poem's title.

The pennant and banner are "insensate," without sensitivity, representing as they do the regional emblems of Northern and Southern armies fighting each other in the Civil War; they are symbols of the sides they represent. The child is attracted to the pennants and banners as children tend to be, yet somewhat afraid; the father tries to calm the child's fears—though moved himself by the war—and convince him (or her, gender is not specific) that the war has nothing to do with the child: "Forward to stand in front of wars—and O, such wars!—what have you to do with them? / With passions of demons, slaughter, premature death?" The father's very explanation may create some of the child's fear.

In his second statement, the child tells his father how "wonderful" are the flags as he sees them cover "the whole sky." His father is disturbed by this attraction, because for the father the flags are "sorrowful," since to him they represent the war, and he would much prefer that the child think not about the flags but about the city's more normal activities, the "solid-wall'd houses," for example.

The Banner and Pennant then ask the poet to speak to the child, explaining that flags are mere "strips of cloth profiting nothing, / Only flapping in the wind."

But the poet believes the flags represent "Liberty," even at the great cost in lives that the war leaves. He says to the Banner and Pennant,

> I hear and see not strips of cloth alone,
> I hear the tramp of armies, I hear the
>   challenging sentry,
> I hear the jubilant shouts of millions of men, I
>   hear Liberty!
> I hear the drums beat and the trumpets
>   blowing,
> I myself move abroad swift-rising flying
>   then, . . .

As in the earlier "Drum-Taps" poem "From Paumanok Starting I Fly Like a Bird," the poet then flies on "the wings of the land-bird and . . . the wings of the sea-bird, and look[s] down as from a height." He sees first the "thirty-eight spacious and haughty States, (and many more to come,)" at peace: "farmers working . . . mechanics working . . . buildings everywhere founded. . . ." The poet suggests again, however, the symbolism: "Side of my banner broad and blue, side of my starry banner, / Discarding peace over all the sea and land."

The Banner and Pennant respond that the "bard" must write poems for the future: "Not for the present alone, for a thousand years chanting through you, / This song to the soul of one poor little child." But the child, who has not yet been persuaded by the father, still thinks that it would be good to be the banner; he says: "That pennant I would be and must be." To be the flag, the father says, means "to gain nothing, . . . to stand in front of wars . . . / With passions of demons, slaughter, premature death."

Then the Banner, as if in defiance of the father's wishes, says: "Demons and death then I sing, / Put in all, aye all will I, sword-shaped pennant for war." To the Banner, it is the symbol that is important, even if it means "devouring the whole" of the nation, a nation at war.

And the poet, though he is sorry for the child afraid and the anxious father, sings finally in the last section of the banner's importance in spite of all that has been said.

> I hear from above O pennant of war your
>   ironical call and demand,
> Insensate! insensate (yet I at any rate chant
>   you,) O banner! . . .
> I see but you, O warlike pennant! O banner so
>   broad, with stripes, I sing you only,
> Flapping up there in the wind.

As earnest as Whitman is throughout *Leaves of Grass* about the democracy he envisions for America, this poem and some other *Drum-Taps* poems may seem to contradict the book's larger theme of American democracy by suggesting the importance of fighting the Civil War in order to resolve the SLAVERY issue and thereby bring a more lasting peace to the evolving nation. In "Song of Myself" Whitman covers this and other seeming contradictions: "Do I contradict myself? / Very well then I contradict myself, / (I am large, I contain multitudes.)."

"Song of the Broad-Axe" (1856)

First published as "Broad-Axe Poem" in the second edition of *Leaves of Grass* (1856); then as "Chants Democratic, No. 2" (1860); it received its present title and was a separate poem (1867); and it was the seventh separate poem following the "Calamus" cluster in the sixth edition of *Leaves* (1881). The poem is in 12 sections and 254 lines.

The broad-axe has a large, broad head for cutting down trees, but it was also one of the weapons of choice in early wars. It is used in this poem primarily as a metaphor for the building of America. The poet reminds readers, however, that in ancient societies it was used to build houses but also to sack cities or to cut off the heads of martyrs for the cause of social principles or of kings and queens who got in the way of those principles.

> The log at the wood-pile, the axe supported by it,
> The sylvan hut, the vine over the doorway, the
>   space clear'd for a garden, . . .
> The house-builder at work in cities or
>   anywhere, . . .

Building houses is only one use for the broad-axe, although clearly the most important one for the poet as he imagines the huge task for the early settlers of America. But the physical building of America is the easy part, the poet suggests, because "nothing endures but personal qualities."

> Do you think a great city endures?
> Or a teeming manufacturing state or a
> prepared constitution? or the best built
> steamships? . . .

> A great city is that which has the greatest men
>   and women,
> If it be a few ragged huts it is still the greatest city
>   in the whole world.

The physical building of anything—city, steamships, or constitution—has no lasting value unless they are built by men and women of greatness.

The poem's last four sections are devoted to the "shapes" that "arise" in the building of the physical

America, which, if built by the right people, becomes a democratic America. Section 9 begins with the poet's declaration of his love for the nation. Then "the axe leaps!" and the building begins: huts, ploughs, shingles, citadels, saloons, academies, boats, capitols of states, hospitals, steamboats, etc. "The shapes arise!"

"The shapes arise!" is a refrain used seven times in these final sections as Whitman CATALOGs the shapes of the individual elements that make the shape of America: factories, arsenals, railroads, coffins, markets, liquor-bars, bedsteads, cradles, court-rooms, gambling boards, exit and entry doors, etc.

Section 11 evokes the image of the American woman: "Her shape arises." She has "no reason to fear," the poet says, "smutty expressions are idle to her as she passes . . . she is possess'd of herself . . . she is strong, / She . . . is a law of Nature—there is no law stronger than she is." She has the quality of greatness necessary to help build the democratic America of Whitman's vision.

The poem's final stanza sums up the value of shapes—what the broad-axe has accomplished.

> The main shapes arise!
> Shapes of Democracy total, result of centuries,
> Shapes ever projecting other shapes,
> Shapes of turbulent manly cities,
> Shapes of the friends and home-givers of the
>   whole earth,
> Shapes bracing the earth and braced with the
>   whole earth.

The shapes of democracy arise, the poet believes, from the hard-working men and women who build it. Even the lazy ones, it turns out, all help to shape democracy; good people and evil people shape democracy, equality and inequality shape democracy, hope and despair.

The poetic style is of some interest in this six-line poem, especially that of the first stanza of accentual lines (see ACCENTUAL VERSE). There is a wave form to the stanza, the first two and last two lines shorter than the middle two of eight accents each. And there is off-rhyme at the ends of the lines: wan, drawn, one, sown, upon, and on.

"Song of the Exposition" (1871)

First read aloud by Whitman at an Exhibition of the American Institute in New York (September 7, 1871); first published in *Leaves of Grass* as "After All, Not to Create Only" in the fifth edition (1871); it received its present title and was a separate poem (1876); and it was the eighth separate poem immediately following the "Calamus" cluster in the sixth edition (1881).

"After All, Not to Create Only" was the title Whitman used for his lecture at the American Institute, but the lecture was badly received, even parodied, by newspaper reviewers. Whitman changed the title to "Song of the Exposition" for the sake of the opening in 1876 of the Centennial Exposition in Philadelphia. The two-volume printing of *Leaves of Grass* (with *Two Rivulets* as the second volume) helped commemorate the nation's 100th birthday, and it was called the "Centennial Edition."

The poem still bothers critics, many of whom think that most of Whitman's best poetry had been written by the early 1870s. This poem was written for a special occasion, and the single focus was lost both on his immediate audience and on many readers to come.

"Song of the Open Road" (1856)

Published first as "Poem of the Road" in the second edition of *Leaves of Grass* (1856); it received its present title and was a separate poem in the fourth edition (1867); and it became the second of 12 separate poems that followed the "Calamus" cluster in the sixth edition (1881). The poem is in 15 sections and 224 lines.

This is one of Whitman's most obviously transcendental poems (see TRANSCENDENTALISM). The "open road" is a metaphor for a mystical journey the poet takes toward a spiritual union with the rest of the world. The mystical journey theme is traveled often in *Leaves of Grass,* the poet constantly searching for ways to improve himself by connecting with other people and with the earth itself. See, for other examples, "Salut au Monde," "Crossing Brooklyn Ferry," and "Starting from Paumanok."

"Song of the Open Road" begins with an objective description of the poet's personal experience on an otherwise unidentified walking tour:

> Afoot and light-hearted I take to the open
>   road,
> Healthy, free, the world before me,
> The long brown path before me leading
>   wherever I choose.

The walker needs nothing more, not even "good-fortune," because, he says, he will provide his own good-fortune; he feels "strong and content" traveling the open road.

He speaks directly to the road itself at the beginning of Section 2, conjuring up a feeling he has that the road is more than has yet met his eye. He envisions others who have walked the same road—"the black," "the felon," "the diseas'd," "the illiterate person," "the escaped youth," "the rich person's carriage," "the eloping couple"—none is denied access to the open road.

The poet's vision expands to include walks in cities, the planks along wharves, "rows of houses," porches, the "gray stones of interminable pavements." At the beginning of Section 4, the earth expands for the poet and becomes open to his imagination: "The picture alive, every part in its best light." He believes that the road he travels speaks to him, asking him not to leave for fear of becoming "lost." And he answers:

> I am not afraid to leave you, yet I love you,
> You express me better than I can express
>   myself,
> You shall be more to me than my poem.

He believes that "heroic deeds were all conceiv'd in the open air, and all free poems also." Perhaps he even thinks that his own poems can only be free of 19th-century poetic restraints if he breaths the open air into them. He feels that he will like the company of everyone he meets and that other walkers will like him; "I think whoever I see must

be happy." Happiness may generate anyone's wish to walk the open road.

In the first line of Section 5 the poet "ordains [himself] loos'd of limits and imaginary lines." He transcends his own body and becomes aware that he is "larger, better than [he] thought, / I did not know I held so much goodness."

The spiritual journey gives him much pause. He sees "the secret of the making of the best persons, / It is to grow in the open air and to eat and sleep with the earth." He sees that "wisdom is not finally tested in schools," that his former ideas about "philosophies and religions" need to be reexamined. "Only the kernel of every object nourishes," he now realizes, and everyone must do his or her own husking. "Here is realization," he says, awake to new ideas: "The past, the future, majesty, love— if they are vacant of you, you are vacant of them."

Whitman speaks of the "efflux of the soul" in the first line of Section 7, the word "efflux" used by the poet to mean to cause the soul to flow from within outward to the Self. And he says in the first line of Section 8 that the "efflux of the soul is happiness," and, he says further that we are "rightly charged" by this manifestation of the soul. In "I Sing the Body Electric" Whitman wrote of the electricity generated by the soul to the body.

In Sections 9–11 the poet invites readers to join him in this spiritual journey: "Allons! whoever you are come travel with me." But he warns that anyone who walks with him "needs the best blood, thews [the bodily power of a man], endurance, / None may come to the trial till he or she bring courage and health."

Sections 12 and 13 catalog the "great Companions" already on the open road; "they are the swift and majestic men—they are the greatest women." These are the "roads for traveling souls." The invitation to join him is for everyone. "Whoever you are," he says, "come forth . . . / You must not stay sleeping and dallying there in the house."

In Section 14, Whitman uses the metaphor of war to encourage followers:

> My call is the call of battle, I nourish active
>   rebellion,
> He going with me must go well arm'd,

He going with me goes often with spare diet,
poverty, angry enemies, desertions.

And the final section offers again the hand of the poet. The "road is before us," he says. "It is safe—I have tried it."

Camerado, I give you my hand!
I give you my love more precious than money,
I give you myself before preaching or law;
Will you give me yourself? will you come travel
with me?
Shall we stick by each other as long as we live?

"Song of the Open Road" is an invitation: to the poet himself to be unafraid of the spiritual values he may find along the road ahead and to others to be a comrade and experience along with the poet whatever life brings.

"Song of the Redwood-Tree" (1874)

First published in HARPER'S NEW MONTHLY MAGA-ZINE (February 1874); first published in Leaves of Grass as "Centennial Songs, No. 2" (1876); then under its present title and as the ninth separate poem following the "Calamus" cluster for the sixth edition (1881). The poem is in three sections and 105 lines.

One of the major themes running through Leaves of Grass is that of Nature and Man working together toward the building of America. In this poem it is the great redwood tree that "sings" of its willingness to give up its long life for the sake of the greater good—for the building of something at once magnificent and with far-reaching values for the world at large:

A chorus of dryads, fading, departing, or
hamadryads departing,
A murmuring, fateful, giant voice, out of the
earth and sky,
Voice of a mighty dying tree in the redwood
forest dense.

"Dryads" are wood nymphs, and "hamadryads" are wood nymphs fabled in mythology to die with the trees they inhabit. In "Song of the Redwood-Tree," the voices of the poet and of the redwood are heard, the wood nymphs speaking for the tree. Only the poet can hear the voice from the tree; the words of the nymphs are printed in italics:

Farewell my brethren,
Farewell O earth and sky, farewell ye neighboring
waters,
My time has ended, my term has come.

The "music" of the axes begins in the deep woods of California, near "the sea in the Mendocino country." The wood-spirits from thousands of years ago rise to join the "refrain" of the hamadryads about to die with their great trees. The wood nymphs recognize the value of giving up the trees to the future of America.

The "choppers" don't hear the wood nymphs, only the poet can hear as they sing "not of the past only but the future":

O the great patient rugged joys, my soul's strong
joys unreck'd by man,
(For know I beat the soul befitting me, I too have
consciousness, identity,
And all the rocks and mountains have, and all the
earth,)
Joys of the life befitting me and brothers mine,
Our time, our term has come.

For thousands of years the trees have been left alone. But now they know it is time to give themselves up for the sake of the new nation. In this poem the redwoods are a symbol of the greatness of that growth. There is a "soul" in nature, Whitman believed, a "consciousness" that allows it to sacrifice itself for the sake of other natural things, including human nature.

This sacrifice, however, doesn't stop at California's coast. The building of America also requires the loosening of bonds to other parts of the world, especially Europe, which the wood nymphs refer to as the "old dynastic slaughter-house . . . of murder-plots . . . with scent left yet of wars and scaffolds everywhere." The nymphs realize the importance of building on "these virgin lands, lands of the Western shore." And they "pledge" themselves to the cause.

The poet responds to this in Section 2 by remembering that a "swarming and busy race" is at work, "settling and organizing everywhere," and, at the same time, even foreign nations are involved in America's future. There are "Ships coming in from the whole round world, and going out to the whole world, / To India and China and Australia and the thousand island paradises of the Pacific."

In Section 3 the poet envisions the future of the "Western shore . . . the promise of thousands of years, till now deferr'd." But the West is beginning to come alive with the great western migration and the fulfilling of promises for "our common kind . . . / The new society at last, proportionate to Nature." California and its redwood trees are symbolic of that proper growth.

> Fresh come, to a new world indeed, yet long
>   prepared,
> I see the genius of the modern, child of the real
>   and ideal,
> Clearing the ground for broad humanity, the
>   true America, heir of the past so grand,
> To build a grander future.

Even nature itself benefits from this cutting of the redwoods. As long, that is, Whitman says, as the "new society" and nature are "proportionate," as long as they take care of one another in the building of that "grander future."

"Song of the Rolling Earth, A" (1856)

First published as "Poem of the Sayers of the Words of the Earth" in the second edition of *Leaves of Grass* (1856); it was then titled "To the Sayers of Words" (1860); as "Carol of Words" (1871); then under its present title and as the 11th separate poem following the "Calamus" cluster in the sixth edition of *Leaves* (1881). The poem is in four sections and 130 lines.

Whitman's poetry has to do with the relationship between words and meaning. This poem in particular, however, focuses on the idea that words

have no meaning in and of themselves, only as they provoke images for the reader or listener. The "rolling earth" is the poet's metaphor for this idea:

> A song of the rolling earth, and of words
>   according,
> Were you thinking that those were the words,
>   those upright lines?
> those curves, angles, dots?
> No, those are not the words, the substantial
>   words are in the ground and sea,
> They are in the air, they are in you. . . .
>
> Human bodies are words, myriads of words, . . .
> Air, soil, water, fire—those are words, . . .
> The workmanship of souls is by those inaudible
>   words of the earth,
> The masters know the earth's words and use them
>   more than audible words.

Poets know that the words they use are mere symbols for meaning that transcend the word itself. EMERSON wrote, in his essay "Nature," Part IV, "Language," (1836), that "Language is a . . . use which Nature subserves to man. Nature is the vehicle of thought. . . . Words are signs of natural facts."

Section 1 in this poem suggests that the source of words is the moving ("rolling") earth, and many of the images connect words to the source. "Air, soil, water, fire—those are words," the poet says. And,

> The earth does not withhold, it is generous
>   enough,
> The truths of the earth continually wait, . . .
> They are calm, subtle, untransmissible by print.

The words are waiting for someone to translate them.

Whitman then turns this idea into a metaphor for the significance of the individual person (Section 2): "Whoever you are! you are he or she for whom the earth is solid and liquid, / You are he or she for whom the sun and moon hang in the sky." He says a few lines later that each individual is "the word of the past and present, and the true word of immortality; / No one can acquire for another—not one, / No one can grow for another—not one."

Each individual must think for him or her self, Whitman offers here; each person is responsible for his or her own destiny. "The song is the singer," he says; the murder is the murderer, the theft is the thief, the love is the lover; and in each case, what he or she does "comes back most" to him or her. "No man understands any greatness or goodness but his own, or the indication of his own." The earth teaches us that who we are is determined by what we do. Whitman connects people to the earth upon which they grow.

Section 3 continues this merger of people and earth: "I swear the earth shall surely be complete to him or her who shall be complete, / The earth remains jagged and broken only to him or her who remains jagged and broken." But the poet begins to see also that there is "little or nothing in audible words," because everything "merges toward the presentation of the unspoken meanings of the earth." There are words, even "dictionaries of words that print cannot touch." The best the earth has to offer, the reality of things that people realize on occasion, cannot be told in words. So, he concludes, it is better to leave "the best untold." At the end of the section, he uses the "soul" as an example of something "real," something "positive and direct," but for which there is no "proof." There are no words to define or even to describe the soul.

Whitman begins Section 4 by summarizing: "I swear I will never henceforth have to do with the faith that tells the best, / I will have to do only with that faith that leaves the best untold." Some things must be taken on faith. But what then about words?

> Say on, sayers! sing on, singers!
> Delve! Mould! Pile the words of the earth!
> Work on, age after age, nothing is to be
>   lost, . . .
> When the materials are all prepared and ready,
>   the architects shall appear.

The architects are the poets, men and women who understand, perhaps by faith only, the relationship of earth and people, and who can discover the proper words to interpret the "real" to readers. Whitman says in the last two lines of the poem that the poets "shall perceive that you are not an iota less than they, / You shall be fully glorified in them."

Getting to the meaning of words is a mystical and transcendental process; meaning transcends what we think of as a normal mental exercise and becomes based on a faith in the often vague relationship of words and meaning.

"Song of the Universal" (1874)

Written as a commencement poem and meant for presentation at Tufts College (June 17, 1874); Whitman was ill, however, and could not deliver the poem himself; it was published the same day in the *New York World* and in the NEW YORK EVENING POST; it was first published in *Leaves of Grass* as one of the "Centennial Songs" in the *Two Rivulets* volume of the 1876 printing of *Leaves;* then under its present title and as the first of seven poems in the "Birds of Passage" cluster for the sixth edition (1881). The poem is in four sections and 65 lines.

Usually it is the poet who asks the muse for help in writing a poem, but in the first line of this poem it is the Muse who asks the poet to "Sing me a song no poet yet has chanted, / Sing me the universal."

"Universal" suggests "unlimited" in meaning and something that is understood by everyone. And no matter the "measureless grossness" and "slag," the negatives that life sometimes brings, at the "heart" of everything is the "seed perfection." And, the poet says, in everyone born, "conceal'd or unconceal'd the seed is waiting." Perfection is in the genes.

How perfection got into the genes, Whitman suggests in Section 2, is part of the "mystic evolution," which scientists have not yet solved. The movement through the evolutionary process has been by "spiral routes" and "long detours, / (As a much-tacking ship upon the sea)." But it has a "permanent flowing" movement, he says, and "for it the real to the ideal tends." To think of perfection as universal is an "ideal," but one that tends toward the real.

A balance of good and evil was always important to Whitman, and in this poem he writes that it is not just "right" which is justified but "evil" too. Where there is perfection, however, there must also be imperfection. The last line of Section 2 makes clear that "only the good is universal," part of perfection.

The second three-line stanza in Section 3 reflects Whitman's constant upbeat attitude. Even in imperfection one may find a "ray of perfect light":

> From imperfection's murkiest cloud,
> Darts always forth one ray of perfect light,
> One flash of heaven's glory.

Whitman suggests that the perfection "gene," which is universal, allows everyone to feel, even in the midst of "the mad Babel-din," that ray of light that allows him or her to feel the good even in the bad. Whitman would have as a simple part of human nature this positive attitude.

The poet turns then, in Section 4, toward America, which becomes a metaphor for this "ideal." It is America, "for the scheme's culmination, its thought and its reality, / For these (not for thyself) thou has arrived." One of America's reasons for existence is, according to Whitman, to act as an example to the world of a place where people believe in this ideal. It is not the "measur'd faiths of other lands, the grandeurs of the past" that matter; America must establish its own "grandeurs."

Whitman asks God for the faith to "sing that thought," to write poems in which this ideal for America becomes "universal." He ends the poem by asking whether all of this is possible.

> Is it a dream?
> Nay but the lack of it the dream,
> And failing it life's lore and wealth a dream,
> And all the world a dream.

Within the America of the poet's dream, preserved by faith, is the seed of perfection. No matter the number of imperfections, the seed is there to cultivate and display to the world.

"Songs Of Parting" (1881)

Cluster title for 17 poems published together for the sixth edition of *Leaves of Grass* (1881). Fifteen of the poems appeared in earlier editions, two were new. "Songs of Parting" is the final group of poems in the 1881 edition of *Leaves*. Whitman will continue to write poems, but they will be included in later editions as "Annexes."

Though Whitman would live another 11 years after publication of this edition, he is clearly concerned in these poems with the idea of his own death and with "parting" from readers. He says, for example, in the cluster's opening poem ("As the Time Draws Nigh"), "Perhaps soon some day or night while I am singing my voice will suddenly cease." The poem was first published as "To My Soul" in the third edition (1860), and, although it was revised for later editions, the line was not revised, which reflects the poet's concern for "departure" as early as 1860.

Five of the poems in this cluster appeared in the *Drum-Taps* edition, all suggesting Whitman's ongoing concern for preserving the memory of the soldiers, North and South, who died in the CIVIL WAR, yet another kind of "parting."

The cluster's 17 poems were presented in the following order: "As the Time Draws Nigh," "Years of the Modern," "Ashes of Soldiers," "Thoughts" (Of these years), "Song at Sunset," "As at Thy Portals Also Death," "My Legacy," "Pensive on Her Dead Gazing," "Camps of Green," "The Sobbing of the Bells," "They Draw to a Close," "Joy, Shipmate, Joy!," "The Untold Want," "Portals," "These Carols," "Now Finalè to the Shore," and "So Long!"

"Soon Shall the Winter's Foil Be Here" (1888)

First published in the *NEW YORK HERALD* (February 21, 1888); then in *November Boughs* (1888); and it was the 49th of 65 poems in the "First Annex: Sands at Seventy" cluster for the "Death-bed" printing of *Leaves of Grass* (1892).

Winter's "foil" is spring. The "icy ligatures unbind and melt," and from the "dead clods and chills" come "dandelions, clover, the emerald grass" and all the things that make for scenes of spring. It is just such scenes the "annual play brings on."

"Sounds of the Winter" (1891)

First published in LIPPINCOTT'S MAGAZINE (March 1891); it was the 18th of 31 poems in *Good-Bye My Fancy* (1891); then in "Second Annex: Good-Bye My Fancy" for the "Death-bed" printing of *Leaves of Grass* (1892).

This seven-line poem is descriptive of winter's sounds: the "cheery railroad train," the "whispering air," the "tones" of women and children. And there is the sound of an old man talking too much and saying little of importance, yet saying it rhythmically. One of the sounds of winter is Whitman's own voice, still sounding his "barbaric yawp over the rooftops of the world. . . . *we keep up yet the lilt.*"

"Spain, 1873–1874" (1873)

First published in the *NEW YORK DAILY GRAPHIC* (March 24, 1873); then in the 1876 printing of *Leaves of Grass;* it was the 14th of 22 poems in the "From Noon to Starry Night" cluster for the sixth edition (1881).

In December 1874 Don Alfonso became king of Spain, defeating an attempt on the part of his opposition to create a democratic nation. The poem suggests that the move toward a constitutional republic was a brave one, and it ends allowing for hope: "Thou hast given us a sure proof, the glimpse of thyself, / Thou waitest there as everywhere thy time."

"Spanish Lady, The" (1840)

First published in the *LONG ISLAND DEMOCRAT* (August 4, 1840); an "early poem" *not* later published in *Leaves of Grass.* It is most accessible now in Francis Murphy (editor), *Walt Whitman: The Complete Poems* (Penguin Books, 1996).

"Sparkles from the Wheel" (1871)

First appeared as one of the "Leaves of Grass" poems in the fifth edition of *Leaves of Grass* (1871); and as the 22nd of 38 poems in the "Autumn Rivulets" cluster for the sixth edition (1881).

Drawing of Whitman by Herbert Gilchrist, 1882
(Library of Congress, Prints and Photographs Division)

It is the "sparkles" from the knife-grinder's wheel that catch the poet's attention as he visualizes himself as a "phantom curiously floating" above the street observing the children's interest in the "diffusing, dropping, sideways-darting, in tiny showers of gold, / Sparkles from the wheel."

Specimen Days (1882)

First published by Rees Welsh Company of Philadelphia in 1882 in a collection of Whitman's prose entitled *Specimen Days & Collect*; reprinted by David McKay in Philadelphia (1892). *Specimen Days* is a book of 189 short journal notes—Whitman called them "diary-jottings, war memoranda of 1862–'65, Nature notes of 1877–'81, with Western and Canadian observations afterward." It is divided unequally into those four basic topics, the "diary-jottings" scattered throughout and including notes on about a dozen people Whitman knew or knew about. Most of the Civil War items had been published in *Memoranda During the War* (1875–76).

These "specimens," or sample essays, from the life of the poet—each one titled, most of them 200 words or less—are organized into five sections. The first 13 items are autobiographical, for the purpose, Whitman says, of satisfying in a recent letter written to "an insisting friend" for information about his birth in West Hills on Long Island and family genealogy; the next 62 items are devoted to his "war memoranda," mostly notes he made during his work in Washington hospitals and on the battlefields of Virginia; the next 57 are devoted primarily to nature, "notes of 1877–'81," with excursions into the natures of the human species; the next 30 notes are jottings he made on his travels west and to Canada from September to December, 1879; and the final section includes a miscellany of reminiscences about people and places he knew and his life and times.

In a special "preface" he wrote for the British edition (1887), Whitman provided in the first two sentences what is probably the best summary anyone has written about his intentions in *Specimen Days*.

If you will only take the following pages, as you do some long and gossipy letter written for you by a relative or friend traveling through distant scenes and incidents, and jotting them down lazily and informally, but ever veraciously (with occasional diversions of critical thought about somebody or something), it might remove all formal or literary impediments at once, and bring you and me close together in the spirit in which the jottings were collated to be read.

You have had, and have, plenty of public events and facts and general statistics of America;—in the following book is a common individual New World *private life*, its birth and growth, its struggles for a living, its goings and comings and observations (or representative portions of them) amid the United States of America the last thirty or forty years, with their varied war and peace, their local coloring, the unavoidable egotism, and the lights and shades and sights and joys and pains and sympathies common to humanity.

With the exception of the items taken from his war memoranda, *Specimen Days* offers an inspection of both the poet's fairly peaceful life and, to an extent, the genesis of his poetry.

But the war notes tend to shock. He writes of a Confederate soldier, for example, who lived three days with the top of his head off, showing "brains partially exuded." He had not been moved from the spot of his wounding, and his constant digging with his heel into the ground "night and day," had left a hole "big enough to put in a couple of ordinary knapsacks." He died a few minutes after some "of our soldiers" moved him into a nearby house.

Whitman probably had not been there to see such horror, but he saw enough of it in hospitals around Washington and on some Virginia battlefields that he didn't need to exaggerate any soldier's story in order to make it his own. These "war memoranda," in fact, represented the best objective description of Civil War devastation available—at least until the publication of Stephen Crane's *The Red Badge of Courage* in 1895. Whitman had the advantage over Crane of having been through the hospital experiences and at least one or two battles. Crane experienced none of the war (he was born in 1871), yet his novel provides an authentic depiction of the war's devastation.

"Spirit That Form'd This Scene" (1881)

First published in CRITIC (September 10, 1881); it was the 20th of 22 poems in the "From Noon to Starry Night" cluster for the sixth edition of *Leaves of Grass* (1881). The poem carries the subtitle, "Written in Platte Cañon, Colorado."

The poem was written on Whitman's trip to Colorado in the late fall of 1879. It is descriptive of the scene, one in which he lets the "Spirit that form'd" the Platte Canyon know that poets "have remember'd thee."

Whitman begins a paragraph in *Specimen Days* titled "An Egotistical 'Find' " by stating, "I have found the law of my own poems," a reference to the effect of his Colorado trip on his poetry.

"Spirit Whose Work is Done" (1865)

First appeared in the *Sequel to Drum-Taps* volume (1865) and under this title throughout its publication history in *Leaves of Grass*; it was the 40th of 43 poems in the "Drum-Taps" cluster for the sixth edition (1881). The parenthetical subtitle, "(*Washington City, 1865*)," was added for the fifth edition (1871).

The poet invites the "spirit of dreadful hours"—the motivation for his CIVIL WAR poems—to

Touch my mouth ere you depart, press my lips
  close,
Leave me your pulses of rage—bequeath them
  to me—fill me with currents convulsive,
Let them scorch and blister out of my chants
  when you are gone,
Let them identify you to the future in these
  songs.

He doesn't want to forget the horrors of the war, even as the "immortal ranks . . . return from the battles." Only if the "scorches and blisters" last, will he be able to remember the horrors. And he wants the same spirit to work in the reader's memory, "the future in these songs."

"Spontaneous Me" (1856)

Titled "Bunch Poem" in the second edition of *Leaves of Grass* (1856), the title taken probably from the poem's second to last line; it was the fifth poem in the "Enfans d'Adam" cluster (1860); it received its present title and was the fifth of 16 poems in the "Children of Adam" cluster for the sixth edition (1881).

In this 45-line poem, Whitman connects each of his five senses to the natural spontaneity of all men and women, especially in the act of procreation. The poem is an elaboration of the first line: "Spontaneous me, Nature."

Each of the senses is imaged through a catalog of sexually explicit moments between the poet and his lover, all meant to confirm the naturalness of love-making.

The poet presents his "oath of procreation" near the end of the poem, "The greed that eats me day and night with hungry gnaw, till I saturate what shall produce boys to fill my place when I am through." The poet recognizes his own "greed" in the act of procreation, but even this greed, he believes, is spontaneous and natural.

The rhythm of "Spontaneous Me" merges with its meaning, making it one of the more artistic poems in the "Children of Adam" cluster, but what may be more interesting to 21st-century readers is its sexual connotation, which was extremely explicit for the mid-19th century.

"Starting from Paumanok" (1860)

First appeared titled "Proto-Leaf" and as the opening poem in the third edition of *Leaves of Grass*

(1860); it received its present title but with a rewritten opening section for the fourth edition (1867); and it was a separate poem, following the "Inscriptions" cluster of poems for the fifth edition (1871) and throughout the rest of its publication history.

The manuscript title for this poem was "Premonition," a not inappropriate title since Whitman devotes much of the poem to encouraging readers to look ahead to the poems that follow this one; many thematic elements for the whole of *Leaves of Grass* are introduced in this poem, which he began writing shortly after the publication of the 1855 edition. The final version contains 272 lines in 19 sections.

The poem begins with autobiographical material: "Starting from fish-shape Paumanok [the Indian name for Long Island] where I was born, / Well-begotten, and rais'd by a perfect mother, . . ." But the poet soon universalizes his own persona. He dwells "in Mannahatta" (Manhattan) but he can dwell in the "southern savannas" just as easily. He can *become* the other people he imagines, including "a soldier camp'd or carrying [his] knapsack and gun, or a miner in California." Whitman will develop this notion that a poet is capable of transcending his own body and soul to become the person he imagines to a much greater extent in later poems, but "Starting from Paumanok" introduces the idea. He says he can become "withdrawn to muse and meditate in some deep recess." Away from the "clank of crowds," he becomes "aware of the buffalo herds grazing the plains"; he becomes aware of "earth, rocks, . . . flowers, . . . stars, rain, snow, my amaze." He is amazed at these experiences, at this mystical transference.

And so he strikes out for the new world:

> Having studied the mocking-bird's tones and
> the flight of the mountain-hawk,
> And heard at dawn the unrivall'd one, the
> hermit thrush from the swamp-cedars,
> Solitary, singing in the West, I strike up for a
> New World.

This last line foreshadows the influence of *Leaves of Grass* on the "New World" of American poetry, of a verse *free* of traditional rhyme and rhythm patterns in favor of an irregular rhythm and a grander scheme more appropriate for the largeness of America and its democratic principles. The mockingbird and the hermit thrush will become of particular value to Whitman in later poems, each bird "solitary," like himself.

"This then is life," he says in Section 2. He awakens to life's prospects and welcomes them. "How curious! how real! / Underfoot the divine soil, overhead the sun." There is a hint of the grass in this line, one of the key images in *Leaves of Grass.*

The word "Libertad" in the second line of Section 3 is a Spanish word meaning "liberty, freedom." *Libertad de cultos* means freedom of worship; *Libertad de palabra* means freedom of speech. Whitman used "Libertad" here and in other poems as a way of personifying these freedoms. It is part of the poet's concept of democracy.

> Americanos! conquerors! marches
> humanitarian!
> Foremost! century marches! Libertad! masses!
> For you a programme of chants.

The "Libertad" is a person who enjoys the concepts of liberty and freedom, is immune from the influence of others, and is independent—the personification of Whitman's ideal American. The "programme of chants" presents images of midwest America: "the prairies," the "long-running Mississippi," the states of the Midwest, all "shooting in pulses of fire ceaseless to vivify all." All of these images help to bring life to America. In Section 5 Whitman offered his respect to the past: "Dead poets, philosophs, priests, / Martyrs, artists, inventors," etc. But at the same time, he says, we must dismiss them in order to concentrate on our own place and time.

The poet has already come a long way from Paumanok. At the end of Section 5 and through Section 6, he introduces his "mistress the soul." The soul is a mistress, he says, because in it he finds a subject—perhaps even a muse—for his poetry:

> I will make the poems of materials, for I think
> they are to be the most spiritual poems,
> And I will make the poems of my body and of
> mortality.

For I think I shall then supply myself with the
    poems of my soul and of immortality.

The "permanent grandeur of these States," Whitman states in Section 7, "must be their religion." It is not a religion with a name (Christianity, for example), but it reaches to the deepest spiritual level of one's being nevertheless. And without religion "there is no life worth the name."

In Section 10 he names Love, Democracy, and Religion as the three chief sources for his poetic themes. "O such themes—equalities! O divine average! . . . / I take to your reckless and composite chords, add to them, and cheerfully pass them forward." Forward to the reader. "Starting from Paumanok" presents these ideas not as complete in themselves but as mere introductions to ideas yet to come.

In the next sections Whitman introduces images which would provide support for various themes in *Leaves of Grass*. The Alabama mockingbird, for example, in Section 11 would return as a "solitary" in "Out of the Cradle Endlessly Rocking," a symbol of what the boy/poet would become. In Section 12 he introduces his fascination with death: "I will show that nothing can happen more beautiful than death." Section 14 presents a catalog of people and places he loves: "Toward the male of the States, and toward the female of the States." And the land: "Land of the pastoral plains, . . . Land of the eastern Chesapeake! . . . Land of Ontario, Erie, Huron, Michigan!" The love between men and women would become the theme of the "Children of Adam" cluster of poems; the love of men for other men would become the theme of the "Calamus" poems.

All of these various thematic ideas *become* his poems in Section 18. "See, pastures and forests in my poems . . . / See, in my poems, cities, solid, vast. . . ." The poems are the land, and the land and people are his poems. And in this poem's final section, he urges his reader, "camerado," to join him, "to haste, haste on with me."

"Starting from Paumanok" foreshadows the America of Whitman's vision, and he urges readers to follow him on his travels into that "New World."

"[States!]" (1860)

Cut from *Leaves of Grass* after appearing as "Calamus No. 5" in the third edition (1860). The brackets indicate the poem's first line. Although the poem was cut, several lines appeared in the *Drum-Taps* volume (1865) in a poem titled "Over the Carnage Rose Prophetic a Voice" and in a poem titled "A Song" (1867, 1871, and 1876), which was retitled "For You O Democracy" for the final edition of *Leaves* (1881).

"Still Though the One I Sing" (1871)

First appeared as part of "Songs of Insurrection" in the fifth edition of *Leaves of Grass* (1871); it received its present title (1881); it was the 20th of 24 poems in the "Inscriptions" cluster for the sixth edition (1881).

The three-line poem suggests that even though someone is full of "contradictions . . . / I leave in him revolt, . . ." Even someone "made" of contradictions has the "right of insurrection" and still deserves to be sung about.

Whitman says of himself in "Song of Myself," "Do I contradict myself? / Very well then I contradict myself, / (I am large, I contain multitudes.)"

"Stronger Lessons" (1860)

First appeared as part of a poem titled "Debris" in the third edition of *Leaves of Grass* (1860); then under its present title and as a separate poem in the fourth edition (1867); it was cut from the next three editions, reappearing in *November Boughs* (1888); and it was the 52nd of 65 poems in the "First Annex: Sands at Seventy" cluster for the "Death-bed" printing of *Leaves of Grass* (1892).

This poem is a two-line "sermon" on the idea that the "stronger lessons" of life may come from enemies rather than from friends.

"Sun-Down Papers from the Desk of a School-Master" (1840)

A series of essays, written while Whitman was teaching school in 1840, though they have little to do with teaching. The first six were published in the *Hempstead Inquirer* between February 29 and August 11, 1840, the last four in the LONG ISLAND DEMOCRAT between September 29, 1840, and July 20, 1841.

The 10 essays were moralistic, even preachy—against smoking and drinking coffee, for example—and so not very popular. They represent some of Whitman's earliest writing, even before the first fiction, which was also intended to be morally instructive.

"Supplement Hours" (1897)

First published as the eighth of 13 poems in the "Old Age Echoes" cluster for the first posthumous printing of *Leaves of Grass* (1897), added by one of Whitman's executors, Horace TRAUBEL.

The "supplement hours" are, for Whitman, those spent with nature, the "sane, random, negligent hours," more important than hours spent with books or art. The importance of nature is a theme that runs throughout *Leaves of Grass*. See, for particular examples of other poems devoted to this theme, "A Noiseless Patient Spider" and "When I Heard the Learn'd Astronomer."

"Tears" (1867)

First published as "Leaves of Grass, No. 2" in the fourth edition of *Leaves of Grass* (1867); then under its present title in the fifth edition (1871); then with a cluster of poems titled "Sea-Shore Memories" (1876); and finally as the third of 11 poems in the "Sea-Drift" cluster for the sixth edition (1881).

As with many poems in *Leaves of Grass*, Whitman uses the sea as a metaphor for an experience in life; in this poem the sea's spindrift becomes the "tears" of the solitary life, probably the life of the poet himself. "Tears! tears! tears! / In the night, in solitude, tears, . . ." The poem ends, however, by wishing them gone: "But away at night as you fly, none looking—O then the unloosen'd ocean, / Of tears! tears! tears!" It is one of Whitman's more sentimental poems.

Perhaps the most interesting thing about this poem is its rhythmic pattern. It is written in ACCENTUAL VERSE, the number of accented syllables in each line creating the rhythm, in a pattern found in ancient Hebrew poetry, especially in the Old Testament. The 13 lines in "Tears" are all one sentence but in three parts, separated by semicolons. Each part begins and ends with lines carrying, roughly, the same number of accented syllables: 3-3-5-5-3; 5-6-5; and 6-6-8-7-3.

There is also an emphasis on alliteration and assonance, perhaps suggesting to readers sounds of the sea. Besides the repeated "t" sound of the opening and closing lines, there are also the following other examples: "dripping, dripping"; "suck'd in by the sand"; "dark and desolate"; "Streaming tears, sobbing tears"; "swift steps"; "with wind"; "shade so sedate"; and "calm countenance."

"Tests" (1860)

First appeared in the third edition of *Leaves of Grass* (1860); it was the 29th of 38 poems in the "Autumn Rivulets" cluster for the sixth edition (1881). It remained virtually unchanged throughout its publication history.

The "tests" of life, particularly those involving the "soul," cannot be analyzed by "outer authorities," the poet suggests in this five-line poem, but only by the individual self.

"Thanks in Old Age" (1887)

First published in the *PHILADELPHIA PRESS* (November 24, 1887); then in *November Boughs* (1888);

and it was the 46th of 65 poems in the "First Annex: Sands at Seventy" cluster for the "Deathbed" printing of *Leaves of Grass* (1892).

This 14-line poem is a thank-you note from Whitman at age 68 for his life, "health, the midday sun, the impalpable air—for life, mere life." He evokes memories of his mother, father, siblings, and friends. And he is grateful to future readers of his poetry: "We never met, and ne'er shall meet—and yet our souls embrace. . . ." All of the poems in *November Boughs* reflect Whitman's concern with his own aging and impending death, perhaps none more than this one.

"That Music Always Round Me" (1860)

First appeared as "Calamus No. 21" in the third edition of *Leaves of Grass* (1860); it received its present title (1867); it was transferred to the "Whispers of Heavenly Death" cluster (1871); and it became the ninth of 18 poems in the "Whispers" cluster for the sixth edition (1881).

Music has not always been an inspiration to the poet, he says in the opening line, but it is now. He hears a chorus and is "elated," and he CATALOGS singers' voices that move him, and he believes that he understands the power of the music better than the singers themselves. See also "Proud Music of the Storm."

"That Shadow My Likeness" (1860)

Titled "Calamus No. 40" in the third edition of *Leaves of Grass* (1860); it received its present title (1867); it was the 38th of 39 poems in the "Calamus" cluster for the sixth edition (1881).

The "shadow" is of the poet himself, sometimes unrecognizable because of its "chattering, chaffering" (ridiculing of others), so that the poet

sometimes doubts "whether that is really me." But he says that "among my lovers and caroling these songs, / O I never doubt whether that is really me."

The poet feels more comfortable when he is with a lover or writing poems than he does going "to and fro," perhaps too frivolously, along the streets of his neighborhood.

"Then Last of All" (1885)

First published with seven other poems under the heading "Fancies at Navesink" in NINETEENTH CENTURY magazine (August 1885); then in *November Boughs* (1888); and, finally, with the "Fancies at Navesink" group as an insert in the "First Annex: Sands at Seventy" cluster for the "Death-bed" printing of *Leaves of Grass* (1892).

This single quatrain sums up the "Fancies at Navesink" poems by suggesting that the poet, now in his mid-60s, has caught the "mystic human meaning" of the sea's tides, the "swell and ebb, enclosing me the same, / The brain that shapes, the voice that chants this song." The ebb and flood tides, the very movement of the waves, suggest to Whitman the meaning of his own life, even the voice for the poems he has written, similar in the theme perhaps but not in the power of "Out of the Cradle Endlessly Rocking."

"Then Shall Perceive" (1897)

First published as the second of 13 poems in the "Old Age Echoes" cluster for the first posthumous printing of *Leaves of Grass* (1897), added by one of Whitman's executors, Horace TRAUBEL.

The three lines of this poem may be a fragment of a slightly longer poem addressed to Spring.

"There Was a Child Went Forth" (1855)

First appeared as the 10th of 12 untitled poems in the first edition of *Leaves of Grass* (1855); it was titled "Poem of the Child That Went Forth, and Always Goes Forth, Forever and Forever" (1856); as "Leaves of Grass, No. 9" (1860); as "Leaves of Grass, No. 1" (1867); then under its present title for the fifth edition of *Leaves* (1871); and as the third of 38 poems in the "Autumn Rivulets" cluster for the sixth edition (1881).

The theme of the poem is that when our senses touch a thing in nature, that thing becomes part of us and makes us more aware of our role both in nature and in society. Everything we touch becomes part of us:

> There was a child went forth every day,
> And the first object he look'd upon, that object
>   he became,
> And that object became part of him for the day
>   or a certain part of the day,
> Or for many years or stretching cycles of
>   years. . . .

The rest of this 39-line poem CATALOGs all of the things the child *is* because of the things he has seen and touched; the last line reads: "These became part of that child who went forth every day, and who now goes, and will always go forth every day." We can't help making those things part of ourselves.

The poem is one of several in *Leaves of Grass* that follow the rhythmic pattern of the Old Testament, including repetition and parallel structure. The catalog of things the child sees, hears, or touches—early lilacs, grass, white and red morning-glories, white and red clover, the phoebe bird's song, the "sow's pink-faint litter," the cow's calf; plus his own father and mother, the "doubts of day-time and the doubts of night-time," the village after sunset, shadows—this entire catalog of people, places, and things are made parallel to the child's awareness that he is part of all that functions around him. The child cannot avoid the influence of these things on his own personality. He becomes one with them.

"These Carols" (1871)

First published in the fifth edition of *Leaves of Grass* (1871); it was the 15th of 17 poems in the "Songs of Parting" cluster for the sixth edition (1881).

In two lines Whitman dedicates "to the Invisible World" "These carols sung to cheer my passage through the world I see." He has written the poems for the "Songs of Parting" cluster in order to encourage himself through the world as he sees it, but he dedicates the poems to the "Invisible World," the world awaiting him in death.

"These I Singing in Spring" (1860)

Titled "Calamus No. 4" in the third edition of *Leaves of Grass* (1860); it received the present title (1867); and it was the fifth of 39 poems in the "Calamus" cluster for the sixth edition (1881).

The poet finds many tokens of love in the Spring: the "lilac, with a branch of pine . . . some moss which I pull'd off a live-oak in Florida . . . some pinks and laurel leaves, and a handful of sage." But it is the "calamus-root," which the poet finds at a pond-side, that becomes his "token of comrades," a token he offers to the other men he loves.

Whereas in "For You O Democracy" (the immediately preceding poem in the sixth edition of *Leaves of Grass*) the poet shows his love for *all* "comrades," "These I Singing in Spring" seems to offer love only to those who return it, and it is to those he presents the calamus-root: "But what I drew from the water by the pond-side, that I reserve, / I will give of it, but only to them that love as I myself am capable of loving."

"Thick-Sprinkled Bunting" (1865)

First appeared as "Flag of Stars, Thick-Sprinkled Bunting" in the *Drum-Taps* volume (1865); then under its present title in the fifth edition of *Leaves of Grass* (1871); and it was the 18th of 22 poems in the "From Noon to Starry Night" cluster for the sixth edition (1881).

The "bunting" is the flag of the United States, "flag of stars," and, the poet believed, the CIVIL WAR was fought not just for this nation but for the world: "For the prize I see at issue at last is the world, / All its ships and shores I see interwoven with your threads greedy banner." Whitman visualizes the importance of a democratic America as an example to the world. The flag is symbolic of that vision.

"Think of the Soul" (1856)

Cut from *Leaves of Grass* after first appearing as the last nine stanzas of "Poem of Remembrances" in the second edition (1856), then as a separate poem entitled "Leaves of Grass, No. 1" (1867), and under its present title (1871).

"This Compost" (1856)

First appeared under the title "Poem of Wonder at the Resurrection of The Wheat" in the second edition of *Leaves of Grass* (1856); under the title "Leaves of Grass, No. 4" (1860); it received its present title (1867); it was the sixth of 38 poems in the "Autumn Rivulets" cluster for the sixth edition (1881).

The first of two sections reflects the poet's fear of the earth as a huge "compost," filled with the dead: "Perhaps every mite has once form'd part of a sick person." But in the second section he notices ("yet behold!") that "The grass of spring covers the prairies, / The bean bursts noiselessly through the mould in the garden," and "Out of its little hill faithfully rise the potato's dark green leaves, / Out of its hill rises the yellow maize-stalk, the lilacs bloom in the dooryard."

"What chemistry," the poet writes, and he connects the earth's compost with his concept of immortality, each death still contributing to life through its process of decay.

"This Day, O Soul" (1865)

Cut from *Leaves of Grass* after appearing in the *Sequel to Drum-Taps* (1865) and fourth and "Centennial" printings of *Leaves* (1867 and 1876).

"This Dust Was Once the Man" (1871)

First appeared with three other LINCOLN poems under the general heading "President Lincoln's Burial Hymn" in the fifth edition of *Leaves of Grass* (1871); all four poems were then moved to the "Memories of President Lincoln" cluster for the sixth edition (1881).

The poem is a four-line tribute to Lincoln, who "Against the foulest crime in history . . . saved the Union of these States."

"This Moment Yearning and Thoughtful" (1860)

Titled "Calamus No. 23" in the third edition of *Leaves of Grass* (1860); it received its title (1867) and remained unchanged throughout the rest of its publication history; it was the 19th of 39 poems in the "Calamus" cluster for the sixth edition (1881).

The poet sits alone, "yearning and thoughtful," and he thinks there also must be "other men in other lands yearning and thoughtful." Whitman visualizes men in Europe or Asia, alone and contemplative, and he knows, he says at the end of the poem, "we should be brethren and lovers, / I know I should be happy with them."

"Thought" [As I sit . . .] (1860)

First appeared as "No. 5" in a cluster titled "Thoughts" in the third edition of *Leaves of Grass*

(1860); it was then a separate poem in the "Passage to India" supplement (1871); and it became the 15th of 18 poems in the "Whispers of Heavenly Death" cluster for the sixth edition (1881).

Following a chilling description of some well-known ships that sank off the "Northeast coast," the poet offers a "veil'd tableau" of "women gather'd together on deck, pale, heroic, waiting for the moment that draws so close—O the moment! / A huge sob—a few bubbles—the white foam spirting up—and then the women gone, . . ."

In the final lines, however, the poet seems unwilling to accept the "thought" that the women are "gone":

Sinking there while the passionless wet flows
    on—and I now pondering, Are those women
    indeed gone?
Are souls drown'd and destroy'd so?
Is only matter triumphant?

No, the poet would say, it is the soul that is triumphant.

"Thought" [Of Equality] (1860)

First published as the second line of "No. 4" of the "Thoughts" poems in the third edition of *Leaves of Grass* (1860); it received its present title and was printed as a separate poem (1871); and it was the 25th of 29 poems in the ""By The Roadside"" cluster for the sixth edition (1881). The poem is one line but 31 words.

The poet wonders whether allowing others "equality" would ever harm him. He says that in fact the equality of others is "indispensable" for his own equality. If one person is not treated as an equal, then none is equal. This poem was written at the beginning of the CIVIL WAR, a time when Whitman felt ambivalent about SLAVERY; he hated slavery, but he hated the thought of a divided Union even more.

"Thought" [Of Justice] (1860)

First appeared as two lines of a four-line poem titled "No. 4" in the "Thoughts" group for the third edition of *Leaves of Grass* (1860); as one of the "Passage to India" poems (1871); then as the 22nd of 29 poems in the "By The Roadside" cluster for the sixth edition (1881).

This two-line poem is a "thought" about American justice. Whitman believed in equal justice for all, brought about by "natural judges and saviors," people who would make unbiased judgments in their interpretation of the law.

"Thought" [Of obedience] (1860)

First published as No. 7 of the "Thoughts" group in the third edition of *Leaves of Grass* (1860); it received its present title and was published as a separate poem (1871); and it was the 20th of 29 poems in the "By The Roadside" cluster for the sixth edition (1881).

This two-line poem is a comment on "large masses of men" following the wrong leaders, especially those leaders who "do not believe in men." It is "obedience, faith, adhesiveness" that are the marks of good leaders, Whitman believes. He uses the word ADHESIVENESS here to mean friendship or companionship; he is looking for leaders who might also make good friends.

"Thought" [Of Persons] (1860)

First appeared as "No. 3" in the "Thoughts" group in the third edition of *Leaves of Grass* (1860); and it was the 20th of 38 poems in the "Autumn Rivulets" cluster for the sixth edition (1881). It remained unchanged throughout its publication history.

This "Thought" is about people who have "arrived at high positions, ceremonies, wealth, scholarships, and the like." If they do not allow these high positions to merge with "their bodies and souls" then they are, for Whitman, "sad, hasty, unwaked somnambules [sleepwalkers] walking the dusk." They are of no value to themselves or to society.

"Thought of Columbus, A" (1892)

First published as a manuscript facsimile in ONCE A WEEK (July 9, 1892); it was the last of 13 poems in the "Old Age Echoes" cluster for the first posthumous printing of *Leaves of Grass* (1897), added by one of Whitman's executors, Horace TRAUBEL. See "Old Age Echoes."

Traubel explained in a story he wrote for the next issue of *Once a Week* that this was Whitman's last poem, handed to Traubel by the poet on March 16, 1892, 10 days before he died. Extant fragments of the poem indicate Whitman might have begun the poem as early as the preceding November.

Four hundred years before Whitman's death in 1892, Columbus landed on America's shores. This is the poet's commemoration of the event ("The mystery of mysteries"), reminding readers of what America had accomplished in that span of time: "As here to-day up-grows the Western World."

"Thoughts" [Of ownership] (1860)

First published as "No. 2" in a cluster of poems titled *Thoughts* in the third edition of *Leaves of Grass* (1860); as "No. 4" (1871); and it was the sixth of 29 poems in the "By The Roadside" cluster for the sixth edition (1881).

This is a one-sentence, five-line poem of "thoughts" about the impact of "ownership" on the owner. "Of ownership—as if one fit to own things

could not at pleasure enter upon all, and incorporate them into himself or herself; . . . / Because all I see and know I believe to have its main purport in what will yet be supplied."

Things that a person owns eventually become a part of that person.

"Thoughts" [Of Public Opinion] (1860)

First appeared as "Thought" in the third edition of *Leaves of Grass* (1860); then as "Thoughts" (1867); it was the 11th of 22 poems in the "From Noon to Starry Night" cluster for the sixth edition (1881).

In a democracy, the poet suggests here, it is public opinion that matters most.

> Of the President with pale face asking secretly
>   to himself, *What will the people say at last?*
> Of the frivolous Judge—of the corrupt
>   Congressman, Governor, Major—of such as
>   these standing helpless and exposed,
> Of the mumbling and screaming priest, (soon,
>   soon deserted,) . . .

All of these will disappear. It is the "intuitions of men and women, and of Self-esteem and Personality," the "resplendent en-masse," the nation's citizens, who will, in the end, keep democracy alive against the corruption of institutionalized systems.

"Thoughts" [Of these years] (1860)

Published as two separate poems, "Chants Democratic, No. 9" and "Chants Democratic, No. 11," for the third edition of *Leaves of Grass* (1860); the two poems were brought together as "Thoughts" (1871); and it was the fourth of 17 poems in the "Songs of Parting" cluster for the sixth edition (1881). It is written in two sections and 33 lines.

Whitman's "thoughts" here reflect the great diversity of the America of his time. America, he writes, "illustrates birth, muscular youth, the promise, the sure fulfilment, the absolute success, despite of people—illustrates evil as well as good."

"Thoughts—1: Visages" (1860)

Cut from *Leaves of Grass* after first appearing as "Thoughts, No. 1" in the third edition (1860), then under its present title (1867).

"Thoughts—2" [Of Waters, Forests, Hills] (1860)

This six-line poem was first published in a cluster of poems titled "Thoughts" for the third edition of *Leaves of Grass* (1860); but it was then broken up, part of it reappearing in "Thoughts" [Of ownership] in the "By The Roadside" cluster for the final version of *Leaves* (1881).

See also "Thoughts—4" [Of Ownership . . .].

"Thoughts—4" [Of Ownership . . .] (1860)

This poem, like "Thoughts—2" above, was first published in a cluster titled "Thoughts" (1860), but was then broken up, part of it reappearing as "Thought" [Of Justice] in the "By The Roadside" cluster for the final version of *Leaves of Grass* (1881).

"Thoughts—6" [Of What I Write] (1867)

Cut from *Leaves of Grass* after first appearing as the sixth poem in a cluster titled "Thoughts" in the fourth edition (1867), and as a separate poem (1876).

"Thou Mother with Thy Equal Brood" (1872)

Delivered under the title "As a Strong Bird on Pinions Free" as the commencement poem at Dartmouth College (June 26, 1872); it was printed as the title poem in a small volume of eight poems, *As a Strong Bird on Pinions Free* (1872); it was then bound into the *Two Rivulets* volume as a supplement to the 1876 printing of *Leaves of Grass*; and it appeared as a separate poem, revised and under its present title, following the "Whispers of Heavenly Death" cluster in the sixth edition (1881). The final version is in six sections and 131 lines.

Whitman's poems from the early 1870s reflect a certain urgency, the poet thinking that he might not live much longer. He lived until 1892, but he suffered a paralytic stroke January 23, 1873, which slowed him considerably and which encouraged him to begin to reorganize *Leaves of Grass* toward a final edition. Most of his last poems, those written during the 1870s and 1880s, tend toward restatements of earlier themes. "Thou Mother with Thy Equal Brood" is one of the early examples, stating as it does Whitman's earlier convictions about American democracy and the future value of that democracy to the world at large.

The first three sections evoke the America of Whitman's vision. The "Mother" in the title is America itself. Whitman reviews here the theme of America's future and its potential for the rest of the world. He won't repeat the poetic interests of poets "of other lands . . . Nor rhyme, nor the classics, nor perfume of foreign court or indoor library; / But an odor I'd bring as from forests of pine in Maine, or breath of an Illinois prairie." It would be a mistake, he believes, to simply imitate the poetry of European traditions. America's poets must create a new "perfume" out of the makings of individual states.

The second stanza opens with the line from which Whitman took the poem's first title, "As a

Strong Bird on Pinions Free." America must fly its own course, free of outside influences, even free to create its own poetry. "Brain of the New World," the poet warns at the beginning of Section 3, "what a task is thine." It is the task for the citizens of the New World "To formulate the Modern—out of the peerless grandeur of the modern." The "Modern" must be a recasting of "poems, churches, art, / Recast, maybe discard them, end them—maybe their work is done, who knows?)."

At the beginning of Section 4, Whitman urges democratic principles on the rest of the world and suggests that the world depends on America's growth:

> Sail, sail thy best, ship of Democracy, . . .
> With thee Time voyages in trust, the
>   antecedent nations sink or swim with
>   thee, . . .
> Theirs, theirs as much as thine, the
>   destination-port trumphant;
> Steer then with good strong hand and wary eye
>   O helmsman, thou carriest great
>   companions, . . .

America, the "Mother," has for its "Equal Brood" the nations of the rest of the world, "priestly Asia" and "royal feudal Europe"; all the great nations sail with America, equal with it perhaps but guided by what Whitman refers to as the "new, Spiritual World." In America he sees "The soul, its destinies," offering a new guidance to the rest of the world.

This new Spiritual World will come out of America's "unparallel'd flight," just as is the flight of "a strong bird on pinions free." And the poem ends with the thought that the "present" can not hold back America; only the "Future" can hold the America of the poet's vision.

"Thou Orb Aloft Full-Dazzling" (1881)

First published in the AMERICAN (June 4, 1881) under the title "A Summer Invocation"; it received its present title and became the first of 22 poems in the "From Noon to Starry Night" cluster for the sixth edition of Leaves of Grass (1881).

The poet evokes the Sun in this poem, and, after honoring its "perturbations," its deviations from a regular course, he asks it to "Prepare the later afternoon of me myself—prepare my lengthening shadows, / Prepare my starry nights." The poet wants to be prepared for his own deviations, his "lengthening shadows" as old age approaches.

"Thou Reader" (1881)

First appeared in the sixth edition of Leaves of Grass (1881) and was the last of 24 poems in the "Inscriptions" cluster.

Here are the poem's two lines: "Thou reader throbbest life and pride and love the same as I, / Therefore for thee the following chants."

All of the poems in the "Inscriptions" cluster are introductory, and this final one urges the reader to read on.

"Time to Come" (1842)

First published in the NEW YORK AURORA (April 9, 1842); an "early poem" not later published in Leaves of Grass. It is most accessible now in Francis Murphy (editor), Walt Whitman: The Complete Poems (Penguin Books, 1996).

"To a Certain Cantatrice" (1860)

First appeared in the third edition of Leaves of Grass as one of the "Messenger Leaves" (1860); it was one of the "Songs of Insurrection" in the third printing of the fifth edition (1876); it then became the 14th of 24 poems in the "Inscriptions" cluster for the sixth edition (1881).

This is one of several poems dedicated to individuals, in this case "to a certain cantatrice," a professional woman singer. "Here, take this gift," the poet says to the otherwise unidentified woman, "I was reserving it for some hero, speaker, or general, . . . / But I see that what I was reserving belongs to you just as much as to any."

The singer may have been Marietta ALBONI, a famous coloratura soprano; Whitman wrote later that he had heard her sing in 10 OPERAS during the 1852–53 New York opera season. There may be a more important idea here, however, one that ties the poem to Whitman's concept of democracy. The woman singer is as deserving of the poet's "gift" as is "some hero, speaker, or general."

"To a Certain Civilian" (1865)

First appeared as "Did You Ask Dulcet Rhymes from Me?" in the *Drum-Taps* volume (1865); then under its present title and with a group titled "Ashes of Soldiers" in the fifth edition of *Leaves of Grass* (1871); and it became the 38th of 43 poems in the "Drum-Taps" cluster for the sixth edition (1881). It was revised often during its publication history.

The 10-line poem is like an angry letter to someone, perhaps a reviewer, who has criticized the poet's work. At the end the poet tells the "Civilian" to "go lull yourself with what you can understand, and with piano-tunes, / For I lull nobody, and you will never understand me."

Perhaps because Whitman included it among his CIVIL WAR poems, readers may see the poem as a comment on the civilian's inability to understand poems about the horrors of the war.

"To a Common Prostitute" (1860)

First appeared as one of the "Messenger Leaves" in the third edition of *Leaves of Grass* (1860); it was the 18th of 38 poems in the "Autumn Rivulets" cluster for the sixth edition (1881). It was censored often by various publications.

Whitman altered this six-line poem slightly between the 1860 and 1881 editions of *Leaves of Grass* by changing "My love" to "My girl" at the beginning of the fourth line and "kiss on your lips" to "significant look" in the sixth line.

The poem is addressed to prostitutes, who are accepted by Whitman as equals, just as is every other human being regardless of his or her position in society: "Be composed—be at ease with me—I am Walt Whitman, liberal and lusty as Nature, / Not till the sun excludes you do I exclude you." Whitman noted, in response to the editorial criticism, that all those who excluded prostitutes, or people in any other profession, from their rightful place in society did not understand one of the major principles of democracy.

"To a Foil'd European Revolutionaire" (1856)

First appeared under the title "Liberty Poem for Asia, Africa, Europe, America, Australia, Cuba, and The Archipelagoes of the Sea" in the second edition of *Leaves of Grass* (1856); it was retitled "To a Foiled Revolter or Revoltress" (1860); then it appeared under its present title (1871); and as the seventh of 38 poems in the "Autumn Rivulets" cluster for the sixth edition (1881).

It is significant that the poem was in a cluster titled "Songs of Insurrection" for the fifth edition (1871), a title then dropped for the sixth edition (1881).

"European Revolutionaire" is a plea to rebels throughout the world to fight for liberty: "Courage yet, my brother or my sister! / Keep on—Liberty is to be subserv'd whatever occurs." Later the poet added: "When Liberty goes out of a place it is not the first to go, nor the second or third to go, / It waits for all the rest to go, it is the last."

Whitman encourages revolutionaries everywhere to fight for liberty against tyranny.

"To a Historian" (1860)

First appeared in *Leaves of Grass* as "Chants Democratic, No. 10" in the third edition (1860); under its present title (1867); then it became the fifth of

24 poems in the "Inscriptions" cluster for the sixth edition (1881).

This is the first of several poems in which Whitman suggests that the sensations he feels as he lives and writes poetry in the middle of the 19th century will be felt by future readers and will help explain the history through which he lives. To the historian, he says: "Chanter of Personality, outlining what is yet to be, / I project the history of the future." These poems are, he says, my vision of the America to come.

Whitman projects himself here as a prophet, one of his duties as a poet; the idea is thematic in *Leaves of Grass*. In later poems, he will project himself as "visiting" past and future places and events, "floating" above the scene and "observing."

"To a Locomotive in Winter" (1876)

First published in the *New York Tribune* (February 19, 1876); it was then printed in the *Two Rivulets* volume of the 1876 printing of *Leaves of Grass*; and it was the fourth of 22 poems in the "From Noon to Starry Night" cluster for the sixth edition (1881).

This is a love song for the early trains, a "recitative" Whitman calls it in the first line—that is, between a song and ordinary speech. Anyone who remembers the steam engine, its "great protruding head-light fix'd in front," its "dense and murky clouds out-belching from [its] smoke-stack," will enjoy this lyrical poem.

"To a President" (1860)

First published as one of the "Messenger Leaves" in the third edition of *Leaves of Grass* (1860); it became the 10th of 29 poems in the "By The Roadside" cluster for the sixth edition (1881). It remained unchanged throughout its publication history.

The four-line poem is directed at President James Buchanan, who was a disappointment to

Whitman. He addresses the president in the first two lines: "All you are doing and saying is to America dangled mirages, / You have not learn'd of Nature—of the politics of Nature you have not learn'd the great amplitude, rectitude, impartiality, . . ." The poet apparently felt that Buchanan did not understand the great issues of a democracy, especially that of the need for equality.

Abraham LINCOLN had become the Republican Party's nominee for president on May 16, 1860, however, so Whitman had hope for the future.

"To a Pupil" (1860)

First appeared as one of the "Messenger Leaves" in the third edition of *Leaves of Grass* (1860); and as the 23rd of 38 poems in the "Autumn Rivulets" cluster for the sixth edition (1881). It remained virtually unchanged throughout its publication history.

This seven-line poem is a simple admonition to young people to develop a "Personalty" that will impress others: "Rest not till you rivet and publish yourself of your own Personality."

"To a Stranger" (1860)

Titled "Calamus No. 22" in the third edition of *Leaves of Grass* (1860); it received its title (1867) and remained unchanged throughout the rest of its publication history; it was the 18th of 39 poems in the "Calamus" cluster for the sixth edition (1881).

It is unusual for one of the Calamus poems to suggest heterosexual love, but this one combines heterosexual and homosexual love in a dream the poet has had in seeing a "passing stranger," with whom he believes he has "lived a life of joy." The "stranger" is undefined, someone the poet has met and loved in the past: "You must be he I was seeking, or she I was seeking."

The poet remembers, in the dream, growing up, "a boy with me or a girl with me, / I ate with you and slept with you." He dreams of the love he had for this boy or girl and ends the poem hoping not to lose the love: "I am to wait, I do not doubt I am to meet you again, / I am to see to it that I do not lose you."

"To a Western Boy" (1860)

Titled "Calamus No. 42" in the third edition of *Leaves of Grass* (1860); it received its present title (1867); it was the 34th of 39 poems in the "Calamus" cluster for the sixth edition (1881).

The poet speaks to a potential *eleve* (pupil) who has sought him out, telling him that "if blood like mine circle not in your veins, / If you be not silently selected by lovers and do not silently select lovers," then it is of no use that you "seek" to become a pupil of mine.

This idea seems to contradict Whitman's stated point of view that it is not necessary for anyone to walk in his footsteps or believe all that he believes. What is more important is for people to think for themselves.

"To Be at All" (1897)

First published as the 10th of 13 poems in the "Old Age Echoes" cluster for the first posthumous printing of *Leaves of Grass* (1897), added by one of Whitman's executors, Horace TRAUBEL.

The parenthetical subhead reads: "(Cf. Stanza 27, 'Song of Myself')," indicating that this is probably a fragment cut from an early version of "Song of Myself." Apparently Whitman encouraged Traubel to include it with his other selections for the "Old Age Echoes" cluster.

"To Be at All" certainly echoes Section 27 of "Song of Myself," the idea that it is great to be alive. He says, "To be at all—what is better than that?" The eight-line Section 27 of "Song of Myself" is about the mystery of being: "To touch my person to some one else's is about as much as I can stand."

"To-day and Thee" (1888)

First published in the *NEW YORK HERALD* (April 23, 1888); then in *November Boughs* (1888); and it was the 15th of 65 poems in the "First Annex: Sands at Seventy" cluster for the "Death-bed" printing of *Leaves of Grass* (1892).

Whitman evokes the writers of the past, the "appointed winners in a long-stretch'd game," allowing the heirs of today to enjoy the "heroes, histories, arts, experiments" of "Egypt, India, Greece and Rome." What we are today, the poet says, converges in the historic past.

"To Foreign Lands" (1860)

First appeared under the title "To Other Lands" in the third edition of *Leaves of Grass* (1860); then under its present title (1871); and it became the fourth of 24 poems in the "Inscriptions" cluster of the sixth edition (1881).

In this three-line poem Whitman suggests to the old world that if it wants to solve the "puzzle" of the "New World," to "define America, her athletic Democracy, / . . . I send you my poems. . . ." In these individual poems in the "Inscriptions" cluster and in the whole of *Leaves of Grass,* Whitman expected to explain America and its democratic principles.

"To Get the Final Lilt of Songs" (1888)

First published in the *NEW YORK HERALD* (April 16, 1888); then in *November Boughs* (1888); and it was the 35th of 65 poems in the "First Annex: Sands at Seventy" cluster for the "Death-bed" printing of *Leaves of Grass* (1892).

It is necessary, Whitman suggests in this six-line poem, that to get "the final lilt of songs," their full value, one must study the music. The songs studied are, however, in this poem a metaphor for life itself.

One must study the songs of "Job, Homer, . . . Shakspere," and others, to get "final" value and appreciation; one must in old age study life to get its final value and appreciation.

"To Him That was Crucified" (1860)

First appeared as one of the "Messenger Leaves" in the third edition of *Leaves of Grass* (1860); it became the 15th of 38 poems in the "Autumn Rivulets" cluster for the sixth edition (1881).

Without naming Christ, the poet suggests that many people are crucified, and all of them are brothers; the opening line reflects this idea: "My spirit to yours dear brother." Later he reflects further: "I specify you with joy O my comrade to salute you, and to salute those who are with you, before and since, and those to come also, / That we all labor together transmitting the same charge and succession."

The "charge" is not specified, but it must certainly be to preach one's serious beliefs to the world, regardless of consequences—as did Christ.

"Tomb Blossoms, The" (1842)

Short story (more a sketch than a traditional story), first published in the *United States Magazine and Democratic Review* (January 1842; see DEMOCRATIC REVIEW, THE). The tale is most accessible now in *Walt Whitman: The Early Poems and the Fiction,* edited by Thomas L. Brasher (New York University Press, 1963).

The unnamed narrator of this sketch tells about meeting an old women in a cemetery spreading flowers over two graves and pausing over each as she does so. She is "an old, a very old inmate of the poor-house. . . . She was a native of one of the West India Islands, and . . . had, with her husband, come hither to settle and gain a livelihood. They were poor, most miserably poor."

The inquisitive narrator learns from the woman, referred to only by her last name, Delaree, that both of the graves belong to her husband. She explains that she was ill when her husband died and so could not attend the burial, that he was buried in a pauper's grave and that the sexton could tell her only that her husband was "positively" in one of the two graves she was now covering with flowers. The narrator passes on to the reader his consequent thought:

> What a wondrous thing is human love! . . . Here is this aged wayfarer—a woman of trials and griefs—decrepit, sore, and steeped in poverty—the most forlorn of her kind, and yet . . . her memory of her love hovers like a beautiful spirit amid the gloom.
>
> And the buried man—he was happy to have passed away as he did. The woman—she was the one to be pitied. Without doubt she wished many times that she were laid beside him. And not only she, thought I, as I cast my eyes on the solemn memorials around me: but at the same time there were thousands else on earth who panted for the long repose, as a tired child for the night. The grave—the grave. What foolish man calls it a dreadful place?

This is one of Whitman's works of fiction that connects most thematically to his poetry. A lot of the poems in *Leaves of Grass* are devoted to the idea that death is one of the great life experiences and should not, therefore, be feared.

CHARACTER

Delaree   An old woman in the story "The Tomb Blossoms." She is an "inmate of the poor-house" from the West India Islands, and had come to this country so her husband could find work and a home for the two of them. "They were poor," the narrator says, "most miserably poor."

"To Old Age" (1860)

First published as one of the "Messenger Leaves" in the third edition of *Leaves of Grass* (1860); it was published as a separate poem (1867); it was one of the "Passage to India" poems in the fifth edition (1871); and it was the 26th of 29 poems in the "By The Roadside" cluster for the sixth edition (1881).

This one-line poem is an evocation to old age: "I see in you the estuary. . . ." Whitman uses the estuary that "spreads itself grandly" out to the "great sea" as a metaphor for what he suggests happens to people as they get older. For Whitman, death is one of life's great adventures, and he sees death as a voyage out to sea.

"To One Shortly to Die" (1860)

First appeared as one of the "Messenger Leaves" in the third edition of *Leaves of Grass* (1860); it became the 13th of 18 poems in the "Whispers of Heavenly Death" cluster for the sixth edition (1881).

The poet has a "message" for the "one shortly to die": "You are to die—let others tell you what they please, I cannot prevaricate, / I am exact and merciless, but I love you—there is no escape for you." It is the strongest medicine, Whitman is saying, to tell the truth to the dying person. And in the last line he says: "I do not commiserate, I congratulate you." The poem presents Whitman's theme of death as the greatest of life's experiences. It should be valued, not feared.

"Torch, The" (1865)

First appeared in the *Drum-Taps* volume (1865); and as the 30th of 38 poems in the "Autumn Rivulets" cluster for the sixth edition (1881). It remained virtually unchanged throughout its publication history.

This four-line imagistic poem is descriptive of a scene of fishermen along the "Northwest coast in the midst of the night," watching from the shore as others "are spearing salmon, / The canoe, a dim shadowy thing, . . . / Bearing a torch ablaze at the prow." This seems to be one of the few poems in *Leaves of Grass* depending entirely for success on a

mental picture created in the mind of the reader—like a Japanese haiku poem.

"To Rich Givers" (1860)

First published as one of the "Messenger Leaves" in the third edition of *Leaves of Grass* (1860); it was printed as a separate poem (1867); as one of the "Songs of Parting" group (1871); and it was the 12th of 29 poems in the "By The Roadside" cluster for the sixth edition (1881).

The poet tells of his acceptance of those who give him things: "What you give me I cheerfully accept, . . ." But he too gives gifts, perhaps the richest gift of all—his poems: "For I myself am not one who bestows nothing upon man and woman, / For I bestow upon any man or woman the entrance to all the gifts of the universe."

As Whitman's reputation grew, he received many gifts, from strangers as well as friends, "a little sustenance" he calls it in this poem. His reciprocal gift was his own poetry, "the entrance to all the gifts of the universe." Whitman saw poetry, and not just his own, as a window on life.

"To Soar in Freedom and in Fullness of Power" (1897)

First published as the first of 13 poems in the "Old Age Echoes" cluster for the first posthumous printing of *Leaves of Grass* (1897), the poems added by one of Whitman's executors, Horace TRAUBEL.

"I have not felt to warble" like the birds, Whitman writes in this five-line poem. He has, instead, "[soared] in freedom and in the fullness of power, joy, volition," a line suggesting the FREE VERSE poetic form for which Whitman is now so well known. The five lines may have been transcribed by Traubel from a fragment of prose, perhaps intended by Whitman as an introductory statement or preface under the title "My Poetry is more the Poetry of Sight than Sound."

"To the East and to the West" (1860)

Titled "Calamus No. 35" in the third edition of *Leaves of Grass* (1860); it received its present title (1867); it was the 32nd of 39 poems in the "Calamus" cluster for the sixth edition (1881).

The brotherhood of men is envisioned in this poem as encompassing all of America, and the poet believes that the "main purport of these States is to found a superb friendship," unknown anywhere else in the world. This friendship waits, he says, "and has been always waiting, latent in all men."

One of Whitman's important ingredients for democracy is brotherly love. The "germs are in all men," he says in this poem, and America was founded in order to present Democracy to the world. The poem is placed in the "Calamus" cluster because Whitman no doubt has in mind homosexual love, but the love of one man for another is a metaphor here for the brotherhood of all men, of all people, an essential ingredient of democracy.

"To Thee Old Cause" (1871)

First appeared in the fifth edition of *Leaves of Grass* (1871); and it was the sixth of 24 poems in the "Inscriptions" cluster for the sixth edition (1881).

Though not mentioned by name, the "cause" in this poem is America and its democratic principles and the CIVIL WAR, which was fought for that cause.

> Thou peerless, passionate, good cause,
> Thou stern, remorseless, sweet idea, . . .
> As a wheel on its axis turns, this book
>   unwitting to itself,
> Around the idea of thee.

In spite of the war, he suggests, I still send out these poems in honor of the "sweet idea" of the America to come. It is the "old cause" that is the central theme of Whitman's time and place, mid-19th century America. He hated SLAVERY, because it turned blacks into unequal members of society, but he hated the split in the Union more, because it tore up the America of his vision. See also *Democratic Vistas.*

"To the Garden the World" (1860)

First poem in the "Enfans d'Adam" cluster for the third edition of *Leaves of Grass* (1860); it was the first of 16 poems in the "Children of Adam" cluster for the sixth edition (1881).

The Garden of Eden is where love is viewed by the poet as a life force; there is innocence in the garden, an innocence lost by Adam and Eve and all their children, because, as Whitman suggests more pointedly in other poems, they see physical love as sin. "To the Garden the World" begins by establishing Adam and Eve in the garden as a "prelude" for the rest of us.

> To the garden of the world anew ascending,
> Potent mates, daughters, sons, preluding
> The love, the life of their bodies, meaning and
>   being, . . .
> Amorous, mature, all beautiful to me, all
>   wondrous, . . .

Adam and Eve are still unashamed, according to the poet, because theirs is the innocence that their children have lost. It is the "life of their bodies" that gives men and women their "meaning and being." And it is "love" that gives meaning to life. For Whitman, the only sin for Adam and Eve (and for their children) was their belief that amorous love was sinful.

"To the Leaven'd Soil They Trod" (1865)

First appeared in the *Sequel to Drum-Taps* pamphlet (1865) and under this title throughout its publication history in *Leaves of Grass;* it was the last of 43 poems in the "Drum-Taps" cluster for the sixth edition (1881).

The soil is "leaven'd" by the blood of soldiers wounded or killed in the CIVIL WAR, and the poet hopes that the blood-stained soil will help to make more fertile his own poetry, now that the war is over. He appeals to the "general Western world to attest [his] songs, . . . the Alleghanian hills and the tireless Mississippi, . . . the far-off sea and the unseen winds." They "answer all," he says: "The Northern ice and rain that began me nourish me to the end, / But the hot sun of the South is to fully ripen my songs."

Out of the blood-stained soil, both North and South, will come a new fertility that will enrich all people. And, the poet believes, that his poems will also gain from the new fertility and become enriched with new meaning for the Nation.

"To the Man-of-War Bird" (1876)

First published as "The Man-of-War Bird" in the London *Athenaeum* (April 1, 1876); then it was inserted in the third printing of the fifth edition of *Leaves of Grass* (1876); it received its present title and was the fourth of 11 poems in the "Sea-Drift" cluster for the sixth edition (1881).

Several critics have noted that this poem was a near paraphrase of French poet Jules Michelet's *The Bird* (first translated into English in 1869) and that Whitman acknowledged his indebtedness to Michelet in a headnote for "To the Man-of-War Bird" when it was reprinted in the Philadelphia *Progress* (November 16, 1878).

Whitman describes in this 21-line poem the toughness of the Man-of-War bird (better known on America's East Coast as the frigate bird). The bird has "slept all night upon the storm," but finds itself "renew'd" the next day. In the second stanza the poet describes the bird as "born to match the gale," capable of surviving "sea and hurricane," a "ship of air that never furl'st thy sails."

Whitman may feel a comparison between himself and the Man-of-War bird. He identifies himself as "a speck, a point on the world's floating vast," a

parenthetical thought in the middle of his description of the bird's strength and ability to survive the great sea's sometimes terrible moods. The last line reflects Whitman's appreciation but also perhaps his jealousy: "What joys! what joys were thine!"

"To the Pending Year" (1889)

First published as "To the Year 1889" in CRITIC (January 5, 1889); it received its present title and was the 10th of 31 poems in *Good-Bye My Fancy* (1891); then in "Second Annex: Good-Bye My Fancy" for the "Death-bed" printing of *Leaves of Grass* (1892).

"Eleemosynary gifts" in the last line are a form of charity, and Whitman seems to be offering this poem as a gift to the new year (1889), the only "shot left" for the poet, who feels the effects of old age and perhaps wonders if this new year will be his last.

"To the Reader at Parting" (1871)

Cut from *Leaves of Grass* after first appearing in the fifth edition and sixth printing (1871 and 1876).

"To the States" (1860)

First appeared as "Walt Whitman's Caution" in the third edition of *Leaves of Grass* (1860); it was one of the "Messenger Leaves" poems (1871); it was one of the "Songs of Insurrection" (1876); and it was transferred under the present title and as the 12th of 24 poems in the "Inscriptions" cluster for the sixth edition (1881).

The three-line poem represents one of Whitman's pleas against SLAVERY—of any kind: "Once fully enslaved, no nation, state, city of this earth, ever afterward resumes its liberty."

"To the States: To Identify the 16th, 17th or 18th Presidentiad" (1860)

First published as one of the "Messenger Leaves" in the third edition of *Leaves of Grass* (1860); it was the last of 29 poems in the "By The Roadside" cluster for the sixth edition (1881). It was unchanged throughout its publication history.

The poet regrets the immediate past three presidential terms of office and hopes that the next three will be better. The presidents are not named, but they are Millard Fillmore, the 13th president (1850–53); Franklin Pierce, the 14th (1853–57); and James Buchanan, the 15th (1857–61).

The eight-line poem suggests that not only did the three presidents sleep through their terms of office, but the nation slept as well.

> Why reclining, interrogating? why myself and
>   all drowsing?
> What deepening twilight—scum floating atop
>   of the waters,
> Who are they as bats and night-dogs askant in
>   the capitol? . . .

The poet cannot believe that the congressmen, judges, and president (representing the three branches of American government) are awake to the realities of nation.

The poet's hope lies, however, in the next three presidents, the "16th, 17th, and 18th Presidentiad." Whitman suggests that the "muttering thunder and lambent shoots" will bring a refreshing rain and perhaps wake the people. Whitman uses the word "lambent" here to suggest that the lightning "shoots" present a soft, clear light that, with the thunder, will wake the people.

"To the Sun-set Breeze" (1890)

First published in *LIPPINCOTT'S MAGAZINE* (December 1890); it was the 15th of 31 poems in *Good-Bye*

My Fancy (1891); then in "Second Annex: Good-Bye My Fancy" for the "Death-bed" printing of *Leaves of Grass* (1892).

Whitman evokes the breeze as it enters his window "late this heated day . . . gently vitalizing" him as he lies in bed "old, alone, sick," sweating and feeling "thy soothing fingers on my face and hands." The poet wonders if the breeze doesn't have a spiritual side as well: "Thou, messenger-magical strange bringer to body and spirit of me" possible cures from other places, "occult medicines, . . . God sent." Whitman, a man who believed that God was in all things and that all things encompassed God, asks at the end of the poem: "Hast thou no Soul? Can I not know, identify thee?" Is there not also a soul in natural things?

"To Think of Time" (1855)

First published as the third of 12 untitled poems in the first edition of *Leaves of Grass* (1855); it was titled "Burial Poem" for the second edition (1856); titled "Burial" (1860); it received its present title (1871); and it was included as a separate poem in the sixth edition (1881). It is in nine sections and 121 lines.

Thinking of "time" can only take one to thoughts of death, and Whitman meditates in this poem on issues raised by most readers sooner or later, issues having to do with the value of life and with the possibilities of an afterlife: "Have you guess'd you yourself would not continue? . . . / Have you fear'd the future would be nothing to you?" Most people have some difficulty coping with the idea that the world will go on as before after they die.

Sections 2 and 3 remind readers that life and death are both facts of life; we are born, we strain at the chains, and then we die. We tend to be "indifferent" to the lives of others, and the "burial lines" never cease: "He that was President was buried, and he that is now President shall surely be buried."

The poet envisions in Section 4 the funeral for "an old Broadway stage-driver": "Steady the trot to the cemetery, duly rattles the death-bell, . . . / The mound above is flatted with the spades—silence."

Is that it then, Whitman asks, just "silence." "Is there any thing more?" And the description of his life is as quickly given as the funeral. "Died, aged forty-one years—and that was his funeral." And the indifference. As in Tolstoy's "The Death of Ivan Ilych," the other drivers in Whitman's poem might well say to their dead comrade, "I'm just glad it's him and not me."

In Section 5 Whitman adds to the irony of "indifference" by reminding readers how seriously we take "The market, the government, the work-ing-man's wages," yet how little they will mean later on. "Yet we lie beyond the difference," he says. "Your farm, profits, crops—to think how engross'd you are, / To think there will still be farms, profits, crops, yet for you of what avail?"

Nothing that happens in life can be avoided, the poet suggests in Section 7. "The law of the past can-not be eluded," he says; nor can the "present and future" or the "law of drunkards, informers, mean persons"; none of these things can be avoided.

The idea of inevitable death is reiterated at the beginning of Section 8: "black lines go ceaselessly over the earth." But the poet raises a new issue in this section, suggesting that if there is nothing after death, then "we are betray'd."

> If all came but to ashes of dung,
> If maggots and rats ended us, then Alarum! for
>   we are betray'd,
> Then indeed suspicion of death.
>
> Do you suspect death? if I were to suspect death I
>   should die now,
> Do you think I could walk pleasantly and
>   well-suited toward annihilation?

As happens often in *Leaves of Grass*, the poet ends this meditation on "time" by expressing his belief in the "eternal soul," not just for humans but for all living things: "I swear I think now that every thing without exception has an eternal soul! / The trees have, rooted in the ground! the weeds of the sea have! the animals!" And through this belief that God is in all things, the poet overcomes his fear of death, his fear of nothingness.

"To Think of Time" immediately precedes in *Leaves of Grass* the next cluster of poems, titled "Whispers of Heavenly Death," in which each of the 18 poems suggests a way of imagining death, what Hamlet referred to as "undiscovered country."

"To Those Who've Fail'd" (1888)

First published in the NEW YORK HERALD (January 27, 1888); then in *November Boughs* (1888); and it was the fourth of 65 poems in the "First Annex: Sands at Seventy" cluster for the "Death-bed" printing of *Leaves of Grass* (1892).

The poem is directed to those many people who had "aspiration[s] vast" and yet failed because of an early death: "unnam'd soldiers fallen" in battle, but other people as well; the poet thinks of them as "High, high above the rest . . . Possess'd by some strange spirit of fire, / Quench'd by an early death." To all of those people the poet would "rear a laurel-cover'd monument." They had no chance to reach their aspirations.

"To You" (1860)

Cut from *Leaves of Grass* after first appearing in the "Messenger Leaves" cluster of the third edition (1860), and under its present title (1876).

"To You" ["Birds of Passage"] (1856)

First published as "Poem of You, Whoever You Are" in the second edition of *Leaves of Grass* (1856); it was "To You, Whoever You Are" (1860); then "Leaves of Grass, No. 4" (1867); it received its present title (1871); and it was the third of seven poems in the "Birds of Passage" cluster for the sixth edition (1881). This poem should not be confused with the two-line poem of the same title in the "Inscriptions" cluster. This "To You" has 47 lines.

The "You" of the title is the individual reader, perhaps off in a corner somewhere, reading this poem. All of *Leaves of Grass* may be explained this way, but there is in "To You" a more immediate demand for attention. The poet "sings" the value of each individual, and he apologizes for not reaching "you" sooner.

> I only am he who places over you no master,
>   owner, better, God, beyond what waits
>   intrinsically in yourself. . . .
> O I could sing such grandeurs and glories about
>   you!
> You have not known what you are, you have
>   slumber'd upon yourself all your life, . . .

Not even God is better than the individual soul, whom the poet loves and now raises in his poem to new levels of importance.

Whitman would shame every American with an inferiority complex to get over it. You have been asleep long enough about your own merits, he says; so wake to the "grandeurs and glories about you." The poet's mystical vision allows him to see the good inside every individual, and he would have everyone carry the seeds of this "good" to the world.

The reader becomes the great cosmic individual:

> There is no endowment in man or woman that
>   is not tallied in you,
> There is no virtue, no beauty in man or
>   woman, but as good is in you,
> No pluck, no endurance in others, but as good
>   is in you,
> No pleasure waiting for others, but an equal
>   pleasure waits for you.

Equal parts of love and psychology work to express Whitman's mystical ideal for democracy, which cannot work well unless every member of its society feels good about him or her self.

"To You" ["Inscriptions"] (1860)

First appeared as part of "Messenger Leaves" in the third edition of *Leaves of Grass* (1860); it became the 23rd of 24 poems in the "Inscriptions" cluster for the sixth edition (1881).

It has two lines and should not be confused with another poem with the same title, a 47-line poem in the "Birds of Passage" cluster. See immediately above. The poem offers a comparatively superficial idea, suggesting that people need not be shy when meeting one another on the street.

"Transpositions" (1856)

First appeared as "Poem of the Propositions of Nakedness" in the second edition of *Leaves of Grass* (1856); it was titled "Chants Democratic, No. 5" (1860); then as "Respondez!" (1867); three lines were taken from the original poem and given the present title for the sixth edition (1881).

Whitman suggests in these three lines that people need to be transposed in order to see how the others live. "Let judges and criminals be transposed—let the prison-keepers be put in prison—let those that were prisoners take the keys."

"Trickle Drops" (1860)

Titled "Calamus No. 15" in the third edition of *Leaves of Grass* (1860); it received its present title (1867); it was the 14th of 39 poems in the "Calamus" cluster for the sixth edition (1881).

This is one of the poems many critics wish Whitman had not included in *Leaves of Grass*. The "trickle drops" represent the blood the poet sheds in writing his poems, at least the sexual poems in "Children of Adam" and "Calamus": "Glow upon all I have written or shall write, bleeding drops, / Let it all be seen in your light, blushing drops." Critics may have been reminded of some of the too-sentimental religious poetry of the mid-17th century and thought Whitman was better than that.

E. Fred Carlisle writes in *The Uncertain Self: Whitman's Drama of Identity*, however, that the poet feels danger in making public his sexual ambiguity. The poem "expresses the overwhelming sense of shame exposure can cause," Carlisle says. The "red drops" are "confession drops," Whitman says in the poem, a confession of his sexual ambiguity.

"True Conquerors" (1888)

First published in the NEW YORK HERALD (February 15, 1888); then in *November Boughs* (1888); and it was the 43rd of 65 poems in the "First Annex: Sands at Seventy" cluster for the "Death-bed" printing of *Leaves of Grass* (1892).

Whitman CATALOGs in six lines the "true conquerors," old people—"farmers, travelers, workmen (no matter how crippled or bent,)"—no matter the vocation, they have struggled and "survived"; they are "long life's unflinching ones!"

"Turn O Libertad" (1865)

First appeared in the *Drum-Taps* volume (1865); it was then moved to a group titled "Marches Now the War is Over" for the fifth edition of *Leaves of Grass* (1871); it was under this title throughout its publication history, and it became the 42nd of 43 poems in the "Drum-Taps" cluster for the sixth edition (1881).

The poet personifies Liberty in this poem. The "feudal world," he writes, has dominated people and nations throughout the war. It is time now to give up that "backward world." Instead, he says,

> . . . turn your undying face,
> To where the future, greater than all the past,
> Is swiftly, surely preparing for you.

"Turn O Libertad," now the war is over, toward the future, when all wars will be wars of Liberty—"wars to come are for you."

"Twenty Years" (1888)

First published in New York's MAGAZINE OF ART (July 1888); then in *November Boughs* (1888); and it was the 54th of 65 poems in the "First Annex: Sands at Seventy" cluster for the "Death-bed" printing of *Leaves of Grass* (1892).

The poet meets a veteran sailor, home after 20 years at sea, home to a number of "changes" to his world, all the things he had once counted on gone, including his parents who died while he was at sea. He has money and a sloop, tied out from shore, but the poet wonders, nevertheless, what the sailor's future will be like, after 20 years away from home.

"Twilight" (1887)

First published in CENTURY MAGAZINE (December 1887); then in *November Boughs* (1888); and it was the 56th of 65 poems in the "First Annex: Sands at Seventy" cluster for the "Death-bed" printing of *Leaves of Grass* (1892).

Wood engraving of Whitman, 1890–94 *(Library of Congress, Prints and Photographs Division)*

The poet compares the twilight, with its "soft voluptuous opiate shades" to "nirwana" (nirvana), the Buddhist belief in the extinction of life at death but a change of the soul into a supreme spirit and, perhaps more important in Whitman's thinking at the time, a condition of great peace. The poet says in his definition, however, as he thinks of his own impending death, "rest and night—oblivion"—a forgetting.

"Twilight Song, A" (1890)

First published in CENTURY MAGAZINE (May 1890); it was the 19th of 31 poems in *Good-Bye My Fancy* (1891); then in "Second Annex: Good-Bye My Fancy" for the "Death-bed" printing of *Leaves of Grass* (1892).

This is one of the most impressive poems in the "Good-Bye My Fancy" cluster, a lyrical hymn of praise for the CIVIL WAR dead.

The poet, "in twilight late alone by the flickering oak-flame," thinks about "long-pass'd war scenes" and of "unknown" and "unreturned" soldiers North and South, East and West, a "million unwrit names." This he says is a "special verse" for them, "unknown names, or North or South," written 25 years after the war but not too late to honor them, "embalm'd with love in this twilight song."

Two Rivulets (1876)

Title of a companion volume to the 1876 printing of *Leaves of Grass,* a volume reprinted virtually unchanged from the fifth edition (1871). *Two Rivulets* included 14 new poems and seven new essays. The poems were as follows: "Two Rivulets," "Or from that Sea of Time," "Eidólons," "Spain, 1873–'74," "Prayer of Columbus," "Out from Behind this Mask," "To a Locomotive in Winter," "The Ox-Tamer," "Wandering at Morn," "An Old Man's Thought of School," "With all Thy Gifts, &c," "From My Last Years," "In Former Songs," and "After the Sea-Ship."

The prose items were "Thoughts for the Centennial," "Nationality (and Yet)," "Origins—Darwinism—(Then Furthermore)," "New Poetry—California, Mississippi, Texas," "Rulers strictly Out of the Masses," "Fine Manners......Transportation," and "Women and Conscience......Freedom."

"Two Rivulets" (1876)

Fourteen-line poem cut from *Leaves of Grass* after appearing in the 1876 printing.

"Unexpress'd, The" (1891)

First published in LIPPINCOTT'S MAGAZINE (March 1891); it was the 28th of 31 poems in *Good-Bye My Fancy* (1891); then in "Second Annex: Good-Bye My Fancy" for the "Death-bed" printing of *Leaves of Grass* (1892).

After all the poetry has been written, all the "cycles, poems, singers, plays," after Homer, Shakespeare and others, Whitman wonders in this poem if there isn't still "something lacking," something "unexpress'd." Perhaps the "best" is yet to come, which may be the poet's glimpse of eternity or his own immortality.

"Unfolded Out of the Folds" (1856)

First appeared as "Poem of Women" in the second edition of *Leaves of Grass* (1856); then as one of the "Leaves of Grass" group (1860); it received its present title (1871); and it was the 24th of 38 poems in the "Autumn Rivulets" cluster for the sixth edition (1881).

This 12-line poem is devoted to the idea that only the best women can produce the best men. "Unfolded out of the folds of the woman man comes unfolded, and is always to come unfolded, / Unfolded only out of the superbest woman of the earth is to come the superbest man of the earth, . . ."

The first 10 of the 12 lines begin with the word "Unfolded," creating a lyrical effect. James E. Miller, Jr., comments about the music of this poem in *A Critical Guide to Leaves of Grass* (1957): "The incantation permitted by the repetition of this single word [Unfolded] constitutes the life-blood of the poem. Quite frequently Whitman's short lyrics employ some form of primitive, bardic chant. Some of his best brief poems are brilliant incantations that hypnotically weave a mystic magic spell."

"United States to Old World Critics, The" (1888)

First published in the *New York Herald* (May 8, 1888); then in *November Boughs* (1888); and it was the 44th of 65 poems in the "First Annex: Sands at Seventy" cluster for the "Death-bed" printing of *Leaves of Grass* (1892).

The poem is a five-line response to those in the "Old World" still critical of America. The "varied, vast, perpetual edifice" that the nation is becoming will "arise inevitable in time . . . / The solid-planted spires tall shooting to the stars."

"Unnamed Lands" (1860)

First appeared in the third edition of *Leaves of Grass* (1860); it was the eighth of 38 poems in the "Autumn Rivulets" cluster for the sixth edition (1881). It was virtually unrevised throughout its printing history.

The poem is written to honor nations and people readers know little or nothing about, "unnamed lands" that existed "ten thousand years before these States, and many times ten thousand years before these States." The poet asks: "Are those billions of men really gone? / Are those women of the old experience of the earth gone?" Those nations and people still exist, "invisible to us"; they await us "in the yet unseen world."

Whitman did not believe in the Christian idea of an afterlife, but he believed that no one was ever "really gone." Their ideas and experiences made them immortal. See also "Song of Prudence," the poem that immediately followed "Unnamed Lands" in the 1881 edition of *Leaves*.

"Unseen Buds" (1891)

First published as the 30th of 31 poems in *Good-Bye My Fancy* (1891); then in "Second Annex: Good-Bye My Fancy" for the "Death-bed" printing of *Leaves of Grass* (1892).

The "unseen buds" in this eight-line poem are perhaps a Whitman metaphor for his own poems, leaves of grass, "buds" of poetic ideas or even of poetic styles which take time to germinate. At his death in 1892, Whitman's ideas and style still had been neither accepted nor appreciated by the general public, and he may envision a time when his poems would become flowers.

"Untold Want, The" (1871)

First published in the fifth edition of *Leaves of Grass* (1871); and it was the 13th of 17 poems in the "Songs of Parting" cluster for the sixth edition (1881).

The "untold want" in this two-line poem is a seeking after what death is like: "Now voyager sail thou forth to seek and find."

"Up, Lurid Stars!" (1973)

This poem was published for the first time in the Sculley Bradley-Harold W. Blodgett text of *Leaves of Grass* (1973). The two editors state that this six-line poem "is related to the five-line poem, 'World Take Good Notice,' in *Drum-Taps* (1865)."

"Vigil Strange I Kept on the Field One Night" (1865)

First appeared in the *Drum-Taps* volume (1865) and under this title throughout its printing history in *Leaves of Grass*; it was the 15th of 43 poems in the "Drum-Taps" cluster for the sixth edition (1881).

The poem is a dramatic monologue, the poet-soldier speaking to his good friend, perhaps his lover, though referred to as "my son," as Whitman often referred to the young men he loved. The poet has carried the wounded soldier into a wooded area, away from the war.

> Vigil strange I kept on the field one night;
> When you my son and my comrade dropt at my
>   side that day,
> One look I but gave which your dear eyes
>   return'd with a look I shall never forget,
> One touch of your hand to mine O boy, reach'd
>   up as you lay on the ground, . . .

It is a moving scene, two soldiers exchanging looks that tell of their deep friendship, even love for one another.

The speaker goes back to the battle, and when he returns that night, his friend is dead: "Found you in death so cold dear comrade, found your body son of responding kisses, (never again on earth responding,)." The soldier stays with his dead comrade through the night: "Vigil of silence, love and death, vigil for you my son and my soldier." He buries his friend at dawn the next day: "I rose from the chill ground and folded my soldier well in his blanket, / And buried him where he fell."

The act of burying the friend in his army blanket where he had died was not unusual in the CIVIL WAR. It was quick and practical. But in this poem Whitman, who must have witnessed such scenes, creates a much more dramatic and ritualistic act on the part of the friend. It is an act of love and farewell by one soldier for another, a close and loving friend. The poem contains some of the most rhythmical lines in all of Whitman's *Drum-Taps* poems.

"Virginia—the West" (1872)

First published under this title in KANSAS MAGAZINE (March 1872); then in a separate publication of Whitman's poems titled *As a Strong Bird On Pinions Free and Other Poems* (1872); it was in the *Two Rivulets* volume in the reprinting of the fifth edition of *Leaves of Grass* (1876); and it was the seventh of 43 poems in the "Drum-Taps" cluster for the sixth edition (1881).

In this 12-line poem Whitman shows his displeasure at Virginia on the state's seceding from the Union for the CIVIL WAR. Virginia was, for Whitman, "the noble sire fallen on evil days." The state's disloyalty to the nation, which it had helped form, is compared unfavorably with the loyalty of the states of the West which had remained with the Union.

> I saw with hand uplifted, menacing,
>   brandishing,
> (Memories of old in abeyance, love and faith in
>   abeyance,)
> The insane knife toward the Mother of All. . . .

The western states include "the land of the prairies, land of Ohio's waters and of Indiana."

Virginia provided four of the first five presidents of the United States, and Whitman is struck by the seeming incongruity of the state's great support by men and ideas at the original building of the nation with its secession from the Union a few years later.

"Visor'd" (1860)

First published as four lines in the poem "Debris" in the third edition of *Leaves of Grass* (1860); it was printed under the present title and as a separate poem (1867); and it was the 21st of 29 poems in the "By The Roadside" cluster for the sixth edition (1881).

This four-line poem is about women wearing masks, "a perpetual natural disguiser," and how the masks present "changes and transformations . . . even when she sleeps." The poet doesn't make it clear whether he likes or dislikes the masks, but the fact that he wrote about them may indicate his biases.

"Vocalism" (1881)

First appeared in the sixth edition of *Leaves of Grass* as the 14th of 38 poems in the "Autumn Rivulets" cluster (1881). The poem is a combination of two earlier poems: the first section of "Chants Democratic, No. 12" (1860) and the second section of "Leaves of Grass, No. 21" (1860).

"Vocalism" is a celebration of the power of voices.

O what is it in me that makes me tremble so at voices?
Surely whoever speaks to me in the right voice, him or her I shall follow,
As the water follows the moon, silently, with fluid steps, anywhere around the globe.

Whitman often spoke of wanting to become a serious orator. He was sometimes involved in party politics and gave speeches in support of candidates. He read his poems aloud to various audiences and occasionally wrote college commencements poems and read them to the graduates. He was perhaps best known, however, for a series of LINCOLN LECTURES after the CIVIL WAR. He had as a child admired the orations of the preacher Elias HICKS and often wished as an adult for a similar voice.

"Voice from Death, A" (1889)

First published in the *New York World* (June 7, 1889); it was the 22nd of 31 poems in *Good-Bye My Fancy* (1891); and in "Second Annex: Good-Bye My Fancy" for the "Death-bed" printing of *Leaves of Grass* (1892). A parenthetical subheading for this poem reads "(The Johnstown, Penn., cataclysm, May 31, 1889.)"

The JOHNSTOWN FLOOD killed an estimated 5,000 people, with property losses estimated at $10,000,000.

The poem is about death itself, however, the "voice" from Johnstown coming as a reminder of how quickly death can enter the lives of ordinary people:

Thou! thou! the vital, universal, giant force resistless, sleepless, calm,
Holding Humanity as in thy open hand, as some ephemeral toy, How ill to e'er forget thee.

It is too easy, the poet says, to get wrapped up in the "little potencies of progress, politics, culture, wealth, inventions, civilization," and forget how quickly death can wake us to its "silent, ever-swaying power, . . . upon which we float, and every one of us is buoy'd."

"Voice of the Rain, The" (1885)

First published in OUTING (August 1885); then in *November Boughs* (1888); and it was the 48th of 65 poems in the "First Annex: Sands at Seventy" cluster for the "Death-bed" printing of *Leaves of Grass* (1892).

The poet asks the rain, "who art thou," and the rain answers that it is the "Poem of Earth." The rain argues that it descends to "lave the drouths" and that without it the earth's seeds would remain "seeds only, latent, unborn." For Whitman the rain is one more manifestation of his belief in the connectedness of all things in Nature.

"Wallabout Martyrs, The" (1888)

First published in the NEW YORK HERALD (March 16, 1888); then in *November Boughs* (1888); and it was the 11th of 65 poems in the "First Annex: Sands at Seventy" cluster for the "Death-bed" printing of *Leaves of Grass* (1892).

There is a prose epigraph longer than the five-line poem which explains that the "Wallabout Martyrs" were the American Revolutionary "patriots" who died in the British prison ships and prisons during 1776–83 and were buried, "many thousands of them—in trenches in the Wallabout sands." Wallabout Bay was on the East River, between the Manhattan and Williamsburg bridges. The prisons were where the BROOKLYN Navy Yard is now located.

The martyred soldiers are "greater" than Achilles, Ulysses, or Alexander, Whitman believed, because they became the "stepping stones" to the America of his day.

Walt Whitman: Daybooks and Notebooks

A three-volume set, edited by William White and published by New York University Press in 1978. Volume 1 contains Whitman's "Daybooks: 1876–1881"; volume 2 contains "Daybooks: December 1881–1891"; and volume 3 contains "Diary in Canada, Notebooks, Index." These volumes are part of a series of books titled *The Collected Writings of Walt Whitman*, edited by Gay Wilson Allen and Sculley Bradley.

Walt Whitman: Notebooks and Unpublished Prose Manuscripts

In six volumes, edited by Edward F. Grier and published in 1984 by New York University Press as part of the series entitled *The Collected Writings of Walt Whitman*. Volume 1 is subtitled "Family Notes and Autobiography, Brooklyn and New York"; volume 2 is subtitled "Washington"; volume 3 is subtitled "Camden"; volumes 4 and 5 are subtitled "Notes"; and volume 6 is subtitled "Notes and Index."

Walt Whitman's Blue Book: The 1860–61 Leaves of Grass Containing His Manuscript Additions and Revisions

This is a two-volume set, published in 1968 by the New York Public Library and containing Whitman's manuscript revisions of the third edition of *Leaves of Grass* (1860). Volume 1 is a facsimile of a unique copy of the manuscript revisions in the Oscar Lion Collection at the New York Public Library. Volume 2 is a textual analysis of the revisions, edited by Arthur Golden. See also *Collected Writings*.

Walt Whitman's Diary in Canada

Includes extracts from other of Whitman's Diaries and Literary Note-Books, edited by William Sloan Kennedy, 1904. The material in this book is included in volume 3 of William White's *Walt Whitman's Day-Books and Other Diaries* in *The Collected Writings of Walt Whitman*.

"Wandering at Morn" (1873)

First published as "The Singing Thrush" in the *NEW YORK DAILY GRAPHIC* (March 15, 1873); then in the *Two Rivulets* volume with *Leaves of Grass* (1876); and it was the 34th of 38 poems in the "Autumn Rivulets" cluster for the sixth edition (1881).

The poet proposes in this poem that evil can evolve into good. As he "Wander[s] at Morn, . . . / Yearning for thee harmonious Union" [of the United States], he watches a "singing bird divine," a thrush who captures and eats "worms, snakes, loathsome grubs," and turns them into "sweet spiritual songs." The result is an enrichment of the earth, and Whitman equates this idea with the evolving Union: "From these your future songs may rise with joyous trills, / Destin'd to fill the world."

"Warble for Lilac-Time"
(1870)

First published in the GALAXY (May 1870); then in the fifth edition of *Leaves of Grass* (1871); it was the 11th of 38 poems in the "Autumn Rivulets" cluster for the sixth edition (1881).

The poem is a song—a "warble"—in celebration of spring: "Warble me now for joy of lilac-time (returning in reminiscence,) / Sort me O tongue and lips for Nature's sake, souvenirs of earliest summer." The poet then CATALOGs the signs of spring, and all of the signs mean, as he suggests in the last lines, "To grace the bush I love—to sing with the birds, / A warble for joy of lilac-time, returning to reminiscence."

The first and last lines no doubt suggest Whitman's recalling his use of lilacs in his great LINCOLN poem, "When Lilacs Last in the Dooryard Bloom'd." He said later that he never lost the connection between the smell of lilacs in the spring and his love for President Lincoln.

"Washington's Monument, February, 1885"
(1885)

First published as "Ah, Not This Granite Dead and Cold" in the PHILADELPHIA PRESS (February 22, 1885); then with its present title in *November Boughs* (1888); it was the 32nd of 65 poems in the "First Annex: Sands at Seventy" cluster for the "Death-bed" printing of *Leaves of Grass* (1892).

The Washington monument, a 555-foot marble shaft, was designed by Robert Mills; its construction began in 1848 and was finished in 1884.

Whitman's poem, published shortly after the monument's completion, argues that it is "not this marble, dead and cold" that is the monument to the nation's first military leader and president, but it is found instead "where patriot wills existed or exist, / Wherever Freedom, pois'd by Toleration, sway'd by Law, / Stands or is rising. . . ." It is there that the true monument exists.

It couldn't have taken long, following Whitman's incorrect identification of the monument's stone as "granite" in the poem's first title, for letters to arrive in Camden, informing the poet of his mistake. He changed the title and got the stone correct for the second publication.

"We All Shall Rest at Last"
(1840)

First published in the LONG ISLAND DEMOCRAT (July 14, 1840); an "early poem" *not* later published in *Leaves of Grass*. It is most accessible now in Francis Murphy (editor), *Walt Whitman: The Complete Poems* (Penguin Books, 1996).

"Weave in, My Hardy Life"
(1865)

First appeared in the *Drum-Taps* volume (1865); then it was transferred to the cluster of poems titled "Marches Now the War is Over" for the fourth edition of *Leaves of Grass* (1867); it was the 13th of 22 poems in the "From Noon to Starry Night" cluster for the sixth edition (1881).

The poet wishes in this poem for the "weaving" into his "hardy life" the best of everything: "Weave yet a soldier strong and full for great campaigns to come, / Weave in red blood, weave sinews in like ropes, the senses, sight weave in." And the weaving should be constant: "We know not why or what, yet weave, forever weave."

The speaker does not know the source for the weavings he wishes for, nor does he feel it is necessary to know, just that all the good things he imagines can become part of the pattern of his life.

"We Two, How Long We Were Fool'd" (1860)

First appeared as the seventh poem in the "Enfans d'Adam" cluster for the third edition of *Leaves of Grass* (1860); it was the ninth of 16 poems in the "Children of Adam" cluster for the sixth edition (1881). The original first line, "You and I—what the earth is, we are," was dropped in the fourth edition (1867).

The "Two" of the title are modern lovers who have learned that they can return to the Garden of Eden and that sex is a purifying force within them, not a sin as they have been "Fool'd" into thinking by modern social mores. And in their return they are able to declare in the final two lines: "We have circled and circled till we have arrived home again, we two, / We have voided all but freedom and all but our own joy."

The dominating theme in the "Children of Adam" poems uses the metaphor of the circling return to the Garden of Eden to mean a new beginning for the America of the mid-19th century.

"We Two Boys Together Clinging" (1860)

Titled "Calamus No. 26" in the third edition of *Leaves of Grass* (1860); it received its present title (1867); it was the 23rd of 39 poems in the "Calamus" cluster for the sixth edition (1881).

The nine-line poem is a description of two boys enjoying excursions together up and down the roads of North and South, full of the "power" that comes from being on the open road and feeling a law unto themselves. They love each other, and they are not bothered by priests—or anyone else—apparently alarmed at seeing the two boys together.

The boys fulfill their "foray," suggesting that they raid places for the spoils of at least food—if not also the pleasure of seeing the expressions on the faces of people they meet, who recognize their HOMOSEXUALITY.

"What Am I After All" (1860)

First appeared as "Leaves of Grass, No. 22" in the third edition of *Leaves of Grass* (1860); and as the 25th of 38 poems in the "Autumn Rivulets" cluster for the sixth edition (1881).

The poet reminds readers in this four-line poem that each person is pleased with the "sound" of his or her name, but it is not the pronunciation that matters so much as the meanings behind the name: "Did you think there was nothing but two or three pronunciations in the sound of your name?"

"What Best I See in Thee" (1881)

First appeared as the 19th of 22 poems in the "From Noon to Starry Night" cluster in the sixth edition of *Leaves of Grass* (1881). The poem's subtitle is "*To U. S. G. return'd from his World's Tour.*" The poem is in honor of Ulysses S. Grant, the 18th president (1869–77).

What "best" Whitman sees in General Grant, who returned to the United States in 1879 after a more than two-year tour of the world—honored everywhere he went—is that American voters were "justified" in electing him president in 1868.

"What Place is Besieged?" (1860)

First appeared as the last four lines of "Calamus No. 31" in the third edition of *Leaves of Grass* (1860); it became a separate poem under the present title for the fourth edition (1867); it was the 19th of 24 poems in the "Inscriptions" cluster for the sixth edition (1881).

The four-line poem suggests that any place "besieged" deserves to be defended with "parks of artillery, / And artillery-men, the deadliest that ever fired gun." Soldiers should defend besieged places and themselves.

"What Ship Puzzled at Sea" (1860)

First appeared as the first four lines of "Calamus No. 31" in the third edition of *Leaves of Grass* (1860); then as a separate, four-line poem titled "Here, Sailor!" (1871); and under its present title as the 10th of 18 poems in the "Whispers of Heavenly Death" cluster for the sixth edition (1881). With the exception of some changes in punctuation, it is the same four lines as in the 1860 version.

The poet offers himself as the "perfect pilot" for guiding ships into port. Whitman means this metaphorically; he would make "the most perfect pilot" for their spiritual lives.

"What Think You I Take My Pen in Hand?" (1860)

Titled "Calamus No. 32" in the third edition of *Leaves of Grass* (1860); it received its present title (1867); it was the 31st of 39 poems in the "Calamus" cluster for the sixth edition (1881).

Whitman asks the reader if he thinks that a poet taking pen in hand will produce a poem about some great ship under sail or of the "splendors" of a day or of some "vaunted glory" in the city. No, he says, "I take my pen in hand" to write merely of "two simple men" saying good-bye to one another on the pier in the midst of a crowd, "parting the parting of dear friends." They hang on to each other, one "passionately" kissing the other.

In his copy of the 1860 edition of *Leaves of Grass*, Whitman marked for deletion this poem

and another Calamus poem "Are You the New Person Drawn Toward Me?" He apparently thought the sexual content was too explicit. But, with only a few revisions in wording, both were reprinted in the fourth edition (1867) and subsequent editions.

"When I Heard at the Close of the Day" (1860)

Titled "Calamus No. 11" in the third edition of *Leaves of Grass* (1860); it received its present title (1867); it was the 10th of 39 poems in the "Calamus" cluster for the sixth edition (1881).

The poet is not satisfied with the "plaudits" he received for his poetry "at the close of the day," because the great love within him for mankind, especially for his "dear friend" is not what it should be to make him happy. But when "the one I love most lay sleeping by me under the same cover in the cool night, . . . / And his arm lay lightly around my breast—. . . that night I was happy."

Most early reviews of Whitman's poetry criticized him for subject and/or style, but he received several favorable reviews, especially one from EMERSON, who wrote a letter to Whitman after receiving a copy of the first edition of *Leaves of Grass*, saying "I greet you at the beginning of a great career." The poet may have had Emerson's now-famous comment in mind when he wrote this poem. Not even "plaudits" from Emerson matter as much, Whitman suggests, as does the love of his lover.

"When I Heard the Learn'd Astronomer" (1865)

First published as one of the *Drum-Taps* poems (1865); then in the "Songs of Parting" cluster for the fifth edition of *Leaves of Grass* (1871); and it was the seventh of 29 poems in the "By The Road-side" cluster for the sixth edition (1881).

Whitman was interested in astronomy and attended a number of lectures on the subject in 1848, particularly those of Ormsby MacKnight Mitchell, who published a book titled *A Course of Six Lectures on Astronomy* (1849). But this one-sentence, eight-line poem reflects every intelligent student's thoughts, sooner or later, about classroom lectures. No matter how great the lecture or the lecturer, nothing is more important to education than experience.

> When I sitting heard the astronomer where he
>   lectured with much applause in the
>   lecture-room,
> How soon unaccountable I became tired and
>   sick,
> Till rising and gliding out I wander'd off by
>   myself,
> In the mystical moist night air, and from time
>   to time,
> Look'd up in perfect silence at the stars.

This is one of Whitman's accentual poems, the number and placement of accented syllables creating the rhythm (see ACCENTUAL VERSE). Note also that the poem begins with lines of three and five syllables and ends with lines of five and three.

"When I Peruse the Conquer'd Fame" (1860)

Titled "Calamus No. 28" in the third edition of *Leaves of Grass* (1860); it was given its title (1867); and it was the 22nd of 39 poems in the "Calamus" cluster for the sixth edition (1881).

The poet does not envy the heroic generals, the president of the United States, nor the rich. What he *does* envy are the "brotherhood of lovers," their long lives of "danger" and "odium," yet "unfaltering" and "affectionate and faithful" to one another. Then, he says, he is "pensive" and walks "away fill'd with the bitterest envy."

"When I Read the Book" (1867)

First appeared in the fourth edition of *Leaves of Grass* (1867); it was the ninth of 24 poems in the "Inscriptions" cluster for the sixth edition (1881).

The "book" in the title refers to biographies in general, but Whitman is concerned also for himself, about what biographers will say of him. The first biography of Whitman was published after the poem, so it is unlikely that the poet had a particular biography in mind, but Whitman felt that the best biography would come from *Leaves of Grass* itself.

"And so will some one when I am dead and gone write my life? / (As if any man really knew aught of my life. / . . . I seek for my own use to trace out here.)" The word "here" suggests the poems he is writing for *Leaves of Grass.*

The early reviews of his book were often unkind, and reviewers sometimes criticized the poet as much as the poem, and Whitman may have had that criticism in mind when he wrote "When I Read the Book."

"When Lilacs Last in the Dooryard Bloom'd" (1865)

First appeared with 17 other poems in the 24-page pamphlet titled *Sequel to Drum-Taps* (1865); *Sequel* was later the same year bound into the back of the 72-page volume *Drum-Taps*, published earlier that year; all the poems from both publications were then added to the fourth edition of *Leaves of Grass* (1867). "Lilacs" became the first of four poems under the collective title "President Lincoln's Burial Hymn" for the fifth edition of *Leaves* (1871); and it was placed under the cluster heading "Memories of President Lincoln" for the sixth edition (1881). The other poems in the LINCOLN cluster are "O Captain! My Captain!," "Hush'd Be the Camps To-day," and "This Dust Was Once the Man."

"When Lilacs Last in the Dooryard Bloom'd" is one of the great elegies in the English language. It has sometimes been mistaken for an "occasional" poem, which it is not. It was written about six months after President Lincoln's death from scattered notes Whitman had made as early as the day after the president died. Nearly all of Whitman's biographers have quoted the English poet Algernon SWINBURNE, who referred to this poem as "the most sweet and sonorous nocturne ever chanted in the church of the world." The poem is written in 16 sections and 206 lines. The first 13 sections are short, 14 lines or less.

Whitman lived in Washington and was working as a volunteer in the hospitals, treating soldiers of both sides of the war. He was at his mother's home in New York, however, when Lincoln died on April 15, 1865. He was shot on Good Friday evening and died the next morning. Whitman arrived in Washington on Monday and attended the funeral services at the White House on Wednesday.

Whitman attempted to sum up his thoughts on Lincoln in notes he made during that historic Easter weekend and the few days that followed. He wrote a paragraph titled "Death of President Lincoln" for *Specimen Days*, published in 1882; the entry is dated "April 16, '65"—Easter Sunday.

"Unionism," Whitman wrote, "in its truest and amplest sense, formed the hardpan of his character." He may have been assassinated, but the Union was not. The nation is "immortal." The importance of "Union" is thematic in a number of Whitman's poems, and the importance of the poet's belief in the unity of all things is thematic in "When Lilacs Last in the Dooryard Bloom'd." It is interesting to note that all of the ideas from *Specimen Days* and other prose sources are nearly always improved when incorporated into the poetry.

SECTIONS 1–3

Lilacs were in full bloom in Washington when Whitman arrived there on April 17, and lilacs were displayed around the casket at the funeral services. The poet would write later that the odor of the lilac bush ever afterward reminded him of the tragedy of Lincoln's death. Whitman also remembered that he had observed a bright evening star during several days in March, and, although at the time he took the star as a sign of good fortune for America, he nevertheless used the star in the poem, as well as

the lilac bush and other springtime images as metaphors for his love and respect for the president. The poem's Section 1 is devoted to them:

> When lilacs last in the dooryard bloom'd,
> And the great star early droop'd in the western
>   sky in the night,
> I mourn'd, and yet shall mourn with
>   ever-returning spring.
>
> Ever-returning spring, trinity sure to me you bring,
> Lilac blooming perennial and drooping star in the
>   west,
> And thought of him I love.

The "trinity" of spring, lilac, and star give form to the subject of the poem—not so much the death of Lincoln as of death itself. Whitman had already shown in "Out of the Cradle Endlessly Rocking" that for him death was one of life's great experiences and a poetic theme that had come to him while he was a child strolling along LONG ISLAND's shores.

The poet develops the star image in the five-line Section 2 of "Lilacs." Lincoln is the "powerful western fallen star," a star now hidden by a "black murk" (murder) and by a "cloud," the symbol of the poet's grief, a cloud that the poet says "will not free my soul."

Whitman develops the lilac bush imagery in Section 3. He finds the lilacs first in the dooryard of an old farmhouse, the lilac bush "tall-growing with heart-shaped leaves of rich green." It will become for the poet a symbol of his love for the president and a way for working out his sorrow. In the section's last line, he breaks off a sprig of the lilac, which he will place later on Lincoln's coffin. And once the poet has reconciled his love of life with his love of death, he will, in the poem's final section, leave another lilac sprig "there in the door-yard, blooming, returning with spring."

SECTIONS 4–8

A new image is introduced in Section 4, that of the hermit thrush, a solitary bird who "Sings by himself a song," the "Song of the bleeding throat, / Death's outlet song of life," the bird a metaphor for the solitary soul. The thrush represents for Whitman the solitary soul of man, and the poet tells the "dear brother" that he understands that "If thou wast not granted to sing thou would'st surely die." The poet connects with the hermit thrush, because he feels that he too would die if he could not sing these poems.

Sections 5 and 6 describe Lincoln's funeral train as it makes its way from Washington to Springfield, Illinois, never out of the sight of the thousands of people along the tracks, eager for a glimpse of the cortege as it rolls slowly by and anxious for the nation's future. Each of the two sections is written as one PERIODIC SENTENCE, the subject of the sentence coming in the last line; and there is a poetic rhythm meant, perhaps, to suggest the rhythm of the train as it rumbles "through old woods . . . passing the endless grass . . . yellow-spear'd wheat . . . Night and day journeys a coffin." Striking in these two sections is the parallel relationship between life and death, between the rebirth imagery of the spring described along the train's route and the coffin itself, carrying the body of the president.

At the end of Section 6, with bells tolling their "perpetual clang," and as the poet imagines the train heading west, he makes an offering of the lilac: "Here, coffin that slowly passes, / I give you my sprig of lilac."

Section 7 provides a transition, Whitman suggesting that it is not merely Lincoln's death he is "singing" but death itself. It is not for Lincoln alone, he says in the opening line, but it is "branches green to coffins all I bring, / For fresh as the morning, thus would I chant a song for you O sane and sacred death." For Whitman the springtime images suggest not death but life. The awareness of death makes it life-affirming; it makes life more brilliant.

The poet's offering of the sprig of lilac on Lincoln's coffin is not meant for the president alone but for all coffins, for all who have died:

> Copious I break, I break the sprigs from the
>   bushes,
> With loaded arms I come, pouring for you,
> For you and the coffins all of you O death.

Whitman must have had in mind especially the more than 600,000 recent deaths of soldiers in the CIVIL WAR; but the idea that death is an affirmation of life echoes throughout *Leaves of Grass.*

The "great star" image of Section 1 is conjured up again in Section 8 as Whitman describes the meaning of the "western orb" that he had seen a month before and which he now understands. He evokes the star again, explaining that he now recognizes its meaning—"how full you were of woe"—as it prepared to disappear over the "rim" of the western horizon, as it "dropt in the night, and was gone." He now recognizes the star as prophesying doom.

SECTIONS 9–13

Sections 9 and 10 return to the hermit thrush, the poet evoking now the thrush itself, telling it to "sing on there in the swamp," that he has been detained by his lingering over the setting star; "my departing comrade holds and detains me." In his agony over Lincoln's death he asks the thrush, "How shall I warble myself for the dead one there I loved?" And he wonders what "perfume" he should use "for the grave of him I love," deciding that since "sea-winds" blow toward the prairies of Illinois from both the eastern and western seas he will use these winds and the "breath of my chant" as perfume for the grave.

Whitman presents a catalog of America in Sections 11–12, pictures which he can "hang on the chamber walls . . . / To adorn the burial-house of him I love." The pictures are of America's "growing spring and farms and homes," rivers and the "ranging hills on the banks," "the city at hand," "all the scenes of life and the workshops, and the workmen homeward returning." The poet wishes to place on the walls of Lincoln's tomb all of these pictures of American life, suggesting comfort for the president in his death chamber. Whitman was influenced by Egyptology early in his career, and he was no doubt impressed by the idea that on the walls of the great pyramids, Egyptian leaders were comforted in the afterlife by artifacts of their life and nation.

All of these images of both country and city life represent for Whitman the life of America at the time of Lincoln's assassination, a nation coping with a war of secession and then with the murder of its leader. But he sees beyond the dark days to the "miracle spreading bathing all, the fulfill'd noon, / The coming eve delicious, the welcome night and the stars, / Over my cities shining all, enveloping man and land." Affirmation is in the pictures of American life he wishes to "hang on the chamber walls" of Lincoln's tomb.

The poet summons the hermit thrush again in Section 13, asking that it "sing on" its "chant from the bushes, / Limitless out of the dusk, out of the cedars and pines." The thrush is a "wondrous singer," even if, as Whitman says, the voice is "of uttermost woe." He says he only hears the hermit thrush, but the poem's two other major symbols return in the section's last two lines: "yet the star holds me, (but will soon depart,) / Yet the lilac with mastering odor holds me."

This gathering together of the bird, star, and lilac images at the end of the section is a reminder of their constant presence and a foreshadowing of the poet's bringing together the poem's major themes.

SECTION 14

The poet describes his coming to awareness of the nature of the relationship of his "love of life" and his "love of death." While he contemplates the meaning of all that he has thought about, he notes "the large unconscious scenery of my land and its lakes and forests." The dark cloud reappears suddenly, however, over the scene and the "long black trail."

The cloud, which in Section 2 he had observed as a symbol of his grief for the death of Lincoln and which would "not free [his] soul," now suggests to him a new understanding of death. "I knew death," he says, "its thought, and the sacred knowledge of death." And the two walk beside him at this moment of insight:

Then with the knowledge of death as walking
    one side of me,
And the thought of death close-walking the
    other side of me,
And I in the middle as with companions, and
    as holding the hands of companions, I fled
    forth . . .
Down to the shores of the water, the path by
    the swamp in the dimness,
To the solemn shadowy cedars and ghostly
    pines so still.

This "knowledge of death" suggests an understanding that death represents for the poet a spiritual rebirth; and "thought of death" suggests that death merely takes life away. On the one hand there is what the poet now "knows" about death, knowledge that comes from the soul; on the other hand there is fear, a fear generated by thoughts of the undiscovered country that death represents. The reconciliation of these two opposites—perhaps best defined as love of life and knowledge of death—is the climactic moment in Whitman's narrative.

The poet will return to his thoughts of Lincoln at the end of the poem, but the president's death has become in Section 14 a mere touchstone for the much larger theme of death.

The three "companions" walk "the path by the swamp" where the "gray-brown bird" resides, and the poet compares himself once again to the solitary thrush: "And the singer so shy to the rest receiv'd me, . . . / And he sang the carol of death, and a verse for him I love." The hermit thrush sings of the reconciliation of the two seemingly conflicting ideas. Section 14 ends with a song of the hermit thrush—seven FREE VERSE quatrains, set in italic type—a song of joy, referring to "lovely and soothing death," to "delicate death," which praises the "fathomless universe,"

> *Prais'd be the fathomless universe,*
> *For life and joy, and for objects and knowledge*
>   *curious,*
> *And for love, sweet love—but praise! praise!*
>   *praise!*
> *For the sure-enwinding arms of cool-enfolding*
>   *death.*

Death, the "Dark mother" of the next line, is referred to four lines later as the "strong deliveress." Death delivers the child of the new birth into a spiritual state—a new life. The poet identifies with the solitary thrush, interpreting the bird's song, furthering his understanding of the spiritual triumph over death. "*I float this carol with joy, with joy to thee O death.*" It is "spiritual" for Whitman not in the traditional religious sense but in the more idealistic sense of a reliance on the ultimate unity of all things and on the importance of intuition in arriving at truth. It is Whitman's version of EMERSON's concept of TRANSCENDENTALISM, something that transcends human experience to create a revelation about life.

SECTIONS 15–16

In Section 15 the poet identifies with the hermit thrush, the "solitary singer," in singing himself of triumph over death.

> To the tally of my soul,
> Loud and strong kept up the gray-brown bird,
> With pure deliberate notes spreading filling the
>   night.

The poet sees "panoramas of visions"—another term perhaps for "mystical insight"—of the armies North and South in the Civil War, the "battle-corpses . . . not as was thought, / They themselves were fully at rest, they suffer'd not." It is the living who suffer, the mother, the wife, the child, "and the armies that remain'd suffer'd." Death brings a peace that is unknown to the living.

In the final section of "Lilacs" (Section 16), the poet presents a reiteration of the poem's most important images, and he evokes once again the trio of lilac, bird, and star: "I leave thee lilac . . ."; "I cease from my song for thee [thrush] . . ."; and, with a "gaze" toward the west, he sees his "comrade lustrous with silver face in the night. . . ." Whitman gathers all of these images into one final summation of his experience of suffering the death of President Lincoln and his comrades during the war, yet gaining the greater, spiritual awakening to the meaning of and reconciliation with death.

All of the poem's key images are evoked in the next five lines:

> The song, the wondrous chant of the
>   gray-brown bird,
> And the tallying chant, the echo arous'd in my
>   soul,
> With the lustrous and drooping star with the
>   countenance full of woe,
> With the holders holding my hand nearing the
>   call of the bird,
> Comrades mine and I in the midst, and their
>   memory ever to keep, for the dead I loved so
>   well.

This reiteration brings him back to the poem's original subject in the final three lines:

> For the sweetest, wisest soul of all my days and
>   lands—and this for his dear sake,
> Lilac and star and bird twined with the chant
>   of my soul,
> There in the fragrant pines and the cedars dusk
>   and dim.

The three images are fused into the one final image of Lincoln resting at last "in the fragrant pines and the cedars dusk and dim" of his Illinois grave.

"When the Full-Grown Poet Came" (1876)

First published in the NEW YORK TRIBUNE (February 19, 1876); it was pasted in at the back of the first volume of the reprinting of the fifth edition of *Leaves of Grass* in 1876 and was the final poem in a cluster titled "Bathed in War's Perfume" of the second issue the same year; it was excluded from the sixth edition (1881); but Whitman revived it, and it became the 20th of 31 poems in *Good-Bye My Fancy* (1891); and it was in "Second Annex: Good-Bye My Fancy" for the "Death-bed" printing of *Leaves of Grass* (1892).

Although both nature and the "Soul of man" claim the poet as their own, the "full-grown poet stood between the two," took each by the hand and stood, he says, "as blender, uniter, tightly holding hands" until he "reconciles the two, / And wholly and joyously blends them." Only as a mature poet, was he able to merge his soul with all of nature, one of Whitman's significant themes in *Leaves of Grass*.

"While Behind All, Firm and Erect" (1897)

First published as the fifth of 13 poems in the "Old Age Echoes" cluster for the first posthumous printing of *Leaves of Grass* (1897), added by one of Whitman's executors, Horace TRAUBEL.

This three-line poem is a PERIODIC SENTENCE, the grammatical subject coming at the end of the sentence. The proud and honored "helmsman" guides the ship through rough waters.

"While Not the Past Forgetting" (1888)

First publication of this poem is uncertain. Whitman has a parenthetical note to the poem, "Publish'd May 30, 1888," but Whitman scholars have not been able to substantiate the date. It was published in *November Boughs* (1888); and it was the 50th of 65 poems in the "First Annex: Sands at Seventy" cluster for the "Death-bed" printing of *Leaves of Grass* (1892).

Although the nation is at peace now, the poet is saying in this six-line poem, let us not forget to lay "wreaths of roses and branches of palm" on the graves of those soldiers North and South who died in the CIVIL WAR.

"Whispers of Heavenly Death" (1868)

First published as the first of five poems under the general heading "Whispers of Heavenly Death" in the *BROADWAY MAGAZINE* (London) (October 1868); it first appeared in *Leaves of Grass* in the fifth edition (1871); then in the *Two Rivulets* volume of *Leaves* (1876); and it was the second of 18 poems in the "Whispers of Heavenly Death" cluster for the sixth edition (1881). It remained virtually unrevised throughout its publication history.

This title poem describes the quiet peace that surrounds the death scene: "Footsteps gently ascending, mystical breezes wafted soft and low." Even nature feels the scene: "great cloud-masses, / Mournfully slowly they roll, silently swelling and

mixing." The poet senses in the last stanza "some solemn immortal birth," as if death were like the birth of a child, only this birth is to immortality. "Some soul is passing over."

"Whispers Of Heavenly Death" (1881)

Cluster of 18 poems which appeared together first in the sixth edition of *Leaves of Grass* (1881). Thirteen of the poems had been published in the "Passage to India" supplement to the fifth edition (1871–72), five of the 13 having appeared first in the *BROADWAY MAGAZINE* (London) (October 1868). Whitman added five more poems from "Passage to India" to make the cluster of 18. The poems in this group have as a common theme the acceptance of death, the willingness to imagine what Hamlet referred to as the "undiscovered country."

For the sixth and all subsequent editions of *Leaves* the poems appeared in the following order: "Darest Thou Now O Soul," "Whispers of Heavenly Death," "Chanting the Square Deific," "Of Him I Love Day and Night," "Yet, Yet, Ye Downcast Hours," "As if a Phantom Caress'd Me," "Assurances," "Quicksand Years," "That Music Always Round Me," "What Ship Puzzled at Sea," "A Noiseless Patient Spider," "O Living Always, Always Dying," "To One Shortly to Die," "Night on the Prairies," "Thought" (As I sit), "The Last Invocation," "As I Watch'd the Ploughman Ploughing," and "Pensive and Faltering."

"Whoever You Are Holding Me Now in Hand" (1860)

Titled "Calamus No. 3" in the third edition of *Leaves of Grass* (1860); it received its present title (1867); and it was the third of 39 poems in the "Calamus" cluster for the sixth edition (1881).

Readers both in Whitman's time and in his future are invited to join the poet in a love relationship. It is the brotherhood-of-man theme that prevails not just in this and most of the Calamus poems but throughout *Leaves of Grass*. The love the poet seeks will not be easy, he says, because I am "far different" from "what you supposed." He does not reject physical love, in fact encourages it, but he also wants readers to understand the larger concept of the need for love in all relationships.

Taking the poet by the hand will also be difficult, the reader is warned, because the idea is bound to be misunderstood—just as are the poet's poems. Whitman's first two editions of *Leaves of Grass* were criticized for sexual innuendo, and he knows that the poems in the "Children of Adam" and "Calamus" clusters first introduced in the third edition will receive even heavier criticism.

> Nor will my poems do good only, they will do
>   just as much evil, perhaps more,
> For all is useless without that which you may
>   guess at many times and not hit, that which
>   I hint at;
> Therefore release me and depart on your way.

The "evil" will be in the response of easily prejudiced people. It is the brotherhood theme, but what is suggested on the surface is the potential for physical love between one man and another, and it is this that the poet feels may be misunderstood, just as are so often his poems about the love he expresses for all people. The poem's final line tells the reader that it would be much safer to reject his offer of love and "depart" while there is still time.

"[Who is Now Reading This?]" (1860)

Cut from *Leaves of Grass* after first appearing as "Calamus No. 16" in the third edition (1860). The brackets indicate the poem's first line.

It is one of Whitman's confessional poems, indicating some guilt over things that puzzle him about himself and that may puzzle others. The only hint for *why* he is "conscience-struck" comes in the eighth line: "Or as if I do not secretly love strangers! (O tenderly, a long time, and never avow it;)." This line, plus the placement of the poem in the "Calamus" cluster, suggests "guilt" over a homosexual relationship.

"Who Learns My Lesson Complete?" (1855)

First appeared as the 11th of 12 untitled poems in the first edition of *Leaves of Grass* (1855); it was titled "Lesson Poem" (1856); then "Leaves of Grass, No. 11" (1860); and "Leaves of Grass, No. 3" (1867); then it was with the "Passage to India" poems (1871); and finally under its present title and as the 28th of 38 poems in the "Autumn Rivulets" cluster for the sixth edition (1881).

The "Lesson" to be learned "Complete" is that not only is the world "wonderful" and beautiful but each person who lives or who has ever lived is just as wonderful. "I am immortal," Whitman says, and so are we all.

> I do not think seventy years is the time of a
>   man or woman,
> Nor that seventy millions of years is the time of
>   a man or woman,
> Nor that years will ever stop the existence of
>   me, or any one else.

He evokes future readers: "And that my soul embraces you this hour, and we affect each other without ever seeing each other, and never perhaps to see each other, is every bit as wonderful."

"Wild Frank's Return" (1841)

Short story, first published in the *United States Magazine and Democratic Review* (November 1841; see DEMOCRATIC REVIEW, THE). The tale is most accessible now in *Walt Whitman: The Early Poems and the Fiction*, edited by Thomas L. Brasher (New York University Press, 1963).

Set in the farmland of eastern LONG ISLAND, this is a tale of a family dispute. Mr. Hall is the head of a large farm family and requires "all his boys to labor in proportion to their age." His "right hand man" is his oldest son, Richard. The other sons do what Richard tells them to do, all that is except Frank, a "capricious, high-temper'd lad," 19 or 20 years old and known around the countryside as "Wild Frank" because of his quick temper and the mischief he so easily gets into. Frank is, nevertheless, the favorite of his mother.

Hall believes that each son should have something around the farm that he can call his own, and "somehow or other," a "fine young blood mare . . . had fallen to Frank's share." Black Nell is "a beautiful creature, large and graceful, with eyes like dark-hued jewels, and her color that of deep night." In spite of Frank's seeming ownership of Black Nell, Richard decides he wants her and so takes upon himself the "privilege of managing and using Black Nell, notwithstanding what Frank consider'd his prerogative." Their father sides with Richard in this dispute, and Frank is so angered by the decision that he leaves home and is not heard of again for two years.

When he returns to Long Island he seeks out Richard first, before going back to the farm. Frank has changed during his absence and wants forgiveness from Richard and the family for his angry response to the dispute two years ago. Richard, who is now married and living 15 miles from the family farm, lends Frank the still beautiful Black Nell for the ride to the farm. Two miles from home Frank stops to rest and ties a piece of "strong cord" to the horse's bridle, with the other end secured to his own wrist. He naps under a tree, but when a thunderstorm comes up and lightning strikes nearby, Black Nell bolts.

The Hall family knows that Frank has returned to Richard's farm, and they await the prodigal son's return home. But they are greeted instead by the still startled Black Nell galloping into the yard. They are even more startled to see on the ground next to the mare "a mangled, hideous mass—the rough semblance of a human form—all batter'd and cut, and bloody." Frank is still attached to the "strong cord" tied to the horse's bridle. And "as the mother gazed—for she could not withdraw her eyes—and the appalling truth came upon her mind, she sank down without a shriek or utterance, into a deep, deathly swoon."

One of the interesting features of this story—by comparison to other Whitman short stories—is

that it is told in flashback. The tale begins with Frank showing up at Richard's farm after two years away from home; then the narrator provides the details of why he had been away and picks up the opening scene again at the point where Frank ties himself to Black Nell under the oak tree for an hour's nap before the final and disastrous leg of the journey home.

CHARACTERS

Mr. Hall   Father of a large farm family in eastern Long Island, who had particular ideas about how the family should participate in the running of the farm. He requires each son, for example, to work on the farm according to his age. And he believes that each boy should have some special thing or animal for which he takes complete responsibility. His oldest son, Richard, is his father's right-hand man, and the sons do what Richard says—all except Frank.

Frank Hall   Known as "Wild Frank" because he is a "capricious, high-temper'd lad," and because his quick temper often gets him into mischief. He is, however, the favorite of his mother. One of his responsibilities on the farm is the care of Black Nell, a fine young mare that Frank's father had given to him to take care of. But the oldest son, Richard, decides that he wants the care of Black Nell for himself, and, when the father sides with Richard, Frank angrily leaves the farm and doesn't return for two years.

Richard Hall   Oldest son and his father's "right hand man." The other sons do what Richard says, except for "Wild Frank." Richard decides that he wants to care for the young mare Black Nell, which has been Frank's responsibility. His father supports Richard in the family argument to follow, which creates an angry feud that ends with Frank leaving home.

"With All Thy Gifts" (1873)

First published in the NEW YORK DAILY GRAPHIC (March 6, 1873); then in the *Two Rivulets* volume of *Leaves of Grass* (1876); and it was the 36th of 38 poems in the "Autumn Rivulets" cluster for the sixth edition (1881).

The poem is an apostrophe to America, the poet wondering if, "With All Thy Gifts" America should lack the gift "of perfect women fit for thee—what if that gift of gifts thou lackest? / The towering feminine of thee? the beauty, health, completion, fit for thee? / The mothers fit for thee?"

The equality of men and women is such a thematic element throughout *Leaves of Grass,* it is not clear what may have generated this seemingly pessimistic poem about the women of America.

"With Antecedents" (1860)

First published as "You and Me and To-Day" in the *SATURDAY PRESS* (New York) (January 14, 1860); then as "Chants Democratic, No. 7" in the third edition of *Leaves of Grass* (1860); it received its present title and was the last of seven poems in the "Birds of Passage" cluster for the sixth edition (1881). The poem is in three sections and 41 lines.

But for "antecedents" of father and mother, Whitman reminds readers, and "the accumulations of past ages," we would not be here today. In Section 1 Whitman CATALOGS the historic antecedents: from "Egypt, India, Phenicia, Greece and Rome, / With the Kelt, the Scandinavian, the Alb [evidently meaning Albion; that is, from England, invented by Whitman] and the Saxon." He includes also "the sale of slaves . . . the troubadour, the crusader, and the monk. . . ." Anyone's list of antecedents is long.

In Section 2 Whitman makes clear the idea that these antecedents are only important because they bring us to the present moment and that we are an accumulation of every influence of the past:

> O but it is not the years—it is I, it is You, . . .
> We stand amid time beginningless and endless,
>   we stand amid evil and good,
> All swings around us, there is as much darkness
>   as light, . . .

The past as introduction to the present is thematic in *Leaves of Grass.* We owe a debt to the past, to antecedents, but it is the present time that matters.

Whitman says in Section 3 that "the past was great and the future will be great," but it is "where I am or you are this present day" that is "the centre of all days." All that matters to us is in the present moment, what T. S. Eliot would refer to 80 years later as "the still point of time," where the "dance" is.

"With Husky-Haughty Lips, O Sea!" (1884)

First published in *HARPER'S WEEKLY* (March 1884); then in *November Boughs* (1888); and it was the 29th of 65 poems in the "First Annex: Sands at Seventy" cluster for the "Death-bed" printing of *Leaves of Grass* (1892).

Listening to the sea's sounds, the poet personifies the sea and believes that he understands its "talk and conference." He wonders why the sea "ever seek'st and seek'st" the "lonely state" yet never gains it. He wonders if there is some "vast heart" or "serpent hiss" or "distant lion roar" at work within the sea, "the first and last confession of the globe." The poet wonders if the sea might be willing to tell its tale of cosmic passion to "a kindred soul"—the poet himself.

"Woman Waits for Me, A" (1856)

Titled "Poem of Procreation" in the second edition of *Leaves of Grass* (1856); it was the fourth poem in the "Enfans d'Adam" cluster (1860); it received its present title and was the fourth of 16 poems in the "Children of Adam" cluster for the sixth edition (1881).

The "Me" of this poem suggests Adam in the Garden of Eden speaking of Eve, but it is also for every man speaking of every woman. "Nothing is lacking," the poet says, "yet all were lacking if sex were lacking, . . . Sex contains all, bodies, souls, / Meanings, proofs, purities, delicacies, results, promulgations, / Songs, commands, health, pride, the maternal mystery, the seminal milk."

The poet wishes to "dismiss" himself from "impassive women," but will stay with the woman who waits for him.

> I see that they understand me and do not deny
> me,
> I see that they are worthy of me, I will be the
> robust husband of those women.
> They are not one jot less than I am.

There is no inequality in these sexual encounters; women are not "one jot less" than men.

The speaker then describes the beginning of a new race of Americans: "I pour the stuff to start sons and daughters fit for these States, I press with slow rude muscle." And it is this attitude toward sexual love that Whitman thinks of as one of the essential ingredients for democracy. It is through love than equality becomes possible.

These amative poems, the poet seems to be saying in "A Woman Waits for Me" and generally throughout the "Children of Adam" cluster, will encourage readers to remain the "Children of Adam" but to move out of the Garden of Eden, away from the idea of sin. The new race of Americans will begin out of the "pent-up rivers" of new Adams and new Eves.

"World Below the Brine, The" (1860)

First published as "Leaves of Grass, No. 16" in the third edition of Leaves of Grass (1860); then as "Leaves of Grass, No. 4" (1867); it received its present title and was published with the "Sea-Shore Memories" cluster (1871); it then became the seventh of 11 poems in the "Sea-Drift" cluster for the sixth edition (1881). At 11 lines, it is the shortest poem in the cluster.

Whitman CATALOGs the natural beauty of the "world below the brine," beginning with its "forests at the bottom of the sea," the "Sea-lettuce, vast lichens, strange flowers and seeds, the thick tangle, . . . / Dumb swimmers there among the rocks." And rising,

almost as if a swimmer were viewing it all, to the surface where the main fighting for food exists:

> The sperm-whale at the surface blowing air and
> spray, . . .
> The leaden-eyed shark, the walrus, the turtle,
> the hairy sea-leopard, and the sting-ray,
> Passions there, wars, pursuits, tribes, . . .

The poet then describes the change at the surface: "The change thence to the sight here, and to the subtle air breathed by beings like us who walk this sphere, / The change onward from ours to that of beings who walk other spheres."

One may read these lines as a description of the continuing evolutionary change taking place, with a thought toward the future of "beings." Or, because the "Sea-Drift" cluster of poems tends toward connections with the soul and its transcendental nature, the soul may be seen in "The World Below the Brine" as "walk[ing] other spheres."

"World Take Good Notice" (1865)

First appeared in the Drum-Taps volume (1865), under this title and unrevised throughout its publication history in Leaves of Grass; it was the 31st of 43 poems in the "Drum-Taps" cluster for the sixth edition (1881).

This five-line poem is a "notice" to the world of the things that "Now and henceforth flaunt from these shores," a bragging, after the CIVIL WAR, of what America will now become.

"Wound-Dresser, The" (1865)

First appeared as "The Dresser" in the Drum-Taps volume (1865); then under its present title in the reprint of the fifth edition of Leaves of Grass (1876); it was the 21st of 43 poems in the "Drum-Taps" cluster for the sixth edition (1881). The final version is in 65 lines and four sections.

In answer to children's questions about his experiences in the CIVIL WAR, the "wound-dresser," now an "old man bending," tells of his experiences helping wounded and dying soldiers at army hospitals during the war.

The old man thinks in Section 1 about what he should say in answer to the questions. He remembers scenes of sitting by wounded soldiers, of "unsurpass'd heroes" on both sides, and now he feels he is "witness again" to "the mightiest armies of earth."

In Section 2 the old soldier begins to relate some of his recalled experiences as a wound-dresser:

> Bearing the bandages, water and sponge,
> Straight and swift to my wounded I go, . . .
> To each and all one after another I draw near,
>   not one do I miss,
> An attendant follows holding a tray, he carries
>   a refuse pail,
> Soon to be fill'd with clotted rags and blood,
>   emptied, and fill'd again.

The speaker's genuine love for the soldiers becomes apparent: "One turns to me his appealing eyes— poor boy! I never knew you, / Yet I think I could not refuse this moment to die for you, if that would save you."

In Section 3 the narrator describes the wounds of several soldiers and, in some cases, wishes for the soldier a "sweet death . . . / In mercy come quickly." He describes a soldier he remembers whose hand had been amputated and who could not bear to look at the stump. He is "faithful," he says, "I do not give out, . . . / These and more I dress with impassive hand, (yet deep in my breast a fire, a burning flame.)" He recalls in this repetition of experiences as a wound-dresser moments of deep grief.

The narrator returns to the present time in Section 4, still remembering—but now in silence— wartime experiences, working in hospitals, pacifying

Harper's Ferry, West Virginia, at the confluence of the Shenandoah and Potomac Rivers, and the site of John Brown's antislavery raid on October 16–18, 1859. Photographed by Alexander Gardner, 1865 *(Library of Congress, Prints and Photographs Division)*

and soothing the wounded, suffering at seeing the wounded and dying. At the end of the poem he returns to the children's questions, which he has answered but now thinking to himself:

> . . . I recall the experience sweet and sad,
> (Many a soldier's loving arms about this neck
>   have cross'd and rested,
> Many a soldier's kiss dwells on these bearded
>   lips.)

Whitman himself was a wound-dresser, working in Washington hospitals throughout the war, carrying out slop buckets, assisting doctors and nurses, writing letters for soldiers both North and South, and holding the hands of the dying.

"Year of Meteors (1859–60)" (1865)

First appeared in the *Drum-Taps* volume (1865); and it was the sixth of seven poems in the "Birds of Passage" cluster for the sixth edition of *Leaves of Grass* (1881).

This poem celebrates the events of the "Year of meteors! brooding year!" During 1859–60 there were several historical events, including the "contest for the nineteenth Presidentiad" in which LINCOLN defeated Stephen A. Douglas to become the 19th president of the United States. But it was also the year that the abolitionist John Brown was hung for treason in Charles Town, Virginia (December 2, 1859), witnessed by Whitman; also the arrival in New York City (June 28, 1860) of the "Great Eastern," a 600-foot steamship, with its immigrant passengers and "cargoes of gold"; and a visit from Edward, Prince of Wales, a "fair stripling" (October 11, 1860). There is also the "meteor-procession," which Whitman describes as "foreboding":

> Nor the comet that came unannounced out of
>   the north flaring in heaven, . . .
> (A moment, a moment long it sail'd its balls of
>   unearthly light over our heads,
> Then departed, dropt in the night, and was
>   gone;)
> Of such, and fitful as they, I sing. . . .

The poet sings of the special events of the "Year of Meteors," suggesting the value of celebrating the idea that one should notice important things because life is short. Perhaps more important, though, Whitman suggests the parallel between this poem and his own life: "As I flit through you hastily, soon to fall and be gone, what is this chant, / What am I myself but one of your meteors?" Whatever value this poem may have—or the poet's life itself—may be compared to the comet, "dropt in the night" and "gone."

"Years of the Modern" (1865)

First published as "Years of the Unperformed" in the *Drum-Taps* volume (1865); it received its present title in the fifth edition of *Leaves of Grass* (1871); and it was the second of 17 poems in the "Songs of Parting" cluster for the sixth edition (1881).

This is an extremely upbeat poem, reflecting Whitman's vision of the American future, the "years of the modern": "I see Freedom, completely arm'd and victorious and very haughty, with Law on one side and Peace on the other."

The world watched as the democratic principles developed, which Whitman saw as vital to America's future, especially after the CIVIL WAR. The poet believed that the "stupendous trio" of Freedom, Law, and Peace would be as important to the rest of the world as it was to America.

"Year that Trembled and Reel'd beneath Me" (1865)

First appeared in the *Drum-Taps* volume (1865) and under this title throughout its printing history; it was the 20th of 43 poems in the "Drum-Taps" cluster for the sixth edition of *Leaves of Grass* (1881).

The poet is depressed by the war, and, although the "year" is not given, the "year that trembled and reel'd beneath me!" is certainly a year of heavy losses, perhaps 1863 when Southern generals Lee and Jackson won in May battles at Chancellorsville. Nearly 18,000 Northern and 13,000 Southern soldiers died during the three days of fighting.

The poet wonders in the final two lines whether, as the poet for the war, he is doomed to write only of death and defeat: "Must I indeed learn to chant the cold dirges of the baffled? / And sullen hymns of defeat?"

"Yet, Yet, Ye Downcast Hours" (1860)

The second and third stanzas of this three-stanza poem appeared first as part of the poem "Debris" in the third edition of *Leaves of Grass* (1860); the stanzas then appeared under the title "Despairing Cries" (1867); a first stanza and the present title were added for the "Whispers of Heavenly Death" cluster for the fifth edition in *Passage to India* (1871); and it was the fifth of 18 poems in the "Whispers" cluster for the sixth edition (1881).

The "Downcast Hours" are those spent by the poem's speaker on his deathbed. He pleads for help: "The sea I am quickly to sail, come tell me, / Come tell me where I am speeding, tell me my destination." But the sea responds: "I understand your anguish, but I cannot help you." The poet in "Old age, alarm'd, uncertain," hears the voices of youth—a woman and a man—and he realizes he cannot escape his loss of time, his impending death.

"Yonnondio" (1887)

First published in the *CRITIC* (November 26, 1887); then in *November Boughs* (1888); and it was the 39th of 65 poems in the "First Annex: Sands at Seventy" cluster for the "Death-bed" printing of *Leaves of Grass* (1892).

Yonnondio is identified in the epigraph to this 12-line poem as an Iroquois term, the sense of which is "lament for the aborigines." Whitman refers to the poem as a "dirge," a song of lamenta-

tion over the loss of the earliest known inhabitants of America, "gone and still, and utterly lost."

"You Felons on Trial in Courts" (1860)

First appeared as "Leaves of Grass, No. 13" in the third edition of *Leaves of Grass* (1860); and it became the 16th of 38 poems in the "Autumn Rivulets" cluster for the sixth edition (1881).

Whitman says to the "felons on trial":

Who am I too that I am not on trial or in prison?
Me ruthless and devilish as any, that my wrists are not chain'd with iron, or my ankles with iron?
You prostitutes flaunting over the trottoirs or obscene in your rooms,
Who am I that I should call you more obscene than myself?

Equality is the theme of this poem, the poet recognizing that he too is "smutch'd and choked," and could just as easily be on trial or in prison. He is "of them," and "henceforth I will not deny them—for how can I deny myself?"

"You Lingering Sparse Leaves of Me" (1887)

First published in *LIPPINCOTT'S MAGAZINE* (November 1887); then in *November Boughs* (1888); and it was the 57th of 65 poems in the "First Annex: Sands at Seventy" cluster for the "Death-bed" printing of *Leaves of Grass* (1892).

Whitman uses in this six-line poem the last leaves of autumn, falling just before winter sets in (November 1887), as a metaphor for his own last "leaves" of poetry, which he believes he is now writing and which will be his last poems before death. He was to live another five years after publication of this poem and of most of the others in *November Boughs*, but he was ill during the late 1880s and felt constantly that he had not much time left. His last poems, he says, however, are the "faithfulest—hardiest."

"Young Grimes" (1840)

First published in the LONG ISLAND DEMOCRAT (January 1, 1840); an "early poem" *not* later published in *Leaves of Grass*. It is most accessible now in Francis Murphy (editor), *Walt Whitman: The Complete Poems* (Penguin Books, 1996).

"Youth, Day, Old Age and Night" (1855)

Poem of four lines, originally lines 19–22 in a 71-line poem, last of the 12 untitled poems in the first edition of *Leaves of Grass* (1855); the longer poem was later titled "Great Are the Myths" but not published after the 1855 edition; the four lines under the present title appeared as the 12th and last separate poem following the "Calamus" cluster for the sixth edition (1881).

The poem is about the three stages of man, the first two lines devoted to youth, the third to maturity, and the fourth to old age and death: The

Night follows close with millions of suns, and sleep and restoring darkness." This is one of Whitman's beautiful images of death, a subject which fascinated him and for which he was always upbeat.

"You Tides with Ceaseless Swell" (1885)

First published with seven other poems under the heading "Fancies at Navesink" in NINETEENTH CENTURY magazine (August 1885); then in *November Boughs* (1888); and, finally, with the "Fancies at Navesink" group as an insert in the "First Annex: Sands at Seventy" cluster for the "Death-bed" printing of *Leaves of Grass* (1892). See "First Annex: Sands at Seventy."

The poet evokes the "power, . . . the unseen force" that creates the ocean's "tides," asking where it comes from. And he wants to know what "messages" it has for people on earth, whether the power "holding the universe with all its parts as one" may be compared to "sailing in a ship," where the helmsman holds all the parts as one. As in "Had I the Choice," which immediately precedes this poem in *Leaves of Grass*, Whitman is asking questions about the great secrets of the universe.

PART III

Related People, Places, Publications, and Topics

A

accentual verse   A metrical system based on the number of accented syllables per line, rather than on the number of syllables per line or on a pattern of accented and unaccented syllables. In accentual verse the total number of syllables is not as important as the number of accented syllables.

Accentual verse is less common in traditional English-language poetry than patterns of accented and unaccented syllables, also known as *accentual-syllabic verse*. The most familiar example of traditional accentual-syllabic verse is basic iambic pentameter, containing lines of 10 syllables each in a fixed pattern of alternating accented and unaccented syllables. This is the rhythm of Shakespeare and of most English language poetry: "No longer mourn for me when I am dead / Than you shall hear the surly sullen bell. . . ." Whitman's lines and stanzas, on the other hand, often follow patterns regarding the number of accented syllables, with the number or placement of unaccented syllables being more irregular.

In the best poetry meter is subtle and often works to merge form and meaning. In Whitman, for example, the merger often takes place when he is using the sea as metaphor. Readers may notice the "wave" movement of many of his stanzas, where the number of accented syllables is smaller in the early and late lines in a stanza or series of stanzas and larger in the middle lines. See, for example, "Out of the Cradle Endlessly Rocking" in Part II. There is a good example of an accentual stanza in lines 41–45, where the female mockingbird disappears, perhaps out over the sea waves:

TILL of a SUDden,
May-be KILL'd, unKNOWN to her MATE,
One FOREnoon the SHE-bird CROUCH'D
    NOT on the NEST.
Nor reTURN'd that afterNOON, nor the
    NEXT.
Nor ever apPEAR'd aGAIN.

The first and fifth lines have two accented syllables (marked in capital letters), the second and fourth lines have three each, and the middle line has five, creating the impression of a wave. The unaccented syllables do not follow the accented syllables in any regular pattern; sometimes one accented syllable follows directly on another (". . . CROUCH'D NOT . . .").

In "Dirge for Two Veterans," a poem of sympathy for the dead soldiers of the Civil War returning on stretchers to hospitals, there is a "death-march" effect created in the rhythm of the lines.

The MOON gives you LIGHT.
And the BUgles and the DRUMS give you
    MUSic,
And my HEART, O my SOLDiers, my
    VETerans,
My HEART gives you LOVE.

In each of the poem's nine stanzas there are two accented syllables in the first and fourth lines and three in the second and third, providing the suggestion of drums beating out the rhythm of the death-march. Here, the placement of the unaccented syllables is more regular, so that the poem mirrors the regular heat of the march.

For other examples of Whitman's accentual verse, see entries for "A Sight in Camp in the Daybreak Gray and Dim," "Passage to India," "By Broad Potomac's Shore," "Beautiful Women," and "Joy, Shipmate, Joy."

Alboni, Marietta (1826–1894) Italian OPERA contralto whom Whitman heard in New York and who became one of his favorite singers. Alboni is named in his poem "Proud Music of the Storm" and is referred to in "To a Certain Cantatrice."

Alboni made her opera debut at La Scala in Milan, Italy, in 1843, and 10 years later she was in New York with the reputation of one of the world's great singers.

During New York's 1852–53 opera season, she performed 10 different operas, 12 concerts of opera music, and Rossini's oratorio *Stabat Mater*. This was her only trip to the United States. Whitman said he heard every one of her performances, which might mean 25 or 30 since it was customary for performers to sing each opera more than once.

The entry for Alboni in *Grove's Dictionary of Music and Musicians* states that "Her voice, a rich, deep, true contralto of fully two octaves, from g to g, was perfectly even throughout its range." Even without knowing perhaps the technical language, Whitman must have been impressed by her voice.

Alcott, Bronson (1799–1888) American philosopher and teacher, a member of the New England transcendentalists (see TRANSCENDENTALISM). He is perhaps best known as the father of Louisa May Alcott, the author of *Little Women*. He contributed a number of philosophical essays to various MAGAZINES, however, including the *DIAL*; his book publications included *Tablets* (1868) and *Observations on the Principles and Methods of Infant Instruction* (1830).

Alcott thought Whitman was a genius and praised *Leaves of Grass* for its "bold, stirring thoughts" and for the poet's "keen appreciation of beauty." The two men met in late 1855, shortly after publication of the first edition of *Leaves of Grass*.

Alcott provides what is perhaps the best written description of Whitman available. In *Journals of Bronson Alcott*, edited by Odell Shepard and pub-

lished in 1938, there is an entry for October 4, 1856, describing a visit he made that afternoon with Henry David THOREAU and Sarah Tyndale to Whitman's home in BROOKLYN: "I pass a couple of hours, and find him to be an extraordinary person, full of brute power, certainly of genius and audacity, and likely to make his mark on Young America—he affirming himself to be its representative man and poet."

He continued in his journal entry:

Broad-shouldered, rouge-fleshed, Bacchus-browed, bearded like a satyr, and rank, he wears his man-bloomer in defiance of everybody, having these as every thing else after his own fashion, and for example to all men hereafter. Red flannel undershirt, open-breasted, exposing his brawny neck; striped calico jacket over this, the collar Byroneal, with coarse cloth overalls buttoned on it; cowhide boots; a heavy roundabout, with huge outside pockets and buttons to match; and a slouched hat, for house and street alike. Eyes gray, unimaginative, cautious yet sagacious; his voice deep, sharp, tender sometimes and almost melting. When talking will recline upon the couch at length, pillowing his head upon his bended arm, and informing you naively how lazy he is, and slow. Listens well; asks you to repeat what he has failed to catch at once, yet hesitates in speaking often, or gives over as if fearing to come short of the sharp, full, concrete meaning of his thought. Inquisitive, very; over-curious even; inviting criticisms on himself, on his poems—pronouncing it 'pomes.'—In fine, an egotist, incapable of omitting, or suffering any one long to omit, noting Walt Whitman in discourse. Swaggy in his walk, burying both hands in his outside pockets. Has never been sick, he says, nor taken medicine, nor sinned; and so is quite innocent of repentance and man's fall. A bachelor, he professes great respect for women. Of Scotch descent by his father; by his mother, German. Age 38, and LONG ISLAND born.

In a journal entry for September 17, 1881, Alcott describes what was apparently his last meeting with Whitman: "He is too brawny and broad to be either high or deep, and must rank with the sensuous school of thought and style. Yet, a majestic presence, and worthy of his fame."

Aldrich, Thomas Bailey (1836–1907) American poet, writer of short stories and novels, and editor, best known perhaps as the author of *The Story of a Bad Boy* (1870) and *Marjorie Daw and Other People* (1873). He was editor of the ATLANTIC MONTHLY from 1881 to 1890.

At one time he was an associate editor of the SATURDAY PRESS under Henry CLAPP and a member of a group of literary Bohemians, including Whitman, who met at PFAFF's beer cellar in New York. Mark Twain called Aldrich the "wittiest man in seven centuries."

Aldrich is quoted as having said that Whitman was a "charlatan," that *Leaves of Grass* was a mere curiosity that would last only if "kept in a glass case."

American, The (1880–1891; 1894–1900) Weekly magazine based in Philadelphia and published by Wharton Barker, initially as a Republican journal, later independent. Barker was the Populist candidate for president in 1900. He lost the election and his magazine folded.

The *American* published news about books and art. Its editors were William R. Balch and Robert Ellis Thompson when two of Whitman's poems were published in its pages: "My Picture-Gallery" (October 30, 1880) and "A Summer Invocation" (June 14, 1881), later titled "Thou Orb Aloft Full-Dazzling."

The writer of an article titled "Literary Life in Philadelphia" for the *American* (July 1887) names as the most "illustrious" writers of Philadelphia Walt Whitman, who was actually living in Camden, New Jersey, at the time, and George H. Boker, dramatist and poet.

American Review, The (1845–1852) Magazine founded to support Henry Clay's political aspirations and continued as a political and literary journal. Edgar Allan Poe contributed several items, including "The Raven," which was first published in its pages.

Whitman's contribution to the magazine was his short story "The Boy Lover" (May 1845). The magazine, which was renamed *American Whig Review* in 1850 for its final two years of publication, was vigorous in encouraging the growth of American literature.

American Revolution (1775–1781) Whitman believed that Independence Day was a sacred holiday, and he wrote essays suggesting better ways of celebrating it. There was a general feeling during Whitman's years of influence that the Fourth of July was a celebration of liberty, and Whitman believed it should celebrate equality and fraternity as well.

Whitman's great uncle had been killed during the Revolutionary War in the Battle of BROOKLYN, and an ancestor on his mother's side had died in a British prison. The poet wrote an "Ode" in honor of Independence Day in 1846, to be sung at Fort Greene in Brooklyn to the tune of "The Star-Spangled Banner." Bad weather interfered with the ceremony, but Whitman had already published the poem in the BROOKLYN DAILY EAGLE (July 2, 1846), for which he was editor at the time, and he was instrumental in turning Fort Greene into a public park, which it still is, at the corner of Myrtle Avenue and Vanderbilt in Brooklyn.

"American Scholar, The" (1837) Oration delivered by Ralph Waldo EMERSON before the Phi Beta Kappa Society, at Harvard University, Cambridge, Massachusetts, August 31, 1837. It was published separately the same year and reprinted in *Nature, Addresses, and Lectures* (1849).

Oliver Wendell Holmes called the speech "our intellectual Declaration of Independence." The founding fathers certainly introduced to America the importance of the "individual" working within society, but "The American Scholar" was in Emerson's time and still is the touchstone for thinking about how individualism works. The idea influenced Whitman among a number of other writers and thinkers, mainly because of its appeal for people who could think not only for themselves but about the nation's future.

The education of scholars, Emerson said, should be divided into three parts: nature, books, and action. What Emerson thought about the influence of nature must have caught Whitman's attention. "Every day, the sun; and, after sunset, Night and her stars. Ever the winds blow; ever the grass grows. The scholar is he of all men whom this spectacle most engages." He ends this discussion by reciting the "ancient precept, 'Know thyself,' and the modern precept, 'Study nature,' which he believes have become 'one maxim'."

The scholar must also know "the mind of the past," and he gets this from books. At the same time, each age "must write its own books; or rather, each generation for the next succeeding. The books of an older period will not fit this [one]." But books can get in the way of "Man Thinking," Emerson said, and the thinking man "must not be subdued by his instruments." No scholar should allow someone else—past or present—to do his thinking for him.

The influence of nature and books, though great, should not, Emerson said, be a substitute for "action," the third ingredient for the education of scholars. "Action is with the scholar subordinate," he said, "but it is essential. Without it he is not yet man. Without it thought can never ripen into truth. . . . Inaction is cowardice, but there can be no scholar without the heroic mind."

Emerson also discusses the three important ages of history—classic, romantic, and philosophic—and believes that each "scholar" goes through all three stages: The boy is Greek; the youth, romantic; the adult reflective. He says that his age is criticized for being "the age of Introversion," but he argues that there is nothing wrong in thinking about the inner self. "Sight is the last thing to be pitied," he says. "Would we be blind? Do we fear lest we should outsee nature and God, and drink truth dry. . . . This time, like all times, is a very good one, if we but know what to do with it."

Emerson's influence on Whitman was described by the latter poet in a letter to John Trowbridge in 1860: "I was simmering, simmering, simmering; Emerson brought me to a boil." Twenty years after the lecture at Harvard, Whitman was to use many of Emerson's ideas as core thoughts in his own writing: particularly in *Democratic Vistas*, the "preface" to the 1855 edition of *Leaves of Grass*, and in the great poem itself.

Aristidean, The (1845–c. 1848) Monthly magazine edited by Thomas Dunn English in New York in 1845. Four of Whitman's short stories were first published in the short-lived journal, which, according to Edgar Allan Poe—writing for a competitive publication at the time—never had more than 50 subscribers. The four Whitman stories are "Arrow-Tip" (March 1845), "Shirval: A Tale of Jerusalem" (March 1845), "Richard Parker's Widow" (April 1945), and "Some Fact-Romances" (December 1845).

Arnold, Matthew (1822–1888) English writer and critic, a contemporary of Whitman, an author best known perhaps for the poems "The Scholar-Gipsy" (1853) and "Dover Beach" (1867) and the critical essay *Culture and Anarchy* (1869).

It was this latter work which irritated Whitman, who said that Arnold "was not in the abstract sense a damned fool, but with respect to the modern—to America—he was the damndest of damned fools—a total ignoramus—knew nothing at all." This quotation is taken from Justin Kaplan's *Walt Whitman: A Life* (1982), Kaplan then adding that "Arnold's brand of 'culture' was almost as hard [for Whitman] to take as his 'anarchy.' "

Art Autograph, The (1880) New York literary arts journal and first publisher of Whitman's poem "The Prairie States" (May 1880).

Atlantic Name of a White Star steamship that wrecked and sank off the Nova Scotia coast, with a loss of 547 passengers and crew (April 1, 1873). Whitman memorialized the event in his poem "Sea Captains, Young or Old," published in the NEW YORK DAILY GRAPHIC (April 4, 1873). The poem's title was later changed to "Song for All Seas, All Ships."

Atlantic Monthly (1857–present) This popular Boston magazine began in 1857 as a journal of literature, art, and politics, with James Russell Lowell as its first editor. The first issue carried "Autocrat of the Breakfast Table" by Oliver Wendell Holmes. Other early contributors included Ralph Waldo EMERSON, Henry Wadsworth Longfellow, Harriet Beecher Stowe, and John Greenleaf Whittier.

Francis H. Underwood was the prime mover at the beginning of the magazine's long and important career. The *Atlantic Monthly* was founded during two afternoons of conferences on May 5 and 6, 1857, at Boston's Parker House by a group that included Underwood, Emerson, Longfellow, Lowell, and Holmes. Holmes named the magazine, and it was decided that there would be no by-lines; Emerson is quoted as saying, "The names of the contributors will be given out when the names are worth more than the articles." Although the founders promised that the magazine would support no political party, the founders were devout abolitionists.

Whitman contributed the following two poems to the *Atlantic Monthly:* "Bardic Symbols" (April 1860), later titled "As I Ebb'd with the Ocean of Life"; and "Proud Music of the Sea-Storm" (February 1869), later titled "Proud Music of the Storm."

B

Baconian Theory (late 1800s) The theory that Francis Bacon wrote some or all of the plays attributed to Shakespeare became somewhat controversial in England during the last quarter of the 19th century, even to the extent of the Shakespeare Memorial Library at Stratford-on-Avon collecting arguments on the Bacon side.

Horace TRAUBEL reports in *Walt Whitman in Camden* a letter from William O'CONNOR to Whitman dated February 1, 1885, informing the poet that "Mr. Gibson," the librarian at the Shakespeare Library "wrote me, very liberally asking me to send to the Library anything I had written in favor of the Baconian theory, saying that the management wished to give houseroom to anything related to the subject (fact is, those fellows over there are beginning to feel the force of the Baconian claim. It is a sign of the rising of the tide, and ten years ago such a request would not have been made.)" O'Connor told Whitman that he had sent a copy of Bucke's biography, which included some of the poet's comments on the subject.

Traubel also writes that, in a conversation with the poet on April 13, 1888, he had asked if Whitman accepted "the whole Bacon proposition." Whitman said, "Not the whole of it: I go so far as to anti-Shakespeare: I do not know about the rest. I am impressed with the arguments but am not myself enough scholar to go with the critics into any thorough examination of the evidences."

In a letter to biographer Richard Maurice BUCKE, dated November 18, 1891, Whitman says, in part, that "the Bacon attribution & cypher are too thin yet—too 'got up' at best—But we will see what time brings out further—at any rate 'probable' or even 'likely' wont do in science or history."

Bellini, Vincenzo (1801–1835) Italian OPERA composer, perhaps best known for the operas *Norma* (1831), *La Sonnambula* (1831), and *I Puritani* (1835). Whitman refers to the first two of these operas in his poem "Italian Music in Dakota."

Bishop, Ann (1810–1884) English OPERA soprano, who became Madame Anna Bishop after she began her professional career in 1831. She performed in America on several tours, and Whitman heard her sing on August 5, 1847, in DONIZETTI's *Linda di Chamounix.*

The poet said, in a review of the opera for the *BROOKLYN DAILY EAGLE,* that Bishop's "voice is the purest soprano—and of as silvery clearness as ever came from the human throat—rich but not massive—and of such flexibility that one is almost appalled by the way the most difficult passages are not only gone over with ease, but actually dallied with, and their difficulty redoubled. They put one in mind of the gyrations of a bird in the air."

Blake, William (1757–1827) English poet, painter, and engraver of his own art and poetry, best known perhaps for *Songs of Innocence* (1789) and *Songs of Experience* (1794).

Blake connects to Whitman because of the similarity of their poetic visions. At the end of English poet and critic Algernon SWINBURNE's work

William Blake: A Critical Essay (1868) the writer makes a favorable comparison between Blake and the American poet. Swinburne wrote that Blake and Whitman were so alike that it might make for a belief in the mystical transition of souls.

At least one other English critic claimed that he could quote lines from Blake and fool people into thinking they had come from *Leaves of Grass*. Swinburne wrote that Whitman's poetry was "more frank and fresh" than Blake's and "[smelled] of sweeter air." Critics in general have believed that Blake's mystical visions were fairly constant, whereas Whitman's were less regular and more controlled. It isn't clear if Whitman knew Blake's works, although he once referred to Blake's "half-mad vision."

Whitman designed the granite tomb for his own burial plot in the Harliegh Cemetery in Camden, New Jersey, and got the idea for one of the design images from Blake's etching *Death's Door*.

Booth, John Wilkes (1838–1865) Whitman saw this actor, son of the great Shakespearean actor Junius Brutus Booth, in a performance of *Richard III* in 1862, three years before Booth shot President LINCOLN at Ford's Theatre. Whitman had seen his famous father, also in *Richard III*, on June 8, 1835, and he wrote of the son's performance that it "is about as much like his father's, as the wax bust of Henry Clay . . . is like the genuine orator in the Capitol, when his best electricity was flashing alive in him and out of him."

Whitman noted that his young friend, Peter DOYLE, had been at Ford's Theatre the night of April 14, 1865, when Booth shot President Lincoln.

Boston Daily Globe, The (1872–present) Founded by Maturin Ballou as a four-cent morning paper in 1872, the *Globe* lost money almost from the beginning. It was rescued by Charles H. Taylor, an experienced journalist who became its publisher in 1873, cut its price to two cents in 1877, and began to make the paper's first profits. Taylor looked for items of interest to a growing and diverse Boston population.

The *Boston Daily Globe* was the first publisher of Whitman's poem "The Sobbing of the Bells" (Sep-

tember 27, 1881). The poem is a memorial to President James Garfield, who had been shot by an assassin in Boston on July 2, 1881, and died September 19. Whitman was in Boston at the time of Garfield's death and wrote the six-line poem for immediate publication.

The newspaper also published a story about Whitman's visit to Boston in 1881, in which he discusses with the reporter the "architecture" of *Leaves of Grass*.

Brignoli, Pasquale (1824–1884) OPERA tenor referred to in Whitman's poem "The Dead Tenor," published in CRITIC (November 8, 1884). Brignoli made his New York debut in 1855 and was one of the popular singers in several of New York's opera houses. The funeral for Signor Brignoli was held in New York City on November 3, 1884.

Brinton, Daniel G. (1837–1899) Member of the University of Pennsylvania teaching faculty during Whitman's years in Camden, New Jersey. He taught Indian languages and archaeology and was a friend of Whitman during his Camden years. Whitman referred to him as a "master-man—stern, resolute, loyal—yes, what I like (in the best sense) to call adhesive: a good comrade, a ripe intellect."

Brinton and Horace TRAUBEL did an interview with Whitman. They asked if he felt himself "a gay lad among the lassies of the village—a beau in the rustic society of his day." Whatever he answered made the two men think that he hated women.

Brinton was one of the pallbearers and speakers at Whitman's funeral.

Broadway Magazine (1867–1868) Monthly London journal of the popular arts and first publisher of five Whitman poems, all in the October 1868 issue: "Darest Thou Now O Soul," "Whispers of Heavenly Death," "A Noiseless Patient Spider," "The Last Invocation," and "Pensive and Faltering."

Brooklyn The Whitman family moved to Brooklyn from West Hills, LONG ISLAND, on May 27, 1823, three days before Walt's fourth birthday. They would live in several different homes during the next 10 years, before moving back to Hempstead,

Long Island, in 1833. Walter Sr. had difficulty keeping a job, and the family was often in money trouble. Walt had a job with the BROOKLYN EVENING STAR, however, and so, at age 14, when the family moved back to Hempstead he stayed on his own in Brooklyn. He took a job as a compositor in New York sometime in 1835 and then rejoined his family the next year and began teaching school in Norwich, near Oyster Bay.

Brooklyn was still a mere Long Island village while the Whitmans were there and did not become a "city" until 1834. It had been Breuckelen until 1816, named by Dutch settlers in the mid-17th century after a village in Holland. By 1896, however, Brooklyn had taken in the whole of Kings County, Long Island, and on January 1, 1898, as a "borough," it became part of New York City. It is now the largest of the five New York boroughs, with more than 3,000,000 citizens.

The Whitmans moved almost once a year during their 10 years in Brooklyn. The first home was a rented house near the FULTON FERRY, just west of the Navy Yard. Walter Sr. was waiting to buy land in order to build a more permanent home. The next house was on Cranberry Street across from the Plymouth Church. The family's first five residences would be in that neighborhood. Walter Sr. built another house at the corner of Tillary and Adams Streets. The family was living on Henry Street in the spring of 1827 when Louisa's fifth child to live (Andrew Jackson WHITMAN) was born on April 7.

Whitman wrote about those early years in *Specimen Days*, saying that "from 1824 to 28 our family lived in Brooklyn on Front, Cranberry, and Johnson Streets. In the latter my father built a nice house for a home, and afterward another in Tillary Street. We occupied them, one after the other, but they were mortgaged, and we lost them."

The steam-frigate *Fulton* blew up in the Brooklyn Navy Yard on July 4, 1829, and "jarred half the city," as Whitman remembered it later. He described being impressed by the military funeral held for the 40 people killed in the accident.

Walt got his first job in the summer of 1830, at age 11, as an office boy in a law firm on Fulton Street. He became a printer's devil (or apprentice) for the LONG ISLAND PATRIOT in 1831, under editor

Samuel E. Clements, who encouraged the boy's interest in print journalism. In the summer of 1832 he took a job with another Brooklyn printer, Erastus Worthington, and in the fall he began work with the LONG ISLAND STAR and its editor Alden Spooner. Walt remained with the *Star* the next year after his family moved to Hempstead, but he rejoined the family in 1836, after his short stint in New York continuing to learn the newspaper trade.

He was back in Brooklyn in 1846 to work as a reporter for the daily *Brooklyn Evening Star* and then for the weekly *Long Island Star,* the newspaper for which he had been a printer's devil 15 years before. He became editor of the *Brooklyn Daily Eagle and Kings County Democrat* on June 1 and was the editor and key reporter until January 21, 1848, when, according to Whitman mythology (often created by the poet himself), he was fired. He became editor and publisher of the *Brooklyn Freeman* in 1848, and, after returning from New Orleans in late 1848, where he had been the editor of the *NEW ORLEANS CRESCENT* for three months, he became editor of another new paper, the *Daily News* (New York), which went out of business two months later.

Brooklyn was known as a city of churches when the Whitmans first moved there from West Hills. They were not a religious family, although Walt's mother attended church and encouraged her children to attend. Walt went to the St. Ann's Episcopal Church Sunday School, but what he remembered most about the experience were the poetic rhythms and imagery of the Old Testament books, apparently read aloud for the class.

In a footnote to his Brooklyn experiences during the 1830s, Whitman wrote in *Specimen Days* that "of the Brooklyn of that time hardly anything remains, except the lines of the old streets. The population was then between ten and twelve thousand. For a mile Fulton Street was lined with magnificent elm trees. The character of the place was thoroughly rural. . . . Who remembers the old places as they were? Who remembers the old citizens of that time? Among the former were Smith & Wood's, Coe Downing's, and other public houses at the ferry, the old ferry itself, Love Lane, the Heights and then, the Wallabout with the wooden bridge, and the road out beyond Fulton Street to the old toll gate. . . ."

See the list of Brooklyn homes rented or owned by the Whitman family in part IV of this volume.

Brooklyn Bridge   Ferry boats of various sorts had been taking people back and forth between BROOK-LYN and New York since 1642, and steamboat service had been available since 1814 when Robert Fulton had first offered his much faster service—faster at least than the rowboats that had been the primary means of transportation before Fulton. By steamboat the half-mile commute took about eight minutes and provided 1,000 crossings a day for people and wagons. The pier at the end of Fulton Street, which became known as Fulton Landing during its steamboat days, is still preserved.

Construction of the Brooklyn Bridge began on the Brooklyn side of the East River in January 1870, and the bridge opened in 1883. Here is the lead paragraph on a newspaper story in the BROOK-LYN DAILY EAGLE (February 2, 1870), under the headline "Work Commenced on the East River Bridge": "The preliminary work of laying the foundation of the Brooklyn tower of the East River Bridge was commenced this morning at the upper slip of FULTON FERRY by tearing up the wood-work of the dock located there. It is intended to push operations with the utmost vigor, and to have the bed clear for the reception of the caisson by the first or tenth of March next. Two steam derricks and fifty laborers are already engaged; and in a few days two steam dredging machines will be put in operation. The bed of the river at this point consisting of stones and heavy boulders, blasting will in some cases have to be resorted to, and the assistance of divers become necessary. The work is being conducted under the supervision of Mr. William C. Kingsley, General Superintendent."

An earlier story had announced that the bridge would be a "Steel Wire Cable Suspension Bridge," 1,600 feet between the towers and 135 feet above the river. It would have the "strength of parts not less that six times the strain to which they will be subjected." Another story described the Fulton Ferry side of the river: "North of Fulton ferry, the tower of the East River Bridge rises to a height of 107 feet, over-looking the warehouses of the shore line with their millions of dollars' worth of merchandise; it rises slowly but surely, and looks as if eagar to aid in joining New York and Brooklyn by the greatest highway of the world; it rises, a monument of Brooklyn's greatness, past, present and future, a wonder of modern times and grand achievement of American engineering science."

The bridge, when completed in 1883 would virtually obliterate the Fulton Ferry village, which is now a small group of dilapidated buildings barely noticeable in the shadow of the great bridge.

Whitman titled one of his best-known poems "Crossing Brooklyn Ferry," which describes the ferry crossing but then turns the ferry system into a metaphor for life's crossings.

Brooklyn Daily Eagle, The (1841–1955; 1976–present)   Daily newspaper founded on October 26, 1841, by Henry Cruse Murphy and Isaac Van Anden as an organ of the Democratic Party, "devoted to the sacred preservation of all the fine old landmarks of the Jeffersonian school." William B. Marsh was editor for its first five years but died February 26, 1846, of a congested liver, brought on, according to the paper's obituary, by overwork at the *Eagle.*

The paper was known officially as *The Brooklyn Eagle and Kings County Democrat,* but when it became a daily on June 1, 1846, the owners changed the name to *The Brooklyn Daily Eagle and Kings County Democrat.*

Whitman replaced Marsh as both editor and chief reporter in early March 1846 and worked in those jobs until January 1848. Even at age 26, when Whitman took the *Eagle* job, he had already worked for 25 newspapers during the previous 15 years, seven as editor. He didn't work for more than two years on any one paper, including the *Brooklyn Daily Eagle.*

The *Eagle* was, when Whitman became its editor, a four-page paper, in a format slightly larger than 15 × 24 inches, and six columns per page. In general, most of the 24 columns were devoted to advertising and legal notices. That left the second page for editorials, news reports, and "the latest intelligence from Europe." The newspaper had only six or seven employees and little circulation.

Whitman was editor, chief reporter, drama critic, and book reviewer.

He wrote more than 1,000 articles and editorials for the *Eagle* during his two-year tenure as editor. His subjects were considerably varied, but he wrote several articles on each of the following topics: democracy and patriotism, local and national politics and politicians, the U.S.-MEXICAN WAR, the economy, prison reform, labor and labor organizations, local newspapers and their editors, education and schools. He reviewed books and local theater performances, particularly OPERA. And he began a series of 25 articles he called "City Intelligence" ("Local Intelligence" for the final two) in which he wrote mostly upbeat stories about BROOKLYN or New York: "City Intelligence: Fulton Street, Brooklyn" began the series on June 4, 1846.

On the occasion of the *Eagle* adding the word *Daily* to its title, Whitman wrote an editorial his first day on the job, titled "Ourselves and the 'Eagle,'" on the relationship of newspaper editors and readers (June 1, 1846). He likes the public relations, but he thinks most editors are too busy:

> Here, in this country, most editors have far far *too much to do,* to make good work of what they do. Abroad, it is different. In London or Paris, the payment for a single "leader" is frequently more than the month's salary of the best remunerated American editor. Crowding upon one individual the duties of five or six, is, indeed, the greatest reason of all why we have in America so very few daily prints that are artistically equal to the European ones. Is it not astonishing, then,—not that the press of the United States don't do better, but that it don't do worse?

Whitman wrote several such editorials for the *Eagle* on the subject of editors and their readers. In another, entitled "American Editing and Editors" (September 29, 1846), he begins by saying, "It is a singular fact that while the people of the United States are a *newspaper-ruled* people, we have in reality few, we may almost say no, newspapers that approach even in the neighborhood of perfect specimens of their kind." Whitman suggests that the one problem may be that editors have "so low a

standard . . . [and that] society has not required more."

Van Anden was sometimes upset by Whitman's free-spirited writing, which eventually made the newspaper not so much a Democratic organ as a showcase for the personality of its editor. Whitman would take long afternoon walks, which might have seemed irresponsible to Van Anden but which produced serious articles about local matters that must have attracted Brooklyn readers. Here is part of an article, for example, entitled "An Hour among the Shipping" (March 9, 1846), published a few days after Whitman had joined the paper but before he was editor:

> We spent an hour or two yesterday afternoon, sauntering along South Street, in New York, and "boarding" some of the lately arrived packet ships. The gales and tempestuous weather, at intervals, since the middle of January, have detained more vessels, and raised anticipations of more marine disasters, than ever before in the same space of time. Within the last five or six days, however—and particularly on Friday, Saturday and yesterday—the fears of our citizens have been nearly altogether allayed. The *Sully* and the *Wellington* are yet due; but the greater part of other ships, for whom fears had begun to grow eager, are safe in the docks.
>
> The *Massachusetts* we found in apparently fine order, notwithstanding her long passage of forty four days, and her battles with the ice and wind. . . . The *Roscius* was really a pitiful sight. . . . She puts one in mind of a dripping, half-drowned Chanticleer. Her spars, sails, and rigging are actually *drooping*—and every thing about her has a kind of bob-tailed look. . . .
>
> The ship *Sea*, we noticed, was obliged, lying as she was in the dock yesterday, to continually work her pumps, and is probably doing so at this moment. . . .
>
> At 1 o'clock, the *Franconia*, from Liverpool, and the *Sartelle*, N. O., came up the bay in handsome style. We went on board both of them. . . .

Another editorial began, "We have been really shocked, during the past two weeks, with the frequent sight of cruelty to horses. . . ." Whitman also wrote frequently on public school education. In one editorial, he states: "There are at this moment about 26,000 youth in courses of education in the Public schools of New York City. A most liberal policy is pursued toward these schools. Books and all the necessary materials of learning, are provided for them— in which respect our Brooklyn schools are behind hand; for here the children have to find their own books, and confusion and delay are thus created."

And the newspaper's circulation steadily increased. In an item, "New Feathers for Our 'Eagle'" (May 21, 1846), Whitman wrote about the new type purchased for the newspaper and that the advertising recommendations of the *Eagle* are fully equal to any of its contemporaries: our circulation being equal to any paper, if not the *best* in Brooklyn."

Much of what Whitman learned in his mixing with the people of New York and Brooklyn would find its way later into the poetry. "There is hardly anything on earth, of its sort," he would write for the paper, "that arouses our sympathies more readily than the cause of a laborer, or a band of laborers, struggling for a competence, (men in luckier situations would call it a mere pittance) and standing out against the exactions of grinding 'bosses' and speculators." This sympathy would become thematic in his poetry a few years later.

In *Specimen Days* (1882), Whitman wrote an item entitled "Starting Newspapers," in which he says of his work with the *Brooklyn Daily Eagle,* "I had one of the pleasantest sits of my life—a good owner, good pay, and easy work and hours." He also provided his own explanation for his dismissal from the paper: "The troubles in the Democratic party broke forth about those times (1848–'49) and I split off with the radicals, which led to rows with the boss [Van Anden] and 'the party,' and I lost my place." Whitman was initially in favor of the War with Mexico (1846–48)—for mostly wrong reasons—but changed his mind when he realized that the Democratic government of President James Polk might allow SLAVERY in the new states of the Southwest. The owners of the *Brooklyn Daily Eagle* did not like Whitman's change of mind. See U.S.-MEXICAN WAR.

When Whitman was fired or quit the *Eagle,* one of its competitors apparently gloated over the

news—to which the *Eagle* responded with the following punning verse:

> It is true, as you say,
> We sent Whitman away,
> But that is a private affair;
> But since you have spoken
> Know by this token,
> You have no *wit, man,* to spare.

Whitman wrote the following sarcastic statement concerning "Thomas's Execution" for the *Brooklyn Daily Eagle* (November 21, 1846): "The hanging of the negro Thomas went off 'beautifully,' according to the N. Y. papers! This choking work seeks to prevent crime in the very spirit which causes and multiplies crime!"

Besides the more than 1,000 articles and editorials Whitman wrote for the *Eagle,* he also published while he was its editor two poems: "The Play-Ground" (June 1, 1846) and "Ode" (July 2, 1846).

All issues of the *Brooklyn Daily Eagle,* from its beginning in 1841 to 1902, are available for free online at http://eagle.brooklynpubliclibrary.org/eagle. The news articles, features stories, and editorials that Whitman wrote for the *Eagle* (and all other newspapers he wrote for through 1848) are available in the two volumes *Whitman: The Journalism,* edited by Herbert Bergman, Douglas A. Noverr, and Edward J. Recchia for Peter Lang Publishers (1998 and 2003). For a list of nearly all of his journalism writings, see William White's "Walt Whitman's Journalism: A Bibliography" (*Walt Whitman Review,* 14, no. 3, September 1968). See also WHITMAN IN JOURNALISM and the appendix in part IV of this book: "Newspapers and Magazines that Published Whitman's Articles and Editorials."

Brooklyn Daily Times, The (1857–1859)

Three men founded the *Williamsburg Daily Times* on February 28, 1848, at 129 Grand Street in Williamsburg, a village that would be consolidated with BROOKLYN in 1855. The paper's owners, George C. Bennett, Aaron Smith, and Dr. Egbert Guernsey, changed the name in 1855, first to the *East Brooklyn Daily Times.* Three days later they dropped the "*East.*"

Although the actual dates during which Whitman worked for the Brooklyn *Times* are somewhat vague, there seems to be general agreement that he began as editor about May 1, 1857, and was released sometime in the spring or early summer of 1859. The paper was at 145 Grand Street when Whitman took over as editor.

Whitman got in trouble with a number of church people in Brooklyn, including the Rev. Henry Ward Beecher, one of the most influential ministers in the city. In an editorial entitled "Beecherroyalty" (May 4, 1857), Whitman accused Beecher of encouraging his parishioners to worship their minister.

> We cannot help regarding hero worship as a great evil, whatever the characteristics and position of the hero himself. . . .
>
> The mission of the age, as many people consider it, is to correct this tendency—to discourage any man or woman from pinning his faith and confidence blindly and unreflectingly to any central authority whatever. To develop and encourage individuality and self-reliance is conceived by many to be the great mission of the present age,—and very great success has attended the efforts made to encourage this tendency of the times.
>
> Mr. Beecher is doubtless a very able and sincere teacher of the people, but if the general effect of his teaching may be judged by the influence which his ministrations produced on the mind of the author of "notes from a Plymouth Pulpit," we may well doubt whether he is not making people Beecherites instead of making them Christians, and teaching them to worship him instead of that Creator whom he so eccentrically defines as "a dim and shadowy effluence."

In an editorial entitled "Unsound Churches" (June 21, 1857) Whitman listed nine Williamsburg churches from a variety of denominations that had been condemned as unsafe by fire inspectors, and he suggested that there were probably several unsafe Brooklyn churches as well. These and other editorials critical of local churches may have been the last straw for the owners of the *Brooklyn Daily Times*. The pressure from irate ministers and church members no doubt contributed to the ultimate firing of the editor.

There is a further note of interest on Whitman's work with the Brooklyn *Times*. He spent as much time or more as editor there as with the BROOKLYN DAILY EAGLE, and yet his biographers devote far more space to his work on the *Eagle*. And if the news items, feature stories, and editorials for which he is given credit is accurate, he wrote more than 1,200 pieces for the *Times* and about 1,000 items for the *Eagle*. It is difficult at best to know exact numbers, because many if not most of Whitman's newspaper items were unsigned, and bibliographers have often to determine authorship on the basis of writing style alone. It is a more difficult decision with Whitman's earlier journalism pieces, one would suppose, because he was developing a prose style in the 1840s when most of his journalism experience took place, and by the time he was editor of the *Brooklyn Times* the style was more mature and so more easily recognizable to bibliographers.

For more detailed information about Whitman's years with the *Brooklyn Daily Times*, see *I Sit and Look Out: Editorials from the Brooklyn Daily Times by Walt Whitman*, selected and edited by Emory Holloway and Vernolian Schwarz (New York: Columbia University Press, 1932). For a more complete listing of items Whitman wrote for the Brooklyn *Times*, see William White's article, "Walt Whitman's Journalism: A Bibliography" (*Walt Whitman Review*, 14, no. 3, September 1968). See also WHITMAN IN JOURNALISM.

It is interesting to note that the Brooklyn *Times* was one of the first newspapers to review the first edition of *Leaves of Grass*. The review (September 29, 1855) states, in part: "Other poets celebrate great events, personages, romances, wars, loves, passions, the victories and power of their country, or some real or imagined incident—and polish their work, and come to conclusions, and satisfy the reader. This poet celebrates himself, and that is the way he celebrates all. He comes to no conclusions, and does not satisfy the reader. He certainly leaves him what the serpent left the woman and the man, the taste of the tree of the knowledge of good and evil, never to be erased again."

Except perhaps for the notion that he did not satisfy readers, Whitman must have appreciated this review.

Brooklyn Evening Star   Whitman wrote 54 articles for this daily newspaper between September 1845 and March 1846, many of them about youth and/or the public schools, or arguing in print with other local editorial writers about various issues.

In one such essay, "Vulgarity of Newspaper Quarrels," in which he seems to take on all of New York's newspaper editors (February 5, 1846), Whitman writes: "The American press is painfully scurrilous. We hardly know a journal which does not occasionally utter language in print, that if spoken by the tongue in a mixed assemblage of ladies and gentlemen, would send its author to coventry for the remainder of his life."

Brother Jonathan   A sometimes monthly, sometimes weekly literary journal, perhaps best known because it pirated novels from England. It was edited at one time by Benjamin H. Day, founder and editor of the (New York) *Sun*. See Whitman's poem "The Death of the Nature-Lover."

The origin of the periodical's name is obscure, but there is a story told that General George Washington ran out of ammunition during the Revolutionary War and, when none of his officers suggested a remedy, he said, "We must consult Brother Jonathan," meaning Jonathan Trumbull, the governor of Connecticut. The problem of the ammunition was resolved, and "to consult Brother Jonathan" became a slogan and "Brother Jonathan" became a name to describe a shrewd Yankee.

The journal was the first publisher of a Whitman article entitled "Boz and Democracy" (February 26, 1842)—"Boz" a reference to Charles Dickens, who was in the U.S. to promote copyright laws—and two poems: "The Death of the Nature-Lover" (March 11, 1843), and "Ambition" (January 29, 1842).

Brown, Lewis K. (Lewy)   (unknown) Beloved soldier friend of Whitman's, whom the latter met on one of his hospital visits. Whitman observed the amputation of Lewis's leg at the Armory Square Hospital on January 5, 1864. The two men carried on a correspondence after the war. See also DOYLE, PETER.

Bryant, William Cullen   (1794–1878) American poet, one of the leading writers during Whitman's lifetime. Bryant was best known for his poems of Nature, especially "Thanatopsis," and as the editor for 50 years of the NEW YORK EVENING POST. "Thanatopsis," published in the *North American Review* (1817), was an influence on Whitman. "Thanatopsis" is Greek for "view of death," a subject Whitman would lean on throughout his own poetic career.

Bryant lived most of his life in New York City and the two men knew and liked one another. They would take city walks together or ride the bus together to various city haunts, Bryant often talking about his most recent travels abroad.

A number of Whitman items were first published in the *Post* while Bryant was editor, but only one poem: "Song for Certain Congressmen" (March 2, 1850), which argues against the move in Congress to compromise on the issue of SLAVERY. And Bryant published a Whitman article in the early 1850s calling for American painters and sculptors to become "ardent, radical, and progressive" and to create "art worthy of America," ideas he would use thematically in *Leaves of Grass*.

Bryant was a regular contributor to the DEMOCRATIC REVIEW, which was for Whitman a "magazine of a profounder quality of talent than any since." It published subjects of much interest to both Whitman and Bryant: American culture, TRANSCENDENTALISM, animal magnetism, capital punishment, etc.

Bucke, Dr. Richard Maurice   (1838–1902) Whitman friend and biographer; they met for the first time in 1877 on Bucke's visit to Whitman's home in Camden, New Jersey. He became one of three Whitman literary executors, along with Thomas HARNED and Horace TRAUBEL.

Bucke, a Canadian physician, psychiatrist, and superintendent of the insane asylum in London, Ontario, was also something of a mystic and had been inspired by a reading of *Leaves of Grass* in 1868. He became extremely interested in Whitman and his poetry and wrote the poet's first biography,

Walt Whitman, published by David McKay in Philadelphia (1883), at that time Whitman's own publisher. He wrote that Whitman's poetry offered the highest form of "cosmic consciousness."

In discussing Whitman's poetry, Bucke wrote about a "marked rise in the moral nature of America and that *Leaves of Grass* is the initiative of such a rise, the preface and creator of a new era. . . . What the Vedas were to Brahmanism, the Law and the Prophets to Judaism, the Avesta and Zend to Zoroastrianism, the Kings to Confucianism and Taoism, the Pitakas to Buddhism, the Gospels and Pauline writings to Christianity, the Qurān to Mohammedanism, will *Leaves of Grass* be to the future of American civilization." For Bucke, "*Leaves of Grass* was the bible of Democracy, containing the highest exemplar of life yet furnished, and suited to the present age and to America. Within it is folded (as the oak in the acorn, or the man in the new-born babe) a new spiritual life for myriads of men and women."

Whitman is quoted as saying at a birthday celebration in 1891 that Bucke's biography "is about the only one that thoroughly radiates and depicts and describes in a way I think thoroughly delineates me." It is not surprising that he should feel that way, since he had read and edited Bucke's book before it went to press.

Bucke also wrote *Man's Moral Nature* (1879) and *Cosmic Consciousness* (1901), both books inspired by Whitman's poetry and by conversations with the poet in Camden. The doctor was also instrumental in the publication of Whitman's announcement about the "completion" of *Leaves of Grass,* written for Bucke two months before Whitman's death in March 1892. Whitman, writing in the third person about *Leaves,* states that "he would like this new 1892 edition to absolutely supersede all previous ones. Faulty as it is, he decides it is by far his special and entire self-chosen poetic utterance." The notice was published in the New York Herald.

Whitman told Bucke in several conversations late in his life that he had produced children, a boy and a girl. Whitman claimed that both children were now adults living somewhere in the South. Bucke made no serious effort after Whitman died to investigate the possibility of children, and, since no facts have ever been confirmed, biographers remain skeptical.

Burroughs, John (1837–1921)   American writer and naturalist and author of two books on Whitman: *Notes on Walt Whitman as Poet and Person* (1867) and *Whitman: A Study* (1896). The two men met in Washington in 1863, while Whitman was working as a hospital assistant during the Civil War.

Burroughs was better known nationally, however, for his love of nature and for his poetic style of writing in more than a dozen books on the subject of nature, including *Wake-Robin* (1871), *Locusts and Wild Honey* (1879), and *Ways of Nature* (1905).

John Burroughs, writer, naturalist, and friend of Whitman's. He wrote *Whitman: A Study* in 1896. *(Library of Congress, Prints and Photographs Division. Edward B. Greene)*

He was drawn toward nature by EMERSON and THOREAU and toward poetry by Whitman. Nearly all of his books reflect these dual influences, especially *Birds and Poets* (1877).

At their first meeting Burroughs and Whitman formed an immediate friendship. Burroughs wrote to a friend that Whitman was "kind, sympathetic, charitable, humane, tolerant, a man I did not suppose was possible. He loves everything and everybody." Burroughs and his wife rented a house in the District of Columbia and then built a house at 1331 Y Street and established the tradition of Sunday breakfasts with Whitman. Burroughs is generally credited with increasing Whitman's interest in ornithology, and there is evidence in a letter the naturalist wrote that his description of the song of the hermit thrush probably encouraged the poet to make the song and the thrush major symbols in "Out of the Cradle Endlessly Rocking."

Burroughs was instrumental in discouraging Whitman from going to England in the early 1870s after he had received an invitation from Alfred Tennyson, England's poet laureate at the time. Burroughs had heard from William Michael ROSSETTI that Whitman did not have the proper reputation in England for a reading tour, that not even Tennyson, Browning, or SWINBURNE had yet done readings in their native land.

Burroughs wrote a review for the *Galaxy* (December 1, 1866) of Whitman's *Drum-Taps* poems, saying that they are poems "that may be slow in making admirers, yet [are] well worth the careful study of every student of literature."

Mr. and Mrs. Burroughs moved to New York State in 1872 and built a home, "Riverby," at Esopus. Whitman visited Riverby at least three times, even after his stroke in January 1873, and Burroughs was a visitor on several occasions to Whitman's house in Camden, where he moved, shortly after his mother's death on May 23. Burroughs was one of the pallbearers at Whitman's funeral on March 30, 1892.

C

"Calamus" Title for a cluster of poems in *Leaves of Grass* (see in part II).

Calamus Title for a book of letters written by Whitman to Peter DOYLE between 1868 and 1880, edited by Richard Maurice BUCKE. It was published in Boston by Laurens Maynard in 1897.

Carlyle, Thomas (1795–1881) Scottish essayist and critic, known in Whitman circles for his article "Shooting Niagara: And After?," a scathing criticism of democracy published in Horace Greeley's NEW YORK TRIBUNE (August 16, 1867). The Scottish writer had argued that democracy would destroy civilization. The editor of the GALAXY, a new literary magazine in New York, who was looking for material, asked Whitman if he would like to respond to the Carlyle essay. As the nation's leading spokesman for democracy, Whitman could not refuse the assignment. He wrote three articles for the *Galaxy*: "Democracy," "Personalism," and "Literature." Only the first two were published by the journal, but the three essays became *Democratic Vistas* in 1871. Whitman was a better poet than writer of prose, but the stimulation of responding to Carlyle helped make *Democratic Vistas* one of the best explanations of and arguments for democracy ever written.

In *Walt Whitman: A Life* (1980), biographer Justin Kaplan quotes Whitman as saying that no one could beat Carlyle for pure "cussedness." Paraphrasing Whitman further, Kaplan says that no one "since Isaiah had voiced so much unrelieved bitterness with the secular world. . . . 'Shooting Niagara'

was a finger in the eye of just about every American of liberal inclinations. Carlyle said that extending the vote to the English working class, as mandated by Disraeli's Reform Bill, merely assured a fresh supply of 'blockheadism, gullibility, bribability, amenability to beer and balderdash, by way of amending the woes we have had from our previous supplies of that bad article.' By allowing an electoral head count to become the Divine Court of Appeal on every question and interest of mankind' (a principle Americans were about to reaffirm in the Fourteenth and Fifteenth Amendments to the Constitution), England was headed over Niagara Falls in a barrel, in emulation of its former colony." Carlyle also summed up the American CIVIL WAR, Kaplan says, by stating that "half a million Northerners and Southerners lost their lives fighting a civil war for the empty purpose of emancipating 'three million absurd Blacks.' "

Carpenter, Edward (1844–1929) English writer and lecturer, who wrote about sexual reform and women's rights in England, but is perhaps best known for his long poem *Towards Democracy* (in four parts, 1883–1902). He wrote a memoir titled *Days with Walt Whitman* (1906), in which he describes the immediate influence the poet had on him as a student at Cambridge University. He was educated for the ministry but apparently changed his mind on a first reading of *Leaves of Grass* while at the university.

Carpenter wrote about a conversation with Whitman in which the American poet talked about the writing of *Leaves of Grass*. It "is something that few, . . . only one here and there, perhaps oftenest women, are at all in a position to seize," Whitman is quoted as saying. "It lies behind almost every line; but concealed, studiedly concealed; some passages are purposely obscure. There is something in my nature *furtive* like an old hen! You see a hen wandering up and down a hedgerow, looking apparently quite unconcerned, but presently she finds a concealed spot, and furtively lays an egg, and comes away as though nothing had happened! That is how I felt in writing 'Leaves of Grass.' "

Carpenter wrote of his first meeting with Whitman on May 2, 1877, after several years of exchanging letters. He wrote that "at first sight [Whitman was] quite an old man with long grey, almost white, beard, and shaggy head and neck, grey dress too; but tall, erect, and at closer sight not so old—a florid fresh complexion, pure grey-blue eye (no sign of age there) and full, strong, well-formed hands." Whitman showed him the area, including visits to meet Anne GILCHRIST and her children in Philadelphia and the Staffords at Timber Lake, just south of Camden.

catalog A stylistic device Whitman used in which sometimes long lists of people, places, and/or things are mentioned or described as a way for the poet to emphasize the ever increasing boundaries of his ideas.

The lists are often used to enhance Whitman's concept of certain principles. It would not be enough, Whitman must have felt, to merely identify his vision of DEMOCRACY, for example, by using as his only samples men and women, or blacks and whites. Democracy could only be explained in terms of the equality of *all* people and in *all* walks of life. It would have been impossible to catalog all the various kinds of people—their ethnic classifications, their colors, their vocations, their genealogies, their social standings, etc.

Yet the impact on the reader of cataloging seems to be twofold: first, it makes him or her aware of the expansiveness of Whitman's idea; and second, in the best poems the very rhythm of the catalog enhances the reader's appreciation for the poet's merger of form and meaning. The rhythm of the

lines, in other words, merges with the meaning Whitman is offering in using the catalog style.

Perhaps the best example of how the rhythm of cataloging works to enhance meaning is in Section 15 of "Song of Myself." The poet identifies, or explains, himself to himself (and to readers) by looking outward to identify with other people. In more than 100 lines Whitman presents a catalog of one-line pictures of Americans either singing at their work or at a work that sings. Here are the first few lines:

> The pure contralto sings in the organ loft,
> The carpenter dresses his plank, the tongue of
>   his foreplane whistles its wild ascending lisp,
> The married and unmarried children ride home
>   to their Thanksgiving dinner,
> The pilot seizes the king-pin, he heaves down
>   with a strong arm,
> The mate stands braced in the whale-boat,
>   lance and harpoon are ready,
> The duck-shooter walks by silent and cautious
>   stretches,
> The deacons are ordain'd with cross'd hands at
>   the altar, . . .

Taken as a whole, Section 15 is Whitman's presentation of the rhythm of America at work. And the reader not only senses the rhythm of these lines but hears the music as well, the "song" of America.

Cattell, Ed See DOYLE, PETER.

Century Magazine (1881–1930) A literary periodical, which had been *Scribner's Monthly* from 1870 to 1881. *Century's* first editor, Richard Watson Gilder, immediately transformed the newly named journal into one of New York's leading publishers of fiction and poetry, including five of Whitman's poems. The editors serialized novels by William Dean HOWELLS, Henry JAMES, and Mark Twain, among others.

The magazine was officially the *Century Illustrated Monthly Magazine* when Gilder accepted for publication the following five poems by Whitman: "Twilight" (December 1887); "Old Age's Lambent Peaks" (September 1888); "My 71st Year" (November 1889); "Old Age's Ship; and Crafty Death's"

(February 1890); and "A Twilight Song" (May 1890).

cholera epidemic (1832)   Cholera reached the U.S. East Coast in 1832, beginning in New York City on June 26. The epidemic killed 100 people a day at its height in July and a total of 3,500 by December, when it finally lessened. A third of the population left New York, carrying the disease into the countryside.

The worst conditions were in the "Five Points" area of the city, a slum district surrounding the intersection of Anthony Street (now Worth Street), Orange Street (now Baxter), and a section of Park Street (later demolished)—the home now of the U.S. District and New York County civil and criminal courthouses. There were five corners at the intersection, thus the name. When its slum conditions were at their worst during the 1820s and 1830s, this area rivaled London's East End for population density, unemployment, crime, infant mortality, and disease, all of which made the area ripe for contributing to the city's cholera epidemic.

There were three other cholera epidemics that hit New York while Whitman was working either in New York or BROOKLYN. One in 1848–49 killed more than 5,000 city residents; another in 1854 killed 2,500; the third occurred in 1866 and killed more than 1,100.

Civil War (1861–1865)   Whitman and many of his contemporaries referred to it as the "Secession War." The poet spent nearly three years of the war serving in Washington, D.C., hospitals, assisting with the wounded and dying soldiers of both North and South. He spoke to the soldiers, heard their war stories, wrote letters to their parents, wives, and sweethearts, and generally acted not as a stranger but as a friend. After the war he received thank-you letters from a number of these soldiers, at least one from a soldier who had since married and whose first child was named Walt Whitman.

The cost of the Civil War was enormous. Statistics are nearly always approximate, because accurate records were not kept—perhaps because neither side thought the war would last long. And it is difficult to find agreement of numbers in any two sets of records. But there seems to be a general consensus about some things. The numbers of Confederate dead are estimated at 258,000, more than a third of the estimated 600,000 to 700,000 soldiers who fought on the side of the South. The numbers of Union dead were approximately 360,000, with another 275,000 wounded, of the estimated 2,000,000 men who enlisted with the Union forces. More men died as a result of the American Civil War than in any other war involving the United States, before or since.

Before Whitman worked in Washington hospitals he had spent the early fall of 1862 in a New York hospital, and in a conversation with a friend, Fred Gray, at PFAFF'S CELLAR, he heard what may have been his first account of battle conditions, this with the 51st New York Regiment, which led an attack on Antietam in the Shenandoah Valley. General George B. McClellan had been chasing General Robert E. Lee down the valley but then let him go, the "worst blunder" of the war, according to Whitman. There were 20,000 dead or wounded soldiers from both sides in that battle.

Whitman wrote in *Specimen Days* (1882) that he first heard the news of the attack on Fort Sumter "late at night (13th April, 1861)" after an OPERA and on his way down Broadway toward his home in BROOKLYN. He heard the newsboys shouting as they came up the street, and he and 30 or 40 other people gathered outside the Metropolitan Hotel at the corner of Broadway and Prince Streets, with someone reading a telegram and newspaper stories aloud to the entire group. "No remark was made by any of the crowd," Whitman wrote; they "all stood a minute or two, I remember, before they dispersed. I can almost see them there now, under the lamps at midnight again." After the telegrams and the stories, he made his way home to Brooklyn.

Of the 188 short essays in *Specimen Days*, 62 are from notes he took during his thinking about and actual experiences in the "secession war." Most of what he knew about the war in its first year and a half he learned from New York newspapers. He was unemployed at the time but contributing poems and essays to several local papers, including 25 articles for the *Brooklyn Daily Standard* under the general heading "Brooklynania."

One of his early essays about the war, written several years later from notes he had taken at the time and published in *Specimen Days* under the title "Battle of Bull Run, July, 1861," offers a few insights into war in general. One is that "All battles, and their results, are far more matters of accident than is generally thought." In writing about Bull Run, Whitman said that "Each side supposed it had won, till the last moment. . . . By a fiction, or series of fictions, the national forces at the last moment exploded in a panic and fled from the field. The defeated troops commenced pouring into Washington over the Long Bridge at daylight on Monday, 22d." In the Willard Hotel that evening, Whitman says, a Northern Colonel, sick with defeat, made a speech declaring that he thought the North should capitulate.

Whitman wrote that "If there were nothing else of Abraham LINCOLN for history to stamp him with, it is enough to send him with his wreath to the memory of all future time, that he endured that hour, that day, bitterer than gall—indeed a crucifixion day—that it did not conquer him—that he unflinchingly stemmed it, and resolved to lift himself and the Union out of it."

Whitman, still from his point of view in the late 1870s, wrote that there were two days during the war that he could not forget: "that first Bull Run defeat and the day of Abraham Lincoln's death."

He read about the early battles in newspapers, and when he read in the NEW YORK HERALD (December 16, 1862) that his younger brother George had been wounded at the battle of Fredericksburg three days earlier he went to Washington where he thought he might get further information. He discovered that George was in a field hospital at Falmouth, Virginia, just northeast of Fredericksburg. Walt was in Falmouth by December 21st and began his first visits to camp hospitals, visits that he would continue there and in Washington, D.C., hospitals for the rest of the war.

In "Down at the Front" (*Specimen Days*) he describes conditions at the hospitals for the "Army of the Potomac." He writes as if copying directly from the original notes taken during the war: "Spend a good part of the day in a large brick mansion on the banks of the Rappahannock, used as a hospital since the battle—seems to have received only the worst cases." He notes that within 10 yards of the building's front door there is a "heap of amputated feet, legs, arms, hands, etc." and several dead bodies nearby, "each covered with its brown woolen blanket." The scene probably inspired Whitman's *Drum-Taps* poem "A Sight in Camp in the Daybreak Gray and Dim":

> Three forms I see on stretchers lying, brought
>   out there untended lying,
> Over each the blanket spread, ample brownish
>   woolen blanket,
> Gray and heavy blanket, folding, covering all.

Whitman returned to Washington in January. He describes the trip north, first by the Aquia Creek Railroad from Falmouth to Aquia Creek Landing (about 12 miles) and then by government steamer from Aquia Creek up the Potomac to Washington (about 40 miles). The landing was at the foot of Sixth Street on the Washington Channel. There were a number of wounded on the boat, and he carried letters from other soldiers not going home and hoping to get messages to loved ones, letters which Whitman mailed from Washington. He had made friends with a number of soldiers in the field hospitals around Falmouth, and he wrote several letters, dictated to him by wounded men.

He wrote a letter to Mr. and Mrs. S. B. Haskell in Breesport, New York, dated August 10, 1863, describing the final days and death of their son. "He is one of the thousands of our unknown American young men in the ranks," Whitman wrote, "about whom there is no record or fame, no fuss made about their dying so unknown." He noted also, "poor dear son, though you were not my son, I felt to love you as a son."

He would write in *Specimen Days* of seeing the wounded from the Battle of Chancellorsville arrive at the landing at the foot of Sixth Street. It was raining, and the "pale, helpless soldiers had been debarked, and lay around on the wharf and neighborhood anywhere." The men "are lying on blankets, old quilts, etc., with bloody rags bound round heads, arms, and legs." He says that even as he writes, "hundreds more are expected, and tomorrow and the next day more, and so on for many days. Quite often they arrive at the rate of 1,000 a day."

Civil War, medical care   At the beginning of the war, medical care was so primitive that almost as many soldiers died from "care" as from wounds. There was only one hospital prepared to take the first soldiers wounded in battle. That was the Washington Infirmary at Judiciary Square on E Street between Fourth and Fifth Streets. Perhaps worse than the lack of hospitals—because other Washington, D.C., buildings were soon made available, 85 altogether—was the lack of transportation for the wounded from battlefields to the city. There was simply no system.

It would be August 1862 before the medical director for the Army of the Potomac, Jonathan Letterman, established an organization of ambulances and trained drivers and stretcher bearers that were assigned to the evacuation of the wounded. Horses and mules pulled wagons and carts, bumping over the roads with their loads of wounded soldiers, first to field stations, then to the hospitals. The animals had to be taken care of as well, so veterinarians became essential even before care could be provided for soldiers. More horses and mules died during the war than men, an estimated 1,000,000 horses and mules to 620,000 soldiers, from North and South. Infirmaries were established to take care of the animals.

Whitman was one of dozens, perhaps hundreds, of untrained volunteer male and female "nurses," dedicated mainly to making wounded and dying soldiers more comfortable in extremely uncomfortable surroundings. For most of three years (1862–65), Whitman spent long hours each day in one of six or seven hospitals in Washington, D.C., visiting the sick and wounded. He also had a paying job as a government clerk, but his bosses could not have seen much of him during the war.

In the hospitals, he carried on long conversations with soldiers, getting them to talk about themselves and their homes; he was always a good listener, and the soldiers must have appreciated such personal interest. He took books and newspapers to the hospital wards and read aloud, sometimes apparently to one soldier but often to groups of soldiers gathered around. And he wrote letters dictated by a soldier to his family at home, letters which sometimes arrived after the soldier had died.

Whitman also made daily notes of the names, wounds, hometowns, and loved ones of the soldiers he talked with, and these notes plus a good memory and a natural tendency to love nearly everyone he met, made him an excellent hospital worker. He did not discriminate between Northern and Southern soldiers. He talked with and wrote letters for soldiers on both sides in the war, reassuring loved ones at home that their soldiers was getting the best treatment possible. Whitman used these notes later for several entries in *Specimen Days* (1882).

Whitman records in *Specimen Days* seeing an ambulance procession "passing up Fourteenth Street, on their way, probably, to Columbian, Carver, and Mount Pleasant Hospitals. This is the way the men come in now [June 25, 1863], seldom in small numbers, but almost always in these long, sad processions. Through the past winter, while our army lay opposite Fredericksburg, the like strings of ambulances were of frequent occurrence along Seventh Street, passing slowly up from the steamboat wharf, with loads from Aquia Creek." Most of the wounded, coming from battlefields in southeast Virginia and points further south, were taken from land points near Aquia Creek up the Potomac River to wharfs near Sixth Street along what is now the Washington Channel.

The Confederate army used a similar system for handling their wounded, and in the battles of northern Virginia, Confederate soldiers were often taken to Washington hospitals along with the federal soldiers.

Even before men became soldiers they were endangered by unsanitary facilities at the training camps to which they were assigned. Diseases spread because there were so many men and so few proper sanitation and washing facilities and because of a lack of proper food, sometimes even of a shortage of food. It has been estimated that nearly two-thirds of the men who died during the CIVIL WAR—North and South—died of diseases, particularly measles, which spread across a campground in a matter of a few weeks.

There were two potential stops for a wounded soldier before he reached a city facility. Wounded were first taken to a field dressing station, usually to the rear of the fighting, where the injured man was examined and his wounds bandaged. He was given whiskey if in shock and morphine for pain. Medical personnel, often poorly trained for such matters, would decide whether a soldier was fit to go back to the battlefield. If not, he would be sent to a field hospital.

Medical personnel at the field hospital, presumably better trained than those at the dressing station, would determine whether the soldier was "slightly wounded," a "surgical case," or "mortally wounded." The latter were usually left to die. The surgical cases were operated on, most operations involving the amputation of arms and legs. Almost all of the amputees received some form of anesthesia, usually chloroform or ether; but the instruments used were hardly ever sterilized and might be used on several soldiers by doctors who had little choice as they moved through a field tent full of wounded, sometimes screaming soldiers. In spite of conditions, reports indicate that 75 percent of the amputees survived.

Amputation was necessary sometimes because of the damage done by rifle shots or explosions of cannon shots in battle and sometimes because it took so long to get a soldier to a field hospital that gangrene had already set in. Tetanus, typhoid fever, and dysentery also killed thousands of soldiers, before they had a chance to get to a city facility. Even at Washington hospitals, the third stop for wounded soldiers, epidemics of tetanus and typhoid fever were common. The White House, which received a number of soldiers at a hospital unit on its grounds, was not immune from disease, and President LINCOLN's son, Willie, died there of typhoid fever in 1862.

Doctors in the mid-19th century had usually completed only two years of medical training, mostly classroom lectures and no practical experience. America was far behind the medical training provided in Europe. France had thermometers, for example, but a report states that there were only 20 thermometers available to the entire federal army

Soldiers standing in front of the Sanitary Commission in Washington, D.C. The main office was at 244 F Street NW. Photographed by Mathew Brady *(Library of Congress, Prints and Photographs Division)*

of the U.S. and that a stethoscope was a mere novelty. Harvard University's Medical School did not even own a microscope until after the war.

Some reports suggested that medical personnel at field hospitals often kept soldiers too long, sending them on to Washington only after they were so ill that it would be impossible to survive the trip.

Whitman wrote about wounded soldiers who died of overdoses of opium pills or laudanum, given by incompetent helpers to relieve pain; and he reports one case where a "wardmaster" gave a soldier lead muriate of ammonia, intended for washing his feet.

He also wrote in *Specimen Days* in a section titled "My Preparations for Visits" of his own way of protecting against infectious diseases: "My habit, when practicable, was to prepare for starting out on one of those daily or nightly tours of from a couple to four or five hours by fortifying myself with previous rest, the bath, clean clothes, a good meal, and as cheerful an appearance as possible."

There were many organizations formed during the war for various purposes, including the improvement of medical treatment. The U.S. Sanitary Commission, founded shortly after the war began, conducted investigations and made improvements in sanitary conditions and medical practices. In charge of the Washington hospitals was Frederick Law Olmsted, Jr., who had an office at 244 F Street NW. His work was primarily devoted to organizing and managing shelters for the recovering wounded and for men who had recovered from wounds but were still unfit for returning to combat. The latter cases were housed at Camp Fry, the present site of George Washington University.

Another organization, the U.S. Christian Commission, was formed to treat the minds and souls of men wounded psychologically as well as physically. It would become the Young Men's Christian Association (YMCA).

Civil War hospitals   On arrival in Washington in January 1863—from his trip to Falmouth, Virginia, to check on his wounded brother—Whitman immediately began to make himself useful around the city's hospitals. There were at least 85 Washington, D.C., buildings used as hospitals during the war, including 14 churches. In *Specimen Days* he

names several of the buildings where soldiers were maintained, most on cots or makeshift beds, in rooms, in hallways, anywhere there was room, none of the buildings built for the purpose.

The "hospitals" mentioned most often by Whitman are the Old Patent Office Building, Armory Square Hospital, Campbell Hospital, the Washington Infirmary (Columbian), Carver Hospital, and Mount Pleasant Hospital. Whitman spent entire days moving from ward to ward and cot to cot, talking to the wounded men, often writing letters for them or reading aloud to individual soldiers or several at a time. See CIVIL WAR.

Louisa May Alcott was a nurse in the Union Hotel Hospital, at the corner of Gay and Washington Streets in Georgetown, and she wrote about her experiences in *Hospital Sketches* (1863). There is no evidence that she and Whitman met.

When the casualties from the First Battle of Bull Run (July 21, 1861) were taken to Washington (about 27 miles), the only available hospital was the Washington Infirmary at Judiciary Square. It was located on E Street between Fourth and Fifth Streets, at the rear of the Court House. The three-story brick building had been built in 1804 as a jail and became a medical facility in 1844, the first teaching hospital in Washington. It was part of Columbian College, which later became George Washington University. The military took it over at the beginning of the war, but its use was short-lived, because the hospital burned in November 1861; it reopened in 1863, still on E Street but between 12th and 13th Streets.

The Armory Square Hospital, which Whitman mentions in *Specimen Days*, was on the National Mall, where the Air and Space Museum is now. The armory had 1,000 beds, with pavilions and tents spread out across the mall as the building itself filled to capacity. In a note for *Specimen Days* dated February 4, 1863, Whitman wrote that he had gone "pretty thoroughly through Wards E and D." He had given out paper and envelopes to a number of wounded soldiers and wrote letters for a few who could not themselves write. He says he talked with two or three members of the BROOKLYN 14th Regiment. He also describes in some detail a lengthy operation he saw performed on a soldier from a New York regiment.

"There was an unusual cluster of surgeons, medical cadets, nurses, etc. around his bed—I thought the whole thing was done with tenderness, and done well." A wife was with another wounded soldier, a mother with another. The mother told Whitman that the boy was her youngest of seven children. Yet another soldier had been at Armory Square Hospital since Bull Run (probably the second battle on August 24, 1862). "A bullet had shot him right through the bladder, hitting him front, low in the belly, and coming out back. . . . There were other disagreeable circumstances. . . . At present comparatively comfortable, had a bad throat, was delighted with a stick of horehound candy I gave him, with one or two other trifles."

The Old Patent Office Building, taking up the two square blocks between F and G Streets and Seventh and Ninth Streets, was turned into military barracks and a hospital/morgue. Cots for the wounded were placed among the display cases, filled with models of patented inventions. Whitman was at the hospital on February 23, 1862, according to a note he wrote then and later used in an item in *Specimen Days* titled "Patent Office Hospital." He refers to it as "that noblest of Washington buildings," and he says that on his first visit it "was crowded close with rows of sick, badly wounded and dying soldiers." He remarks on the strangeness of mixing the cots with the glass cases full of "every kind of utensil, machine, or invention it ever entered into the mind of man to conceive."

Campbell Hospital, on Boundary Street, at the northern end of Fifth and Sixth Streets, NW, was another facility in which Whitman spent many hours. It had been built as a barracks for cavalry and was located at the northern extremity of the city, near the end of Seventh Street. It was at the end of a horse railway route, which is how Whitman got there. There were 11 wards with a capacity of 600 beds. There were several small buildings nearby the main buildings that served as nurses' quarters, guard rooms, "Negro quarters," and a dead house. Whitman wrote a note about a visit to Campbell dated January 30, 1863, for *Specimen Days* about "cleaning up the ward, and giving the men all clean clothes— through the ward (6), the patients dressing or being dressed—the naked upper half of the bodies—the

good humor and fun—the shirts, drawers, sheets of beds, etc. and the general fixing up for Sunday." In a later note he wrote that the wounded were "largely from the West. Most of them are entirely without friends or acquaintances here—no familiar face, and hardly a word of judicious sympathy or cheer, through their sometimes long and tedious sickness, or the pangs of aggravated wounds."

The United States Capitol itself was used as a hospital, with 2,000 cots set up in the House and Senate chambers, even in the Rotunda. The first wounded arrived at the Capitol building after the second battle of Bull Run (August 24, 1862) and after Antietam (September 17, 1862). In the two battles there were approximately 26,000 federal troops killed and about 18,000 confederates. At one time during the war there were more wounded soldiers in Washington hospitals than there were citizens.

F Street from the White House to Sixth Street was where many of Washington's upscale stores were located during the 1860s, but there were a number of medical offices as well, including the Georgetown University Medical Department at the corner of 10th Street, used throughout the war as a hospital. Dr. Robert Stone, President LINCOLN's doctor, had his office in his home at the corner of F and 14th, not far from Ford's Theatre. Several other medical organizations would move to F Street after the war.

Another important Civil War hospital was the Lincoln General Hospital, on East Capitol at 15th Street. It opened in December 1862 as a facility for more than 2,500 beds; it included 20 elongated buildings that formed a V on the grounds, plus 25 tent wards.

St. Elizabeths Hospital, located at what is now 2700 Martin Luther King, Jr., Avenue, was called the Government Hospital for the Insane when it was built in 1855. During the Civil War, the soldiers treated there called it St. Elizabeths (the name of the land on which it stood) in order to avoid the stigma of "insane asylum." The name was officially changed by an Act of Congress in 1916. Three hundred Civil War soldiers, federal and confederate, are buried in a cemetery at St. Elizabeths.

The Armed Forces Institute of Pathology was founded as a museum in 1862, the purpose of which was to collect pathological information from Civil War casualties in order to confirm army pension records.

The Army Medical Museum was founded in 1862 as a source of information for improving Civil War medical conditions. Now called the National Museum of Health and Medicine at 6900 Georgia Avenue, the museum has more than a million items of archival materials and medical research collections, including items from the Civil War.

Columbia Hospital for Women was not opened until 1870, but it had an important connection to the war: 20 of the 50 beds in the hospital were reserved for the wives and widows of federal soldiers who had fought in the war. The hospital was also needed as a medical facility for the hundreds of women who went to Washington after the war looking for missing family members.

Ford's Theatre, at 511 10th Street, was not used as a hospital during the war, but after Lincoln's assassination it was closed, remodeled, and used by the army for postwar medical work of the Surgeon General's Office, including the Civil War medical records archives, the Army Medical Museum, and offices for the preparation for publication of *The Medical and Surgical History of the War of the Rebellion.*

Clapp, Henry (1814–1875) New York City journalist, editor of the SATURDAY PRESS and one of the leaders of the PFAFF'S CELLAR group of Bohemian writers, including Whitman, who gathered regularly at the restaurant at 653 Broadway in New York. Clapp was called the "King of Bohemia."

He was one of the few editors who reviewed favorably Whitman's *Leaves of Grass* in its early editions. Clapp, who often wrote under the name "Figaro," wrote *Leaves from an Editor's Portfolio* (1846). He was referred to by a friend as "one of the most sparkling cynical wits that ever worked on the American press."

Clare, Ada (1836–1874) Pseudonym of Jane McElheney, a New York City writer, nicknamed the "Queen of Bohemia," because she was a "beautiful" member of the group of writers who met regularly at PFAFF'S CELLAR in New York to talk about writing and literature. She wrote poetry and short stories for city magazines and newspapers, and when the Pfaff's group began to drift away or die off, she became a Broadway actress.

cluster A term Whitman used to describe a group of poems under a particular heading and with similar subject matter. There were 12 "clusters" of poems in the sixth and final edition of *Leaves of Grass* (1881): "Inscriptions" (24 poems), "Children of Adam" (16 poems), "Calamus" (39 poems), "Birds of Passage" (7), "Sea-Drift" (11), "By The Roadside" (29), "Drum-Taps" (43), "Memories of President Lincoln" (4), "Autumn Rivulets" (38), "Whispers of Heavenly Death" (18), "From Noon to Starry Night" (22), and "Songs of Parting" (17).

The "cluster" idea apparently came to Whitman during a rush of poetic activity between 1857 and 1859. The second edition of *Leaves of Grass* (1856) contained 20 new poems, plus the 12 poems of the first edition (1855). But by the time he was prepared to go to press with the third edition (1860), he had added 146 new poems and had organized some of the poems into clusters. From the beginning, however, the clusters were only roughly organized by single themes. One could argue that the whole of the finished *Leaves of Grass* is a single cluster of approximately 400 poems, all on the theme of America, a new nation with its democratic ideals on display for Americans and for the world. Yet even that suggestion of a general theme oversimplifies and perhaps even diminishes the poetic value of *Leaves of Grass* and of individual poems. The book and its poems were in an almost constant state of revision, Whitman adding, subtracting, and rearranging during the next several printings of *Leaves,* arriving at the final form only with the 1881 edition.

The "Calamus" cluster was probably the most successful in the 1860 edition, but by the fifth edition (1871) even it had been reduced to 39 poems from the original 45. The poems were generally about the sensual love of men for one another, the subject of homosexuality causing a great deal of controversy. There is little evidence, however, that the changes Whitman made to the Calamus poems during the next several years were the result of the controversy. The poems in the "Children of Adam" cluster, titled "Enfans d'Adam" for the third edition, were about heterosexual love, the sensuality of those poems also controversial. But the early criticism of the poems in both of these clusters tended to miss the larger thematic idea of the importance of love itself as central to a working DEMOCRACY.

There were also in the final edition 25 poems published separately from the clusters. And there were three "Annexes," groups of poems (but not referred to as clusters) published in later printings of *Leaves of Grass* but added only at the back of the book: "Sands at Seventy" (58 poems), "Good-Bye My Fancy" (31 poems), and "Old Age Echoes" (13 poems), the latter group added by Whitman executor Horace Traubel (with the poet's permission) for the first posthumous printing of *Leaves of Grass* (1897).

Columbian Magazine (1786–?) Philadelphia literary monthly magazine, founded in 1786 by a local group of writers, including Mathew Carey and Francis Hopkinson. In its early history it was known as the most attractive journal of its time, using copperplate engravings to illustrate its stories.

In its later history it became the UNIVERSAL ASYLUM AND COLUMBIAN MAGAZINE and carried three of Whitman's short stories: "Eris: A Spirit Record" (March 1844), "Dumb Kate: An Early Death" (May 1844), and "The Little Sleighers" (September 1844). It also published an early Whitman essay on New York City, "A Sketch of a Winter Morning on the Battery" (September 1844).

Cooper Public School Whitman read "An Old Man's Thought of School" at the inauguration of Cooper Public School in Camden, New Jersey, October 31, 1874. The school was located at the corner of Third and State Streets in Camden, the site today of the Coopers Poynt School.

The poem was published in the NEW YORK DAILY GRAPHIC (November 3, 1874) with a note of explanation: "The following poem was recited personally by the author Saturday afternoon, October 31, at the inauguration of the fine new Cooper Public School, Camden, New Jersey." The subtitle

in the final version reads, *"For the Inauguration of a Public School, Camden, New Jersey, 1874."*

In the poem the poet reminds his audience that just as a church is not a "pile of brick and mortar," but a preacher and the people, so a school is not just a building but a teacher and the pupils.

Cosmopolitan (1886–present) Magazine founded by Paul J. Schlicht and first published in Rochester, New York, by the firm of Schlicht & Field. It was advertised as a "first-class family magazine," a monthly, edited for the first three years by Frank P. Smith.

Schlicht and Smith moved the publication to New York in its second year and Smith almost immediately accepted for publication Whitman's poem "Shakspere—Bacon's Cipher" (October 1887). A decade or so later *Cosmopolitan* would accept for first publication H. G. Wells's novels *The War of the Worlds* (1897) and *The First Man in the Moon* (1900–01).

Critic (1881–1906) Founded as a New York politically independent biweekly magazine by Jeannette and Joseph Gilder, who were also its editors. Their primary interest was in articles about American culture. Whitman was a leading contributor, writing a series of articles titled "How I Get Around at Sixty, and Take Notes," which began with the *Critic*'s first issue. He also wrote "Walt Whitman in Camden" for the journal, but signed it "George Selwyn."

Jeannette Gilder is quoted as saying in a letter that "one of the things of which I am most proud is that the *Critic* was the first publication of its class to invite Walt Whitman to contribute to its pages."

The journal published no fiction but used short poems as fillers, including the following six poems by Whitman: "Spirit That Form'd This Scene" (September 10, 1881); "The Dead Tenor" (November 8, 1884); "Yonnondio" (November 26, 1887); "To the Year 1889" (January 5, 1889), later titled "To the Pending Year"; and "The Pallid Wreath" (January 1891).

D

Daily Plebeian (1842–1845) This Democratic organ had bought out the *NEW YORK AURORA* and the *NEW YORK DEMOCRAT,* among other papers, and was absorbed itself by the *New York Morning News* in 1845. During its three-year life span, it published three of Whitman's essays, in 1842 and 1843.

Davis, Mary O. (1837–1908) Housekeeper of Whitman's home at 328 Mickle Street in Camden, New Jersey, for the last six years of his life. In his will, Whitman gave Mrs. Davis permission to "occupy" the Mickle Street house for a year after his death, "free of rent, provided, however, that she pay the taxes for said year on said premises."

democracy, Whitman's vision of Perhaps the most important key to understanding Whitman's *Leaves of Grass* is to understand his vision for American democracy. His idea encompassed three basic principles.

First, people must be individualistic, capable of thinking for themselves, yet at the same time act as an integral part of the whole fabric of society. "One's-Self I sing, a simple separate person, / Yet utter the word Democratic, the word En-Masse." The poet did not make these the first lines of the first poem in *Leaves of Grass* without reason; they could pass for the theme of the book. Individualism, Whitman wrote in *Democratic Vistas* gives "character to the idea of the aggregate." And "it is mainly or altogether to serve independent separatism that we favor a strong generalization, consolidation."

Second, equality was for Whitman an essential ingredient of democracy. Without it the first principle would mean nothing. The SLAVERY issue and the lack of women's rights were constant reminders for Whitman that democracy did not yet exist in

Whitman's home at 328 Mickle Street, Camden, New Jersey *(Library of Congress, Prints and Photographs Division)*

the growing nation and that it would not exist until all people were equal, educated so they could think for themselves and be a part of the whole of American society. The poems reflect the poet's attitude toward WOMEN better than they do his attitude toward slavery. There are few lines in the poetry that mention the word "man" or a derivative of it without the word "woman" or a derivative. In "A Song of Joys," for example, he writes, "O the horseman's and horsewoman's joys!" "I am the poet of the woman the same as the man," he says in "Song of Myself."

On the slavery issue, Whitman was considerably more ambivalent. From the early 1850s he feared that slavery might divide the nation, and the preservation of the Union was more important to him than was the slavery issue by itself. The CIVIL WAR was devastating, both for the nation and for Whitman's concept of democracy. He must have recognized the paradox: How could the black man or woman be "equal" as long as they were enslaved? Yet how could the "Union" survive a war of secession?

Third, America could not make an important contribution to world history without developing a national literature. American literature to the middle of the 19th century had remained English; American writers, especially the poets, were still under the influence of the romantic movement, which was alive and well in the British Isles. The need for a national literature was one of the elements of *Leaves of Grass* that so caught EMERSON's attention and which initiated his letter to Whitman declaring his admiration for the poems. He said in the letter, "I find it [*Leaves of Grass*] the most extraordinary piece of wit and wisdom that America has yet contributed."

In *Democratic Vistas* Whitman wrote that a national literature was essential if America was to become a world leader.

> The problems of the achievements of this crowning stage through future first-class National Singers, Orators, Artists, and others—of creating in literature an *imaginative* New World, the correspondent and counterpart of the current Scientific and Political New Worlds—and the perhaps distant, but still delightful prospect, (for our children, if not in our own day,) of delivering America, and, indeed, all Christian lands everywhere, from the thin, moribund, and watery, but appallingly extensive nuisance of conventional poetry—by putting something really alive and substantial in its place. . . .

If America was to achieve democracy through equality it must break from the European class system, which he considered one of the great concerns to people everywhere. "There can be no greater [danger] than having certain portions of the people set off from the rest by a line drawn—[having some people] not privileged as others, but degraded, humiliated, made of no account." It is the "average man of a land at last," Whitman says, who is important. And he writes that it is the "average" individual who is "of greatest concern only in a democratic society."

The best way to express these principles of democracy, he says, is through imaginative literature—written or oral stories. The "songs [that is, poems], aesthetics, etc., of a country are of importance principally because they furnish the materials and suggestions of personality for the women and men of that country, and enforce them in a thousand effective ways."

Whitman wrote in the preface to the first edition of *Leaves of Grass* (1855) that the "United States themselves are essentially the greatest poem. . . . Here is not merely a nation but a teeming nation of Nations. . . . The attitude of great poets is to cheer up slaves and horrify despots. . . . Liberty relies upon itself, invites no one, promises nothing, sits in calmness and light, is positive and composed, and knows no discouragement."

The poet was not naïve enough to believe that his vision for democracy would ever become reality, and during the Civil War he must have found it difficult to stay "positive and composed." The notes he made during the war—most of them while he worked as a hospital attendant in Washington, D.C., and which would appear in his *Memoranda During the War* (1875–76) and *Specimen Days* (1882)—show little "discouragement"; yet the notes are full of so many one-on-one experiences with severely wounded and dying men that he must have felt the weight of a failed social system, the core of which allowed for an underclass of blacks and women.

Whitman's ambivalence and the potential national conflicts aside, however, the idea of democracy has never been better explained than in Whitman's essays on democracy and in *Leaves of Grass.*

Democratic Review, The (1837–1859) Journal devoted primarily to public affairs, published first in Washington and then moved to New York in 1841. Its official title was *United States Magazine and Democratic Review.* John L. O'Sullivan, founder and editor, was most noted for coining the phrase "manifest destiny." He published literary contributions from such mid-19th century writers as Hawthorne, Longfellow, Whittier, BRYANT, Lowell, Poe, and Whitman.

The *Democratic Review* published nine of Whitman's short stories: "Death in the School-Room (A Fact)" (August 1841), "Wild Frank's Return" (November 1841), "Bervance: or, Father and Son" (December 1841), "The Tomb Blossoms" (January 1842), "The Last of the Sacred Army" (March 1842), "The Child-Ghost: A Story of the Last Loyalist" (May 1842), "A Legend of Life and Love" (July 1842), "The Angel of Tears" (September 1842), and "Revenge and Requital; A Tale of a Murderer Escaped" (July–August 1845).

Dial, The (1840–1844) A quarterly journal published in support of the New England transcendentalist movement from July 1840 to April 1844 (see TRANSCENDENTALISM). It was edited first by Margaret Fuller and later by Ralph Waldo EMERSON. Contributions included essays and poems by Henry David THOREAU and Bronson ALCOTT as well as works by Fuller and Emerson. The magazine was restarted in 1888 in Chicago, continuing its support of the transcendental system of thought.

Donizetti, Gaetano (1797–1848) Italian OPERA composer, perhaps best known for *Lucia di Lammermoor* (1835). In "Italian Music in Dakota," Whitman makes a brief reference to the "ecstatic chorus" in Donizetti's lesser-known opera *Poliuto,*

which he revised and retitled *Les Martyrs* (1840). Whitman loved opera and lived during a great period of New York City opera venues and traveling opera companies (see NEW YORK OPERA HOUSES).

Doyle, Peter (1847–1907) An Irish immigrant and Confederate soldier, he was employed in Washington after the war as a streetcar conductor and railroad worker. He was 18 years old and living in Alexandria, Virginia, when he and Whitman first met in Washington in December 1865. He became Whitman's "beloved male friend." Doyle had been captured by Northern troops during the war and imprisoned in Washington. He was at Ford's Theatre on April 14, 1865, when President LINCOLN was shot.

After the war Doyle took a job as horse-car conductor on the Washington-Georgetown Line in the District of Columbia, and Whitman was his only customer on a December evening ride, the poet heading back to his apartment. According to a letter Doyle wrote to Whitman biographer John BURROUGHS, the two men were "familiar at once" and Whitman did not get off at his own stop but, instead, he "went all the way back with me"— "back" meaning, perhaps, back to the horse-car barns at the Navy Yard on the Anacostia.

Doyle was uneducated but in need of a father figure, and Whitman filled that role during the next 27 years. He often referred to Pete as his "darling son." But Doyle was not interested in Whitman's poetry, a constant source of disappointment for the poet.

Once, when they both thought Pete might have syphilis (but which turned out to be a shaving rash), Whitman told him he was a "little too fond . . . of the women."

The poet wrote a letter from BROOKLYN, dated August 21, 1869, in which he says that he "was unspeakably shocked and repelled from you by that talk and proposition of yours—you know what— there by the fountain. It seemed indeed to me, (for I will talk out plain to you, dearest comrade) that the one I loved, and who had always been so manly and sensible, was gone, and a fool and intentional suicide stood in his place. I spoke so sternly and cutting. (Though I see now that my words might have appeared to have a certain other meaning, which I didn't dream of—insulting to you, never for one moment in my thoughts.) But will say no more of this—for I know such thoughts must have come when you was not yourself but in a moment of derangement,—and have passed away like a bad dream." It is clear here that Doyle had threatened suicide, which "shocked" Whitman, but it is not clear what the poet meant by his parenthetical acknowledgement that his "cutting" words might have carried "a certain other meaning." This is one of several ambiguous statements in letters Whitman wrote to young male friends that may contain "code" words implying HOMOSEXUALITY.

Later, in Camden, Whitman told some friends that Pete was "a great big hearty full-blooded everyday divinely generous working man: a hail fellow well met—a little too fond of his beer, now and then, and of the women." Doyle was one of four friends who sat up with Whitman after his stroke in 1873, and he was present in Camden for the "viewing" of Whitman's body on March 30, 1892, the day of the poet's funeral. Doyle referred to Whitman as his "affectionate father and comrade."

There were several other young men with whom Whitman corresponded with affection, including Jack Flood, Lewy BROWN, Harry STAFFORD, Ed Cattell, Thomas SAWYER, Bill Duckett, Fred VAUGHAN, and Johnny Lee, all laborers and barely literate. In a letter to Doyle, Whitman referred to Lee as "my dear darling boy." Whitman's relationship with Doyle lasted longer, however, and seemed stronger than that with any of the other young men.

Peter Doyle is something of an enigma. There was affection between the two men that biographers believe went beyond the "normal," and some quote letters between Whitman and Doyle as evidence of a homosexual relationship. Whitman wrote "love letters" to both men and women— though mostly to young men—and the poetry of *Leaves of Grass* makes clear that he had great love for all people, regardless of gender, race, or station in life.

There may well have been a sexual relationship between Doyle and Whitman, but there is no evidence beyond the letters. Whitman bragged about

Whitman with his Confederate friend Peter Doyle, 1865 *(Library of Congress, Prints and Photographs Division)*

having fathered children, six by at least one report, but there is no further evidence there either. Nor is there evidence of more than a platonic relationship with Anne GILCHRIST, who certainly loved Whitman and kept a bedroom for him during her three-year stay in a rented house in Philadelphia while she was visiting from England—a bedroom he used often. See also Ellen EYRE, a "mysterious" woman who wrote a passionate love letter to Whitman but who is otherwise virtually unknown.

It is just as well perhaps that there is no concrete evidence of a sexual relationship with Peter Doyle. It might diminish the value of the love Whitman shows in his poetry for all humankind. Whitman was his own best example of the ultimate democratic persona, the main character in the poems of the "Children of Adam" and "Calamus" clusters in *Leaves of Grass.*

Duckett, Bill (unknown)   One of Whitman's young male admirers. See DOYLE, PETER.

E

Eakins, Thomas (1844–1916) Philadelphia artist, best known for his paintings of sports, especially rowing. In July 1887 he painted Whitman's portrait. Whitman said that Eakins was not just a mere painter but "a force." The day after Whitman died on March 26, 1892, Eakins and one of his pupils did a death mask.

Eldridge, Charles (unknown) Of THAYER & ELDRIDGE Publishers in Boston, one of Whitman's longtime friends. During the CIVIL WAR, Eldridge, who was an assistant to the Union Army paymaster, and another Whitman friend, William O'CONNOR, a clerk on the Light-House Board in Washington, lent Whitman money and managed a military pass

Horse and carriage donated to Whitman by friends in 1885. He hired Bill Duckett to drive it, and in spite of several illnesses, Walt was able to get around Camden fairly easily. *(Library of Congress, Prints and Photographs Division)*

so he could go to Virginia in search of his brother George, who had been wounded but was still with his regiment in Falmouth. Eldridge even hired Whitman as a part-time copyist in the army paymaster's office. He was one of the four Whitman friends (with Peter DOYLE, Nelly O'Connor, and John BURROUGHS) who sat up with the poet after his stroke in 1873.

Emerson, Ralph Waldo (1803–1882)   American essayist, poet, and philosopher, the leading interpreter of TRANSCENDENTALISM for Americans. He is perhaps better known generally, however, for his philosophical essay "Self-Reliance" and his oration at Harvard University in 1837, titled "The AMERICAN SCHOLAR." He is best known in Whitman studies, however, for his letter to the poet after reading *Leaves of Grass* in 1855. Emerson had written in 1850 that "the Poet of America is not yet come. When he comes he will sing differently." When he read *Leaves of Grass* five years later he thought his wish might already have come true, and he wrote a letter to Whitman immediately (perhaps the most famous letter in American literary history), saying to him, "I greet you at the beginning of a great career," a statement Emerson would later regret but not retract.

He was a Harvard graduate and became an ordained Unitarian minister in 1829 but resigned from the ministry three years later, in part because of the death of his wife in 1831 which brought about doubts concerning some Christian doctrines, but he had by that time also become particularly disenchanted with Unitarian ideas about the role of the spirit in human lives.

Emerson traveled in Europe during 1832–33 and met Thomas CARLYLE, William Wordsworth, and Samuel Taylor Coleridge, all of whom were enthusiastic about transcendentalism, a philosophy of idealism based in sources among German writers, especially Johann Wolfgang Goethe.

Emerson became the "father" of American transcendentalism with the publication of a 96-page book titled *Nature* (1836). The essay reveals Emerson's reevaluation of the traditional ideas about God and nature. He argues that people have the ability to "transcend" the material world of the senses and

Ralph Waldo Emerson, leader of the New England philosophers and one of the few readers of the first edition of *Leaves of Grass* (1855) who understood the depth of Whitman's book *(Library of Congress, Prints and Photographs Division)*

become aware of the all-pervading spirit of the universe and the potential it offers for human freedom. No wonder he and Whitman connected so easily. Nearly everything Emerson wrote after 1836 was an extension of the ideas explored in *Nature*. And *Leaves of Grass* is full of similar ideas, especially about the transcendent spirit of the universe.

The New England poet was one of few critics who praised *Leaves of Grass* when it was published in 1855; luckily for Whitman, he was also the most important critic, since his influence on other poets, both in America and abroad, was substantial. His famous letter to Whitman is dated July 21, 1855, written not more than two weeks after the book's publication.

The letter began, "Dear Sir—I am not blind to the worth of the wonderful gift of *Leaves of Grass*. I find it the most extraordinary piece of wit and wisdom that America has yet contributed. I am very happy in reading it, as great power makes us happy. . . ."

Here are more excerpts:

I give you joy of your free and brave thought. I have great joy in it. I find incomparable things said incomparably well, as they must be. I find the courage of treatment which so delights us, and which large perception only can inspire.

I greet you at the beginning of a great career, which yet must have had a long foreground somewhere, for such a start. I rubbed my eyes a little, to see if this sunbeam were no illusion; but the solid sense of the book is a sober certainty. It has the best merits, namely, of fortifying and encouraging.

I did not know until I last night saw the book advertised in a newspaper that I could trust the name as real and available for a post-office. I wish to see my benefactor, and have felt much like striking my tasks and visiting New York to pay you my respects.

The letter was signed, R. W. Emerson.

Leaves of Grass had not received particularly good reviews, so it is no wonder that Whitman not only treasured Emerson's letter but caused it to be printed in full in the NEW YORK TRIBUNE. He used quotations from it in promoting the second edition a year later and reprinted it at the back of the book, along with a thank-you letter addressed to "dear Friend and Master." He also had the printers place at the bottom of the book's spine the key quotation: "I Greet You at the / Beginning of A / Great Career / R W Emerson."

Whitman had not, however, asked Emerson for permission to reprint or quote the letter, certainly an unmannerly act on Whitman's part. The Concord poet, though certainly enchanted by *Leaves of Grass*, was not pleased at being used by Whitman in order to brag about himself and his poetry. Emerson told a friend that if he had known his letter would be published he would have toned down some of his enthusiasm. A Boston newspaper editor referred to Whitman's self-publicity at Emerson's expense as "the grossest violation of literary comity and courtesy that ever passed under our notice."

Emerson had written to Longfellow that Whitman had "done a strange rude thing in printing in the Tribune . . . my letter of thanks for his book."

There is some dispute over just how angry Emerson was, but, once he realized that many of his friends did not understand Whitman's poetry and so found it easy to criticize, Emerson certainly defended the poems. He wrote a letter to Thomas CARLYLE (May 6, 1856) in which he refers to *Leaves of Grass* as a "nondescript monster" that "was indisputably American. . . . It is called *Leaves of Grass,*—was written and printed by a journeyman printer in BROOKLYN, New York, named Walter Whitman," and he promised to send a copy to Carlyle, telling him, "and after you have looked into it, if you think, as you may, that it is only an auctioneer's inventory of a warehouse, you can light your pipe with it."

One of Emerson's friends, Charles Norton, thought the book was too graphic and coarse, but he also understood why Emerson liked it. He told their mutual friend, James Russell Lowell, that Emerson liked it because Whitman had evidently read Emerson and so was a mix of "Concord philosopher and New York fireman." Emerson thought that *Leaves of Grass* was "the American poem." He referred to *Leaves* as "that wonderful book—with all its formlessness & faults."

In a later lecture Emerson would speak of the "oversoul" of *Leaves of Grass*; he had written an essay entitled "The Oversoul" (1841) in which he discusses the great "Unity within which every man's particular being is contained and made one with all other." This concept of the soul was certainly one of Whitman's major poetic themes.

Emerson was so respected in New England that his excitement over *Leaves of Grass* apparently generated train tickets into New York for a number of writers curious to meet the "journeyman printer."

The more liberal of New England writers went to New York almost immediately. ALCOTT, THOREAU, and Moncure Conway, one of the younger "radicals," were among the early visitors to Whitman's Brooklyn home. Emerson was in New York in December 1855 and invited Whitman to his hotel for dinner—this first meeting of the two men is dated by Emerson biographer Gay Wilson Allen as December 11.

The influence of Emerson on Whitman is clear. Allen, who also wrote a critical biography of Whitman, summed up the two men: "Walt Whitman, Emerson's disciple, later wanted to make his own life a poem. Emerson set the example by wanting to make his life a sermon." Whitman wrote about the influence in a letter to John Trowbridge in 1860, "I was simmering, simmering, simmering; Emerson brought me to a boil."

Eyre, Ellen (unknown) The "mysterious" New York actress, who was in Whitman's life for not longer than three months in 1862 but who left a love letter as evidence of a "relationship," if not a sexual encounter. The letter is dated March 25, 1862, and reads, in part:

> My Dear Mr. Whitman: I fear you took me last night for a female privateer. It is time I was sailing under my true colors,—but then today I assume you cared nothing piratical though I would joyfully have made your heart a captive. . . . A gold mine may be found by the divining rod, but there is no such instrument for detecting in the crowded streets of a great city the unknown mine of latent affection a man may have unconsciously inspired in a woman's breast. I make these explanations in extenuation not by way of apology. . . .

Hypocrisy is said to be the homage that sin pays to virtue, and yet I can see no vice in that generous sympathy in which we share our caprices with those who inspired us with tenderness. I trust you will think well enough of me soon to renew the pleasure you afforded me last p.m. and I therefore write to remind you that this is a sensible head as well as a sympathetic heart, both of which would gladly evolve with warmth for your diversion and comfort. You have already my whereabouts and hours. It shall only depend on you to make them yours and me the happiest of women.

The letter is signed: "I am always your sincerely, Ellen Eyre."

She was a married actress, but that and the letter are all anyone seems to know about the "mysterious" woman. Whitman mentions having told a Frank Sweeney the "whole story" about Ellen Eyre, but Sweeney apparently kept to himself whatever secret there was to keep, and Whitman does not mention her in any of his letters. Apparently there was a photograph of an actress on his mantel at the Mickle Street house in Camden, a woman he referred to as an "old sweetheart of mine," but biographers can only guess at her identity or at her relationship with Whitman. By the time he was in Camden he also bragged about having fathered six children.

F

Fern, Fanny (1811–1872)   The pen name of Sara Parton (Sara Payson Willis; her original name was Grata Payson Willis). She was one of the most popular American women writers of the 19th century and one of the first women journalists. She published essays of a domestic nature for Boston and New York periodicals. Her book of these articles, *Fern Leaves from Fanny's Port-Folio* (1853), sold more than 100,000 copies. She also wrote several best-selling books, including a biting satire, *Ruth Hall* (1855), and *A New Story Book for Children* (1865).

In 1856 she married James PARTON, who had published a popular biography of the NEW YORK TRIBUNE's Horace Greeley the year before. He was her third husband. James and Whitman were friends, and Sara soon became enamored of the poet. She praised *Leaves of Grass* in one of her articles and offered to Whitman "the cordial grasp of a woman's hand."

The Partons became involved in the only legal case taken against Whitman and one that damaged further the poet's moral character, already diminished in the minds of many because of his poems. In early 1857 Whitman had some financial problems, and James Parton offered to lend the poet $200. The friendship ended sometime before the note came due in the late spring, probably, biographers believe, because of Parton's jealousy over Whitman's relationship with Sara.

One of Sara's lawyers, Oliver Dyer, accepted the note at her request, went to Whitman's house on Classon Avenue in BROOKLYN, and took several items (books and at least one painting) in what

Whitman believed to be full payment of the loan. It isn't clear whether Dyer failed to give the receipt to Parton or even if there was a receipt, or if Parton was still angry at Whitman. He sued nevertheless, and it became something of a scandal and a significant embarrassment for Whitman.

When Whitman biographer William Sloane KENNEDY looked at the details shortly after the poet's death, he concluded that Sara had been "sweet" on Whitman but had suddenly developed for him an "unquenchable spite," perhaps because he had rejected her. Ellen O'Connor, a friend of Whitman and one of Kennedy's sources, told him he should read the Potiphar story in the Bible. The story is in both the Bible and the Koran: Potiphar was Joseph's master in Egypt, and when Joseph rejected the advances of Potiphar's wife, she accused him of attempted rape, and Potiphar put him in prison (Genesis 39).

In May Whitman had become editor of the BROOKLYN DAILY TIMES, and he wrote an editorial (July 9, 1857) stating that "one genuine woman is worth a dozen Fanny Ferns." What anger Whitman showed as a result of the embarrassment over the loan was clearly directed not at Parton but at his wife.

fiction, Whitman's   Whitman is credited with writing a novel, *Franklin Evans*, and 24 short stories, 23 for publication between 1841 and 1847. According to Thomas L. Brasher in *Walt Whitman: The Early Poems and the Fiction* (1963), another Whitman story, "Lingave's Temptation," which may have been the first chapter of a novel, has not been identified by place or date of publication but was thought to have been published also during the 1840s.

Whitman's attempts at writing fiction mostly failed, at least by 21st-century standards. The stories carried rather obvious moral meanings that would pass as sermons today. Readers familiar with the author's poetry, almost none of which is as superficial or sentimental as the fiction, must wonder at the difference between the two genres.

There is also a fairy-tale feeling to nearly all of the short stories. Story openings tend to establish this atmosphere. Here is the opening, for example, to "Dumb Kate": "It was a quaint, comfortable, ancient house, that tavern. Huge buttonwood trees embow-er'd it round about, and there was a long porch in front, the trellis'd work whereof, though old and moulder'd, had been, and promised still to be for years, held together by the tangled folds of a grape vine wreath'd about it like a tremendous serpent."

Whitman changed the titles of several of his stories in later printings; in part II, the novel is entitled *Franklin Evans; or the Inebriate: A Tale of The Times*. The short stories are listed as follows: "The Angel of Tears," "Bervance: or, Father and Son," "The Boy Lover," "The Child and the Profligate," "Death in the School-Room," "Dumb Kate," "The Love of Eris: A Spirit Record," "The Half-Breed: A Tale of the Western Frontier," "The Last Loyalist," "The Last of the Sacred Army," "A Legend of Life and Love," "Lingave's Temptation," "The Little Sleighers," "The Madman," "My Boys and Girls," "One Wicked Impulse!," "Reuben's Last Wish," "Richard Parker's Widow," "The Shadow and the Light of a Young Man's Soul," "Shirval: A Tale of Jerusalem," "The Tomb Blossoms," "Wild Frank's Return," and "Some Fact-Romances." Two other stories, "The Death of Wind-Foot" and "Little Jane" are included also in part II of this book, although both were embedded in Whitman's novel, *Franklin Evans*.

Flood, Jack (unknown)   One of Whitman's young admirers. See DOYLE, PETER.

Florida War (1836–1843)   Started by the U.S. government as a way to remove the Indian tribes in Florida to land west of the Mississippi River. By the end of the war nearly 5,000 Indians had been moved—at the cost of the lives of 1,500 U.S. soldiers, $20 million, and a great deal of suffering on the part of the Seminole, Cherokee, and Mikasukis tribes.

Osceola, a leader of the Seminoles, was captured during the war and sent to Fort Moultrie on Sullivan's Island near Charleston, South Carolina. Osceola died on January 30, 1838, of what Whitman called a broken heart in his poem "Osceola."

Forney's Progress (1871–1875)   Founded as a powerful Republican weekly magazine in Philadelphia by John W. Forney, a famous politician and newspaper editor in that city. Its format was attractive, but it was not able to establish much of a literary reputation. Whitman published one poem in its pages, "A Riddle Song" (April 17, 1880).

Fowler, Lorenzo Niles (1811–1896)   Brother of Orson Squire FOWLER, the founder of FOWLER & WELLS Co. in Brooklyn during the second quarter of the 19th century. The brothers were phrenologists, a subject that interested Whitman for a time, and he had his head read by Lorenzo Fowler during the summer of 1849. He produced a "chart of bumps" for Whitman that indicated "amativeness" (sexual love), "philoprogenitiveness" (love of mankind), and "adhesiveness" (lasting friendship, especially with other men), all of which were types of love that Whitman incorporated into his poetry.

Fowler, Orson Squire (1809–1887)   Founder of FOWLER & WELLS Co. He and his brother, Lorenzo Niles FOWLER, took in a partner, Samuel R. Wells, in 1844. The Fowlers were phrenologists, and most of the books published by the firm were about phrenology. Orson Fowler wrote two books on the subject: *Physiology, Animal and Mental* and *Memory and Intellectual Development*.

Fowler & Wells Co.   Orson FOWLER and Samuel Wells were BROOKLYN distributors of the first edition of *Leaves of Grass* (1855) and publishers of the second edition (1856). Whitman told a friend,

Sarah Tyndale, that he was trying to find someone else to publish the second edition, that "Fowler and Wells are bad persons for me. They retard my book very much."

Because of the publicity of the first edition—a Boston legal officer declared the poems to be immoral—Fowler & Wells took no credit in print as publishers of Whitman's book. The firm's founder, Orson Squire Fowler was a phrenologist, and phrenology was the subject of most of the books under the Fowler & Wells imprint. A brother, Lorenzo Niles FOWLER, helped start the company circa 1840, which took on Samuel R. Wells as a partner in 1844. The publishers went out of business in 1863.

The two brothers were also editors and publishers of the *American Phrenological Journal*.

Fox, George (1624–1691)   English religious reformer and founder of the Religious Society of Friends on Cape Cod in 1657. He is quoted by Whitman in the poem "An Old Man's Thought of School" as having "rais'd his warning cry" that a church is not the "brick and mortar," but the people in it. So it is with a school building, Whitman says in the poem: the teachers and students are more important than the building. The poem was read by the poet at the inauguration of the COOPER PUBLIC SCHOOL in Camden, New Jersey, October 31, 1874.

free verse   The term *free verse* originated from the French term *vers libre*, coined by French poets of the symbolist movement during the last 30 years of the 19th century. Free verse is poetry "free" of the traditional rules of versification, and it has been one of the major verse forms in English since World War I. It is the poetic form used most often by Whitman.

The *Oxford English Dictionary* defines free verse as "Poetic writing in which the traditional rules of prosody, esp. those of metre and rhyme, are disregarded in favour of variable rhythms and line lengths." It gives as the first use of the term a quotation from the 1902 *Encyclopaedia Britannica*, stating that "M. Vielé-Riffin and M. Gustave Kahn gave us vers libres which, but for their typographi-

cal arrangement, are indistinguishable from prose." Free verse is as old as the Hebrew poetry of the Old Testament, particularly the Psalms and Song of Solomon, and was used by a number of 19th- and 20th-century poets, particularly Whitman, but also including, among others, Stephen Crane, Ezra Pound, Carl Sandburg, William Carlos Williams, Marianne Moore, D. H. Lawrence, E. E. Cummings, and T. S. Eliot.

Free verse is described by William Flint Thrall, Addison Hibbard, and C. Hugh Holman in *A Handbook to Literature* as having an "irregular metrical pattern, [and a] use of cadence rather than uniform metrical feet. Even though free verse does not follow the regular rhythm of the usual poetry, it has great possibilities for subtle effects; in fact this freedom to secure a variety of rhythmical effects instead of one is the chief justification for the existence of the form. Free verse lives in greater rhythmical units than conventional verse. In conventional verse the unit is the foot, or, perhaps, the line; in free verse the unit is the stanza. . . ." The essay ends with the statement that "free verse in the twentieth century has done much to free poetry from certain formal conventions which might, conceivably, have mechanized it beyond all spontaneity and life."

Free verse was something of a shock to most mid-19th-century readers of Whitman's poetry, accustomed as they were to a uniform metrical pattern and a rhyme scheme. Whitman presented instead stanzaic patterns, familiar perhaps only to readers who knew the ancient Hebrew patterns, especially those used by the poets of the Old Testament. Emerson recognized what Whitman was doing and referred to him as the first truly American poet.

The caesura breaks in the following quotation from Whitman's "preface" to the 1855 edition of *Leaves of Grass* show perhaps that Whitman is already thinking about the poetry to come, even as he writes prose:

> He [the American poet] is the seer . . . he is individual . . . he is complete in himself . . . the others are as good as he, only he sees it and they do not. He is not one of the chorus . . . he does

not stop for any regulations . . . he is the president of regulation.

It is almost as if Whitman were warning readers that his poetry will be different, that it establishes new "regulations" which open poetry to larger, greater verse possibilities. But there are important qualifications, ideas about poetic form that kept what would later be known as "free verse" from allowing the poet to feel "free" to do anything he or she wanted. Robert Frost's statement that free verse is like playing tennis with the net down, meant to be a criticism of the form, may be, nevertheless, fairly close to a workable analogy for "free verse." One might answer, for example, that the lack of a net allows the player more freedom, but he or she must play still within the lines set down on the court, even though it may be the poet who determines where the lines go.

This freedom is the "soul" of America, Whitman says in the 1855 "preface":

> The poetic quality is not marshalled in rhyme or uniformity or abstract addresses to things nor in melancholy complaints or good precepts, but is the life of these and much else and is in the soul. The profit of rhyme is that it drops seeds of a sweeter and more luxuriant rhyme, and of uniformity that it conveys itself into its own roots in the ground out of sight. The rhyme and uniformity of perfect poems show the free growth of metrical laws and bud from them as unerringly and loosely as lilacs or roses on a bush, and take shapes as compact as the shapes of chestnuts and oranges and melons and pears, and shed the perfume impalpable to form.

And he adds, as a sort of apology, "What ever satisfies the soul is truth."

Whitman is arguably America's most influential free verse poet, although the term was not yet used during Whitman's lifetime. According to many critics, the rhythmical quality of Whitman's poetry is unsurpassed.

In one of the last poems Whitman wrote, "To Soar in Freedom and in Fullness of Power," the poet says: "I have not felt to warble" like the birds. He has, instead, "[soared] in freedom and in the fullness of power, joy, volition," a line suggesting the free verse poetic form for which Whitman is now so well known.

Fugitive Slave Act (1850) The Fugitive Slave Act of 1850 was an attempt by Southern congressmen to strengthen federal laws against helping slaves escape to the North. Anyone "harboring, concealing or rescuing" a runaway slave could be fined $1,000 and put in jail for six months. On May 26, 1854, a vigilance committee against the new law tried to rescue the runaway slave Anthony Burns from the Boston courthouse, killing a marshall in the process. U.S. Commissioner Edward G. Loring remanded Burns to his Virginia owner in spite of the protests, and he left for Alexandria on June 2. Boston citizens collected $1,300 and brought Burns back to the city in 1855.

Whitman was incensed by the news of the slave's forced return to Virginia and wrote the poem "A Boston Ballad" as a satirical protest against the incident. In the poem he raises from their graves the American soldiers who had died during the Revolutionary War and King George III of England as well, so he could explain to the soldiers that they had all died in vain and to the king that he had won the war after all.

Fulton Ferry A waterfront settlement in BROOKLYN's earliest days, when it was not called Brooklyn but Breuckelen, settled by the Dutch in 1646. The village was formed around a ferry landing on the East River, begun by Cornelis Dircksen, who, as early as 1642, used rowboats to get people to and from New York City. Robert Fulton began his steamboat ferry service in 1814, running boats from the foot of what is now Old Fulton Street in Brooklyn to the present Pier 11 ferry stop in New York. He was the first to make steam navigation successful seven years earlier. The distance for the ferryboat run was and still is slightly less than a half-mile, and even in Whitman's time took only eight minutes to get across. Several boat lines operated the run until the New York and Brooklyn Ferry Company formed in 1839 and bought up all the smaller companies.

Fulton Ferry boat on a run from Brooklyn across the East River to New York City, 1890 *(Library of Congress, Prints and Photographs Division)*

During the early part of the 19th century, Fulton Ferry was a fairly thriving community of small houses and shanties, taverns, stables, and stores. The BROOKLYN BRIDGE, which was under construction from January 1870 and completed in 1883, was begun on the Brooklyn side of the East River just north of Fulton Ferry, the tower rising to a height of 107 feet. The bridge would virtually obliterate the Fulton Ferry village, which is now a small group of dilapidated buildings barely noticeable in the great shadow of the bridge.

When Whitman was editor of the BROOKLYN DAILY EAGLE, he wrote dozens of articles about local places, not the least of which was Fulton Ferry. Here is an excerpt from an article titled "Our Ferries—A Word to Ferry Directors and Officers—The Contemplated New Ferries for South and East Brooklyn" (March 28, 1846):

To a place situated like Brooklyn, nothing, of course, can be more important than having plenty of cheap ferries. Deprive us of them and we are without the strongest artery of our circulation; we lose that which not enriches the robber, but "makes us poor indeed."

The *Fulton Ferry*, as it is the oldest in age, and the most liberal in all its arrangements, deserves the first mention in the list of these important establishments. In the way of large, commodious, swift boats, and the obliging demeanor of the officials attached to it, the old Fulton has borne, and still bears, a most irreproachable character. But there is one thing in which we think the directors miss it materially. They should reduce the commutation prices to *six* and *five dollars* a-year, instead of ten as heretofore. . . . The objection to reduction, is, as we understand, that they pay so high a rent to the Corporation of New York—that disgraceful and extortionate body charging them $35,000 a year! But we think their receipts would not fall away materially . . . if they were to reduce. . . .

As things are, we cheerfully bear testimony to the handsome management of the concern, and consider that—with the above exception—the public owe all good will to the Fulton extablishment.

Ferryboats still operate daily from Fulton Ferry Landing, with boats running to the original New York landing site at what is now the South Street Seaport (Pier 11), and to Battery Park (Pier A), the World Financial Center (North Cove), West 23rd Street (Pier 63), and West 44th Street (Pier 84). There are now as many as 14 northbound ferry crossings a day, but tickets are $4 one-way for commuters (almost as much as a year-long ticket when Whitman wrote the above article), $8 one-way for tourists ($15 for an all-day pass).

For the *Brooklyn Daily Eagle* (April 17, 1846), Whitman wrote a one-paragraph article titled "A Word to the Fulton Ferry Company," criticizing the owners for not controlling "tobacco smokers and spitters." He writes: "As to the spitters, there is perhaps no deliverance from them—but the smokers (who are the worst) should be stopped altogether. No person ought to be allowed on the boats, at all, smoking a cigar. This is the rule in some of the best conducted lines of passage in the country."

In another article, "Women's Tickets for the Fulton Ferry" (May 14, 1846), for the same newspaper, Whitman suggests that the company reduce the price of women's annual tickets to $5 from $10. "With hardly an exception [the young women commuters] are persons of moderate circumstances, to whom every dollar is a consideration. . . . We are refreshed every day by the sight of their pleasant faces blooming with health and intelligence; and if *we* were the toll-taker, we couldn't have the face to charge them any thing more than a look into their bright eyes, for the privilege of passage. . . .—for women *are* citizens, though they don't vote."

One of Whitman's best poems in *Leaves of Grass* is "Crossing Brooklyn Ferry," in which the poet uses the ferryboat crossing of the East River as a metaphor for a mystical journey into spiritual discoveries. Whitman set type and published the first edition of *Leaves of Grass* (1855) out of a print shop at 70 Fulton Street, at the southwest corner of Cranberry Street. There is a bronze plaque there now commemorating the spot.

G

Galaxy, The (1866–1878)   Short-lived New York literary magazine set up by the brothers William C. and Francis P. Church in early 1866 to compete with the ATLANTIC MONTHLY in Boston. The *Galaxy* lasted 12 years and then was merged with its Boston rival. During the 12 years the Church brothers published four of Whitman's poems and two of the three essays that later became *Democratic Vistas*.

In their August 1867 issue the Churches published Whitman's poem "A Carol of Harvest for 1867" and, in its December issue, a review by John BURROUGHS of Whitman's *Drum-Taps*. So when Thomas CARLYLE published his "Shooting Niagara" in the NEW YORK TRIBUNE (August 1867), a scathing attack against democracy, the Church brothers knew that Whitman would provide the best response. Carlyle had argued that democracy would eventually destroy civilization, and Whitman could not resist writing a rebuttal.

The poet wrote three articles for the *Galaxy*: "Democracy," "Personalism," and "Literature." The editors accepted and published the first two but rejected the third on vague grounds but perhaps because of reader complaints about the first two essays.

"Democracy" was published in the December 1867 issue of the *Galaxy* and "Personalism" in the May 1868 issue. The three appeared together as *Democratic Vistas* in an 84-page pamphlet in 1871.

Whitman poems first published in *Galaxy*, along with "A Carol of Harvest for 1867," were "Brother of All with Generous Hand" (January 1870), later titled "Outlines for a Tomb," "Warble for Lilac-Time" (May 1870), and "O Star of France" (June 1871).

Gilchrist, Anne (1828–1885)   English widow of Alexander Gilchrist, a biographer of William BLAKE before the English poet's reputation was established. Alexander died in 1861 with the biography unfinished, and Anne, with the help of William Michael ROSSETTI, completed the work. She also wrote several literary articles and a biography of Mary Lamb (1883).

Following the death of her husband from scarlet fever at age 33 (Anne's age as well), she moved from London to a small cottage in the Hampshire village of Shottermill, where she completed her husband's *Life of Blake*. She was a close friend of Thomas and Jane Carlyle, Alfred and Emily Tennyson, and Dante Gabriel, William Michael, and Christina Rossetti.

In 1869 W. M. ROSSETTI, who with Algernon Charles SWINBURNE had recognized the likenesses between Whitman's poetry and Blake's, lent Mrs. Gilchrist a copy of his edited book, *Selections from Walt Whitman*. She had heard the criticism about the obscenity, so she began reading in skepticism but finished in "delight and wonder."

When she wrote a thank-you note to Rossetti two weeks later, she told him: "I can read no other book. It holds me entirely spellbound, and I go through it again and again with deepening delight and wonder. . . . There is nothing in him that I shall ever let go my hold of. For me the reading of his poems is truly a new birth of the soul." She was particularly impressed by Whitman's idea of a "sane and sacred death," and she quoted other lines from poems in later letters to Rossetti. She admired the poet's "fearlessness at the beauty of Death," quoting: "O vast and well-veiled Death! / O the beautiful touch of Death, soothing and benumbing."

She said that for the first time she understood the "meaning of democracy—of individuality, and, as never before," she realized the glory of being a woman and mother. For this she quoted lines from "Song of Myself": "I am the poet of the woman the same as of the man, / And I say it is as great to be a woman as to be a man, / And I say there is nothing greater than the mother of men."

Rossetti was pleased with her response to a poet for whom he too had such respect, and so he lent her a copy of the complete *Leaves of Grass*, probably the fourth edition (1867), telling her that anyone who was so appreciative of the "glorious man Whitman, one day to be known as one of the greatest sons of the Earth," should have access to the poet's entire work. He told her that the sound of *Leaves of Grass* was to him "like a portentous roll of chorus, such as 'The Lord God Omnipotent Reigneth' in Handel." When he warned her about the passages that had been most often criticized—no doubt the poems in the "Children of Adam" and "Calamus" clusters—she wrote back that such a "great and divinely beautiful nature could not infuse any poison into the wine he had poured out for them. . . . What I like, I grasp firmly and silently; what I do not like, I prefer to let go silently too."

Later, she wrote that none of the poems troubled her "even for a moment," because it was not, as some critics had suggested, that the "heights brought down to the depths, but the depths lifted up level with the sunlit heights, that they might become clear and sunlit too."

In another letter, she told Rossetti: "I had not dreamed that words could cease to be words and become electric streams like these. I do assure you that, strong as I am, I feel sometimes as if I had not bodily strength to read many of these poems. In some of them there is such a weight of emotion, such a tension of the heart, that mine refuses to

Anne Gilchrist, an Englishwoman who fell in love with Whitman's poetry and then with the poet himself
(Library of Congress, Prints and Photographs Division)

beat under it—stands quite still—and I am obliged to lay the book down for a while; . . . then there is such calm wisdom and strength of thought, such a cheerful breadth of sunshine, that the soul bathes in them, renewed and strengthened. Living impulses flow out of these that make me exult in life, and yet look longingly towards the 'superb vistas of Death' " (see "Song at Sunset," line 21).

Rossetti was impressed enough with Gilchrist's letters to encourage her to let him put them together and send them as an essay to Whitman's friend William O'CONNOR, with whom he had been corresponding, to see if it could be published. She approved of the idea and "A Woman's Estimate of Walt Whitman" was published in Boston's the *Radical* (May 1870). It was one of the most insightful reviews of *Leaves of Grass* that the poet would read.

She said of Whitman in the article: "Happy America, that he should be her son! One sees, indeed, that only a young giant of a nation could produce this kind of greatness, so full of the ardor, the elasticity, the inexhaustible vigor and freshness, the joyousness, the audacity of youth."

She wrote further:

Those who admire [one] poem, and don't care for [another], and talk of formlessness, absence of metre, etc., are quite as far from any genuine recognition of Walt Whitman as his bitter detractors. . . . We criticize a palace or a cathedral; but what is the good of criticizing a forest? Are not the hitherto-accepted masterpieces of literature akin rather to noble architecture; built up of material rendered precious by elaboration; planned with subtile art, that makes beauty go hand-in-hand with rule and measure, and knows where the last stone will come before the first is laid; the result stately, fixed, yet such as might, in every particular, have been different from what it is (therefore inviting criticism), contrasting proudly with the careless freedom of Nature—opposing its own rigid adherence to symmetry to her willful dallying with it? But not such is this book. Seeds brought by the winds from north, south, east, and west, lying long in the earth, not resting on it like the stately building, but hid in it and assimilating it, shooting upwards to be nourished by the air and the sunshine and the rain which beat idly against that,—each bough and twig and leaf growing in strength and beauty its own way, a law to itself, yet with all this freedom of spontaneous growth, the result inevitable, unalterable (therefore setting criticism at naught)—above all things, vital—that is, a source of ever-generating vitality: such are these poems.

On Whitman's FREE VERSE poetic form, Gilchrist wrote: "I see that no counting of syllables will reveal the mechanism of the music; and that this rushing spontaneity could not stay to bind itself with the fetters of metre. But I know that the music is there, and that I would not for something change ears with those who cannot hear it."

No critic in America or abroad, not even EMERSON, wrote in such detail of his or her understanding of Whitman's themes of love and death. After Gilchrist quotes the poet on the "beauty of death," she writes:

He who can thus look with fearlessness at the beauty of Death may well dare to teach us to look with fearless, untroubled eyes at the perfect beauty of Love in all its appointed realizations. Now none need turn away their thoughts with pain or shame; though only lovers and poets may say what they will—the lover to his own, the poet to all, because all are in a sense his own. None need fear that this will be harmful to the woman. How should there be such a flaw in the scheme of creation that, for the two with whom there is no complete life, save in closest sympathy, perfect union, what is natural and happy for the one should be baneful to the other? The utmost faithful freedom of speech, such as there is in these poems, creates in her no thought of feeling that shuns the light of heaven, none that are not as innocent and serenely fair as the flowers that grow; would lead, not to harm, but to such deep and tender affection as makes harm or the thought of harm simply impossible.

No wonder Whitman was impressed by Anne Gilchrist.

He wrote to Rossetti in response to the article, stating that "nothing in my life, or my literary fortunes, has brought me more comfort and support every way—nothing has more spiritually soothed me—than the warm appreciation of friendship of that true, full-grown woman."

Gilchrist understood his poetry, as is unmistakable from the essay quoted above and from other letters she continued to write to Rossetti and the long, first letter she wrote to the poet himself. It is very much a love letter.

Her letter to him (September 3, 1871) indicates something of the depth of sexual frustration she had felt in her marriage. She refers to a love "slumbering—undeveloped. For, dear Friend, my soul was so passionately aspiring—it so thirsted & pined for light, it had not power to reach alone and he [Alexander] could not help me on my way. And a woman is so made that she cannot give the tender, passionate devotion of her whole nature save to the great conquering soul, stronger in its powers, though not in its aspirations, than her own, that can lead her forever & forever up and on." The implication is that Whitman was, for her, that "conquering soul." She boldly stated her love for him and a "proposal" of marriage, or at least of a sexual relationship: "Try me for this life," she wrote. "I am yet young enough to bear thee children, my darling, if God should so bless me. And would yield my life for this cause with serene joy if it were so appointed, if that were the price for thy having a 'perfect child.'" Whitman must have been surprised if not shocked at such a declaration, but he must have taken it, at least in part, as a love similar to his own, that is, a simple, sensual love for people.

His answering letter (November 3, 1871) is short, pleasant, and politically correct. After explaining that he had waited for the proper moment to respond, a special day, "a sort of Sabbath or holy day apart to itself, under serene & propitious influences—confident that I could then write you a letter which would do you good, & me too." He tells her that he must "show, without further delay, that I am not insensible to your love. I too send you my love. And do you feel no disappointment because I now write but briefly. My book is my best letter, my response, my truest explanation of all. In it I have put my body & spirit. You understand this better & fuller & clearer than any one else. And I too fully & clearly understand the loving & womanly letter it has evoked. Enough that there surely exists between us so beautiful & delicate a relation, accepted by both of us with joy."

Gilchrist and Whitman continued to correspond, and in August 1876, she wrote that she had booked passage on a boat to Philadelphia, with her three children—Beatrice ("Bee"), 22; Herbert, 19; and Grace ("Giddy"), 17. Whitman, no doubt somewhat intimidated, wrote to try to discourage the trip, but she wrote back that her children were

now old enough to enjoy the trip and that she no longer had any significant responsibilities in England. She had made up her mind.

They arrived in early September and rented a house in Philadelphia at 1929 North 22nd Street, across the river from Camden, New Jersey, where Whitman was living with his brother George and his wife. The living arrangement with his brother was not working out, so Whitman spent most of his time with Anne and her children, all of whom he soon came to love. She made up a spare bedroom for him.

She spent the next three years in Philadelphia and established what was apparently a platonic relationship with Walt.

The Gilchrists left New York for Glasgow, Scotland, on June 9, 1879. Anne lived out the last six years of her life at 12 Well Road in Hampstead. She continued to write to America, not only to Whitman but to many others whom she had met in the three years she was in the country. She also had visits from at least two of those friends, William O'CONNOR and Edward CARPENTER, both of whom were friends of Whitman's and had written memoirs.

Grace Gilchrist later recalled, in an article she wrote for England's *Temple Bar* (February 1898), that after supper at their home in Philadelphia, they would take chairs out onto the sidewalk in front of the house on 22nd Street, "American fashion, beside the stoop," and discuss mostly literary topics, Whitman preferring to not read his own poems aloud. Grace also remembered that he had tea with them every day but Sunday.

Whitman's poem "Going Somewhere" is a "memory-leaf for her dear sake," written upon hearing of Anne's death in England in 1885.

Good Gray Poet, The

Good Gray Poet, The (1866) Title of a pamphlet by William Douglas O'CONNOR, published in January 1866 as a defense of Whitman, who had been fired as a government clerk the summer before by James Harlan, the secretary of the interior. Harlan had found a copy of *Leaves of Grass* in Whitman's desk and condemned it as immoral.

The monograph, subtitled "A Vindication," defended Whitman's poetry on the principle of freedom in literature. O'Connor argues that all great literature may contain material that may be offensive to some people, but that literature is deemed great in part because even those things that seem offensive to some are meant to be uplifting to all, to affirm rather than negate life.

O'Connor noted Whitman's patriotism in serving wounded soldiers during the CIVIL WAR. He wrote that "He has been a visitor of prisons, a protector of fugitive slaves, a constant voluntary nurse, night and day, at the hospitals, from the beginning of the war to the present time; a brother and friend through life to the neglected and the forgotten, the poor, the degraded, the criminal, the outcast, turning away from no man for his guilt, nor woman for her vileness. His is the strongest and truest compassion I have ever known."

The Good Gray Poet, however, went beyond O'Connor's defense of the poet or his right to publish his poetry. As Gay Wilson Allen writes in *The Solitary Singer* (1955), "O'Connor not only created a mythical poet, ten times larger than life and as majestic as a Greek statue, but he also made him a veritable reincarnation of Christ; and not unconsciously either, for two years later O'Connor underscored this interpretation in his short story 'The Carpenter,' in which Whitman by his compassionate love performs a miracle on Christmas Eve." Whitman was embarrassed by this description, but he nevertheless wrote a preface for a posthumous collection of O'Connor's *Three Tales,* which contained "The Carpenter."

In spite of the extensive defense of Whitman as a man and as a poet, *The Good Gray Poet* is still best known for its title, from which Whitman got his assumed name. Whitman would write later that the name of "Good Gray Poet" has "stuck—stuck."

H

Harned, Thomas B. (1851–1921)   One of three
Whitman literary executors, with Horace TRAUBEL
and Dr. Richard BUCKE. Harned was a Camden,
New Jersey, lawyer and Traubel's brother-in-law. He
liked Whitman and his poetry and often invited
him to his Camden home to meet notable American and foreign guests.

The three executors received upon Whitman's
death portions of the poet's personal notes, letters,
and manuscripts. In 1917 Harned sent his collection of approximately 3,000 items to the Library of
Congress. The collection was among the first Whitman materials received by the library. It contains
early versions of poems which were later printed in
Leaves of Grass.

Harper's New Monthly Magazine (1850–
present)   Whitman wrote for BROOKLYN newspapers several reviews of the early issues of *Harper's
New Monthly Magazine* (renamed *Harper's Monthly
Magazine* in 1900 and *Harper's Magazine* in 1925);
and, after Whitman established himself as the poet
of *Leaves of Grass,* the editors published six of his
poems.

The magazine was founded in New York City in
June 1850 by the five Harper brothers who ran the
largest book publishing firm in the city. They
picked Henry J. Raymond, who would start the
NEW YORK TIMES in 1852, as their first editor, and,
for three years after he started the *Times* he edited
both publications.

Harper's New Monthly had 144 pages and a first
printing of 7,500 copies at 25 cents each. The first

issue carried the first installments of two serials and
three short stories, including two by Charles Dickens. The connection with Harper Bros. Publishers
gave the *New Monthly* access to all the larger firm's
authors. All the earliest material published was
pirated, and there was no pay for reprints until the
late 1850s.

The magazine published works by William
Makepeace Thackeray, Anthony Trollope, Thomas
Hardy, George Eliot, Mark Twain, Ralph Waldo
EMERSON, Nathaniel Hawthorne, and Herman
Melville and illustrations by Frederic Remington
and Winslow Homer, among others.

One of the great editors of the period, Alfred H.
Guernsey, a classics scholar, succeeded Raymond as
editor in 1855 and edited the magazine through the
CIVIL WAR years. W. D. HOWELLS was an editor
during the 1880s and instrumental in getting
poems from Whitman.

From 1874 to 1892 *Harper's New Monthly* carried six poems by Whitman: "Song of the Redwood-Tree" (February 1874); "Prayer of Columbus"
(March 1874); "Patroling Barnegat" (April 1881);
"Of That Blithe Throat of Thine" (January 1885);
"With Husky-Haughty Lips, O Sea!" (March
1884); and "Death's Valley" (April 1892). The latter poem was published in the issue following
Whitman's death on March 26.

Harper's Weekly (1857–1916)   Founded   in
1857 by Fletcher Harper, who, with his brother
James, had been running HARPER'S NEW MONTHLY
MAGAZINE, founded in 1850. Although the *Weekly*

carried both literature and literary essays, it offered a greater accent on politics than did the *Monthly*, and there were more illustrations in the *Weekly*. The *Weekly* also published some of Whitman's poetry.

The *Weekly* was Fletcher Harper's "pet enterprise," as his grandson J. Henry Harper was to write years later. Fletcher died in the late 1890s, and the magazine nearly went bankrupt in 1899 and finally died in 1916. *Harper's Weekly* had a circulation of 60,000 in its first year, 75,000 the following year, and 90,000 at its peak in 1861. The magazine was subtitled *A Journal of Civilization*, and scholars and historians have enjoyed searching through its complete run for what is still the best illustrated record of the nation between 1857 and 1916. Thomas Nast joined the staff in 1862 and developed fame for the magazine and himself with caricatures of New York's corrupt Tweed Ring, plus his cartoons, from which we get the Republican Party elephant and the Democratic Party donkey. It carried a number of fictional serials, including Dickens's *Tale of Two Cities* and Willkie Collins's *The Woman in White*.

Harper's Weekly published four of Whitman's poems, including "Beat! Beat! Drums!" (September 28, 1861); the poem was published simultaneously in the NEW YORK LEADER, and in the *Boston Evening Transcript*; Whitman also read the poem aloud the same evening at PFAFF'S CELLAR restaurant in New York. Other Whitman poems published in the *Weekly* were: "As One by One Withdraw the Lofty Actors" (May 16, 1885), later titled "Death of General Grant"; and "Bravo, Paris Exposition!" (September 28, 1889).

Hartshorne, William (c. 1790–1859) Printer for the LONG ISLAND PATRIOT, when Whitman became a printer's devil (apprentice) for the weekly newspaper at age 11, his first newspaper job. Hartshorne taught Walt typesetting, and he and other apprentices boarded with Hartshorne's granddaughter during the young Whitman's year with the paper. He liked Hartshorne and later wrote of the older man's influence on him to become a journalist.

Hicks, Elias (1748–1830) Quaker preacher and evangelist, who is said to have traveled 40,000 miles on behalf of his beliefs. He split from the Quakers in 1827 over doctrinal differences. He thought that the traditional view of Christ as a meek and mild prophet got in the way of Christ's more practical value as an example for all people. Hicks was a liberal, and his beliefs were too close to Unitarian ideas to be acceptable to orthodox Quakers.

After the split, Hicks and his followers were known as "Hicksites," first used as a negative description of maverick Quakers, but it soon became favored by the Elias Hicks followers, who are today recognized as "Friends." Hicksville, LONG ISLAND, is named after the preacher.

Hicks was both a friend of the Whitman family and a major influence on their religious beliefs as Walt was growing up; the poet carried many of Hicks's beliefs into his own adulthood. Walt, as a small child, heard Hicks preach, and although what

Elias Hicks, Quaker preacher and friend of the Whitman family. Walt remembered in later years how impressed he was as a child hearing Hicks preach, not so much for what he said but how he said it. Engraving by Peter Maverick *(Library of Congress, Prints and Photographs Division)*

he said probably had little influence on the boy, his manner of oratory, the rhythm of his prose, apparently left an impression. Whitman valued more than the Scriptures what Hicks called "obedience to the light within," an idea that Whitman would accept and use as a guiding principle in his own thinking, the idea appearing, often thematically, in *Leaves of Grass.*

Whitman was also influenced by the severe attitude Hicks took against SLAVERY. A writer of antislavery books and a friend of Hicks named Lydia Maria Child (1802–80) wrote about an incident in which a Virginia farmer who heard Hicks preach against slavery was "so filled with wrath, that he swore vehemently he would blow out the preacher's brains, if he ventured near his plantation." Apparently Hicks heard about the threat, walked out to the plantation, identified himself, and argued with him about slavery. Child writes that the farmer did not kill Hicks, "by reason of a restraining power within." Each man made his case, and they shook hands at the end of the visit. Six months later, according to Child, the "Virginian emancipated all his slaves."

Hicks was known for his oratory, attracting to his sermons working-class families like the Whitmans, but also city politicians and other dignitaries. In 1829, two years after the split from Quakerism, Hicks was often openly critical of the church, stating for example, that the blood of Christ was "no more effectual than the blood of bulls and goats." This was, according to orthodox believers, pure heresy. But Hicks was trying to place an emphasis on the importance of an individual going directly to God, who connects to the soul through the "Inner Light." This contact with God provided moments of spiritual exaltation and could not be reached through an intermediary, such as a priest or preacher. Whitman would later write that RELIGION must be taken out of the church, away from ministers and priests and given back to the people, who must learn to think for themselves.

Whitman wrote that there was an "unnameable constitutional something" that "emanated from [Hicks's] very heart to the hearts of his audience" and that could be "launch'd out only by a powerful human magnetism." Whitman wrote a short biography of Hicks, stating at one point that he was "the democrat in religion as Jefferson was the democrat in politics."

The preacher produced several books, including *Observations on Slavery* (1811), *Sermons* (1828), *Elias Hicks's Journal of his Life and Labors* (1828), *The Letters of Elias Hicks* (1835), and *The Quakers* (1832), a four-volume history that included some of Hicks's sermons. Elias Hicks's followers founded Swarthmore College in 1864.

Home Journal, The (1846–1901) Founded in New York as the *National Press: A Home Journal,* but it was the *Home Journal* when Whitman's poem "New Year's Day" was published in its pages (March 30, 1892), a month after the poet's death. The periodical was published by Morris Phillips & Company in New York and edited by Morris Phillips during Whitman's last years.

The *Home Journal* became *Town and Country* in 1901 and still publishes under that title.

homosexuality As with nearly all matters concerning a person's sexual orientation, there is little evidence of Whitman's private preferences other than in letters. Nothing he wrote for publication provides evidence; one of his most important contributions to American literature was a vision of democracy that insisted on the love of people for one another, regardless of gender, race, or ethnic beliefs. Nevertheless, he was probably homosexual and perhaps bisexual. There are a dozen or so young men with whom he may have had sexual relations, or at least a manly love that is made clear in letters he wrote to them. And there were also several women, all closer to his own age, whom he loved dearly, though probably platonically.

The poetry of *Leaves of Grass* is full of the love Whitman felt for everyone he met, which he wanted to communicate to readers. There are two clusters of poems in *Leaves* devoted to sexual love: the "Children of Adam" cluster, 16 poems devoted to heterosexual love; and the "Calamus" cluster, 39 poems devoted to homosexual love. All of these poems got the poet in trouble with readers, especially newspaper critics and reviewers, most of whom could not see through the sexual images to the larger theme.

His letters to the soldiers he attended in hospitals during the CIVIL WAR are full of his love for them, referring to them most often as "son" or "comrade," or "my darling boy." He wrote a letter, dated November 8, 1863, in which he urges "Lewis Kirk BROWN and Hospital Comrades," to "give my love to Charley Cate and all the boys in ward K, and to Benton if he is there still—I wish you would go in ward C and see James O. Stilwell, and also Thomas Carson in same ward, and Chambers that lays next to him, and tell them I sent them my love." He continues to list soldiers by name and by ward, telling "Lewy" to tell them, "I send my love." Whitman ends the letter by asking Brown to pass the letter around: "I wish each of the boys I have mentioned to have my letter that wishes it, & read it at leisure for themselves, & then pass to another." It seems unlikely that these letters would have been made so public in the hospital wards if Whitman had been having sexual relations with these men, as a few biographers have suggested.

Whitman kept almost daily notes of names and places while visiting in hospitals, which reinforced his memory as he wrote letters to these young men and to their loved ones at home. He seemed always to know the location of the soldier's cot in hospital wards, the wounds he had suffered, often his hometown and something of his family life. "I send my love to little Billy the Ohio boy in ward A, and to Miss Gregg herself—and if Miss Doolittle is in ward B [both women were nurses], please ask her to tell the boys in the ward I sent them my love, and to her too, and give her this letter some evening to read to the boys, and one of these days I will come back and read to them myself."

Whitman's letters to the young men he became closest to indicate a much deeper love relationship, often beginning, "How are you my dearest boy"; often ending, "From your loving comrade, Walt" (see DOYLE PETER; HARRY STAFFORD). Whitman often hints in his letters of more intimate feelings in these relationships. Many of the letters offer evidence of homosexual relationships, yet without overt statements of a sexual nature, and all of this is further complicated by the vocabulary of the letters, words that do not mean now what they meant then. Even the word "lover" was used then between men and women for a relationship beyond a handshake but not yet holding hands.

There is little question that Whitman showed throughout his life an interest in young, working-class men, nearly all of whom were uneducated. He had little formal education himself, having left school at age 11; and he too was from a working-class background, so it might be argued that it was natural for him to enjoy the company of boys with a similar background to his own. It may be that he had a greater understanding of and appreciation for what these boys were going through, most of them in their adolescent years. Yet there must have been more than that; Whitman found it easy to love them, and—perhaps precisely because he knew their backgrounds so well—to arrange sexual meetings.

Perhaps the most telling note on the subject was one written to himself, in which he wishes

> to give up absolutely and for good, from the present hour, this feverish, fluctuating, useless undignified pursuit of 16.4—too long, (much too long) persevered in,—so humiliating——It must come at last and had better come now . . .—avoid seeing her, or meeting her, or any talk or explanations—or any meeting whatever, from this hour forth, for life.

Critic Oscar Cargill suggested that the "16.4" is code that represents the 16th and fourth letters of the alphabet, P and D for Peter Doyle, and French scholar Roger Asselineau noted that Whitman had changed masculine pronouns in an early draft to feminine in the above quotation.

The English writer Edward CARPENTER (1844–1929), who wrote about sexual reform and women's rights, was greatly influenced by Whitman and wrote *Towards Democracy*, a book about what he called "spiritual democracy" and the goal of "freedom and joy." He wrote to Whitman in July 1874 to thank him for encouraging "a ground for the love of men," providing men with pride in their noble instincts. He wrote that "Women are beautiful, . . . but, to some, there is that which passes the love of women."

See also GILCHRIST, ANNE; WOMEN, WHITMAN AND.

Howells, William Dean (1837–1920) American novelist and critic, who once said that *Leaves of Grass* was "not poetry but the materials of poetry." He wrote a review of *Drum-Taps* for the ROUND TABLE (November 1865), saying that *Drum-Taps*, in terms of decency, was an improvement over the "preponderant beastliness" of the whole of *Leaves of Grass*.

Howells was editor of the ATLANTIC MONTHLY (1871–81), and although Whitman contributed two poems to the famous Boston periodical, they were accepted for publication before Howells became editor.

Howells wrote an article for *Conservator* (June 1895), describing his first meeting with Whitman at PFAFF'S CELLAR. He wrote that he didn't care much for Whitman's poetry but "I like his prose, if there is a difference, much better: there he is of a genial and comforting quality, very rich and cordial, such as I felt him to be when I met him in person."

I

influence of Whitman   An argument could be made that nearly all American poets after Whitman were influenced by him. One of the most obvious examples is in the poetry of Carl Sandburg (1878–1967), whose celebration of America was a constant theme in his poems; examples include "Chicago" (1914), "Good Morning, America" (1928), "The People, Yes" (1936), "The American Songbag" (1937), and "New American Songbag" (1950).

Vachel Lindsay (1879–1931), who was said to have learned prosody from hymn books, not unlike Whitman, also wrote poems with strong rhythmic patterns, as well as patriotic poems such as "General William Booth Enters into Heaven" (1913) and "Lincoln Walks at Midnight." Both Lindsay and Sandburg were Illinois poets.

Hart Crane (1899–1932) celebrated the American experience and wrote a poem titled "The Bridge" (1930) very much in the style of Whitman and using the BROOKLYN BRIDGE also as a metaphor for the strength of America's potential for uniting past and present.

Robinson Jeffers (1887–1962) followed Whitman's poetic style but not his subject matter, though his poems show his fondness for California's scenic coasts.

Allen Ginsberg (1925–97) was a popular poet of the beat movement, best known for "Howl" (1956) and for his influence on the young men and women of the 1950s. *Beat* was first defined as meaning "tired" or "worn down" by the America of the years following World War II and including the Vietnam War; later *beat* took on the more spiritual significance of "beatific." Ginsberg and other beat poets, many of whom were influenced also by Whitman, felt alienated from American society and filled their poetry with their anger. Ginsberg wrote "A Supermarket in California," which invokes the "lonely old courage-teacher":

> What thoughts I have of you tonight, Walt
>   Whitman, for I walked down the sidestreets
>   under the trees with a headache self-
>   conscious looking at the full moon. . . .
> I saw you, Walt Whitman, childless, lonely old
>   grubber, poking among the meats in the
>   refrigerator and eyeing the grocery boys. . . .
> Ah, dear father, graybeard, lonely old courage-
>   teacher, what America did you have when
>   Charon quit poling his ferry and you got out on
>   a smoking bank and stood watching the boat
>   disappear on the black waters of Lethe?

Except for the run-on sentences, which Ginsberg did *not* get from Whitman, the FREE VERSE rhythm is much the same. The supermarket becomes for Ginsberg a metaphor for all that is wrong with the America of his own time; he wonders what happened to the America about which Whitman wrote so optimistically.

Ingersoll, Robert G. (1833–1899)   Lawyer, orator, and agnostic, known as an outspoken defender of free-thinking in religious matters. He disliked

Leaves of Grass on a first reading but changed his mind after friends had urged him to reread the book. "The Great Agnostic" is known for his religious aphorisms—for example, "With soap, baptism is a good thing," and "An honest God is the noblest work of man."

Ingersoll gave an oration during Whitman's funeral at Harleigh Cemetery, saying, in part, "death is less terrible that it was before. Thousands and millions will walk into the dark valley of the shadow, holding Walt Whitman by the hand."

J

James, Henry (1843–1916) Edith Wharton wrote a marvelous tribute to both Whitman and her good friend Henry James in her chapter on James in *A Backward Glance* (1934). She writes that she "had never before heard poetry read as [James] read it." She describes a gathering of friends and the mentioning of Whitman's name, and she describes the "joy" of discovering that James thought Whitman, "as I did," she writes, "the greatest of American poets."

James was handed a copy of *Leaves of Grass,* and, she says, "all that evening we sat rapt while he wandered from 'The Song of Myself' to 'When lilacs last in the door-yard bloomed' (when he read 'Lovely and soothing Death' his voice filled the hushed room like an organ adagio), and thence let himself be lured on to the mysterious music of 'Out of the Cradle,' reading, or rather crooning it in a mood of subdued ecstasy till the fivefold invocation to Death tolled out like the knocks in the opening bars of the Fifth Symphony."

Wharton continues her description of further conversation with James about Whitman. "We talked long that night of 'Leaves of Grass', tossing back and forth to each other treasure after treasure; but finally James, in one of his sudden humorous drops from the heights, flung up his hands and cried out with the old stammer and twinkle: 'Oh, yes, a great genius; undoubtedly a very great genius! Only one cannot help deploring his too-extensive acquaintance with the foreign languages.'"

Johnston, Dr. John (?–1927) One of the leaders of a group of Whitman admirers in Bolton, England. He visited the poet at his home in Camden, New Jersey, in 1890 and later published a pamphlet, with J. W. WALLACE, titled *Visits to Walt Whitman in 1890–1891 by Two Lancashire Friends,* printed in Bolton (1890) and reprinted in Boston (1897). This short memoir provides what William Sloan KENNEDY refers to as "one of the best pen-portraits of Whitman ever made." Johnston also took a photograph of Whitman seated in a wheelchair along a Delaware River wharf, the photograph known as the "wharf photograph."

Johnstown Flood (May 31, 1889) Caused by the collapse of the Conemaugh Reservoir Dam, built in 1852 as part of the Pennsylvania canal system and rebuilt in 1879–81. Engineers began warning Johnstown area residents the morning of May 31 but were generally ignored. The dam broke at 3:30 P.M. and an estimated 5,000 people died. Property losses were estimated at $10 million. Donations totaling $3,742,818 from all over the world were sent to relief agencies.

Whitman's poem "A Voice from Death" uses the disaster as a metaphor for death itself, the "voice" coming as a reminder of how quickly it can enter the lives of ordinary people.

K

Kansas Magazine (1872–1873) Published in Topeka for its short life by owner and editor Thomas Gregg, who owned eight other local newspapers and magazines around the Midwest. Two of Whitman's poems were published in *Kansas Magazine*, which the poet described in 1872 as a new magazine in the style of ATLANTIC MONTHLY intended for "Western thought & reminiscences." The poems were "The Mystic Trumpeter" (February 1872) and "Virginia—the West" (March 1872), both of which would be reprinted in *As a Strong Bird on Pinions Free* (1872).

Whitman also wrote an article titled "Walt Whitman in Europe," extolling his European reputation, and asked his journalist friend Richard Hinton to sign his own name to it and mail it off to *Kansas Magazine* for publication in January 1873. Hinton was known in Kansas as one of John Brown's "Free Soil" guerrillas, and, since the editors had already published two poems by Whitman, they gave their okay to the article.

Kennedy, William Sloane (1850–1929) Harvard divinity student who became a journalist and literary critic. His early response to *Leaves of Grass* was to use the terms "bad taste," "coarse indecencies," and "moral repulsiveness" in describing the poems. He even wrote a letter to Whitman asking if he thought "in a thousand years from now people will be celebrating the birth of Walt Whitman as they are now the birth of Christ?"

In his books *Reminiscences of Walt Whitman* (1896) and *The Fight of a Book for the World: A Companion Volume to Leaves of Grass* (1926), Kennedy showed a significant change of mind. Kennedy also wrote a number of articles on Whitman and edited a book titled *Walt Whitman's Diary in Canada* (1904). He also wrote two biographies, *Henry W. Longfellow* (1882) and *John G. Whittier* (1892).

In 1887, Kennedy was instrumental in raising $800 from Whitman's friends in Boston toward the building of a cabin at TIMBER CREEK. Whitman was too weak at the time, however, and the money was used for other purposes.

A Kennedy "lecture" is quoted by Richard Maurice BUCKE in his biography of Whitman (1883) in which Kennedy compares Whitman and EMERSON. Bucke quotes the lecture: "Emerson is the 'knight-errant of the moral sentiment;' Whitman accepts the whole 'relentless kosmos,' and theoretically, at least, seems to blur the distinction between right and wrong. Emerson's pages are like beds of roses and violets; Whitman's like masses of sun-flowers and silken-tasselled maize. . . ."

Bucke includes an excerpt from another lecture Kennedy gave, in which he said, in part: "Walt Whitman is not a man who can be described by comparison or by antithesis. No genius can be so described. If you will give me an adequate account of a cubic mile of sea-water or blue ether, measure the work of the sun, the beauty of the morning star, or the influence of the starry midnight upon the soul, then I will give you an adequate account of this man. He is not immoral, but unmoral, as a faun or a satyr; a dynamic force, an animate fragment of the universe, a destroyer of shams, a live fighter upon the stage."

L

Lee, Johnny See DOYLE, PETER.

Libby Prison Confederate stockade during the CIVIL WAR, near Richmond, Virginia, where Walt's brother George was kept for most of five months, September 30, 1864, to late February, 1865.

The Libby Prison was second only to Andersonville, Georgia, in notoriety for its treatment of

Richmond, Virginia, at the corner of Carey and Governor Streets, at the end of the Civil War, May 1865 *(Library of Congress, Prints and Photographs Division)*

prisoners. It was not abuse by prison guards that made Libby (and Andersonville) notorious, but lack of food and medical aid. When Union prisoners from the battle of First Bull Run (July 21, 1861) arrived in Richmond, the local Confederate officer, General John Winder, commandeered several vacant tobacco warehouses, including one owned by the firm of Libby and Son. Records indicate there were 1,000 wounded Union troops and 1,200 missing from the war's first battle, so a place for the Confederate soldiers to keep prisoners was needed immediately.

The prison had eight warehouses, each 103 by 42 feet and containing a wood stove and little else in the way of prisoner comfort. The stove was used for heating the building and for cooking food. The Confederacy attempted to exchange some of its prisoners, but U.S. government officials refused, creating more crowding at Libby and, eventually, shortage of food and medical supplies, following by the deaths of soldiers.

By the time George WHITMAN was captured, Libby Prison was being used more as a stopover on the prisoners' way to points south. By that time too, prisoner exchange agreements had been worked out, so George and a number of his New York comrades were on their way home.

Lincoln, Abraham (1809–1865)   Sixteenth president of the United States, credited with preserving the union of the states during the CIVIL WAR and for emancipating the slaves. He was shot by John Wilkes BOOTH on Good Friday (April 14, 1865), and died the next morning.

Whitman and Lincoln never met to shake hands, although in *Specimen Days* (1882–83) the poet describes a poignant moment on a Washington street when he watched as the president and Mrs. Lincoln passed by in their barouche, "on a pleasure ride through the city. . . . They passed me . . . very close, and I saw the President in the face fully, as they were moving slowly, and his look, though abstracted, happened to be directed steadily in my eye. He bowed and smiled, but far beneath his smile I noticed well the expression I have alluded to (the eyes, always to me with a deep latent sadness in the expression). None of the

artists or pictures has caught the deep, though subtle and indirect, expression of this man's face."

William Sloan KENNEDY wrote about the parallel lives of the two men in his preface to *The Fight for a Book for the World: A Companion Volume to Leaves of Grass* (1926): "Abraham Lincoln and Walt Whitman, the one a moral giant in the political field, the other in that of the prophet-bard; fashioned by the life-force, in apparent scorn of heredity, out of the middle clay; large-molded, rich-juiced; hewers out of their own fortunes; the one the child of the prairies, the other of the sea; towering both, as we look back, above the welter of commonplace humanity around them." Kennedy said further that whereas Lincoln had given America a "firm civil foundation," Whitman had given it a "soul."

Whitman wrote a letter from Washington during the Civil War (dated March 19, 1863) to New York friends Nat and Fred Gray, describing the Lincoln he saw on the streets of the Capital:

> He has a face like a Hoosier Michael Angelo, so awful ugly it becomes beautiful, with its strange mouth, its deep cut, criss-cross lines, and its doughnut complexion.—My notion is too, that underneath his outside smutched mannerism, and stories from third-class county barrooms (it is his humor), Mr. Lincoln keeps a fountain of first-class practical telling wisdom. I do not dwell on the supposed failures of his government; he has shown, I sometimes think an almost supernatural tact in keeping the ship afloat at all, with head steady, not only not going down, and now certain not to, but with proud and resolute spirit, and flag flying in sight of the world, menacing and high as ever. I say never yet captain, never ruler, had such a perplexing dangerous task as his, the past two years. I more and more rely upon his idiomatic western genius, careless of court dress or court decorum.

Whitman was at home in New York when Lincoln died at 7:22 A.M., April 15, 1865. Whitman arrived in Washington on Easter Monday (April 17) and attended the funeral services on the 19th. After millions of people had viewed the casket on its train ride to the Midwest, Lincoln was buried in Oak Ridge Cemetery, near Springfield, Illinois, on May 4. Newspaper reports stated that from Washington to Springfield, Illinois, the train was never out of the sight of people standing by the side of the tracks waiting for a chance to view the cortege.

Whitman wrote a paragraph titled "Death of President Lincoln" for *Specimen Days*; the entry is dated "April 16, '65"—Easter Sunday. It is written from notes he had made that day:

> He leaves for America's history and biography, so far, not only its most dramatic reminiscence—he leaves, in my opinion, the greatest, best, most characteristic, artistic, moral personality. Not but that he had faults, and showed them in the Presidency; but honesty, goodness, shrewdness, conscience, and (a new virtue, unknown to other lands, and hardly yet really known here, but the foundation and tie of all,

as the future will grandly develop), Unionism, in its truest and amplest sense, formed the hardpan of his character. . . . He was assassinated—but the Union is not assassinated. . . . One falls, and another falls. The soldier drops, sinks like a wave—but the ranks of the ocean eternally press on. Death does its work, obliterates a hundred, a thousand—President, general, captain, private—but the Nation is immortal.

The importance to America of "Union" is a major theme in *Leaves of Grass*. And the use of the "eternal ocean" as a metaphor for life and the immortality of the nation is also a constant in *Leaves*.

Whitman's greatest memorial to Lincoln, however, was his poem "When Lilacs Last in the Dooryard Bloom'd." Lilacs were in full bloom in Washington when Whitman arrived there on April

Battery of cannons lining a street in Washington, D.C., during the Civil War *(Library of Congress, Prints and Photographs Division)*

17, and lilacs were displayed around the casket at the funeral services two days later. The poet was to write later that the odor of the lilac bush ever afterward reminded him of the tragedy of Lincoln's death. Whitman also remembered that he had observed a bright evening star during several days in March, and, although at the time he took the star as a sign of good fortune for America, he nevertheless used the star in the poem—along with the lilac bush—as metaphors for his love and respect for the president:

> When lilacs last in the dooryard bloom'd,
> And the great star early droop'd in the western
>   sky in the night,
> I mourn'd, and yet shall mourn with
>   ever-returning spring.

Lincoln is memorialized in this great poem, but the subject is death itself. Whitman uses Lincoln's death as a metaphor for a spiritual awakening to the meaning of and reconciliation with death.

Lincoln lectures Whitman gave at least eight Lincoln lectures between 1879 and 1890, the first in New York City at Steck Hall on 14th Street, April 14, 1879, 14 years to the day of Abraham LINCOLN's assassination. He gave what was basically the same lecture in Boston at the St. Botolph Club (April 15, 1881); in Philadelphia four times in 1886, most notably on April 15 at the Chestnut Street Opera House; in New York's Madison Square Theatre (April 14, 1887) with several famous people in the audience, including Mark Twain, Andrew Carnegie, José Martí, (the Cuban revolutionist), James Russell Lowell, and Charles Eliot Norton (the famed Harvard professor). Whitman's final Lincoln lecture was at the Contemporary Club in Philadelphia in 1890. The poet was ill at the time and needed help to and from the stage.

The lectures usually included a reading of "O Captain! My Captain!," a poem of which he had already grown tired. It had been written in a hurry, and Whitman knew that it was popular in spite of its inferiority.

His introductory remarks to the subject of Lincoln, however, were detailed and dramatic. He described the times he had seen Lincoln, what he looked like and how he interpreted the president's character. His New York lecture (April 14, 1879), for example—similar to all the lectures—began as follows:

> How often since that dark and dripping Saturday—that chilly April day, now fifteen years bygone—my heart has entertain'd the dream, the wish, to give of Abraham Lincoln's death, its own special thought and memorial. Yet now the sought-for opportunity offers, I find my notes incompetent, (why for truly profound themes, is statement so idle? Why does the right phrase never offer?) and the fit tribute I dream'd of, waits unprepared as ever. My talk here indeed is less because of itself or anything in it, and nearly altogether because I feel a desire, apart from any talk, to specify the day, the martyrdom. . . .

Whitman provided a summary of the years leading up to the CIVIL WAR, and he described the first time he saw the president, newly elected and on a stopover in New York on his way from Illinois to Washington, D.C.:

> In the height of all this excitement and chaos [of the coming war], hovering on the edge at first, and then merged in its very midst, and destined to play a leading part, appears a strange and awkward figure. I shall not easily forget the first time I ever saw Abraham Lincoln. It must have been about the 18th or 19th of February, 1861. It was rather a pleasant afternoon, in New York City, as he arrived there from the West, to remain a few hours, and then pass on to Washington, to prepare for his inauguration. I saw him in Broadway, near the site of the present Post-office. He came down, I think from Canal street, to stop at the Astor House. The broad spaces, sidewalks, and streets in the neighborhood, and for some distance, were crowded with solid masses of people, many thousands. The omnibuses and other vehicles had all been turn'd off, leaving an unusual hush in that busy part of the city. Presently two or three shabby hack barouches made their way

with some difficulty through the crowd, and drew up at the Astor House entrance. A tall figure step'd out of the centre of these barouches, paus'd leisurely on the sidewalk, look'd up at the granite walls and looming architecture of the grand old hotel—then, after a relieving stretch of arms and legs, turn'd round for over a minute to slowly and good-humoredly scan the appearance of the vast and silent crowds. . . .

Whitman presented details of the presidency, then the dramatic details of the assassination: "A moment's hush—a scream—the cry of *murder*—Mrs. Lincoln leaning out of the box, with ashy cheeks and lips, with involuntary cry, pointing to the retreating figure, '*He has kill'd the President.*' "

And the poet would end by evoking the "leading historians and dramatists" of the future, "centuries hence," who in seeking "some special event, incisive enough to mark with deepest cut . . . this turbulent Nineteenth century of ours . . . those historians will seek in vain for any point to serve more thoroughly their purpose, than Abraham Lincoln's death. Dear to the Muse—thrice dear to Nationality—to the whole human race—precious to this Union—precious to Democracy—unspeakably and forever precious—their first great Martyr Chief."

Lind, Jenny (1820–1887) Swedish OPERA soprano, known as "the Swedish Nightingale," one of the most famous opera performers to sing in New York during the 19th century. She toured America with P. T. Barnum (1850–52), and gave at least 25 performances during the tour; she gave all of the approximately $30,000 she made on the tour to Swedish art scholarships and various charities.

Whitman was not particularly impressed by Lind, to some extent because of the heavy-handed publicity Barnum provided before her arrival. Twenty thousand people showed up on the street in front of Irving House on September 1, 1850, for her first performance. Whitman heard her sing at Castle Garden on September 24, noting that "she was dressed in pink satin, with black lace flounces and cape—great, green cockades in her hair—white kid gloves, fan, handkerchief. . . ." The poet wrote:

"She simply has a clear, shrill voice, of wonderful fluency, which will perhaps make you think of rich plate glass."

The writer of the entry on Jenny Lind in *Grove's Dictionary* makes it clear that the publicity for her performances, both in England and in America, was overdone, but he also acknowledges that she was one of the great opera singers. She "was a soprano of bright, thrilling and remarkably sympathetic quality. . . . She had also a wonderfully developed 'length of breath', which enabled her to perform long and difficult passages with ease. . . ."

Lippincott's Magazine (1868–1916) House publication of J. B. Lippincott & Company of Philadelphia. It was published monthly and was edited in its first 17 years by John Foster Kirk, an author and bibliographer in his own right. William Shepherd Walsh (1885–89) and Henry Stoddart (1889–96) were editors, however, during the years when Whitman published eight poems in *Lippincott's* pages. Unlike a number of its competitors during those years, *Lippincott's* paid its contributors.

The journal had several titles during its history, including *Lippincott's Magazine: A Popular Journal of General Literature, Science and Politics*. It was in those years that it published the following Whitman poems: "Going Somewhere" (November 1887); "You Lingering Sparse Leaves of Me" (November 1887); "Not Meagre, Latent Boughs Alone" (November 1887); "After the Supper and Talk" (November 1887); "Sail Out for Good, Eidólon Yacht!" (March 1891); "To the Sun-set Breeze" (December 1890); "Sounds of the Winter" (March 1891); and "The Unexpress'd" (March 1891).

Long Island Whitman was born in West Hills, in Huntington Township, Suffolk County, Long Island, New York, and lived—with the exception of his time in Washington, D.C., during the CIVIL WAR—in Long Island homes until 1873, when he moved to Camden, New Jersey.

Long Island is approximately 120 miles long, 12 to 20 miles wide, and 1,682 square miles in area. West Hills was a farming village when Whitman was born there on May 31, 1819. The birthplace home has become a museum and is located a mile south of what is now the village of South Huntington, on Walt Whitman Road, across from the Walt Whitman Mall.

There were people on Long Island for thousands of years before the Dutch first arrived in the 1630s. Tribes of hunters were probably the first settlers, arriving shortly after the ice age ended 10,000 years ago. In general, the Dutch settled on the western half of the island; the English settled on the eastern half. Dutch farms spread along the shore across from what is now Manhattan and the East River. Dutch and English settlements came later in the 17th century, the English in Hempstead, Flushing, Gravesend, Newtown, and Jamaica; the Dutch in Breuckelen (which became BROOKLYN in 1834), Midwout (Flatbush), Amersfoort (the Flatlands), New Utrecht and Boswyck.

Long Island was known during Whitman's lifetime as a region for agriculture, fishing, and shipbuilding. During the 20th century industrial development continued, and it is one of the most prosperous areas of its size in the United States. Its two westernmost counties include two of the five New York City boroughs, Brooklyn and Queens.

Whitman's description in *Specimen Days* of Long Island and his life there provides readers not only with some of the poet's best prose writing but also with hints at sources for many of his poems.

Worth fully and particularly investigating indeed, this Paumanok [the Indian name for Long Island], stretching east through Kings, Queens and Suffolk Counties, 120 miles altogether. On the north, Long Island Sound, a beautiful, varied and picturesque series of inlets, "necks," and sealike expansions, for a hundred miles to Orient Point. On the ocean side the great south bay dotted with countless hummocks, mostly small, some quite large, occasionally long bars of sand out two hundred rods to a mile and a half from the shore, while now and then, as at Rockaway and the east along the Hamptons, the beach makes right on the island, the sea dashing up without intervention. Several lighthouses on the shores east; a long history of wrecks tragedies, some even of late years. . . .

Whitman referred to two of these wrecks in *Leaves of Grass*. One was the *Mexico*, lost off Hempstead Beach in 1840; the other was the brig *Elizabeth*, which Whitman describes as a "fearful affair, in one of the worst winter gales, where Margaret Fuller went down with her husband and child." The poet continues his description of Long Island.

Inside the other bars or beach this south bay is everywhere comparatively shallow; of cold winters all thick ice on the surface. As a boy I often went forth with a chum or two, on those frozen fields, with hand sled, axe, and eel-spear, after messes of eels. We would cut holes in the ice, sometimes striking quite an eel bonanza, and filling our baskets with great, fat, sweet, white-meated fellows. . . . The shores of this bay, winter and summer, and my doings there in early life, are woven all through *L. of G.* One sport I was very fond of was to go on a bay party in summer to gather sea gulls' eggs. (The gulls lay two or three eggs, more than half the size of hens' eggs, right on the sand, and leave the sun's heat to hatch them.)

The eastern end of Long Island, the Peconic Bay region, I knew quite well, too—sailed more than once around Shelter Island, and down to Montauk—spent many an hour on Turtle Hill by the old Lighthouse, on the extreme point, looking out over the ceaseless roll of the Atlantic. I used to like to go down there and fraternize with the bluefishers, or the annual squads of sea-bass takers. Sometimes, along Montauk peninsula (it is some 15 miles long, and good grazing), met the strange, unkempt, half-barbarous herdsmen, at that time living there entirely aloof from society or civilization in charge, on those rich pasturages, of vast droves of horses, kine, or sheep owned by farmers of the eastern towns. . . .

More in the middle of the island were the spreading Hempstead plains, then (1830–1840) quite prairielike, open, uninhabited, rather sterile, covered with kill-calf and huckleberry bushes, yet plenty of fair pasture for the cattle, mostly milch cows, who fed there by hundreds, even thousands, and at evening . . . might be seen taking their way home, branching off regularly in the right places. . . .

As Wordsworth wrote, the child is father to the man. Whitman's boyhood experiences shaped the poetry of his adulthood.

Long Island Democrat (1835–1912)   James Brenton, called "Dr. Franklin" by friends, was editor of the *Democrat* when Whitman joined the staff in 1839 at age 20. He worked as a typesetter for two years, and Brenton published nine of Whitman's poems and several articles during the short time he worked for it.

He was teaching school and helping Brenton in off hours. The 20-year-old Whitman lived with the Brentons, and what they remembered most about him, according to Whitman biographer Emory Holloway, was that he spent a lot of time "loafing" in their backyard under an old apple tree.

The articles published by the *Long Island Democrat* were part of Whitman's series of "Sun-Down Papers: From the Desk of a Schoolmaster." There were 10 numbered essays in the series, the first three published in the *Hempstead Inquirer* (February and March 1840), the next six in the *Democrat* (April 1840–July 1841), and the 10th in the *Long-Island Farmer and Queens County Advertiser* (July 1841).

The essays have little to do with school teaching but are, instead, discourses on smoking, the difference between the death of an old person and the death of a young one, the nature of philosophy, the search for truth, etc. In the essay on smoking, Whitman writes:

There is something very majestic, truly, in seeing a human being with a long roll of black leaves held between his teeth, and projecting eight or ten inches before him. It has been said by some satirical individual, that a fishing-rod is a thing with a hook at one extremity, and a fool at the other; it may with much more truth be affirmed, that a segar, generally has a *smoky fire* at one end, & a *conceited spark* at the other. Weak, and silly indeed, must be that youth, who thinks that these are the characteristics of

manhood, they are much oftener the proofs of empty brains, and a loaferish disposition.

Perhaps the best that came from the "Sun-Down Papers" was that there was inspiration for Whitman, perhaps just in the title, to later write "Sun-Down Poem," which later became "Crossing Brooklyn Ferry," one of Whitman's great poems.

The poems published in the *Long Island Democrat* were "Our Future Lot" (October 31, 1839), "My Departure" (November 27, 1839), "Young Grimes" (January 1, 1840), "The Inca's Daughter" (May 5, 1840), "The Love That Is Hereafter" (May 19, 1840), "We All Shall Rest at Last" (July 14, 1840), "The Spanish Lady" (August 4, 1840), "The End of All" (September 22, 1840), "Fame's Vanity" (October 23, 1840), and "The Columbian's Song" (October 27, 1840).

Long-Islander, The (1838–present)   Whitman, at age 19, was founder and editor of this weekly newspaper in Huntington, LONG ISLAND. Today's *Long-Islander* includes a credit line under its masthead, "Founded by Walt Whitman in 1838." Its Web site has a head shot of Whitman in its upper left-hand corner. None of the weekly issues that Whitman produced in the year he ran the paper still exists, although seven of his articles were reprinted in the *Hempstead Inquirer* and the *Long Island Democrat*. Whitman would write in *Specimen Days* about this first experience as editor:

My first real venture was the *Long Islander*, in my own beautiful town of Huntington, in 1839. . . . I had been teaching, . . . but liked printing; . . . I went to New York, bought a press and types, hired some little help, but did most of the work myself, including the presswork. . . . I bought a good horse, and every week went all around the country serving my papers, devoting one day and night to it. I never had happier jaunts. . . . The experience of those jaunts, the dear old-fashioned farmers and their wives, the stops by the hayfields, the hospitality, nice dinners, occasional evenings, the girls, the rides through the brush, come up in my memory to this day."

Walt's earliest known poem, "Our Future Lot," was probably published in the *Long-Islander*. It was reprinted in the *Long Island Democrat* (October 31, 1839) and later retitled "Time to Come."

Issues of the *Long-Islander*, though meant to be a weekly, were irregular, sometimes once a week, sometimes once every two or three weeks, and eventually the financial backers stopped the money, and Whitman was forced to stop publication. The next editor resumed publication on July 12, 1839.

Whitman returned to Huntington in 1881 and visited the newspaper office. The paper ran a story about the visit (August 5, 1881), stating, in part: "After more than forty years' absence, the author of *Leaves of Grass,* and founder of this paper, has been visiting our town the past week in company with Dr. R. M. BUCKE, of London, Canada, who is engaged in writing a life of 'THE GOOD GRAY POET.'"

Dr. Bucke was a friend of Whitman and one of his executors. "The good gray Poet" reference is a name given to Whitman in the title of a short biography by William Douglas O'CONNOR.

Long Island Patriot, The (1821–?)   Whitman's "career" in journalism began in the summer of 1831 on this four-page weekly newspaper, just after his 11th birthday. The paper's offices were located on Fulton Street in what would three years later become "officially" BROOKLYN. Whitman worked as a printer's devil and apprentice for the paper's owner and editor, Samuel E. Clements. William HARTSHORNE taught him typesetting, and Walt wrote what he later called "sentimental bits," small items of local interest, although none of those articles has been found.

The *Patriot* was politically extremist on the side of the Democratic Party and New York's Tammany Hall. Clements was fired shortly after the young Whitman started work. The editor and a friend had dug up the body of the famous preacher Elias HICKS shortly after he was buried in 1830; they wanted to make a death mask of his face, but—so the story goes—they argued over ownership of the mask and it was broken. Hicks's family sued, and Clements was forced to leave Long Island.

Whitman certainly would have taken notice of these events, because his father and Hicks were close friends, and Walt had been moved as a child by the sermons he had heard Hicks preach and remembered them in later years as his introduction to oratory.

Long Island Star, The (1809–1968)   Whitman began working for the *Star* in the fall of 1832 at age 12, following his first newspaper job with the LONG ISLAND PATRIOT the previous summer. The *Star* was also a four-page weekly, owned and edited by Alden Spooner, who published poetry and reviews of books and plays, all of which was of interest to his young apprentice.

Spooner was as politically extreme on the side of the Whig Party as Samuel Clements, editor of the *Patriot,* had been prejudiced in favor of the Democrats. The difference of political opinion could not have been lost on the young Whitman. His later Federal-Union-first attitude may have developed in part as a result of the dangers he recognized in the extremes represented by the first two men for whom he worked.

M

Magazine of Art (1878–1904) The London publishing house of Cassell & Company produced this monthly art magazine as a New York edition of its London *Magazine of Art*, using the same articles and illustrations.

Whitman's poem "Twenty Years" was first published in New York's *Magazine of Art* (July 1888).

magazines in Whitman's time Magazine production flourished in America from the mid-1830s to the end of the century, publishing fiction, poetry, plays, and essays for thousands of readers. HARPER'S NEW MONTHLY had a circulation of 200,000 shortly after its founding in 1850, featuring short stories and novels with woodcut illustrations. *Godey's Lady's Book* was founded in 1830; it had a circulation of 25,000 in 1839 but 150,000 in 1860 at the beginning of the CIVIL WAR.

Magazines were most often short-lived, but Whitman benefited greatly from the Golden Age of magazine production in the United States. See the list of newspapers and magazines in part IV that published Whitman's works.

Manhattan and New York City Whitman makes no distinction between New York City, named Manhattan, and the entire city of what would later become the five boroughs.

McKay, David (?–1918) He took over publication of the fifth edition of *Leaves of Grass* (1871) when the Boston publisher James Osgood failed to fight the censorship of the book by the Massachusetts attorney general.

McKay, who worked for Rees Welsh and Company in Philadelphia in 1871, not only became publisher for the fifth edition but was Whitman's publisher for all subsequent printings of *Leaves of Grass*. The David McKay Publishing house was at 1022 Market Street in Philadelphia.

Mickle Street Review, The (1979–1992; 2002–present) Electronic journal of Whitman and American Studies, sponsored by the Walt Whitman Program in American Studies at Rutgers University in Camden, New Jersey. Its Web site is http://www.micklestreet.rutgers.edu.

The *Mickle Street Review* began as an annual print publication in 1979. It ceased publication in 1992 but was revived in 2002 as an e-text journal. The stated mission of the first series, as described on the Web site, "was to provide common ground for poets, writers, teachers, students, and readers with an interest in Walt Whitman or the subjects that he wrote about." The second, e-text, series "will be even broader in scope," according to its online statement of purpose, "seeking to initiate a dialogue among diverse speakers and audiences who might otherwise not come into contact with each other."

Munyon's Magazine (1884–1894) Founded by J. M. Munyon in Philadelphia as a monthly family magazine, originally named *Munyon's Illustrated World*, but changed to *Munyon's Magazine* in 1887.

Ice wagon in front of the Whitman house at 328 Mickle Street in Camden, New Jersey *(Library of Congress, Prints and Photographs Division)*

It had a circulation of 100,000 in 1890 at an annual subscription fee of $1.50, but Munyon ended publication in 1894.

Whitman published two poems in the journal: "Osceola" (April 1890) and "The Commonplace," published as a manuscript facsimile (March 1891).

music and Whitman's poetry   Whitman considered all of his poetry to be musical, singable, certainly to be read aloud. The story is told of French composer Claude Debussy once telling French poet Stéphane Mallarmé that he had put Mallarmé's poem "L'Après-midi d'un faune" to music, to which Mallarmé responded, "I thought I had already done that." Whitman would have appreciated this story. He referred to his poems as "songs" and to himself as a "singer of songs."

During his journalism career, Whitman wrote several articles about music, often adding remarks concerning the importance of establishing American music as stock in trade for concerts. In "American Music, New and True!" for the BROOKLYN EVENING STAR (November 5, 1845), Whitman wrote that

> for the first time we, on Monday night, heard something in the way of American music, which overpowered us with delightful amazement.—We allude to the performances of the Cheney family at Niblo's Saloon. They certainly, to our taste, excel all the much vaunted foreign artists, not excepting Templeton, whom we saw there. Simple, fresh, and beautiful, we hope no spirit of imitation will ever induce them to engraft any 'foreign airs' upon their 'native graces.' We want this sort of starting point from which to mould something new and true in American music. . . .

He lists some of the songs the Cheneys sang: "The Irish Mother's Lament," "Nature's Nobleman," "Farewell to Naxos," and "Vermonters' Song."

A week later Whitman wrote again about the Cheneys' singing, in a performance the night before "at the Institute." And he would scold the BROOKLYN audience for its response: "How strangely stiff and formal they are! How chary of their applause! Or rather how chary of their hands—for our brain has not yet got over that jarring discord produced by kicking and stamping with heavy boots and thumping with canes! Let us whisper in their ear, that kicks are poor tokens of kindness, and no thorough-bred person now-a-days, ever expresses approbation with his *feet*."

Whitman returned to his criticism of Templeton a year later in an article for the BROOKLYN DAILY EAGLE, entitled "Templeton the Singer," (June 19, 1846). "It is astonishing how the public in America, can swallow superannuated third-rate artistes from the Old World, merely through a few prodigiously silly newspaper puffs! Templeton's voice is inferior to many a man's singing in our Brooklyn church choirs. He may at one time of his life have done very well; but he is now old and withered."

Whitman was so caught up in the need to create American art forms that it is difficult to know whether the European singers he criticizes were as bad as he says or whether his American biases simply dominated his every thought when he attended concerts.

Whitman begins another article, "The Oratorio of St. Paul" (November 28, 1845): "Good music certainly strikes the subtle chords of the soul in a way which no other influence possesses."

In perhaps the most famous article Whitman wrote on the subject of the importance of defining American music, he criticizes the current interest of the New World in music from the Old ("Art-Singing and Heart-Singing," written for the *Broadway Journal*, November 29, 1845). He says, "we have long enough followed obedient and child-like in the track of the Old World. We have received her tenors and her buffos, her operatic troupes and her vocalists, of all grades and complexions; listened to and applauded the songs made for a different state of society—made, perhaps, by royal genius, but made to please royal ears likewise; and it is time that such listening and receiving should cease."

He wrote that "with all honor and glory to the land of the olive and the vine, fair-skied Italy—with no turning up of noses at Germany, France, or England—we humbly demand whether we have not run after their beauties long enough."

There are "two kinds of singing," he says, "heart-singing and art-singing." The former "touches the soul" and can come from any society, . . . but "nearly every nation has its peculiarities and its idioms, which make its best intellectual efforts dearest to itself alone, so that hardly any thing which comes to us in the music and songs of the Old World, is strictly good and fitting to our own nation."

There is a footnote to "Art-Singing and Heart-Singing," which Whitman probably wrote himself, stating that he "pretends to no scientific knowledge of music," merely an appreciation. There is no evidence that he ever had any formal study, but there is certainly evidence in the number of articles he wrote about music—plus the poetry of *Leaves of Grass*—that he had a great amount of music appreciation.

Whitman carried the idea of the need for America to sing its own songs over into his own poetry. The "Poet of Democracy" urged other poets to break away from European roots and create a poetry for America, a poetry rich in the images of a great new nation and the democratic ideals for which it was built.

He wrote several other articles on music, including the following: "Educating the Young—Brooklyn Schools—Effect of Music on Children" (*Brooklyn Evening Star*, January 7, 1846); " 'True American' Singing" (*Brooklyn Evening Star*, January 13, 1846); "Are Your Children Taught Singing?" (*Brooklyn Evening Star*, February 9, 1846); "Music for the 'Natural Ear' " (*The Brooklyn Eagle*, April 3, 1846); "Mr. Bradbury's Concert at the N.Y. Tabernacle Tomorrow Night" (a pre-concert blurb) (*The Brooklyn Eagle*, April 16, 1846); "Templeton the Singer" (a scathing review) (*The Brooklyn Daily Eagle*, June 19, 1846); "City Intelligence: Music at Midnight" (*The Brooklyn Daily Eagle*, July 11, 1846); and "Mrs. Bishop's Singing" (*The Brooklyn Daily Eagle*, August 5, 1847).

Whitman wrote a short, one-paragraph item for the *Eagle* (December 8, 1847), entitled "Vocal Music in the Brooklyn Schools," in which he said: "The teaching of vocal music is not only commendable, but, in the opinion of the best teachers, absolutely *necessary* in public schools. It would be well if this branch were more thoroughly fostered and encouraged. Music should be taught in the schools as a *science*. Why not give an exhibition of the scholars in music?"

He also wrote at least three articles about "New and Beautiful Music," written about a local owner of a music store, "Mr. Charles Holt, of 156 Fulton Street, near Broadway, New York." The items are clearly meant to encourage more songs about America. One of the songs cited is by Holt himself, "A bark has moored, &c.," a song of the landing of the Pilgrims at Plymouth in the winter of 1620, for four voices; another song mentioned is "I'd like to live in yonder star," a ballad, according to Whitman, "composed by John Undermer, of Albany."

A recent Whitman biographer Justin Kaplan uses a quotation about the poetry from one of Whitman's earliest friends and biographers John BURROUGHS: "The rhythms and harmonies of 'Lilacs' as well as its method ('a constant interplay—turning and re-turning of images and sentiments') could best be understood through 'the analogy of music.' Swamp-wild like the hermit thrush's, Whitman's music also derived from OPERA and oratorio. 'Art-singing and Heart-singing,' as he distinguished them twenty years earlier, had become synonymous."

Emory Holloway also discusses music in his *Whitman: An Interpretation in Narrative*. "[Whitman] must find relief in song," Holloway says, "and in doing so composed what SWINBURNE, a master of melody himself, described as the 'most sonorous nocturne ever chanted in the church of the world.' 'When Lilacs Last in the Dooryard Bloom'd' is just that, national religious music, and no mere occasional poem. Whitman's lines must be read as music is read. Fragmentary quotation here would only do violence to its delicate interwoven *motifs* of lilac scent and singing thrush and symbolical star, to its incremental repetitions, to its haunting, uplifting suggestiveness."

Gay Wilson Allen writes in *The New Whitman Handbook* that Whitman's method of organizing long poems was symphonic. Allen names as examples, "The Sleepers," "Proud Music of the Storm," "Mystic Trumpeter," and "Song of the Redwood-Tree." "[Whitman] likes to advance a theme," Allen says, "develop it by enumeration and representative symbols, advance other themes and develop them in similar manners, then repeat, summarize, and emphasize. Thus Whitman's repetition of thought, of words, of cadences—playing variations on each out of exuberance and unrestrained joy both in the thought and form—all combine to give him the satisfaction and conviction that he has 'expressed' himself, not logically or even coherently, but by suggestion and by sharing his own emotions with the reader."

music settings   There are a least 400 settings for Whitman's poetry—that is, music composed for a particular poem or poems or music "suggested" to the composer by the poems. There are simple songs taken directly from a Whitman poem, and there are major works of composition, not the least of which are two oratorios by Ralph Vaughan Williams and a requiem by Paul Hindemith.

Here are some examples:

Paul Angerer: "Gesang von mir selbst (after Walt Whitman)" (oratorio for tenor, bass, chorus, and boys' voices)
William Bergsma: "On the Beach" (choral work)
Sir Arthur Bliss: "Morning Heroes" (song)
Eugene Bonner: "Whispers of Heavenly Death" (for voice and orchestra)
Rutland Boughton: "Pioneers" (choral work)
Robert Ernest Bryson: "Drum Taps" (for chorus and orchestra)
Jarmil Burghauser: "The Mystic Trumpeter" (cantata)
Elliott Carter: "Warble for Lilac Time" (for soprano and orchestra)
Mario Castelnuovo-Tedesco: "Leaves of Grass" (song)
Samuel Coleridge-Taylor: "Sea Drift" (choral rhapsody)
Frederick Converse: "The Mystic Trumpeter" (orchestra fantasy) and two orchestra poems

Frederick Delius: "Sea Drift" and "Songs of Farewell" (choral works) and "Idyll" (for voice and orchestra)

Brian Easdale: "Leaves of Grass" (song cycle)

Charles Tomlinson Griffes: "Salut au monde" (stage work)

Howard Hanson: "Drum Taps" (for baritone, chorus, and orchestra) and three songs with orchestra: "The Untold Want," "Portals," and "Joy! Shipmate, Joy!"

Roy Harris: "Whitman Triptych" (for women's chorus) and "Walt Whitman Suite" (choral work)

Fritz Hart: "Gods" (for chorus and orchestra)

Hans Werner Henze: "Whispers of Heavenly Death" (cantata)

Paul Hindemith: "When Lilacs Last in the Dooryard Bloom'd" (American requiem for chorus and orchestra) and five songs

Gustav Holst: "Dirge for Two Veterans" and "Ode to Death" (both choral works) and "Whitman Overture" (for orchestra)

Charles Martin Loeffler: "Drum Taps: A Soldier's March Song" (for orchestra and men's choir)

Harl McDonald: "Dirge for Two Veterans" (women's chorus and orchestra)

Johanna Müller-Hermann: "In Memoriam" (oratorio)

Robert Sanders: "Mystic Trumpeter" (for narrator, baritone, chorus, and orchestra)

William Schuman: "Pioneers" (for eight-part chorus) and "A Free Song" (Secular Cantata No. 2)

Roger Sessions: "Turn O Libertad" (choral work)

Sir Charles Stanford: "Elegiac Ode" (choral work) and three songs

Randall Thompson: "A Ship Starting" (song)

Ralph Vaughan Williams: "Toward the Unknown Region" (for chorus and orchestra), "A Sea Symphony" (for soprano, baritone, chorus, and orchestra), and four songs "Darest thou now, O soul," "Nocturne," "A Clear Midnight," and "Joy, Shipmate, Joy!"

Charles Wood: "Dirge for Two Veterans" (choral work) and one song: "Ethiopia Saluting the Colours"

N

New Orleans Crescent (1848–?) Founded by J. E. McClure in 1848 with Whitman as its first editor. Whitman accepted the job on a casual meeting with McClure during intermission of a play they were attending in New York on February 9, 1848. Two days later, Walt and his brother Jeff, a printer's apprentice, left for New Orleans. The first issue of the *Crescent* was published on February 28.

In an item entitled "Starting Newspapers" in *Specimen Days* (1882), Whitman describes meeting one of the *Crescent*'s owners "between the acts one night in the lobby of the old Broadway theater near Pearl Street, New York City." The two men met, and "after fifteen minutes' talk (and a drink) we made a formal bargain, and he paid me two hundred dollars down to bind the contract and bear my expenses to New Orleans." Whitman and Jeff were on the job two days later. He writes that he "had a good leisurely time, as the paper wasn't to be out [for] three weeks."

A combination of problems, particularly dysentery on Jeff's part and homesickness for both brothers, led to the Whitmans lasting such a short time in New Orleans. McClure and Whitman disagreed politically also, and, with elections coming up later in the year, McClure decided he did not want to face political arguments with his editor. So Whitman was on his way back to New York on May 27, three months after first arriving in the Crescent City.

Whitman published 60 of his own articles in the *Crescent* during the three months, and one poem, "The Mississippi at Midnight" (March 6, 1848).

Most of the articles were on subjects of local interest, the result of Whitman's habit of walking the streets—and in New Orleans the levees—of the city to get a feel for the people and places.

New World, The (c. 1840–?) Journal published in New York City at 30 Ann Street, with Park Benjamin as editor and J. Winchester as publisher.

One of Whitman's first published poems appeared in the *New World*, "The Punishment of Pride" (December 18, 1841), but it was not later included in *Leaves of Grass*. Two of the author's fictional works were also published in the magazine: his novel, *Franklin Evans; or The Inebriate. A Tale of the Times* (November 1842), and a short story, "Child's Champion" (November 20, 1841).

New York Aurora (1841–?) For less than three months during the spring of 1842 Whitman became chief editor of the *Aurora*, the position offered to him after a "trial" as a freelance writer. He was 23 years old at the time. The paper's owners were Anson Herrick and John F. Ropes, and the four-page, two-penny daily had a circulation of about 5,000 readers.

Whitman was in charge of a team of "penny-a-line" writers, and both the owner and Whitman wrote essays claiming that the *Aurora* was the best newspaper in the city.

A number of articles expressed some of Whitman's democratic principles. One in particular (March 16, 1842) elaborated on the idea summarized in an epigraph to the article, "The best government is that which governs least." (He might have been paraphrasing Jefferson here, because THOREAU would not publish his famous statement, "That government is best which governs least," for another seven years; and yet, according to a note in Bergen Evans's *Dictionary of Quotations,* no one has ever found the statement in Jefferson's writings.)

It did not take long, however, for Whitman to become disenchanted with the *Aurora.* Herrick and Ropes accused Whitman of writing biased articles, in particular one about the "serpent tongued," "hypocritical scoundrel" Bishop John Hughes. He referred to Irish priests as "sly, false, deceitful villains." In another essay he wrote that the Irish were "ignorant" about American democracy. Bishop Hughes had petitioned the government for money for Catholic schools, and Whitman reminded him about the separation of church and state. In yet another editorial attacking Bishop Hughes, Whitman accused the "villainous priests" of persuading Irish parents to "keep their boys and girls from school [in order to put pressure on the government to provide the funds for Catholic schools]. . . . In the whole course of American history, no example of foreign insolence can be pointed to, which can parallel this proceeding of these sly and dangerous traitors to the land and to all integrity."

He wrote an editorial statement of principle for the *Aurora:* "There are a thousand dangerous influences operating among us—influences whose tendency is to assimilate this land in thought, in social customs, and, to a degree, in government, with the moth eaten systems of the old world. Aurora is imbued with a deadly hatred to all these influences; she wages open, heavy, and incessant war against them."

Whitman wrote "To a Common Prostitute" for the third edition of *Leaves of Grass* (1860), adding to its censorship problems, but he had preceded it with a sympathetic essay for the *Aurora* (March 24, 1842, writing sarcastically that two justices "last evening . . . made a descent upon Broadway, and in the course of a couple of hours caught and caged . . . upwards of fifty of the most dashy and beautiful of the *'evening belles.'* These women will be paraded before the police justices this morning, at ten o'clock."

The friction between owners and editor notwithstanding, the newspaper published more than 130 of Whitman's essays, plus two poems. He was editor for only three months (February, March, and April, 1842), but some of these articles must have been written before he was named editor when he was doing what he calls in *Specimen Days* "free lance" work.

The two poems were "Time to Come" (April 9, 1842) and "The Death and Burial of McDonald Clarke" (March 18, 1842).

New York Daily Graphic, The (1873–1889)

Founded in 1873 by a group of Canadian engravers under the leadership of Stephen H. Horgan, with David Croly as editor. It was the first illustrated daily newspaper in the United States, launched on March 4, 1873. There had been weekly illustrated newspapers—*Frank Leslie's Weekly* and HARPER'S WEEKLY, for example—but not a daily.

The *Graphic* began with eight pages each day and a tabloid-size format, necessary because of press requirements for engravings. The 1870s were years when the engraving process was getting faster and producing pictures of quality, and the *Daily Graphic* relied heavily on picture appeal. Horgan was instrumental in producing experimental engravings for the paper by the early 1880s.

Croly made lavish use of photographs, mixing them with a recently developed engraving process developed in France. Issues of the *Daily Graphic* would often carry a front-page montage of several photo reproductions of a single news event. Eventually, the newspaper's artists and photographers were able to develop the first "linecuts" and "halftones.

Although the tabloid lasted only 16 years, the popularity of its illustrations paved the way for further experimentation on other New York newspapers. The paper is often remembered for promoting an attempt in 1873 to cross the Atlantic by balloon.

In a general article of review, "By Matador" (November 25, 1873), an unidentified author writes that "it takes seven years to learn to appreciate Walt Whitman's poetry. At least it took me precisely that time, and I divided it as follows: For four years I ridiculed *Leaves of Grass* as the most intricate idiocy that a preposterous pen had ever written. During the next two years I found myself occasionally wondering if, after all, there might not be some glimmer of poetic beauty in Whitman's ragged lines. And then during the last year of my Walt Whitman novitiate the grandeur and beauty and melody of his verse, its vast and measureless expression of all human thoughts and emotions, were suddenly revealed to me. I understand it now. I have learned its purpose and caught the subtle melody of its lines."

The paper was known for its no-fear approach to crime news, sometimes running parallel with items of a literary nature, including the following poems by Whitman: "Nay, Tell Me Not To-Day the Publish'd Shame" (March 5, 1873); "With All Thy Gifts" (March 6, 1873); "The Singing Thrush" (March 15, 1873) [see "Wandering at Morn"]; "Spain, 1873–1874" (March 24, 1873); "Sea Captains Young and Old" (April 4, 1873) [see "Song for All Seas, All Ships"]; "A Kiss to the Bride" (May 21, 1874); "An Old Man's Thought of School" (November 3, 1874); "In the Wake Following" (December 25, 1874) [see "After the Sea-Ship"]; "The Ox-Tamer" (December 25, 1874); and "Come Said My Soul" (December 25, 1874).

New York Democrat, The (1844–?)   Competitive New York newspapers wrote announcements of the birth of this morning daily newspaper in July 1844, stating, according to one paper, that it was "established to support the principles, measures, and candidates of the democratic party." Whitman was the paper's first editor.

The *Democrat* owners (perhaps it was the editor) wrote in its August 12, 1844, issue that the paper was not going to carry a political bias, but would be independent and write about the importance of democratic principles, including a "strict construction" of the Constitution.

New York Evening Post, The (1801–c. 1951)   Founded by the Federalist Party shortly after Thomas Jefferson became president in 1801. Alexander Hamilton raised $10,000 to finance the paper, mostly from Federalist politicians who had just been dismissed from office and from rich business people who felt disenfranchised.

The first editor of the *Post* was William Coleman, a lawyer and occasional journalist who lacked the business acumen to run a daily newspaper in New York. Hamilton, on the other hand, had a genuine claim both as a journalist and as a businessman. He published the "Federalist" papers in the *Independent Journal* during the political debate over the adoption of the U.S. Constitution. He was also sponsor and one of the founders of another newspaper, Fenno's *Gazette of the United States.* And for the first three years of the life of the *Evening Post* he was, until his death in 1804, the editorial director of the *Evening Post.*

The New England poet William Cullen BRYANT became editor of the *Post* in 1829 and for the next 50 years. Five of Whitman's articles were first published in the *Post* while Bryant was editor and one poem: "Song for Certain Congressmen" (March 2, 1850), a poem which argues against the move in Congress to compromise on the question of SLAVERY. An apparently lost CIVIL WAR article entitled "A War-Time Letter, Washington March 19, 1863" was also published by the *Post* in 1918.

New York Evening Tattler (1839–?)   Whitman was editor of this newspaper for a short time in the summer of 1842 and published four articles, one while he was still editor of the NEW YORK AURORA.

In an essay entitled "Boz's Opinion of Us" (August 11, 1842), Whitman criticizes Charles Dickens, who, following a trip to the United States, wrote letters to American newspapers berating the treatment he had received. Whitman seemed to ignore the purpose of Dickens's visit, which was to make a case to publishers and politicians to pass copyright laws. All foreign literary works were reprinted in the United States without permission or pay.

In most of Whitman's articles about Dickens, however, he discussed the importance of the English author's democratic principles. The name "Boz" in Whitman's title came from Dickens's *Sketches by Boz: Illustrative of Every-Day Life and Every-Day People* (1836–37), one of the English author's earliest works, which attracted a large audience.

New York Herald, The (1835–1924)   Founded by James Gordon Bennett in 1835 as competition for the New York SUN, the *Herald* became known as a somewhat radical and independent penny daily newspaper, reflecting Bennett's abilities for hiring people who could gather the news and write it in interesting, often humorous ways. He also bought the technology for producing daily copies quickly, cheaply, and in great quantities. The newspaper began as the *Herald*, but by the mid-1840s it became the *New York Herald.*

Bennett had failed as a publisher of other newspapers and had even been turned down for a job with the *Sun*, but he was a success with the *Herald.* The first editorial offices were in a cellar at 20 Wall Street, where the first edition (a "specimen" copy) was published on May 6, 1835. By the late 1840s, Bennett moved to a large brick building at the corner of Nassau and Fulton streets.

Bennett's son, James Gordon Bennett, Jr., was the paper's proprietor from 1867 to 1918 and responsible for publishing 33 of Whitman's poems. Bennett was something of a playboy, living mostly either on yachts in the United States or in expensive hotels in Europe. As a result of his travels, he decided that Europe needed an English-language newspaper, which he founded as the *Paris Herald* in 1887.

All but one of the Whitman poems for the *Herald* were published in 1888: "Mannahatta" (February 22); "Paumanok" (February 29); "From Montauk Point" (March 1); "To Those Who've Fail'd" (January 27); "A Carol Closing Sixty-Nine" (May 21); "The Bravest Soldiers" (March 18); "As I Sit Writing Here" (May 14); "My Canary Bird" (March 2); "Queries to My Seventieth Year" (May 2); "The Wallabout Martyrs" (March 16); "The First Dandelion" (March 12); "America" (February 11); "To-day and Thee" (April 23); "After the Dazzle of Day" (February 3); "Abraham Lincoln, Born Feb. 12, 1809" (February 12); "Out of May's Shows Selected" (May 10); "Halcyon Days" (January 29); "Broadway" (April 10); "To Get the Final Lilt of Songs" (April 16); "Old Salt Kossabone" (February 25); "Continuities" (March 20); "Life" (April 15); "True Conquerors" (February 15); "The United States to Old World Critics" (May 8); "The Calming Thought of All" (May 27); "Life and Death" (May 23); "Soon Shall the Winter's Foil Be Here"

(February 21); "A Prairie Sunset" (March 9); "Orange Buds by Mail from Florida" (March 19); "The Dead Emperor" (March 10); "The Dismantled Ship" (February 23); and "Interpolation Sounds" (August 12). "As the Greek's Signal Flame" was published December 15, 1892.

New York Leader (1856–1871) Whitman wrote a series of articles he called "City Photographs" for the *Leader* during the first years of the CIVIL WAR, articles similar to those he wrote on New York City for NEW YORK AURORA and on BROOKLYN for the *Brooklyn Standard.* His first four articles for the *Leader* were each titled "The Broadway Hospital." It was during Whitman's journalism work for the *Leader* in 1862 that he may have had an affair with Ellen EYRE.

The *Leader* did not pay well, so Whitman wrote for a number of other papers as well in order to earn a few dollars a week from his writing. During the early years of the war he was continuing to work on a new edition of *Leaves of Grass*, an edition that turned out to be *Drum-Taps* (1865).

The *Leader* also published three of Whitman's poems: "Beat! Beat! Drums!" (September 28, 1861; published simultaneously in HARPER'S WEEKLY and *The Boston Evening Transcript*); "Little Bells Last Night" (October 12, 1861; see "I Heard You Solemn-Sweet Pipes of the Organ"); and "Old Ireland" (November 2, 1861).

New-York Mirror: A Weekly Journal Devoted to Literature and Fine Arts (1823–1860) Whitman's first published and extant article appeared in this newspaper on November 29, 1834. It was titled "The Olden Time," a three-paragraph piece about two "very aged persons" who remembered New York City "as a little *dorp* or village; all fresh and green as it was, from its beginning." The article begins as follows:

> In December, 1758, there died at Smithtown, in Suffolk county, LONG ISLAND, a *Negro Harry*, aged at least one hundred and twenty years when he died. He remembered New-York, he said, when there were but three houses in it. He could do a good day's work when he had passed

one hundred years. He was purchased at New York by Richard Smith, the first proprietor of Smithtown, and descended down to his grandson, Captain Richard Smith, who was still alive at Smithtown, when Harry died. He had been a slave in that family one hundred years. Some of the Smith family, or some of the ancients of Smithtown, ought to have some traditions from such an old oracle.

For *Specimen Days,* Whitman wrote an item titled "Starting Newspapers," in which he describes the thrill of finding the above article in print:

I had a piece or two in George P. Morris's then celebrated and fashionable *Mirror,* of New York City. I remember with what half-suppressed excitement I used to watch for the big, fat, red-faced, slow-moving, very old English carrier who distributed the *Mirror* in Brooklyn; and when I got one, opening and cutting the leaves with trembling fingers. How it made my heart double-beat to see *my piece* on the pretty white paper, in nice type.

New York opera houses   There were at least a dozen theaters in New York City performing operas during the 1840s and 1850s when Whitman was working for several different newspapers and getting free theater tickets. He heard OPERAS in all of them. Following is a list of the most important opera houses and some history.

THE ACADEMY OF MUSIC
The Academy of Music is perhaps the best-known of the mid-19th-century New York opera houses. It was located on 14th Street between Third Avenue and Irving Place when it opened October 2, 1854, with Giulia Grisi and Giuseppe Mario as the principals in Bellini's *Norma.* Whitman was present on opening night. The Academy was New York's operatic center for nearly 30 years.

A fire destroyed the original building in 1866. It was rebuilt and the new lavish theater continued its reputation for grand performances until the neighborhood began to take on an ugly look late in the century. It then was turned into a vaudeville

and movie theater until 1926, when the building was demolished.

In February of the 1854–55 season it offered Pasquale BRIGNOLI in his New York operatic debut, in *William Tell* and *Il Trovatore.* The 16-year-old Adelina Patti made her debut at the Academy, singing in *Lucia* on November 24, 1858. Patti would become one of the city's leading prima donnas and a rival of the popular Jenny LIND, who gave her "farewell" performances at the Academy on May 18, 21, and 24, 1852. Shortly after Lind's farewell, Marietta ALBONI made her New York debut on June 23, a contralto many thought was the greatest performer of her time.

Whitman was at the Academy of Music the night Fort Sumter was attacked, the first battle of the CIVIL WAR (April 13, 1861). The opera may have been Gaetano DONIZETTI's *Linda di Chamounix.*

PALMO'S OPERA HOUSE
Palmo's was founded in 1844 at 39-41 Chambers Street between Broadway and Centre Streets. Restaurant owner Ferdinando Palmo built the theater but lost a fortune and was bankrupt after two years.

It opened on February 3, 1844, with the first performance in New York of Bellini's *I Puritani* and continued to prefer Italian operas—as did most of the theaters performing opera.

Following Palmo's financial difficulties the theater was converted into Burton's Theater and then demolished in 1876.

NIBLO'S GARDEN THEATRE
Located at the corner of Broadway and Prince Streets, Niblo's played host to the French opera company of New Orleans in its first appearance in New York (May 1843). It was also where Señor Marty's Havana Opera Company performed at the beginning of the 1850 opera season—in the newly rebuilt 3,000-seat theater after an enormous fire gutted the original building in 1846. Some of the best singers were in the Havana company; some of them—Bosio, Badiali, and Marini in particular—stayed in New York after the 1850 season and later developed international reputations in Europe.

Whitman wrote about stopping on Broadway after an opera and reading the news of the attack on Fort Sumter, the first battle of the Civil War. *(Library of Congress, Prints and Photographs Division)*

During the fall of 1852 Niblo's offered what is considered to be its greatest season, with established performers, headed by Anna BISHOP. In January of that season Henrietta Sontag, one of Europe's famous singers, made her operatic debut in *La Fille du Regiment,* and through the rest of the winter she appeared more than 30 times, primarily in works by Rossini and DONIZETTI. Whitman's favorite opera singer, Marietta ALBONI, also sang at Niblo's through the spring season that year.

By the summer of 1853 Niblo's had become the leading opera house in New York City. William Niblo, the original owner, retired in 1858, though the opera house retained his name and reputation.

PARK THEATER

Built at 21-25 Park Row (opposite City Hall Park) in 1798 and destroyed by fire in 1848. Manuel Gar-

cia's famous opera company gave its New York debut in a performance of Rossini's *Barbiere di Siviglia* at the Park on November 29, 1825, one of the earliest operas at the theater. Garcia himself sang Almaviva and his daughter Maria Felicita (later Malibran) sang Rosina.

The Park opened the 1841–42 opera season with a local cast of performers. Balfe's *Bohemian Girl* had its premier at the Park on November 25, 1844. A New Orleans opera company, led by Mme. Julie Calvé, was at the Park during the summer, 1845, performing Meyerbeer, Auber, Rossini, and Donizetti. Donizetti's *La Favorita* and Meyerbeer's *Robert le Diable* had their New York debuts at the Park Theater.

In April 1847 an Italian opera company from Havana opened at the Park and became more famous than any other group performing at New

York opera houses during that period. Don Francesco Marty y Torrens ("Señor Marty") was the company's manager.

And in the fall of 1847 the Park introduced Anna BISHOP, who made an overnight success and continued developing her career until the opera house burned in December 1848.

In *Specimen Days*, Whitman names several of the opera houses that he frequented during the 40s and 50s, but he emphasizes the Park by listing the names of several singers and actors he had seen there:

> The old Park Theater—what names, reminiscences, the words bring back! Placide, Clarke, Vernon, Fisher, Clara F., Mrs. Wood, Mrs. Sequin, Ellen Tree, Hackett, the younger Kean, Macready, Mrs. Richardson, Rice—singers, tragedians, comedians.

The Park was not as famous as the Academy of Music, probably because it did not last as long, yet it produced the best of the classic repertory, plays and operas.

ASTOR PLACE OPERA HOUSE

Located on East Eighth Street at Astor Place, the theater opened its doors on November 22, 1847, with Verdi's *Ernani* and rapidly developed a reputation as the most beautiful theater in New York. The European conductor Max Maretzek made his New York debut at the Astor in the 1848–49 season and was for several years one of the most important music personalities in America. The theater had a seating capacity of 1,800.

Maretzek had enough financial support to take several performers away from the Havana Opera Company, which was producing at that time a number of great singers, including Bosio, Bettini, and Badiali. Nevertheless the Astor Place closed in 1852.

In spite of its reputation for good opera, Astor Place is probably best remembered for the 1849 riot of jingoistic immigrants in front of the theater. They were protesting the appearance of a British actor, and were fired at by the police, with at least 18 killed and hundreds injured. The Astor Place

manager became unwilling to book important singers and actors, forcing it to close. In 1854 it became the Clinton Hall Library.

CASTLE GARDEN

Better known as "the Battery," Castle Garden was the site of Havana Opera Company performances during the summers of 1846 and 1849. Conductor Maretzek managed the house in 1850 and often attracted several excellent performers. Giulia Grisi, who, with her husband Giuseppe Mario, an internationally famous couple, performed at the Castle Garden in, among other operas, *Lucrezia Borgia*.

Whitman writes of having heard Jenny Lind sing at the Battery. "The Battery—its past associations—what tales those old trees and walks and sea wall could tell!"

BROADWAY THEATRE

The Broadway opened in 1847, with performances by ANNA BISHOP in *Lucrezia Borgia*, *Linda di Chamounix*, and *La Sonnambula*.

ITALIAN OPERA HOUSE

At the corner of Church and Leonard Streets in New York, the "Italian Opera House" opened on November 18, 1833. It was the first theater built in New York specifically for opera, but it lasted only two seasons.

BOWERY THEATER

Whitman writes in an essay titled "The Old Bowery" about hearing Giuseppe Mario at the Bowery Theater; in fact, "many times, and at his best," the poet says. He heard the tenor in *Lucrezia Borgia* and refers to him as "inimitable."

In the short essay in *Specimen Days* titled "Plays and Operas, Too," Whitman writes that "All through these years [the 1840s and 1850s], off and on, I frequented the old Park, the Bowery, Broadway, and Chatham Square Theaters, and the Italian operas at Chambers Street, Astor Place, or the Battery—many seasons was on the free list, writing for papers even as quite a youth." Also in *Specimen Days* he writes about three of "life's rare and blessed hours": "the wild sea storm I once saw one winter day off Fire Island—the elder Booth in

Richard, that famous night nearly forty years ago in the Old Bowery—or ALBONI in the children's scene in *Norma.*"

In *November Boughs,* he described the Bowery as "packed from ceiling to pit with its audience mainly of alert, well dress'd, full-blooded young and middle-aged men . . . bursting forth in one of those tempests of hand clapping peculiar to the Bowery."

RICHMOND HILL THEATRE

Mozart's librettist, Lorenzo Da Ponte, was one of several sponsors of the 1832–33 opera season at the Richmond Hill—all operas from the Italian repertory.

CHAMBERS STREET OPERA HOUSE

In an article for the *BROOKLYN DAILY EAGLE* while he was editor, Whitman wrote of Chambers Street Opera House that "they are continuing the representation of a narrow few [operas]—those not even the second best—of the Italian operas; tonight 'Lucrezia Borgia.' On Wednesday night it will be pleasanter to go, for then they give 'Lombardi.'"

OLYMPIC THEATER

The following passage is from an article Whitman wrote when he was editor of the *Brooklyn Daily Eagle* (February 24, 1847): "At the Olympic Theatre, they are giving a run, after the old sort, of the popular operas, very neatly got up on a small scale; Miss Taylor appears tonight as Zorlina in 'Fra Diavolo' (the best played parts at this theatre are Diavolo's two fellow robbers)."

New York Statesman (1843–?) This newspaper was founded in March 1843, with Whitman as its editor. No copies exist.

New York Times, The (1851–present) Founded as a penny paper in 1851 by three men: Henry J. Raymond, George Jones, and Edward B. Wesley. Raymond, who had been one of Horace Greeley's editors at the *NEW YORK TRIBUNE*, was editor of the new paper, and Jones was business manager. They realized the need for a new conservative Whig newspaper in New York and promised for the *New York Times* a wider coverage of the news and greater

editorial content in support of Whig political candidates and policies. The new daily was an immediate success. It had a circulation of 20,000 within 10 weeks; but it was also an expensive operation, costing $78,000 in its first year. To help offset costs, Raymond raised the price from one cent to two. He also sold 100 shares of stock in the paper for $1,000 per share and within five years was able to pay a total of $20,000 a year back to stockholders.

Raymond also promised better coverage of literary events, including reviews of books and plays. The newspaper covered a speech delivered by Whitman at a Japanese embassy reception in New York on June 16, 1860, and printed a poem, "The Errand-Bearers," which the poet read aloud to the audience. See "A Broadway Pageant," the title given to the poem for the *Drum-Taps* volume (1865).

New York Tribune (1841–1924) Founded on April 19, 1841, by Horace Greeley, this "penny" newspaper became a popular advocate of the Whig Party and had a circulation of 10,000 by the end of the first year. Whitman was one of Greeley's first editors. The *Tribune* was started shortly after the election of William Henry Harrison as president in November 1840. He was the first Whig president, and the paper supported the Whig agenda for labor. Greeley announced the conditions for founding the paper: "I had been incited to this enterprise by several Whig friends, who deemed a cheap daily, addressed more specifically to the laboring class, was eminently needed in our city." The paper's prolabor bias helped to sell copies.

Greeley was so immediately successful with the daily that he founded the *New York Weekly Tribune* on September 29, 1841, a paper meant for readers west of the Mississippi. It reprinted material, including Greeley's editorials, from the daily *Tribune* and included articles of interest to people in the West or headed west. The *Weekly Tribune* reached a circulation of 200,000 during the 1860s, largest of any U.S. newspaper.

Whitman, at age 22 and without much editorial experience, became Greeley's chief editor in March 1842. He was a "bold, energetic and original writer" and responsible for getting out the four-page daily which included news and editorials aimed primarily at a New York City audience.

In the early 1850s Greeley's continued success forced him to hire Charles A. Dana as managing editor for what had become a newspaper with more than 100 employees and hundreds of thousands of dollars in operating costs. The *Tribune* became the *New York Herald-Tribune* in 1924.

Ten of Whitman's poems were first published in the *New York Tribune*: "Blood-Money" (March 22, 1850); "The House of Friends" (June 14, 1850); "Resurgemus" (June 21, 1850); "Eidólons" (February 19, 1876); "Out from Behind This Mask" (February 19, 1876); "When the Full-Grown Poet Came" (February 19, 1876); "The Beauty of the Ship" (February 19, 1876); "After an Interval" (February 19, 1876); "To a Locomotive in Winter" (February 19, 1876); and "From Far Dakota's Cañons" (June 25, 1876).

Whitman apparently did not publish any articles in the *Tribune* while he was editor, but he wrote 11 articles for the paper between 1877 and 1885. One was entitled "Walt Whitman on Thomas Paine," reprinted in *Specimen Days* as "In Memory of Thomas Paine." It was a speech Whitman delivered at Lincoln Hall in Philadelphia on January 28, 1877, the 140th anniversary of Paine's birthday. One sentence, in particular, sums up Whitman's tribute to the importance of Paine in the forming of the country: "He served the embryo Union with most precious service—a service that every man, woman and child in our thirty-eight states is to some extent receiving the benefit of today—and I for one here cheerfully, reverently throw my pebble on the cairn of his memory."

Two other Whitman-related items were published by Greeley in the *Tribune*: Thomas CARLYLE's "Shooting Niagara" (August 16, 1867) and EMERSON's letter to Whitman in 1855 complimenting him on *Leaves of Grass.* Carlyle had argued in the *Tribune* that democracy would "destroy civilization." The editor of the GALAXY magazine asked Whitman if he would like to respond, and the chief spokesman for democracy could not resist. He wrote *Democratic Vistas*, two-thirds of which was first published in the *Galaxy* (December 1867 and May 1868).

Emerson's letter, which Whitman gave to Dana for publication in the *Tribune*, was published without Emerson's permission. In the letter, Emerson provided Whitman with a line that was to be repeated often in advertisements for *Leaves of Grass*, even on the spine of the second edition of *Leaves of Grass*: "I greet you at the beginning of a great career."

In an unsigned story in the *Tribune*, published November 19, 1881, during a time when the newspaper was also printing the poet's own articles, the writer presents a scathing review of Whitman's poetry to that time. He begins by saying that "after the dilettante indelicacies of William H. Mallock and Oscar WILDE, we are presented with the slop-bucket of Walt Whitman." He later acknowledges some poetic qualities in *Leaves of Grass* but writes that the "chief question raised by this publication [*The Tribune*] is whether anybody—even a poet—ought to take off his trousers in the market-place. Of late years we believe that Mr. Whitman has not chosen to be so shocking as he was when he had his notoriety to make, and many of his admirers—the rational ones—hoped that the *Leaves of Grass* would be weeded before he set them out again. But this has not been done: and indeed Mr. Whitman could hardly do it without falsifying the first principle of his philosophy, which is a belief in his own perfection, and the second principle, which is a belief in the preciousness of filth."

New York Weekly Graphic, The Whitman published a series of six "war memoranda" essays in this newspaper, the last three of which were later published together as "Army Hospitals and Cases: Memoranda at the Time, 1863–66" and published in CENTURY MAGAZINE (October 1888).

The six earlier essays were published in the *Weekly Graphic* as follows: "'Tis But Ten Years Since [First Paper]" (January 24, 1874), "'Tis But Ten Years Since [Second Paper]" (February 7, 1874), "'Tis But Ten Years Since [Third Paper]" (February 14, 1874), "'Tis But Ten Years Since [Fourth Paper]" (February 21, 1874), "'Tis But Ten Years Since [Fifth Paper]" (February 28, 1874), and "'Tis But Ten Years Since [Sixth Paper]" (March 7,

1874). And they were all part of Whitman's pamphlet *Memoranda during the War,* published in 1875–76.

Nineteenth Century   Journal of the arts that published eight poems by Whitman in its August 1885 issue: "Had I the Choice," "The Pilot in the Mist," "You Tides with Ceaseless Swell," "Last of Ebb, and Daylight Waning," "And Yet Not You Alone," "Proudly the Flood Comes In," "By That Long Scan of Waves," and "Then Last of All."

Nore, the   Part of the Thames River estuary, an anchorage, southeast of London, made famous by a mutiny in the British fleet there in 1797, which resulted in the hanging of its leader, Richard PARKER. The incident served, however, to expose the fleet commander's brutality. Whitman used the incident in his short story "Richard Parker's Widow."

Northfleet   British steamship that sank in a collision off Dungeness, England, in the Straits of Dover, at a loss of 300 passengers and crew on January 22, 1873. Whitman commemorated the event, as well as the sinking of another ship, ATLANTIC, on April 1, 1873, in his poem "Sea Captains, Young and Old," published in the NEW YORK DAILY GRAPHIC (April 4, 1873). The poem's title was later changed to "Song for All Seas, All Ships."

O

O'Connor, William Douglas (1832–1889)   A political radical and journalist and one of Whitman's close friends; they met in Boston in 1860 when Whitman was preparing for publication his third edition of *Leaves of Grass*, and the friendship developed later, when both men were government employees in Washington, D.C.

Whitman wrote in later life, remembering the first meeting, that O'Connor "was a . . . gay-hearted, fine-voiced, glowing-eyed man; lithe-moving on his feet, of healthy and magnetic atmosphere and presence, and the most welcome company in the world. He was a thorough-going anti-slavery believer, speaker, and writer, (doctrinaire,) and though I took a fancy to him from the first, I remember I fear'd his ardent abolitionism—was afraid it would probably keep us apart." The friendship lasted until O'Connor's death three years before Whitman's.

Whitman spent a lot of time at the O'Connor house in Washington. The poet felt at home there, and they were, he said, "my understanders, my lovers: they more than any others. I was nearer to them than any others—oh! Much nearer." Nelly O'Connor was in love with Whitman in her own way, offering to move in with Whitman at his Camden, New Jersey, home when her husband died in 1889.

O'Connor published the GOOD GRAY POET (1866) in part as a defense of Whitman, who had been dismissed as a government clerk. It was also written to defend the principle of freedom in literature. The book is best known, however, because of its title, from which Whitman got his assumed name. Whitman later wrote a preface for a posthumous collection of O'Connor's stories titled *Three Tales*, containing "The Carpenter," a story with a Christ-like depiction of Whitman.

Henry Raymond, owner and editor of the NEW YORK TIMES, did not like *Leaves of Grass*, but he liked *The Good Gray Poet* well enough to offer O'Connor a job as reporter for the *Times*. Raymond invited O'Connor to write a review of the 1860 edition of *Leaves*, but told him to keep it short. O'Connor responded with a 6,000-word review that spread over four columns of the newspaper's six-column format. Five years later, Raymond rejected a review of *Drum-Taps* by O'Connor, in which O'Connor wrote that *Drum-Taps* proved that Whitman belonged "among the chief poets of the world." Raymond evidently disagreed.

Whitman once made the statement that he would "rather hear O'Connor argue for what I consider wrong than hear most people argue for what I think right."

O'Connor also wrote an abolitionist novel, *Harrington: A Story of True Love* (1860) and two pamphlets arguing that Sir Francis Bacon had written Shakespeare's plays.

Once a Week (1888–1895)   Founded by Peter Fenelon Collier, an Irish immigrant at age 17, who became an American publisher at 24. Originally titled *Collier's Once a Week*, it advertised in its first issue that it was a magazine of "fiction, fact, sensation, wit, humor, news." The name was changed to *Collier's Weekly, An Illustrated Journal* in 1895.

The first editor was Nugent Robinson, who published Whitman's poem "A Thought of Columbus" (July 9, 1892) as a manuscript facsimile.

opera, Whitman and Whitman learned to enjoy opera just at a time when New York City was rich in opera companies and the means to attract the best performers who were then singing in the great European houses. This was during the 1840s and 1850s while he was a journalist, working as a reporter or editor for several different newspapers and getting free tickets to NEW YORK OPERA HOUSES and theaters.

The influence of opera on Whitman is impossible to measure, but it is clear that he felt that his own "songs" were often inspired by operas and operatic styles. He was fascinated by every aspect of opera: the voices of singers, the instruments of the orchestra, the dramatic story-lines, even audience responses. He was interested in the magic of the drama, what it did to his imagination, and how the drama merged with the MUSIC. Late in his life he remembered that his first "mystical experience" had its origins in opera.

Whitman's "Out of the Cradle Endlessly Rocking" states clearly that the source of the poet's inspiration and subject matter came from the sea; yet it is also quite possible—especially because the poem may be analyzed for its musical, even operatic style of presentation—that some mystical experiences derived from opera carried over into the poetry.

During the late 1840s and early 1850s Whitman was developing his own poetic techniques, and there is little doubt that what he learned from his interest in opera inspired the "music" of his poetry.

He attended opera regularly. He stated that he had heard the Italian contralto Marietta ALBONI every time she sang in New York. Her only performances in the city were during the 1852–53 season, when she sang in 10 different operas, in 12 concerts of mostly opera music, and in Rossini's oratorio *Stabat Mater.* Alboni probably sang in each opera more than once, and—even allowing for Whitman's noted exaggeration—he must have heard one of the greatest of all opera contraltos sing at least 25 or 30 times.

Whitman wrote reviews of a number of opera performances, and, late in life, he remembered the names of the singers and the operas he had heard. If his memory was accurate, he heard all or nearly all of the major opera performers who sang in New York from 1840 until 1861, when he rushed off to Washington at the beginning of the CIVIL WAR. There were at least a dozen theaters open at various times during those years that performed opera, and they brought to New York a who's who of mostly European opera companies and their singers.

Besides Marietta Alboni, the list of singers includes: the famed Swedish soprano Jenny LIND, who toured the United States in the period 1850–52 under the auspices of circus impresario P. T. Barnum (Whitman once wrote about Lind that "with all her blandishments, [she] never touched my heart in the least"); the Italian tenor Allesandro Bettini, who made his New York debut in 1852; Italian bass Ignazio Marini, who made his debut in 1850; Italian soprano Balbina Steffanone, in her New York debut in 1850; Italian tenor Pasquale BRIGNOLI, who made his New York debut in 1855 and was the subject of Whitman's poem "The Dead Tenor" (written after Brignoli's death); Italian soprano Giula Grisi, who, with her husband Giuseppe Mario, was famous for her previous performances at London's Covent Garden, particularly in *Norma;* Italian baritone Cesare Badiali, probably the best-known baritone of his day, who made his New York debut in 1850; Italian soprano Angiolina Bosio, in her New York debut in 1850; and soprano Adelina Patti, who made her New York opera debut on November 24, 1859, at age 16, singing Lucia. Adelina (1843–1919) was from a family of opera performers; her sister, Carlotta, also sang opera, and their brother, Carlo, was a violinist with the New Orleans Opera Company. They were the children of Salvatore Patti and Caterina Barili, both of whom sang with Italian opera companies.

Whitman heard 25 operas performed—according to his own notes and published works—some of them several times: Auber's *Masaniello;* BELLINI's *I Puritani, La Sonnambula,* and *Norma;* DONIZETTI's *La Favorita, La Fille du Regiment, Linda di Chamounix, Lucia di Lammermoor, Lucrezia Borgia, Marino Faliero,* and *Poliuto*; Gounod's *Faust*; Meyerbeer's *Le Pro-phète, L'Etoile du Nord,* and *Robert le Diable*; Mozart's *Don Giovanni*; Verdi's *Ernani, I Lombardi, Il Trova-tore,* and *Rigoletto*; Rossini's *Guillaume Tell, Il Barbi-ere di Siviglia, La Cenerentola,* and *La Gazza Ladra*; and Von Weber's *Der Freischütz.*

There is no evidence that Whitman attended any opera in New Orleans during the three months he was there in 1848, during which time operas were performed almost daily. Yet he was certainly aware that the city had two major opera houses and that the New Orleans Opera Company performed regularly in New York. It seems unlikely that he did not attend some performances.

In an article for the NEW YORK AURORA (April 15, 1842) entitled "Italian Opera in New Orleans," Whitman criticizes the NEW YORK HERALD editor James Gordon Bennett for running a favorable blurb on a New Orleans performance by "Mrs. Sutton" in *Sonnambula*. Whitman calls the item "stupid hum-bug. . . . No other paper in the country but his ever attempted to soft soap La Signora Fatoni Sutton . . . into a *prima donna. . . .* The fact is, La Signora *Fat-*oni [sic] is only a second rate singer, and about a third rate musician. She had a fair chance at the [New York] Park [Theatre], in Norma, and could not succeed in drawing even the expenses. As a concert singer, she was thrown into the shade by [Euphrasia] Borghese, and yet she had the temerity to go to Havana and New Orleans to test the public favor with that accomplished artist." The review is as much a criticism of Whitman's rival editor James Gordon Bennett as it is of Mrs. Sutton.

In an article entitled "The New Opera" (the BROOKLYN DAILY EAGLE, March 6, 1847), Whitman reviews a performance of Verdi's *I Lombardi,* per-formed by an Italian opera company in New York. "[Francesco] Beneventano's voice in no previous opera has so fully developed its powers; those pow-ers are indeed wonderful, . . . and in his bursts of musical furor he seems to possess the ability of drowning the entire orchestra! . . . Rapetti plays a violin solo in the third act, which alone is worth going from the ninth ward of BROOKLYN to hear; and the solo is backed by one of the sweetest songs Barili ever sang."

In a review of *The Barber of Seville* two weeks later, he recommends that Sesto Benedetti be allowed to sing "the part Signor Patti at present fills." Whitman never hesitated to apply heavy crit-icism to singers he thought deserved it. On the other hand, he was far less critical of the operas he heard during the 1860s and early 1870s.

Three of Whitman's poems in particular name operas or key roles: "Italian Music in Dakota" men-tions *La Sonnambula, Norma,* and *Poliuto*; "Proud Music of the Storm" names characters in *Lucia di Lammermoor, Norma, Ernani, I Puritani, La Favorita,* and *La Sonnambula* and refers also to *William Tell, Huguenots, The Prophet, Robert le Diable, Faust,* and *Don Juan*; "The Dead Tenor" is a tribute to the tenor Pasquale Brignoli, and mentions three roles for which he was famous: Fernando in *La Favorita,* Manrico in *Il Trovatore,* the lead role in *Ernani,* and Gennaro in *Lucrezia Borgia.*

Outing (1882–1923) Founded as a monthly periodical in Albany, New York, by William Bailey Howland. It had several titles and breaks in its pub-lication history, and it moved first to Boston (1884) and then to New York (1886). *Outing* was prima-rily a gentleman's sports publication and had among its earliest writers Walter Camp, the father of American football, and among its artists Frederic Remington. Jack London's *White Fang* was serialized in 1906. Whitman's poem "The Voice of the Rain" was first published in *Outing* (August 1885).

P

pantheism A philosophical belief that God is in all things. The pantheist believes that nature is both the revelation of deity and deity itself. Whitman believed in the spirit of "soul" in every living thing. See, for example, "Song at Sunset," where the poet states in line 37: "Surely there is something more in each of the trees, some living soul."

In *The Solitary Singer* (1955), Gay Wilson Allen says of "When Lilacs Last in the Dooryard Bloom'd" that it is one of the "great pantheistic elegies, such as Shelley's 'Adonais,' EMERSON's 'Threnody.' " Allen says that Whitman compares physical love to a kind of death. "To the woman he says that earthly life is of short duration; but, 'Be not impatient—a little space,' and we shall be absorbed into 'the air, the ocean and the land' forever. The solution is, in fact, a symbolical death—the path to eternal happiness."

In "Song of Myself," which explains Whitman's concept of pantheism as well perhaps as any poem in *Leaves of Grass,* he tries to answer a child's question about the meaning of "grass." He describes it as "the beautiful uncut hair of graves," a metaphor he probably got from Homer. The image suggests Whitman's developing fascination with death. The last stanza of Section 6 pushes this grass/death image a step further:

> The smallest sprout shows there is really no
>   death,
> And if ever there was it led forward life, and
>   does not wait at the end to arrest it,
> And ceas'd the moment life appear'd.

This is pantheistic, a philosophy Whitman readily accepted: The belief that God is not a personality, but that the spirit of God is in all things and that all things reflect that spirit.

Parker, Richard (1767–1797) Admiral of the British navy, accused of mutiny at the NORE anchorage of the Thames River in 1797 and hanged for the incident. Whitman's short story "Richard Parker's Widow" is based on the incident.

Parton, James (1822–1891) One of the most successful and respected American biographers of the mid-1800s. He established his reputation with *The Life of Horace Greeley* (1855), and he wrote also the lives of Aaron Burr (1857), Andrew Jackson (three volumes, 1859–60), Benjamin Franklin (two volumes, 1864), John Jacob Astor (1865), Thomas Jefferson (1874), and Voltaire (two volumes, 1881).

He was a friend of Whitman for a time, but the friendship was broken during the early months of 1857, apparently by his wife's relationship with Whitman. Sara Parton was a popular writer also, using the pen name Fanny FERN for articles she wrote on domestic issues.

Parton brought a strange legal case against Whitman on June 17, 1857. Parton had lent the poet $200, and when he failed to pay off the short-term loan, he sent a lawyer, Oliver Dyer, to Walt's house to claim the money. Walt could not pay but gave up several books and paintings to Dyer in lieu of the $200, which apparently Dyer failed to give to

Parton, who then sued Whitman in default of the debt. Whitman thought the loan had been paid. The entire affair was something of a scandal in New York and certainly an embarrassment for Whitman.

Whitman biographer William Sloane KENNEDY, who tried to check out further details about the scandal shortly after the poet died in 1892, had only one significant source of information, a close Whitman friend, Ellen O'Connor. She told Kennedy to look up the story of Potiphar in the Old Testament. Potiphar was Joseph's master in Egypt, and when Joseph rejected the advances of Potiphar's wife, she accused him of attempted rape, and Potiphar put him in prison (Genesis 39). The inference here is that Whitman rejected Sara, and she got revenge by telling her husband that the poet had abused her.

Parton, Sara   See FERN, FANNY.

periodic sentences   A sentence in which the most important element comes at the end. Here is an example: Because of his great good looks and the obvious joy with which he tackled various academic subjects, the boy was passed on to the next grade.

Whitman uses periodic sentences for poetic emphasis, holding the most important idea until the end of the sentence to give it prominence. See, for example, the opening stanza of "Out of the Cradle Endlessly Rocking"; there are 22 lines, all one sentence, leading to the final, key idea. Here are the last five lines:

> A man, yet by these tears a little boy again,
> Throwing myself on the sand, confronting the
>   waves,
> I, chanter of pains and joys, uniter of here and
>   hereafter,
> Taking all hints to use them, but swiftly leaping
>   beyond them,
> A reminiscence sing.

Many of Whitman's poetic stanzas—some 10 or more lines in length—are all one sentence, and several of those sentences are presented with the grammatical subject at the end.

personalism   A philosophy that teaches, according to Odell Shepard in his biography of Bronson ALCOTT, that "the ultimate reality . . . is a Divine Person who sustains the universe by a continuous act of creative will." Alcott, who had been influenced by Whitman, wrote about the importance of becoming "one with the Person dwelling in every breast" as a way of understanding the idea that "all souls have a Personal identity with God and abide in him."

In *The Journals of Bronson Alcott*, edited by Shepard (1938), Alcott is quoted as writing in a letter: "I can only ask you to distinguish finely that in yourself which differences you from other persons essentially and that which unites and makes them one with yourself, also makes you one with them, indissolubly and forever. The unity is the Personality; the difference is the Individuality. . . . We must grow into and become one with the Person dwelling in every breast, and thus come to apprehend the saying 'I and my Father are one'—that is, perceive that all souls have a Personal identity with God and abide in him."

Whitman may have been the first American to use the term; his essay "Personalism" was published in the GALAXY (May 1868) and was reprinted as one of his three main points in an 84-page pamphlet on democracy in *Democratic Vistas* (1871). Alcott's definition of Personalism is certainly echoed throughout Whitman's works.

Pfaff's Cellar   Established at 653 Broadway in New York at a chophouse owned by Charles Ignatius Pfaff. It was a gathering place for New York bohemians—newspaper editors and reporters, theater people, musicians, critics, and writers of fiction and poetry. Whitman enjoyed the freethinking aspect of the collection of interesting contemporaries. Henry CLAPP, founder of SATURDAY PRESS in 1858, reigned at Pfaff's as "prince of the bohemians." Ada CLARE, mistress of composer Louis Moreau Gottschalk, was known as the "queen of Bohemia."

Other "Pfaffians" included William Dean HOWELLS, John Swinton, Joseph E. Chamberlin, Fitz-Greene Halleck, Edwin Einstein, William Winter, Charles D. Gardette, Thomas Bailey ALDRICH, and Fitz-James O'Brien. The last four were editors or writers at one time or another under Henry Clapp at *Saturday Press*. Halleck is quoted as saying that Whitman "ought to write his poems seated on the back of an elephant." Einstein wrote to Whitman in 1875 asking if he needed money as an article in the Sun indicated; Walt wrote back about his various ailments but that money was not then a problem.

Clapp enlisted a number of contributions for his newspaper at Pfaff's, including two of Whitman's most familiar poems: "A Child's Reminiscence," the early version of "Out of the Cradle Endlessly Rocking," and "O Captain! My Captain."

Chamberlin, who wrote a column called "Listener" for the *Boston Evening Transcript* and was a member of the Pfaffians, wrote the paper's obituary on Whitman (March 28, 1892), in which he quotes a "chant" that was sung at Pfaff's Cellar in honor of Whitman:

And here's to the genial philosopher, too,
At Pfaff's,
Who glows for the many as well as the few,
At Pfaff's,
Who don't want to put a green shade on the
    sun,
Or try to make two look as if they were one
At Pfaff's, at Pfaff's, at Pfaffs,
For nature is nature at Pfaff's!

Whitman would write in *Specimen Days* about a trip he took back to Pfaff's during a stay in Manhattan.

Then an excellent breakfast at Pfaff's restaurant, 24th Street. Our host himself, an old friend of mine, quickly appeared on the scene to welcome me and bring up the news, and, first opening a big fat bottle of the best wine in the cellar, talk about antebellum times, '59 and '60, and the jovial suppers at his then Broadway place, near Bleecker Street. Ah, the friends and names and frequenters, those times, that place. Most are dead—Ada Clare, Wilkins, Daisy Sheppard, O'Brien, Henry Clapp, Stanley, Mullin, Wood, Brougham, Arnold—all gone. And there Pfaff and I, sitting opposite each other at the little table, gave a remembrance to them in a style they would have themselves full confirmed, namely, big, brimming, filled-up

champagne glasses, drained in abstracted silence, very leisurely, to the last drop. (Pfaff is a generous German *restaurateur*, silent, stout, jolly, and I should say the best selector of champagne in America.)

Whitman visited Pfaff's during the spring of 1862 while he was volunteering as an assistant at one of New York's hospitals during the Civil War. Some of the doctors frequented Pfaff's after work and would question Whitman about his choice of "friends" among the hospital wounded, friends with nicknames such as "Balky Bill," "Old Elephant," "Broadway Jack," "Pop Rice," "Yellow Joe," etc. Whitman merely replied to the doctors' questions by saying that he felt sorry for the wounded soldiers and enjoyed listening to their stories. He received a love letter from a woman identified only as "Ellen Eyre," addressed to him at Pfaff's Restaurant, Broadway, New York.

John Swinton once described Whitman's place in Pfaff's society as someone who would "sit by Pfaff's privy and eat sweet-breads and drink coffee, and listen to the intolerable wit of the crack-brains."

Philadelphia Press (1857–c. 1920) Founded by John W. Forney as a Democratic newspaper, but it became Republican in 1860 when Forney felt betrayed by President Buchanan, who favored the admission of Kansas as a slave state. The *Press* supported Lincoln and antislavery issues throughout the Civil War.

During Forney's tenure as publisher, the *Press* published four of Whitman's poems: "Election Day, November, 1884" (October 26, 1884); "Red Jacket (from Aloft)" (October 10, 1884); "Washington's Monument, February, 1885" (February 22, 1885); and "Thanks in Old Age" (November 24, 1887).

Philadelphia Public Ledger (1836–?) Founded on March 25, 1836, by three New York printers: William M. Swain, Arunah S. Abell, and Axariah H. Simmons, all of whom had worked on the Sun and saw the possibilities of success with a penny daily newspaper in Philadelphia. George W. Childs and the Drexel brothers, Anthony and Francis, bought the paper in 1864 and turned it into the largest circulation newspaper in Philadelphia.

The *Public Ledger* had a tendency toward sensationalism and for its attacks on local corruption. But it also published literary items, including a poem by Whitman, entitled "For Queen Victoria's Birthday" (May 22, 1890).

Price, Abby H. (unknown)   She was a good friend of Walt's mother when they first lived in BROOKLYN on Front Street. Her husband, Edmund, owned a pickle factory at 314 Front Street. Abby was active in several reform movements: abolition of slavery, women's rights, and dress reform.

R

Radical, The (1865–1872) Publication of the Radical Club, an informal group of New England ministers and laymen, who fought against Christian "supernaturalism." The group included a number of Unitarian and transcendentalist New England thinkers. One of the finest and fullest appreciations of Whitman's *Leaves of Grass* was printed in the journal's May 1870 issue, an essay by Anne GILCHRIST entitled "An Englishwoman's Estimate of Walt Whitman."

religion, Whitman and Whitman did not single out one religion as more valuable than another, any more than he singled out any one person or occupation or section of the country or state as more worthy than another.

He also clarified in his "preface" to the 1872 edition of *Leaves of Grass* what he calls "the Religious purpose" underlying the poems. He refers to the poems as "the New Theology—heir of the West—lusty and loving, and wondrous beautiful. . . . As there can be, in my opinion, no sane and complete Personality, nor any grand and electric Nationality, without the stock element of Religion imbuing all the other elements, (like heat in chemistry, invisible itself, but the life of all visible life,) so there can be no Poetry worthy the name without that element behind all. . . ." And Religion, Whitman believed, must be taken out of the church, away from ministers and priests and given back to the people:

It [Religion] is, indeed, too important to the power and perpetuity of the New World to be consigned any longer to the churches, old or new, Catholic or Protestant—Saint this, or Saint that. . . . It must be consigned henceforth to Democracy *en masse,* and to Literature. It must enter into the Poems of the Nation. It must make the Nation. . . .

This latter idea is not new to *Leaves of Grass*; it had been filtered through the poetry all along. But it helps to clarify previous statements expressing his religious beliefs. He had said as early as the 1855 "preface" to *Leaves:*

There will soon be no more priests. Their work is done. They may wait awhile . . . perhaps a generation or two . . . dropping off by degrees. A superior breed shall take their place . . . the gangs of kosmos and prophets en masse shall take their place. A new order shall arise and they shall be the priests of man, and every man shall be his own priest. The churches built under their umbrage shall be the churches of men and women. Through the divinity of themselves shall the kosmos and the new breed of poets be interpreters of men and women and of all events and things. They shall find their inspiration in real objects today, symptoms of the past and future. . . . They shall not deign to defend immortality or God or the perfection of things or liberty or the exquisite beauty and reality of the soul. They shall arise in America and be responded to from the remainder of the earth.

Whitman was certainly wrong here. The priests and churches have not gone away, and the "new breed of poets" are arguably weaker than ever—in Whitman's terms—certainly not strong enough to encourage the thought that people should become the priests of themselves. But this was part of his vision for religion in the democracy of the future.

In "Song of Myself," Whitman argues for the acceptance of the best thoughts from all religions and the avoidance of religious "hucksters."

> Taking myself the exact dimensions of Jehovah,
> Lithographing Kronos, Zeus his son, and
>   Hercules his grandson,
> Buying drafts of Osiris, Isis, Belus, Brahma,
>   Buddha,
> In my portfolio placing Manito loose, Allah on
>   a leaf, the crucifix engraved,
> With Odin and the hideous-faced Mexitli and
>   every idol and image,
> Taking them all for what they are worth and
>   not a cent more,
> Admitting they were alive and did the work of
>   their days,
> (They bore mites as for unfledg'd birds who
>   have now to rise and fly and sing for
>   themselves.)

None of the beliefs of any one religion is accepted at face value but must have its "exact dimensions" taken before acceptance. And the last line of the quoted passage sums up Whitman's own attitude toward religion: In a democracy, people must learn, like the "unfledg'd birds," to "rise" from the nest and "sing" for themselves. Later in "Song of Myself," the poet sums up his faith in a God of all religions: "My faith is the greatest of faiths and the least of faiths, / Enclosing worship ancient and modern and all between ancient and modern." Sections 48 and 49 sum up the pantheistic theme of transcendent reality: God is no more important than any human Self.

> I have said that the soul is not more than the
>   body,
> And I have said that the body is not more than
>   the soul,
> And nothing, not God, is greater to one than
>   one's self is, . . .

> I hear and behold God in every object, yet
>   understand God not in the least,
> Nor do I understand who there can be more
>   wonderful than myself.

Because in Whitman's philosophy God is everywhere, his spirit encompassing everyone and everything, the poet wishes instead to focus on the love for all things that he feels as a result of that spirit. "Why should I wish to see God better than this day," he asks. The day is the very reflection of God: he sees God "in the faces of men and women" and in his own "face in the glass"; he "finds letters from God dropt in the street, and every one is sign'd by God's name." For the poet, God is no greater than this.

Whitman wrote a letter to an unnamed correspondent from BROOKLYN, dated July 20, 1857, with an interesting anecdote.

> A minister, Rev. Mr. Porter, was introduced to me this morning,—a Dutch Reformed minister, and editor of the Christian Intelligencer, N.Y.— Would you believe it,—he had been reading Leaves of Grass, and wanted _more_? He said he hoped I retained the true Reformed faith which I must have inherited from my mother's Dutch ancestry.—I not only assured him of my retaining faith in that sect, but that I had perfect faith in all sects, and was not inclined to reject one single one—but believed each to be about as far advanced as it could be, considering what had preceded it—and moreover that every one was the needed representative of _its_ truth—or of something needed as much as truth.—I had quite a good hour with Mr. Porter—we grew friends—and I am to go dine with the head man of the head congregation of Dutch Presbyterians in Brooklyn, Eastern District!

Rome, James and Thomas (unknown)   BROOKLYN printers hired by Whitman to print the first edition of Leaves of Grass (1855). Their job printing shop was located on the southwest corner of Fulton and Cranberry Streets in Brooklyn.

Rossetti, William Michael (1829–1919)   English author and art critic, best known in Whitman studies as the man who introduced Anne GIL-CHRIST to Whitman's poetry. Rossetti was a friend of Anne's, and when her husband, Alex, died in 1861, he helped her finish Alex's biography of William BLAKE.

Rossetti sent Gilchrist a copy of his edited, first British publication of selected Whitman poems, and she began a series of letters to him extolling their value. Rossetti was so impressed that he suggested to her that she let him put the letters together as an article, titled "A Woman's Estimate of Walt Whitman," which he then sent to Whitman's friend, William O'CONNOR. The article was published in Boston's RADICAL (May 1870).

William Michael was the brother of Dante Gabriel Rossetti and their sister, Christina, both well-known English poets.

Round Table, The   New York literary journal, perhaps better known for its attacks on other periodicals than for its own literary merit. It had a semireligious agenda, which attracted articles by the clergy.

It published a review of Whitman's *Drum-Taps* by William Dean HOWELLS (November 1865), in which Howells wrote that *Drum-Taps*, at least in terms of decency, was an improvement over the "preponderant beastliness" of the whole of *Leaves of Grass*.

Rover, The   Literary journal that published Whitman's short story "My Boys and Girls" (April 20, 1844).

S

Saturday Press (1858–1860; 1865–1866) Founded by Henry Clapp and Edward Howland as a New York weekly publication of miscellaneous literary items. It was a magazine of sophisticated humor, best known perhaps as the first publisher of Mark Twain's short story "The Jumping Frog of Calaveras County" (November 18, 1865); the humorist "Josh Billings" was introduced in the same issue. Clapp is also "famous" for describing Horace Greeley as a "self-made man who worships his creator."

Clapp and Howland published three of Whitman's poems: "A Child's Reminiscence" (December 24, 1859), which later became "Out of the Cradle Endlessly Rocking"; "You and Me and To-Day" (January 27, 1860) (see "With Antecedents"); and "O Captain! My Captain!" (November 4, 1865).

Other editors of the short-lived newspaper included William Winter, Fitz-James O'Brien, Thomas Bailey Aldrich, Ada Clare, and Charles D. Gardette. All of these people knew Whitman through informal gatherings at Pfaff's Cellar in New York, where, with a lot of other bohemian writers and artists, they held animated discussions on the arts.

Sawyer, Thomas P. (unknown) Wounded at the Second Battle of Bull Run (August 29, 1862), Sawyer, a sergeant from Massachusetts, was still recovering at Washington's Armory Square Hospital when Whitman arrived in early 1863 and began work as a self-appointed medical assistant, making daily rounds of the hospitals. Sometime in early spring Sawyer was released and returned home.

Whitman wrote a number of affectionate letters to Sawyer, stating in one that "My love you have in life or death forever." Apparently Sawyer did not write as many letters to Whitman as he received, but he signed a letter, received by Walt on April 26, 1863, that began, "Dear comrade & brother." See Doyle, Peter.

self-reliance One of the most important bits of knowledge the speaker in "Song of Myself" describes. His own self-reliance is described in Section 46:

> No friend of mine takes his ease in my chair,
> I have no chair, no church, no philosophy,
> I lead no man to a dinner-table, library,
>   exchange,
> But each man and each woman of you I lead
>   upon a knoll,
> My left hand hooking you round the waist,
> My right hand pointing to landscapes of
>   continents and the public road.
>
> Not I, not any one else can travel that road for
>   you,
> You must travel it for yourself. . . .
>
> You are also asking me questions and I hear you,
> I answer that I cannot answer, you must find out
>   for yourself.

Critic James E. Miller, Jr., says of this section of "Song of Myself" that the poet "is presenting the essence of his transcendent knowledge or 'supreme perception.' It is not a static knowledge that can be codified for church or philosophy, expressed in a book, or conveyed through logic. Rather it is a dynamic, intuitive insight that each man must gain for himself. The poet can only point the way." See also EMERSON, RALPH WALDO.

Sheridan, General Philip H. (1831–1888) American soldier and West Point graduate, he was appointed by General Grant as commander of cavalry for the Army of the Potomac in 1863.

Whitman wrote a poem, "Interpolation Sounds," in honor of Sheridan who died on August 5, 1888; the poem was published in the NEW YORK HERALD (August 12, 1888). Whitman added a note to the poem, saying, in part that "in the grand constellation of five or six names, under LINCOLN's Presidency, that history will bear for ages in her firmament as marking the last life-throbs of secession, and beaming on it dying gasps, Sheridan's will be bright. . . . If the war had continued any long time these States, in my opinion, would have shown and proved the most conclusive military talents ever evinced by any nation on earth."

short stories   See FICTION, WHITMAN'S.

slavery   Whitman was somewhat ambivalent about slavery, in favor on the one hand of "free soil"—an antislavery movement during the mid-19th century, opposed to allowing slavery in new U.S. Territories—and, on the other hand, afraid that eliminating slavery altogether might generate enough southern anger to start a civil war.

After the U.S.-MEXICAN WAR (1846–48), President James K. Polk asked Congress for $2 million with which to negotiate a peace with Mexico and the cost of new territory acquired in the war. Congress voted for the money but added the "WILMOT PROVISO," which stipulated "neither slavery nor involuntary servitude shall ever exist in any part of said territory." The proviso passed and generated a bitter debate over the issue of slavery, not just in the southwest territories but east of the Mississippi River as well.

Whitman wrote an editorial for the BROOKLYN DAILY EAGLE (December 21, 1846), urging the Democratic Party to vote for "free soil." He was afraid of the extremes on both sides of the ongoing debate, thinking that they might destroy the principles of democracy, which he was in the process of formulating for himself and which would become one of the major themes in his writing. The "free-soil" stand taken by Whitman as editor of the *Eagle* probably cost him his job and certainly became a turning point in his life. He had been a Democrat, writing for and/or editing several Democratic newspapers. And although he had always believed in the moral principles behind the antislavery movement, he was afraid that the slavery issue might split the Union, and nothing was more important to Whitman than preservation of the Union of states.

Shortly after the U.S.-Mexican War, slavery became the major national issue. Whitman's seeming ambivalence created a stance that made it seem as if he favored slavery. But the poet saw a larger picture than slavery and felt that it justified his mostly middle-of-the road editorials. His *Brooklyn Eagle* editorial favoring "free-soil," however, angered the newspaper's owner and Whitman was gone by late January 1848.

The most significant principle upon which Whitman built his concept of democracy was the equality of all people: men and women, black and white, all religious beliefs, all ethnic backgrounds. He "sings" himself in his poetry because he sees in himself the image of everyone else, past, present, and future, longing for that equality. Whitman brags not for himself, in other words, but for humankind, and he shows in the bulk of *Leaves of Grass* his kinship not only with other people but with all of Nature as well. In "Song of Myself," he says, "Whoever degrades another degrades me, / And whatever is done or said returns at last to me." Whitman's poetry is constant in its appeal for the equality of all people in all places in all time.

Equality is the key to Whitman's attitude toward slavery; the external circumstances were more important than the internal. The preservation of the Union was the primary issue, slavery secondary.

And it was not just Negro slavery that Whitman hated, but slavery of any kind. And, he expresses the importance of the poet in freeing individuals under any kind of bondage. At the end of Section

10 of "By Blue Ontario's Shore," the poet explains the poet's role in the slavery issue:

> For the great Idea, the idea of perfect and free
> individuals,
> For that, the bard walks in advance, leader of
> leaders,
> The attitude of him cheers up slaves and
> horrifies foreign despots.
>
> Without extinction is Liberty, without retrograde
> is Equality,
> They live in the feelings of young men and the
> best women,
> (Not for nothing have the indomitable heads of
> the earth been always ready to fall for Liberty.)

In a poem called "Thought" [Of Equality], Whitman expresses this idea again: "Of Equality—as if it harm'd me, giving others the same chances and rights as myself—as if it were not indispensable to my own rights that others possess the same." I am not free, the poet suggests, as long as there is slavery of any kind.

Several poems are written directly to the slavery issue. "A Boston Ballad," for example, ridicules the trial and return to the state of Virginia of a slave caught in Boston. The slave is not mentioned in the poem, though it is clear that he is the subject matter. That he is not mentioned lends support to the poem's more universal appeal for the elimination of "slavery" everywhere, and not just in America, but worldwide.

In "Ethiopia Saluting the Colors" Whitman describes a "Negro" woman along the roadside as Sherman's army marches through Carolina. She understands none of what is going on around her. Readers see the "fateful" slave failing to understand anything of what is going on, but because the poet cannot separate himself from the slave the reader also sees the universal appeal against slavery.

"To the States," one of the "Inscriptions" poems, presents a plea against slavery: "Once fully enslaved, no nation, state, city of this earth, ever afterward resumes its liberty."

As concerned as he was about the Union—or, perhaps because of it—Whitman showed little bias during the CIVIL WAR. He spent most of the war in Washington and northern Virginia hospitals comforting the wounded and dying soldiers of both sides, writing letters to homes North and South, from soldier sons and husbands to their mothers, wives, and sweethearts.

The song Whitman sang of himself was the song he sang for all people, and he catalogued those people throughout *Leaves of Grass*. That is why he insisted so strongly in "Song of Myself" that "Whoever degrades another degrades me. . . ." Slavery was abominable to Whitman because it degraded not only the slave and the slaveholder, but all Americans. One of the most moving passages in the poem is in Section 33:

> I am the hounded slave, I wince at the bite of
> the dogs,
> Hell and despair are upon me, crack and again
> crack the marksmen,
> I clutch the rails of the fence, my gore dribs,
> thinn'd with the ooze of my skin,
> I fall on the weeds and stones,
> The riders spur their unwilling horses, haul
> close,
> Taunt my dizzy ears and beat me violently over
> the head with whip-stocks.

In "Song of Myself" and in other poems and prose Whitman shows his concern that equality be the first principle of a democratic society. That is why he was so ambivalent about slavery; he was against slavery at any cost save one: the Union of the states was more important than the single issue of slavery. Democracy could withstand slavery for a while longer, he felt, but if the Northern forces won the war, not only would the Union be preserved but slavery might also then be abolished.

soul and body Whitman believed that the body and soul were separate, which allowed the soul to become immortal. The idea is thematic in many of his poems, but the following stanza from "Pioneers! O Pioneers!" adds an element of mystical interest:

> I too with my soul and body,
> We, a curious trio, picking, wandering on our
> way,

Through these shores amid the shadows, with
   the apparitions pressing,
Pioneers! O pioneers!

The "curious trio" here is the "I," the "soul," and
the "body." Whitman is identifying the "I" as separate also, allowing him to observe his own "Self"
walking the streets of New York or at work on his
poetry.

This mystical union in disunion has a history in
mythology. In Thomas Cahill's *Sailing the Wine-
Dark Sea: Why the Greeks Matter* (2003), the author
notes that "Psyche was, to begin with, a Greek
word for 'life,' in the sense of individual human life,
and occurs in Homer in such phrases as 'to risk
one's life' and 'to save one's life.' . . . In the works of
the early scientist-philosophers, psyche can refer to
the ultimate substance, the source of life and consciousness, the spirit of the universe. By the fifth
century B.C., psyche had come to mean the 'conscious self,' the 'personality,' even the 'emotional
self,' and thence it quickly takes on, especially in
Plato, the meaning of 'immortal self'—the soul, in
contrast to the body."

This separation of soul and body was Whitman's
idea in the major poems, especially the idea that
only by separation can the soul become "immortal."

See, especially, "When Lilacs Last in the Dooryard Bloom'd," "Out of the Cradle Endlessly Rocking," and "Passage to India."

Southern Literary Messenger, The (1834–1864)
Founded in 1834 by Thomas Willis White and
edited for its first several issues by James Ewell
Heath. Edgar Allan Poe worked for the *Messenger*
during the period 1835–37, writing book and article reviews and contributing three original stories
of his own. White appointed Poe editor in December 1835 and fired him a year later.

The Richmond, Virginia, publication carried
mostly the literature of southern writers. The editors published one of Whitman's poems: "Longings
for Home" (July 15, 1860), later titled "O Magnet-
South."

Southwest Review (1815–present)   The *Southwest Review* is published at Southern Methodist

University and is, according to its Web site, the
fourth oldest continuously published literary quarterly in the United States. One of Whitman's biographers, Emory Holloway, published a Whitman
poem entitled "Pictures" in an essay Holloway
wrote, entitled "Whitman's Embryonic Verse," for
the July 1925 issue of *Southwest Review.* The poem
had not been previously published.

Stafford,   Harry (1858–?)   One   of   several
young men with whom Whitman was especially
affectionate. Stafford took Peter DOYLE's place in
the poet's esteem when he and Harry met after
Whitman moved to Camden, New Jersey. Stafford
was the son of Susan and George Stafford, who
furnished Whitman with a place to stay in 1876,
following several illnesses and a stroke. They
owned a house near TIMBER CREEK, a beautiful
stream about 400 yards downhill from the house,
just southeast of Camden. Whitman loved the
place and made notes on the surrounding nature,
which he entered as short essays into his book
Specimen Days (1882).

Harry was 18 when Whitman first visited the
Stafford farmstead in 1876; Whitman was 57.
Harry was working as an errand boy at the Camden
print shop where Whitman was seeing his *Two
Rivulets* volume through the press. Sometime in
1877 Whitman tried to get Harry to accept a
friendship ring, but he refused. Later, however, he
wrote to Walt, saying that he was the only "true
friend" he had and wished that he would offer the
ring again, which apparently Whitman did.

Stoker,   Bram (1847–1912)   Irish novelist and
short story writer, best known for his novel *Dracula*
(1897). He was a drama critic for the Dublin *Mail*,
met the Shakespearean actor Henry Irving, and
became Irving's manager. On one of the actor's
tours in the United States, Irving and Stoker met
Whitman (April 1884). The three were to remain
good friends for the rest of the poet's life.

Whitman was apparently eager to meet Stoker,
whose short stories the poet had read and liked,
and Stoker had been introduced to Whitman's
poetry, apparently while a student at Trinity College, Dublin.

Subterranean, The Published Whitman's essay "Lesson of the Two Symbols" (July 15, 1843).

Sun, The (1833–1950) Considered the first successful penny daily newspaper in New York, founded by Benjamin H. Day; the first issue was printed (September 3, 1833) in a $7^{1}/_{2}$-by-10-inch format, four pages of three columns each. It was immediately popular, according to Frank Luther Mott in his *American Journalism* (1950), particularly because of its "humorous treatment of police-court news."

Whitman wrote 14 articles for the *Sun* between October 1842 and September 1843, many of them concerning public education.

Sunday Times & Noah's Weekly Messenger (1843) Whitman helped to edit this New York newspaper in early 1843 and published five articles during the year he was employed. The *Sunday Times* combined with *Noah's Weekly Messenger* in July 1843.

Swinburne, Algernon Charles (1837–1909) English poet and critic, known for his interest in a variety of verse forms and for his love of the sea, in common with Whitman. Biographers and critics alike have referred to Swinburne's comment on Whitman's "When Lilacs Last in the Dooryard Bloom'd" that it is the "most sonorous nocturne ever chanted in the church of the world." In comparing Whitman and William BLAKE, Swinburne wrote that Whitman's poetry was "more frank and fresh" than Blake's and "[smelled] of sweeter air."

T

Terry, Ellen (1847–1928) English actress, who played leading Shakespeare roles opposite Henry Irving in England and then toured the United States, giving readings and lectures on Shakespeare. Bram STOKER, who would later publish *Dracula* (1897) and was a friend of Terry as well as Whitman, sent her a copy of *As a Strong Bird on Pinions Free and Other Poems* in 1877, and she wrote a thank-you note to Whitman:

> Honored Sir—and Dear Poet—I beg you to accept my appreciative thanks for your great kindness in sending me by Mr. Stoker the little big book of poems—As a Strong Bird, etc., etc.
>
> Since I am not personally known to you I conclude Mr. Stoker 'asked' for me—it was good of him—I know he loves you very much.
>
> God bless you dear sir—believe me to be with much respect Yours affectionately, Ellen Terry.

Whitman gave the letter to his friend Horace TRAUBEL in a conversation on March 30, 1888, and Traubel printed it in his biography of Whitman. Whitman told Traubel that "these actor people always make themselves at home with me and always make me easily at home with them. I feel rather close to them—very close—almost like one of their kind."

Thayer & Eldridge Boston publishers W. W. Thayer and Charles ELDRIDGE, who published the third edition of *Leaves of Grass* (1860). Whitman referred to them as his first "real" publishers. They wrote to him in February 1860 almost begging him to let them print the next edition of his book. He accepted and they printed, free of charge to Whitman, a 64-page brochure full of blurbs about the edition of *Leaves of Grass* they were about to produce, somewhat embarrassing apparently even to Whitman, who was an expert on publicizing his own work.

The third edition of *Leaves* was an attractive book of 456 pages, published in mid-May and sold out of its 1,000 copies by July. In spite of Whitman's good thoughts about the Thayer & Eldridge Publishing House, it overextended itself financially and was bankrupt by the end of the year. Thayer & Eldridge sold the printer's plates to the third edition, and the buyers printed several unauthorized editions.

Thoreau, Henry David (1817–1862) Philosopher and essayist, best known for his book *Walden* (1854), his major contribution to American TRANSCENDENTALISM, a belief that, among other things, a person's own insights were better for discovering "truth" than either logic or experience. Thoreau is credited for having attempted to "live" his own philosophic beliefs.

Thoreau disliked some of the passages in *Leaves of Grass* yet liked the book as a whole and praised Whitman as a "great fellow." The two men met for the first time in 1856 at the poet's home in

BROOKLYN. Thoreau was in the company of Bronson ALCOTT and Sarah Tyndale, the abolitionist.

Thoreau's philosophic ideas are prevalent in *Leaves of Grass,* maybe especially in the importance of the internal over the external. Whitman would have related, for example, to Thoreau's comment in *A Week on the Concord and Merrimack Rivers* (1849) that "friendship is . . . a relation of perfect equality," or to "our vices always lie in the direction of our virtues, and in their best estate are but plausible imitations of the latter." Whitman wrote about the equal nature of opposites.

Whitman must also have felt some comfort in Thoreau's statement in *Walden,* published less than a year before *Leaves of Grass,* that "If I seem to boast more than is becoming, my excuse is that I brag for humanity rather than for myself; and my shortcomings and inconsistencies do not affect the truth of this statement." Whitman's "Song of Myself" was criticized for its author's seeming to brag too much for himself.

Timber Creek   Timber Creek serves now as the border between Camden and Gloucester Counties in New Jersey, and runs more or less parallel to the Atlantic City Expressway. It is still—130 years after Whitman admired it and spent the better part of two summers living just above it—a tidal stream running through a beautiful, mostly wooded area, that empties into the Delaware River at Westville, about three miles south of Camden. There are two branches of Timber Creek, the north branch with headwaters in Winslow Township and the south branch in Washington Township.

For Whitman it was a bucolic spot for rest from his recent illnesses, including a stroke. He was invited in 1876 by his friends George and Susan Stafford to spend some time at their farm above Timber Creek. Whitman was also glad for a chance to get away from the too close ties he had in Camden, living as an upstairs guest of his brother George and his sister-in-law, Louisa, in their house on Stevens Street. The arrangements were not working well, yet Walt had little money at the time for renting a house elsewhere. So the invitation from the Staffords came at the right time.

The Stafford house was 12 or 13 miles upstream from Westville and about 400 yards above Timber Creek. Walt made notes while he was at the Stafford farmhouse that would later become parts of several essays on nature in *Specimen Days* (1882). He wrote about those "restoration hours" as if they were the beginning of a new life. He describes the lane from the farmhouse down to the creek as his new "hobby, . . . a real farm lane fenced by old chestnut rails gray-green with dabs of moss and lichen, copious weeds and briers growing in spots athwart the heaps of stray-picked stones at the fence bases." And he wrote about the "spring under the willows—musical as soft-clinking glasses—pouring a sizable stream, thick as my neck, pure and clear . . . gurgling, gurgling ceaselessly—meaning, saying something . . . (if I could only translate it). . . ."

A note dated June 2, 1878, was apparently written under an oak tree during a rain storm.

This is the fourth day of a dark northeast storm, wind and rain. Day before yesterday was my birthday. I have now entered on my sixtieth year. Every day of the storm, protected by overshoes and a waterproof blanket, I regularly come down to the pond and ensconce myself under the lee of a great oak.

I am here now writing these lines. The dark smoke-colored clouds roll in furious silence athwart the sky; the soft green leaves dangle all around me; the wind steadily keeps up its hoarse, soothing music over my head Nature's mighty whisper.

Seated here in solitude I have been musing over my life connecting events, dates, as links of a chain, neither sadly nor cheerily, but somehow to-day here under the oak, in the rain, in an unusually matter-of-fact spirit.

But my great oak sturdy, vital, green five feet thick at the butt. I sit a great deal near or under him. Then the tulip tree near by the Apollo of the woods tall and graceful, yet robust and sinewy, inimitable in hang of foliage and throwing-out of limb, as if the beauteous, vital leafy creature could walk, if it only would. (I had a sort of dream-trance the other day, in which I saw my favorite trees step out and promenade up, down and around very curiously, with a whisper from one, leaning down as he passed me: We do all this on the present occasion exceptionally, just for you.

While at Timber Creek Whitman met the Staffords' five children, including their 18-year-old son, Harry, who immediately became an intimate friend with the 57-year-old poet. He tended to replace Peter DOYLE in Whitman's esteem. Harry was working for the print shop in Camden that was setting type for Whitman's *Two Rivulets,* so the two men saw each other often during that time. Walt introduced Harry to friends as "my son" or "my nephew," and Whitman told John BURROUGHS that they shared a room and bed. He later told Harry in a letter how much he regarded the Timber Creek experiences as a life-saving period of time for himself and that Harry was "the central figure of . . . all."

transcendentalism A philosophical ideal that recognizes the unity of all things, the innate good in human beings, and the greater importance of intuition over logic and experience. The world comes alive in the mind, the New England transcendentalists believed, so that is where *truth* may be found.

American transcendentalism originated in Concord, Massachusetts, and had its best years between 1830 and 1855. Ralph Waldo EMERSON and Theodore Parker were two of its major proponents. Others included Margaret Fuller, Bronson ALCOTT, William Ellery Channing, and Henry David THOREAU, all of whom wrote essays in support of transcendental ideas. Although Whitman did not write essays helping to define transcendentalism, the movement's ideas were one of the poet's chief influences, and nearly all of his poetic themes fit well with the transcendental system of thought. Many of the articles by the New England writers were published in the DIAL magazine, a short-lived (1840–44) publication associated with transcendentalism and edited first by Fuller and then by Emerson. Alcott, Parker, and Channing were all

ministers, providing strong moralistic or religious involvement, both for transcendentalism and for the *Dial.*

The New England transcendentalists were reacting to the British Empirical School of philosophers who believed, with English philosopher John Locke, that the mind is passive and accepts things passively. Locke argued in his *Essay Concerning Human Understanding* (1690) that no knowledge is innate, that all knowledge is based on experience. Parker, a Unitarian minister, was the first to attack the empiricists; and he was dismissed from the ministry because of his beliefs. He argued that Locke's ideas did not account for ethics or morality, that the mind not only receives but creates reality; he believed that the mind conditions experience.

Whitman's major poems take readers on mystical voyages into a spiritual world where the soul communicates directly with God; to get to that spiritual world, one must "transcend" his or her own mental image of the world. John Locke believed that everything was independent of God; Whitman believed that God was in everything.

Traubel, Horace (1858–1919) Friend of Whitman's from 1873 to Whitman's death in 1892 and one of three executors of his estate. Traubel kept notes of his almost daily conversations with Whitman during the last four years of the poet's life, beginning on "Wednesday, March 28, 1888," four years almost to the day before Whitman's death. The notes were later published in nine volumes, between 1906 and 1996, the entire work titled *With Walt Whitman in Camden.* The notes are meticulously dated and annotated. Only the first three volumes were published during the writer's lifetime. It is this biographical work for which Traubel is best known.

He met Whitman in 1873 when the poet moved to Camden, New Jersey, where his brother George and his wife, Louisa, lived. It was just after Whitman's stroke, and the poet needed the rest that he thought he would get at the Stevens Street house. Traubel was 15 years old at the time of his meeting with Whitman, and the boy's parents were upset that he would be associating with the somewhat disgraced man.

Horace Traubel, friend of Whitman who kept notes of conversations with the poet during his last four years and author of the nine-volume *With Walt Whitman in Camden* (Library of Congress, Prints and Photographs Division)

In the preface to the first volume of his notes, Traubel writes: "My story is left as it was originally written. I have made no attempt to improve it." He says that Whitman did not know that he was "keeping such a record, . . . Yet he knew I would write of our experiences together." And as an epigraph to the first volume, he quotes Whitman as telling him to "Be sure to write about me honest: whatever you do do not prettify me: include all the hells and damns." It's interesting to note that John BURROUGHS, another friend and biographer, once reacted to Traubel's quotations by saying that he had never heard Whitman utter the words "hell" or "damn."

Traubel, who had been influenced by Whitman's poetry long before he met him, spent the 27 years of his life after Whitman's death working to promote the poet. Traubel founded and edited the *Conservator* (1890–1919) and the *Artsman* (1903–07), both publications devoted to keeping Whitman's poetry alive. Traubel also wrote three volumes of his own poetry, *Chants Communal* (1904), *Optimos* (1910), and *Collects* (1914), his poems reflecting Whitman's poetic influence. He also kept up a correspondence with Whitman friends and followers, particularly in England and western Europe, where the American poet was well known and perhaps better appreciated than in America.

Truth (1881–c. 1920s) A weekly periodical in the beginning of an off-and-on publication history, known in its best years as a leader in journalistic social satire. Blakely Hall was editor during Whitman's connection with the magazine near the end of the poet's life. *Truth* may have had an odd history but it was generally considered to be a lively, innovative, and attractive journal.

Hall accepted for publication Whitman's poem "Old Chants" (March 19, 1891).

U

Union Magazine of Literature and Art (1847–1852) New York monthly journal, which published Edgar Allan Poe's "To Helen" and "The Bells." Whitman's contribution was his short story "The Shadow and the Light of a Young Man's Soul" (June 1848).

United States Magazine and Democratic Review, The See DEMOCRATIC REVIEW, THE.

Universal Asylum and Columbian Magazine, The See COLUMBIAN MAGAZINE.

Universalist Union (1835–1847) Published Whitman's essay titled "Greenwood Cemetery" (November 16, 1839), one of the poet's earliest writings. The subject interested Whitman, because the cemetery was in the process of being readied for its first occupants. "Having received a very polite invitation from the Committee of the 'American Institute Fair' to accompany them to this future repository of the dead, I gladly availed myself of the favorable opportunity, and was constrained to exclaim with the Queen of Sheba, 'the half was not told me.'"

Whitman wrote that the Greenwood offers beautiful views of "BROOKLYN, the bay and harbor of New York, Staten Island, and the Quarantine. It is, indeed, a second 'Mount Auburn' [another local cemetery], and is destined at no very distant period to become its rival." And it cost $130,000 for the 200 acres.

U.S.-Mexican War (1846–1848) There were several reasons for the American war with Mexico, but distrust between the two nations began when the United States annexed Texas and gave it statehood (December 29, 1845). Mexico withdrew its ambassador. After negotiations broke down, including the offer of nearly $40 million by the United States to appease Mexico for the addition of New Mexico and California as well as Texas, President Polk sent troops across the Rio Grande into Mexico.

Whitman's editorship of the BROOKLYN DAILY EAGLE coincided almost exactly with the two years of the U.S.-Mexican War, but it took him a year to finally understand that it might be the intention of Polk and the Democratic Party to make SLAVERY legal in any newly annexed southwestern states. He was still biased against Mexico for its atrocities during the battle of the Alamo 10 years earlier and so failed to see the U.S. government's hidden agenda. Emory Holloway writes in *Whitman: An Interpretation in Narrative* (1926) that Whitman "was in a mood to declare war at once, without that delay which was being counseled by [John C.] Calhoun and the Abolitionists alike. With [Whitman] it was a war of revenge, at least at the beginning. . . . Accepting every move of the Democratic president without question . . . Whitman was arguing, a year before the war was won, that the annexation of a large part of Mexico was a foregone conclusion." The abolitionists believed, with good reason, that the U.S. government would allow slavery in the new states.

Holloway described Whitman's change of attitude. "By January, 1847, he had had enough. Declaring that he had upheld the President and the Army from the start in a just cause, he insisted, nevertheless, that 'the time has arrived when all citizens should speak candidly and firmly on this subject of the Mexican War.'" This was the beginning of his "free soil" editorials for the *Eagle:*

> If there are any States to be formed out of territory lately annexed, or to be annexed, by any means to the United States, let the Democratic members of Congress, (and Whigs too, if they like,) plant themselves quietly, without bluster, but fixedly and without compromise, on the requirement that *Slavery be prohibited in them forever.* We wish we could have a universal straightforward setting down of feet on this thing, in the Democratic Party.

The *Brooklyn Daily Eagle* was an organ of the Democratic Party, and Whitman's change of editorial mind no doubt was the major reason he lost his position.

V

Van Velsor, Major Cornelius (1768–1837) Walt's maternal grandfather. He was one of the descendants of the early Dutch settlers, who settled much of the western half of LONG ISLAND. The Van Velsor farm—good, fertile land—was located in Woodbury, about halfway between Cold Spring Harbor and the major road running east and west across Long Island. He also bred and raised horses.

Whitman remembered how much fun he had visiting his Van Velsor grandparents. His grandfather made weekly trips into BROOKLYN to sell his crops and often took Walt and one or two of his brothers along. Walt described the home in *Specimen Days* under the title "The Maternal Homestead":

[The home] stood there a long, rambling, dark gray, shingle-sided house, with sheds, pens, a great barn, and much open road-space. . . . The whole scene, with what it aroused, memories of my young days there half a century ago, the vast kitchen and ample fireplace and the sitting room adjoining, the plain furniture, the meals, the house full of merry people, my grandmother Amy's sweet old face in its Quaker cap, my grandfather "the major," jovial, red, stout, with sonorous voice and characteristic physiognomy, with the actual sights themselves, made the most pronounced half-day's experience of my whole jaunt.

Whitman wrote, regarding his Van Velsor grandfather that "the old race of the Netherlands, so deeply grafted on MANHATTAN Island and in Kings and Queens Counties, never yielded a more marked and full Americanized specimen than Major Cornelius Van Velsor."

Van Velsor, Naomi (Amy) Williams (d. 1826) Walt's maternal grandmother and a favorite of Walt's. She and her Williams ancestors practiced the Quaker religion. She had seven sisters and one brother, a sailor like his father, both of whom died at sea.

Her father, Captain John Williams, had fought with John Paul Jones on the *Bonhomme Richard* in its famous Revolutionary War battle against the *Serapis* off the English coast (September 23, 1779). He died at sea, but apparently not in this battle, which means he would have boarded the *Serapis* along with his captain and the American sailors left alive, because the *Bonhomme Richard* sank after the British surrender. Walt would write in his later years of how much he enjoyed the stories his grandmother told him about the adventures of her father.

Vaughan, Fred (unknown) Met Whitman in the early 1860s, and at least one biographer suggests that Fred may have been Whitman's first homosexual lover. See also DOYLE, PETER; HOMOSEXUALITY.

W

Wallace, J. W. (1855–1926) Leader of the Bolton, England, group of Whitman followers, who visited the poet in Camden, New Jersey, during the last year of the poet's life. He coauthored, with Dr. John JOHNSTON, a pamphlet titled *Visits to Walt Whitman in 1890–1891 by Two Lancashire Friends*, referred to by William Sloane KENNEDY as "one of the best pen-portraits of Whitman ever made."

Wallace kept notes on his visits to Whitman's home and wrote the following about the poet's death: "on the evening of Saturday, March 26th—the daylight fading and a gentle rain falling outside—the end came, simply and peacefully—Whitman conscious to the last, calm and undisturbed, his right hand resting in that of Horace Traubel."

Walt Whitman Arts Center (1976–present) A nonprofit, multicultural literary, performing and visual arts center, located on the campus of Rutgers University in Camden, New Jersey. It was established in 1976 as the Walt Whitman International Poetry Center.

According to a statement of purpose, posted on its Web site, the arts center is dedicated to continuing Whitman's legacy of artistic excellence in literature while also encouraging the enjoyment of a variety of performing and visual arts. See http://www.waltwhitmancenter.org.

Walt Whitman Birthplace and Museum (1957–present) The farmhouse in West Hills, near Huntington, LONG ISLAND, built by Walter WHITMAN, SR., in 1816, where the poet was born in 1819. The Walt Whitman Birthplace Association was established in 1949 to preserve the house, and the building was designated a New York State Historic Site in 1957 and listed on the New York State and National Registers of Historic Places in 1985. The museum Web site is http://www.waltwhitman.org.

The birthplace house was renovated during the 1990s and restored, based on historic records and an 1890 photograph. Restoration was completed in 2000. Almost half of the 200 objects on display at the site are from the original house.

An Interpretive Center opened in 1997 near the original farmhouse; it includes a classroom, library, offices, a gift shop, and storage facilities for museum collections. Changing exhibits include Whitman memorabilia, photographs, and books. There are regularly scheduled poetry readings at the center, as well as lectures, educational programs, an arts and crafts festival, and a Whitman birthday celebration each year. Guided tours include an audiovisual presentation titled "The Good Grey Poet."

A full year of events was planned in celebration of the 150th anniversary of the first edition of *Leaves of Grass* (1855), culminating in the 2005 Walt Whitman Birthday Celebration on June 5, 2005.

Walt Whitman Quarterly Review (1955–present) Scholarly journal with essays of criticism on the works of Whitman, as well as biographical essays, bibliography, news items, and announcements of meetings and conferences devoted to the poet or in which sessions on him are included. *WWQR* is sponsored by the Graduate College and the Department of English at the University of Iowa and is the official journal of the Walt Whitman Studies Association. The publication's Web site is http://www.uiowa.edu/~wwqr/.

The *WWQR* was founded by Gay Wilson Allen as the *Walt Whitman Newsletter* in 1955, published by the New York University Press. It moved to the Wayne State University Press in 1956 and became the *Walt Whitman Review* in 1959; it became the *Walt Whitman Quarterly Review* in June 1983.

Washingtonian (1842–1843)   Changed to *Washingtonian and Organ* for the issue published January 28, 1843. Whitman's short story "Reuben's Last Wish" (May 21, 1842) was published before the publisher changed the name. Apparently only one issue was published under the new name; it included the first installment of Whitman's short story "The Madman" (January 28, 1843), but neither further issues of the magazine nor the rest of Whitman's story have been found.

Wells, Samuel R.   See FOWLER & WELLS CO.

Whitman, Andrew Jackson (1827–1863)   Walt's brother was with the Union army during the CIVIL WAR. He and his wife, Nancy, had two children, the daughter named Mannahatta, after her uncle's poem and his interest in the Indian name for New York City. Andy died of a throat ailment on December 3, 1863, during Walt's time in Washington, D.C. Nancy had become a New York prostitute. Their two children were taken care of by their grandmother, Louisa Whitman.

Whitman, Edward (1835–1892)   Walt's youngest sibling, called "Ed" or "Eddie." He had mental and physical problems and lived with his mother until she died in 1873 and then with other family members until he was institutionalized at Blackwoodtown in southeast New Jersey.

Walt always felt sorry for Eddie and once told friend and biographer John BURROUGHS that he blamed Eddie's mental retardation on his father's addiction to alcohol, saying that he had been "a poor stunted boy almost from the first. He had the convulsions" and practically no "mental life at all."

Whitman, George Washington (1829–1901)   Walt's younger brother by 10 years, joined the Union army during the CIVIL WAR and was listed as missing following the battle of Fredericksburg (December 13, 1862). Walt read a notice in the *NEW YORK HERALD* (December 16), naming "G. W. Whitmore" as one of the wounded from New York's 51st Regiment and assumed the name was a misprint. He went to Washington to see if he could get further information and found that George was recovering in a field hospital at Falmouth, Virginia, near Fredericksburg.

In *Specimen Days* Whitman writes that George had been "in active service . . . four years, re-enlisting twice—was promoted, step by step (several times immediately after battles)," eventually to "lieut. Colonel—was in the actions at Roanoke, Newbern, 2d Bull Run, Chantilly, South Mountain, Antietam, Fredericksburg, Vicksburg, Jackson, the bloody conflicts of the Wilderness, and at Spotsylvania, Cold Harbor, and afterward around Petersburg; at one of these latter was taken prisoner, and passed four or five months in secesh [secessionist] military prisons, narrowly escaping with life, from a severe fever, from starvation and half-nakedness in the winter."

The Confederate stockades were known for their bad conditions—26,000 Union soldiers died in them during the war. George was captured on September 30, 1864, and taken to LIBBY PRISON, which, after Andersonville, was the most notorious of all the Confederate prisons. Libby was near Richmond, Virginia, made up of vacant tobacco warehouses, one of which belonged to the tobacco firm of Libby and Son.

George suffered from his wounds and poor care but was lucky to be in a group of soldiers exchanged for Confederate soldiers and so was returned to his home in BROOKLYN. Prisoners were usually returned

George Washington Whitman, the poet's brother. He fought in the Civil War, was wounded, then was traded with other Northern soldiers by the Confederates for wounded of their own. *(Library of Congress, Prints and Photographs Division)*

to the north by boat, and George wrote home from Annapolis on February 24, 1865, where his group of Union prisoners landed, that he had just arrived "from the Hotel de Libby, and if ever a poor devil was glad to get in a Christian Country it was me." He was back in Brooklyn in early March.

George had not been an admirer of LINCOLN, once saying about the "Emancipation Proclamation," which had been heavily criticized by newspaper editors and opposing politicians, that Lincoln would have "to lick the south before he [could] free the niggers."

George married Louisa Orr Haslam on April 14, 1871, and moved to Camden, New Jersey. They had one son, named Walter Orr, who died within his year of birth.

George never quite understood his famous brother's poetry; yet, with so many famous visitors

to Camden in the later years, he must have understood the fame. Walt moved to Camden in 1873 to live with George and his wife on Stevens Street.

Whitman, Hannah Louisa (1823–1899)   The younger of two Whitman sisters, Walt's favorite, she was named after her grandmother Hannah Brush Whitman. Hannah Louisa married the artist Charles L. Heyde on March 16, 1852, and moved to Burlington, Vermont. Walt was closer to his two sisters and his mother than he was to his father or brothers.

Hannah and her husband did not get along well, and, at one point Walt was tempted to go to Vermont and bring her home. Hannah told Walt that Charley was tyrannical, abusive, and unfaithful; Charley told Walt that Hannah "makes a half barbarous life for herself and almost baffles all my efforts at times to humanize her." Charley was eventually taken to a hospital, and diagnosed with chronic dementia; Hannah spent the rest of her life in a darkened room.

Walt referred to Charley as "the bed-buggiest man on earth, . . . almost the only man alive who can make me mad; a mere thought of him, an allusion, the least word, riles me." He was, with the exception of Walt's brother Jeff, the only member of Walt's family who seemed to understand and like *Leaves of Grass*; he wrote a favorable letter about it to the NEW YORK TIMES (December 2, 1866).

Whitman, Jesse (1749–1803)   Walt's grandfather. He inherited 500 acres of good central LONG ISLAND farmland and the slaves who helped farm it.

Whitman, Jesse (1818–1870)   Walt's older brother by 14 months. Jesse, named for his paternal grandfather, was mentally ill and, after a serious outbreak of violence in 1864, was institutionalized. He was committed by the family on December 5 to the Kings County Lunatic Asylum. The admission statement reads:

Admitted December 5th 1864. Born in New York, aged 48 years. Single. A seafaring man. Temperate. About sixteen years ago had a fall from the mast which injured his head. He remained in City Hosp. N.Y. about six months, and went out apparently well. He has been considered somewhat insane by his friends for the last four years. For the last year he had been worse, at times violent, usually in the night on awaking from sleep.

Walt signed it as "brother." There is no evidence that Jesse had an accident at sea. His brother Jeff believed that Jesse had a serious case of syphilis.

Walt received a letter from an "E. Warner, "Assist. Phys.," dated March 22, 1870, informing him that Jesse had died "very suddenly yesterday from the rupture of an aneurism."

Whitman, Louisa Van Velsor (1795–1873)   Walt Whitman's mother, the stronger and more influential of his two parents. When she died, on May 23, 1873, Whitman thought it was the "great tragedy" of his life. She was of Dutch and Welsh descent. Her father was Cornelius VAN VELSOR and her mother was Naomi (Amy) Williams VAN VELSOR; they owned a horse farm near Cold Spring, LONG ISLAND, about four miles from West Hills, where Walt was born.

Whitman wrote about his mother's parents in *Specimen Days,* stating that "The later years of the last century [1700s] found the Van Velsor family, my mother's side, living on their own farm at Cold Spring, Long Island . . . near the eastern edge of Queens County, about a mile from the harbor."

One of Louisa's ancestors was "Old Salt Kossabone," a sailor who had died at sea under circumstances which turned him into a family legend, a tale that Whitman related in his poem titled "Old Salt Kossabone."

Walt remembered playing at the Van Velsor homestead when a child and as a young man. After visiting the "ancient grave place eighty or ninety rods" from the home, he writes in *Specimen Days* that he remembered the old house: "a long, rambling, dark gray, shingle-sided house, with sheds, pens, a great barn, and much open road-space." He remembers also that the "Van Velsor people were noted for fine horses, which the men bred and trained from blooded stock. My mother, as a young woman, was a daily and daring rider."

Louisa Van Velsor Whitman, the poet's mother. She was probably the most influential woman in Whitman's life. *(Library of Congress, Prints and Photographs Division)*

Walt had great respect for his mother. She had borne nine children, six boys, two girls, and a child born in 1825 but who died six months later. The surviving children were Jesse (1818); Walt (1819); Mary Elizabeth (1821); Hannah Louisa (1823); Andrew Jackson (1827); George Washington (1829); Thomas Jefferson (1833); and Edward (1835). Jesse was mentally retarded, and Eddie was both mentally and physically handicapped, both ending their lives in institutions. Andy was at least unstable, getting into constant trouble; when he died at age 36 in 1863, his wife, Nancy, had become a prostitute, and their two children were taken to their grandmother, who was 68 years old at the time.

In 1872, arthritic, and within a year of her death, Louisa was still taking care of her house, the seriously retarded Eddie, and Andy's two children.

Whitman, Mary Elizabeth (1821–1899)   Walt's sister. She married a shipwright, Ansel Van

Nostrand, on January 2, 1840, and moved with him to Greenport, LONG ISLAND, where Walt visited on several occasions.

Bertha Funnell, in her book *Walt Whitman on Long Island*, writes that a direct descendant of Mary Elizabeth was present on September 27, 1956, at the opening of the Great South Bay Shopping Center in West Babylon, site of a former home of the Whitmans in 1836.

Whitman, Nehemiah (c. 1705–1789) Walt's great-grandfather, a successful farmer of the 500-acre land near West Hills on LONG ISLAND, owned by the Whitmans for several generations. Whitman slaves helped farm the land, which made the family prosperous during those years. Succeeding Whitman farmers were not as prosperous however, and, eventually, the land was sold off.

Whitman, Phoebe (Sarah) White (c. 1713–1803) Walt's great-grandmother on his father's side. She was well known in the community near West Hills, LONG ISLAND, where she and her husband, Nehemiah, ran a farm of 500 acres.

According to John BURROUGHS in his *Notes on Walt Whitman as Poet and Person*, the poet had told him legendary stories about Phoebe, the great-grandmother who had died 15 years before he was born. She lived to be about 86. Whitman told Burroughs that "She smoked tobacco, rode on horseback like a man, managed the most vicious horses, and becoming a widow in later life, went forth every day over the farmlands, frequently in the saddle, directing the labor of her slaves, with language in which on exciting occasions, oaths were not spared." She was certainly one of the poet's most interesting ancestors.

Whitman, Thomas Jefferson (1833–1890) Walt's brother. Jeff was 14 years younger than Walt but was always considered by the poet his only "real brother," the others all with various psychological problems. Walt once said of Jeff that he "was a very handsome, healthy, affectionate, smart child. . . . O, how we loved each other—how many jovial times we had!"

Jeff, who had learned typesetting in BROOKLYN, went with Walt to New Orleans in 1848, where they worked for three months on the *NEW ORLEANS CRESCENT*. He complained in letters home of the boardinghouse where they first stayed as having floors with "dirt an inch thick." He worked as a printer's devil and general office boy; he was 15 at the time.

He later became interested in civil engineering, especially land surveying, and went to work for the New York municipal water system. He then became a city engineer in St. Louis. He married Martha Emma Mitchell (Mattie), and they had two daughters, Mannahatta (Hattie) (1860–86) and Jessie Louisa (1863–1957). Walt loved Mattie and once declared that she and his mother were "the two best and sweetest women I have ever seen or known or ever expect to see."

Thomas Jefferson Whitman, 14 years younger than Walt and the latter's favorite sibling, probably because he was the only member of his family who seemed to understand and appreciate *Leaves of Grass (Library of Congress, Prints and Photographs Division)*

Jeff was also the only member of Walt's immediate family who seemed to both like and understand *Leaves of Grass.* He was also interested in music, especially OPERA, and these common interests must have enhanced the fondness that Walt felt for his brother.

Whitman, Walter, Sr. (1789–1855)   Walt Whitman's father was born on the day French peasants stormed the Bastille in Paris—July 14, 1789. He was born on land his ancestors had owned on LONG ISLAND through six generations. His English parents, Jesse WHITMAN and Hannah Brush Whitman, and the Whitman ancestors before them were landowners in Huntington Township. Joseph W. Whitman, the poet's great-great-great-grandfather, settled with his family near Commack, about 10 miles east of West Hills, where the poet was born at least 100 years later.

Walter Sr. was a carpenter by trade and built a number of houses in the Huntington area, including the house in West Hills sometime before 1816 where he took his bride. He would later build houses in BROOKLYN, sometimes living in them with his family until they were sold and then moving into another, just built.

Walt reminds readers in a note to "Genealogy—Van Velsor and Whitman" in *Specimen Days* that "Long Island was settled first on the west end by the Dutch, from Holland, then on the east end by the English—the dividing line of the two nationalities being a little west of Huntington, where my father's folks lived, and where I was born." Walt's mother, Louisa Van Velsor WHITMAN, was from the Dutch side of the line.

He says in the essay on genealogy:

The Whitman name in the eastern states, and so branching west and south, starts undoubtedly from one John Whitman, born 1602, in Old England, where he grew up, married, and his eldest son was born in 1629. He came over in the *True Love* in 1640 to America, and lived in Weymouth, Mass., which place became the mother hive of the New Englanders of the name; he died in 1692. His brother, Rev. Zechariah Whitman,

also came over in the *True Love,* either at that time or soon after, and lived at Milford, Conn. A son of this Zechariah, named Joseph, migrated to Huntington, Long Island, and permanently settled there. Savage's *Genealogical Dictionary* (Vol. iv., p. 524) gets the Whitman family established at Huntington, per this Joseph, before 1664. It is quite certain that from that beginning, and from Joseph, the West Hill Whitmans, and all others in Suffolk County, have since radiated, myself among the number.

The Whitmans owned slaves at West Hills to help farm the 500 acres. Walter Sr. was known for his strong opinions, especially toward a radical concept of democracy, and he was a friend of Thomas Paine and the Quaker minister Elias HICKS, who greatly influenced the Whitman family's religious

Walt Whitman, Sr., the poet's father   *(Library of Congress, Prints and Photographs Division)*

beliefs. The family also knew about the lectures of Frances WRIGHT, the radical free-thinker, who helped found the *New Harmony Gazette* in 1825, a weekly socialist and agnostic publication.

Walter Sr. also owned a copy of *Ruins of Empire* (*Les Ruines, ou meditation sur les revolutions des empires*) (1791; translation 1795), a history of the decline of ancient civilizations and the rise of modern ones, by Count Constantin de Volney (1757–1820), French historian and philosopher. In the book de Volney argues that with the guidance of Nature and Reason people would come to understand their own best interests; they would put aside the dual tyranny of religious superstition and political des-

potism, which will then lead to freedom, equality, and justice.

All three of these radical thinkers—Hicks, Wright, and de Volney—were vilified by editors and politicians, but their beliefs would become a significant influence on the beliefs of Walter Sr.'s poet-son, Walt Whitman, their philosophies if not their names appearing in *Leaves of Grass*. Whitman was to say in old age that he was "perhaps . . . the only one living . . . who [could] throw an authentic sidelight upon the radicalism of those post-Revolutionary decades."

The Whitman family moved to Brooklyn on May 27, 1823, driving into the village just as people

The original carpenter's shop on Cumberland Street, near Atlantic Avenue in Brooklyn, owned by Whitman's father *(Library of Congress, Prints and Photographs Division)*

were returning from one of the most famous horse races in racing history—at the Union Race Track near Jamaica—between a famous Long Island horse named American Eclipse and a horse named Sir Henry, "the pride of the South." Eclipse won the race, and citizens in Brooklyn village and most of Long Island celebrated throughout the night. Eclipse is named in *The Encyclopedia Americana*, along with Seabiscuit, Equipoise, and six other horses as the most important race horses not to have run in the Triple Crown races—the Kentucky Derby, the Preakness, and the Belmont Stakes. Walter Sr. was apparently unimpressed by the race or its aftermath celebration, but Louisa was excited, in spite of being three months pregnant with Hannah Louisa. She had been raised on a horse farm and no doubt knew about the race at the Jamaica track.

Brooklyn was still a mere Long Island village while the Whitmans were there the first time and did not become a "city" until 1834. It had been Breuckelen until 1816, named by Dutch settlers in the mid-17th century after a village in Holland. The Whitmans moved almost once a year during the 10 years in Brooklyn. The first was a rented house on Front Street, near the settlement/village of Fulton Ferry, while Walter Sr. waited to buy land to build a more permanent home. He was employed as a carpenter at $1 a day. The new house was built on Cranberry Street across from the Plymouth Church, but they lived there only a short time at the end of 1824. Walter built another house at the corner of Tillary and Adams Streets. The family was living on Van Dyke Street in the spring of 1827 when Andrew Jackson WHITMAN was born on April 7.

See the appendix listing of the Whitman Brooklyn residences in part IV.

Whitman as teacher   After Whitman's first job in journalism as an apprentice printer (1832), he had eight teaching positions from 1836 to 1841 before giving up teaching entirely to get back to the newspaper business.

He taught in LONG ISLAND schools at East Norwich, in the summer of 1836; near Babylon, in the winter of 1836–37; in Long Swamp, in the spring of 1837; Smithtown, in autumn and winter, 1837–38; in Little Bay Side, near Jamaica, in winter 1839–40; at Trimming Square, in the spring of 1840, and Woodbury, in the summer of 1840, both near his birthplace in West Hills; and in Whitestone, in winter and spring of 1840–41.

In "Growth—Health—Work" in *Specimen Days* (1882), Whitman writes about his first teaching experience:

> 1836–7, worked as compositor in printing offices in New York City. Then, when little more than eighteen, and for a while afterward, went to teaching country schools down in Queens and Suffolk Counties, Long Island, and 'boarded round.' (This latter I consider one of my best experiences and deepest lessons in human nature behind the scenes, and in the masses.)

"Boarding round" meant living in the homes of the students two or three days at a time, and was, as he says above, one of his "best experiences." The pay was poor, in Whitman's case perhaps $40 for a three-month term. Whitman most likely taught in the primary grades, which would have included reading and writing, and perhaps geography. Each student's parents had to provide the textbooks, so independent study was the method in each classroom.

According to his brother George, Walt was respected as a teacher, though he was often criticized for what might be called today his laid-back nature in the classroom.

Whitman in journalism   Whitman felt that the 14 or 15 years during the 1840s and 1850s which he spent working in journalism were his years of "especial education." The years between about 1830 and 1860 were tremendous boom years for American journalism. It was the period of the growth of penny newspapers in New York City, together with a flourishing economy. It was the time of the Industrial Revolution and of the "party press," when most newspapers were founded to support political candidates. There were about

1,200 American newspapers in 1833 and about 3,000 by 1860. And the attraction to newspaper journalism was great enough that owners had little trouble finding editors and reporters.

During the years between 1831 and 1848 Whitman was a paid reporter or editor for 27 different newspapers, and during his lifetime he published news items, feature articles, or editorials for more than 80 newspapers, nearly all of them in the New York City area. The longest tenure Whitman had as a reporter or editor on any one newspaper was about two years, mostly because his liberal editorial views often grated against the political views of the owners. But even after letting him go, owners or editors would still invite him to submit articles.

Whitman's first job in journalism was as a printer's devil and compositor, beginning at age 11 (1831) with the LONG ISLAND PATRIOT; the next year he worked as an apprentice for the LONG ISLAND STAR. Whitman would write in *Specimen Days* an item entitled "Starting Newspapers," in which he remembers his earliest newspaper job and his first serious article:

> I commenced when I was but a boy of eleven or twelve writing sentimental bits for the old Long Island *Patriot*, in BROOKLYN; this was about 1832. Soon after, I had a piece or two in George P. Morris's then celebrated and fashionable *Mirror*, of New York City. I remember with what half-suppressed excitement I used to watch for the big, fat, red-faced, slow-moving, very old English carrier who distributed the *Mirror* in Brooklyn; and when I got one, opening and cutting the leaves with trembling fingers. How it made my heart double-beat to see *my piece* on the pretty white paper, in nice type.

The *Mirror* article is the first known to have been written by Whitman. Titled "The Olden Times," it appeared in the *NEW-YORK MIRROR: A Weekly Journal Devoted to Literature and Fine Arts* (November 29, 1834).

In 1838, at age 19, he became the founder, publisher, and editor of the Huntington weekly the LONG-ISLANDER, a newspaper that still exists.

The first issue was distributed on June 5, 1838. Apparently none of the issues from Whitman's one year as editor still exist, but seven of the articles he wrote that year were reprinted in the *Hempstead Inquirer* and the LONG ISLAND DEMOCRAT. Three of the articles are two sentences long, and the longest is three paragraphs. One of the short items is entitled "Fishing": "This sport is said to be excellent the present season. A small party the other day, in the bay, caught 61 black fish some of them weighing over 6 pounds, and several but little under."

In the same *Specimen Days* item quoted above, Whitman writes:

> My first real venture was the *Long Islander*, in my own beautiful town of Huntington, in 1839. . . . I had been teaching, . . . but liked printing; . . . I went to New York, bought a press and types, hired some little help, but did most of the work myself, including the presswork. . . . I bought a good horse, and every week went all around the country serving my papers, devoting one day and night to it. I never had happier jaunts. . . . The experience of those jaunts, the dear old-fashioned farmers and their wives, the stops by the hayfields, the hospitality, nice dinners, occasional evenings, the girls, the rides through the brush, come up in my memory to this day.

During the years between 1841 and 1848, he was editor of seven New York area newspapers: the NEW YORK AURORA (1842), the NEW YORK EVENING TATTLER (1842), the SUNDAY TIMES (coeditor, 1842), the NEW YORK STATESMAN (1843), the NEW YORK DEMOCRAT (1844), the *Evening Mirror* (1844), and the BROOKLYN DAILY EAGLE (1846–48). And he was a paid reporter for several other papers: the NEW WORLD, BROTHER JONATHAN, the SUN (New York), the SUBTERRANEAN, the SUNDAY TIMES & NOAH'S WEEKLY MESSENGER, the *Evening Mirror*, the *Broadway Journal*, the *United States Magazine and Democratic Review* (see DEMOCRATIC REVIEW, THE), the AMERICAN REVIEW, and the BROOKLYN EVENING STAR.

He moved to Brooklyn in 1846 so he could take newspaper jobs, first for the *Brooklyn Evening Star* and then for the weekly *Long Island Star.*

In March 1946, at age 26, Whitman was named editor-in-chief of the *Brooklyn Eagle and Kings County Democrat,* which became on June 1, 1846, the *Brooklyn Daily Eagle and Kings Count Democrat.* He was editor and chief reporter for the *Eagle* until January 21, 1848, when, according to Whitman, he "lost [his] place." He says of this latter experience:

. . . for two years I had one of the pleasantest sits of my life—a good owner, good pay, and easy work and hours. The troubles in the Democratic party broke forth about those times (1848–'49) and I split off with the radicals, which led to rows with the boss and 'the party,' and I lost my place.

He became editor and publisher of the *Brooklyn Freeman* in 1848, after returning from New Orleans, where he had been the editor of the NEW ORLEANS CRESCENT for three months. Apparently no issues of the *Freeman* survive. During the spring of 1850 he wrote a number of articles for the *Daily Advertiser* in New York. And after he published his first edition of *Leaves of Grass* in 1855, he took one more turn at newspaper journalism with a job as editor of the BROOKLYN DAILY TIMES. It isn't clear how long he was employed there, but he is credited with editorials from May 1, 1857, to June 26, 1859, which means he worked longer at the *Times* than he did at the *Brooklyn Eagle,* and he published 1,200 articles and editorials with the *Times* to 1,000 for the *Eagle;* yet it is the *Eagle* for which he is better known.

It would be difficult to find topics of interest to the readership during his years in journalism that he did not write about. Whether feature stories or editorials, Whitman seems to have covered the territory. Education, especially in the local public schools, seemed to dominate his interest during those years, with literature and music perhaps next. The following list gives a fair idea of the great variety of his subjects: politics (mostly reform); justice, or, more accurately, injustice; the press (including criticism of other newspaper editors); crime; women; marriage; neighborhoods; SLAVERY and abolition of slavery; foreign affairs; the U.S.-MEXICAN WAR; public tastes (not just in art, but also in public affairs); holidays; religion; weather; and sports.

His first biographer, Dr. Richard BUCKE, in writing about the importance of journalism in Whitman's career, said that "only those who know *Leaves of Grass* can understand the full meaning of [the 'especial education' the newspaper experience provided]. . . . It was perhaps the most comprehensive equipment ever attained by a human being, though many things that the schools prescribe were left out. It consisted in absorbing into himself the whole city and country about him, New York and Brooklyn, and their adjacencies; not only their outside shows, but far more their interior heart and meaning. In the first place he learned life—men, women, and children; he went on equal terms with every one, he liked them and they liked him, and he knew them far better than they knew themselves. Then he became thoroughly conversant with the shops, houses, sidewalks, ferries, factories, taverns, gatherings, political meetings, carousing, etc. . . . He knew the hospitals, poorhouses, prisons, and their inmates. He passed freely in and about those parts of the city which are inhabited by the worst characters; he knew all their people, and many of them knew him; he learned to tolerate their squalor, vice, and ignorance; he saw the good (often much more than the self-righteous think) and the bad that was in them, and what there was to excuse and justify their lives. . . . He knew and was sociable with the man that sold peanuts at the corner, and the old woman that dispensed coffee in the market. He did not patronize them, they were to him as good as the rest, as good as he, only temporarily dimmed and obscured."

It was the perfect education for a New York newspaper reporter and editor. And in the nearly 3,000 articles and editorials he wrote, the growth of the writer is evident, and the prose is clearly a precursor to his poetry. There are sentences in the journalism that could have been transferred directly into *Leaves of Grass.* The journalism years were essential preparation for the poetry years.

The following excerpt is from an editorial Whitman published while with the *Brooklyn Eagle* in which he discusses the relationship between journalist and readers; he might have written the same paragraph a few years later as he established himself as a poet.

There is a curious kind of sympathy (haven't you ever thought of it before?) that arises in the mind of the newspaper conductor with the public he serves. He gets to love them. Daily communion creates a sort of brotherhood and sisterhood between the two parties. As for us, we like this. We like it better than the more "dignified" part of editorial labors—the grave political disquisition, the contests of faction, and so on. And we want as many readers of the *Brooklyn Eagle*—even unto the half of Long Island—as possible, that we may increase the number of these friends. For are not those who listen to us friends?—Perhaps no office requires a greater union of rare qualities than that of a *true editor*. No wonder, then, that so few come under that flattering title! No wonder, that we are all derelict, in some particular! In general information, an editor should be complete, particularly with that relating to his own country. He should have a fluent style: elaborate finish we do not think requisite in daily writing. His articles had far better be earnest and terse than polished; they should ever smack of being uttered on the spur of the moment, like political oratory. . . . An editor needs, withal, a sharp eye, to discriminate the good from the immense mass of unreal stuff floating on all sides of him—and always bearing the counterfeit presentment of the real. . . .

The importance for a journalist of being able to tell the difference between the real and the counterfeit is what Ernest Hemingway would call, 50 years later, a personal, built-in "shit detector."

Whitman wrote a short item entitled "How to Write for Newspapers" (*The Brooklyn Eagle*, April 24, 1846), listing six requisites for the writer: "1. Have something to write about. 2. Write plain; dot your i's; cross your t's; point sentences; begin with capitals. 3. Write short; to the point; stop when you have done. 4. Write only on one side of the leaf. 5. Read it over, abridge and correct it, until you get it into the shortest space possible. 6. Pay the postage."

For a comprehensive listing and reprinting of Whitman's newspaper articles and editorials, see *The Collected Writings of Walt Whitman: The Journalism*, edited by Herbert Bergman, Douglas A. Noverr, and Edward J. Recchia, in two volumes (New York: Peter Lang, 1998). At the end of Whitman's life (1892), the profession of journalism had grown to such an extent that there were 16 daily newspapers in New York City, nine morning and seven evening, plus 13 foreign-languages dailies.

See part IV for "Newspapers and Magazines That published Whitman's Articles and Editorials." It includes dates for each of the newspapers for which Whitman held a paid position.

Wilde, Oscar (1854–1900)   Irish dramatist and poet, best known for his comic plays *Lady Windermere's Fan* (1893) and *The Importance of Being Earnest* (1899), and for his novel *The Picture of Dorian Gray* (1891). He was known also for his flamboyance, especially his dandified costumes.

He was on a lecture tour of the United States in 1882 when he met Whitman. Wilde visited the poet in Camden, upsetting Walt's brother George and his wife, who had difficulty enough understanding Walt, to say nothing of the various visitors to the Stevens Street house, and Oscar Wilde in particular.

Whitman later wrote that Wilde drank elderberry wine and hot toddies that evening and then wrote a thank-you note, stating, "There is no one in this great wide world of America whom I love and honor so much."

Wilde's relations with Lord Alfred Douglas caused a scandal in England during the 1890s, and Douglas's father, the marquess of Queensberry, accused Wilde of sodomy. Wilde sued for libel but lost and spent two years in jail (1897–98).

Wilmot Proviso (1846)   President Polk sent to Congress a bill proposing to spend $2 million to negotiate a peace with Mexico, the money to pay for land the president assumed would be acquired from Mexico. David Wilmot, a member of the president's own Democratic Party, proposed an amendment (August 8, 1846) that would provide that "as an express and fundamental condition to the acquisition of any territory from the Republic of Mexico by the United States, by virtue of any treaty which may be negotiated between them, and to the use by the Executive of the moneys herein appropriated, neither SLAVERY nor involuntary servitude shall ever exist in any part of said territory. . . ."

This Wilmot Proviso created serious and bitter debate among the members of Congress and in their states. It was eventually defeated in Congress, but the sectional debate was one of the major factors for the establishment of the Republican Party and, in 1860, for the election of Abraham LINCOLN.

It was also a factor in making Whitman aware that he had been on the wrong side of the debate. He was editor of the *BROOKLYN DAILY EAGLE* at the time and had supported President Polk and the Democratic Party in the U.S.-MEXICAN WAR. He had not been alert enough to the slavery issue involved in the war, however, or to the government's intention to allow for slavery in the new territories. Whitman wrote an editorial for the *Eagle* in favor of the Wilmot Proviso, which angered the newspaper's owners and resulted in the dismissal of their editor.

women, Whitman and It is difficult to find lines in *Leaves of Grass* which mention *men* in any of the word's manifestations that do not include *women* or one of its manifestations. Whitman had no apparent difficulty with pronoun references either; his "his and her" references seemed to come easily from his pen.

See the "Children of Adam" poems and "A Woman Waits for Me" in particular. He says of women:

> I will go stay with her who waits for me, and
>   with those women that are warm-blooded
>   and sufficient for me,
> I see that they understand me and do not deny
>   me,
> I see that they are worthy of me, I will be the
>   robust husband of those women.
> They are not one jot less than I am.

Whitman wrote a letter to the Washington, D.C., postmaster in 1872 urging a change of the postal law that would allow books and manuscripts a special rate. He argued that the word "books" in the present law should be allowed a broader definition in the way Jefferson had used the word "man" in its generic sense of men and women in the *Declaration of Independence.*

Gender equality was just one of the equalities that helped form Whitman's concept of democracy.

WOMEN IN LOVE WITH WHITMAN

Several women fell in love with Whitman. The most often named by biographers are Susan Garnet Smith, Juliette Beach, Ellen EYRE, Ellen O'Connor, and an unnamed "young lady" who "sized up Walt as a good bedfellow." Most important, however, was Anne GILCHRIST, one of the most outspoken in her love for the poet but also in her love and respect for his poetry. Both Eyre and Gilchrist offered to bear Whitman's children, within or without marriage.

World, The (1860–1931) Founded in New York by Alexander Cummings, a Philadelphia newspaper reporter and founder of the *Philadelphia Evening Bulletin* in 1847. Cummings started the *World* as a religious daily yet was censored in 1864 for publishing a forged presidential proclamation ordering the drafting of 400,000 men to fight in the CIVIL WAR.

Joseph Pulitzer bought the *World* in 1882 for $346,000 and immediately turned it into a first-rate daily newspaper, doubling its circulation to 40,000 in four months and to 100,000 by the fall of 1884. Pulitzer starting an evening edition and a Sunday *World,* and the three papers provided more income than any of the other leading New York dailies. Pulitzer died in 1911, and in 1931 Roy W. Howard of the Scripps-Howard newspaper chain bought the *World,* closed the morning and Sunday papers, and combined the evening paper with the New York *Telegram* to make the *World-Telegram.*

One of Whitman's poems was published under Pulitzer's direction, "A Voice from Death" (June 7, 1889).

Wound-Dresser, The (1898) Title for a book of letters written by Whitman from Washington hospitals during the CIVIL WAR, edited by Richard Maurice BUCKE, one of Whitman's estate executors; published in Boston by Small, Maynard and Company in 1898. Only 60 copies were printed. The book is subtitled "A Series of Letters Written from the Hospitals in Washington During the War of the Rebellion." It includes the poem "The Wound-Dresser," plus several previously published essays about his hospital duties, and letters he wrote to the loved ones of soldiers from both North and South.

Wright, Frances (1795–1852)   Scottish-born free-thinker, who spent two years in America at the time of Whitman's birth (1819) and whose writings were influential on the poet's parents and later on the poet himself. She was a feminist and reformer, who came back to the United States in 1824 with the Marquis de Lafayette, met retired presidents Jefferson and Madison, who encouraged her in setting up the Nashoba Community (1825–28) in Tennessee with a plan to emancipate the slaves.

She helped found, with Robert Dale Owen, the *New Harmony Gazette* (1825–35), a socialist and agnostic weekly retitled the *Free Enquirer* in 1829. Wright gave public lectures on women's rights, including birth control; also on free education, equitable distribution of wealth, and on the mistaken beliefs of organized religion. Her lectures were later published in two volumes as *Course of Popular Lectures* (1829 and 1836), probably Whitman's sources for her ideas. She also wrote *A Few Days in Athens* (1822), a work of fiction about a student of Epicurus, which Whitman later referred to as his "daily bread."

PART IV

Appendices

CHRONOLOGY

1816
Personal: Walter Whitman, Sr., and Louisa Van Velsor marry (June 8).

Other Literary Events: Transatlantic shipping begins.

1818
Personal: Jesse Whitman born (March 2).

Other Literary Events: William Cullen Bryant's "To A Waterfowl" published.

Historical Events: North boundary of the Rocky Mountains set at 49th parallel.

1819
Personal: Walt Whitman born (May 31), at West Hills, in Huntington Township on Long Island, New York. His father, Walter Whitman, Sr., and mother, Louisa Van Velsor Whitman, were among the earliest white settlers of Huntington Township.

Other Literary Events: James Russell Lowell born (Feb. 22). Herman Melville born (Aug. 1). James Fenimore Cooper's *The Spy* published. Bryant's *Poems* published.

Historical Events: Florida purchased. University of Virginia founded by Thomas Jefferson.

1821
Personal: Mary Elizabeth Whitman born (Feb. 3).

Other Literary Events: The *Saturday Evening Post* founded (1821–1967). English poet John Keats dies (Feb. 23).

Historical Events: Hurricane hits New York (Sept. 3), causing tide to rise 13 feet in one hour, with widespread flooding south of Canal Street. Mary Baker Eddy born (1821–1910).

1823
Personal: Whitman family moves to Brooklyn (May 27). They rent a house on Front Street, near the Fulton Ferry settlement. Hannah Louisa Whitman born (Nov. 28).

Other Literary Events: Cooper's *The Pioneers* and *The Pilot* published. Clement Moore's *A Visit from St. Nicholas* published. The *New-York Mirror* founded (1823–60).

Historical Events: Monroe Doctrine adopted (Dec. 2).

1824
Personal: Walter Whitman, Sr., buys property at corner of Washington and Johnson Streets in Brooklyn (Sept. 1). At a ceremony in July honoring Revolutionary War hero Lafayette, Walt is lifted up by the general and kissed on the cheek.

Other Literary Events: Washington Irving's *Tales of a Traveller* published. The *Springfield Republican* founded (1824–present). English poet George Gordon, Lord Byron dies (April 19).

Historical Events: National Republican Party founded (1824–32). Stonewall Jackson born (Jan. 21). French general Lafayette tours America.

1825
Personal: Whitman begins elementary school. He will attend until 1830. Walter Sr. buys lot at corner of Tillary and Adams Streets in Brooklyn and builds a house. Walt later writes that both lots his father purchased "were mortgaged and we lost them." A fourth child is born to the Whitmans (March 2) but dies unnamed (Sept. 14).

Historical Events: John Quincy Adams is U.S. president (1825–1829). England's first railway line opens. Erie Canal completed in October.

1826
Personal: Whitman's "Quaker" grandmother, Naomi (Williams) Van Velsor, dies (February). The Whitman family lives on Van Dyke Street, Brooklyn.

Other Literary Events: Cooper's *The Last of the Mohicans* published. Bryant's "A Forest Hymn" published.

Historical Events: Thomas Jefferson (83) and John Adams (90) both die within few hours of each other on July 4, the 50th anniversary of the Declaration of Independence.

1827
Personal: Andrew Jackson Whitman born (April 7). Whitmans live in house on Adams Street until November and then move to a house on Tillary Street, where they are relatively stable for four years.

Other Literary Events: Edgar Allan Poe's *Tamerlane and Other Poems* published. Cooper's *The Prairie* published. *Youth's Companion* founded (1827–1929).

Historical Events: Greek War of Independence fought.

1828
Personal: Whitmans live on Tillary Street in Brooklyn.

Other Literary Events: Noah Webster's *Dictionary of the English Language* (American) published. Count Lev Tolstoy born (Sept. 9).

Historical Events: American Peace Society founded.

1829
Personal: Walt spends a number of days during summer visiting his grandparents and the beaches of Long Island. George Washington Whitman born (Nov. 28). Walt is taken by his parents to hear the Quaker preacher Elias Hicks at Morrison's Hotel in Brooklyn (November). Walt later wrote a short biography of Hicks.

Other Literary Events: Poe's *Al Aaraaf, Tamerlane, and Minor Poems* published.

Historical Events: Andrew Jackson is president (1829–37). Steamship *Fulton* explodes in the Brooklyn Navy Yard (June 4), killing 40 people. Typewriter invented, (probably) by William Burt.

1830
Personal: Walt quits school and takes job as office boy in the law firm of James B. Clark & Son on Fulton Street in Brooklyn. Edward Clark, the son, provides Walt with a subscription to a circulating library in Brooklyn so he can continue his education.

Other Literary Events: Oliver Wendell Holmes's "Old Ironsides" published; Sarah Hale's "Mary Had a Little Lamb" published. Boston's *Daily Evening Transcript* founded (1830–1941). Emily Dickinson born (Dec. 10).

Historical Events: U.S. population is 12.8 million. Mormon church founded. Bourbons overthrown in France, following restoration of the monarchy in 1814.

1831
Personal: Walt works as a printer's devil at the *Long Island Patriot*, under editor Samuel E. Clements. This is the beginning of his lifelong interest in printing and journalism.

Other Literary Events: John Greenleaf Whittier's *Legends of New England* published.

Historical Events: Electromagnetic telegraph invented by Joseph Henry (though not of practical use until Samuel Morse developed it 13 years later). New England Anti-Slavery Society founded.

1832
Personal: Walt begins work during the summer for Brooklyn printer Erastus Worthington. In the fall he works on the *Long Island Star* for editor Alden Spooner.

Other Literary Events: Nathaniel Hawthorne's "Roger Malvin's Burial" published. Louisa May Alcott born (Nov. 29). Johann Wolfgang von Goethe, whose works Whitman would later admire, dies (March 22).

Historical Events: Cholera pandemic hits New York City (June 26). English first reform bill passes

Parliament. Charles Darwin's voyage of the *Beagle* begins (1832–36).

1833

Personal: Whitman family moves to central Long Island in May; Walt stay in Brooklyn to continue work on the *Star*. Thomas Jefferson Whitman born (July 18).

Other Literary Events: Poe's "MS Found in a Bottle" published. The *Sun* (New York) founded. Honoré de Balzac's *Eugénie Grandet* is published, one of 20 works he wrote between 1832 and 1835.

Historical Events: American Anti-Slavery Society founded. New York University founded.

1834

Personal: Whitmans move to Norwich, near Oyster Bay, Long Island. Walt works for various newspapers in New York.

Other Literary Events: The *Southern Literary Messenger* founded (1834–64). English poet Samuel Taylor Coleridge dies (July 25).

Historical Events: Cyrus H. McCormick patents reaping machine, turning subsistence farming into mass production. Brooklyn, which until this year was officially considered a village, becomes a city. It will not become part of New York City (as a "borough") until 1898.

1835

Personal: Edward Whitman born (Aug. 9). Walt takes job (May 12) as apprentice printer in Manhattan; during summer he becomes "journeyman printer."

Other Literary Events: Mark Twain born as Samuel L. Clemens (Nov. 30). Hawthorne's "Young Goodman Brown" published. The *New York Herald* founded (1835–1966).

Historical Events: August fire destroys most of Paternoster Row, New York's printing center.

1836

Personal: Walt takes his first teaching position in Norwich, near his grandfather's farm in Cold Spring. He moves in May to Hempstead, Long Island, to be

with his family. Whitman family then moves to Babylon, Long Island, and Walt teaches there for three months.

Publications: Walt writes his first short story, "My Boys and Girls."

Other Literary Events: Ralph Waldo Emerson's essay "Nature" is published. William Holmes McGuffey's *Eclectic Readers* published. Charles Dickens's *Pickwick Papers* published. Thomas Carlyle's *Sartor Resartus* is published. Bret Harte born (Aug. 25).

Historical Events: Battle of the Alamo fought (Feb. 23–March 6). Whig Party formed. Colt revolver manufactured. Mt. Holyoke Seminary for women founded.

1837

Personal: Walt teaches in Long Swamp, Long Island, during the spring term. He teaches the fall term at Smithtown.

Other Literary Events: Emerson's *The American Scholar* published. Hawthorne's *Twice-Told Tales* published. The *Baltimore Sun* founded (1837–present). *New Orleans Picayune* founded (1837–present). *Democratic Review* founded (1837–59).

Historical Events: Martin Van Buren president (1837–41). Financial panic hits New York. Victoria becomes queen of Great Britain and Ireland.

1838

Personal: Walt starts his own weekly newspaper, the *Long-Islander* in Huntington, Long Island (June). He writes, edits, sets type, prints, and delivers the paper. His brother George is printer's devil, and they live together above the print shop.

Publications: Walt publishes "Our Future Lot" in the *Long Island Democrat* (Oct. 31), his earliest-known published poem.

Other Literary Events: Emerson's "Divinity School Address" published. Whittier's *Ballads and Anti-Slavery Poems* published.

Historical Events: Underground Railroad established to help slaves escape to the North.

1839

Personal: Walt sells the *Long-Islander* and looks for work in New York. He takes a job at the *Long Island*

Democrat (August). He takes a teaching position for the fall term at Jamaica Academy, in Flushing Hill. In December he begins teaching at Little Bay Side school near Jamaica.

Publications: Walt writes a series of articles for the *Long-Islander* under the general heading "The Sun-Down Papers." He publishes the poem "Fame's Vanity" in the *Long Island Democrat* (Oct. 23) and "My Departure" (Nov. 27).

Other Literary Events: Count Alexis de Tocqueville's *Democracy in America* is published. Henry Wadsworth Longfellow's *Hyperion and Voices of the Night* published.

Historical Events: Darwin publishes his journals on his *Beagle* voyage (1832–36).

1840

Personal: Whitman family moves to Dix Hills, Long Island (May). Walt teaches spring term at Trimming Square, Long Island; the summer term in Woodbury; and the fall term in Whitestone, near Jamaica. Walt's sister Mary Elizabeth marries Ansel Van Nostrand (Jan. 2) and moves with him to Greenport, Long Island.

Publications: During the year, Walt publishes a number of poems in the *Long Island Democrat*.

Other Literary Events: Richard Henry Dana's *Two Years Before the Mast* published. Cooper's *The Pathfinder* published. First *Dial* magazine founded (1840–44). English novelist Thomas Hardy born (June 2).

Historical Events: U.S. population is 17 million.

1841

Personal: Walt gives a speech on July 29 at a Democratic Party rally in City Hall Park in New York. He is still teaching in Whitestone. In May he takes job in the printing office of the (New York) *World*.

Publications: Walt publishes five short stories during the fall and early winter.

Other Literary Events: Cooper's *The Deerslayer* published. Poe's "Murders in the Rue Morgue" published. Emerson's *Essays: First Series* published. Brook Farm established in West Roxbury, Massachusetts, and lasts six years. The *New York Tribune* founded (1841–24).

Historical Events: William Henry Harrison is president (1841). John Tyler is president (1841–45).

1842

Personal: Walt becomes a reporter for the New York daily, the *Aurora* (February). He becomes editor (late March), the first of several New York editorial posts he will hold during the next 20 years. He leaves the *Aurora* (May) over disagreements with the owners

Publications: Walt hears lecture by Emerson, "Nature and the Powers of the Poet," at the New York Historical Library and reviews it for the *Aurora*. One of Whitman's first assignments for the *Aurora* is a series of articles titled "Walks in Broadway." He writes for the *New York Evening Tattler* (May and June) and publishes a number of poems and essays in various journals during the year, including the short story "The Last Loyalist" in the *Democratic Review* (May).

Other Literary Events: Dickens's *American Notes* published. Poe's "Masque of the Red Death" published. Alfred Tennyson's *Poems* published in England.

1843

Personal: Walt becomes editor of the *New York Statesman*. The publication is short-lived, however, and he will spend most of the year writing and publishing poems and essays.

Publications: Whitman's *The Madman*, an incomplete novel, is published in the *Washingtonian and Organ* (Jan. 28).

Other Literary Events: Poe's "The Gold Bug" and "The Black Cat" published. Scottish essayist Thomas Carlyle's *Past and Present* published in England. Henry James born (April 15).

1844

Personal: Walt becomes editor of the *New York Democrat* during the summer but disagrees with management over the fall's political candidates and is fired.

Publications: Walt writes articles for the *New Mirror* (October). He publishes several short stories, including "The Love of Eris: A Spirit Record" in the *Columbian Magazine* (March); "My Boys and Girls" in the *Rover* (April 20); "Dumb Kate" in the *Columbian*

(May); and "The Little Sleighers" in the *Columbian* (September).

Other Literary Events: Emerson's *Essays: Second Series* published.

1845

Personal: Without permanent work during the summer, Walt rejoins his family in Brooklyn. His father is building a house in the Dix Hills area of the village.

Publications: "Arrow-Tip," one of Whitman's better short stories, is published in the *Aristidean,* along with "Shirval: A Tale of Jerusalem," both in the March issue. Late in the year, Walt writes theatre/music reviews for the *Long Island Star.* He becomes interested in opera and publishes "Art-Music and Heart-Music" in the *Broadway Journal* (Nov. 29), edited by Poe.

Other Literary Events: Poe's *The Raven and Other Poems* published. Margaret Fuller's *Woman in the Nineteenth Century* published. Richard Wagner's *Tannhauser* first performed, Dresden Court Opera (Oct. 19).

Historical Events: James Polk is president (1845–49). Texas annexed. U.S. Naval Academy founded.

1846

Personal: Whitman becomes editor of the *Brooklyn Daily Eagle* (March). He will hold the position for nearly two years, one of his longest tenures as editor.

Publications: Whitman publishes his poem "Ode-By Walter Whitman" in the *Eagle* (July 2), meant to be sung to the tune of "The Star-Spangled Banner" at the July 4 celebration at Fort Greene in Brooklyn.

Other Literary Events: Melville's *Typee* published. Hawthorne's *Mosses from an Old Manse* published. Poe's "Cask of Amontillado" published.

Historical Events: U.S.-Mexican War (1846–48). Oregon annexed. Wilmot Proviso passed in Congress. Smithsonian Institution established. England repeals its "Corn Laws."

1847

Personal: Walt supports editorially the "Free-Soil" position, which prohibits new states from allowing slavery. He also supports in *Eagle* editorials the Wilmot Proviso, which prohibits slavery in any territories gained by the United States after the U.S.-Mexican War.

Publications: Whitman becomes enthusiastic opera-goer and writes an overview of the Brooklyn opera season for the *Eagle* (Feb. 28); he writes his first opera review, after hearing a performance of *Il Barbiere di Siviglia* (March 23).

Other Literary Events: Longfellow's *Evangeline* published. Melville's *Omoo* published.

Historical Events: Free-Soil Party formed (1847–54).

1848

Personal: Walt argues with *Eagle* editors over political issues and leaves (or is fired from) the paper (late January). In mid-February, without work but not without luck, Whitman meets J. E. McClure, part owner of the *New Orleans Crescent* and accepts offer to edit the *Crescent.* He becomes editor of the *New Orleans Daily Crescent* (Feb. 25); the job lasts three months. Walt and Jeff, who accompanied his brother to New Orleans, arrive back in Brooklyn (June 15). Walt is elected (August 5) as one of 15 delegates for the Free-Soil Party, in support of Martin Van Buren for president. Walt has his head "read" by phrenologist Lorenzo Fowler, who sees in Whitman amativeness (love for women) and adhesiveness (love for men) and combativeness. Walt publishes first issue of the *Brooklyn Daily Freeman* (Sept. 9). The next day, a fire destroys the Freeman building, and further publication is delayed two months.

Other Literary Events: Lowell's *Biglow Papers* published. Karl Marx and Friedrich Engels publish *Communist Manifesto.*

Historical Events: Gold discovered in California. War with Mexico ends. College of the City of New York founded. University of Wisconsin founded. Seneca Falls woman suffrage meeting held. Associated Press founded; begins with election results. Irish potato famine results in boatloads of Irish citizens migrating to America.

1849

Personal: Whitman resigns as editor of the *Brooklyn Daily Freeman* (Sept. 11), which effectively kills the hard-luck newspaper after less than a year of publication.

Other Literary Events: Francis Parkman's *Oregon Trail* published. Melville's *Mardi* and *Redburn* published. Henry David Thoreau's *A Week on the Concord and Merrimack Rivers* and "Civil Disobedience" published. Sarah Orne Jewett born (Sept. 3). James Whitcomb Riley born (Oct. 7). Poe dies (Oct. 7).

Historical Events: Zachary Taylor is president (1849–50). Gold rush begins in California. Astor Place riot takes place in New York.

1850

Personal: Walt is without formal newspaper work.

Publications: Walt publishes several poems and essays, including: "Song for Certain Congressmen" in the *New York Evening Post* (March 2); the poems "Blood-Money," "The House of Friends," and "Resurgemus" in the *New York Tribune* (March 22, June 14, and June 21, respectively).

Other Literary Events: Hawthorne's *The Scarlet Letter* is published. Tennyson's *In Memoriam* published. Wordsworth dies (April 23).

Historical Events: U.S. population is more than 23 million. Millard Fillmore is president (1850–53). Compromise of 1850 passes Congress. Jenny Lind's opera tour of America.

1851

Personal: Walt writes letter to William Cullen Bryant, editor of the *New York Evening Post*, describing pride in the growth of Brooklyn, which had become a "city" in 1834. He also writes about the Brooklyn Art Union, where he presents a lecture "Art and Artists" (March 31).

Publications: Walt writes a series of "letters from Paumanok" (Long Island) for Bryant's *Evening Post*. One of the articles is devoted to opera.

Other Literary Events: Melville's *Moby-Dick* published. Hawthorne's *The House of Seven Gables* published. Stephen Foster composes "Old Folks at Home." Kate Chopin born (Feb. 8).

Historical Events: Maine's liquor prohibition becomes law. Northwestern University founded.

1852

Personal: Whitman's sister Hannah marries Charles Heyde (March 16). Walter Sr. spends several months

during 1851 and 1852 as carpenter, including the building of two houses for his own family. He sells the Myrtle Avenue house in Brooklyn (May), and they move into a house he has built on Cumberland Street (Sept.).

Other Literary Events: Harriet Beecher Stowe's *Uncle Tom's Cabin* published. Hawthorne's *The Blithedale Romance* published.

Historical Events: Antoinette-Louisa Brown Blackwell becomes first American woman ordained as church minister. Louis Napoleon becomes Napoleon III, emperor of France.

1853

Personal: Walter Sr. sells the Cumberland Street house (March), and the family moves into a smaller house on the same street (April).

Other Literary Events: *Putnam's Monthly Magazine* founded (1853–1910).

Historical Events: Franklin Pierce is president (1853–57). Gadsden Purchase sets U.S.-Mexican border. Matthew Calbraith Perry voyages to Japan. Railroad connection established from New York to Chicago. The Crystal Palace Exhibition opens in New York City.

1854

Personal: Whitman family living in a house on Skillman Street (May). Gabriel Harrison takes photograph of Walt in Brooklyn (July) that is used the next year as the frontispiece for the first edition of *Leaves of Grass*. Walt writes a letter protesting the Brooklyn City Council's enacting of Sunday blue laws (including the prohibition of the running of streetcars and railroads on Sunday), published in the *Brooklyn Evening Star* (Oct. 20).

Publications: Walt writes "Poem of Apparitions in Boston, the 78th Year of These States," later titled "A Boston Ballad."

Other Literary Events: Thoreau's *Walden* is published. Timothy Shay Arthur's *Ten Nights in a Barroom* published.

Historical Events: United States signs trade treaty with Japan. Kansas-Nebraska Act establishes territories. Crimean War begins.

1855

Personal: This is one of the most important years in Whitman's life, although it will take time for him to realize it. Emerson sends Whitman a letter (July 21) congratulating him for *Leaves of Grass* and saying, "I greet you at the beginning of a great career." Walt's father, Walter Whitman, Sr., dies (July 11).

Publications: First edition of *Leaves of Grass* published (c. July 4), some of it handset by Whitman himself in Rome Brothers Print Shop, Brooklyn. Walt's essay "A Visit to the Opera" is published in New York's *Life Illustrated,* and he begins a series of articles in *Life Illustrated,* titled "New York Dissected."

Other Literary Events: Longfellow's poem *Hiawatha* is published. John Bartlett's *Familiar Quotations* published. Irving's *Life of Washington* published. Boston's "Saturday Club" founded (1855–present). The *New York Ledger* founded (1855–1903).

Historical Events: John Brown's antislavery forces in violent action with slavery forces in Kansas.

1856
Personal: Whitman family moves (May 1) to a brownstone house on Classon Avenue in Brooklyn. Walt's mother takes in boarders. Fanny Fern, the highest paid and one of the most popular New York columnists, reviews *Leaves of Grass* for the *New York Ledger* (May 10); refers to Walt as "this glorious Native American." Bronson Alcott and Thoreau visit Whitman in Brooklyn (Oct. 4). They return (Nov. 10) with Sarah Tyndale, a strong abolitionist and an advocate of women's rights.

Publications: Second edition of *Leaves of Grass* published (on or near Sept. 1) by Fowler & Wells. Whitman, unashamedly and without permission, publishes Emerson's letter of July 21, 1855, congratulating the poet for *Leaves of Grass.* Walt publishes "The Slave Trade" in *Life Illustrated* (August 2), an exposé describing the use of the New York harbor by slave ships.

Other Literary Events: German poet Heinrich Heine dies (Feb. 17). Sigmund Freud born (May 6). George Bernard Shaw born (July 26).

Historical Events: "Know-Nothing" movement established. Copyright law passed by Congress.

1857
Personal: Strange legal case is brought against Whitman (June 17): Oliver Dyer, a lawyer representing James Parton (Fanny Fern's husband) arrives at Walt's house to claim $200 owed to Parton. Walt cannot pay but gives up books and paintings in way of payment, which apparently Dyer fails to give to Parton, who then sues Whitman in default of debt.

Publications: Walt takes job (May) with the *Brooklyn Daily Times.* It is not clear that he is the editor, but he writes more than 200 articles/editorials for the newspaper in the two years he is employed.

Other Literary Events: *Atlantic Monthly* founded (1857–present). *Harper's Weekly* founded (1857–16). Gustave Flaubert's *Madame Bovary* published. Charles Baudelaire's *Flowers of Evil* published.

Historical Events: James Buchanan is president (1857–61). Dred Scott decision issued. Financial panic in New York.

1858
Personal: Whitman's first stroke occurs during the summer. He calls it "sunstroke," but there is dizziness and weakness, which may be a precursor to the serious strokes several years later.

Other Literary Events: Longfellow's *Courtship of Miles Standish* published. Holmes's *Autocrat of the Breakfast-Table* published.

Historical Events: Lincoln-Douglas debates begin (Aug. 21). First transatlantic cable laid.

1859
Personal: Walt leaves work with the *Brooklyn Daily Times* (late spring) and spend the summer working on the next edition of *Leaves of Grass.* Walt's brother Jeff marries Martha E. Mitchell ("Mattie") (Feb. 23). They move in for a time with the Whitman family when it moves to a house on Portland Avenue, Brooklyn (May).

Publications: "A Child's Reminiscence" (later "Out of the Cradle Endlessly Rocking") is published in the *Saturday Press* (Dec. 24). *Vanity Fair* founded (1859–1963).

Other Literary Events: Darwin's *Origin of Species* published. William Makepeace Thackeray's *The Virginian* published.

Historical Events: John Brown leads raid on Harpers Ferry (Oct. 16–18). Cooper Union founded.

1860
Personal: Whitman goes to Boston (March 15) to help publishers Thayer & Eldridge work on third

edition of *Leaves of Grass*. He meets William and Ellen O'Connor, who will become good friends and supporters of his poetry.

Publications: Third edition of *Leaves of Grass* published (late spring) by Thayer & Eldridge. The poems include "Sun-Down Poem" (later "Crossing Brooklyn Ferry").

Other Literary Events: Hawthorne's *The Marble Faun* published. Holmes's *Professor at the Breakfast-Table* published. Hamlin Garland born (Sept. 14).

Historical Events: U.S. population is 31.5 million. Tweed Ring formed. Pony Express begins. South Carolina secedes from the Union.

1861

Personal: Publishers Thayer & Eldridge declare bankruptcy (Jan. 10). The 1860 *Leaves of Grass* plates are sold to Boston publisher Richard Worthington, who prints a "pirated edition" of *Leaves*. Whitman sees Lincoln in New York, apparently for the first time; the president is on his way to Washington for his inauguration. Walt's brother George enlists in Brooklyn's 13th Regiment (April 19). He reenlists for three years in the New York 51st Volunteers and leaves for camp in Virginia (Oct. 30).

Publications: Whitman's poem "Beat! Beat! Drums!" is published in *Harper's Weekly* and in the *New York Leader* (Sept. 28). Walt contributes to various publications, including 25 articles under the general heading "Brooklyniana" for the *Brooklyn Daily Standard;* he produces another series titled "City Photographs" for the *New York Leader.*

Other Literary Events: Longfellow's "Paul Revere's Ride" published.

Historical Events: Abraham Lincoln is president (1861–65). Ten more Southern states secede: Mississippi, Florida, Alabama, Georgia, Louisiana, Texas, Virginia, Tennessee, Arkansas, and North Carolina. Civil War begins "officially" (April 15). First Battle of Bull Run (July 21). Kingdom of Italy proclaimed. Czar Alexander II frees Russian serfs.

1862

Personal: Walt sees brother George's name on list of war wounded in the *New York Herald* (Dec. 14) and goes to Washington for more information. He travels to Falmouth, Virginia, near Fredericksburg (Dec. 17), where George is recovering from facial wounds.

Other Literary Events: Julia Ward Howe's "Battle Hymn of the Republic" published. Edith Wharton born (Jan. 24).

Historical Events: Civil War battles: Shiloh, second Bull Run, Harpers Ferry, Antietam, and Fredericksburg. The *Monitor,* the Union Army's ironclad ship, is lost at sea (Dec. 30) in a battle with the *Merrimac.* Sioux and U.S. Army battle in Minnesota. France invades Mexico.

1863

Personal: Walt returns to Washington (Jan. 2) and begins work in Washington hospitals (late Feb.). Whitman sees procession of "about" 100 Confederate soldiers marched down Pennsylvania Avenue to prison. He later writes of them as "brothers," still Americans, "silent proud young fellows." He meets John Burroughs, the naturalist, who becomes a close friend. Walt's brother Andrew dies (Dec. 3).

Other Literary Events: Edward Everett Hale's "The Man Without a Country" published.

Historical Events: Union Army victorious at Gettysburg (July 4) and Vicksburg. Other battles at Chancellorsville, Chickamauga, and Chattanooga. Lincoln's "Gettysburg Address" delivered (Nov. 19). Emancipation Proclamation issued. Draft riots in New York City (July 13–16) over Lincoln's military draft policies.

1864

Personal: Walt travels to Culpeper, Virginia (Jan.), where he is a firsthand witness to a battle. Suffering from constant work with wounded and dying soldiers, Walt has breakdown in June and goes to his mother's home in Brooklyn for six months. He commits his brother Jesse to the Kings County Lunatic Asylum (Dec. 5).

Other Literary Events: Jules Verne's *Journey to the Center of the Earth* published. Henry James's first published story, "A Tragedy of Error," appears. Elizabeth Gaskell's *Wives and Daughters* published. Hawthorne dies (May 19).

Historical Events: Civil War battles: Wilderness, Spotsylvania, Cold Harbor; siege of Petersburg; Sherman's march through Georgia to the sea. First Pullman railroad car becomes active. Maximilian installed by France as ruler of Mexico (1864–67).

1865

Personal: Rents a room at 468 M Street in Washington (Jan.). Letter (Jan. 20) from George stating that he is military prisoner at Danville, Virginia. With help from Walt, George is released (Feb). Walt appointed clerk in Indian Bureau of the Department of Interior (Jan.); is fired by Secretary James Harlan (June 30) when he learns that Walt is author of *Leaves of Grass;* Walt then becomes clerk at the attorney general's office (July). Whitman hears news of Lincoln's assassination on April 15, leaves for Washington April 17, and attends funeral services April 19.

Publications: *Drum-Taps* and *Sequel to Drum-Taps* published, the Sequel containing "When Lilacs Last in the Dooryard Bloom'd." "O Captain! My Captain!" published in *Saturday Press* (Nov. 4).

Other Literary Events: Thoreau's *Cape Cod* published. Tolstoy's *War and Peace* published. Lewis Carroll's *Alice's Adventures in Wonderland* published. Elizabeth Gaskell dies (Nov. 12).

Historical Events: President Lincoln shot (Apr. 14, "Good Friday") by John Wilkes Booth. Lincoln dies the next morning. Lee surrenders to Grant at Appomattox (Apr. 9). Vice President Andrew Johnson becomes president (1865–69). Thirteenth Amendment passes in Congress (prohibits slavery). Ku Klux Klan founded.

1866

Personal: Whitman's friend William O'Connor publishes *The Good Gray Poet*, a "vindication" of Walt after his being fired by Secretary of the Interior Harlan for having written *Leaves of Grass*. Walt is promoted and gets pay increase at the attorney general's office (Nov.).

Publications: Fourth edition of *Leaves of Grass* published (late Nov.). It carries an 1867 publication date.

Other Literary Events: Whittier's *Snowbound* published. Fyodor Dostoyevsky's *Crime and Punishment* published. The *World* (New York) founded (1866–1931). New York's Metropolitan Museum of Art founded. *Galaxy* magazine founded (1866–1878).

Historical Events: Reconstruction begins. Alfred Nobel invents dynamite. Marquess of Queensberry lists rules of boxing.

1867

Personal: Walt moves to 472 M St. in Washington. Burroughs publishes *Notes on Walt Whitman, as Poet and Person.* Family now lives at 1194 Atlantic Street in Brooklyn. Jeff takes job in St. Louis and he and wife Martha move there during the summer.

Publications: This is the announced and generally accepted publication year for the fourth edition of *Leaves of Grass.* There are six new poems plus "Drum-Taps" and "Sequel to Drum-Taps" as annexes. *Galaxy* publishes Whitman's essay *Democracy.*

Other Literary Events: Emerson's poems *May-Day, and Other Pieces* published. Matthew Arnold's poem "Dover Beach" published. Ivan Turgenev's *Smoke* published.

Historical Events: Nebraska becomes state. U.S. buys Alaska from Russia.

1868

Personal: Correspondence between Walt and Anne Gilchrist begins. Walt's nephew Andy is run over and killed by a cart in New York. Walt had ignored his mother's request that Andrew and Nancy's children be taken away from them because of neglect.

Publications: Rossetti publishes selections from *Leaves of Grass* in England. Walt's poem "Whispers of Heavenly Death" published.

Other Literary Events: Louisa May Alcott's *Little Women* published. Bret Harte's "The Luck of Roaring Camp" published. Robert Browning's *The Ring and the Book* published. *Lippincott's Magazine* founded (1868–1916). Magazine for women's rights, *The Revolution*, founded by Elizabeth Cady Stanton and Susan B. Anthony (1868–70).

Historical Events: President Johnson impeached; survives close Senate vote. Benjamin Disraeli becomes British prime minister.

1869

Personal: Louisa Whitman and Edward move to Portland Avenue in Brooklyn (May 1). Walt works on new edition of *Leaves of Grass.*

Other Literary Events: Twain's *Innocents Abroad* published. Arnold's *Culture and Anarchy* published. Richard Doddridge Blackmore's *Lorna Doone* published. Booth Tarkington born (July 29). E. A. Robinson born (Dec. 22).

Historical Events: Ulysses S. Grant is president (1869–77). Fifteenth Amendment passes Congress (establishes universal male vote). Women win voting rights in Wyoming.

1870
Personal: Walt's brother Jesse dies (March 21) at the Kings County Lunatic Asylum and is buried in a pauper's grave. Mrs. Gilchrist's "An English-Woman's Estimate of Walt Whitman" published in Boston's *Radical Review* (May).

Publications: Poem "Passage to India" is rejected by Bret Harte at *Overland Monthly* in San Francisco, but will become one of Whitman's major poems when published in the 1871 edition of *Leaves.*

Other Literary Events: Emerson's "Society and Solitude" published. Charles Scribner begins *Scribner's Monthly.* Charles Dickens dies (June 9).

Historical Events: U.S. population is 38.8 million. Standard Oil Co. founded. Franco-Prussian War fought (1870–71).

1871
Personal: Mrs. Gilchrist writes love letter to Walt, offering to have his children with or without marriage. Brother George marries Louisa Orr Haslam, and they move to 322 Stevens Street in Camden, New Jersey. New York newspapers run story about Whitman's death in a train accident but refuse to run the poet's denial.

Publications: Fifth Edition of *Leaves of Grass* published. Includes "Passage to India" in supplement. *Democratic Vistas* published. Walt delivers poem "After All, Not to Create Only" at the National Industrial Exhibition (Sept. 7).

Other Literary Events: Edward Eggleston's *Hoosier Schoolmaster* published. William Ellery Channing's *The Wanderer* published. George Eliot's *Middlemarch* published. James McNeill Whistler's painting *Whistler's Mother* exhibited.

Historical Events: Chicago fire destroys great portion of the city. New York Tweed Ring defeated. Smith College founded. Barnum Circus first performs.

1872
Personal: Walt and O'Connor have bitter argument over the slavery issue, which breaks the friendship. Louisa Whitman and Eddie move in with George and his wife, Louisa, in Camden, New Jersey.

Publications: Walt delivers reading at Dartmouth College titled "As a Strong Bird on Pinions Free," which becomes "Thou Mother with thy Equal Brood" in 1881 edition of *Leaves of Grass.*

Other Literary Events: Mark Twain's *Roughing It* published. Paul Laurence Dunbar born (June 27).

Historical Events: Scandal hangs over Crédit Mobilier (1872–73).

1873
Personal: Walt has stroke (Jan. 22), following several spells of dizziness. He is bedridden for a month and finds his left leg useless. Moves in with brother George and his wife, Louisa (plus his mother and Eddie) in Camden, New Jersey. Jeff's wife, Martha, dies in St. Louis. Walt's mother dies (May 23). He would later refer to her death as the "great dark cloud of my life." He returns to Camden and his brother's house, staying in his mother's two-room apartment. George and Louisa move to 431 Stevens Street, and Walt takes a third-floor room.

Other Literary Events: Thomas Bailey Aldrich's "Marjorie Daw" published. *Woman's Home Companion* founded (1873–1957). Willa Cather born (Dec. 7).

Historical Events: Nevada silver rush.

1874
Personal: Peter Doyle visits Walt in Camden for the first time (end of May). Walt buys a lot at 460 Royden Street for $460, but he never builds a house there.

Publications: Walt's series of articles on the Civil War begins in the *New York Daily Graphic* and will be included in *Memoranda During the War* (1875). Walt's poem "The Song of the Universal" is read by proxy at Tufts College; he is too ill to attend. *Democratic Vistas* is translated into Danish.

Other Literary Events: Gertrude Stein born (Feb. 3). Amy Lowell born (Feb. 9). Robert Frost born (March 26). Ellen Glasgow born (April 22). Clarence Day born (Nov. 18).

Historical Events: Women's Christian Temperance Union founded.

1875

Personal: Walt has another stroke, this time on the right side. He fears that he will never regain full use of his legs. He attends, however, the reburial of Poe and the dedication of a Poe Memorial in Baltimore.

Other Literary Events: Mary Baker Eddy's *Science and Health* published. *Chicago Daily News* founded (1875–1978).

Historical Events: Greenback Party founded. Brigham Young University founded.

1876

Personal: Spends almost half the year at Timber Creek. Stays with George and Susan Stafford and establishes loving relationship with their son Harry. William Rossetti and Mrs. Gilchrist sell copies of the two-volume collection of Walt's poems in England and send the money for the poet's medical expenses. Mrs. Gilchrist arrives in Philadelphia with three grown children (Sept.) and rents a house that includes a bedroom for Walt.

Publications: Publishes centennial volume of *Leaves of Grass* as vol. 1 (using the plates from the 1872 edition) of a two-volume set, the second volume titled *Two Rivulets*, which includes the *Passage to India* annex.

Other Literary Events: Twain's *Tom Sawyer* published. *Frank Leslie's Popular Monthly* founded. Jack London born (Jan. 12). O. E. Rölvaag born (April 22). Sherwood Anderson born (Sept. 13).

Historical Events: Bell Telephone Co. formed. Battle of Little Big Horn fought. University of Texas founded.

1877

Personal: Dr. Richard Bucke, head of an insane asylum in London, Ontario, visits Whitman in Camden. Bucke would later write a biography of Whitman, edited by the poet himself. Walt continues to visit the Staffords at Timber Creek and Anne Gilchrist across the river in Philadelphia.

Other Literary Events: James's *The American* published.

Historical Events: Rutherford B. Hayes is president (1877–81). End of Reconstruction. Thomas Edison develops phonograph.

1878

Personal: Whitman visits the neurologist Dr. S. Weir Mitchell in April and learns that his paralysis is the result of a ruptured blood vessel in the brain. Walt attends funeral of Bryant in New York City (June 14). He visits John and Ursula Burroughs in the Catskill Mountains in June.

Other Literary Events: James's *Daisy Miller* published. Carl Sandburg born (Jan. 6). Don Marquis born (July 29). Upton Sinclair born (Sept. 20).

Historical Events: Egyptian-Abyssinian War fought (1875–79). Uprisings of Ottoman forces in Bosnia and Herzegovina fail.

1879

Personal: Walt presents first Lincoln lecture in New York (April 14). There would be 10 Lincoln lectures before illness stops the poet after 1890. Anne Gilchrist and her three children sail for England (June 9). Walt begins western trip (Sept. 10), including a stop in St. Louis for a visit with brother Jeff and his family. He continues west as far as Denver; because of a relapse of his illness on his way home, he stops in St. Louis again for nearly three months before returning to New York in January.

Other Literary Events: Émile Zola's *Nana* published in France. James Branch Cabell born (April 14). Wallace Stevens born (Oct. 2). Vachel Lindsay born (Nov. 10).

Historical Events: Edison invents lightbulb. First Madison Square Garden opens in New York. Chicago Art Institute opens.

1880

Personal: Walt delivers Lincoln address, this year in Boston (April 14). He lectures (April 15) in Philadelphia on Lincoln's death. He rewrites his will, making George and Louisa executors; different executors would be named later. Visits Dr. Bucke in Canada, staying at his home near the insane asylum, at which Bucke is director. Walt returns to Camden in October and spends much of the remainder of the year at Timber Creek.

Publications: Whitman publishes "Summer Days in Canada" in the *London* (Ontario) *Advertiser* and two

Camden newspapers. "The Dalliance of Eagles" is published in *Cope's Tobacco Plant.*

Other Literary Events: Lew Wallace's *Ben-Hur* published. Henry Adams's novel *Democracy* published. Second *Dial* magazine founded (1880–1929). H. L. Mencken born (Sept. 12). Sholem Asch born (Nov. 1).

Historical Events: U.S. population is 50 million. Louis Pasteur presents his germ theory of disease.

1881

Personal: Walt gives a Lincoln lecture April 15 at the St. Botolph Club in Boston. He stays at the Revere House and is entertained by a number of New England friends, including William Dean Howells and Henry Wadsworth Longfellow. Whitman visits and gets visits from Harry Stafford a number of times during the year. Harry is one of Walt's young male friends.

Publications: "Patroling Barnegat" published in *Harper's Monthly* (April). Sixth edition of *Leaves of Grass* published in Boston by Osgood Publishing House (Nov.). It contains 20 new poems, with a lot of rearranging of other poems. The book's longest poem gets its final title, "Song of Myself." This edition of *Leaves* becomes the final version, the remaining printings containing additional poems as "annexes."

Other Literary Events: Joel Chandler Harris's *Uncle Remus* published. *Century Magazine* founded (1881–1930).

Historical Events: James Garfield is president (1881). Chester Arthur is president (1881–85). American Federation of Labor (A. F. of L.) formed. Tuskegee Institute founded.

1882

Personal: Society for Suppression of Vice claims that *Leaves of Grass* is immoral. In a letter to Osgood, Walt rejects outright most of the publisher's revisions. Osgood, the Boston publisher, quits and sells the plates to Whitman. William O'Connor letter defending *Leaves* is published in *New York Tribune* (May 25). Oscar Wilde visits Walt in Camden, and the two men like each other from the start. Walt continues to visit the Staffords often at Timber Creek.

Publications: *Specimen Days & Collect* published (Sept. 8). Rees Welsh & Co. in Philadelphia takes

over publication of the new edition of *Leaves of Grass,* then sells firm to David McKay, who remains Whitman's publisher for the rest of the poet's life.

Other Literary Events: Frank R. Stockton's "The Lady or the Tiger" published. Twain's *Prince and Pauper* published. Susan Glaspell born (July 1). Longfellow dies (March 24).

Historical Events: Jesse James is shot dead.

1883

Personal: Dr. Bucke publishes *Walt Whitman*, a biography that Walt helped to write (June 20). Walt visits John Burroughs in Philadelphia for two weeks (Feb.). Harry Stafford visits Whitman in Camden (Oct. 30), and before the end of the year is working in Dr. Bucke's insane asylum in London, Ontario. Peter Doyle visits in Camden (Dec. 7) reestablishing his long friendship with Walt.

Other Literary Events: James Whitcomb Riley's *Old Swimmin'-Hole* published. Edward Eggleston's *Hoosier Schoolboy* published. Twain's *Life on the Mississippi* published. Robert Louis Stevenson's *Treasure Island* published. *Ladies' Home Journal* founded (1883–present).

Historical Events: Civil Service reform enacted. Brooklyn Bridge completed. Metropolitan Opera founded.

1884

Personal: Walt is ill during much of February. He attends the funeral (March 12) of 19-year-old friend Tasker Lay, who died of consumption. Lay's parents are tenants of Walt's on Mickle Street until the next January. Walt buys house at 328 Mickle Street in Camden (April 3); moves in March 26. He pays $1,750 cash for the new residence. He will live in this house until his death in 1892. Harry Stafford marries Eva Westcott (June 25); Walt attends Camden wedding.

Publications: "A Backward Glance on My Own Road" published in the *Critic* (Jan. 5); the poem later becomes "A Backward Glance O'er Travel'd Roads." "The Dead Tenor" published (Nov. 4), in honor of Whitman's favorite opera tenor, Pasquale Brignoli.

Other Literary Events: Twain's *Huck Finn* published. Jewett's *A Country Doctor* published. Lowell's essay "On Democracy" published. Sara Teasdale born (Aug. 8). Damon Runyon born (Oct. 4).

Historical Events: National Equal Rights Party nominates Bella A. Lockwood as first woman U.S. presidential candidate.

1885

Personal: Mary Davis becomes Walt's housekeeper (Feb. 24). Walt suffers another stroke in July; several friends buy him a horse and phaeton so he can still get around. He suffers yet another stroke (late Sept.). Whitman visits ophthalmologist Dr. William Osler, who later founded Johns Hopkins Medical School in Baltimore, who provides him with positive results of eye tests. Whitman gets around fairly easily in his new horse and buggy, driven by his young friend Bill Duckett. Walt's good friend Mary Whitall Smith takes her family to England, where she visits a number of Walt's English friends, including Anne Gilchrist. Mary's article "Walt Whitman in Camden" is published in the *Pall Mall Gazette* (Dec. 23). Anne Gilchrist dies (Nov.).

Publications: "Francies at Navesink" published in London's *Nineteenth Century* magazine (August).

Other Literary Events: Howells's *Rise of Silas Lapham* published. Sinclair Lewis born (Feb. 7). Ezra Pound born (Oct. 30).

Historical Events: Grover Cleveland's first administration (1885–89). Washington Monument in D.C. and Statue of Liberty in New York dedicated.

1886

Personal: Whitman gives Lincoln Lecture at the Pythian Club, Elkton, Maryland (Feb. 2), in Camden (March 1), in Philadelphia at the Chestnut Street Opera House, and in Haddonfield, New Jersey (May 18). Walt receives money collected in England on his behalf by friends, including William Rossetti, Robert Louis Stevenson, Henry James, and John Addington Symonds.

Publications: "A Thought on Shakspere" published in the *Critic* (Aug. 14).

Other Literary Events: Jewett's *A White Heron* published. Frances (Eliza) Burnett's *Little Lord Fauntleroy* published. Stevenson's *Dr. Jekyll and Mr. Hyde* published in England. *Cosmopolitan* founded (1886–present). Van Wyck Brooks born (Feb. 16). Emily Dickinson dies (May 15).

Historical Events: Haymarket Riots in Chicago. Sears Roebuck founded. Coca-Cola sold for first time.

1887

Personal: Whitman delivers Lincoln Lecture at the Madison Square Theatre in New York, before a large audience that includes Andrew Carnegie, James Russell Lowell, and José Martí. During summer, Herbert Gilchrist, son of Anne, returns to America and does an oil portrait of Walt. In December, Thomas Eakins begins his portrait.

Publications: Walt reads aloud his poems "The Mystic Trumpeter" and "A Word Out of the Sea" in Philadelphia at the Contemporary Club. "Shakspere-Bacon's Cipher" published in *Cosmopolitan* (Oct.).

Other Literary Events: *Scribner's Magazine* founded (1887–1939). Robinson Jeffers born (Jan. 10). Edna Feber born (Aug. 15).

Historical Events: First electric streetcar. Interstate Commerce Act passes Congress.

1888

Personal: Horace Traubel begins taking notes of conversations with Walt; it will later become *With Walt Whitman in Camden* in nine volumes. Walt suffers a series of strokes in early June. He writes a revised will, naming Traubel, Dr. Richard Maurice Bucke, and Thomas Harned as his executors. Eddie Whitman, Walt's retarded brother, is placed by his mother and brother Jesse in the Blackwoodtown, New Jersey, insane asylum (Aug. 1). Walt sells his horse and buggy and remains in his room on Mickle Street from September to May 1889.

Publications: *November Boughs* published, including 62 new poems and a preface, "A Backward Glance O'er Travel'd Roads" (fall). *Complete Poems and Prose* also published (fall).

Other Literary Events: Edward Bellamy's *Looking Backward* published. James's *Aspern Papers* published. *Collier's* magazine founded (1888–1957). T. S. Eliot born (Sept. 26). Eugene O'Neill born (Oct. 16). Maxwell Anderson born (Dec. 15) Louise May Alcott dies (March 6).

Historical Events: Germany's Wilhelm I dies in Berlin (March 9). *National Geographic* founded (1888–present).

1889

Personal: William O'Connor dies in Washington (May 9). A 70th birthday celebration is given for Whitman at the Morgan Hall in Philadelphia (May 31); Walt is onstage in a wheelchair while entertained by speeches in his honor. The speeches are collected and published as *Camden's Compliment to Walt Whitman* (Oct.). Whitman visits Harleigh Cemetery to choose a burial spot, a lot 20′ × 30′ on a slight hill.

Publications: "A Voice from Death" about the Johnstown, Pennsylvania, flood published in the *World* (New York) (June 7).

Other Literary Events: Henry Adams's *History of the United States* published. Eugene Field's *A Little Book of Western Verse* published. *Munsey's Magazine* founded (1889–1929). Conrad Aiken born (Aug. 5).

Historical Events: Benjamin Harrison is president (1889–1893). Department of Agriculture established. Johnstown Pennsylvania flood. Oklahoma settlement begins.

1890

Personal: Walt gives Lincoln Lecture at the Contemporary Club in Philadelphia (April 15). He leaves the Mickle Street house for a carriage-ride visit to Harleigh Cemetery and his own gravesite (May 14). Whitman's 71st birthday is celebrated with friends at Reisser's Restaurant in Philadelphia (May 31). Walt's brother Jeff (Thomas Jefferson Whitman) dies in St. Louis (Nov. 25).

Other Literary Events: Dickinson's *Poems* published. Howell's *A Hazard of New Fortunes* published. *Literary Digest* founded (1890–1938). *Smart Set* founded (1890–1930). Christopher Morley born (May 5). Katherine Anne Porter born (May 15). Conrad Richter born (Oct. 13).

Historical Events: U.S. population is 63 million. Sherman Anti-Trust Act passes Congress. Sioux villagers massacred by U.S. troops at Wounded Knee. Nelly Bly completes 72-day round-the-world tour. Daughters of American Revolution (DAR) formed. "New" Madison Square Garden completed.

1891

Personal: Thomas Eakins's portrait of Whitman displayed in the Pennsylvania Academy of Fine Arts exhibition (January). Traubel married to Anne Montgomerie at the Mickle Street house (May 28). Whitman is ill with lung congestion, and his doctors do not expect him to recover (mid-Dec.).

Publications: Final printing of *Leaves of Grass* during Whitman's lifetime published at end of this year and beginning of 1892. Walt completes the final version of *Leaves*, and a hurried proof-copy is presented to him (Dec. 13), but publication takes place in 1892 and is commonly known as the Death-bed edition. *Good-Bye My Fancy* published (May). Four poems that will become part of "Old Age Echoes" (1897) published in *Lippincott's Magazine* (March).

Other Literary Events: Hamlin Garland's *Main-Travelled Roads* published. Howells's *Criticism and Fiction* published. Dickinson's *Poems: Second Series* published. Henry Miller born (Dec. 26). Lowell dies (Aug. 12). Melville dies (Sept. 28).

Historical Events: Congress passes bill on International Copyright (March 5). Forest Reserve Act passes Congress.

1892

Personal: Whitman writes codicil to his will, making several small changes. Ellen O'Connor remarries (March). Whitman dies March 26 in the early evening, five days before his 73rd birthday. He is buried in Camden's Harleigh Cemetery on March 29. The tomb is of his own design.

Publications: "Death-bed Edition" of *Leaves of Grass* published. It is technically a reprinting of the sixth edition (1881). A second, matching, volume of Whitman's prose was also published.

Other Literary Events: Ambrose Bierce's poems *Black Beetles in Amber* published. Kipling's *Barrack-Room Ballads* published. Edna St. Vincent Millay born (Feb. 22). Archibald MacLeish born (May 7). Pearl Buck born (June 26).

Historical Events: Ellis Island first used as immigrant station. University of Chicago founded.

JOURNALISM CHRONOLOGY

Note: Below are the years of tenure for paid jobs Whitman held as reporter and/or editor. See the next appendix for a chronological listing of journals that published his articles.

1831–1834

Worked as printer's devil for the *Long Island Patriot* and as an apprentice for the *Long Island Star;* he also contributed an article to the *New York Mirror,* entitled "The Olden Time," apparently his first published work.

1838–1839

Became the founder and editor of the *Long-Islander* in Huntington; he worked as a typesetter for the *Long Island Democrat.*

1840–1841

Published a series of articles in the *Hempstead Inquirer,* the *Long Island Democrat,* and the *Long-Island Farmer and Advertiser.*

1841

Worked as a printer and reporter for the *New World* (New York); he also contributed articles for *Brother Jonathan* and his first fiction for the *United States Magazine and Democratic Review.*

1842–1843

Edited the *New York Aurora* for a few weeks in the spring of 1842 and for the *New York Evening Tattler* during the summer months. During the spring of 1843 he edited the *New York Statesman* and coedited the *New York Sunday Times.* He also contributed articles for the *New York Sunday Times,* the *New World, Brother Jonathan,* and the (New York) *Sun.*

1844

Edited the *New York Democrat* during the summer and fall and contributed articles during the year for the *New York Sunday Times & Noah's Weekly Messenger.*

1845–1846

Contributed articles for the *Broadway Journal,* the *United States Magazine and Democratic Review,* and the *American Review;* he returned to Brooklyn in August 1845 and contributed articles for the *Brooklyn Evening Star* from September to March 1846.

1846–1848

Edited the *Brooklyn Daily Eagle* from March 1846 to January 1948. The newspaper's official title was the *Brooklyn Eagle and Kings County Democrat.* It became the *Brooklyn Daily Eagle and Kings County Democrat* in June 1846.

1848

Dismissed as editor of the *Brooklyn Daily Eagle* in January. Whitman and his brother Jeff took a job with the *New Orleans Crescent* for three months, from February to May 27.

1848–1849

Edited the *Brooklyn Freeman* from September 9, 1848, to September 11, 1849.

1849–1854

Ran a print shop in Brooklyn; contributed articles for the *New York Sunday Dispatch,* the *Brooklyn Daily Advertiser,* the *National Era,* the *New York Evening Post.* In summer 1851 he edited the weekly *Statesman and Traveller's Director for Long Island.*

1855

The first edition of *Leaves of Grass* was printed in Brooklyn at the Rome Brothers shop at 70 Fulton Street.

1857–1859

Whitman accepted a position as editor of the *Brooklyn Daily Times,* beginning about May 1, 1857, and ending sometime in the late spring or early summer of 1859. He wrote approximately 1,200 news items, feature stories, and editorials for the *Times.*

NEWSPAPERS AND MAGAZINES THAT PUBLISHED WHITMAN'S ARTICLES AND EDITORIALS

Note: The list below is chronological by publication. The dates in parentheses are years when Whitman was a paid reporter and/or editor or years when articles by him were published by the journal named. The number of items published by the journal follows the colon.

The journals in which Whitman published nonfiction prose items are well documented, but some caution must be taken with the numbers. Articles published in newspapers during Whitman's years of writing for them often provided no by-line, making it difficult if not impossible for scholars to determine authorship, especially for the earliest items. Once Whitman's style became familiar it was easier to detect his authorship, but even then some guessing was inevitable.

The best sources for titles of articles and other details about Whitman's journalism are Herbert Bergman's *The Collected Writings of Walt Whitman: The Journalism* in two volumes; Thomas Brasher's *Whitman as Editor of the Brooklyn Daily Eagle*; William White's *Walt Whitman's Journalism: A Bibliography*; and Joel Myerson's *Walt Whitman: A Descriptive Bibliography*. See "Bibliography of Secondary Sources" for publication details.

Long Island Patriot (1831–1832):?
Long Island Star (1832–1833):?
New-York Mirror: A Weekly Journal Devoted to Literature and Fine Arts (1833): 1 ("The Olden Time," Nov. 29; Whitman's first published item still extant)
Long-Islander, The (1838–1839): 7
Universalist Union (1839): 1

Long Island Democrat (1838–1841): 9
New York *Christian Messenger* (1839): 1
Rural Repository (1839): 1
Hempstead Inquirer, The (1840): 3
Long Island Farmer and Queens County Advertiser (1840–1841): 2
New Era (1841): 1
Brother Jonathan (1842): 1
New York Aurora (1842): 136
Evening Tattler (New York) (1842): 4
New World, The (1842): 2
Sunday Times (New York) (1842–1943): 5
Daily Plebian, The (New York) (1842–1843): 3
Sun, The (New York) (1842, 1876): 14
Subterranean, The (1843): 1
New York Statesman (1843): ?
Sunday Times & Noah's Weekly Messenger (New York) (1844): 1
New York Democrat, The (1844): 7
New Mirror (New York) (1844): ?
Brooklyn Evening Star (1845–1846, 1854): 52
Democratic Review (1845): 1
American Review: A Whig Journal of Politics, Literature, Art and Science (1845): 1
Broadway Journal, The (1845): 2
Brooklyn Evening Star (1845–1846): 54
Brooklyn Daily Eagle (1846–1848, 1863): 808
New Orleans Daily Crescent (1848): 60
Brooklyn Freeman (1848–1849): 18
Brooklyn *Salesman* (1849?): ?
Brooklyn Daily Advertiser (1850–1851): 4
National Era (Washington) (1850): 3
New York Evening Post (1851, 1918): 6
United States Review (1855): 1

Brooklyn Daily Times, The (1855–1859, 1885): 1,229

New York *Life Illustrated* (1855–1856): 13

American Phrenological Journal (1856): 1

Brooklyn Register (1859): 1

Saturday Press (New York) (1859–1860): 2

Brooklyn City News (1860, 1862): 1

Brooklyn Standard (1860–1862): 25

New York Leader (1862): 7

New York Times (1863–1865): 8

Brooklyn Daily Union (1863–1865): 2

Amory Square Hospital Gazette (Washington) (1864): 1

The Galaxy (1867–1868): 2

Sunday Morning Chronicle (Washington) (1868): 1

Washington *Sunday Herald* (1872): 1

New York Daily Graphic (1873–1874): 3

New York Weekly Graphic (1874): 6

New Republic (Camden) (1874): 1

West Jersey Press (Camden) (1876): 1

Daily Post (Camden) (1877–1891): 9

Washington Star (1875, 1879): 2

New York Tribune (1877–1885): 11

Philadelphia *Times* (1879, 1884): 2

Philadelphia *Progress* (1879): 2

Cope's Tobacco Plant (Liverpool, England) (1879): 1

Denver *Daily Tribune* (1879): 1

Philadelphia Press (1880–1886): 9

Literary World (Boston) (1880): 2

Advertiser (London, Ontario) (1880): 3

The Critic (1881–1890): 28

North American Review (1881–1891): 7

American, The (Philadelphia) (1881): 1

Camden Daily Courier (1882): 1

World (New York) (1881): 1

Baldwin's Monthly (New York) (1884–1885): 2

Star (New York) (1885): 1

Lippincott's Magazine (1887, 1891): 4

Picayune (New Orleans) (1887): 1

Century Magazine, The (1887–1888): 2

New York Herald (1887–1888): 5

London (England) *Literary World* (1888): 1

Pall-Mall Gazette (London) (1890): 2

Boston Transcript (1890): 1

New York Morning Journal (1890): 1

Poet-Lore (1890): 1

Munyon's Illustrated World (1890): 1

Engineering Review (1890): 1

Frank Leslie's Popular Monthly (1892): 1

WHITMAN ADDRESSES

Whitman Family Home Addresses in Brooklyn (and Other Brooklyn Addresses of Interest)

1823
Front Street near the Fulton Ferry (residence).

1824
Cranberry Street opposite the Plymouth Church (residence).

Henry Street north of Fulton Avenue (residence).

1825
Johnson Street north of Adams Street (residence).

Johnson Street across from the previous address (residence).

Cranberry and Henry Streets (the Apprentices Library where Walt witnessed the cornerstone ceremony and where Lafayette kissed him on the cheek).

1825–1829
Public school (District School Number 1, at corner of Concord and Adams Streets in Brooklyn).

1826
251 Adams Street (residence).

1827
41 Tillary Street (residence).

1831
149 Fulton Street (office of the *Long Island Patriot,* where Whitman worked).

1832
Henry Street near Cranberry Street (residence).

10 Liberty Street (residence).

1833
120 Front Street (residence).

1844
71 Prince Street (residence, sold five years later at a profit of $600).

Skillman Street (residence).

1846–1848
30 Fulton Street (office of the *Brooklyn Daily Eagle,* when Whitman was editor).

Adams Street near Myrtle Avenue (Whitman rented a room).

1848
110 Orange Street (office of the *Brooklyn Freeman,* a newspaper for which Whitman was the first editor; after a fire the office was moved to 96 Myrtle Avenue, then to the corner of Fulton and Middagh Streets, then to 335 Fulton, south of Myrtle).

1849
106 Myrtle Avenue (residence and print shop).

1852
Cumberland Street north of Atlantic Avenue (residence).

1854
142 Skillman Street (residence).

1855
Ryerson Street north of Myrtle Avenue (residence).

1856
91$^1/_2$ Classon Avenue (residence).

1857–1859
145 Grand Street (office of the *Brooklyn Daily Times*, where Whitman was editor).

1859–1863
107 Portland Avenue north of Myrtle Avenue (residence).

Whitman Addresses in Washington, D.C.

1862
Rents a room in a boardinghouse at 456 Sixth Street, where the O'Connors also had an apartment.

1863
Boardinghouse at 501 Pennsylvania Avenue, near Third Street.

1864
Rents room at 468 M Street.

1865
Moves to 472 M Street.

1866
Moves to 535 15th Street.

Whitman Addresses in Camden

June 1873
Moves from Washington to 322 Stevens Street (lives with George and Louisa Whitman).

September 29, 1873
George and Louisa move to 431 Stevens Street; Walt takes third-floor room.

July 1874
Walt buys lot for $450 at 460 Royden, but does not build on it.

1884–1892
328 Mickle Street (lives out his life at this residence).

GLOSSARY OF WHITMAN TERMS

Note: Whitman sometimes used words with unusual meanings or words made up for poetic purposes. Following are some examples. Not included below are two of the poet's language idiosyncrasies that readers will often see in his works: the apostrophe-d ('d) instead of the past tense form of a verb, as in "bloom'd" for bloomed; and the Quaker style of referring to months by their number rather than by name, as in "the fourth month" for April.

accouchement "Childbirth." See, for example, "To Think of Time" (Section 2): "Not a day passes, not a minute or second without an accouchement."

adhesiveness Defined as "sticking together," "devoted attachment," "joining together." Whitman uses the word to indicate a fraternal friendship or love relationship. Adhesiveness is used to describe the brotherhood of men, comradeship, a love sometimes physical (though not necessarily sexual), and often spiritual, a love he uses often as a metaphor for democracy.

The poet apparently got the term from his interest in phrenology, a system for analyzing character by measuring the shape and protuberances of a person's skull, adhesiveness indicating an emotional attachment between or among men.

The "Calamus" poems are about adhesiveness, though they are not the only poems about fraternity or that use the idea of the love of men for one another as a metaphor. The Calamus poems were misunderstood in Whitman's time, because readers seemed incapable of reading past the sexual connotations to a concept of democracy that emphasizes the importance of love in all relationships.

Equality, the essential ingredient for a working democracy, Whitman believed, could exist only if people loved one another. He used the word "amativeness" (as in the poems in the "Children of Adam" cluster) for the love between men and women, but it rarely has the depth of meaning that adhesiveness carries.

For examples of the poet's use of "adhesiveness," see "Not Heaving from My Ribb'd Breast Only": "Not in any or all of them O adhesiveness! O pulse of my life!" See also "Song of the Open Road" (Section 6), "Thought" [Of obedience], and "So Long!": "I announce adhesiveness, I say it shall be limitless, unloosen'd."

alembic Any container that purifies what it contains. Used by Whitman to mean a still, as in the distillation of a beverage. See "From Noon to Starry Night" (Section 5) where the word is used as a metaphor: "I see the vast alembic ever working, I see and know the flames that heat the world."

amativeness Another word Whitman got from his interest in phrenology (see "adhesiveness" above). Amativeness means an inclination to love, but it carries a sexual connotation for the love between men and women; whereas "adhesiveness" is used for a love of one man for another which may be sexual but which is most often used as a metaphor for the kind of love that is essential to a democratic society.

Whitman referred to his "Children of Adam" poems as "amative."

atomies   Dust mites, used by Whitman as a metaphor in "The Voice of the Rain": "I descend to lave the drouths, atomies, dust-layers of the globe."

camerado   From "comrade" or "friend," probably made up by Whitman to emphasize the need of friendship, especially among men, for a democratic society. It can carry a sexual connotation. See in "Song of Myself," for example (last line in Section 45), where he uses it to describe God as a comrade and lover to men:

> My rendezvous is appointed, it is certain,
> The Lord will be there and wait till I come on
>   perfect terms,
> The great Camerado, the lover true for whom I
>   pine will be there.

See also in the poem titled "As I Lay With My Head in Your Lap Camerado."

chansonnier   French for "song writer," used by Whitman in "France, The 18th Year of These States" and "Terminus" in the "Drum-Taps" cluster: "I myself as connector, a chansonnier of a great future, am now speaking."

comity   Courteous or polite, civil; as in "Starting from Paumanok" (Section 6): "And I will make a song that there shall be comity by day and by night between all the States, and between any two of them."

douceurs   French word meaning "sweets," "sweetness," or pleasant manner. Whitman uses the word in "The Sleepers" (Section 1): "I am the ever-laughing—it is new moon and twilight, / I see the hiding of douceurs, I see nimble ghosts whichever way I look." According to the *Oxford English Dictionary*, the word can also mean "a gratuity" or "bribe."

effuse   To pour forth, as in "Why should not a man or woman do as much as the seasons, and effuse as much?" (in "On Journeys through the States") or in "Sometimes with One I Love," line 1: "Sometimes with one I love I fill myself with rage for fear I effuse unreturn'd love."

en-masse   A French term, meaning "people banding together as a unified force." Whitman believed that democracy depended on people who were individuals, capable of thinking for themselves, but at the same time a part of the whole of society. He used the term in the first two lines of the first poem in *Leaves of Grass*, "One's Self I Sing": "One's-self I sing, a simple separate person, / Yet utter the word Democratic, the word En-Masse."

These two lines offer Whitman's simple definition of democracy and becomes the theme for *Leaves of Grass*. See also "Song of Myself" (Section 23), "A Broadway Pageant" (Section 2), "Long, Too Long America," "Thou Mother with Thy Equal Brood" (Section 5), and "Thoughts" (of public opinion, in the "From Noon to Starry Night" cluster). He uses the term also in *Specimen Days* in a section titled "Down at the Front." Referring to soldiers marching after a battle at Culpepper, Virginia, he writes: "Along and along they filed by me, with often a laugh, a song, a cheerful word, but never once a murmur. It may have been odd, but I never before so realized the majesty and reality of the American people *en masse*."

In a discussion of his own religious beliefs, he uses the term again to indicate the importance of people working out their own religion without the help of the churches or their leaders: "It [Religion] is, indeed, too important to the power and perpetuity of the New World to be consigned any longer to the churches, old or new, Catholic or Protestant— Saint this, or Saint that. . . . It must be consigned henceforth to Democracy *en masse*, and to Literature. It must enter into the Poems of the Nation."

eidólon   An eidolon is, according to the *Oxford English Dictionary*, an "unsubstantial image, spectre, phantom." It is the phantom ideal attached to every "real" object, experience, or idea. See the poem "Eidólons," and also the last line of "Sail Out for Good, Eidólon Yacht!": "Sail out for good, eidólon yacht of me!"

emulous Imitative or to emulate. Whitman uses the word in "The Ship Starting": "The pennant is flying aloft as [the ship] speeds she speeds so stately—below emulous waves press forward."

fancy Whitman uses this word to mean the "creative imagination." The *Oxford English Dictionary*, however, distinguishes "fancy" from "imagination" (for usage after about the mid-16th century). In literary usage, according to the *OED*, *fancy* is used to "express aptitude for the invention of illustrative or decorative imagery," whereas *imagination* "is the power of giving to ideal creations the inner consistency of realities." See, in particular, both of Whitman's poems entitled "Good-Bye My Fancy."

feuillage French for "foliage," "leafage." Whitman uses it to relate to his leaves of grass: "Always our old feuillage! / Always Florida's green peninsula—always the priceless delta of Louisiana—always the cotton-fields of Alabama and Texas" ("Our Old Feuillage," lines 1–2).

float See "Crossing Brooklyn Ferry." Then, in further description, he uses the word "float" to describe the state of his body's suspension as it transcends the physical state for the spiritual. "Float" is used here and in other Whitman poems to indicate a state of suspension, of levitation, that the poet feels in this mystical merging of his body and soul with the bodies and souls of others. See also "Darest Thou Now O Soul": "Then we burst forth, we float, / In Time and Space O soul, prepared for them" (that is, for things that otherwise bind us to earth).

imperturbe Whitman coined the word "imperturbe," as he did a number of other words, in order to fit a rhythm pattern. The most common reading of this coinage is that the poet means "imperturbable," that is, not easily disturbed or excited—in this case with nature and natural things: "Me imperturbe, standing at ease in Nature" (from "Me Imperturbe").

inhalement As in Whitman's short story "The Shadow and the Light of One Man's Soul": "Ah, for how many the morose habit which Archie rooted *out* from his nature, becomes by long usage and indulgence rooted *in*, and spreads its bitterness over their existence, and darkens the peace of their families, and carries them through the spring and early summer of life with no inhalement of sweets, and no plucking of flowers!"

inure To become accustomed to, especially something difficult. See, for example, "Not Youth Pertains to Me":

> Beauty, knowledge, inure not to me—yet there
>   are two or three things inure to me,
> I have nourish'd the wounded and sooth'd
>   many a dying soldier,
> And at intervals waiting or in the midst of
>   camp,
> Composed these songs.

Kanuck Whitman means Canuck, a Canadian, or, more specifically, a French Canadian.

libertad Spanish word used by Whitman to mean "liberty or freedom." Whitman used the word as a way of personifying various freedoms. See "Starting from Paumanok" (Section 3, line 2): "Foremost! Century marches! Libertad! Masses! / For you a programme of chants." Or as in "Proud Music of the Storm" (Section 3): "The clear electric base and baritone of the world, / The trombone duo, Libertad forever." Or in "As I Walk These Broad Majestic Days": "Libertad and the divine average, freedom to every slave on the face of the earth."

livraisons French word meaning the presentation of the parts of a novel for serial publication in a magazine. Whitman uses the term first in *Memoranda During the War* and then as a footnote to the first entry in *Specimen Days*, referring to the "dozens" of "little notebooks" he had kept over time and from which he has written the short, memoranda "jottings."

ma femme French for "my wife." Whitman uses it to personify American democracy, as in the last line of his poem praising the French for seeking freedom from tyranny during their revolution, making it analogous to America's freedom. "I will yet sing a song for you ma femme" ("France, The 18th Year of These States").

maya   Sanskrit word, meaning "illusion" or "illusory." Whitman was interested in Hindu philosophy. See the last two lines of "Are You the New Person Drawn Toward Me?" in the "Calamus" cluster: "Do you suppose yourself advancing on real ground toward a real heroic man? / Have you no thought O dreamer that it may be all maya, illusion?"

presidentiad   Apparently Whitman's own word, meaning the four-year term of American presidents.

promulge   To declare publicly. See "On Journeys Through the States": "We say to ourselves, Remember, fear not, be candid, promulge the body and the soul."

querilities   The poet's word for "querulous," meaning to complain or be peevish. See in "As I Sit Writing Here": "As I sit writing here, sick and grown old, / Not my least burden is that dullness of the years, querilities."

resurgemus   The original title for "Europe: The 72d and 73d Years of These States." It is probably taken from the Latin word *resurgo*, meaning resurgence, as in the rising up of citizens against unjust governments, the subject of the poem.

"So long"   An expression meaning "good-bye" or "until we meet again," which Whitman probably invented. The *Oxford English Dictionary* (1973) lists him as having used it in 1868, after an English writer used it in 1865. The *OED* editors, however, have the Whitman citation year wrong. He used it in his third edition of *Leaves of Grass*, published in 1860. It is repeated almost as a refrain in his poem titled "So Long!"

Sufi   A member of a sect of Muslim mystics. In his poem "A Persian Lesson," Whitman refers to a "greybeard sufi," giving his "last lesson . . . On the slope of a teeming Persian rose-garden."

windrows   A row of hay raked up for drying. Whitman uses the term in reference to his own poems. See, for example, "As I Ebb'd with the Ocean of Life," where he refers to both himself and his poems as "loose windrows . . . little corpses," one of the most pessimistic of his poems.

Whitman's Last Will
and Testament

William Sloane Kennedy adds the following comment in a note to his printing of Whitman's will in *The Fight of a Book for the World,* reprinted below:

"In Traubel's *With Whitman in Camden,* Volume I, there is a facsimile of what is given without explanation as Whitman's last will and testament, but which is dated over three years previous to the one given [in Kennedy's book] (i.e. June 29, 1888) and reads quite differently; is, in fact, a wholly different will, has no codicil and different witnesses. I had the above will verified by the deputy surrogate of the County of Camden.

—W. S. K."

The last will and testament of Walt Whitman, of Camden, N.J.

I order all my just debts and funeral expenses paid as soon as conveniently can be after my decease.

I give $1000 to my sister, Mrs. Mary Elizabeth Van Nostrand, of Greenport, Suffolk County, New York State.

I give $1000 to my sister, Mrs. Hannah Louisa Heyde, of Burlington, Vt.

I give $250 to Mrs. Susan Stafford, wife of George Stafford, of Glendale, Camden County, N.J.

I give $1000 to Mrs. Mary O. Davis, now of 328 Mickle Street, Camden, N.J.

I give to Mrs. Mapes $20.

I give to Mrs. Nancy Whitman, my brother Andrew's widow, $50.

I give to my brother, George W. Whitman, the portraits of my father and mother (two small oil paintings and one framed photograph) and one old large Dutch portrait, four altogether, also the big mahogany table.

I give to Thomas Donaldson the big arm chair presented to me by his children.

I give to Harry Stafford, of Marlton, N.J., my gold watch.

I give to my friend, Peter Doyle, my silver watch.

I give to J. H. Johnston, jeweler of New York City, my second arm chair, rattan seated.

I hereby appoint my friends Dr. R. M. Bucke of [London] Ontario, Canada; Thomas B. Harned, of Camden, N.J., and Horace L. Traubel, of the same place, my literary executors and immediately upon my decease I direct that they shall take absolute charge and possession of all my literary effects of every kind whatever, including my library, manuscripts, letters, correspondence, also all my books in stock or otherwise, publications, copyrights, plates and to manage and control the same and the future publications of my writings and make all and every use of the aforesaid property as in their judgment they deem proper—provided and subject to only one restriction, to wit, that they pay over from time to time to my executrix any profits arising from the publication of my books.

All the rest and residue of my property of every kind and description, including the house No. 328 Mickle Street, Camden, N.J., where I now reside, I give, bequeath and devise to my brother, Edward L. Whitman, absolutely forever.

As my said brother Edward L. Whitman is mentally incapacitated, I hereby appoint Mrs. Louisa Orr Whitman, wife of my brother, George W. Whitman, his sole guardian of his person and property and I direct that no bonds shall be required of her in her discharge of said guardianship.

I hereby appoint the said Louisa Orr Whitman, wife of my brother, George W. Whitman, executrix of this my last will and testament, and I direct that she shall not be required to furnish bonds.

I give to Warren Fritzinger (my nurse) $200.

I order and direct that Mary O. Davis be permitted to occupy my said house, 328 Mickle Street, Camden, for one year after my decease free of rent, provided, however, that she pay the taxes for said year on said premises.

The last two items are written after the apparent conclusion of my said will, but I direct that said items shall have the same force and effect as if they were written before the residuary clause.

In witness whereof I have hereto set my hand and seal this twenty-fourth day of December, eighteen hundred and ninety-one.

Walt Whitman [Seal]

Signed, published, and declared by the said Walt Whitman to be his last will and testament in the presence of us, who were present at the same time and subscribed our names as witnesses in the presence of the testator.

Henry Hollinshead, Jr.
Thomas B. Hall
Camden, N.J.

Codicil

This is a codicil, to be added to the last will and testament of me, Walt Whitman, which will bear date the twenty-fourth day of December, eighteen hundred and ninety-one.

I do hereby ratify and confirm my said will in all respects save so far as any part thereof shall be revoked or altered by this present codicil.

I give to Mrs. Susan Stafford two hundred dollars instead of two hundred and fifty dollars.

I give to Mrs. Mary E. Van Nostrand two hundred dollars instead of one thousand dollars.

I give to Walt Whitman Fritzinger (a new-born son of Harry Fritzinger) the sum of two hundred dollars to be invested for him.

I give my gold watch to Horace L. Traubel instead of to Harry Stafford.

I give my silver watch to Harry Stafford instead of Peter Doyle.

Walt Whitman.

Dated January 1st, 1892.

Signed, published and declared by the said Walt Whitman as a codicil to his last will and testament in the presence of us who were present at the same time and subscribed our names as witnesses in his presence.

Augusta A. Harned,
Mrs. Elizabeth Keller.

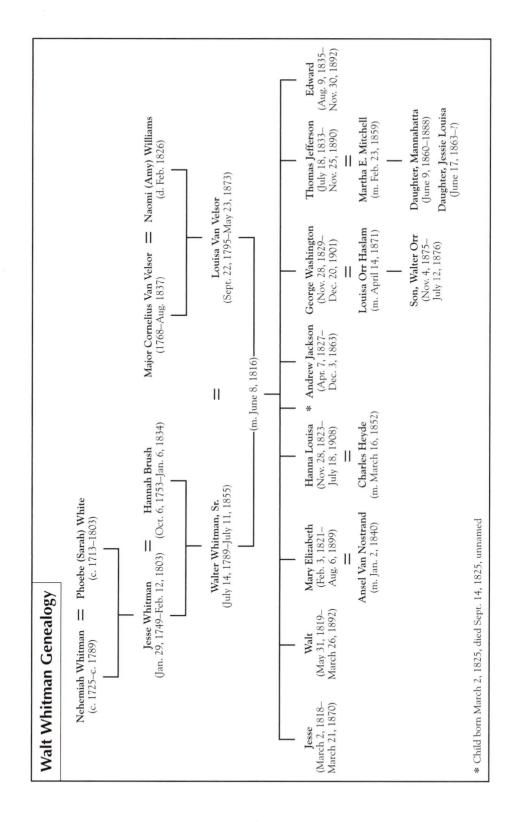

Walt Whitman Genealogy

Nehemiah Whitman = Phoebe (Sarah) White
(c. 1725–c. 1789)   (c. 1713–1803)

Jesse Whitman = Hannah Brush
(Jan. 29, 1749–Feb. 12, 1803)   (Oct. 6, 1753–Jan. 6, 1834)

Walter Whitman, Sr.
(July 14, 1789–July 11, 1855)

Major Cornelius Van Velsor = Naomi (Amy) Williams
(1768–Aug. 1837)   (d. Feb. 1826)

Louisa Van Velsor
(Sept. 22, 1795–May 23, 1873)

(m. June 8, 1816)

Jesse
(March 2, 1818–
March 21, 1870)

Walt
(May 31, 1819–
March 26, 1892)

Mary Elizabeth
(Feb. 3, 1821–
Aug. 6, 1899)
=
Ansel Van Nostrand
(m. Jan. 2, 1840)

Hanna Louisa
(Nov. 28, 1823–
July 18, 1908)
=
Charles Heyde
(m. March 16, 1852)

* Andrew Jackson
(Apr. 7, 1827–
Dec. 3, 1863)

George Washington
(Nov. 28, 1829–
Dec. 20, 1901)
=
Louisa Orr Haslam
(m. April 14, 1871)

Son, Walter Orr
(Nov. 4, 1875–
July 12, 1876)

Thomas Jefferson
(July 18, 1833–
Nov. 25, 1890)
=
Martha E. Mitchell
(m. Feb. 23, 1859)

Daughter, Mannahatta
(June 9, 1860–1888)
Daughter, Jessie Louisa
(June 17, 1863–?)

Edward
(Aug. 9, 1835–
Nov. 30, 1892)

* Child born March 2, 1825, died Sept. 14, 1825, unnamed

Bibliography of Primary Sources (in Chronological Order)

Leaves of Grass. 1st ed. Brooklyn: Rome Brothers, 1855.

Leaves of Grass. Introduction by Clifton Joseph Furness. Facsimile of 1855 edition. New York: Columbia University Press, 1939.

Leaves of Grass. Facsimile of 1855 edition. New York: Eakins Press, 1966.

Leaves of Grass. Introduction by Richard Bridgman. Facsimile of 1855 edition. San Francisco: Chandler, 1968.

Walt Whitman's Leaves of Grass: The First (1855) Edition. Edited, with introduction by Malcolm Cowley. New York: Viking, 1959.

Leaves of Grass. 2d ed. Brooklyn: Fowler & Wells, 1856. The 1855 "preface" is omitted; the 12 poems from the 1855 edition are revised and titled. Includes Emerson's congratulatory letter to Whitman and Whitman's thank-you letter to Emerson.

Leaves of Grass. 3d ed. Boston: Thayer & Eldridge, 1860. Had at least two printings; includes 152 poems, 146 of them new; poems are grouped in clusters.

Leaves of Grass. Introduction by Roy Harvey Pearce. Facsimile edition of 1860 text. Ithaca, N.Y.: Cornell University Press, 1961.

Walt Whitman's Drum-Taps. New York: Peter Eckler, printer, 1865.

Sequel to Drum-Taps. New York: Peter Eckler, printer, 1865. Includes "When Lilacs Last in the Dooryard Bloom'd."

Walt Whitman's Drum-Taps. New York: Peter Eckler, printer, 1865. Second printing of *Drum-Taps* with "Sequel to Drum-Taps" appended.

Leaves of Grass. 4th ed. New York: William E. Chapin, printer, 1867. Includes separate pagination for "Drum-Taps" and "Sequel to Drum-Taps" poems, plus "Songs before Parting."

Democratic Vistas. New York: J. S. Redfield, publisher, 1871.

Leaves of Grass. 5th ed. Washington, D.C.: J. S. Redfield, 1871. Second printing (1872) includes "Passage to India"; 13 new poems.

Memoranda during the War. Camden, N.J.: Whitman Publication, 1875–76.

Leaves of Grass. Camden, N.J.: Author's ed., 1876. Reprinted from 1871 plates.

Two Rivulets. Vol. 2 of Centennial Edition. Camden, N.J.: Author's ed., 1876. Includes *Democratic Vistas*, *Centennial Songs*, and *Passage to India*.

Leaves of Grass. 6th ed. Boston: James R. Osgood & Co., 1881; Philadelphia: Rees Welsh & Co., 1882; Philadelphia: David McKay, 1888. Poems in final order; only additions in later printings will be "annexes."

Specimen Days & Collect. Philadelphia: Rees Welsh & Co., 1882; Philadelphia: David McKay, 1882–83.

November Boughs. Philadelphia: David McKay, 1888. Includes essay "A Backward Glance O'er Travel'd Roads."

Complete Poems and Prose of Walt Whitman, 1855 . . . 1888. Philadelphia: Ferguson Brothers, printers, 1888. Reprint of 1881 *Leaves of Grass*, plus *Specimen Days*; includes poems from *November Boughs* and the essay "A Backward Glance O'er Travel'd Roads" in an annex.

Leaves of Grass. Philadelphia: David McKay, 1892. Reprinted from 1881 plates; includes two annexes, "Sands at Seventy" and "Good-Bye My Fancy";

Whitman considered this volume to be his authorized text for all future reprintings.

Complete Prose Works. Philadelphia: David McKay, 1892. Includes *Specimen Days & Collect, November Boughs*, and *Good-Bye My Fancy*. Considered to be volume 2 of Whitman's *Leaves of Grass*, 1892 (above).

Leaves of Grass. Boston: Small, Maynard, 1897. Reprinted from 1881 plates; edited by Whitman friend and one of his executors, Horace Traubel, and includes the cluster "Old Age Echoes," which Whitman authorized.

The Collected Writings of Walt Whitman. Edited by Gay Wilson Allen and Sculley Bradley. New York: New York University Press, 1963 and ongoing.

Prose Works 1892. Edited by Floyd Stovall. Vol. 1, *Specimen Days*, 1963; vol. 2, *Collect and Other Prose*, 1964. New York: New York University Press.

The Early Poems and the Fiction. Edited by Thomas L. Brasher. New York: New York University Press, 1963.

Leaves of Grass. Edited by Harold W. Blodgett and Sculley Bradley. New York: New York University Press, 1965. Includes annexes, prefaces, "A Backward Glance O'er Travel'd Roads," "Old Age Echoes," excluded poems and fragments, and uncollected poems and fragments.

The Correspondence. Edited by Edwin Haviland Miller. New York: New York University Press. Vol. 1: 1842–67, 1961; vol. 2: 1868–75, 1961; vol. 3: 1876–85, 1964; vol. 4: 1886–89, 1969; vol. 5: 1890–92, 1969.

Daybooks and Notebooks. Edited by William White. Vol. 1: Daybooks, 1876–November 1881; vol. 2: Daybooks, December 1881–91; vol. 3: Diary in Canada, Notebooks. New York: New York University Press, 1978.

Leaves of Grass: A Textual Variorum of the Printed Poems. Edited by Sculley Bradley, et al. Vol. 1: Poems, 1855–56; vol. 2: Poems, 1860–67; vol. 3: Poems, 1870–91. New York: New York University Press, 1980.

Notebooks and Unpublished Prose Manuscripts. Edited by Edward F. Grier. 6 vols. New York: New York University Press, 1984.

The Collected Writings of Walt Whitman: The Journalism. Edited by Herbert Bergman, Douglas A. Noverr, and Edward J. Recchia. Vol. 1 (1834–46);

vol. 2 (1846–48). New York: Peter Lang, 1998, 2003.

Uncollected Works

Calamus. Edited, with introduction, by Richard M. Bucke. Boston: Laurens Maynard, 1897. Letters by Whitman to Peter Doyle for the period 1868–80.

The Wound-Dresser. Edited by Richard M. Bucke. Boston: Small, Maynard, 1898. Letters by Whitman, written from Washington hospitals during the Civil War.

Notes and Fragments. Edited by Richard M. Bucke. London, Ontario, 1899. Printed privately. Manuscript fragments of poetry and prose.

Letters Written by Walt Whitman to His Mother from 1866 to 1872. Edited by Thomas B. Harned. New York: G. P. Putnam's Sons, 1902.

Walt Whitman's Diary in Canada. Edited by William Sloane Kennedy. Boston: Small, Maynard, 1904. Included in William White's *Daybooks* volume, above.

An American Primer. Edited by Horace Traubel. Boston: Small, Maynard, 1904. Included in William White's *Daybooks* volume, above.

The Letters of Anne Gilchrist and Walt Whitman. Edited by Thomas B. Harned. New York: Doubleday, Doran, 1918.

The Gathering of the Forces. Edited by Cleveland Rodgers and John Black. New York: G. P. Putnam's Sons, 1920. Editorials, essays, literary and drama reviews, and other material written by Whitman as editor of the *Brooklyn Daily Eagle*, 1846–47.

The Uncollected Poetry and Prose of Walt Whitman. Edited by Emory Holloway. 2 vols. New York: Doubleday, Doran, 1921.

The Half-Breed and Other Stories. Edited by Thomas Ollive Mabbott. New York: Columbia University Press, 1927.

I Sit and Look Out. Edited by Emory Holloway and Vernolian Schwarz. New York: Columbia University Press, 1932. Editorials by Whitman for the *Brooklyn Daily Times*.

Walt Whitman's Blue Book. Vol. 1: Facsimile of the unique copy in the Oscar Lion Collection at the New York City Public Library; vol. 2: Textual analysis by Arthur Golden. New York: New York Public Library, 1968.

SELECTED BIBLIOGRAPHY OF
SECONDARY SOURCES

Alcaro, Marion Walker. *Walt Whitman's Mrs. G: A Biography of Anne Gilchrist.* Rutherford, N.J.: Fairleigh Dickinson University Press, 1991.

Allen, Gay Wilson, and Charles T. Davis, eds. *The New Walt Whitman Handbook.* New York: New York University Press, 1975.

———. *A Reader's Guide to Walt Whitman.* New York: Farrar, Straus & Giroux, 1970.

———. *The Solitary Singer: A Critical Biography of Walt Whitman.* New York: Grove Press, 1955.

———. *Waldo Emerson.* New York: Penguin, 1982.

———. *Walt Whitman's Poems: Selections with Critical Aids.* New York: New York University Press, 1955.

Asselineau, Roger. *The Evolution of Walt Whitman: The Creation of a Book.* Cambridge, Mass.: Harvard University Press, 1962.

Benton, Megan, and Paul Benton. "Typographic Yawp: *Leaves of Grass,* 1855–1992." *Bookways: A Quarterly for the Book Arts* (1994–1995): 22–31.

Bloom, Harold. "Walt Whitman: *Song of Myself.*" In *How to Read and Why.* New York: Scribner, 2000.

———. "Walt Whitman as Center of the American Canon." In *The Western Canon: The Books and School of the Ages.* New York: Harcourt Brace, 1994.

Bowers, Fredson, ed. *Whitman's Manuscripts: Leaves of Grass (1860).* Chicago: University of Chicago Press, 1969.

Bradley, Sculley, and John A. Stevenson. *Walt Whitman's Backward Glances: A Backward Glance O'er Travel'd Roads and Two Contributory Essays Hitherto Uncollected.* Freeport, N.Y.: Books for Libraries Press, 1947.

Bradley, Sculley, John A. Stevenson, and Harold W. Blodgett, eds. *Leaves of Grass: A Norton Critical Edition.* New York: W. W. Norton, 1973.

Brasher, Thomas L., ed. *Whitman as Editor of the Brooklyn Daily Eagle.* Detroit: Wayne State University Press, 1970.

Broderick, John C., ed. *Whitman the Poet: Materials for Study.* Belmont, Calif.: Wadsworth, 1962.

Bucke, Richard Maurice. *Walt Whitman.* Philadelphia: David McKay, 1883.

Buckley, John Wells. "The War Hospitals." In *Washington during War Time: A Series of Papers Showing the Military, Political, and Social Phases during 1861 to 1865,* edited by Marcus Benjamin. Washington, D.C.: National Tribune Press, 1902, 138–153.

Burroughs, John. *Whitman: A Study.* Boston: Houghton, Mifflin, 1896.

Carlisle, E. Fred. *The Uncertain Self: Whitman's Drama of Identity.* East Lansing: Michigan State University Press, 1973.

Chase, Richard. *Walt Whitman: Reconsidered.* New York: William Sloane, 1955.

Crawley, Thomas Edward. *The Structure of Leaves of Grass.* Austin: University of Texas Press, 1970.

de Selincourt, Basil. *Walt Whitman: A Study.* New York: Mitchell Kennerley, 1914.

Eitner, Walter H. *Walt Whitman's Western Jaunt.* Lawrence: Regents Press of Kansas, 1981.

Emery, Edwin, and Henry Ladd Smith. *The Press and America.* New York: Prentice-Hall, 1954.

Faner, Robert D. *Walt Whitman & Opera.* Philadelphia: University of Pennsylvania Press, 1951.

Fausset, Hugh I'Anson. *Walt Whitman: Poet of Democracy.* New Haven, Conn.: Yale University Press, 1942.

Funnell, Bertha H. *Walt Whitman on Long Island.* Port Washington, N.Y.: Kennikat Press, 1971.

Giantvalley, Scott. *Walt Whitman, 1838–1939: A Reference Guide*. Boston: G. K. Hall, 1981.

Glazener, Nancy. *Reading for Realism: The History of a U.S. Literary Institution, 1850–1910*. Durham, N.C.: Duke University Press, 1997.

Gould, Elizabeth Porter. *Anne Gilchrist and Walt Whitman*. Philadelphia: David McKay, 1900.

Grier, Edward F., ed. *Notebooks and Unpublished Prose Manuscripts: Washington*. Vol. 2 of *The Collected Writings of Walt Whitman*, edited by Gay Wilson Allen and Sculley Bradley. New York: New York University Press, 1984.

Hicks, Elias. *Journal of the Life and Religious Labours of Elias Hicks*. New York: Arno Press, 1969.

Holloway, Emory. *Whitman: An Interpretation in Narrative*. New York: Alfred A. Knopf, 1926.

Holloway, Emory, and Vernolian Schwarz, eds. *I Sit and Look Out: Editorials from the Brooklyn Daily Times by Walt Whitman*. New York: Columbia University Press, 1932.

Kaplan, Justin. *Walt Whitman: A Life*. New York: Bantam Books, 1982.

Kennedy, William Sloane. *The Fight of a Book for the World: A Companion Volume to Leaves of Grass*. West Yarmouth, Mass.: Stonecroft Press, 1926.

———. "Notes on the Pfaffians." *The Conservator* March 1897: 9.

Kobre, Sidney. *Development of American Journalism*. Dubuque, Iowa: Wm. C. Brown, 1969.

Krieg, Joann P. *A Whitman Chronology*. Iowa City: University of Iowa Press, 1998.

Kronenberger, Louis, and Emily Morison Beck, eds. *Atlantic Brief Lives: A Biographical Companion to the Arts*. Boston: Little, Brown, 1971.

Lewis, R. W. B., ed. *The Presence of Walt Whitman: Selected Papers from the English Institute*. New York: Columbia University Press, 1965.

Lowenfels, Walter, and Nan Braymer, eds. *Walt Whitman's Civil War*. New York: Alfred A. Knopf, 1961.

Miller, Edwin H. *Walt Whitman's Poetry: A Psychological Journey*, 1954.

Miller, James E., Jr. *A Critical Guide to Leaves of Grass*. Chicago: The University of Chicago Press, 1966.

———, ed. *Whitman's "Song of Myself"—Origin, Growth, Meaning*. New York: Dodd, Mead, 1964.

Miller, Perry, ed. *The American Transcendentalists: Their Prose and Poetry*. Garden City, N.Y.: Doubleday, 1957.

Mott, Frank Luther. *American Journalism: A History of Newspapers in the United States Through 260 Years: 1690 to 1950*. Rev. ed. New York: Macmillan, 1950.

Myerson, Joel, ed. *Walt Whitman: A Descriptive Bibliography*. Pittsburgh Series in Bibliography. Pittsburgh, Pa.: University of Pittsburgh Press, 1993.

Priestley, J. B. *Literature and Western Man*. New York: Harper & Brothers, 1960.

Rodgers, Cleveland, and John Black, eds. *The Gathering of the Forces: Editorials, Essays, Literary and Dramatic Reviews and Other Material Written by Walt Whitman as Editor of the Brooklyn Daily Eagle in 1846 and 1847*. 2 vols. New York: G. P. Putnam's Sons, 1920.

Rubin, Joseph Jay, and Charles H. Brown, eds. *Walt Whitman of the New York Aurora*. State College, Pa.: Penn State University Press, 1950.

Rusk, Ralph L. *The Life of Ralph Waldo Emerson*. New York: Charles Scribner's Sons, 1949.

Schmidgall, Gary, ed. *Intimate with Walt Whitman: Selections from Whitman's Conversations with Horace Traubel, 1888–1892*. Iowa City: University of Iowa Press, 2001.

Schwarzlose, Richard A. *Newspapers: A Reference Guide*. New York: Greenwood Press, 1987.

Shepard, Odell, ed. *The Journals of Bronson Alcott*. Boston: Little, Brown, 1938.

Shively, Charles, ed. *Calamus Lovers: Walt Whitman's Working-Class Camerados*. San Francisco: Gay Sunshine Press, 1987.

Sill, Geoffrey M., ed. *Walt Whitman of Mickle Street*. Knoxville: The University of Tennessee Press, 1994.

Stovall, Floyd. "Main Drifts in Whitman's Poetry." *American Literature* 4 (March 1932): 3–21.

Strauch, Carl F. "The Structure of Walt Whitman's 'Song of Myself.'" *English Journal* 27 (September 1938): 597–607.

Tassin, Algernon. *The Magazine in America*. New York: Dodd, Mead, 1916.

Tebbel, John, and Mary Ellen Zuckerman. *The Compact History of the American Newspaper*. New York: Hawthorn Books, 1963.

———. *The Magazine in America: 1741–1990*. New York: Oxford University Press, 1991.

Traubel, Horace. *Walt Whitman, Schoolmaster: Notes of a Conversation with Charles Roe*. Walt Whitman Fellowship Paper No. 14 (April 1895).

————. *With Walt Whitman in Camden (March 28–July 14, 1888)*. 9 vols. Boston: Small, Maynard, 1906.

Weathers, Willie T. "Whitman's Poetic Translations of His 1855 Preface." *American Literature* 19 (March 1947): 21–40.

White, William, ed. *Walt Whitman's Journalism: a Bibliography*. Detroit: Wayne State University Press, 1969.

Wood, James Playsted. *Magazines in the United States.* New York: Ronald Press, 1956.

Selected Foreign Critical Editions

Allen, Gay Wilson, editor. *Walt Whitman Abroad: Critical Essays from Germany, France, Scandinavia, Russia, Italy, Spain and Latin America, Israel, Japan, and India.* Syracuse, N.Y.: Syracuse University Press, 1955.

Asselineau, Roger, and William White. *Walt Whitman in Europe Today: A Collection of Essays.* Detroit: Wayne State University Press, 1972.

Baldensperger, F. "Walt Whitman in France." *Columbia University Quarterly* 21 (October 1919): 298–309.

Carpenter, Edward. *The Upanishads and Leaves of Grass.* London: George Allen, 1906.

Clark, Grace Delano. "Walt Whitman in Germany." *Texas Review* 6 (January 1921): 123–137.

De Moshinski, Elena Aizén. *Walt Whitman y la América Latina.* Mexico City: Universidad Nacional Autónoma de México, 1950.

Grippi, Charles S. "The Literary Reputation of Walt Whitman in Italy." Unpublished Ph.D. diss., New York University, 1971.

INDEX